Also in the Variorum Collected Studies Series:

WILFERD MADELUNG
Religious Schools and Sects in Medieval Islam

GEORGES VAJDA
La transmission du savoir en Islam (VIIe-XVIIIe siècles)

GEORGES VAJDA
Etudes de theologie et de philosophie arabo-islamiques à l'époque classique

M. J. KISTER
Studies in Jāhiliyya and Early Islam

R. B. SERJEANT
Studies in Arabian History and Civilisation

S. M. STERN
Coins and Documents from the Medieval Middle East

ROBERT BRUNSCHVIG
Etudes sur l'Islam classique et l'Afrique du Nord

J. D. LATHAM
From Muslim Spain to Barbary
Studies in the History of Culture of the Muslim West

DONALD P. LITTLE
History and Historiography of the Mamlūks

JEAN-CLAUDE GARCIN
Espaces, pouvoirs et idéologies de l'Egypte médiévale

DAVID AYALON
Outsiders in the Lands of Islam
Mamlūks, Mongols and Eunuchs

A. K. S. LAMBTON
Theory and Practice in Medieval Persian Government

DAVID A. KING
Islamic Astronomical Instruments

BERNARD R. GOLDSTEIN
Theory and Practice in Ancient and Medieval Astronomy

Society and Religion from Jāhiliyya to Islam

M. J. Kister

Society and Religion from Jāhiliyya to Islam

VARIORUM

British Library CIP Data

Kister M.J.
Society and religion from Jahiliyya to Islam. – (Collected studies series; CS327)
1. Arabia. Tribes. Cultural processes, history
I. Title II. Series
305.8009394

ISBN 0-86078-277-8

Published by

Variorum
Gower Publishing Group
Gower House, Croft Road, Aldershot
Hampshire GU11 3HR
Great Britain

Gower Publishing Company
Old Post Road
Brookfield
Vermont 05036
USA

Printed in Great Britain by

Galliard (Printers) Ltd
Great Yarmouth, Norfolk

COLLECTED STUDIES CS 327

CONTENTS

This volume contains viii + 342 pages.

PREFACE

The collected papers in this volume are based mainly on early Arabic sources, partly in manuscripts hitherto unpublished. This material preserves a vast amount of information concerning the life of the tribes in the Arabian peninsula and their contacts with the sedentary population. The transformations affecting the conduct of society in the first period of Islam and the adaptation of the law to the new requirements of the community also form the subject of some of the articles. The emergence of new popular religious customs and beliefs is touched upon as well. It was my aim to add the material accumulated since the first publication of the articles as appendices. Unfortunately I have only managed to prepare Addenda for three of the articles. In the case of one article, "On Concessions and Conduct" it has not been possible to reproduce the text as it was originally printed, for technical reasons. The index refers, of course, to the present layout of the article.

I wish to thank the editors and publishers of the journals and books in which these studies originally appeared for their generous agreement to this reprint. I am also indebted to Mr Ze'ew Klein for the preparation of the index. Mr John Smedley has been most kind and encouraging and deserves my sincere gratitude.

M.J. KISTER

Jerusalem 1990

PUBLISHER'S NOTE

The articles in this volume, as in all others in the Collected Studies Series, have not been given a new, continuous pagination. In order to avoid confusion, and to facilitate their use where these same studies have been referred to elsewhere, the original pagination has been maintained wherever possible.

Each article has been given a Roman number in order of appearance, as listed in the Contents. This number is repeated on each page and quoted in the index entries.

It has not been possible to reproduce all the illustrations originally included in these articles; in some cases new illustrations have been substituted.

I

LABBAYKA, ALLĀHUMMA, LABBAYKA . . .

On a monotheistic aspect of a Jāhiliyya practice

In memory of Dr. Isaiah Shachar

In his article *Talbiyāt al-Jāhiliyya*[1] S.M. Ḥusain recorded twenty five formulae of ritual invocation, *talbiyāt*, uttered by the tribes in the period of the Jāhiliyya during their pilgrimage to Mecca. He mentions that Abū l-ʿAlāʾ al-Maʿarrī had given in his *Risālat al-ghufrān* seven such formulae of tribal *talbiyāt*, classifying them by prosody and metre. Ḥusain supposes that the *labbayka allāhumma labbayka* "was probably adopted from the first responders to the call of Abraham,"[2] and emphasizes that the Prophet changed the Jāhilī formula: *labbayka allāhumma labbayka, lā sharīka laka illā sharīkun huwa laka, tamlikuhu wa-mā malaka* ("Here I am, O God, here I am; Thou hast no partner except such partner as Thou hast; Thou possessest him and all that is his")[3] into the Muslim one: *labbayka allā-humma labbayka, lā sharīka laka; inna l-ḥamda wa-l-niʿmata laka wa-l-mulka, lā sharīka laka* ("Here I am, O God, here I am, Thou hast no partner; the praise and

---

1 *Proceedings of the 9th All India Or. Conference*, 1937, pp. 361-369.

2 *Ibid.*, p. 362.

3 See this Jāhilī *talbiya* e.g.: Ibn al-Kalbī, *al-Aṣnām*, ed. Aḥmad Zakī Pasha, Cairo 1343/1924, p. 7; al-Azraqī, *Akhbār Makka*, ed. F. Wüstenfeld, p. 134; al-Kalāʿī, *al-Iktifāʾ fī maghāzī rasūli llāhi wa-l-thalāthati l-khulafāʾ*, ed. Muṣṭafā ʿAbd al-Wāḥid, Cairo 1387/1968, I, 94; al-Ṭabarī, *Tafsīr*, ed. Shākir, Cairo 1969, XVI, 289, no. 19973; al-Suyūṭī, *al-Durr al-manthūr*, Cairo 1314, IV, 40, 359; al-Bayhaqī, *al-Sunan al-kubrā*, Hyderabad 1352, V, 45 inf.; Ibn Ḥazm, *Ḥajjat al-wadāʿ*, ed. Mamdūḥ Ḥaqqī, Beirut 1966, pp. 349 inf. –350; al-Naysābūrī, *Gharāʾib al-Qurʾān*, ed. Ibrāhīm ʿAṭwa ʿAwaḍ, Cairo 1384/1965, XVII, 96; al-Khāzin, *Lubāb al-taʾwīl*, Cairo 1381, III, 261, V, 13; al-Baghawī, *Maʿālim al-tanzīl* (on margin of *Lubāb al-taʾwīl*), *ibid.*; al-Shahrastānī, *al-Milal wa-l-niḥal*, ed. Muḥammad Sayyid Kaylānī, Cairo 1387/1967, II, 238, 247; Ibn Saʿīd al-Andalusī, *Nashwat al-ṭarab fī taʾrīkhi jāhiliyyati l-ʿarab*, Ms. Tübingen I, fol. 194, inf.; Nūr al-Dīn al-Haythamī, *Majmaʿ al-zawāʾid*, Beirut 1967, III, 223; Abū l-ʿAlāʾ al-Maʿarrī, *Risālat al-ghufrān*, ed. ʿĀʾisha ʿAbd al-Raḥmān, Cairo 1382/1963, p. 535 (with an additional hemistich: *abū banātin bi-fadak;* it is explained by Abū l-ʿAlāʾ as pointing to the idols that were in that time in Fadak); Ibn al-Athīr, *Jāmiʿ al-uṣūl*, ed. Muḥammad Ḥāmid al-Fiqī, Cairo 1368/1949, III, 444, no. 1377; ʿUmar b. Muḥammad al-Mauṣilī, *Kitāb al-wasīla*, Hyderabad 1392/1973, III_{II}, 196; A. Guthrie, The Significance of Abraham, *MW*, 1955, p. 116.

the grace are Thine and the empire; Thou hast no partner.")[4] Ḥusain points out that the tribes performing the pilgrimage acknowledged in their *talbiyāt* a supreme God who was the Master of their gods, giving Him such names as al-Raḥmān, al-Maʿbūd, al-Dayyān, al-Mustajīb, al-Qahhār, al-Ṣamad, and emphasizes the Muslim character of some of the utterances of the *talbiya*. The Prophet used in his prayer the utterance: *in taghfir allāhumma taghfir jammā, wa-ayyu ʿabdin laka lā alammā*, a phrase which, according to Ḥusain, occurs in the *talbiya* of the Ashʿariyyūn.[5] This idea of the presence of an all-powerful and all-pervading Divinity, concludes Ḥusain, was working amongst the Arabs preparing the field for the propagation of the sublime monotheism as preached by Muḥammad.

Ḥusain, although he carefully collected and edited the valuable text of the *talbiyāt*, did not, however, record the sources from which he derived his material. It may be of some importance to trace the sources of the *talbiyāt* and to examine more closely their content and purport. The *talbiyāt* of certain tribes are given in al-Yaʿqūbī's (d. 248 H) *Taʾrīkh.*[6] Al-Yaʿqūbī's account of the *talbiyāt* is preceded by a short account of the gods and idols worshipped by the Arabs. More detailed is the account of *talbiyāt* in Muḥammad b. Ḥabīb's (d. 145 H) *al-Muḥabbar,*[7] followed by a list of idols worshipped by the different tribes. The complete text of several *talbiyāt* is given in the commentary to the phrase: . . . *wa-jtanibū qaula l-zūri* (Sūra XXII, 31) in Muqātil b. Sulaymān's (d. 150 H) *Tafsīr*[8] and this is followed by a list of idols worshipped by the various tribes. *Zūr* is

[4] See the various forms of the Muslim *talbiya*: Abū Yūsuf al-Anṣārī, *Kitāb al-āthār*, ed. Abū l-Wafā, Cairo 1355, nos. 456-458; al-Shāfiʿī, *al-Umm*, Cairo 1321 (reprint 1388/1968) II, 132-133; al-Ṭayālisī, *Musnad*, Hyderabad 1321, p. 232, no. 1668; Ibn Ḥazm, *Ḥajjat al-wadāʿ*, p. 350; Nūr al-Dīn al-Haythamī, *op. cit.*, III, 222-223; al-Ṭaḥāwī, *Sharḥ maʿānī l-āthār*, ed. Muḥammad Zuhrī l-Najjār, Cairo 1388/1968 II, 124-125; Ibn al-Athīr, *Jāmiʿ al-uṣūl*, III, 438-443, nos. 1371-1375; al-Zurqānī, *Sharḥ al-muwaṭṭaʾ*, ed Ibrāhīm ʿAṭwa ʿAwaḍ, Cairo 1381/1961, III, 34; Amīn Maḥmūd Khaṭṭāb, *Fatḥu l-maliki l-maʿbūd, takmilatu l-manhali l-ʿadhbi l-maurūd, sharḥ sunan abī dāwūd*, Cairo 1394/1974, I, 109-111; al-Bayhaqī, *al-Sunan al-kubrā*, V, 44-45; al-Khaṭīb al-Baghdādī, *Taʾrīkh Baghdād*, Cairo 1349/1931, V, 55; Muḥibb al-Dīn al-Ṭabarī, *al-Qirā li-qāṣidi ummi l-qurā*, ed Muṣṭafā l-Saqā, Cairo 1390/1970, pp. 173-175, 415; al-ʿAynī, *ʿUmdat al-qārī*, Cairo 1348, IX, 172-174; al-Qasṭallānī, *Irshād al-sārī*,, Cairo 1323, III, 114-115; Ibn Ḥajar, *Fatḥ al-bārī*, Cairo 1300, III, 324-326; al-Ḥarbī, *Kitāb al-manāsik*, ed. Ḥamad al-Jāsir, al-Riyāḍ 1389/1969, p. 429; ʿUmar b. Muḥammad al-Mauṣilī, *op. cit.*, III_{II}, 193-195; IV_{I}, 183; Ibn Bābūyah al-Qummī, *ʿIlal al-sharāʾiʿ*, Najaf 1385/1966, pp. 416-418; Muḥammad b. abī l-Qāsim al-Ṭabarī, *Bishārat al-muṣṭafā li-shīʿat al-murtaḍā*, Najaf 1383/1963, pp. 213-214; al-Majlisī, *Biḥār al-anwār*, Tehran 1388, XLIX, 92, 93, 183, 339; Murtaḍā l-Zabīdī, *Itḥāf al-sāda al-muttaqīn bi-sharḥ asrār iḥyāʾ ʿulūmi l-dīn*, Cairo 1311, IV, 336; Muḥammad Nāṣir al-Dīn al-Albānī, *Ḥajjat al-nabī*, Damascus 1387, p. 60, nos. 14-15; G.E. von Grunebaum, *Muhammadan Festivals*, New York 1951, p. 28.

[5] Ḥusain, *op. cit.*, pp. 362-364; text no. 3.

[6] Ed. M. Th. Houtsma, Leiden 1883, I, 296-297.

[7] Ed. Ilse Lichtenstaedter, Hyderabad 1361/1942, pp. 311-315; the list of the idols *ibid.* pp. 315-318.

[8] Ms. Ahmet III, 74/II, fols. 22a-24a; the list of the idols is given on fol. 24a, inf.-24b.

rendered by Muqātil by *kadhib*, lie, and identified with the falsehood inherent in the Jāhilī *talbiyāt*, that associate gods and idols with God. *Zūr* is thus defined as *al-shirku fī l-talbiya*,[9] attribution of a partner to God in the *talbiya*.

Muqātil's list, in which fifty six forms of *talbiya* are recorded, is however a composite affair. Several of the *talbiyāt* are in fact duplicates with certain variations. The first eight *talbiyāt* give the utterances of the tribes without referring to the names of the gods. The ninth relates the utterances of the women who perform the circumambulation of the Kaʿba while naked. The tenth gives the *talbiya* of Adam. The following twenty *talbiyāt* (nos. 11-31) are listed by the names of the gods worshipped by the different tribes, without however giving the names of the tribes. This series of *talbiyāt* is preceded by the heading: *talbiyatu l-ʿarabi fī l-jāhiliyyati* and ends with the phrase: *wa-hādhihi ruʾūsu ṭawāghītihim* . . . The forms of *talbiya* which constitute this series correspond to those which occur in the report of Muḥammad b. Ḥabīb. The close relation between the text of Muqātil and that of Ibn Ḥabīb is evident. In the *talbiya* of the tribes worshipping Saʿīda (no. 23) the last line of the *talbiya* breaks the chain of *sajʿ*-rhymes: *miyāḥa* and *raqāḥa* are followed by *ṭāʿa*. This same wording is recorded in Ibn Ḥabīb's *al-Muḥabbar*, where however a marginal gloss in the Ms. of *al-Muḥabbar* replaces the last word by *al-naṣāḥa*.[10] The lacuna in the *talbiya* of the worshippers of al-Munṭabiq (Muqātil, no. 19) can clearly be seen in the Mss., indicating that some phrases of the utterance are missing; the text is identical with that given in *al-Muḥabbar* (p. 313, 1.1), but the printed edition of *al-Muḥabbar* has no note about a lacuna in the Ms. The heading missing in the *talbiya* no. 25 (Muqātil, fol. 23a sup.): *wa-kānat talbiyata man nasaka li-yaghūtha* can be supplied from the account of *al-Muḥabbar* (p. 314, 1.1). Furthermore Ibn Ḥabīb's account of the idols worshipped by the Arabs also shows close similarity with that of Muqātil, though it is more detailed.[11]

In another series of *talbiyāt* (nos. 32-56) only the name of the tribe in which the invocation was used is given, or else both the name of the tribe and that of the idol of the tribe are specified. Three of the *talbiya* invocations in this series (nos. 33, 34, 36) are reported on the authority of Ibn Isḥāq (d. 150 H); one *talbiya* (no. 35) is recorded on the authority of al-Shaʿbī (d. 109 H).

The divergent versions of the *talbiyāt* as recorded in the chapter of Muqātil's *Tafsīr*, the variously formulated utterances, the three traditions on the authority of Ibn Isḥāq and the one of al-Shaʿbī – all this seems to indicate that the chapter was put together by the combination of several sources. This conjecture is corroborated by the fact that two out of the five consulted Mss. (Köprülü 143, fols. 175b penult.-176a; Hamīdiyya 58, fol. 255a.-255b) contain only the first ten

[9] Muqātil, *op. cit.*, fol. 22a, sup.
[10] *Al-Muḥabbar*, p. 313, note 5.
[11] See Muqātil, *op. cit.*, fol. 24b; and see another short account *ibid.*, fol. 210b.

talbiyāt. One may venture to say that some parts of the account were inserted by the transmitter of the *Tafsīr*, al-Hudhayl b. Ḥabīb al-Dandānī.[12]

An examination of the *talbiyāt* mentioned above together with a few more from other sources may shed some light on certain significant aspects of these ritual invocations.

I

The well known Jāhilī *talbiya* associating a partner with God[13] is recorded in Muqātil's account as the *talbiya* of Quraysh, who were worshippers of Isāf.[14] This very *talbiya* is however recorded as the ritual invocation of the Ḥums, a group of tribes including Quraysh, Khuzāʿa, Kināna and ʿAmīr b. Ṣaʿṣaʿa, as stated in this report.[15] In another form of the *talbiya* of the Ḥums they invoke God, addressing Him as the Lord of Sirius (*rabbu l-shiʿrā*) and ask His aid against the offenders. They address Him as the Lord of Manāt,[16] al-Lāt and al-ʿUzzā and as the Lord of the sanctuary of the Kaʿba (*rabbu l-kaʿbati l-ḥarām*). They came to Him riding on lean camels – having evidently made an ardous journey – and left the idols forsaken and desolate, (*khilwan ṣifran*), as they say in their invocation.[17]

It is, of course, of some importance to find the *talbiya* of the Ḥums, a group closely connected by ties of loyalty and allegiance with the Kaʿba, observing distinctive ritual practices during the *ḥajj* and enjoying a special privileged position in Mecca. While the Jāhilī *talbiya* with regard to associating a partner is usually attibuted to Quraysh, or to Quraysh and Kināna,[18] the latter *talbiya* attributed to the Ḥums seems to be congruous with their religious ideas and their duties during the *ḥajj*. The *talbiya* expounds clearly their belief in the authority of Allah over the principal Arab deities al-Lāt, al-ʿUzzā and Manāt. God is the Lord of the Kaʿba and the idols of the gods had been left behind void and insignificant. This may be quite a faithful exposition of their belief. Moreover, the arduous journey fits in well with the fact that they exercised exertions in worship during the *ḥajj*.

---

12 See Sezgin *GAS*, I, 37 (...*"Dieser fügte an manchem Stellen dem Text von Muqātil Überlieferugen von anderen hinzu"*). On the transmission of the *Tafsīr* see al-Khaṭīb al-Baghdādī, *Ta'rīkh Baghdād*, VII, 143, no. 3591, IX, 426, no. 5039; and see Muqātil, *op. cit.*, fol. 33a.

13 See above, note 3.

14 Muqātil *op. cit.*, fol. 22b (no. 11); Ibn Ḥabīb, *al-Muḥabbar*, p. 311; al-Yaʿqūbī, *op. cit.* I, 296; Ḥusain, *op. cit.* p. 367, no. 15 (with the addition: *abū l-banāt bi-fadak*, like in *Abū l-ʿAlā' 's Risālat al-ghufrān*, p. 535).

15 Muqātil, *op. cit.*, fol. 22a (no. 1); a following comment says that the partner attached by the Ḥums to God referred to the angels worshipped by them; this is the *zūr*, the falsehood (mentioned in the verse of the Qur'ān).

16 The phrase in the text: *rabbu l-thālithati l-ukhrā* denotes, of course, Manāt.

17 Muqātil *op. cit.*, fol. 23b (no. 45).

18 See the *talbiya* uttered by Quraysh and Kināna on the Day of ʿArafa, containing the declaration of the associate partner: Muqātil, *op. cit.*, fol. 23a (no. 32).

Their invocation of God to aid them against those who transgress seems to point to these tribal groups who did not observe the sanctity of the Kaʿba and violated the peace of the holy months of the *ḥajj*. No clear answer can be given why their *talbiya* stressed that Allah was the Lord of Sirius. This very expression occurs in the Qurʾān only once (Sūra LIII, 49). Early commentators attribute the worship of Sirius to the tribe of Ḥimyar, or to some ancestor of the Prophet or to the tribe of Khuzāʿa. This could explain the naming of God as the Lord of Sirius, as Khuzāʿa were a part of the Ḥums. But the expression "the Lord of Sirius . . . the Lord of al-Lāt and al-ʿUzzā" recurs as well in the *talbiya* of Madhḥij.[19]

Quite different was the *talbiya* of Ghassān. They invoke God on behalf of their kings, addressing Him as the Lord of their people.[20] In the same vein is cast the very short *talbiya* of Rabīʿa. They uttered their invocation, addressing God as the Lord of Rabīʿat al-Qashʿam.[21] In both forms of the *talbiya* God is perceived as the Lord of the tribe.

Another version of the *talbiya* of Rabīʿa (the worshippers of Muḥarriq[22]) reflects sincere devotion and servitude and expresses the request that the pilgrimage be correct and sound: *labbayka ḥajjan ḥaqqan taʿabbudan wa-riqqan.*[23] A third relation has some additional phrases describing the race of the pilgrims towards Mecca so that they may shave their heads.[24] A fourth version shows some divergence: the Bakr b. Wāʾil stress in their *talbiya* on behalf of Rabīʿa their obedience to the Lord who is not worshipped in a church or in a synagogue. Their idols, they say, they have left protected and safe.[25] A fifth report adds to the concise form of the devotion and servitude a phrase stating the Rabīʿa did not come to Mecca to ask for gifts nor for reasons of trade.[26]

This expression, stating that the pilgrims did not come for trade or profit, recurs in the *talbiyāt* of other tribes.[27] It confirms the early traditions that the tribes refrained from trade activities during their pilgrimage. This was changed by

---

19 Muqātil, *op. cit.*, fol. 23b (no. 41); al-Yaʿqūbī, *op. cit.*, I, 297; and comp. H.A.R. Gibb, "Pre-Islamic Monotheism in Arabia," *Harvard Theological Review*, 1962, pp. 275 inf. -276.

20 Muqātil, *op. cit.*, fol. 24a (no. 54).

21 Ibn Hishām, *Kitāb al-tījān*, Hyderabad 1347, p. 219; and see on *qashʿam* as the sobriquet of Rabīʿa *L'A*, s.v. q sh ʿm.

22 See Muqātil, *op. cit.*, fol. 24b: *wa-kāna al-muḥarriq bi-salmāna li-bakri bni wāʾilin wa-sāʾiri rabīʿata*; Ibn Ḥabīb, *op. cit.*, p. 317.

23 Muqātil, *op. cit.*, fol. 22b (no. 17); Ibn Ḥabīb, p. 312; Abū l-ʿAlāʾ al-Maʿarrī, *op. cit.*, p. 536.

24 Muqātil, *op. cit.*, for 23b (no. 38).

25 Muqātil, *op. cit.*, fol. 24a (no. 50).

26 Muqātil, *op. cit.*, fol 22a (no. 4); cf. *L'A*, s.v. r q ḥ: some people used to utter in their *talbiya* in the period of the Jāhiliyya: *jiʾnāka li-l-naṣāḥa wa-lam naʾti li-l-raqāḥa.*

27 See e.g. Muqātil, *op. cit.*, fol. 22b (no. 23), fol. 23b (nos. 36, 39, 44); Ibn Ḥabīb, *op. cit.*, p. 313.

th revelation (Sūra II, 198) which gave Muslims permission to carry out business transactions during the *ḥajj*.[28]

The description of the hardship of travel during the pilgrimage, the lean camels, the race to reach Mecca, the exertion of performing the *ḥajj* by foot as exposed in the *talbiyāt*[29] – all these features are in agreement with the reports about the pilgrimage in the period of the Jāhiliyya and with the stories about exertions during the *ḥajj* in Islamic times.

The *talbiyāt* reflect the ideas of the tribes about the supreme God as well as their perception of the relation between the lesser gods and the supreme God. The idea that the gods are inferior and dependent upon God is expressed in the *talbiya* of Kinda, Ḥaḍramaut and Sakūn. To the Jāhilī *talbiya* of association (above note 3) they added: . . ."Thou possessest him (i.e. the partner – K) whether Thou destroyest or leavest him; Thou art the Forbearing (*al-ḥalīm*), therefore leave him.[30] Judhām prided themselves in their *talbiya* of their royal descendance, of their forbearing minds and addressed God as "the God of the idols" (*ilāhu l-aṣnāmi*), naming Him al-Raḥmān.[31] In the *talbiya* of Daus God is named "the Lord of the idols" (*rabbu l-aṣnāmi*).[32] Tamīm mentioned in their *talbiya* God the Creator; it is He whom they singled out by their invocation (*wa-akhlaṣat li-rab-bihā duʿāhā*).[33] Qays ʿAylān describe themselves as being together with their idols, in humble submission to al-Raḥmān.[34] Thaqīf, asking for forgiveness of their sins, stated that their goddesses, al-Lāt and al-ʿUzzā, were in the hands of God and that the idols yielded obediently to Him.[35] Asad named God "the One," "the Subduer" and asserted that they did not worship the idols;[36] they also mentioned Him in the *talbiya* as "*al-rabbu l-ṣamad*." The meaning of the word *al-ṣamad*, which occurs only once in the Qurʾān,[37] as one of God's attributes is usually explained as "the Lord to whom people direct themselves in their needs;"[38] there

---

[28] See e.g. Muqātil, *op. cit.*, I, 31b; Ibn al-ʿArabī, *Aḥkām al-qurʾān*, Cairo 1387/1967, I, 135 inf. -136; al-Ṭabarī. *Tafsīr*, ed. Shākir, IV, 164-168, nos. 3763, 3771, 3775, 3777, 3781 (noteworthy is the expression of the commentator: *fa-rukhkhisa lahum* . . . "and they were granted concession") 3787 (and see another version of the verse: no. 3766); al-Suyūṭī, *al-Durr an-manthūr*, I, 222; al-Rāghib al-Iṣfahānī, *Muḥāḍarāt al-udabā*', Beirut 1961, II, 465; and see *JESHO XV* (1972) 76, note 4.

[29] See e.g. Muqātil, *op. cit.*, fol. 22a (nos. 3,7), 23a (no. 34), 23b (no. 44), 24a (no. 49).

[30] Muqātil, *op. cit.*, fol. 24a (no. 53); al-Yaʿqūbī, *op. cit.*, I, 297, 11. 4-5.

[31] Muqātil, *op. cit.*, fol. 24a (no. 52); comp. the fragmentary *talbiya* in al-Yaʿqūbī, *op. cit.*, I, 297.

[32] Muqātil, *op. cit.*, fol. 24a (no. 56).

[33] Muqātil, *op. cit.*, fol. 23a (no. 33); comp. al-Yaʿqūbī, *op. cit.*, I, 296.

[34] Muqātil, *op. cit.*, fol. 23b (no. 37); and comp. the *talbiya* of ʿAkk and the Ashʿariyyūn (ib. no. 40): *ḥajjun li-l-raḥmān, dhallat lahu l-aṣnām*.

[35] Muqātil, *op. cit.*, fol. 24a (no. 48).

[36] Muqātil, *op. cit.*, fol. 23a (no. 35).

[37] Sūra CXII, 2.

[38] See e.g. Abū Misḥal, *Kitāb al-nawādir*, ed. ʿIzzat Ḥasan, Damascus 1380/1961, pp. 122-123 (and see the references of the editor, *ib.*, note "35"); *LʿA* s.v. ṣ m d; Aḥmad b. Ḥamdān al-Rāzī, *al-Zīna*, ed. Ḥusayn al-Hamdānī, Cairo 1958, II, 43-45; and comp. Jirān al-ʿAud,

are however other explanations and some of them seem to have been introduced together with the later ideas about the attributes of God.

The *talbiya* of Ḥimyar is significant. They stress in their invocation that they address God on behalf of the kings and the petty rulers (*ʿani l-mulūki wa-l-aqwāl*) [of people – K] of prudence and forbearing minds, who practise piety towards their kinsmen, staying away from sins by self-withdrawal (from shame – k) and out of Islam (*tanazzuhan wa-islām*). They declare that they humbly submit to the Lord of mankind, yielding to Him on every elevated place [they and their – K] idols and gods.[39] The word *islām* and its meaning need elucidation. It occurs only once in the *talbiyāt*, in the quoted invocation of Ḥimyar; it is preceded by the phrase of eschewing sins, coupled with the word *tanazzuh* denoting keeping aloof from shameful and wicked deeds, and followed by the statement of obedience to the God of mankind. It is apparent that the word *islām* placed between a word which denotes abstention from sin and another one, which talks of submission to God, both terms bearing as they do a religio-ethical connotation, also belongs to the same semantic field. It probably denotes the idea of exclusive devotion to one God, as assumed by the late D.Z. Baneth. In his illuminating discussion of the social and religious background of the Prophet's activity, Baneth made the following observation:

> . . . The fundamental change required by Muḥammad was the abandonment of polytheism, to serve one god only, the same god which they had already previously known under the name of Allah. Does not the idea suggest itself to seek this very meaning of adopting monotheism in the words *aslama, islām*?[40]

This meaning proposed for *islām* by Baneth, is indeed confirmed by the definition given by Muqātil in his *Tafsīr*: *muslim* is consistently interpreted by *mukhliṣun bi-l-tauḥīdi* (or: *bi-tauḥīdi llāhi*);[41] *Islām* and *ikhlāṣ* are here given as identical in connotation. H. Ringgren, analyzing the meaning of *ikhlāṣ* and *mukhliṣ* states that "the context indicates that making one's religion *khāliṣ* to God is contrary to choosing patrons apart from Him,"[42] and finds fit Bell's translation: "making Him the exclusive object of religion."[43] One may venture to assume

Dīwān, ed. Aḥmad Nasīm, Cairo 1350/1931, p. 39, 1. 12; Ibn Muqbil, *Dīwān*, ed. 'Izzat Ḥasan, Damascus 1381/ 1962, p. 51, 1. 3; al-Rāghib al-Iṣfahānī, *al-Mufradāt fī gharībi l-qur'ān*, Cairo 1324, p. 288.

39 Muqātil, *op. cit.*, fol. 23b (no. 43).

40 D.Z.H. Baneth, "What did Muhammad mean when he called his religion *Islām*? The original meaming of *Aslama* and its derivatives," *Israel Oriental Studies* I (1971) 184.

41 See e.g. Muqātil, *op. cit.*, I, 51a (*aslamtu ya'nī akhlaṣtu*), I, 57a (*kuntum muslimīna ya'nī mukhliṣīna lahu bi-l-tauḥīdi*), II, 58b, ult.-59a, 1. 1 (*qabla an ya'tūnī muslimīna, ya'nī mukhliṣīna bi-l-tauḥīdi*), II, 59b, 1. 3 (*wa-kunnā muslimīna ya'nī mukhliṣīna bi-l-tauḥīdi min qablihā*) II, 61b, 1. 4 from bottom, II, 62a, 1. 5 from bottom, II, 73b, II, 83a, b, 1. 2, II, 123a, II, 211a, 1. 6.

42 H. Ringgren, "The Pure Religion," *Oriens* XV (1962), 93-96.

43 *Ibid.*, p. 94 inf.

that *islām* here denotes the idea ascribed to it in the Qur'ān. This may change to some extent the accepted views about the beliefs of the people of the Jāhiliyya and provide a clue for an evaluation as to how monotheistic ideas were adopted and transmitted from the Jāhiliyya period to Islam.

The *talbiya* of Jurhum[44] is of an altogether different content and purport. This tribe was already extinct by the advent of Islam, and traditions as to their origin and ancestors were shrouded in a web of miracles and legend. The *talbiya* of Jurhum is thus merely a reminiscence of an early *talbiya* of an ancient tribe perpetuated in the invocation of the worshippers of Dhū l-Kaffayn;[45] this idol was worshipped by Daus[46] and Khuzā'a.[47] Muqātil records two versions of the *talbiya* of Jurhum: a short one, the *talbiya* of the worshippers of Dhū l-Kaffayn, who utter the invocation of Jurhum, and a longer one referred to above (note 44), recorded as the *talbiya* of Jurhum. They invoke God, stating that they are his servants; that people are (like) newly acquired property, while they are (like) the hereditary property of God; that they have dwelt in God's land and caused it to flourish and that to be remote from God is something which one cannot stand. Further they say in their invocation that they are the first to come to God's meeting place; they will oppose anyone who shows hostility towards God until they set the faith straight in His valley.[48]

The first three hemistichs of this *rajaz* are often quoted in the sources and attributed to 'Amr b. al-Ḥārith (or 'Āmir b. al Ḥārith) b. Muḍāḍ;[49] they became incorporated into the *talbiya.* The concept of man assisting God against His enemies is of considerable antiquity in Islam, recurring as it does in the Qur'ān and in early Islamic literature. The contrasting pair of notions "*ṭirf*" (or *ṭurf*) and "*tilād*", current in ancient Arabic poetry is here interpreted as pointing to the heavenly origin of Jurhum, "*tilāduka*", "Thy hereditary property"; their ancestor is said to have been an angel who, having sinned, was sent down to earth.[50] It is noteworthy that al-Ṭufayl b. 'Amr al-Dausī pulling down the idol of Dhū l-Kaffayn uttered his denunciation of the pagan worship of the idol in the same metre, *rajaz,* and with the same rhyme.[51]

---

44 See on this tribe *EI²*, s.v. Djurhum (W.M. Watt).

45 Muqātil, *op. cit.*, fol. 23a (no. 30).

46 Al-Ya'qūbī, *op. cit.*, I, 296; al-Baghdādī, *Khizānat al-adab (ed. Būlāq)*, III, 246 sup.

47 Muḥammad b. Ḥabīb, *op. cit.*, p. 318.

48 Muqātil, *op. cit.*, fol. 22a (no. 6); comp. Ibn Ḥabīb, *op. cit.*, p. 314.

49 Al-Ṭabarī, *Ta'rīkh*, ed. Muḥammad Abū l-Faḍl Ibrāhīm, Cairo 1961, II, 285; al-Fāsī, *Shifā' al-gharām*, Cairo 1956, I, 357, 374; al-'Iṣāmī, *Simṭ al-nujūm al-'awālī*, Cairo 1380, I, 174; al-Māwardī, *A'lām al-nubuwwa*, Cairo 1319, p. 120; Abū l-Baqā', *al-Manāqib al-mazyadiyya*, Ms. Br. Mus., Add. 23, 296, fol. 79b.

50 Al-'Iṣāmī, *op. cit.*, I, 174 inf. – 175.

51 Ibn Hishām, *al-Sīra al-nabawiyya*, ed. al-Saqā, al-Abyārī, Shalabī, Cairo 1355/1936, II, 25; al-Kalbī, *al-Aṣnām*, p. 37; Ibn Ḥabīb, *op. cit.*, p. 318 (with the variant in the first hemistich: *yā dhā l-kaffayni lastu min tilādikā*): al-Wāqidī, *al-Maghāzī*, ed. Marsden Jones, London 1966, p. 923; Ibn Ḥajar, *al-Iṣāba*, ed. 'Alī Muḥammad al-Bijāwī, Cairo 1392/1972, III, 521; al-Dimyāṭī, *al-Mukhtaṣar fī sīrati sayyidi l-bashar*, Ms. Chester Beatty 3332, fol. 106b.

The phrase "*wa-humu l-awwalūna ʿalā mīʿādika*" deserves attention. Although the word *mīʿād* occurs several times in the Qurʾān, the use of the word with the preposition *ʿalā* is not attested in the Qurʾān. It occurs however with the preposition *ʿalā* in the famous poem of al-Aswad b. Yaʿfur.[52] In the *talbiya* of Jurhum the word seems to denote an appointed time or an appointed place of meeting; in this case it is the time of the *ḥajj* as established by God or the place appointed by God for the pilgrimage, Mecca.[53]

To the sphere of Jāhilī custom also belongs the invocation by women who used to perform the circumambulation naked. To the usually recorded *rajaz* – verse[54] Muqātil adds three *rajaz* hemistichs about the spectators who watch the corpulent women.[55] The body-features mentioned in the last hemistich resemble the details provided about Ḍubāʿa when she circumambulated the Kaʿba in the nude.[56]

II

Abū l-ʿAlāʾ al-Maʿarrī remarks, classifying the different forms of the *talbiyāt*, that there is no *talbiya* (scil. from the period fo the Jāhiliyya – K) cast in one of the *qaṣīda* – metres. He remarks with caution that *talbiyāt* may have perhaps been uttered in one of the *qaṣīda* metres, but they were not recorded by the transmitters. Most of them are utterances cast in *sajʿ* or *rajaz* form.[57] Goldziher analyzed thoroughly the role of *sajʿ* and *rajaz* and their occurrence in invocations, curses, wisdom sayings and in oracular utterances.[58] Gibb succintly referred to *sajʿ* and *rajaz* in connection with the style of the Qurʾān, assuming that there was an estab-

[52] Al-Ḍabbī, *al-Mufaḍḍaliyyāt*, ed. Lyall, XCIV, 11, rendered by Lyall: "Now sweep the winds over all their dwellings: empty they lie, as though their lords had been set a time and no more to be"; al-Aʿshā, *Dīwān*, ed. Geyer (Aʿshā Nahshal XVII, 11) p.296 (and see the references of the editor).

[53] My son, Menahem Kister, provided me with the following note: "The word *mo'ed* in Hebrew has, in addition to its current meanings in the Scriptures, two other denotations: (1) a holy place, a sanctuary (see e.g. Ps. LXXIV, 4, 8, Lam. II, 6; cf. *ohel mo'ed* in this sense; and cf. *pḫr m'd* in the Ugaritic myths indicating the place of the meeting of the gods); (2) a festival, a holiday (see e.g. Lev. XXIII, 37). One of these two meanings suits perhaps the phrase here. The expression *bā'ey mo'ed* (Lam. I, 4) which seems to denote "pilgrims" is probably derived from one of these 2 meanings (see the commentary of Ibn Ezra on this verse)". I have failed to trace this meaning in the Arabic sources.

[54] Al-Azraqī, *op. cit.*, pp. 124-125; al-ʿIṣāmī, *op. cit.*, I, 219; cf. the story of Ḍubāʿa bint ʿĀmir: Ibn Ḥabīb, *al-Munammaq*, ed. Khursheed Aḥmad Fāriq, Hyderabad 1964, p. 272.

[55] Muqātil, *op. cit.*, fol. 22a (no. 9); cf. Mughulṭāy, *al-Zahr al-bāsim*, Ms. Leiden Or. 370, fol. 100a.

[56] Cf. Ibn Saʿd, *op. cit.*, VIII, 153 inf.; Ibn Ḥajar, *al-Iṣāba*, VIII, 6; Mughulṭāy, *op. cit.*, fols. 99b-100a; al-Wāḥidī, *op. cit.*, pp. 151-152.

[57] Abū l-ʿAlāʾ, *op. cit.*, p. 537.

[58] J. Goldziher, *Abhandlungen zur Arabischen Philologie*, Leiden 1896.

lished style of religious discourse in the period of the Jāhiliyya.[59] Tradition stresses the efficacy of *sajʿ* invocations uttered in the *ḥaram* of Mecca in the period of the Jāhiliyya and directed against wrong-doers and oppressors. The *Sīra* of Ibn Isḥāq in the transmission of Yūnus b. Bukayr has a special chapter recording cases of this kind.[60] In early Islam *sajʿ* and *rajaz* were considered a product of the Bedouin mind and it was deemed especially odious to link the Qurʾān with *rajaz*.[61] The Prophet is said to have prohibited the use of *sajʿ* in invocations.[62]

Some *sajʿ* invocations of the Jāhiliyya period were indeed utterly forgotten. According to the report of al-Fākihī the people performing the *ṭawāf* between al-Ṣafā and al-Marwa in the period of the Jāhiliyya used to utter the following short invocation:

al-yauma qirrī ʿaynā: bi-qarʿi l-marwataynā[63]

This invocation is never encountered again in the Islamic period. Some of the invocations of the *talbiya* in their *sajʿ* or *rajaz* forms did, however, survive and were adopted by the Prophet; he used to utter them during his pilgrimage. The invocation *labbayka ḥajjan haqqā*: *taʿabbudan wa-riqqā* mentioned above[64] was uttered by the Prophet in his *talbiya*.[65]

Ibn Manẓūr records the verses uttered by Abū Khirāsh al-Hudhalī during running (*saʿy*) between al-Ṣafā and al-Marwa:

lāhumma hādhā khāmisun in tammā:
atammahu llāhu wa-qad atammā:

---

[59] H.A.R. Gibb, *Arabic Literature*, Oxford 1963, pp. 14-15, 34-35; *idem*, "Pre Islamic Monotheism in Arabia," *Harvard Theological Review*, 1962, pp. 278-279.

[60] A. Guillaume, "New Light on the Life of Muḥhamad," *JSS*, Monograph No. 1, Manchester n.d., pp. 15-18 ("The Potency of Invocations Pronounced in Saj'"). Guillame remarked that he had been unable to find this passage elsewhere. The stories of this passage can, however, be traced in al-Kalāʿī's *al-Iktifāʾ*, I, 66-69; Ibn al-Athīr, *Usd al-ghāba*, Būlāq 1280, III, 150-151; Ibn Ḥajar, *al-Iṣāba*, IV, 752-753; Ibn Abī l-Dunyā, *Kitāb mujābī l-daʿwa*, Bombay 1389/1969, pp. 10-14, no. 5; Abū l-Baqāʾ Muḥammad b. al- Ḍiyāʾ al-Makkī al-ʿAdawī, *Aḥwāl makka wa-l-madīna*, Ms. Br. Mus., Or. 11865, fols. 119b-121a; Ibn Zuhayra, *al-Jāmiʿ al-laṭīf fī faḍli makkata wa-ahlihā wa-bināʾi l-bayti l-sharīf*, Cairo 1357/1938. p. 61.

[61] See al-Balādhurī, *Ansāb al-ashrāf*, Ms. fol. 1211b: .. *ʿani l-ṣalti bni dīnārin qāla: samiʿtu l-ḥajjāja ʿalā minbari wāsiṭin yaqūlu: qātala llāhu ʿabda hudhaylin, wa-llāhi mā qaraʾa mimmā anzala llāhu ʿalā muḥammadin ḥarfan, wa-mā huwa illā rajazu l-ʿarabi, wa-llāhi lau adraktuhu la-saqaytu l-arḍa min damihi;* Ibn Abī l-Dunyā, *al-Ishrāf fī manāzil al-ashrāf*, Ms. Chester Beatty 4427, fol. 62b (al-Ḥajjāj refers to the version of the Qurʾān of Ibn Masʿūd).

[62] See *L'A*, s.v.s j ʿa; ʿAlī al-Qārī, *al-Asrār al-marfūʿa fī l-akhbār al-mauḍūʿa*, ed. Muḥammad al-Ṣabbāgh, Beirut 1391/1971, p. 140, no. 109 (see the comments of the editor); cf. ʿAbd al-Malik b. Ḥabīb, *al-Taʾrīkh*. Ms. Bodleian, Marsh. 288, p. 167, 1. 17. (*. . . qālū; aqbalnā min al-fajji l-ʿamīq naʾummu l-bayta l-ʿatīq; fa qāla ʿumaru: qad waqaʿū fī hādha, yaʿnī sajʿa l-kalām wa-taḥsīnahu.*

[63] Al-Fākihī, *Taʾrīkh makka*, Ms. Leiden, Or. 463, fol. 380a, 11. 2-3.

[64] Note 22.

[65] Abū ʿAbdallāh al-Ṣūrī, *Juzʾ*, Leiden, Or. 2465, fols. 7a-b, 8b; Nūr al-Dīn al-Haythamī, *op. cit*., II, 223; al-Muttaqī l-Hindī, *Kanz al-ʿummāl*. Hyderabad 1374/1954, V, 16, 77-78, nos. 138, 634-635; Murtaḍā l-Zabīdī, *op. cit*., IV 337 inf.

in taghfiri llāhumma tagfir jammā:
wa-ayyu ʿabdin laka lā alammā:[66]

Al-Ṭabarī who reports on the authority of Mujāhid that the people used to circumambulate the Kaʿba uttering the second verse: *in taghfiri llāhuma* . . .[67] records however another tradition saying that the Prophet recited this verse.[68] According to a tradition recorded by Ibn Manẓūr the second verse (*in taghfir* . . .) was composed by Umayya b. abī l-Ṣalt.[69] The verse is indeed ascribed to Umayya b. abī l-Ṣalt in the *Kitāb al-Aghānī* and two versions are related about the circumstances in which Umayya composed the verse: according to al-Zuhrī he uttered it during the miraculous opening of his breast; according to Thābit b. al-Zubayr he recited it before his death.[70] According to a tradition reported by Ibn al-Kalbī the verse was uttered by al-Dayyān (the ancestor of the Banū l-Dayyān)[71] during his prayer.[72] These verses (with the variant: *allāhumma hādhā wāḥidun in tammā* . . .) are recorded by Ḥusain as the *talbiya* of the Ashʿariyyūn.[73] Muqātil records a talk between ʿUmar and Abū Burda (the son of Abū Mūsā al-Ashʿārī) in which he asked him about the *talbiya* of the Ashʿariyyūn. Abū Burda quoted the following form of their Jāhilī *talbiya: allāhumma hādhā wāḥidun innamā:*[74] *athamahu llāhu wa-qad athimā: in taghfiri llāhumma* . . .[75] It is thus a divergent version with a different intent: God knows the sins of the men who commit them (and will certainly punish them – K); if God forgives He will forgive them all together, as there is no believer who has not sinned.

The four hemistichs seem to have been a widely current popular invocation and their authorship was, as usually in such cases, ascribed to different poets, or recorded as a ritual invocation of individuals or groups.[75a]

---

[66] *L'A* s.v. l m m; al-Suyūṭī, *Sharḥ shawāhid al-mughnī*, ed. al-Shanqīṭī, rev. Aḥmad Ẓāfir Kūjān, Damascus 1386/1966, p.625, no.388 (with the variant in the first hemistich: *hādhā rābi'un*); Aḥmad b. Ḥamdān al-Rāzī, *op. cit.*, II, 15.

[67] Al-Ṭabarī, *Tafsīr* (Būlāq) XXVII, 40; al-Suyūṭī, *Sharḥ shawāhid*, p. 625.

[68] Al-Ṭabarī, *Tafsīr*, XXVII, 39; al-Qurṭubī, *Tafsīr*, XVII, 107; al-Suyūṭī, *al-Durr al-manthūr*, VI, 127 inf.; al-Munāwī, *Fayḍ al-qadīr*, Cairo 1391/1972, III, 28, no. 2662; cf. *L'A*, s.v. jmm.

[69] *L'A*, s.v. l m m.

[70] *Aghānī* (Būlāq) III, 190-191; al-Damīrī, *Ḥayāt al-ḥayawān*, Cairo 1383/1963, II, 402-403; al-Jumaḥī, *Ṭabaqāt fuḥūl al-shu'arā'*, ed. Maḥmūd Shākir, Cairo 1952, pp. 223-224 (and see the references of the editor, p. 224, note 3); and see Ṣadr al-Dīn al-Baṣrī, *al-Ḥamāsa al-baṣriyya*, ed. Mukhtār al-Dīn Aḥmad, Hyderabad 1383/1964, II, 431, no. 53 (and see the references recorded by the editor); 'Abd al-Qādir al-Baghdādī, *Khizānat al-adab*, ed. 'Abd al-Salām Hārūn, Cairo 1388/1968, II, 295-296 (and see the references given by the editor); Ibn Ḥajar, *al-Iṣāba*, I, 252.

[71] See on him Ibn Ḥazm, *Jamharat ansāb al-'arab*, ed. 'Abd al-Salām Hārūn, Cairo 1962, p. 416.

[72] *Aghānī*, X, 146, penult.

[73] Ḥusain, *op cit.*, p. 365, no. 3.

[74] The metre here is defective. Perhaps: *lāhumma* has to be read.

[75] Muqātil, *op. cit.*, 24a (no. 51).

[75a] Cf. 'Abd al Qādir al-Baghdādī, *op. cit.*, II, 295.

The two last hemistichs were adopted by the Prophet and uttered by him in his invocation. This is another instance for the way in which Jāhilī pious ideas tainted by a shade of monotheism were taken up by Islam.

The delegation of Najrān, who journeyed to Medina to meet the Prophet, was preceded by Kurz b. ʿAlqama who uttered the following *rajaz* verses:

ilayka taʿdū qaliqan waḍīnuhā:
muʿtariḍan fī baṭnihā janīnuhā:
mukhālifan dīna l-naṣārā dīnuhā[76]

Several traditions report that ʿUmar recited these verses when driving his riding beast swiftly through the Wādī Muḥassir during his *ḥajj.*[77] Another tradition relates that the Prophet uttered these verses when on his *ifāḍa* from ʿArafa.[78]

It is quite significant that these *rajaz* verses, marked as a piece of Yamanī poetry, are recorded as the *talbiya* of the Asad and Ghaṭafān.[79] These *rajaz*-verses are yet another case of the absorption of Jāhilī material, whereby it was transformed into a part of the Muslim ritual invocation.

According to current tradition the tribal *talbiyāt* were prohibited and were substituted by a Muslim formula. This is clearly reflected in the story of ʿAmr b. Maʿdīkarib, reported on the authority of Sharqī b. Quṭāmī: the old tribal *talbiya*, telling about the strenuous efforts of the journey and about the idols left void behind them, was replaced by the prescribed Muslim *talbiya.*[80] The case of the *talbiya* of Zubayd, as recorded by Muqātil, is however different. The Jāhilī *talbiya* mentioned above was replaced by a new one in which God is addressed as "the Lord of the lords" (*rabbu l-arbāb*) and "the Subduer of every idol and graven image in the land" (*qāhiru kulli wathanin wa-ṣanamin fī l-bilād*).[81] It is the only

---

[76] Ibn Sa'd, *op. cit.*, I, 357; Ibn Ḥajar, *al-Iṣāba*, V, 586, no. 7403; al-Kalāʿī, *al-Iktifā*, I, 259.

[77] Al-Bayhaqī, *al-Sunan al-kubrā*, V, 126; al-Bakrī, *Muʿjam mā staʿjam*, ed. Muṣṭafā l-Saqā, Cairo 1368/1949, pp. 1191 inf. – 1192; Ibn Abī Shayba, *al-Muṣannaf*, ed. ʿAbd al-Khāliq al-Afghānī, Hyderabad 1386/1966, IV, 81; Nūr al-Dīn al-Haythamī, *op. cit.*, III, 256; *L'A*, s.v. wḍn; al-Muttaqī l-Hindī, *op. cit.*, V, 116, no. 866, 111, no. 837 (with the hemistich: *wa-ayyu ʿabdin laka lā alammā*, added); Muḥibb al-Dīn al-Ṭabarī, *op. cit.*, p. 414; Ibn al-Athīr, *al-Nihāya, s.v. wḍn; cf.* al-Fākihī, *op. cit.*, fol. 531a; and see Abū ʿUbayda, *Majāz al-Qur'ān*, ed. F. Sezgin, Cairo, 1381/1962, II, 249, no. 898, Murtaḍā l-Zabīdī, *op. cit.*, IV, 386.

[78] Ibn al-Athīr, *al-Nihāya*, s.v. wḍn; *L'A*, s.v. w d n; Muḥibb al-Dīn al-Tabarī, *op. cit.*, p. 414; Nūr al-Dīn al-Haythamī, *op. cit.*, III, 156.

[79] Muqātil, *op. cit.*, 22a (no. 8).

[80] Al-Ṭabarānī, *al-Muʿjam al-ṣaghīr*, ed. ʿAbd al-Raḥmān ʿUthmān, Cairo 1388/1968, I, 59; Nūr al-Dīn al-Haythamī. *op. cit.*, III, 111; al-Ṭaḥāwī, *Sharḥ maʿānī l-āthār*, II, 124-125; Ibn al-Athīr, *Usd al-ghāba*, IV, 133; Ibn Ḥajar, *al-Iṣāba*, IV, 690; Ibn ʿAbd al-Barr, *al-Istīʿab*, ed. ʿAlī Muḥammad al-Bijāwī, Cairo 1380/1960, p. 1203; al-Khaṭīb al-Baghdādī, *Ta'rīkh*, V, 282.

[81] Muqātil, *op. cit.*, 24a (no.49).

case in which a separate *talbiya* of a tribe is mentioned in the period of Islam. It is interesting to note that this *talbiya* stresses the struggle of God against the gods and the idols and His subjugation of them, thus giving a clear idea how Islam was conceived by the tribes in its nascent period.

The animosities between the tribes are reflected in the *talbiyāt* of ʿAbd al-Qays and Qays ʿAylān. The Qays ʿAylān in their *talbiya* make the complaint that Bakr (scil. b. Wāʾil) interpose between them and God; people obey God, while Bakr disbelieve Him. Were it not for Bakr b. Wāʾil people would set out in crowds for the pilgrimage.[82] The worshippers of Dhū l-Lība (i.e. the ʿAbd al-Qays) invoke God that He may turn Muḍar away from them, make the journey safe and relieve them from the lords of Hajar.[83]

The complaint of the ʿAbd al-Qays recurs in fact in another setting: when the delegation of ʿAbd al-Qays came to the Prophet they complained that they were unable to reach Medina, save during the holy months, because the Muḍar-tribes stood in their way.[84]

Different in content and in setting is the *talbiya* of Adam. Adam mentions that God created him with His own hand, bestowed on him graces and attests that God is the Lord of the House (i.e. the Kaʿba).[85] It is apparent that this *talbiya*, in contradistinction to the other Jāhilī ones, is rooted in the Muslim concept of the role of Adam and of other prophets in establishing the *ḥajj* and its rites. Adam built the Kaʿba;[86] he is said to have performed the *ḥajj* from India seventy times.[87] Prophets

---

82 Muqātil, *op. cit.*, fol. 22a (no. 5), 22b (no. 22, given as the *talbiya* of the worshippers of Manāt; and so Ibn Ḥabīb, *al-Muḥabbar* p. 313); see Abū l-ʿAlāʾ, *op. cit.*, p. 536 (recorded as the *talbiya* of Tamīm).

83 Muqātil, *op. cit.*, fol. 23a (no. 27); Ibn Ḥabīb, *al-Muḥabbar*, p. 314.

84 See e.g. al-Zurqānī, *Sharḥ al-mawāhib al-laduniyya*, Cairo 1327, IV, 13-14; Ibn Kathīr, *al-Sīra al-nabawiyya*, ed. Muṣṭafā ʿAbd al-Wāḥid, Cairo 1385/1966, IV, 88; ʿAlī b. Burhān al-Dīn, *Insān al-ʿuyūn* (= *al-Sīra al-ḥalabiyya*), Cairo, 1382/1962, III, 251. The animosity between Tamīm and Rabīʿa was reflected in certain *ḥajj*-practices: the tribes used to rally in al-Muḥaṣṣab and would leave according to an established order, to avoid clashes among them. Ibn ʿAbbās remarked that Tamīm and Rabīʿa used to fear each other (*kānat banū tamīmin wa-rabīʿatu takhāfu baʿḍuhā baʿḍan*). See al-Fākihī, *op. cit.*, fol. 481b.

85 Muqātil, *op. cit.*, fol. 22b (no. 10).

86 See e.g. Muḥibb al-Dīn al-Ṭabarī, *op. cit.*, p. 47 inf.; al-Ṣāliḥī, *Subul al-hudā wa-l-rashād*, ed. Muṣṭafā ʿAbd al-Wāḥid I, 167 (1.4 from bottom) I, 167, 168 (1.3 from bottom), 168, (1.3 from bottom), 171-172; al-Khuwārizmī, *Ithāratu l-targhīb wa-l-tashwīq ilā l-masājidi l-thalāthati wa-ilā l-bayti l-ʿatīq*, Ms. Br. Mus., Or. 4584, fol. 17a, 1.4; cf. Murtaḍā l-Zabīdī, *op. cit.*, IV, 356 sup.

87 Al-Isfarāʾīnī, *Zubdatu l-aʿmāl*, Ms. Br. Mus., Or. 3034, fol. 35a (or 40 times as *Ibid.*, fol. 36a); Muḥibb al-Dīn al-Ṭabarī, *op. cit.*, p. 48 sup.; al-Ṣāliḥī, *op. cit.*, I, 242-243; and see al-Daylamī, *Firdaus*, Ms. Chester Beatty 3037, fol. 117a, inf.: *qad atā ādamu hādhā l-bayta alfa utyatin mina l-hindi ʿalā rijlayhi, lam yarkab fīhinna min dhālika thalātha miʾati ḥajjatin wa-sabʿa miʾati ʿumratin, wa-awwalu ḥajjatin ḥajjahā ādamu wa-huwa wāqifun bi-ʿarafātin atāhu jibrīlu fa-qāla yā ādamu burra nuskuka, amā innā qad ṭufnā bi-hādhā l-bayti qabla an tukhlaqa bi-khamsīna alfa sanatin.*

and saints used since then to perform the pilgrimage, mostly walking, and used to utter the *talbiya* in various forms.[88] It is evident that the Muslim *talbiya* is, according to Muslim concepts, an adequate extension of the *talbiyāt* uttered by the prophets while performing their *ḥajj* to the Kaʿba in Mecca.

III

Muslim scholars differ in their assessment of the position of the *talbiya*: whether it has to be considered a *sunna*, an obligatory practice (*wājib*), a recommended practice (*mandūb*), or an essential part of the *iḥrām*.[89] Neither are they unanimous concerning the form of the *talbiya*: some of them approve of an addition to the widely circulated *talbiya* of the Prophet and adduce various versions of the *talbiya*, others recommend to adhere to the accepted wording of the *talbiya*.[90] A rather liberal opinion is given by al-Ḥarbī: the *muḥrim* utters his *talbiya* in whatever way he likes.[91]

According to a widely current tradition the Prophet was ordered by the angel Jibrīl to enjoin his Companions to utter the *talbiya* in a loud voice; the best pilgrimage was considered to be one which combined the loud cry of the *talbiya* with the slaughter of the sacrifice (*afḍalu l-ḥajj al-ʿajj wa-l-thajj*). The Companions used to recite it in such a loud voice that they would become hoarse.[92] There

[88] See e.g. Aḥmad b. Ḥanbal, *Kitāb al-zuhd*, Beirut 1396/1976, pp. 58, 74, 87; al-Bayhaqī, *al-Sunan al-kubrā*, V, 42; al-Ṣāliḥī, *op. cit.*, I, 243-247; Muḥibb al-Dīn al-Ṭabarī, *op. cit.*, pp. 49-56; al-Mundhirī, *al-Tarhīb*, ed. Muḥammad Muḥyī l-Dīn ʿAbd al-Ḥamīd, Cairo 1380/1961, III, 20-22, nos. 1657-1662; al-Muttaqī l-Hindī, *op. cit.*, V, 78, no. 636; al-Qasṭallānī, *Irshād al-sārī*, III, 115; Nūr al-Dīn al-Haythamī, *op. cit.*, III, 220-222; al-ʿAynī, *op. cit.*, IX, 173; al-Nuwayrī, *Nihāyat al-arab*, Cairo n.d. I, 309-310; al-Majlisī, *Biḥār al-anwār*, XCIX, 44, no. 33; Ibn Bābūyah, *ʿIlal al-sharāʾiʿ*, pp. 418-419.

[89] Al-Zurqānī, *Sharḥ al-muwaṭṭaʾ*, III, 44, al-Shaukānī, *Nayl al-auṭār*, Cairo 1380/1961, IV, 359 ult. – 360; Amīn Maḥmūd Khaṭṭāb, *op. cit.*, I, 111-112 sup.; al-ʿAynī, *op. cit.*, IX, 171 inf.; al-Qasṭallānī, *op. cit.*, III, 113; Ibn Ḥajar, *Fatḥ*, III, 326 inf. – 327.

[90] Al-Shāfiʿī, *op. cit.*, II, 132-133, 186; al-Zurqānī, *Sharḥ al-muwaṭṭaʾ*, III, 34-37; Nūr al-Dīn al-Haythamī, *op. cit.*, III, 222; al-Shaukānī, *op. cit.*, IV, 359; Muḥibb al-Dīn al-Ṭabarī, *op. cit.*, pp. 173-174 (and see pp. 424, 430); Amīn Maḥmūd Khaṭṭāb, *op. cit.*, I, 109, 112-113; al-ʿAynī, *op. cit.*, IX, 173; Ibn Ḥajar, *Fatḥ*, III, 325-326; al-Qasṭallānī, *op. cit.*, III, 114-115.

[91] Al-Ḥarbī, *op. cit.*, p. 429: . . . *wa-kayfamā shāʾa l-muḥrimu an yulabbiya labbā*.

[92] See e.g. Abū Yūsuf, *op. cit.*, p. 95, no. 459; al-Shāfiʿī, *op. cit.*, II, 133; al-Ḥarbī, *op. cit.*, p. 429; al-Shaukānī, *op. cit.*, IV, 360 inf. –361; Muḥibb al-Dīn al-Ṭabarī, *op. cit.*, pp. 171-172; Amīn Maḥmūd al-Khaṭṭāb, *op. cit.*, I, 114-115; al-Zurqānī, *Sharḥ al-muwaṭṭaʾ*, III, 44-45; al-Mundhirī, *op. cit.*, III, 23 (no. 1663), 25 (nos. 1667-1668, 1670); al-Ḥākim, *al-Mustadrak*, I, 450-451; al-Munāwī, *Fayḍ al-qadīr*, II, 31, no. 1248; Ibn Qayyim al-Jauziyya, *Iʿlām al-muwaqqiʿīn*, Beirut 1973, IV, 299; Ibn al-Athīr, *al-Nihāya*, s.v. ʿajj; Ibn Ḥajar, *Fatḥ*, III, 324; al-Qasṭallānī, *op. cit.*, III, 113; *LʿA*, s.v. th j j, ʿa j j; Murtaḍā l-Zabīdī, *op. cit.*, IV, 338; cf. Muḥammad Nāṣir al-Albānī, *Silsilat al-aḥādīth al-ṣaḥīḥa*, Damascus 1392/1972, p. 504, no. 830; and see Gaudefroy Demombynes, *op. cit.*, p. 184.

were, however, other traditions, mitigating ones, which warned of too loud cries which might cause harm to the pilgrims.

It was recommended that the pilgrim utter the *talbiya* at every spot and in various positions: riding, alighting, lying, ascending a hill or a mountain, descending into a valley, at meeting of caravans, in markets and in mosques; some scholars however tried to confine the permission to utter the *talbiya* to certain mosques in Mecca. It is advisable, according to some, that the *talbiya* be followed by an invocation for the Prophet (*al-ṣalāt ʿalā l-nabiyyi, ṣallā llāhu ʿalayhi wa-sallam*).[93] It was permitted to utter the *talbiya* in foreign languages too, even by a person with a good knowledge of Arabic.[94]

Scholars were not unanimous with regard to the place where the Prophet commenced the utterance of the *talbiya* nor about the time and the place where he concluded it.[95]

The divergencies of scholarly opinions about the various practices of the *talbiya* bear evidence that the mandatory forms of the *talbiya* had not been established by the end of the second century of the *hijra*, as already pointed out by Gaudefroy Demombynes.[96] The *talbiya* was however incorporated in the rites of the pilgrimage by the unanimous opinion of Muslim scholars, and its merits and rewards were recorded in the compilations of *ḥadīth*.[97]

IV

The chapter of the *talbiyāt* in Muqātil's *Tafsīr* gives us a clue for a better understanding of the religious ideas of the tribes during the period of the Jāhiliyya. The tribes of course had their gods and the places of worship of these gods were usually shared by other tribes allied with them or living in their neighbourhood. They believed however in a supreme God, who had His House in Mecca. On their pilgrimage to Mecca they directed themselves to this God, who held supremacy over their tribal gods. The relation between God and their gods, as perceived by the tribes, is reflected in the report of al-Yaʿqūbī: when intending to perform the

---

93 Al-Shāfiʿī, *op. cit.*, II, 133-134, 186; al-Zurqānī, *Sharḥ al-muwaṭṭa'*, III, 46; Muḥibb al-Dīn al-Ṭabarī, *op. cit.*, pp. 172-180; al-Ḥarbī, *op. cit.*, p. 429; Amīn Maḥmūd Khaṭṭāb, *op. cit.*, I, 111, 115; and see Gaudefroy Demombynes, *op. cit.*, 181, 183-184; Murtaḍā l-Zabīdī, *op. cit.*, IV, 339.

94 Amīn Maḥmūd Khaṭṭāb, *op. cit.*, I, 111; Gaudefroy Demombynes, *op. cit.*, p. 180.

95 See e.g. Ibn Ḥajar, *Fatḥ*, III, 317 inf. –318; al-ʿAynī, *op. cit.*, IX, 159-160; al-Zurqānī, *Sharḥ al-muwaṭṭa'*, III, 37-38, 43; Nūr al-Dīn al-Haythamī, *op. cit.*, III, 221; al-Ṭaḥāwī, *Sharḥ maʿānī l-āthār*, II, 120-123; al-Shaukānī, *op. cit.*, IV, 360-361; Muḥibb al-Dīn al-Ṭabarī, *op. cit.*, pp. 180-184 (and see pp. 415-416); Amīn Maḥmūd Khaṭṭāb, *op. cit.*, I, 31-35, 116-121; Gaudefroy Demombynes, *op. cit.*, pp. 181-183.

96 Gaudefroy Demombynes, *op. cit.*, p. 183.

97 See e.g. al-Mundhirī, *op. cit.*, III, 24-26, nos. 1665-1666, 1669, 1671; al-Ḥākim, *op. cit.*, I, 451; al-Tibrīzī, *Mishkāt al-maṣābīḥ*, Karachi 1350, p. 223 inf.; Nūr al-Dīn al Haythamī, *op. cit.*, III, 223 ult.; Muḥibb al-Dīn al-Ṭabarī. *op. cit.*, pp. 41, 70; see al-Daylamī, *Firdaus*, Ms. Chester Beatty 3037, fol. 157b: *man labbā sabʿīna marratan fī iḥrāmihi ashhada llāhu ʿazza wa-jalla sabʿīna alfa malakin lahu bi-barāʾatin min al-nāri wa-barāʾatin min al-nifāqi.*

pilgrimage to the Sanctuary at Mecca every tribe would come to (the abode of) their idol and pray there; then they would set out uttering the *talbiya* (on their journey – K) until they reached Mecca.[98] This report demonstrates to what extent there prevailed harmonious co-existence and co-operation between the tribal deities and the supreme God of Mecca. The Jāhiliyya tribes cannot be said to have been straightforward polytheists; they were *mushrikūn*, i.e. while accepting and admitting the existence and supreme authority of God, they associated other deities with Him.

The *talbiyāt* expose a remarkably rich religious vocabulary and terminology. The attributes of God are well attested in the two monotheistic faiths preceding Islam and are recurring in the Qurʾān.[99] It is the merit of Brockelmann, who in his study of the religious terms in the extant compilations of ancient Arabic poetry, adduced an abundant body of references to Allāh and Raḥmān in the Jāhilī poetry. Brockelmann also pointed out the various expressions pertaining to the conception of Allāh in the Jāhiliyya: God the Creator, the Lord of the creatures, the Omnipotent; God punishes and grants rewards; this is why He ought to be feared, revered, and praised. Brockelmann shows that expressions like *ḥamd*, *khashya, hudā, taqwā* occurring in the Jāhilī poetry suggest a kind of religious perception of a High God akin to that of *El-ʿOlam* and *El-ʿElyon*. Admitting that some details of the Genesis-story of creation might have reached Arabia, Brockelmann refutes definitely the assumption that the concept of Allāh might have been borrowed from one of the religions of Revelation or originated from animism.[100] Gibb, starting from a quite different point and using different material arrives at a rather similar conclusion, stressing the original Arabian concepts of monotheism which developed in the Arab peninsula and denying the hypothesis of a Jewish or Christian source for the Qurʾān.[101] In another article Gibb analyses the process of the rededication of the Jāhilī religious symbolism and the re-interpretation of the religious terms of the Jāhiliyya into the monotheistic, Muslim ones.[102] They are moulded in the genuine old Arabic forms of *sajʿ* and *rajaz* and expose the belief in the supreme God of the Kaʿba, Allāh, associated with tribal gods; this was an indigenous religious tradition, developed in the Arabian peninsula,

---

[98] Al-Yaʿqūbī, *op. cit.*, I, 296.

[99] See W. Montgomery Watt, "Belief in a 'High God' in Pre-Islamic Mecca," *JSS* 16(1971) pp. 35-40; the assumption on p. 40 about the pre-nomadic agriculture times in which the deities represented the neutral forces, thus forming "a vigorous paganism" in contradistinction to the Bedouin for whom "it was not incongruous that Allah rather than the pagan deities should send rain and supply man with his *rizq* or provision," seems, however, not to be based on solid textual evidence.

[100] C. Brockelmann, "Allah und die Götzen, der Ursprung des islamischen Monotheismus," *Archiv für Religionswissenschaft* 21 (1922) 99-121.

[101] H.A.R. Gibb, "Pre-Islamic Monotheism in Arabia", pp.269, 271, 277 inf.-278; and see *idem, Studies on the Civilization of Islam,* ed. S.J. Shaw and W.R. Polk, Boston 1962, p. 192; Cf. C. Torrey, *The Jewish Foundation of Islam*, New York 1933, pp. 54-56; W. Montgomery Watt, *Muhammad at Mecca,* Oxford 1953, pp. 158-161.

[102] H.A.R. Gibb, *Studies on the Civilization of Islam,* pp. 176-192.

and reflecting the peculiar setting of co-operation between the tribes and Mecca. It was against the people who recited these *talbiyāt*, the *mushrikūn*, that Muḥammad preached his exclusive monotheistic ideas. It is thus not surprising that some of the expressions and terms in these *talbiyāt* found their way into the Qurʾān. Re-interpreted and transformed they coalesced with other elements to form the body of ideas represented by the religious literature of Islam.

Addenda

Note 3: See: al-Samarqandī, *Tafsīr*, Ms. Chester Beatty 3668/II, fol. 37a; Muqātil, *Tafsīr*, Ms. Ahmet III, 74/II, fol. 78a; Ibn Qayyim al-Jauziyya, *Ighāthat al-lahfān min maṣāyid al-shayṭān*, ed. Muḥammad Ḥāmid al-Fiqī, Cairo 1358/1939, II, 210, 245.

Note 4: See Ibn Qayyim al-Jauziyya, *Badāʾiʿ al-fawāʾid*, Beirut, n.d. (repr.) II, 214–215; Ibn Abī Ḥātim al-Rāzī, *ʿIlal al-ḥadīth* , ed. Muḥibb al-Dīn al-Khaṭīb, Cairo 1343, I, nos. 842, 843, 876, 888; al-Nawawī, *al-Adhkār*, Cairo 1324, p. 87; Ghulām Thaʿlab, *Juzʾ*, Ms. Chester Beatty 3495 (*majmūʿa*), fol. 96b; Abū Nuʿaym, *Ḥilyat al-auliyāʾ*, IX, 28; al-Ṭabarī, *Tafsīr*, ed. Shākir, XIII, 512, No. 16000; al-Ṭabarānī. *al-Muʿjam al-ṣaghīr*, ed. ʿAbd al-Raḥmān ʿUthmān, al-Madīna al-munawwara 1388/1968, I, 87.

Note 38: See F. Rosenthal, "Some Minor Problems in the Qurʾān", *The Joshua Starr Memorial Volume*, New York 1953, pp. 72–83; Rudi Paret, "Der Ausdruck *ṣamad* in Sure 112,2," *Der Islam* 1979, pp. 294–295.

Note 55: Cf. Ibn Abī l-Dunyā, *al-Ishrāf fī manāzil al-ashrāf*, Ms. Chester Beatty 4427, fol. 43a: . . . *kānat imraʾatun jāhiliyyatun taṭūfu bi-l-bayti wa-lahā sittatu banīna yasturūnahā min al-nāsi wa-hiya taqūlu fī ṭawāfihā* . . .

Note 76: Cf. Ibn Ḥajar, *al-Iṣāba*, V, 586, No. 7403.

Note 80: See Ibn Athīr, *Usd al-ghāba*, IV, 133.

I [ج ٢,و ٢٢ أ] واجتنبوا قول الزور ، يقول : اتقوا الكذب ، وهو الشرك • حدثنا ابومحمد قال حدثني أبي قال حدثنا الهذيل عن مقاتل عن محمد بن علي في قوله تعالى واجتنبوا قول الزور قال : الكذب وهو الشرك في التلبية •

(١) وذلك أن الحمس ، قريشاوخزاعة وكنانة وعامر بن صعصعة ، في الجاهلية كانوا يقولون في التلبية : لبيك اللهم لبيك ، لبيك لا شريك لك الا شريكا هو لك تملكه وما ملك ؛ يعنون الملائكة التي تعبد ؛ هذا قول الزور لقولهم : الا شريك هو لك •

(٢) وكان اهل اليمن في الجاهلية يقولون في التلبية : نحن غرابا ١ عكّ ، عكّ اليك ٢ عانيه عبادك اليمانيه ، كيما نحج الثانيه ، على القلاص الناجيه •

(٣) وكانت تميم ١ تقول : لبيك ما نهارنا نجرّه ، ادلاجه وبرده وحرّه ، لانتقي شيئا ٢ ولانضرّه ، حجّا لربّ مستقيم برّه •

(٤) وكانت ربيعة تقول : لبيك اللهمّ حجّا حقّا ، تعبدا ورقّا ، لم نأتك للمناحه ، ١ ولا حبّا ٢ للرباحه •

(٥) وكانت قيس عيلان تقول : لبيك لولا أن بكرا دونكا ، ١ بنو غفار ٢ وهم يلونك ، ٣ يبرك الناس ويفجرونكا ، مازال منّا عجيج ٤ يأتونكا •

(٦) وكانت جرهم تقول : لبّيك انّ جرهما عبادك ، والناس طرف وهم تلادك ، ١ وهم لعمري عمروا بلادك ، لايطاق ربّنا بعادك ، وهم الاولون على ميعادك ، فان (١) يعادوا ٢ كلّ من يعادك ، حتى يقيموا الدين في وادك ٣ •

ألرموز:

أح = Saray, Ahmet III, 74I-II
ك = Köprulu[143]
ح = Hamīdiyya 58
حس = H. Hüsnü 17

[I] (١) ١ قارن ابن الكلبي ، الاصنام ص ٧ •

(٢) ١ كوح : نحن ام عكا؛ س وحس وأح : نحن ابا عك ؛ والنص الذى اورداه هو عن المحبر ص ٣١٣. ٢ اليك ــ محذوف في ك و ح •

(٣) ١ في كوح : وكانت تيم ٢ في كوح : سنا ولا يضره.

(٤) ١ في ك و ح : للمناجه •••• للرقاحه ؛ ويبدو أنّ النص الصحيح هو الذي ورد في المحبر ص ٣١٣ ، السطر الاخير : للمياحه •••• للرقاحه • قارن حسين رقم ٤،٦،٢٥ • ٢ أح وسوحس : ولاجا.

(٥) ١ الى هنا في أحوحس وس؛والزيادة في النص الذياورداه من كوح. ٢ كذا في كوح ؛ وقارن رقم ٢٢ أدناه : بني غطفان • ٣ في كوح : يلوك • ٤ في ك و ح : على عجيجا؛في المحبر: حجّ ، عثج ؛ في رسالة الغفران : عثج ؛ وانظر لسان العرب : عثج •

(٦) ١ مي كوح : وهم عبادك وهم الدين سسل (؟) وادك • ٢ في كوح : وهم يعادوا كل من عاداك • ٣ في كح : في فادك ولا يطاق ربنا بعادك.

(٧) وكانت قضاعة تقول : لبيك ربّ الحلّ والاحرام ، ارحم مقام أعبد ١ وآم ، أتوك يمشون على الاقدام .

(٨) وكانت أسد وغطفان تقول في احرامها بشعر اليمن١ : لبّيك اليك ٢ تعدو قلقا وضينها ، معترضا في بطنها جنينها ، ٣ مخالفا لدين ٤ النصارى دينها .

(٩) وكنّ النساء يطفن بالبيت ١ عراة ، تأخذ احداهن حاشية برد تستتر به وتقول : اليوم يبدو بعضه أو كله ، وما ٢ بدا منه فلا احله ، كم من ٣ لبيب عقله يضله ، وناظر ٤ ينظر فما يمله ، ضخم من الجثم ٥ عظيم ظلّه .

[و ٢٢ ب](١٠) وكانت تلبية آدم عليه السلام ١ : لبيك اللهمّ لبيك ، لبيك عبدا خلقته بيديك ، كرمت فأعطيت ، قربت فأدنيت ، تباركت وتعاليت ، أنت ربّ البيت .

فأنزل الله تعالى : واجتنبوا قول الزور حين قالوا : لا شريك لك الا شريكا هو لك ، تملكه وما ملك . ٢

. تلبية العرب في الجاهلية .

(١١) وكانت قريش تنسك لاساف ، وكانت تلبيتها : لبيك اللهمّ لبيك ، لبيك لا شريك لك ، الاشريك هو لك ، تملكه وما ملك .

(١٢) وكانت تلبية من نسك للعزى : لبيك اللهمّ لبيك ، لبيك ١ وسعديك،لبيك ما أحبّنا اليك .

(١٣) وكانت تلبية من نسك للات ١ : لبيك اللهمّ لبيك ، كفى ٢ ببيتنا بنيه ، ليس بمهجور ولا بليه ، لكنه من تربة زكيه ، أربابه من أصلح ٣ البريه .

(١٤) وكانت تلبية من نسك لجهار: لبيك اللهم لبيك، ١ اجعل ذنوبنا جبارا ،واهدنا لاصلح المنارا ٢ ، ومتعنا وملنا جهارا . ٣

---

(٧) ١ في أحوس : عبد . ومي كوح : أعبد ؛ قارن أدناه رقم ٤٦ .

(٨) ١ بشعر اليمن محذوف في كوح. ٢ اليك حذف في أحوس وحس .
٣ في كوح : في بطنها معترضا جنينها. ٤ في أحوس وحس : لذي النصارى ؛ في كوح : مخالفا دين النصارى دينها .

(٩)١ في كوح : بالبيت بالليل. ٢ في كوح : فما. ٣ "من" حذف في كوح. ٤ في كوح :أو ناظر. ٥ في أحوس وحس: من الحشم؛ ك و ح من الحد(!).

(١٠) في ك و ح :آدم صلى الله عليه وسلم. ٢ في كوح : فأنزل الله : واجتنبوا قول الزور،وهو الشرك في التلبية ؛حدثنا عبد الله قال : حدثنا ابي قال ، حدثنا الهذيل عن مقاتل عن الضحاك في قول الله عز وجل :واجتنبوا قول الزور قال: يقال هو اعياد المشركين ، الشعانين (في النص : السعانين) وغيره ؛ فذلك قول الله للحمس : اجتنبوا قول الزور حين قالوا : الا شريكا هو لك ؛ وأنظر مقاتل أ ح و٢٤ب .

(١٢) ١ لبيك حذف في أح وس وحس؛والزيادة عن المحبر ص ٣١١ .

(١٣) ١ في أح وس وحس: للاب . ٢ في أح وس وحس: كفا . ٣ في المحبر ص ٣١٢ : من صالحي .

(١٤) ١ في المحبر ص ٣١٢ : ... لبيك ، لبيك اجعل . ٢ في المحبر: جبار ، واهدنا لاوضح المنار . ٣ في المحبر : وملنا بجهار .

(١٥) وكانت تلبية من نسك لسواع : لبيك اللهمّ لبيك ، لبيك أنبنا١ اليك ، ان سواعا طليق ٢ اليك •

(١٦) وكانت تلبية من نسك للشمس ١ : لبيك اللهمّ لبيك، لبيك ما نهارنا نجره ، ادلاجه وحرّه وقرّه ، لا نتقي شيئا ولا نضره ، حجّا مستقيما برّه ٢٠

(١٧) وكانت تلبية من نسك لمحرق : لبيك اللهمّ لبيك ، لبيك حجّا حقّا ، تعبدا ورقّا •

(١٨) وكانت تلبية من نسك لودّ : لبيك اللهم لبيك ، لبيك معذرة اليك.

(١٩) وكانت تلبية من نسك لذي الخلصة ١ : لبيك اللهمّ لبيك ، لبيك لما هو واجب اليك ٢٠

(٢٠) وكانت تلبية من نسك لمنطبق : لبيك اللهمّ لبيك ١٠

(٢١) وكانت تلبية عكّ اذا بلغوا مكة يبعثون غلامين يسيران على جمل مملوكين قد جردا عرايا ، ١ فلا يزيدان على ان يقولا : نحن غرابا ٢ عكّ ، فاذا نادى الغلامان ذلك صاح من خلفهما من عك : عك اليك عانيه ، عبادك اليمانيه ، كيمانحجّ الثانيه ، على القلاص ٣ الناجيه ٤٠

(٢٢) وكانت تلبية من نسك مناة : لبيك اللهم لبيك ،لبيك لولا ان بكرا دونكا ، بني غطفان وهم يلونكا ،١ تبرّك الناس ويفجرونكا ، ٢ ما زال منّا عجيجا٣ يأتونكا، انا على عدوتهم ٤ من دونكا •

(٢٣) وكانت تلبية من نسك لسعيد ١ : لبيك اللهمّ لبيك ، لم نأتك للمياحه ،٢ ولا لطلب الرباحه ، ٢ ولكن جئناك للطاعه ٣٠

---

(١٥) ١ في المحبر ص ٣١٢ : ابنا • ٢ في المحبر: طُلِبن •

(١٦) ١ في هامش أ ح ملاحظة الناسخ : " يوخذ من كلامه الاتي أن الشمس هنا وثن وكان لبني تميم • الكاتب " • ٢ في المحبر ص ٣١٢ : حجا لرب مستقيم بره •

(١٩) ١ في المحبر ص ٣١٢ : ذا الخلصة • ٢ في المحبر : بما هو احب اليك.

(٢٠) ١ في المحبر ص ٣١٣ س ١ : ••• لبيك ، لبيك •

(٢١) ١ في المحبر ص٣١٣ : ••• قد جردا فهما عريانان.٢ في أ ح و س وحس : عرايا. ٣ في المحبر : على الشداد • ٤ راجع تلبية عكّ : ابن الكلبي،الاصنام ص٧ •

(٢٢) ١" بني غطفان وهم يلونكا " محذوف في نص المحبر ص ٣١٣ • ٢ في المحبر : ويهجرونك • ٣ في المحبر : ما زال حجّ عثج ;وانظرملاحظة محمد حميد الله رقم ٣ • ٤ في المحبر : على عدوائهم ; وقارن رسالة الغفران ص ٥٣٦ •

(٢٣) ١ في المحبر ص ٣١٣ : لسعيدة ٢٠ في أح وس وحس: للنياحه ; في المحبر :للمياحه ولا طلبا للرقاحه ; ويبدو أن هذا النص هو الاصح • ٣ آنظر ملاحظة رقم ٥ لمحمد حميد الله •
•

(٢٤) وكانت تلبية من نسك ليعوق : لبيك اللهمّ لبيك ،لبيك بغّض الينا الشر،وحبّب الينا الخير ، ولا نبطر ١ فنأشر ٠ ٢

(٢٥) [و٢٣أ] [وكانت تلبيةمن نسك ليغوث]١ :لبيك اللهم لبيك ، احببنا لديك ،٢ فنحن عبادك قد صرنا اليك ٠

(٢٦) وكانت تلبية من نسك لنسر : لبيك اللهمّ لبيك ،لبيك اننا عبيد ، وكلـّـنا ميسر ١ عتيد ،٢ وأنت ربّنا الحميد ، ارددنا ٣ الينا ملكنا والصيد ٠

(٢٧) وكانت تلبية من نسك ذا اللبا :لبيك اللهمّ لبيك ، ربّا صرفت عنّـا مضر ، وسلم ١ لنا هذا السفر ، وارعنا فيهما المزدجر ، ٢ ثم اكفنا ٣ اللهم ارباب هجر ٠

(٢٨) وكانت تلبية من نسك لمرحب : لبيك اللهمّ لبيك ، اننا لديك ، لبيك حببنا اليك ٠

(٢٩) وكانت تلبية من‌نسك لذريح : لبيك اللهم لبيك ،لبيك كلنا كنود ، وكلّنا لنعمة جحود ، فاكفنا كلّ حية رصود ٠

(٣٠) وكانت تلبية من نسك ذا الكفين : لبيك اللهم لبيك ، لبيك ان جرهما عبادك ، والناس طرف وهم تلادك،ونحن أولى بولائك ٠ ١

(٣١) وكانت تلبية من نسك هبل : لبيك اللهم لبيك ، لبيك انّنا لقاح، حرمتنا [على]١ أسنّة الرماح ، يحسدنا ٢ الناس على النجاح ٠

فهذه روؤس طواغيتهم التي كانوا يقصدون ٣ اليها من حجهم ولا يأتون بيوتهم حتى يمرّوا بها فيعظمونها ويتقربون اليها وينسكوا ٤ (١) لها ، يعني يسجدون لها ٠

(٣٢) وكانت تلبية كنانة وقريش : لبيك اللهم لبيك ، لبيك يوم التعريف ويوم الدعاء والوقوف ، ١ لبيك لا شريك لك الا شريكا هو لك ، تملكه وما ملك ٠

---

(٢٤) ١ في المحبر ص٣١٤:ولا تبطرنا ٠ ٢ في المحبر جملة زائدة: ولاتفدحنا بعثار ٠

(٢٥) ١ [ ] محذوف في أح، س‌حس؛ والزيادة من نصّ المحبر ص ٣١٤.
٢ في المحبر : احببنا بما لديك ٠

(٢٦) ١ في المحبر ص ٣١٤: ميسرة؛ في أح‌وس‌وحس : عبيد ؛ في المحبر: عتيد ٠ ٣ في المحبر : اردد الينا ٠

(٢٧) ١ في المحبر ص ٣١٤ : ربّ فاصرفن عنا مضر وسلّمنْ ... ٢ في المحبر : ان عما فيهم لمزدجر ٠ ٣ في المحبر : واكفنا ٠

(٣٠) ١ في أح وس وحس : ونحن أولا بهم اولائك ؛ والنص الذي أوردناه مأخوذ من المحبر ص ٣١٤ ، السطر الاخير – ص ٣١٥ س ١ ٠

(٣١) ١[على]؛ الزيادة عن المحبر ص ٢.٣١٥ في أ ح وحس وس : لحسدتنا.
٣ قارن المحبر ص ٣١٩ س٢ : يصدرون اليها ٠ ٤ في المحبر : فيعظموها ويتقربوا اليها وينسكوا لها؛" يعني يسجدون لها " لم يرد في المحبر ٠

(٣٢) ١ قارن اليعقوبي ، تاريخ ج١ص٢٩٦ ٠

(٣٣) وقال ابن اسحق : وكانت تلبية تميم وأسد وضبّة ومزينة، فكانت تميم تقول : لبيك اللهم لبيك ، لبيك عن تميم قد تراها قد خلفت أوثانها وراها ، وأخلصت لربّها دعاها ، قد افردت حجّ (إ) لمن براها ، قد فاز بالقدرة وابتناها ، مكة للربّ ومن براها ١ .

(٣٤) قال ابن اسحق : وكانت خندف ، تميم واسد وضبة ومزينة ، يعظمون هبل ويقولون : لبيك اللهم لبيك ، ما نهارنا نجره ، ادلاجه وبرده وصره ، لايتقي شيئا ولايضره ، حجّا لرب مستقيم بره ١ .

(٣٥) قال وقال الشعبي : كانت تلبية بني اسد اذا حجوا : لبيك اللهم لبيك ، اليك ربّ اقبلت بنو اسد ، أهل العوالي والوفاء والجلد ، والمـال فينا والبنون والمدد ، وأنت ربّ المشعرين والبلد ، الواحد القهار والربّ الصمد، ما نعبد الاوثان مع من قد عبد ١ .

(٣٦) قال ابن اسحق : كانت هذيل[و ٢٣ ب]تعظم سواعاوكانت تلبيتهم : لبيك عبادك هذيل ، حجّ اليك كالسيل ، نسير النهار والليل ، لم نأت للمياحه ، ١ وجئنا للنصاحه ٢ .

(٣٧) وكانت قيس عيلان تعظم الالهة،وكانت تلبيتهم اذا اهلوا : لبيك اللهم لبيك ، لبيك انت الرحمن ، أتتك قيس عيلان ، راجلها والركبان ١ وشيخها والولدان ، ذليلة للرحمن جميعها والاوثان ٢ .

(٣٨) وكانت تلبية ربيعة بن نزار : لبيك حجّـا حقّـا ، تعبدا ورقّـا، نركب اليك طرقا، مستبقين سبقا ، لحلق روؤس حلقا .

(٣٩) قال ،وكانت تلبية عكّ : لاحجّ الا حجك ، نسألك ونستغيث بك ، فاسق غيثا ربّنا ضكا ، ١ وزاد زكا ، لم نأت للرقاحه،واوجبنا النصاحه .

(٤٠) قال ،وكانت تلبية عكّ والاشعريين ،١ اذا حجوا البيت : لبيك اللهم لبيك ، حجّ للرحمن ، ذلت له الاصنام ، فاغفر ما أحصيت منا عددا .

(٤١) وكانت تلبية مذحج في الجاهلية ، وكانوا يعظمون يغوث ويهلّون له : لبيك اللهم لبيك ، لبيك ربّ الشعرى ، ربّ السموات العلى ، ربّ اللات والعزى ١ .

---

(٣٣) ١ قارن اليعقوبي ، تاريخ ص ٢٩٦ ، تلبية بني تميم .

(٣٤) ١ انظر رقم ٣ أعلاه .

(٣٥) ١ قارن اليعقوبي ، تاريخ ص ٢٩٦ ، تلبية بني أسد ؛ وأنظر حسين ، تلبيات ص ٣٦٥ رقم ٢ .

(٣٦) ١ في أح ، حس وس : للنياحه. ٢ قارن اليعقوبي ، تاريخ ص ٢٩٦ وحسين ، تلبيات ص ٣٦٨ رقم ٢٣.

(٣٧) ١ الى هنا في تاريخ اليعقوبي ص ٢٩٦. ٢ في مقالة حسين ، تلبيات رقم ١٧ : ... بشيخها والولدان ، مذللة للديان .

(٣٩) ١ كذا أحوس وحس؛ولعله : منكا .

(٤٠) ١ في أح وس وحس :والاشعريون .

(٤١) ١ في أح وس وحس :.... الشعرا ... العلا ... والعزا .

(٤٢) تلبية همدان ١ وخولان ؛ وكانت همدان ١ تعظم يعوق ، وكانت تلبيتهم : لبيك رب البنيان ، هذا حجيج همدان ، قد أتاك ركبان ، تريد ربّ غفران ، قد أوجبت النصاحه .

(٤٣) تلبية حمير ، وكانت تعبد نسرا : لبيك اللهم لبيك عن الملوك والاقوال ١ ذوي النهى والاحلام ، والواصلين الارحام ، لم يقربوا٢ للاثام ، تنزّها واسلام ، ذلّوا لرب الانام ، ٣ دانوا له في اعلام ، أوثانها والاصنام ٤ .

(٤٤) وكانت تلبيتهم أيضا : لبيك اللهم لبيك ، لبيك حمير عبادك اليمانيه ، قد أتتك شعثا عانيه ، على قلاص ناجيه ، كيما تحجّ الثانيه ، لم نأت للرباحه، وأوجبنا النصاحه .

(٤٥) وكانت تلبية الحمس : لبيك اللهم لبيك ، لبيك انت رب الشعرى فا[نصر]هم ممن تعدى ، ربّ الثالثة الاخرى ، ورب اللات والعزى ، والكعبة الحرام وحيث تدعا ، جئناك على طريق من يخشى ، تهدي بنا المضمرات تتمادى ، قد خلفوا الاوثان خلوا صفرا .

(٤٦) تلبية كعب(!) بن وبرة ، وكانت تعبد ودا ، وتلبيتهم وتلبية قضاعة : لبيك رب الحلّ والحرام ، اغفر خطايا أعبد وآم ، أتوك يمشون على الاقدام .

(٤٧) وكانت تلبية قضاعة [و ٢٤ أ] خاصة : لبيك اللهم لبيك ، لبيك عن قضاعه ، ذلت لرب الساعه ، سمعا له وطاعه ، يقدمها وداعه .

(٤٨) وكانت تلبية ثقيف في الجاهلية : لبيك اللهم لبيك ، هذه اياد ١ قد أتوك ، قد عطلوا ٢ المال وقد رجوك ، ٣ واللات والعزى في يديك ، ٤ دانت لك الاصنام تعظيما اليك ، قد اذعنت بسلمها اليك ، فاغفر لنا ٥ فطال ما عفوت. ٦

(٤٩) قال ، وكان عمرو بن معديكرب في الاسلام يقول :لقد رأيتنا قبل الاسلام ونحن اذا حججنا نقول:لبيك تعظيما اليك عذرا،هذه زبيد قد اتتك قصرا ، تعدو ١ بها مضمرات شزرا ، يقطعن خبتا وجبالا وعرا ، قد خلفوا الانداد خلوا صفرا؛ ونحن، والحمد لله ، نقول اليوم : لبيك اللهم لبيك ، تلبية صدق ، لبيك اللهم لبيك ، ربّ الارباب ، تعدو بنا سرر غلاب ، لبيك مخلصة الجواب ، العجيج والدماء والاسباب ، قاهر كلّ وثن وصنم في البلاد .

(٥٠) تلبية بكر بن وائل : لبيك اللهم لبيك ، لبيك عن ربيعه ، سامعة مطيعه ، لربّ ما يعبد في كنيسة وبيعه ، قد خلفت أوثانها في عصمة منيعه ١٠

---

(٤٢) ١ أحو سوحس : همذان .

(٤٣) ١ في تلبيات لحسين رقم ١٠ : والاقيال . ٢ حسين : لايقربون. ٣ حسين : كرّام ٤ " دانوا ....والاصنام " ــ لم يرد في نص تلبيات حسين .

(٤٨) ١ اليعقوبي ص ٢٩٦ : ان ثقيفا قد اتوك . ٢ اليعقوبي : وأخلفوا المال ؛ حسين رقم ٨ : وقد عظموا المال . ٣ الى هنا في نص اليعقوبي . ٤ حسين : عزاهم واللات في يديك . ٥ حسين:لها . ٦ حسين:غفرت .

(٤٩) ١ في أح : تعدوا .

(٥٠) ١ قارن : حسين ، تلبيات رقم ١٢ واليعقوبي ص ٢٩٦ .

I

(٥١) وقال عمر بن الخطاب رضي الله عنه لابي بردة بن ابي موسى : أتدري كيف كانت تلبية قومك ١ في الجاهلية ؟ قال : كانوا يقولون : اللهم هذا واحد انما ، أثمه الله وقد أثما ، ٢ ان تغفر اللهم تغفر جمّا وأى عبد لك لا ألمّا .

(٥٢) وكانت تلبية جذام : لبيك اللهم لبيك ، لبيك عن جذام ذوي ١ النهى والاحلام ، بني الملوك العظام ، هم الفروع والاعلام ، واتوا اله الاصنام، مشاتها والركبان ، تعظيما للرحمن ٢ .

(٥٣) تلبية كندة وحضرموت والسكون ١ : لبيك اللهم لبيك ،لبيك لا شريك لك ، الا شريكا تملكه ، ٢ ان تهلكه أو تتركه ، أنت الحليم ١ فاتركه .

(٥٤) تلبية غسان : لبيك اللهم لبيك ، لبيك عن ملوكنا، فأنت ربّ قومنا، لك النداء وعجّنا وثجّنا وحجّنا .

(٥٥) تلبية بجيلة : لبيك اللهم لبيك عن بجيله ، فانها لنعمت القبيله،١ حتى ترى طائفة بكعبة جليله ، قد خلفت أوثانها في واسط القبيله ٢ .

(٥٦) تلبية دوس : لبيك اللهم لبيك ربّ الاصنام ، مشاتها والركبان ، أتتك دوس سامعة مطيعه ، ورب كل واصل ومظهر قطيعه .

II وكانت الاصنام كلها في بلاد العرب ؛ وكانت العزى شجرة بنخلة عندها وثن تعبدها غطفان وكانت غني وباهلة تعبدها معهم[و ٢٤ ب]وكان عندها وثن فقطعها خالد بن الوليد رحمه الله . وكانت اللات بالطائف لثقيف فبعث النبي صلى الله عليه وسلم أبا سفيان والمغيرة بن شعبة فهدماها . وكانت جهار لهوازن بعكاظ . وكانت سواع بنعمان ١ تعبده (١) كنانة وهذيل ومزينة وحيّ من قيس عيلان . وكانت شمس لبني تميم وكانت لها بيت ، وكانت تعبده (١) بنو ٣ ود كلها وضبة وتميم وغني وثور وعكل . وكان ودّ لبني وبرة وكان موضعه بدومة الجندل . وكان الفلس بنجد تعبده طيء، وكان قريبا من فيد . وكانت الانصار وأزد شنوءة وغيرهم من الازد يعبدون المناة وكان (١) بسيف ٤ البحرين (١) . وكانت سعد هذيم ٤أ وسائر قضاعة ، الا بني وبرة ، يعبدون السعيدة ومناة ، وكانت الازد يعبدون السعيدة . وكان ذو الخلصة له بيت يعبده بجيلة وخثعم وحارث بن كعب وجرم وزبيد وغوث من مراد وبنو هلال ابن عمارة . وكان يغوث لمذحج . وكان يعوق لخولان وهمدان . وكان نسر ٥ لحمير

---

(٥١) ١ في أح وس وحس : قوم ؛ وعلى هامش أح : قومى . ٢ حسين رقم ٣ : هذا واحد ان تما ، أتمّه الله وقد أتما .

(٥٢) ١ في أح وحس :ذي . ٢ قارن اليعقوبى ص ٢٩٧ .

(٥٣) ١ اليعقوبي ص ٢٩٧ : كندة وحضرموت . ٢ اليعقوبي :لا شريك لك تملكه أو تهلكه. ٣ حكيم .

(٥٥) ١ قارن أليعقوبي ص ٢٩٧ : لبيك عن بجيلة في بارق ومخيلة.
٢ قارن حسين ، تلبيات رقم ٥ ورسالة ألغفران ص ٥٣٦ .

II (١) أح وس وحس: لنعمان . (٢) في أح وس وحس: بليت (!)
(٣) في أح وس وحس: بني . (٤) في أح وس وحس: لسيف .
(٤أ) في أح وس وحس: سعد وهذيم. (٥) في أح وس وحس: نسرا

وكان في دار قصر باليمن • وكان ذو ٦ لبا لعبد القيس • وكان المحرق بسلمان ٧ لبكر بن وائل وسائر ربيعة • وكان لكندة ذريح بالنجير ٨ باليمن نحو حضرموت. وكان للسلف ولعكّ والاشعريين المنطبق وكان صنما ٩ من نحاس يتكلمون من جوفه بكلام لم يسمع بمثله • وكان يساف ونائلة لقريش والاحابيش • وكان هبل لبني بكر وملك وملكان وسائر كنانة ، وكانت قريش تعبد صاحب كنانة وكانت كنانة تعبد صاحب قريش•

III [ج ٢ و ٢١٠ ب]واما اسماء الالهة فأما ودّ فلكلب بدومة الجندل وأما سواع فلهذيل بساحل البحر ، وأما يغوث فلبني غطيف وهم حي من مراد ، وأما يعوق فلهمدان ، وأما نسر فلحمير لذي كلاع من حمير ، فكانت هذه الالهة يعبدها قوم نوح حتى عبدتها العرب بعد ذلك ؛ وأما اللات فلثقيف وأما العزى فلسليم وغطفان وجشم ١ ونصر بن معاوية وسعد بن بكر • وأما مناة فكانت بقديد ٢ منزل بين مكة والمدينة • وأما يساف ونائلة وهبل لاهل مكة ؛ فكان يساف حيال الحجر الاسود ، ونائلة حيال الركن اليماني ، وهبل في جوف الكعبة ، وكان طوله ثمانية عشر ذراعا • ٣

---

(٦) في أح وس وحس: ذا. (٧) في أح وس وحس: بسيمان.
(٨)في أح وس وحس: بالحر. (٩) في أح وس وحس: صنم.

III (١) في أح : وغشم : وانظر : الفاسي ، شفاء الغرام ج ٢ ص ٢٨٢س٥.
(٢) في أح : لقديد • (٣) راجع : الطبرى ، تفسير (بولاق)ج٢٧ص٣٤–٣٦: السيوطي ، الدر المنثور ج٦ ص ١٢٦–١٢٧ ؛ الزرقاني ، شرح المواهب اللدنية (القاهرة ١٣٢٥) ج٢ ص ٣٤٧ – ٣٤٩ ، ج٣ ص ٢٧ ، ٥٢ – ٥٤ ؛ الصالحي ، سبل الهدى والرشاد في سيرة خير العباد ، ج٢ ص ٢٤٢ – ٢٤٤ ؛ ابن ابي الحديد ، شرح نهج البلاغة ، (تحقيق محمد ابو الفضل ابراهيم ، القاهرة ١٣٨٥/ ١٩٦٥) ج١ ص ١١٩ – ١٢٠ ؛ القرطبي ، تفسير ج ١٨ ص ٣٠٧ – ٣١٠ •

ADDITIONAL NOTES

ad note 3: Ibn Taymiyya, *Iqtiḍā' al-ṣirāt al-mustaqīm mukhālafatu aṣḥāb al-jaḥīm*, ed. Muḥammad Ḥāmid al-Fiqī, Cairo 1369, p. 442. And see the comments of Ibn Taymiyya as to the Jāhilī *talbiya* [*ibid.* p. 442]: ... *fa-inna l-mushrikīna lam yakun aḥadun minhum yaqūlu inna l-'ālama lahu khāliqāni wa-lā inna llāha ma'ahu ilāhun yusāwīhi fī ṣifātihi, hādhā lam yaqulhu aḥadun mina l-mushrikīna, bal kānū yuqirrūna bi-anna khāliqa l-samāwāti wa-l-arḍi wāḥidun* ....

al-Kalā'ī, *al-Iktifā' fī maghāzī rasūli llāhi wa-l-thalāthati l-khulafā'*, ed. Muṣṭafā 'Abd al-Wāḥid, Cairo 1387/1968, I, 94 [and see the comment of al-Kalā'ī, *ibid.*: *fa-yuwaḥḥidūnahu bi-l-talbiya, thumma yudkhilūna ma'ahu aṣnāmahum wa-yaj'alūna mulkahā bi-yadihi*].

Ibn Isḥāq, *Kitāb al-siyar wa-l-maghāzī*, ed. Suhayl Zakkār, Damascus 1398/1978, p. 120: ... *fa-kānat al-ḥumsu, quraysh wa-kināna wa-khuzā'a wa-man waladat qurayshun min sā'iri l-'arab yuhillūna bi-ḥajjihim, fa-min ikhtilāfihim an yaqūlū: labbayka lā sharīka laka illā sharīkun huwa laka, tamlikuhu wa-mā malak. fa-yuwaḥḥadu fīhi bi-l-talbiyati, thumma yudkhilūna ma'ahu aṣnāmahum wa-yaj'alūna mulkahā bi-yadihi.*

ad note 4: al-Ṭabarānī, *al-Mu'jam al-ṣaghīr*, ed. 'Abd al-Raḥmān Muḥammad 'Uthmān, al-Madīna al-munawwara 1388/1968, I, 59, 87.

al-Fasawī, *al-Ma'rifa wa-l-ta'rīkh*, ed. Ḍiyā' al-'Umarī, Beirut 1401/1981, I, 332 inf.-333 sup.

Ibn 'Adiyy [=Abū Aḥmad 'Abdallah b. 'Adiyy al-Jurjānī], *al-Kāmil fī ḍu'afā'i l-rijāl*, Beirut 1405/1985, I, 282.

al-Ṭabarānī, *al-Mu'jam al-kabīr*, ed. Ḥamdī 'Abd al-Majīd al-Silafī, n. p., 1404/1983, XVII, 47, no. 100.

al-Muttaqī l-Hindī, *Kanz al-'ummāl*, Hyderabad 1374/1954, V, 78, no. 638, 80, no. 650.

'Abdallah b. 'Umar, *Musnad* [*takhrīj* abī umayya muḥammad b. ibrāhīm al-ṭarsūsī], ed. Aḥmad Rātib 'Armūsh, Beirut 1393/1973, pp. 42–43, no. 75, 48–49, no. 97 [and see *ibid.* the additional formula of the *talbiya* of Ibn 'Umar: *labbayka labbayka labbayka wa-sa'dayka wa-l-khayr bi-yadayka wa-l-raghbā'u ilayka wa-l-'amal*].

Ghulām Tha'lab, *Juz'*, MS. Chester Beatty 3495, fol 96 b.

'Alā'u l-Dīn 'Alī b. Balabān, *al-Iḥsān bi-tartīb ṣaḥīḥ ibn ḥibbān*, ed. Kamāl Yūsuf al-Ḥūt, Beirut 1407/1987, VI, 41 inf.–42 sup., no. 3788 [with the additional invocation of Ibn 'Umar].

Ibn Ḥajar al-'Asqalānī, *al-Maṭālib al-'āliya bi-zawā'id al-masānīd al-thamāniya*, ed. Ḥabīb al-Raḥmān al-A'ẓamī, Beirut, n. d. , I, 354, no. 1196, 355, no. 1201.

'Abd al-Ghanī al-Jumā'īlī al-Maqdisī l-Ḥanbalī, *Matn 'umdat al-aḥkām min kalām khayri l-anām*, Cairo 1375, p. 64, no. 267 [and see *ibid.* the addition of Ibn 'Umar].

Ibn Bābūyah al-Qummī, *Man lā yaḥḍuruhu l-faqīh*, ed. Ḥasan al-Mūsawī al-Kharsān, Beirut 1401/ 1981, II, 210, no. 959 [with the addition *labbayka dhā l-ma'ārij labbayka*], 211, no. 966. [And see the *talbiya* of the souls of the believers who are in the backs of their fathers [the location of the semen-k] and the wombs of their mothers; this is uttered in the presence of Moses, during the conversation of Moses with God: *ibid.* pp. 209–210, no. 957].

About the significance of the *talbiya* see al-Sayyid al-Bakrī b. Muḥammad Shaṭā al-Dimyāṭī, *I'ānat al-ṭālibīn 'alā ḥalli alfāẓi fatḥi l-mu'īn*, Beirut [reprint], n. d., II, 274: ... *wa-ammā l-ḥikmatu fī l-talbiya fa-inna l-insān idhā nādāhu insān jalīlu l-qadr ajābahu bi-l-talbiya wa-ḥusni l-kalām, fa-kayfa bi-man nādāhu maulāhu l-malik al-'allām wa-da'āhu ilā janābihi li-yukaffira 'anhu l-dhunūb wa-l-āthām; wa-inna l-'abd idhā qāla labbayka yaqūlu llāhu ta'ālā: hā anā dānin ilayka wa-mutajallin 'alayka fa-sal mā turīdu fa-anā aqrab ilayka min ḥabli l-warīd.* And see the exposition of this subject *ibid.* p. 309 inf.

And see Maurice Gaudefroy-Demombynes, *Le pèlegrinage à la Mekke*, Philadelphia 1977, p. 179.

I

3

Muḥammad Ḥabībullāh al-Shanqīṭī, *Zād al-muslim fīmā ttafaqa 'alayhi al-bukhārī wa-muslim*, Beirut, n. d., I, 378-380, no. 573.

Nūr al-Dīn al-Haythamī, *Mawārid al-ẓam'ān ilā zawā'idi bni ḥibbān*, ed. Muḥammad 'Abd al-Razzāq Ḥamza, Cairo, n. d., p. 242, no. 975 [the *talbiya* uttered by the Prophet was: *labbayka ilāha l-ḥaqqi labbayka*].

And see Abū Bakr Muḥammad b. Isḥāq b. Khuzayma, *Ṣaḥīḥ*, ed. Muḥammad Muṣṭafā l-A'ẓamī, Beirut 1399/1979, IV, 172, no. 552 [the *talbiya: labbayka ilāha l-ḥaqqi*, recorded on the authority of Abū Hurayra]

Nūr al-Dīn al-Haythamī, *al-Maqṣad al-'aliyy fī zawā'id abī ya'lā l-mauṣiliyy*, ed. Nāyif b. Hāshim al-Da'īs, Judda 1402/1982, p. 509, no. 557; and see *ibid.* no. 556: ... *anna sa'd b. mālik sami'a rajulan yaqūlu: labbayka dhā l-ma'ārij. qāla: inna llāha dhū l-ma'ārij wa-lākin lam nakun naqūlu dhālika ma'a nabiyyinā.* [Compare the version in Nūr al-Dīn al-Haythamī's *Majma' al-zawā'id*, III, 223]; and see the references given by al-Da'īs in his edition.

And see the discussion as to the permissibility of the additions to the version of the *talbiya*: Ibn Khuzayma, *Ṣaḥīḥ*, IV: the *talbiya* of the Prophet is recorded on p. 171; an addition of Ibn 'Umar is also recorded [no. 551, 2621-2622]. The problem of the additions is discussed on pages 172-173: *bāb dhikri l-bayān anna l-ziyāda fī l-talbiya 'alā mā ḥafiẓa bnu 'umara 'ani l-nabiyyi*, ṣallā llāhu 'alayhi wa-sallam, *jā'izun, wa-l-dalīl 'alā anna ba'ḍa aṣḥābi l-nabiyyi* ṣallā llāhu 'alayhi wa-sallam *qad yaḥfaẓu 'anhu mā yaghrubu 'an ba'ḍihim, li-anna abā hurayrata qad ḥafiẓa 'ani l-nabiyi ṣallā llāhu 'alayhi wa-sallam fī talbiyatihi mā lam yaḥki 'anhu ghayruhu.* [The *talbiya* recorded is: *labbayka ilāha l-ḥaqqi*] The heading of the following chapter [no. 553] runs as follows: *bābu ibāḥati l-ziyādati fī l-talbiyati "dhā l-ma'āriji" wa-naḥwihi ḍiddu qauli man kariha hādhihi l-ziyādata wa-dhakara annahum lam yaqūlūhu ma'a l-nabiyyi* ṣallā llāhu 'alayhi wa-sallam *ma'a l-dalīl 'alā anna man taqaddamat ṣuḥbatuhu li-l-nabiyyi* ṣallā llāhu 'alayhi wa-sallam *wa-kāna a'lama qad kāna yakhfā 'alayhi al-shay'u min 'ilmi l-khāṣṣati, fa-'alimahu man huwa dūnahu fī l-sinni wa-l-'ilmi, li-anna sa'da bna abī waqqāṣin ma'a makānihi mina l-islāmi wa-l-'ilmi ma'a taqaddumi ṣuḥbatihi khabbara annahum lam yaqūlū "dhā l-ma'āriji" ma'a l-nabiyyi* ṣallā llāhu 'alayhi wa-sallam *wa-jābiru bnu 'abdi llāhi dūnahu fī l-sinni wa-l-'ilmi wa-l-makāni ma'a l-nabiyyi* ṣallā llāhu 'alayhi wa-sallam *qad a'lama annahum kānū yazīdūna "dhā l-ma'ārij" wa-naḥwahu wa-l-nabiyyu* ṣallā llāhu 'alayhi wa-sallam *yasma'u lā yaqūlu shay'an, fa-qad khafiya 'alā sa'di bni abī waqqāṣin ma'a mauḍi'hi mina l-islāmi wa-l-'ilmi mā 'alimahu jābiru bnu 'abdi llāhi.*

ad note 19: al-Balādhurī, *Ansāb al-ashrāf*, ed. Muḥammad Ḥamīdullah, Cairo 1959, I, 91 [... *hind bint abī qayla, wa-huwa wajzu bnu ghālib min khuzā'a. wa-kāna abū qayla yud'ā abā kabsha. wa-kāna qad istakhaffa bi-l-ḥaram wa-ahlihi fī fi'latin fa'alahā. fa-kānat quraysh taqūlu li-l-nabiyy ṣallā llāhu 'alayhi wa-sallam: "fa'ala ibn abī kabsha kadhā", yushabbihūnahu idhā khālafa dīnahum* ; and see *ibid.* another tradition: *wa-yuqālu inna zauja ḥalīmata, ẓi'rihi, kāna yuknā abā kabsha* ; and see other traditions *ibid.: wa-yuqālu inna wahban, jaddahu li-ummihi, kāna yuknā abā kabsha; wa-yuqālu inna 'amra bna zaydin, jadda 'abdi l-muṭṭalibi li-ummihi, kāna yuknā abā kabsha.* And see the final phrase: *wa-llāhu a'lam.*
al-Fākihī, *Ta'rīkh makka*, MS. Leiden, Or. 463, fol. 448 b.: ... *ibn al-kalbī: kāna nāsun min khuzā'a min banī mulayḥ ya'budūna l-shi'rā fī l-jāhiliyya ...*
Muṣ'ab b. 'Abdallah al-Zubayrī, *Nasab quraysh*, ed. Levi Provencal, Cairo 1953, pp. 261-262.
Ibn 'Asākir, *Ta'rīkh* [*tahdhīb*], VI, 224-225.
al-Zubayr b. Bakkār, *Jamharat nasab quraysh wa-akhbārihā*, MS. Bodleiana, Marsh 384, fol. 90 a, inf.-90 b. sup.
al-Khāzin, *Tafsīr* [=*Lubāb al-ta'wīl fī ma'ānī l-tanzīl*], Cairo 1381, VI, 224 ult.-225 sup.

ad note 38: See Abū Ḥudhayfa Isḥāq b. Bishr, *Kitāb al-mubtada'*, MS. Ẓāhiriyya 359, [*al-juz' al-khāmis*], fol. 128 b.: ... *wa-kāna qaumu hūdin wa-hum 'ādun aṣḥāba authānin ya'budūnahā min dūni llāhi jalla wa-'azza....fa-ttakhadhū ṣanaman yuqālu lahu ṣamūdun wa-ṣanaman yuqālu lahu l-habbār....* ; and comp. al-Mas'ūdī, *Murūj al-dhahab*, ed. Ch. Pellat, Beirut 1964, II, 277 [ʿĀd worshipped three idols: Ṣamūd, Ṣadā and al-Habā {sic !}; and see U. Rubin, "The *Ṣamad* and the high God, An interpretation of *sūra* CXII", *Der Isla*, LXI (1984) 213, note 97; and see Arne A. Ambros, "Die Analyse von Sure 112, Kritiken, Synthesen, neue Ansaetze", *Der Islam*, LXIII, 232.

ad note 50: Ḥamza al-Iṣfahānī, *al-Durra al-fākhira fī l-amthāli l-sāʾira*, ed. ʿAbd al-Majīd Qaṭāmish, Cairo 1972, II, 555: *wa-zaʿamū anna jurhuman min nitāji mā bayna l-malāʾikati wa-l-insi; qālū: wa-l-sabab fī dhālika anna l-malak mina l-malāʾikati lladhīna ʿinda l-raḥmān kāna idhā ʿaṣā rabbahu ahbaṭahu mina l-samāʾi ilā l-arḍi fī ṣūrati rajulin wa-fī ṭabīʿatihi kamā ṣanaʿa bi-hārūt wa-mārūt ḥattā kāna min shaʾnihimā wa-shaʾni l-zuhara mā kāna. qālū: fa-ʿaṣā llāha malakun mina l-malāʾikati fa-ahbaṭahu ilā l-arḍi fī ṣūrati rajulin, fa-tazawwaja umma jurhum, fa-waladat lahu jurhuman. qāla l-shāʿir yadhkuru dhālika:*
*lā-humma inna jurhuman ʿibādukā * al-nāsu ṭirfun wa-hum tilādukā.*
Ibrāhīm b. Muḥammad al-Bayhaqī, *al-Maḥāsin wa-l-masāwī*, ed. Muḥammad Abū l-Faḍl Ibrāhīm, Cairo 1380/1961, I, 166.
al-Fāsī, *Tuḥfat al-kirām fī akhbāri l-baladi l-ḥarām*, MS. Leiden, Or. 2654, fol. 135 b-136 a:
... fa-lammā aḥassa ʿamr b. al-ḥārith b. muḍāḍ bi-l-hazīmati kharaja bi-ghazālayi l-kaʿba wa-ḥajari l-rukni yaltamisu l-tauba wa-huwa yaqūlu:
*inna jurhuman ʿibādukā * al-nāsu ṭirfun wa-hum tilādukā * wa-hum qadīman ʿamarū bilādakā.*
fa-lam tuqbal taubatuhu....
al-Maqrīzī, *Kitāb fīhi dhikru mā warada fī bunyāni l-kaʿbati l-muʿaẓẓama*, MS. Leiden, Or. 560, fol. 171 a, inf.: ... *fa-lammā ʿaṣā llāha baʿḍu l-malāʾikati wa-ahbaṭahu ilā l-arḍi fī ṣūrati rajulin tazawwaja umma jurhumin fa-waladat minhu jurhuman; wa-li-dhālika qāla shāʿiruhum:*
*lā humma inna jurhuman ʿibādukā * al-nāsu ṭirfun wa-hum tilādukā * wa-hum qadīman ʿamarū bilādakā.*

al-Fāsī, *al-ʿIqd al-thamīn fī taʾrīkhi l-baladi l-amīn*, ed. Muḥammad Ḥāmid al-Fiqī, Cairo 1378/1958, I, 131: ... *wa-qīla inna jurhuman ibnu malakin mina l-malāʾikati adhnaba dhanban fa-uhbiṭa ilā makkata fa-tazawwaja mraʾatan mina l-ʿamālīqi fa-waladat lahu jurhuman. fa-dhālika qaulu l-ḥārithi bni muḍāḍini l-jurhumiyyi:*
allāhumma inna jurhuman ʿibāduka *
al-nāsu ṭirfun wa-hum tilāduka.

ad note 61: See Abū Bakr Aḥmad b. Muḥammad al-Khallāl, *Kitāb al-musnad min masāʾil aḥmad b. ḥanbal*, MS. Br. Mus. Or. 2675, fol. 86 a, inf.: ... *ḥaddathanā al-ṣalt b. dīnār qāla: samiʿtu l-ḥajjāj ʿalā minbari wāsiṭ yaqūlu: ʿabdu llāhi bnu masʿūdin raʾsu l-munāfiqīna lau adraktuhu la-saqaytu l-arḍa min damihi.*

ad note 62: al-Qurṭubī, *Tafsīr* [=*al-Jāmiʿ li-aḥkāmi l-qurʾān*], Cairo 1387/1967, V, 322: ... *fa-khtaṣama ilā l-nabiyyi* ṣallā llāhu ʿalayhi wa-sallam *al-rajulāni fa-qāla aḥadu l-rajulayni* [the version of Abū Dāwūd -k]: *nadī* [but preferable: *a-nadī-k*] *man lā ṣāḥa wa-lā akal * wa-lā shariba wa-lā stahall * fa-mithlu dhālika yuṭall * ? fa-qāla: a-sajʿun ka-sajʿi l-aʿrāb?* And see this tradition: al-Dāraquṭnī, *Sunan*, ed. ʿAbdallah Hāshim Yamānī l-Madanī, al-Madīna l-munawwara, 1386/1966, III, 198, nos. 341-343; and see Anonymous, A fiqh compilation, [no title], in possession of Dr. P. S. van Koningsveld, fol. 73a; and see this tradition: Abū Ṭālib al-Makkī, *Qūt al-qulūb*, Cairo 1351/1932, II, 49 [and see *ibid.* other utterances of the Prophet against *sajʿ*].

Comp. ʿIzz al-Dīn b. ʿAbd al-ʿAzīz al-Sulamī, *Kitāb al-fatāwā*, ed. ʿAbd al-Raḥmān b. ʿAbd al-Fattāḥ, Beirut 1406/1986, p. 67, no. 38 [the *fatwā* refers to the utterance of the Prophet mentioned above]; and see other other *fatwās* of ʿIzz al-Dīn against *sajʿ* in preaching in mosques and in speeches of the *khaṭīb* during ritual performances: *ibid.* pp. 59, no. 27, 75-78, no. 47.

al-Zarkashī, *al-Ijāba li-īrādi mā stadrakathu ʿĀʾishatu ʿalā l-ṣaḥāba*, Cairo n. d., [*dhayl*], p. 91: ʿAʾisha enjoining Ibn Abī l-Sāʾib, the *qāṣṣ* of Medina: ... *ijtanibi l-sajʿa mina l-duʿāʾi fa-innī ʿahidtu rasūla llāhi* [ṣ] *wa-aṣḥābahu lā yafʿalūna dhālika* ...

See further al-Ṭurṭūshī, *Kitāb al-ḥawādith wa-l-bida'*, ed. Muḥammad al-Ṭālibī, Tunis 1959, p. 145: *qāla: wa-yukrahu l-saj'u fī l-du'ā'i wa-ghayrihi, wa-laysa min kalāmi l-māḍīn. wa-rawā ibn wahb 'an 'urwata bni l-zubayri annahu kāna idhā 'uriḍa 'alayhi du'ā'un fīhi saj'un 'ani l-nabiyyi* ṣallā llāhu 'alayhi wa-sallam *wa-'an aṣḥābihi qāla: "kadhabū, lam yakun rasūlu llāhi* ṣallā llāhu 'alayhi wa-sallam *wa-lā aṣḥābuhu sajjā'īna".*

And see 'Umar b. Shabba al-Baṣrī, *Ta'rīkh al-madīnati l-munawwara*, ed. Fahīm Muḥammad Shaltūt, n. p. , 1399, p. 13: ['Ā'isha warned the *qāṣṣ* to refrain from using *saj'* in preaching].

Compare also the impressive invocation of the Prophet with the numerous phrases of *saj'*: al-Ṭabarānī, *al-Mu'jam al-kabīr*, X, 343–344, no. 10668.

Further see the arguments in favour of *saj'* and the negative opinions about *saj'*: Ibn Abī l-Ḥadīd, *Sharḥ nahji l-balāgha*, ed. Muḥammad Abū l-Faḍl Ibrāhīm, Cairo 1385/1965, I, 128-130. [See e. g. p.128: ... *wa-'lam anna l-saj'a lau kāna 'ayban la-kāna kalāmu llāhi ma'īban li-annahu masjū'un, kulluhu dhū fawāṣila wa-qarā'ina....fa-inna akthara khuṭabihi* [i. e. of the Prophet-k] *masjū'un....* and p. 129: ... *wa-ḥtajja 'ā'ibū l-saj'i bi-qaulihi 'alayhi l-salāmu li-ba'ḍihim munkiran 'alayhi: "a-saj'an ka-saj'i l-kuhhāni"....fa-qāla qā'ilun:" a-adī man lā shariba wa-lā akal * wa-lā naṭaq wa-lā stahall * wa-mithlu hādhā yuṭall" * fa-ankara 'alayhi l-salāmu dhālika, li-anna l-kuhhāna kānū yaḥkumūna fī l-jāhiliyyati bi-alfāẓin masjū'a...wa-lau kāna 'alayhi l-salāmu qad ankara l-saj'a la-mā qālahu...*]

ad note 65: See Ibn Balabān, *al-Iḥsān*, VI, 42, no. 3789.

ad note 66: See Ibn Isḥāq, *Kitāb al-siyar wa-l-maghāzī*, pp. 96 ult.-97.

'Abd al-Qādir al-Baghdādī, *Khizānat al-adab*, ed. 'Abd al-Salām Hārūn, Cairo 1399/1979, VII, 190, penult. [the verse *in taghfir allāhumma* attributed to Abū Khirāsh].

Ibn Ḥamza al-Ḥusaynī, *al-Bayān wa-l-ta'rīf fī asbāb wurūdi l-ḥadīthi l-sharīf*, Beirut 1400/1980, II, 152, no. 771 [the verse *in taghfiri llāhumma* uttered by the people of the Jāhiliyya during the circumambulation of the Ka'ba; the Prophet used to recite this verse, which is attributed to Umayya b. Abī l-Ṣalt].

A tradition recorded by Ibn 'Asākir, *Ta'rīkh* [*tahdhīb*], III, 128 inf.–129 sup. says that Umayya b. Abī l-Ṣalt uttered the verse *in taghfiri llāhumma* on his deathbed after lifting his eyes against the ceiling and invoking:

*labbaykumā, labbaykumā * hā anā dhā ladaykumā * lā dhū barā'atin fa-a'tadhir * wa-lā dhū 'ashīratin fa-antaṣir.*

ad note 76: See al-Ṭabarānī, *al-Mu'jam al-ṣaghīr*, I, 59; and see *idem, al-Mu'jam al-kabīr*, XVII, 46, no. 100 [and see the references of the editor].

ad note 77: Cf. al-Sayyid al-Bakrī b. Muḥammad Shaṭa al-Dimyāṭī, *I'ānat al-ṭālibīn*, II, 308 [with an additional verse: *qad dhahaba l-shaḥmu lladhī yazīnuhā*].

ad note 85: Cf. Ibn Abī Dunyā, *al-Ishrāf fī manāzili l-ashrāf*, MS. Chester Beatty 4427, fol. 5 a, l.10.

al-Bayhaqī, *al-Jāmi' li-shu'abi l-īmān*, ed. 'Abd al-'Aliyy 'Abd al-Ḥamīd Ḥāmid, Bombay 1409/1988, VII, 544–546, no. 3699.

ad note 87: See al-Maqrīzī, *Bunyān al-ka'ba*, MS.Leiden Or. 560, fols. 163 b., 164 a–b.

ad note 88: al-'Āqūlī, *'Arfu l-ṭīb min akhbāri makkata wa-madīnati l-ḥabīb*, MS. Leiden Or. 493, fol.70 b sup.: In response of the *talbiya* of Mūsā between Ṣafā and Marwa God called from Heaven: *labbayka 'abdī anā ma'aka*. Then Mūsā fell down prostrating himself. The *talbiya* of Mūsā was: *labbayka anā 'abduka ladayka labbayka.*

The *talbiya* of Yūnus b. Mattā was: *labbayka farrāja l-karbi labbayka.*

'Isā uttered in his *talbiya*: *anā 'abduka bnu amatika binti 'abdika labbayka.*

And see the *talbiya* of Yūnus: Aḥmad b. Ḥanbal, *Kitābu l-zuhd*, Beirut 1396/1976, p. 34: *labbayka kāshifa l-karbi labbayka.*

9

Ibn Balabān mentions in his *al-Iḥsān* [VI, 42, no. 3790] the *talbiya* uttered by Yūnus on the narrow pass of Harshā.

And see al-Bayhaqī, *al-Jāmiʿ li-shuʿabi l-īmān*, VII, 546-548, nos. 3700-3702.

ad note 92: Ibn Khuzayma, *Ṣaḥīḥ*, IV, 174-175, no. 556 [2631]

Ibn Ḥajar al-ʿAsqalānī, *al-Maṭālib al-ʿāliya*, I, 355, no. 1200.

Ibn Bābūyah al-Qummī, *Man lā yaḥḍuruhu l-faqīh*, II, 210, no. 960.

al-Bayhaqī, *al-Jāmiʿ li-shuʿabi l-īmān*, VII, 573-575, no. 3733.

ad note 94: Zakariyyā al-Marwazī,

Juz' sufyāna bni ʿuyayna, ed. Aḥmad b. ʿAbd al-Raḥmān al-Ṣuwayān, al-Kharj 1407/1987, p. 84, no. 20 [and see the numerous references of the editor; the *talbiya* was performed in Persian].

ad note 95: Muḥammad b. al-Ḥasan al-Shaybānī, *Kitābu l-ḥujja ʿalā ahli l-madīna*, ed. Mahdī Ḥasan al-Kaylānī al-Qādirī, Beirut 1403/1983, II, 80-113.

al-Suyūṭī, *Jamʿu l-jawāmiʿ*, II, 471.

Ibn Balabān, *al-Iḥsān*, VI, 43, no. 3793.

al-Muttaqī l-Hindī, *Kanz al-ʿummāl*, V, 79, nos. 643-644, 649.

ad note 96: al-Suyūṭī, *Jamʿu l-jawāmiʿ*, II, 471: Ibn ʿAbbās cursed the person who forbade uttering the *talbiya* on the Day of ʿArafa;ʿAlī used to utter the *talbiya* on that Day. And see this tradition: al-Muttaqī l-Hindī, *Kanz al-ʿummāl*, V, 79, nos. 646, 648. One may assume that Ibn ʿAbbās referred in his curse to Muʿāwiya.

II

MECCA AND THE TRIBES OF ARABIA: SOME NOTES ON THEIR RELATIONS

Reports about the relations between Mecca, Medina and the various tribal units of the Arabian peninsula are scarce. A scrutiny of some of these reports may contribute to a better understanding of certain events in the Arabian peninsula in the second half of the sixth century and the beginning of the seventh century. Certain data supplied by early transmitters may be helpful in elucidating the peculiar methods used by the Meccan clans in their attempts to gain the sympathy of other tribal units and acquire their cooperation in order to secure the continuity of the Meccan mercantile activities and the performance of the ritual practices at the Kaʿba. Some accounts indicate that clashes broke out from time to time between certain Meccan clans and the tribal groups; others point to the involvement of the Meccan and Medinan leaders in the efforts to solve intertribal conflicts. A few reports give information concerning the activities of the tribal groups at Mecca itself, their share in the politics of Mecca, and their involvement in the erection of the building of the Sanctuary at Mecca. Some aspects of these relations will be discussed in the following pages.

I

A clash which took place between a tribal faction and a Qurashī clan comes to light in a story recorded by al-Zubayr b. Bakkār[1] on the authority of Muḥammad b. al-Ḍahhāk al-Ḥizāmī,[2] a Fazārī transmitter Ḥurayth b. Riyāḥ "and others": Everybody who performed the pilgrimage from among the Bedouins used to stop by one of the clans of Quraysh and that clan supplied them garments in which they used to perform the circumambulation of the Kaʿba; at their arrival at Mecca they (i.e. the Bedouin pilgrims – K) threw away the clothes which they wore. The Qurashī clan in whose abode they

[1] Al-Zubayr b. Bakkār, *Jamharat nasab quraysh*, MS. Bodley, Marsh 384, fol. 128b.

[2] See on him: al-Zubayr b. Bakkār, *op. cit.*, ed. Maḥmūd Muḥammad Shākir (Cairo, 1381), I, 402, 494; al-Fāsī, *al-ʿIqd al-thamīn fī taʾrīkhi l-baladi l-amīn*, ed. Fuʾād Sayyid (Cairo, 1385/1966), V, 47–48, no. 1421; al-Bukhārī, *al-Taʾrīkh al-kabīr* (rpt. Hyderabad, n.d.), IV, 334, no. 3030; al-Samʿānī, *al-Ansāb*, ed. ʿAbd al-Raḥmān al-Muʿallimī (Hyderabad, 1384/1964), IV, 148; Fuat Sezgin, *GAS*, I, 266, no. 2.

sojourned, used to take from them (a part of – K) what they slaughtered. The Fazāra, the report continues, used to alight with al-Mughīra b. ʿAbdallah b. ʿUmar al-Makhzūmī. The first who denied al-Mughīra the (lots of the – K) slaughtered beasts was Khushayn b. Laʾy al-Fazārī al-Shamkhī. Al-Mughīra threatened him and Khushayn refrained from performing the pilgrimage. He said:

Yā rabbī hal ʿindaka min ghafīrah: uṣliḥu mālī wa-adaʿ naḥīrah
inna minan māniʿuhu l-mughīrah: wa-māniʿun baʿda minan thabīrah
wa-māniʿun baytaka an azūrah

"O Lord, is there forgiveness with you: I shall set my herds right and leave their slaughter
Indeed I am prevented from coming to Minā by al-Mughīra:
and prevented by him to come to Thabīr after Minā.
And he prevents me from visiting thy House."

The report recorded by Ibn Abī l-Ḥadīd is a shorter version of al-Zubayr's account; it contains however some peculiar divergencies; it is told within the frame of a series of utterances and anecdotes which emphasize the virtues and laudable deeds of the members of the clan of Makhzūm; among the eminent men of Makhzūm there is mentioned "the leader of Quraysh" (*sayyid quraysh fī l-jāhiliyya*), who was the man who debarred (the tribe of – K) Fazāra from performing the ḥajj (*wa-huwa lladhī manaʿa fazārata mina l-ḥajji*). This happened, the report says, when Khushayn b. Laʾy blamed "a people of Quraysh" (*ʿayyara qawman min quraysh*) of having taken (a share of – K) the camels slaughtered by the Bedouins (*al-ʿarab*) during the period of the pilgrimage (*al-mawsim*). Then Khushayn recited the verses about al-Mughīra's action.[3]

A more detailed report is recorded by al-Balādhurī[4] on the authority of Abū l-Yaqẓān.[5] The Fazārī who refused to give al-Mughīra the required share of the slaughtered beasts was Ẓuwaylim b. ʿArīn b. Khushayn, the grandson of Khushayn. Ẓuwaylim, according to the tradition, set out in the period of the Jāhiliyya in order to perform the pilgrimage and alighted at the court of al-Mughīra b. ʿAbdallah al-Makhzūmī. Al-Mughīra bade him pay the *ḥarīm*, i.e. the pay rendered to Quraysh by the men of the tribes who alighted in their dwellings in the period of the Jāhiliyya; this *ḥarīm* consisted of a part of the

[3] Ibn Abī l-Hadīd, *Sharḥ nahj al-balāgha*, ed. Muḥammad Abū l-Faḍl Ibrāhīm (Cairo, 1382/1963), XVIII, 297 (read in the first hemistich *ghafīra*, not *ʿaqīra*; in the third hemistich read *minan māniʿuhu* instead of *minnā māniʿun*; in the fourth read *thabīrah* instead of *bathīrah*.

[4] Al-Balādhurī, *Ansāb al-ashrāf*, MS. Ashir Efendi 597/8, fol. 1161a.

[5] See on him, *GAS*, I, 266, no. 3.

clothes (of the Bedouins whom the Qurashites acommodated – K) and a share of the meat of the slaughtered beasts. Then Ẓuwaylim recited the verses in which he complained of al-Mughīra's iniquitous demands and of his actions which prevented him (i.e. Ẓuwaylim – K) from performing the rites of pilgrimage.[6] A shortened version of this report is given by Ibn Durayd.[7]

Ẓuwaylim's deed was praised by one of his relatives, the Fazārī poet Jabbār b. Mālik b. Ḥimār b. Ḥazn b. ʿAmr b. Jābir b. Khushayn.[8] Jabbār said:

> *wa-naḥnu manaʿnā min qurayshin ḥarīmahā : bi-makkata ayyāma l-taḥāluqi wa-l-naḥri.*
> "We denied Quraysh their *ḥarīm* : at Mecca on the days of the shaving [of heads – K] and of the slaughter [of victims – K]."[9]

But Ẓuwaylim revolted not only against the iniquitous rules and payments imposed on his tribe by some of the Meccan leaders; he also rebelled against the unjust deeds of his relatives, the leaders of his tribe. According to some reports Khushayn b. Laʾy, the grandfather of Ẓuwaylim, was one of the famous warriors of Fazāra; he was nicknamed *dhū l-raʾsayn*, "The Man with the Two Heads," and nobody in Fazāra equalled him in the number of raids carried out by him.[10] His grandson ʿAmr b. Jābir b. Khushayn regarded it as his privilege to get two young camels from every captive captured by Ghaṭafān (to whom Fazāra belonged – K) and freed on ransom.[11] Ẓuwaylim decided to prevent him from unjustly levying this share of the ransom. The motives of his action are clearly expounded in two of his verses:

> *arā ʿamran yasūmu l-nāsa khasfan : lahu min kulli ʿānin bakratāni*
> *fa-innī dāfiʿun mā kunta tuʿṭā : fa-hal laka bi-ntizāʿihimā yadāni*
> "I see ʿAmr wronging the people : to him [belongs the right – K] to take from every captive two young camels.

[6] The verses recorded by al-Balādhurī differ slightly from those recorded by al-Zubayr b. Bakkār; they read as follows: *yā rabbī hal ʿindaka min ghafīrah : inna minan māniʿuhā l-mughīrah. wa-māniʿun baʿda minan thabīrah : wa-māniʿī rabbī an azūrah : aḥbisu mālī wa-adaʿ tanḥīrah.*

[7] Ibn Durayd, *al-Ishtiqāq*, ed. ʿAbd al-Salām Hārūn (Cairo, 1378/1958), p. 282 (the final hemistich, as recorded by al-Balādhurī, is missing).

[8] On Mālik b. Ḥimār see Caskel, *Ǧamharaṭ an-nasab* (*Das Genealogische Werk des Ibn al-Kalbī*) (Leiden, 1966), II, 389.

[9] Al-Balādhurī, MS., fol. 1161b, sup.; on Jābbār b. Mālik see al-Āmidī, *al-Muʾtalif wa-l-mukhtalif*, ed. ʿAbd al-Sattār Farrāj (Cairo, 1381/1961), pp. 128, 138.

[10] Al-Balādhurī, MS., fol. 1161, quoting it on the authority of Ibn al-Kalbī. This assessment is indeed recorded in Ibn al-Kalbī, *Jamharat al-nasab*, MS. Br. Mus., Add. 23, 297, fol. 175b.

[11] Ibn al-Kalbī, *Jamhara*, MS. Br. Mus., fol. 175b; Ibn Ḥazm, *Jamharat ansāb al-ʿarab*, ed. ʿAbd al-Salām Hārūn (Cairo, 1382/1963), p. 259; al-Balādhurī, MS., fol. 1161a.

But I am repudiating what you have been given : do you have the power to snatch them [from my hands – K]? [12]

The leadership of one of the sons of Khushayn (Jābir? – K) was apparently anything but benign; he killed a man who dared to compose verses against him. This deed was praised by a Fazārī poet, Ibn al-ʿAnqā, who extolled the strength and glory of the "Son of the Man with Two Heads." [13]

The few details about Ẓuwaylim give us some insight into the struggle for justice waged by certain courageous tribal rebels against the iniquitous actions of tribal leaders and the oppressive deeds of members of the Meccan nobility.

According to a peculiar tradition even the fundamental event of the transfer of custody over the Kaʿba to Quṣayy came about as an outcome of struggle against the iniquity of Quṣayy's predecessor, Abū Ghubshān. According to an account traced back to Ibn Jurayj and recorded by al-Fākihī from a compilation of al-Wāqidī, the slaughter of the *baḥīra* camels (i.e. lope-eared she camels set free – K) was carried out (scil. in the period of the Jāhiliyya – K) at the Kaʿba, close to Isāf and Nāʾila (who were at that time located close to the Kaʿba – K).[14] Abū-Ghubshān used to take for himself the head and the neck of every *baḥīra* slaughtered; later he considered this to be insufficient and ordered to add to it the shoulders, and people obeyed. But afterwards Abū Ghubshān required in addition the hind part of the victim; however, people were reluctant to obey this. When a man of the Banū ʿUqayl, Murra b. Kathīr (or Kabīr), slaughtered the victim at the Kaʿba, Abū Ghubshān demanded to hand over to him the parts of the animal which he regarded as his due. The ʿUqaylī disobeyed and "people from Quraysh and others" supported the argument of the ʿUqaylī and pronounced the bid of Abū Ghubshān as *ʿabath*, "a wicked deed". Consequently Abū Ghubshān declared that he would not stay in Mecca if people did not accede to his demands, and decided to give up his prerogative at the Kaʿba for a wine skin. In this way Quṣayy acquired control of the Kaʿba.[15]

[12] Al-Balādhurī, MS., fol. 1161a.

[13] Al-Balādhurī, MS., fol. 1161b:

abā li-bni dhī l-raʾsayni majdun muqaddamun:
wa-sayfun idhā massa l-ḍarībata yaqṭaʿu
fa-qultu li-shawwālin tawaqqa dhubābahā:
wa-lā-taḥmi anfan an yusabba muraqqaʿu

The name of the executed man was Shawwāl b. Muraqqaʿ.

[14] About the location of Isāf and Nāʾila see U. Rubin, "The Kaʿba. Aspects of its ritual functions and position in pre-Islamic and early Islamic times," *JSAI* (forthcoming) ad notes 49–50, 121, 172–173, 175.

[15] Al-Fāsī, *Shifā al-gharām bi-akhbāri l-baladi l-ḥarām* (Cairo, 1956), II, 54.

The stories concerning Abū Ghubshān and Quṣayy, or Ẓuwaylim and Mughīra, are but two instances in a chain of reports relating to the incessant struggle of some tribal groups associated with Quraysh to establish fair and honest relations with Meccan clans and the strenuous efforts of some Meccan leaders to secure justice at Mecca itself. Terms like *baghy, khasf, ẓulm* and *jawr* appearing in reports of this kind enable us to reach an understanding of the character of the struggle against iniquity and oppression.

*

The period of the end of the sixth and the beginning of the seventh century was characterized by intertribal conflicts and by the pressure of the Byzantine and Persian Empires (through their vassal states) on the tribal divisions aimed at widening their influence and tightening their control over the Arabian peninsula. Mecca extended in that period its commercial relations, becoming a centre of economic activity for the tribes of the Arabian peninsula, and strengthened its ties with other centres like Medina and Ṭāʾif; transactions of considerable extent involving the purchase of landed property and financial enterprises were carried out by Meccan businessmen.[16]

The commercial co-operation of the merchants of the cities (like Mecca and Medina) with the tribes called for acumen, flexibility and close knowledge of intertribal relations. This can be seen in the story of Qays b. Zuhayr al-ʿAbsī:[17] when he decided to prepare a raid against the Banū ʿĀmir in order to avenge the murder of his father, he set out to Medina and approached Uḥayḥa b. al-Julāḥ al-Awsī, asking that he should sell him weapons. He inquired especially about a strongly built coat of mail owned by Uḥayḥa; he wished to buy it or to receive it as a gift. Uḥayḥa's answer was a shrewd one: "A man like me does not sell weapons; would I know that the Banū ʿĀmir will not claim that I extended help against them to their enemies I would present it to you as a gift." Uḥayḥa was grateful to the Banū ʿĀmir for the praises by which he was lauded in the poem of Khālid b. Jaʿfar of the ʿĀmir b. Ṣaʿṣaʿa; he extolled him as the man of Yathrib who was capable of granting shelter and protection. Uḥayḥa was not ready to forfeit his friendly relations with the ʿĀmir.[18] He nevertheless

[16] See e.g. *JSAI*, 1 (1979), 8–10, 17.

[17] See on him e.g. Caskel, *Ğamhara*, II, 464.

[18] Al-Balādhurī, MS., fol. 1154a:

wa-kāna uḥayḥatu yaḥfaẓu li-banī ʿāmirin anna khālida bna jaʿfarin madaḥahu bi-abyātin awwaluhā:

idhā mā aradta l-ʿizza fī ahli yathribin : fa-nādi bi-ṣawtin
yā-uḥayḥatu tumnaʿu

fa-tuṣbiḥu bi-l-awsi bni ʿamri bni ʿāmirin:
ka-annaka jārun li-l-yamāniyyi tubbaʿi

handed over to Qays the coat of mail and Qays succeeded in acquiring at Medina the needed weapons: spears and coats of mail.[19]

It was indeed Uḥayḥa's coat of mail which brought about a serious clash between Qays b. Zuhayr and one of his relatives, al-Rabīʿ b. Zuyād al-ʿAbsī.[20] Qays drove away 400 pregnant camels belonging to al-Rabīʿ b. Ziyād; he brought them to Mecca and sold them to Ḥarb b. Umayya, ʿAbdallah b. Judʿān and Hishām b. al-Mughīra in exchange for horses and weapons. Qays remained for some time in Mecca (seeking asylum there – K); then he went to the Banū Badr of Fazāra and was granted their protection.[21] It is interesting to note that Qays b. Zuhayr bought in Mecca the ominous horse, Dāḥis, out of the money which he received for the plundered camels of Rabīʿ b. Ziyād.[22] The keen interest of the Medinan notables in the feud between the quarrelling and clashing tribes of ʿAbs and Fazāra and their attempt to bring about a peace agreement between them can be gauged from the report stating that a delegation of the people of Yathrib including the leading personalities of the city – ʿAmr b. al-Iṭnāba, Uḥayḥa b. al-Julāh, Qays b. al-Khaṭīm, Abū Qays b. al-Aslat and the Jew Kaʿb (perhaps Kaʿb b. al-Ashraf – K) – came in order to reconcilie the fighting tribes.[23]

The fact that Qays b. Zuhayr asked for protection of the Banū Badr of Fazāra is instructive. This family became at that time the leading and influential family-group of Fazāra, played a decisive role in the tribal clashes and established close relations with Mecca. ʿAbd al-Raḥmān b. Ḥassān put the clan of the Banū Badr on a par with that of the Makhzūmī clan of the Banū Mughīra as to pride and glory.[24] Ḥudhayfa b. Badr was nicknamed *rabbu*

[19] Al-Balādhurī, MS., fol. 1154a: ... *thumma btāʿa qaysun min yathriba rimāḥan wa-adrāʿan*; this report bears evidence that Yathrib was not merely a rural centre of agricultural activity; there seem to have been a considerable amount of commercial transactions.

[20] See on him g.e., Caskel, *Ǧamhara*, II, 475.

[21] Al-Balādhurī, MS., fol. 1154a: ... *fa-lammā balagha dhālika qaysan aghāra ʿalā l-naʿam fa-ṭarada li-l-rabīʿi* (text: *al-rabiʿ*) *arbaʿa miʾ ati nāqatin laqūḥin fa-marra bihā ilā makkata fa-bāʿahā min ḥarbi bni umayyata wa-ʿabdi llāhi bni judʿāna wa-hishāmi bni l-mughīrati bi-l-khayli wa-l-silāḥi, wa-aqāma bi-makkata, thumma innahu laḥiqa bi-banī badri bni ʿamrin* ...

[22] Al-Balādhurī, MS., fol. 1154b, l. 20: ... *wa-kāna qaysu bnu zuhayrin btāʿa dāḥisan bi-makkata min thamani ibli l-rabīʿi, fa-anzāhu ʿalā farasin lahu fa-jāʾat bi-muhratin sammāhā l-ghabrāʾa.*

[23] Al-Balādhurī, MS., fol. 1156a: ... *wa-qadimat jamāʿatun min ahli yathriba li-l-iṣlāḥi bayna l-ḥayyayni : ʿamru bnu l-iṭnābati, wa-uḥayḥatu bnu l-julāḥi, wa-qaysu bnu l-khaṭīmi wa-abū qaysin bnu l-aslati wa-kaʿbun l-yahūdī* ...

[24] Ibn Abī l-Ḥadīd, XVIII, 287:
inni ṭamiʿtu bi-fakhri man law rāmahu :
ālu l-mughīrati aw banū dhakwāni

maʿaddin, the "Lord of Maʿadd."[25] Abū l-Yaqẓān reports that Ḥiṣn b. Ḥudhayfa was one of the greatest leaders of the federation of Ghaṭafān; he commanded all the allied forces of Ghaṭafān and Asad. A man attending the council (*majlis*) of Muʿāwiya said: "We have never seen a Bedouin who, while leaning on his bow between the two allies, Asad and Ghaṭafān, and dividing the spoils among them, was more dignified (*aʿẓamu qadran*) than Ḥiṣn b. Ḥudhayfa."[26]

Two Fazārī chiefs are highly praised by the poet of ʿĀmir b. Ṣaʿṣaʿa, ʿĀmir b. al-Ṭufayl: they granted him protection when he was captured during a clash with the Fazāra and the Fazārī leader ʿUyayna b. Ḥiṣn demanded to decapitate him; he extols them in one of his poems saying:

1. When thou desirest to meet with a sure defence, seek the protection of Khidhām son of Zayd, if Khidhām will grant it thee.
2. I called upon Abū l-Jabbār, specially naming Mālik; and from aforetime he whom thou tookest under thy shield was never scathed (Lyall's translation).[27]

The competition between tribal leaders to gain rank, position and recognition of governors and rulers is fairly clear in the report about the meeting of Ḥudhayfa b. Badr al-Fazārī and al-Ḥakam b. Marwān b. Zinbāʿ al-ʿAbsī at the court of Ḥīra. Ḥudhayfa used to frequent the court of al-Nuʿmān b. al-Mundhir; the king (al-Nuʿmān) treated him with honour and kindness. Ḥudhayfa used to bring gifts to al-Mutajarrida.[28] Al-Ḥakam also used to visit the court of al-Nuʿmān and bring him gifts. When Ḥudhayfa and al-Ḥakam met some day in al-Ḥīra, al-Ḥakam said to Ḥudhayfa: "May God curse a dignity gained through [the intercession of] women". Al-Mutajarrida became enraged when she heard the words of al-Ḥakam and decided to send to Ḥudhayfa a songstress and wine. When al-Ḥakam attended the council (*majlis*) of Ḥudhayfa the latter asked the girl to sing some poems of Imruʾ l-Qays in

la-malaʾtuhā khaylan taḍibbu lithātuhā :
mithla l-dabā wa-kawāsiri l-ʿiqbāni

Banū Dhakwān are explained to denote Banū Badr b. ʿAmr b. Juwayya b. Dhakwān of the Banū ʿAdiyy of Fazāra; to this clan belong Ḥudhayfa, Ḥamal and their families. See on the descendants of Dhakwān: Ibn al-Kalbī, *Jamhara*, MS. Br. Mus., fol. 172a, ult.

25 Al-Balādhurī, MS., fol. 1153b: ... *wa-kāna yuqālu lahu rabbu maʿaddin* ...: and see: Labīd, *Dīwān*, ed. Iḥsān ʿAbbās (Kuwayt, 1962), p. 55; Ibn Abī l-Ḥadīd, XVIII, 295; Muḥammad b. Ḥabīb, *al-Muḥabbar*, ed. Ilse Lichtenstaedter (Hyderabad, 1361/1942), p. 461; Ibn Qutayba, *al-Maʿārif*, ed. Tharwat ʿUkāsha (Cairo, 1969), pp. 83, 402, 592.

26 Al-Balādhurī, MS., fol. 1158b.

27 ʿĀmir b. al-Ṭufayl, *Dīwān*, ed. Ch. Lyall (Leiden, 1913), p. 141, no. XXVI (Arabic text); see *ibid.*, "Introduction," pp. 81, 114; and see al-Mufaḍḍal al-Ḍabbī, *al-Mufaḍḍaliyyāt*, ed. Ch. Lyall (Oxford, 1921), p. 33.

28 See on her e.g. *Aghānī*, index.

which he mentioned love-affairs with ʿAbsī women. Al-Ḥakam became furious and hit the songstress. Ḥudhayfa rebuked him, saying that he had lost his mind and hurt the honour of al-Nuʿmān. When the two leaders returned to their tribes they related the event; this accident widened the rift between the two leaders and increased the animosity between their tribal divisions.[29]

The position of the Fazārī leaders among the federation of Ghaṭafān caused some tribal divisions to attempt at concluding agreements or alliances with them. The ʿĀmir b. Ṣaʿṣaʿa tried to persuade Ḥiṣn b. Ḥudhayfa and his son ʿUyayna to withdraw from their alliance with the Asad, to enable Asad to return to their relations with Kināna, and to conclude an alliance of the Ghaṭafān with ʿĀmir b. Ṣaʿṣaʿa. ʿUyayna b. Ḥiṣn considered the offer and consulted about it the Banū Dhubyān (one of the main branches of Ghaṭafān – K); they however refused and ʿUyayna had to give up the idea of the alliance with ʿĀmir.[30]

ʿUyayna and his tribal division, the Fazāra, played a very important role in the struggle of the Prophet and the Muslim community with Quraysh at Mecca. An agreement of non-aggression was concluded between the Prophet and ʿUyayna for a limited period; when the Muslim forces left Medina for the raid of Muraysīʿ they feared that ʿUyayna may attack the city in which there were no warriors left, because the treaty was to expire at that time; the Prophet allayed their fears, assuring them that ʿUyayna would not attack the city.[31] ʿUyayna attended the Battle of the Ditch commanding a fighting body of a thousand warriors of Fazāra; it was the strongest force of the allies of Quraysh. Smaller units numbering about 400 warriors each were recruited from among the relatives of Fazāra, Ashjaʿ and Murra.[32] When the situation of the besieged Muslim community became serious, the Prophet sent to ʿUyayna offering him a third of the date harvest of Medina if he withdrew with his force, thus causing disarray among the other forces of the allies of Quraysh. ʿUyayna asked for half the harvest, but consented later to accept the proposal of the Prophet to accept a third of it. However, when the agreement had to be signed, the Companions of the Prophet opposed it and persuaded the Prophet to annul it.[33] The failure of ʿUyayna to gain profits and success on the "Day of the Ditch" (i.e. the siege of Medina) recurred in the siege of Khaybar. ʿUyayna promised to hurry to help the besieged Jews against the besieging Muslims in

[29] Al-Balādhurī, MS., fol. 1154b.

[30] Al-Nābigha al-Dhubyānī, *Dīwān*, ed. Muḥammad Jamal (Beirut, 1347/1929), p. 98.

[31] Al-Wāqidī, *al-Maghāzī*, ed. Marsden Jones (London, 1966), p. 422.

[32] See e.g. al-Wāqidī, p. 443.

[33] Al-Wāqidī, pp. 477–480; Ibn Hishām, *al-Sīra al-nabawiyya*, ed. Muṣṭafā l-Saqā, Ibrāhīm al-Abyārī, ʿAbd al-Ḥafīẓ Shalabī (Cairo, 1355/1936), III, 234.

return for half of the date harvest of Khaybar; he negotiated, however, at the same time with the Prophet the withdrawal of his force of 400 warriors in return for half of the date harvest. In one of the stages of the Muslim attack on Khaybar the Fazārī force withdrew forsaking the besieged Jews. ʿUyayna did not get his half of the date harvest and had to satisfy himself with the grant bestowed on him by the Prophet: a mountain at Khaybar called Dhū l-Ruqayba.[34]

There were some clashes between troops of the Prophet and some Fazārī units, but ʿUyayna was shrewd enough to appear at the conquest of Mecca (although without his tribe) and to accompany the Prophet at his entrance to the city;[35] he is counted among "those whose hearts had to be reconciled" (*al-muʾallafa qulūbuhum*) and was indeed granted by the Prophet a gift of a hundred camels.[36] In spite of his treacherous behaviour when he was sent as messenger of the Muslim forces to al-Ṭāʾif,[37] he was dispatched by the Prophet against a group of Tamīm who prevented their neighbours, the Khuzāʿa, from paying taxes.[38] Finally the Prophet appointed ʿUyayna as tax-collector of Fazāra, an influential and responsible office.[39]

This short sketch of the role of ʿUyayna and his tribal division, the Fazāra, in the Prophet's period indicates clearly that they had close relations with Mecca.[40] They joined the Prophet only after his victory. The high position acquired by ʿUyayna in the period of the Prophet can be seen from the fact that the Caliph ʿUthmān b. ʿAffān married his daughter, Umm al-Banīn bint ʿUyayna b. Ḥiṣn.[41] Only two wives of ʿUthmān attended his clandestine

[34] See e.g. al-Wāqidī, pp. 650–652, 676; and see Yāqūt, *Muʿjam al-buldān* (Beirut, 1376/1957), s.v. Ruqayba.

[35] See e.g. al-Wāqidī, pp. 803–804.

[36] See e.g. Ibn Hishām, IV, 136–137; al-Maqrīzī, *Imtāʿu l-asmāʿ*, ed. Maḥmūd Muḥammad Shākir (Cairo, 1941), I, 424.

[37] See al-Wāqidī, pp. 932–933.

[38] Al-Wāqidī, pp. 974–975.

[39] Al-Balādhurī, *op. cit.*, I (ed. Muḥammad Ḥamīdullah, Cairo 1959) 530.

[40] The Fazāra seem to have taken part in certain ritual practices at the Kaʿba since very early times: see e.g. Ibn Hishām, I, 128:

naḥnu dafaʿnā ʿan abī sayyārah : wa-ʿan mawālīhi banī fazārah

and see al-Fāsī, *Shifā*, II, 32–34 and 35 l. 15; al-ʿIṣāmī, *Simṭ al-nujūm al-ʿawālī* (Cairo, 1380), I, 217; al-Kalāʿī, *al-Iktifāʾ fī maghāzī rasūli llāhi wa-l-thalāthati l-khulafā*, ed. Muṣṭafā ʿAbd al-Wāḥid (Cairo, 1287/1968), I, 77; al-Balādhurī, MS., fol. 1180b.

[41] Al-Balādhurī, MS., fol. 1158a, sup.; Ibn Saʿd, *Ṭabaqāt*, (Beirut, 1377/1957), III, 54; Muḥammad b. Yaḥyā al-Māliqī, *al-Tamhīd wa-l-bayān fī maqtali l-shahīd ʿuthmān*, ed. Maḥmūd Yūsuf Zāʾid (Beirut, 1964), p. 4; Umm al-Banīn was before that offered by ʿUyayna to the Prophet as wife (see Ibn ʿAbd al-Barr, *al-Istīʿāb fīmaʿrifati l-aṣḥāb*, ed. ʿAlī Muḥammad al-Bijāwī [Cairo, 1380/1960], p. 1249 ult.)

funeral: the Kalbite Nāʾila and the Fazārite Umm al-Banīn.[42]

The prophet rightly characterized ʿUyayna as "the fool obeyed by his people."[43] He got indeed the allegiance and loyalty of his people when he decided to fight the body politic of Medina, leading the troops of the Fazāra against the Muslim forces after the death of the Prophet in the "War of the Ridda."[44]

II

Another division of Ghaṭafān, the Banū Murra b. ʿAwf, seem to have had close relations with Mecca. Some clans of Murra claimed that their ancestor was ʿAwf b. Luʾayy, the ancestor of Quraysh.[45] Al-Ḥārith b. Ẓālim al-Murrī asked for the protection of ʿAbdallah b. Judʿān, denied his descent from Ghaṭafān and stated that he was from Quraysh.[46] ʿUmar is said to have justified their claim and was even ready to accept them into the fold of Quraysh.[47] It is of interest that the Meccan notable, ʿAbdallah b. Judʿān,[48] interceded with the king of al-Ḥīra, al-Nuʿmān, on behalf of al-Ḥārith b. Ẓālim and asked that the protection of the king be renewed for him.[49]

A distinctive feature of the religio-economic system of the Banū Murra was the institution of the *basl.* They observed eight months as the trucial period during the year and travelled during these months through the territories of the Bedouins undisturbed; the Bedouin tribes accepted this order and granted them security during these months.[50] One may assume that this *basl* order was designed to bring about a competition between Mecca with its four trucial months and the *basl* system of the Banū Murra.

[42] Ibn Saʿd, III, 78 inf.–79 sup.

[43] See e.g. Ibn ʿAbd al-Barr, pp. 1249 inf.–1250; al-Jāḥiẓ *al-Bayān wa-l-tabyīn*, ed. ʿAbd al-Salām Hārūn (rpt. Beirut of Cairo, 1367/1948), II, 253.

[44] See e.g. Ella Landau–Tasseron, *Aspects of the Ridda Wars*, Ph.D. Diss., Hebrew University, 1981 (in Hebrew), Chapter III (Ghaṭafān) ad notes 137–149.

[45] See e.g. al-Suhaylī, *al-Rawḍ al-unuf*, ed. ʿAbd al-Raḥmān al-Wakīl (Cairo, 1387/1967), I, 410–412; al-Balādhurī, I, 42–43; Ibn Kathīr, *al-Bidāya wa-l-nihāya* (Riyāḍ–Beirut, 1966), II, 204.

[46] Al-Balādhurī, MS., fol. 1143b; *idem*, I, 42 inf.; al-Suhaylī, I, 411; al-Jāḥiẓ, *al-Burṣān wa-l-ʿurjān*, ed. Muḥammad Mursī l-Khūlī (Beirut, 1392/1972), p. 298; Abū l-Baqā Hibatullāh, *al-Manāqib al-mazyadiyya fī akhbāri l-mulūki l-asadiyya*, MS. Br. Mus. add. 23, 296, fol. 43a.

[47] Al-Suhaylī, I, 411, 412.

[48] See on him *EI*², s.v. ʿAbd Allāh b. Djudʿān (Ch. Pellat); and see above ad notes 18, 43.

[49] Al-Balādhurī, MS., fol. 1143b: *thumma innahu ṭalaba lahu l-amāna mina l-nuʿmāni fa-āmanahu wa-qadima fa-aqāma ʿindahu.*

[50] See e.g. al-Suhaylī, I, 414, 421; Ibn Hishām, i, 106–107; and see additional sources in *JESHO*, 8 (1965), 141, n. 4.

The conflict between Mecca and the Banū Murra is reflected in the report about a building erected by the Manū Murra at Buss.[51] An explanatory note on a verse of al-Ḥuṣayn b. al-Ḥumām says: "Buss is a building erected by the Ghaṭafān; they built it in a shape similar to that of the Kaʿba, performed pilgrimage to it, revered it an called it *al-ḥaram*. Zuhayr b. Janāb al-Kalbī raided them and destroyed it."[52] An anonymous report recorded by al-Fayrūzābādī gives more details: Buss is a *House* of Ghaṭafān, built by Ẓālim b. As'ad. He saw that Quraysh circumambulated the Kaʿba and performed the *saʿy* between al-Ṣafā and al-Marwa; he therefore measured the Kaʿba, took a stone from al-Ṣafā and a stone from al-Marwa, returned to his people and built a *House* like the Kaʿba; he laid down the two stones and said: "These are the Ṣafā and the Marwa". So they (i.e. his people) became satisfied with it instead of the pilgrimage to Mecca. Subsequently Zuhayr b. Janāb al-Kalbī raided (scil. the Ghaṭafān – K), killed Ẓālim and destroyed his building.[53] Al-Balādhurī's report is concise: al-Muthallam b. Riyāḥ b. Ẓālim b. Asʿad (in text: Saʿd) b. Rabīʿa b. ʿĀmir was a noble man (*kāna sharīfan*). His grandfather, Ẓālim, was the man who built Buss; Buss is the *House*, which Ghaṭafān worshipped. Zuhayr b. Janāb said:

> Thus Ghaṭafān left afterwards Buss : and what has Ghaṭafān (to do) with a spacious tract of land?[54]

This report corresponds to that of Ibn al-Kalbī.[55]

Another report in Ibn al-Kalbī's *Jamhara* contains details similar to those given in the account of al-Fayrūzābādī (the two stones of al-Ṣafā and al-Marwa, the *House* erected in the territory of Ghaṭafān, Zuhayr b. Janāb destroyed the *House* and [buildings? – K] around it), but has a significant passage, not recorded in other sources: when the Prophet heard about Zuhayr

[51] In text *"lubs"* which is an error. See *L. ʿA.* s.v. bss (correctly Buss); and see the correction in Wellhausen, *Reste Arabischen Heidentums* (Berlin, 1887), p. 33, n. 2; and see Iḥsān ʿAbbās, "Two Hitherto Unpublished Texts on Pre-Islamic Religion," *La Signification du Bas Moyen Age dans l'Histoire et la Culture du Monde Musulman, Actes du 8me Congrès de l'Union Européenne des Arabisants et Islamisants* (Aix-en-Provence, 1976), pp. 7–16; and see Iḥsān ʿAbbās, "Naṣṣāni jadīdāni ʿani l-dīni fī l-jāhiliyyati," *al-Abḥāth*, 1973–1977, pp. 27–34.

[52] *Aghānī*, XII, 126; see on Buss: Yāqūt, *Muʿjam al-buldān*, s.v. b.s.s.: . . . *wa-buss ayḍan baytun banat-hu ghaṭafānu muḍāhātan li-l-kaʿba.*

[53] Al-Fayrūzābādī, *al-Qāmūs al-muḥīṭ*, s.v. bss; and see Wellhausen, pp. 33–34; this report is recorded in al-Sinjārī's, *Manāʾiḥ al-karam*, MS. Leiden, Or. 7018, fols. 13b, ult.–14a.

[54] Al-Balādhurī, MS., fol. 1146b–1147a sup.

[55] Ibn al-Kalbī, *Jamhara*, MS. Br. Mus., fol. 168b, sup.: . . . *al-Muthallam b. Riyāḥ b. Ẓālim b. Asʿad b. Rabīʿa b. ʿĀmir kāna sharīfan, wa-abūhu riyāḥun lladhī qāla lahu zuhayru bnu janābin: fa-khallā baʿdahā ghaṭafānu . . .; wa-kāna banāhu jadduhu ẓālimun . . .*

b. Janāb's action he said: "Of the matters of the Jāhiliyya nothing is in agreement with Islam except that which Zuhayr b. Janāb did."[56] It was no doubt an act of great significance as it helped to preserve the Kaᶜba as the only sanctuary of the Arabian peninsula and spoiled a bold attempt at erecting a tribal sanctuary in competition with the Kaᶜba at Mecca. The intention to imitate the Kaᶜba comes out even in the name of Ghaṭafānī sanctuary, *Buss*, which is derived from the root *bss* and is reminiscent of the name of the Meccan sanctuary, which is called al-Bāssa.[57] The destruction of Buss served indirectly the cause of Islam and the utterance attributed to the Prophet undoubtedly reflects a historical truth.

It is worthwhile mentioning that Buss was not the only sanctuary which was erected by a tribe or a governor: such was for instance the case of the sanctuary of Abraha which was erected in order to compete with the Kaᶜba[58] and the sanctuary erected in Qawdam.[59]

*

The reasons for the enmity between Zuhayr b. Janāb and the Banū Murra, his position in his tribe, the Kalb, his role in the intertribal contests on the background of the rivalry of the petty kingdoms and the struggle of the Byzantine and Sassanian powers for control of the tribes of the Arabian peninsula, all these data are recorded in reports which are often obscure, blurred, divergent or contradictory. A scrutiny of these reports may provide a clue for the elucidation of, at least, some aspects of these events.

According to a tradition traced back to Ibn al-Aᶜrābī (d. ca. 230 AH) the Banū Baghīḍ were attacked by the Ṣudā᾽ (a division of Madhḥij) when they were on their way from Tihāma. The Banū Baghīḍ succeeded however in repelling the attack, gained a sweeping victory and took rich booty. Then they decided to build a *ḥaram*, like that at Mecca, in which no hunted beast would be kiiled, no tree would be felled and no man seeking refuge would be troubled (*lā yuhāju ᶜā᾽idhuhu*). The plan was carried out by the tribal division of Ghaṭafān, the Banū Murra; the man in charge of the *ḥaram* and the builder of

[56] Ibn al-Kalbī, *Jamhara*, MS. Br. Mus., fol. 191a inf.–191b sup.: . . . *fa-hadama* (i.e. Zuhayr b. Janāb) *l-bayta wa-mā ḥawlahu, fa-balagha dhālika l-nabiyya* (ṣ) *fa-qāla: "lam yakun shay᾽un min amri l-jāhiliyyati wāfaqa l-islāma illā mā ṣanaᶜa zuhayru bnu janābin".*

[57] See *L. ᶜA.*, s.v. bss; Ibn Ẓuhayra, *al-Jāmiᶜ al-laṭīf fī faḍli makkata wa-ahlihā wa-binā᾽i l-bayti l-sharīf* (Cairo, 1357/1938), p. 160, penult.; al-Azraqī, *Kitāb akhbāri makkata*, ed. F. Wüstenfeld (rpt. Beirut), p. 50, l. 8; Ibn Nāṣir al-Dīn al-Dimashqī, *Jāmiᶜ al-āthār fī mawlidi l-nabiyyi l-mukhtār*, MS. Cambridge Or. 913, fol. 269a.

[58] See e.g. *EI*², s.v. Abraha (A.F.L. Beeston).

[59] See Yāqūt, *Muᶜjam al-buldān*, s.v. Qawdam.

its walls was Riyāḥ b. Ẓālim (not his father, Ẓālim – K). They built it when staying at a well called Buss. When the news reached Zuhayr b. Janāb, who was then the *sayyid* of Kalb, he vowed to prevent the Ghaṭafān from carrying out their plan. He summoned his tribal relatives to aid him in the noble enterprise (*akram ma'thura*) of the destruction of the Fazārī *ḥaram*, but the Banū l-Qayn from Jusham refused to participate in the raid; he carried out the raid with his people only and defeated the Ghaṭafān. He captured a rider (*fāris*) of the Ghaṭafān in the *ḥaram* of Buss and ordered to kill him; his order was however disobeyed by one of his warriors, who argued that the man was a *basl.*[60] Zuhayr stated that for him there was no obligation to refrain from harming a *basl* (i.e. to take his life – K; *mā baslun ʿalayya bi-ḥarāmin*) and he himself decapitated him. He desecrated the *ḥaram* (*ʿaṭṭala dhālika l-ḥaram*), generously released the captured women and returned them to their tribe.[61] The passage about the decapitation of the *basl* and the desecration of the *ḥaram* of Buss is of importance. It may be deduced that this event put an end to the free and undisturbed traffic of the Banū Murra during eight months in the Arabian peninsula and did away with the sanctity of the *ḥaram* of Buss; the only sacred months to remain were thus the four months of the Pax Meccana; the only sanctuary which continued to be venerated was the *ḥaram* of Mecca. Zuhayr's deed appears to be the reason why the group of Janāb b. Hubal were included in the organization of the Ḥums.[62]

Some of the accounts link the person of Janāb with that of Dāwūd b. Hubāla,[63] whose kingdom was conquered by the Byzantines and who fought at that time on their side. He later embraced Christianity and became reluctant to shed blood; he was however compelled to obey the order of the Byzantines to raid the Arab tribes. In his force was (according to this report) Zuhayr b. Janāb. Zuhayr went out, fought and killed Haddāj b. Mālik of the ʿAbd Qays and Haddāj b. Mālik b. Taymallāh b. Thaʿlaba b. ʿUkāba.[64]

Some reports connect Zuhayr b. Janāb with the expedition of Abraha.[65] When the Abyssinians went out on their expedition to destroy the sanctuary at Mecca they were approached by Zuhayr; he met their king, was welcomed by

[60] See on *basl* n. 50 above.

[61] *Aghānī*, XXI, 63.

[62] See *JESHO*, 8 (1965), 133, n. 4, 134, n. 3; and see Caskel, *Ǧamhara*, II, 77 inf.–78 sup.

[63] Caskel, *Ǧamhara*, II, 232 (Dāwūd b. Habāla).

[64] See on him Ibn Ḥabīb, *"Asmā' al-mughtālīn min al-ashrāf"* in ʿAbd al-Salām Hārūn's *Nawādir al-makhṭūṭāt* (Cairo, 1374/1954), II, 127–128; on the two Haddāj see Caskel, *Ǧamhara*, II, 276.

[65] See on Abraha: *EI*², s.v. Abraha (A.F.L. Beeston); and see R. Paret, *Der Koran, Kommentar und Konkordanz* (Stuttgart, 1980), ad Sura 105; and see *JESHO*, 15 (1972), 61–76.

him and was sent as his messenger to (the tribes in – K) the vicinity (*nāḥiya*) of Iraq in order to summon them to submit to his authority (*ilā l-dukhūli fī ṭāʿatihi*). When he was in the territory of Bakr b. Wāʾil, he was attacked by a man of the tribe and seriously wounded, but managed to escape.[66] A similar report is given in the *Aghānī* on the authority of Abū ʿAmr al-Shaybānī; there are, however, several differences which may be noted: Abraha appointed Zuhayr b. Janāb over the tribes of Bakr and Taghlib; he ruled them for a time until they were afflicted by a drought. Zuhayr prevented them from pasturing their herds unless they paid the taxes imposed upon them; their situation worsened and they were on the brink of perishing. One of the Taymallah b. Thaʿlaba[67] decided to assassinate Zuhayr; he attacked him in his sleep and pierced his belly with a sword; he left the tent of Zuhayr with the conviction that he had killed him. Zuhayr remained however alive, and a group of his people wrapped him in a shroud and were given permission to leave with what was supposed to be his corpse in order to bury him in the territory of his tribe. The stratagem succeeded: Zuhayr returned to his tribe, recovered and ordered to prepare a raid against the Bakr and Taghlib. The raid was successful and Zuhayr returned with a rich booty. Kulayb and Muhalhil were captured and many warriors from Taghlib were killed.[68]

Zuhayr's appointment over the Bakr and Taghlib is explicitly mentioned in a poem of al-Musayyib b. al-Rifall, a descendant of Zuhayr:

1. *wa-abrahatu lladhī kāna ṣṭafānā : wa-sawwasanā wa-tāju l-mulki ʿālī*
2. *wa-qāsama niṣfa imratihi zuhayran : wa-lam yaku dūnahu fī l-amri wālī*
3. *wa-ammarahu ʿalā ḥayyay maʿaddin : wa-ammarahu ʿalā l-ḥayyi l-muʿālī*
4. *ʿalā bnay wāʾilin lahumā muhīnan : yarudduhumā ʿalā raghmi l-sibāli*
5. *bi-ḥabsihimā bi-dāri l-dhulli ḥattā : alammā yahlikāni mina l-huzāli*

1. And Abraha, he who had chosen us : and invested us with authority : and high is the crown of kingdom.
2. And he gave half of the rule to Zuhayr : nobody except him was a ruler of the affairs.
3. And he invested him with power over the two tribes of Maʿadd: and he gave him authority over the tribe competing for superiority

[66] Ibn Qutayba, *al-Shiʿr wa-l-shuʿarāʾ*, ed. M. J. de Goeje (Leiden, 1904), pp. 223–225.
[67] A group of Bakr b. Wāʾil; see Caskel, *Ǧamhara*, II, 543.
[68] *Aghānī*, XXI, 64.

4. Over the two sons of Wāʾil (i.e. their descendants) treating them with contempt : turning them humbled and abased.
5. Detaining them in the abode of vileness : until they would perish out of emaciation.[69]

Some reports tell about his visits to the court of the Ghassānī ruler and his stratagems in spreading false accusations against his opponents and foes in order to keep the favours of the ruler al-Ḥārith b. Māriya exclusively to himself.[70] Some accounts relate anecdotes about the attendance of Zuhayr at the courts of governors and rulers in company of certain fools of his family; Zuhayr succeeds in saving the people from the fateful results of their stupid words.[71]

The sources are unanimous about the strength and power of Zuhayr; he is said to have been one of the *jarrārūn* (i.e. commanding more than thousand warriors – K) and one who succeeded in uniting the whole tribe of Kalb, or even the whole federation of Quḍāʿa.[72] Ibn al-Kalbī reports a conflict between Zuhayr and Rizāḥ (a half brother of Quṣayy, the leader of ʿUdhra – K) concerning their attitude towards the tribal divisions of Nahd, Ḥawtaka and Jarm; these tribal divisions were driven out by Rizāḥ from the federation of Quḍāʿa, and were compelled to migrate and join other tribes. Rizāḥ's action was severely censured by Zuhayr.[73] Al-Bakrī records the story of the conflict. mentions the role of Nahd and their strength in the past and draws the line of succession of that power: Ḥanẓala b. Nahd, the ancestor of Nahd, was the arbiter of Tihāma and the leader of the Bedouins (*al-ʿarab*) at ʿUkāẓ during the period of the markets. Then the leadership went over to the Kalb b.

[69] Abū Ḥātim al-Sijistānī, *Kitāb al-muʿammarīn*, ed. Goldziher, (Leiden, 1899), p. 29 (Ar. text); al-Marzubānī, *Muʿjam al-shuʿarāʾ*, ed. F. Krenkow (Cairo, 1354), p. 386 (only 4 verses).

[70] *Aghānī*, IV, 175–176; Ibn ʿAsākir, *Tahdhīb taʾrīkh* (Beirut, 1399/1979), V, 321–322.

[71] *Aghānī*, XXI, 65 (the fool was his brother, Ḥāritha); Abū Hilāl al-ʿAskarī, *Jamharat al-amthāl*, ed. Muḥammad Abū l-Faḍl Ibrāhīm and ʿAbd al-Majīd Qaṭāmish (Cairo, 1384/1964), I, 151 (the fool was his brother, ʿAdiyy. According to Ibn al-Kalbī, *Jamhara*, Escurial 1968, p. 380 ʿAdiyy was considered a fool: *kāna yuḥammaqu*). Another fool in his family was his son Khidāsh (Ibn al-Kalbī, *Jamhara*, Esc. p. 405 ult.–406; see the utterance of al-Samawʾal about him: *laysa li-qalbi khidāshin udhunānī*).

[72] See Muḥammad b. Ḥabīb, *al-Muḥabbar*, p. 250 (Zuhayr and Rizāḥ b. Rabīʿa al-ʿUdhrī); *Aghānī*, XXI, 65 (Zuhayr and Ḥunn b. Zayd); al-Bakrī, *Muʿjam mā staʿjam*, ed. Muṣṭafā l-Saqā (Cairo, 1364/1945), p. 39 (Zuhayr and Rizāḥ b. Rabīʿa); Abū Ḥātim al-Sijistānī, p. 28 (Zuhayr and Rizāḥ); and see al-Majlisī, *Biḥār al-anwār* (Teheran, 1392), LI, 268; al-Murtaḍā, *Amālī*, ed. Muḥammad Abū l-Faḍl Ibrāhīm (Cairo, 1373/1954), I, 240; Ibn al-Kalbī, *Jamhara*, Esc. p. 514 (Zuhayr and Rizāḥ).

[73] Ibn al-Kalbī, *Jamhara*, Esc., p. 514; al-Bakrī, *Muʿjam mā staʿjam*, p. 39.

Wabara, afterwards to ʿAwf b. Kināna b. ʿAwf.[74] After some generations it passed over to Zuhayr b. Janāb, then to ʿAdiyy b. Janāb and finally it remained in the family of al-Ḥārith b. Ḥiṣn b. Ḍamḍam b. ʿAdiyy b. Janāb.[75] The conflict between Rizāḥ and the two tribes, Nahd and Ḥawtaka, is mentioned in Ibn Hishām's *Sīra*: but in this account it was Quṣayy who censured Rizāḥ for his expulsion of these two tribal divisions of Quḍāʿa. He said the following verses:

1. Who will tell Rizāḥ from me : that I blame you on two accounts:
2. I blame you for the Banū Nahd b. Zayd : because you drove a wedge between them and me.
3. And for Ḥawtaka b. Aslum : verily, he who treats them badly has badly treated me. (A. Guillaume's translation, slightly modified).

It is of great importance that Quṣayy wanted Quḍāʿa to increase and to be united because of "their goodwill to him when they responded to his appeal for help."[76] The account confirms that there were contacts between Quraysh and the Quḍāʿī divisions and shows the help extended by some Quḍāʿī groups to Quṣayy.

Al-Āmidī records a story in which Zuhayr is connected with the person of Muhalhil, the legendary leader of Taghlib during the wars of Basūs.[77] Zuhayr is said to have attacked the Taghlib, succeeded in getting away with booty, was however pursued by Muhalhil, who tracked down one of the attackers (Imruʾ l-Qays b. Ḥumām al-Kalbī) and wounded him.[78]

The reports about contacts between Zuhayr and Muhalhil are however refuted by a statement saying that Zuhayr preceded Muhalhil.[79]

The amusing story about the capture of Zuhayr by Hammām b. Murra[80] also belongs to the period of the war of Basūs. Zuhayr offered as ransom for his release a hundred camels, but Hammām refused; he consented however to free him on condition that Zuhayr would mention his name and make an invocation for his life before every drink.[81]

[74] Al-Bakrī, *Muʿjam*, p. 56: ʿAuf b. Kināna b. ʿAuf b. ʿUdhra . . . b. Kalb was the first to whom the idol of Wadd was handed over and a tent was pitched over him; and see Caskel, *Ğamhara*, II, 210.

[75] See e.g. al-Bakrī, *Muʿjam*, pp. 30, 39, 49, 51.

[76] Ibn Hishām, I, 136 (=A. Guillaume, *The Life of Muhammad* [Karachi, 1967], p. 55); the verses are attributed to Zuhayr in Bakrī's *Muʿjam*, p. 39.

[77] See on him Caskel, *Ğamhara*, II, 421; and see above ad n. 68.

[78] Al-Āmidī, *al-Muʾtalif*, pp. 7–8; Ibn al-Kalbī, *Jamhara*, Esc., pp. 413 inf.–414.

[79] Abū Aḥmad al-Ḥasan b. ʿAbdallah al-ʿAskarī, *Sharḥ mā yaqaʿu fīhi l-taṣḥīf wa-l-taḥrīf*, ed. ʿAbd al-ʿAzīz Aḥmad (Cairo, 1383/1963), p. 427.

[80] See on him e.g. Caskel, *Ğamhara*, II, 278.

[81] Al-Maghribī, *Nashwat al-ṭarab*, MS., Tübingen 1, fol. 52 r.

According to some reports Zuhayr's brother ʿUlaym introduced the *mirbāʿ* in the tribal division of Kalb (i.e. the fourth of the booty, paid to the leader of the tribe; in this case paid to ʿUlaym – K).[82] His son, ʿAbdallah b. ʿUlaym, is said to have opposed Zuhayr and bade the people disobey his orders. Zuhayr became embittered and angry over the loss of his position in the tribe and decided to drink unmixed wine until his death.[83]

*

There are divergent traditions about the life-span of Zuhayr; he was included in the list of the *muʿammarūn,* men distinguished for their longevity, and unusual periods of life were attributed to him. Accounts vary from 450 years,[84] 420 years,[85] 350 years,[86] 250 years,[87] 220 years,[88] 200 years[89] to 150 years.[90] The list is confusing and does not give any clue for establishing the period in which the events happened. It may therefore be useful to cast a brief glance at the other persons mentioned in the preceding accounts.

Al-Mughīra b. ʿAbdallah al-Makhzūmī who caused the rebellious action of the Fazārī chief is known as the father of the wealthy and influential family of the Banū l-Mughīra. His son Hishām b. al-Mughīra died, according to some accounts, in the last decade of the sixth century.[91] The grandsons of al-Mughīra, the sons of Hishām, took active part in the struggle between the Prophet and the Meccan unbelievers.[92] The period of the activity of al-Mughīra, the father of Hishām, may be put in the middle of the sixth century.

[82] Ibn al-Kalbī, *Jamhara,* Esc., p. 380; and see *ibid.,* the verse of Zuhayr:
sannahā rābiʿu l-juyūshi ʿulaymun:
kulla yawmin taʾtī l-manāyā bi-qadri

[83] Muḥammad b. Ḥabīb, *al-Muḥabbar,* p. 471; Ibn al-Kalbī, *Jamhara,* Esc., p. 394; Abū Ḥātim al-Sijistānī, pp. 28–29; *Aghānī,* III, 17, XXI, 66; Ibn Qutayba, *al-Shiʿr,* p. 224.

[84] *Aghānī,* XXI, 65 penult.

[85] Abū Ḥātim al-Sijistānī, p. 25.

[86] Abū Ḥātim al-Sijistānī, *ibid.*

[87] *Aghānī,* XXI, 65.

[88] Ibn al-Kalbī, *Jamhara,* Esc., p. 380; al-Majlisī, *Biḥār,* LI, 267.

[89] Abū Ḥātim al-Sijistānī, p. 28.

[90] *Aghānī,* III, 17.

[91] See on him: al-Zubayr b. Bakkār, MS., fol. 129a–b; Ibn Abī l-Ḥadīd, XVIII, 285 seq. (and see the utterance attributed to the Prophet about him p. 293: *law dakhala aḥadun min mushrikī qurayshin al-jannata la-dakhalahā hishāmu bnu l-mughīrati; kāna abdhalahum li-l-maʿrūfi wa-aḥmalahum li-l-kalli*); Muṣʿab b. ʿAbdallah al-Zubayrī, *Nasab quraysh,* ed. Lévi-Provençal (Cairo, 1953), p. 301; and see *Le Muséon,* 78 (1965), 427 (according to this report he died AD 598).

[92] See e.g. on the Banū l-Mughīra and their relatives: Muʾarrij b. ʿAmr al-Sadūsī, *Kitāb ḥadhf min nasab quraysh,* ed. Ṣalāḥ al-Dīn al-Munajjid (Cairo, 1960), pp. 66–75; and see Muṣʿab b. ʿAbdallah, pp. 301–303; on al-Ḥārith b. Hishām see e.g. Ibn al-Athīr, *Usd al-ghāba fī maʿrifati*

This was the period of the growth of the Meccan body politic and the incubation of the opposition of certain Fazārī clans against their Makhzūmī hosts at Mecca.

As to Zuhayr b. Janāb, it is plausible to give credence to the reports about the relations between Zuhayr and Abraha. Abraha, when on his expeditions against Mecca, was evidently interested in the collaboration with Kalb in order to gain control over the Bakr and Taghlib when he would continue his march against al-Ḥīra. The appointment of Zuhayr as tax-collector seems to have taken place when Abraha went out against Mecca; this may be dated to the middle of the sixth century.[93] The failure of Abraha's expedition and his retreat to the Yaman stimulated the Bakr and Taghlib to rebel against Zuhayr, the merciless tax-collector. The destruction of the sanctuary of Buss must have taken place after the strength of Abraha was crushed and Zuhayr renewed close relations with Mecca; these relations began already in the period of Quṣayy, which is said to have preceded that of Zuhayr: Quṣayy was active in the first half of the sixth century.[94] Quṣayy succeeded in gaining control of Mecca and expelled the former ruler of Khuzāʿa, aided by his Quḍāʿī half-brother (from the ʿUdhra) and probably by a Byzantine troop sent by the governor of Syria.[95] The tradition that he rebuilt the Kaʿba[96] seems plausible.

l-ṣaḥāba (Cairo, 1280), I, 351–352; on ʿAmr b. Hishām (Abū Jahl) see al-Balādhurī, I, index (esp. pp. 125–130); on al-ʿĀṣ b. Hishām see al-Balādhurī, I, 292, 299; on Salama b. Hishām see e.g. Ibn al-Athīr, *Usd*, II, 341. The hostile attitude of the Shīʿa towards the Makhzūm is exposed in the interpretation of verses 28–29 of Sūrat Ibrāhīm: "Hast thou not seen those who exchanged the bounty of God with unthankfulness and caused their people to dwell in the abode of ruin? Gehenna wherein they are roasted, an evil establishment." (Arberry's translation). According to an utterance attributed to ʿAlī and ʿUmar the verses refer to the Banū l-Mughīra and to the Banū Umayya; they are meant by "those who exchanged the bounty of God with unthankfulness" and "caused their people to dwell in the abode of ruin." The Banū l-Mughīra were killed on the Day of Badr; the Banū Umayya were given some period of time to enjoy life. (*... wa-qīla: nazalat fi-l-afjarayni min qurayshin : banī makhzūmin wa-banī umayyata; fa-ammā banū umayyata fa-muttiʿū ilā ḥīnin, wa-ammā banū makhzūmin fa-uhlikū yauma badrin; qālahu ʿalī b. abī ṭālib wa-ʿumaru bnu l-khaṭṭābi ...*) See: al-Qurṭubī, *al-Jāmiʿ li-aḥkāmi l-qurʾān* (Cairo, 1387/1967), IX, 364; ʿAlī b. Mūsā b. Jaʿfar b. Muḥammad b. Ṭāwūs, *al-Malāḥim wa-l-fitan* (Najaf, 1382/1962), p. 98; Hāshim b. Sulaymān al-Tawbali al-Katakānī, *al-Burhān fī-tafsīri l-qurʾān* (Qumm, 1393), II, 316–317; al-ʿAyyāshī, *Tafsīr al-qurʾān*, ed. Hāshim al-Rasūlī al-Maḥallātī (Qumm, 1385), II, 229–230, nos. 22–23, 27–28.

93 See *EI*², s.v. Abraha (A.F.L. Beeston); and see Khālid al-ʿAsalī, *"Aḍwāʾ ʿalā kitāb al-mufaṣṣal fī taʾrīkhi l-ʿarab qabla l-islām", al-ʿArab*, 1971, pp. 37–38, no. 14.

94 See *EI*², s.v. Ḳuraysh (Montgomery Watt): "... On the death of Ḳuṣayy, probably in the first half of the sixth century AD ..."

95 See Ibn Qutayba, *Kitāb al-maʿārif*, ed. Tharwat ʿUkāsha (Cairo, 1969), pp. 640 ult.–641: *... wa-aʿānahu qayṣar ʿalayhā*

96 See Muḥammad b. Yūsuf al-Ṣāliḥī, *Subul al-hudā wa-l-rashād fī sīrat khayri l-ʿibād* (=*al-*

Quṣayy introduced substantial changes in the sanctuary of Mecca, ordered to build houses in areas in which building was hitherto forbidden and permitted to fell trees in the sacred territory.[97] The changes introduced by Quṣayy in Mecca, the repatriation of the dispersed Qurashī factions and their unification into a coherent tribal body at Mecca[98] opened a new era of development and expansion for Mecca. The crucial event of the defeat of the army of Abraha enhanced the growth of the power of Mecca and strengthened the prestige of Quraysh. The activity of Zuhayr can be estimated to have taken place in the period following the "Day of the Elephant."

The date of the destruction of Buss can further be conjectured by the examination of the data about the persons who are mentioned in the accounts about this event. Al-Muthallam b. Riyāḥ b. Ẓālim, the grandson of the builder of Buss, killed a man named Ḥubāsha who was under the protection of al-Ḥārith b. Ẓālim al-Murrī. Al-Muthallam asked the protection of al-Ḥuṣayn b. Ḥumām al-Murrī; when al-Ḥārith b. Ẓālim heard about it he demanded of al-Ḥuṣayn b. al-Ḥumām to pay the blood-wit of the slain Ḥubāsha.[99] According to an account traced back to Abū ʿUbayda the poet al-Ḥuṣayn b. al-Ḥumām reached the time of Islam.[100] This opinion is indeed recorded in the compilations about the Companions of the Prophet.[101] His son is said to have visited the court of Muʿāwiya.[102] The ill-famed commander sent by Yazīd b.

Sīra al-shāmiyya), ed. Muṣṭafā ʿAbd al-Wāḥid (Cairo, 1392/1972), I, 192: ... *al-marrata l-sābiʿata: ʿimāratu quṣayyi bni kilābin; naqalahu l-zubayru bnu bakkārin fī Kitābi l-Nasabi wa-jazama bihi l-imāmu Abū Isḥāqa al-Māwardiyyu l-aḥkāmi l-sulṭāniyya* ...; and see al-Maqrīzī, *Dhikru mā warada fī bunyāni l-kaʿbati l-muʿaẓẓama*, MS. Leiden, Or. 560, fols. 175b: ... *dhakara l-zubayru bnu bakkārin wa-ghayruhu anna quṣayya bna kilābin banā l-bayta, wa-lam yadhkur dhālika l-azraqī*... fol. 176b, l. 10: *wa-banā quṣayyun al-kaʿbata ʿalā khamsin wa-ʿishrīna dhirāʿn* ... Fol. 178a, l. 17: *fa-lammā stabadda quṣayyun bi-amri makkata akhadha fī bunyāni l-bayti wa-jamʿi nafaqatihi thumma hadamahu wa-banāhu bināʾan lam yabnmi aḥadun mimman banāhu mithlahu wa-jaʿala yaqūlu wa-huwa yabnī:*

abnī wa-yabnī llāhu yarfaʿuhā : wa-l-yabni ahlu wirāthihā baʿdī;
bunyānuhā wa-tamāmuhā wa-ḥijābuhā : bi-yadi l-ilāhi wa-laysa bi-l-ʿabdi;
fa-banāhā wa-saqqafahā bi-khashabi l-daumi l-jayyidi wa-bi-jarīdi l-nakhli wa-banāhā ʿalā khamsatin wa-ʿishrīna dhirāʿan ...

al-Zurqānī, *Sharḥ al-mawāhib al-laduniyya* (Cairo, 1325), I, 206, l. 18: ...*fa-banat-hu jurhum, thumma quṣayy b. kilāb, naqalahu l-zubayr b. bakkār wa-jazama bihi l-māwardī*...

97 See e.g. Ibn Hishām, I, 132; and see *JESHO*, 8 (1965), 126.

98 See e.g. al-Balādhurī, I, 50; Ibn Kathīr, *al-Sīra al-nabawiyya*, ed. Muṣṭafā ʿAbd al-Wāḥid (Cairo, 1384/1964), I, 97.

99 See *Aghānī*, XII, 126.

100 *Aghānī*, XII, 128.

101 See e.g. Ibn Ḥajar, *al-Iṣāba fī tamyīzi l-ṣaḥāba*, ed. ʿAlī Muḥammad al-Bijāwī, (Cairo, 1392/1972), II, 84–85, no. 1735.

102 *Aghānī*, XII, 123.

Muᶜāwiya to attack Medina on the "Day of the Ḥarra" (63 AH), the aged Muslim b. ᶜUqba al-Murrī (he went out to Medina at the age of more than 90 years), is listed with the same number of genealogical links as Muthallam.[103] The demolition of Buss may thus be dated to the third quarter of the sixth century.

Some other reports may be scrutinized as well. A tradition says that Zuhayr b. Janāb remained alive until he met a man of the fifth generation of the descendants of his brother; it was Abū l-Aḥwaṣ ᶜAmr b. Thaᶜlaba b. al-Ḥārith b. Ḥiṣn b. Ḍamḍam b. ᶜAdiyy b. Janāb.[104] Ibn al-Kalbī reports that ᶜAmr b. Thaᶜlaba captured al-Aᶜshā when he was on his way to the king of the family of Jafna.[105] He was released according to the request of Shurayḥ b. Ḥiṣn b. ᶜImrān b. Samawʾal.[106] This report, as recorded in the commentary of a *qaṣīda* of al-Aᶜshā, is corroborated by an account in Abū l-Baqā's *Manāqib*.[107] The accounts quoted above seem to indicate that the activity of Zuhayr b. Janāb and the strengthening of the ties of Quḍāᶜa with Mecca took place in the second half of the sixth century and that Zuhayr died in the late decades of that century.

III

Authority and rule were based in the Meccan body politic on mutual agreements concluded between the various tribal factions and clans. Duties were imposed and privileges were established after intertribal struggles ceased; the stipulations in the agreements were laid down according to the balance of strength of the negotiating tribal groups. According to such agreements or pacts, usages upheld by custom turned into customary law, administratively bidding taxes became obligatory payments, customary religious practices became mandatory regulations. The struggle for power of the different tribal factions on the one hand and the necessity to prevent disorder in Mecca on the other hand originated the institution of the *ḥukkām*, the arbitrators. Al-Maqrīzī provides a list of the arbiters of Quraysh in the period of the Jāhiliyya (in fact at the end of the sixth and the beginning of the seventh century – K): ᶜAbd al-

[103] See Ibn Ḥajar, *al-Iṣāba*, VI, 294, no. 8420; al-Balādhurī, MS., fol. 1147a; Ibn al-Kalbī, *Jamhara*, MS. Br. Mus., fol. 168b (in all these sources; Muslim b. ᶜUqba b. Riyāḥ b. Asᶜad b. Rabīᶜa b. ᶜĀmir.)

[104] Abū Ḥātim al-Sijistānī, p. 29.

[105] Ibn al-Kalbī, *Jamhara*, Esc., p. 384, l. 1; Caskel, *Ğamhara*, II, 185.

[106] See *al-Aᶜshā, Dīwān*, ed. R. Geyer (Wien, 1928), pp. 125–126, (nos. XXIII–XXIV) commentary.

[107] Abū l-Baqā, *al-Manāqib al-mazyadiyya*, MS., fol. 141a.

Muṭṭalib and his two sons, al-Zubayr and Abū Ṭālib; Abū Sufyān and his father Ḥarb on behalf of the Banū Umayya; al-Walīd b. al-Mughīra on behalf of the Makhzūm; al-ʿĀṣ b. Wāʾil and Qays b. ʿAdiyy on behalf of Banū Sahm; Nawfal b. ʿAbd al-ʿUzzā on behalf of the Banū ʿAdiyy and al-ʿAlāʾ b. Ḥāritha al-Thaqafī on behalf of the Banū Sahm; Naufal b. ʿAbd al-ʿUzzā on behalf of the Banū Zuhra.[108] A passage quoted by al-Maqrīzī from al-Fākihī's *Taʾrīkh Makka* sheds some light on the position of the arbiters and on the way in which they were elected: in order to avoid wickedness they were chosen by mutual consent and none of them would strive to overpower the rest of Quraysh (... *wa-lam yakun minhum aḥadun mutamallikan ʿalā baqiyyati qurayshin. wa-innamā dhālika bi-tarāḍīhim ʿalayhi ḥasman li-māddati l-sharri; qālahu l-fākihiyyu...*).[109] Quṣayy's innovations and regulations (taxes imposed on aliens entering Mecca [scil. with merchandise – K], food provided for the pilgrims, fire lit on Muzdalifa, practices in the *dār al-nadwa* etc.) became binding and obligatory, as the different clans agreed to carry them out: the *ḥukkām* of Mecca seem to have acted according to that tradition. This is reflected in the following passage recorded by Maqrīzī: *wa-inna amra quṣayyin fī qawmihi ka-l-dīni l-muttabaʿi lā yuʿmalu bi-ghayrihi fī ḥayātihi wa-min baʿdihi.*[110]

The mutual agreements between the chiefs of the different tribal factions of Quraysh are reflected in the story of the rebuilding of the Kaʿba by Quraysh. The different factions and clans agreed upon to allot every faction its share in the erection of the building: the Banū ʿAbd Manāf and the Banū Zuhra were entrusted with the side of the door; the space between the Black Stone and the southern corner was assigned to the Banū Makhzūm and groups of Quraysh who joined them; the back of the Kaʿba was entrusted to the Banū Jumaḥ and Banū Sahm; the section of the *ḥijr* was given to the ʿAbd al-Dār b. Quṣayy, the Banū Asad b. ʿAbd al-ʿUzzā and the Banū ʿAdiyy b. Kaʿb; the *ḥijr* is the *ḥaṭīm* – says an attached note.[111]

According to tradition Quraysh planned to rebuild the Kaʿba and to cover

[108] Al-Maqrīzī, *Dhikru mā warada fī bunyān al-kaʿba*, MS., fols. 177b inf.–178a sup.; al-Sinjārī, *Manāʾiḥ al-karam*, MS., fol. 59b.

[109] Al-Maqrīzī, *Dhikru mā warada*, MS., fol. 178a sup.; al-Sinjārī, *Manāʾiḥ*, MS., fol. 59b.

[110] Al-Maqrīzī, *Dhikru mā warada*, MS., fol. 176b.

[111] Ibn Hishām, I, 207; al-ʿIṣāmī, *Simṭ al-nujūm*, I, 166; al-Sinjārī, *Manāʾiḥ*, MS., fol. 62a; Ibn Ruzayq, *al-Ṣaḥīfa al-ʿadnāniyya*, MS. Br. Mus. Or. 6569, fol. 259b; al-Shāṭibī, *al-Jumān fī akhbāri l-zamān*, MS. Br. Mus. Or. 3008, fol. 58b; al-Maqrīzī, *Dhikru mā warada*, MS., fol. 180a–b; al-Ṣāliḥī, *Subul al-hudā*, II, 229; Ibn Kathīr, *al-Sīra al-nabawiyya*, I, 277 penult.–278 sup. Ibn Kathīr, *Tafsīr* (Beirut, 1385/1966), I, 318; ʿAlī b. Burhān al-Dīn al-Ḥalabī, *Insān al-ʿuyūn (=al-Sīra al-ḥalabiyya)* (Cairo, 1382/1962), I, 159 inf.–160 sup.

the building with a roof; their calculation of the expenditure seems to have been inaccurate[112] and they were compelled to limit the size of the building; they did not include in the building the space of the *ḥijr*; the *ḥijr* remained outside the Ka^cba.[113] The exclusion of the *ḥijr* led later to a heated discussion in connection with the circumambulation of the Kaʿba; the question posed was whether the believers should during the *ṭawāf* disregard the area of the *ḥijr* excluded from the building or to circumambulate behind it, considering it as part of the Sanctuary. The Prophet's answer was clear: the *ḥijr* is part of the Kaʿba and the circumambulation has to be performed from behind the space of the *ḥijr*.[114] The reason for this decision is said to have been that the *ḥijr* was part of the House erected by Abraham.[115]

This fact was taken into consideration by ʿAbdallah b. al-Zubayr when he decided to rebuild the Kaʿba (anno 64/683); although he was advised to confine himself to the repairing of the building "as built by Quraysh," he decided to pull down the Kaʿba and to erect the building of the Sanctuary in its original "Abrahamian" dimensions (i.e. to include the *ḥijr*, which was excluded by Quraysh – K); he indeed carried out his plan.[116] Al-Ḥajjāj changed the building of the Kaʿba: he left Ibn al-Zubayr's extension of the building, but ordered to pull down the part of the *ḥijr* built by Ibn al-Zubayr.[117]

[112] See the references provided by U. Rubin, *The Kaʿba*, n. 26; and see al-Suyūṭī, *Jamʿ al-jawāmiʿ* (Cairo, 1978), I, 1218.

[113] See e.g. Ibn Kathīr, *al-Sīra al-nabawiyya*, I, 281–282; al-Zurqānī, *Sharḥ al-mawāhib*, I, 206, l. 20; al-Maqrīzī, *Dhikru mā warada*, MS., fol. 181b; al-Shāṭibī, *al-Jumān*, MS., fol. 59a; ʿAlī b. Burhān al-Dīn, *Insān al-ʿuyūn*, I, 189; and see the thorough scrutiny of the problem in U. Rubin, *The Kaʿba*.

[114] See e.g. al-Shāṭibī, *al-Jumān*, MS., fol. 59a: ... *wa-suʾila rasūlu llāhi* (ṣ) *ʿani l-ḥijri, hal huwa mina l-kaʿbati am lā, fa-qāla huwa mina l-kaʿbati wa-lā yajūzu l-ṭawāfu illā khalfahu* ...; and see al-Muḥibbu l-Ṭabarī, *al-Qirā li-qāṣidi ummi l-qurā*, ad. Muṣṭafā l-Saqā (Cairo, 1390/1970), p. 507: ... *fa-inna l-ḥijra mina l-bayti fa-dhhabī fa-ṣallī fīhi* ...

[115] See U. Rubin, *The Kaʿba*, chapter 2: "the ritual functions" ... esp. n. 54.

[116] See e.g. al-Ḥarbī, *al-Manāsik wa-amākin ṭuruqi l-ḥajj*, ed. Ḥamad al-Jāsir (Riyāḍ, 1389/1969), pp. 488–491 (see esp. p. 488 penult.: ... *fa-adkhala fīhā naḥwan min sabʿi adhruʿin mina l-ḥijri* ... and 489: ... *fa-in badā li-qawmiki min baʿdiki an yabnūhu fa-halummī urīki mā tarakū fa-arāha naḥwan min sabʿi adhruʿin* ...); Muḥibb al-Dīn al-Ṭabarī, *al-Qirā*, pp. 508–509; and see al-Shāṭibī, *al-Jumān*, MS., fol. 59a (seven cubits of the *ḥijr* not included in the building erected by Quraysh; according to a tradition recorded by Muḥibb al-Dīn, *al-Qirā*, p. 509, ʿAbdallah b. al-Zubayr included five cubits of the *ḥijr* in the Kaʿba erected by him).

[117] See e.g. Muḥibb al-Dīn al-Ṭabarī, *al-Qirā*, p. 509 (... *ammā mā zāda fī ṭūlihi fa-aqirrahu, wa-ammā mā zāda fīhi mina l-ḥijri fa-ruddahu ilā bināʾihi* ...); Ibn Ẓuhayra, *al-Jāmiʿ al-laṭīf*, p. 92 has an erroneous reading: ... *ammā ma zāda fī ṭūlihi fa-akhkhirhu* ...; al-Maqrīzī, *Dhikru mā warada*, MS., fol. 184a: ... *thumma hadama* (i.e. al-Ḥajjāj) *mā banāhu bnu l-zubayri fī l-kaʿbati min nāḥiyati l-ḥijri, thumma aʿādahu ʿalā mā kāna ʿalayhi wa-akhraja l-*

Tradition says that the Prophet attended the building of the Kaʿba by Quraysh; when the chiefs of the Qurashī clans quarrelled as to who would put the Black Stone in its place the Prophet was unanimously chosen by the contending factions to put the Stone in its place.[118] Traditions are however divergent about the age of the Prophet at the time of the building of the Kaʿba: whether he was a youth, a boy who had reached virility, 15 years old, 25 years, 30 years, 35 years, 15 years before he got his revelation, five years before revelation or before he was employed by Khadīja.[119] All the traditions are unanimous that he participated in the building. An important role in the erection of the Kaʿba was allotted to al-Walīd b. al-Mughīra al-Makhzūmī,[120] a noble member of Quraysh; he was a courageous man and did not fear to start the demolition of the old building of the Sanctuary.

According to a tradition recorded by Ibn al-Kalbī when the Meccans were engaged in building the Kaʿba and realized that they lacked the necessary funds for accomplishing of the building, they were surprised by a generous offer for help from a wealthy tribal leader of the Kalb. It was Ubayy b. Sālim al-Kalbī who came to Mecca and asked the Meccans to allow him to get a share in the building. They agreed and he built the right side of the Kaʿba. Al-Jawwās b. al-Qaʿṭal said about that:

> *Lanā aymanu l-bayti lladhī taḥjubūnahu :*
> *wirāthatu mā abqā ubayyu bnu sālimi*
> To us belongs the right side of the House which you cover with curtains :
> an inheritance left by Ubayy b. Sālim.[121]

This tradition is quoted (with few variants) by Ibn Qutayba.[122] Al-Maqrīzī records the tradition on the authority of Ibn al-Kalbī and gives the full name of the Kalbī leader: Ubayy b. Sālim b. al-Ḥārith b. al-Wāḥid (Mālik) b. ʿAbdallah

ḥijra min al-kaʿbati, wa-kāna dhālika fī sanati arbaʿin wa-sabʿīna; fa-laysa fī l-kaʿbati al-āna min bināʾi l-ḥajjāji ghayru l-jidāri lladhī yalī l-ḥijra faqaṭ.

118 See e.g. Ibn Isḥāq, *al-Siyar wa-l-maghāzī*, ed. Suhayl Zakkār, (Damascus, 1398/1978), pp. 107–108; al-Ḥarbī, *al-Manāsik*, p. 487; al-Ṣāliḥī, *Subul al-hudā*, II, 231–232; ʿAlī b. Burhān al-Dīn al-Ḥalabī, *Insān al-ʿuyūn*, I, 161; Ibn Nāṣir al-Dīn al-Dimashqī, *Jāmiʿ al-āthār fī mawlidi l-nabiyyi l-mukhtār*, MS. Cambridge Or. 913, fol. 268a.

119 See e.g. al-Ṣāliḥī, *Subul al-hudā*, II, 233–234; al-Zurqānī, *Sharḥ al-mawāhib*, I, 203; al-Ḥarbī, *al-Manāsik*, pp. 494–495; Ibn Nāṣir al-Dīn, *Jāmiʿ al-āthār*, MS., fol. 268a; Ibn Isḥāq, *al-Siyar wa-l-maghāzī*, p. 109; and see the references given by U. Rubin, *The Kaʿba*, n. 16.

120 See e.g. Ibn Hishām, I, 206–207.

121 Ibn al-Kalbī, *Jamhara*, Esc., MS., pp. 414–415; *inṭalaqa ubayyun maʿahu mālun kathīrun fa-atā qurayshan ḥīna arādū bināʾa l-kaʿbati fa-qāla: daʿūnī ushrikkum fī bināʾihā, fa-adhinū lahu, fa-banā jānibahā l-aymana ...*

122 Ibn Qutayba, *Kitāb al-maʿārif*, p. 561.

b. Hubal b. ʿAbdallah b. ʿUlaym b. Janāb.[123] He was thus a descendant of ʿUlaym, the brother of Zuhayr b. Janāb.

There is nothing to make us doubt the soundness of this tradition; it is indeed credible that the Qurashites were glad to allot a share of the building to a Kalbite tribal group.

*

The memory of Janāb b. Hubal remained alive among the Kalb. The troops levied from among his descendants are praised in the poems of al-Jawwās b. al-Qaʿṭal, himself a descendant of Janāb:

Daʿā bi-silāḥin, thumma aḥjama idh raʾā : suyūfa janābin wa-l-ṭiwāla l-madhākiyā

He called for weapons, then he turned back as he saw : the swords of Janāb and the long-bodied horses, which had reached full age and complete strength.[124]

In a verse in which al-Jawwās describes the march of the divisions of Janāb and ʿAuf he says that they are filling the high mountains formed of one mass of rocks.[125] Ibn Saʿd recorded a letter sent by the Prophet to the Banū Janāb and their allies.[126]

*

Kalb were famous for their wealth and the multitude of their flocks. The Prophet is reported as saying that God would grant forgiveness to a countless multitude of believers on the night of mid-Shaʿbān as numerous as the hairs of the flocks of the tribe of Kalb.[127] The close ties of Kalb with the Umayyad rulers seem to be reflected in a saying reported by ʿAwāna in which the

[123] Al-Maqrīzī, *Dhikru mā warada*, MS., fol. 180a inf.–180 sup.

[124] Al-Balādhurī, *op. cit.*, V (ed. Goitein, Jerusalem, 1936), 142; al-Ṭabarī, *Taʾrīkh*, ed. Abū l-Faḍl Ibrāhīm (Cairo, 1971), V, 542; al-Masʿūdī, *al-Tanbīh wa-l-ishrāf*, ed. de Goeje (rpt. Baghdad), p. 310.

[125] *Aghānī*, XVII, 112:
idhā sārat qabāʾilu min janābin : wa-ʿawfin ashḥanū shumma l-hiḍābi.

[126] Ibn Saʿd, *Ṭabaqāt*, I, 285.

[127] See e.g. al-Naysābūrī, *Gharāʾib al-qurʾān wa-raghāʾib al-furqān*, ed. Ibrāhīm ʿAṭwa ʿAwaḍ (Cairo, 1388/1968), XXV, 65; Muḥammad Ḥasanayn Makhlūf al-ʿAdawī, *Risāla fī faḍli laylati l-nisfi min shaʿbān*, ed. Ḥasanayn Muḥammad Makhlūf (Cairo, 1394/1974), p. 20 (and see *ibid.*, the explanation of the Prophet: ... *qultu: yā nabiyya llāhi, mā bālu ghanami banī kalbin? qāla: laysa fī l-ʿarabi qawmun aktharu ghanaman minhum* ...); and see the references given in Kister, "Shaʿbān is my month," in *Studia Orientalia Memoriae D.H. Baneth Dedicata* (Jerusalem, 1979), p. 26, n. 52.

position of different tribes was assessed. "The kingdom was never aided by a tribe (stronger – K) than that of Kalb."[128] It is not surprising that they attracted the enmity of the opposition-groups of the Umayyads. Apocalyptic tradition has gloomy things to say about the fate of Kalb during the crucial clash between the Mahdī and his enemy, the Sufyānī. The Kalb will be attacked by the forces of the Mahdī and plundered. The event will be named: "The Day of the Plunder of the Bedouins" or "The Day of the Plunder of Kalb." "The man who will be disappointed on that Day will [indeed] be disappointed."[129]

*

The few accounts discussed above may provide us with a clue for a better understanding of the relations of Mecca with certain tribal groups. These reports seem to reflect the ingenious and sagacious policy of the Meccan leaders, who succeeded in their wisdom and flexibility to establish friendly relations with influential tribal leaders and to win them over to a peaceful co-operation with Mecca. The wise leaders of Mecca did not hesitate even to attach them as partners in the erection of the Sanctuary of Mecca.

[128] Ibn Abī l-Dunyā, *al-Ishrāf fī manāzil al-ashrāf*, MS. Chester Beatty 4427, fol. 43b: . . . *akhbaranā l-ḥakamu bnuʿawānata l-kalbiyyu ʿan abīhi, qāla, lam yuʾayyadi l-mulku bi-mithli kalbin, wa-lam tuʿla l-manābiru bi-mithli qurayshin, wa-lam tuṭlabi l-tirātu bi-mithli tamīmin, wa-lam turʿa l-riʿāya bi-mithli thaqīfin, wa-lam tusadda l-thughūru bi-mithli qaysin, wa-lam tuhaji l-fitanu bi-mithli rabīʿata, wa-lam yujba l-kharāju bi-mithli l-yamani.*

[129] Nuʿaym b. Ḥammād, *Kitāb al-fitan*, MS. Br. Mus. Or. 9449, fol. 95b: . . . *thumma yasīru ilā kalbin fa-yanhabuhum fa-l-khāʾibu man khāba yawma nahbi kalbin* . . .; fol. 96a: . . . *ʿan kaʿbin qāla: wadidtu annī udriku nahba l-aʿrābi wa-hiya nahbatu kalbin fa-l-khāʾibu man khāba yawma kalbin* . . .; fol. 96b: . . . *fa-yaqtatilu huwa wa-jayshu l-sufyāniyyi ʿalā sabʿi rāyāt, kullu ṣāḥibi rāyatin minhum yarjū l-amra li-nafsihi fa-yahzimuhumu l-mahdiyyu; qāla abū hurayrata: fa-l-maḥrūmu man ḥurima nahba kalbin* . . .; fol. 97b: . . . *fa-l-khāʾibu man khāba yawma kalbin, ḥattā tubāʿa l-jāriyatu l-ʿadhrāʾu bi-thamāniyati darāhima*. And see Yūsuf b. Yaḥyā l-Maqdisī l-Shāfiʿī, *ʿIqd al-durar fī-akhbāri l-muntaẓar*, ed. ʿAbd al-Fattāḥ al-Ḥilw (Cairo, 1399/1979), pp. 69–70, 85, 86 (and see the references provided by the editor).

III

NOTES ON CASKEL'S ǦAMHARAT AN-NASAB

M. J. Kister and *M. Plessner*

Martin Plessner, der am 27. November 1973 kurz vor Vollendung seines 73. Lebensjahres in Jerusalem gestorben ist, übernahm ,,auf dringenden Wunsch" des am 28. Januar 1970 verstorbenen Werner Caskel die Besprechung seines letzten Werkes:

WERNER CASKEL, *Ǧamharat an-nasab, Das genealogische Werk des Hišām ibn Muḥammad al-Kalbī.* Band I: Einleitung von Werner Caskel; die Tafeln von Gert Strenziok. Band II: Erläuterungen zu den Tafeln von Werner Caskel; Das Register, begonnen von Gert Strenziok, vollendet von Werner Caskel. — Leiden, E. J. Brill 1966. I: xvi, 132 S., 334 Taf., 2 S. Nachträge und Berichtigungen; II: 614 S., 2 S. Nachträge und Berichtigungen, 4°

und zwar ,,nach langem Sträuben" — denn er sah sich zu einer Rezension ,,dieses monumentalen Werkes" in ,,keiner Weise qualifiziert" — und nachdem er ,,sich der Beteiligung von M. J. Kister versichert hatte" (aus einem Brief an die Redaktion). Zunächst folgen hier (bis S. 50, 18) Plessner's Bemerkungen:

Die Wissenschaft von der Genealogie, d.h. der Verwandtschaftsverhältnisse der alten Araber, ist von Hišām ibn Muḥammad al-Kalbī begründet worden. So sagt wenigstens Ḥāccī Xalīfa, Nr. 1345 s.v. *ʿilm al-ansāb*, der auf die Vorarbeiten von Hišām's Vater, Muḥammad ibn as-Sāʾib, nicht eingegangen ist, weil diese nicht zu einer vollendeten literarischen Form gediehen sind. (In den Enzyklopädien wird die Wissenschaft verschiedentlich erwähnt, z.B. in den persischen *Nafāʾis al-funūn fī ʿarāʾis al-ʿuyūn* des Muḥammad b. Maḥmūd al-Āmulī [ca. 740/1340], Lith. Teheran 1309, I, 245-49; trotzdem fehlt sie bei Ṭašköprüzāde, was Ḥāccī Xalīfa zu einer kritischen Bemerkung veranlasst hat.) Ausser der *Camhara* führt er an dieser Stelle vier weitere Werke Ibn al-Kalbī's an, *al-Mnzl* (von Flügel *Munzil* vokalisiert), *al-Wacīz*, *al-Farīd* und *al-Mulūkī* (zweifellos ist diese Lesart der Istanbuler Edition von 1943 die richtige; Flügel schreibt *Mulūk*). Von diesen erscheinen aber nur *al-Farīd* und *al-Wacīz* an ihrer Stelle im Alphabet (9049 bzw. 14184); von den beiden anderen hatte der Bibliograph also wohl nur indirekt Kenntnis. Yāqūt, *Iršād*, ed. Margoliouth, VII, 253 setzt *al-Mnzl* mit *k. an-Nasab al-kabīr* (s. zu diesem Titel Caskel's Einleitung) gleich und führt die anderen drei Titel (statt *al-Wacīz* schreibt er *al-Mūcaz*) am Ende der von ihm übernommenen Liste des *Fihrist* auf. (Caskel I, 79 Anm. 4 nennt nur zwei, *Farīd* und *Mulūkī*, und möchte sie als Prunktitel bezweifeln; man vergleiche über diese Frage die nachfolgenden Ausführungen Kister's; Yāqūt nennt unter Ibn al-Kalbī's Gewährsmännern Ibn Saʿd kātib al-Wāqidī, während das Verhältnis doch umgekehrt war, vgl. Caskel, I, 114 f.)

Ibn al-Kalbī hat sein Werk, wie gesagt, auf der Grundlage eines von seinem Vater begonnenen *Ansāb*-Buches verfasst. Laut Caskel's ansprechender Vermutung (I, 75) hat der Vater bis in die Zeit des Chalifen al-Manṣūr gearbeitet, woraus sich erklärt, dass die meisten ,,Zeitgenossen", also die auf den Tafeln zu unterst stehenden Personen, in die Zeit dieses Chalifen fallen. Der Sohn, der ca. 204/819 starb, fügte dann weitere Namen bis in die Zeit al-Maʾmūn's hinzu, soweit sie ihm zugänglich waren. Auch Ibn al-Kalbī hat das Werk nicht selbst publiziert; wir lesen es nur — teilweise — in der *riwāya* des Muḥammad Ibn Ḥabīb (I, 122).

Das Werk Ibn al-Kalbī's zu kommentieren ist die Aufgabe, die sich Caskel gestellt hatte. Zu einer Edition reichte das Material nicht aus. Deshalb finden wir in Caskel's Werk keinen arabischen Text, sondern genealogische Tabellen und ein Register, wie wir sie — man muss jetzt sagen: en miniature — seit 120 Jahren von Wüstenfeld's Hand besitzen. Während jedoch Wüstenfeld nur die arabischen Stämme und Familien erfassen wollte und daher mit ca. 50 Tafeln auskam, enthalten Caskel's Tafeln alle Namen, incl. der Personennamen; die einzige Bedingung ist, dass sie als in Ibn al-Kalbī's Werk stehend nachgewiesen werden konnten. Es sind also in den neuen 334 Tafeln ca. 35000 Namen enthalten, unter denen die der Zeitgenossen Ibn al-Kalbī's noch bei weitem nicht alle damals lebenden echten Araber innerhalb der erfassten Gebiete darstellen. Aber auch die vorigen Generationen sind keineswegs voll erfasst; z.B. hören die Aliden (Tafel 5) in der Generation nach ʿAlī auf. Die Umaiyaden gehen bis zur Generation der Söhne ʿAbd al-Malik's (Tafel 10), während auf derselben Tafel Vettern verschiedenen Grades noch 1-2 Generationen weiter verzeichnet sind. Die Abbasiden erscheinen überhaupt nicht, während z.B. der berühmte Abū Yūsuf genannt ist (Tafel 223).

Die sowohl auf Caskel's wie auf Wüstenfeld's Tafeln stehenden Stammbäume stimmen nicht in allen Gliedern überein. Das ist natürlich; denn Wüstenfeld hat eine Vielfalt von Quellen benutzt, die entgegen seiner Versicherung im Vorwort zum *Register* unmöglich in allem übereinstimmen konnten, da sie sich auf verschiedene Zeiten bezogen und nicht alle auf ihre Integrität geprüft werden konnten. Caskel dagegen hat eine einzige konkrete Quelle benutzt, deren Rekonstruktion eben der Inhalt seines Buches ist. In seinem Register, zu dem bei jedem Namen die Quellen, d.h. Handschriften, Abschriften und spätere Benutzer der *Ğamhara*, angegeben werden, stehen überall zuerst die Stellen, an denen er in den Handschriften und ihren Derivaten vorkommt. Der Versuchung, Ibn al-Kalbī's Material zu ergänzen, d.h. Namen aufzunehmen, die zwar bekannt, aber eben nicht in dieser Quelle nachweisbar sind, hat er konsequent widerstanden.

Von Caskel's Mitarbeitern ist einer, G. Strenziok, so weitgehend an der Arbeit beteiligt, dass er auf den Titelblättern erscheint. Seine Dissertation *Die Genealogien der Nordaraber nach Ibn al-Kalbī* liegt dem entsprechenden Teil der Tafeln zugrunde, für die er denn auch als Verfasser erscheint. Strenziok hat auch das Register begonnen, d.h. nicht nur die Stammeskartothek in eine alphabetische umgewandelt, sondern auch die historischen Bemerkungen zu den historisch oder sonstwie bedeutenden Personen zu schreiben angefangen. Aber der Plan des Ganzen, die beiden grossen Einleitungen und der weitaus grösste Teil des Registers sind Caskel's Werk.

Es ist nicht leicht, die Summe von Gelehrsamkeit, die in diesem Register steckt, zu ermessen. Allein die Datierungen von Dichterversen und die Urteile über deren Echtheit spiegeln das Lebenswerk eines Mannes, dessen ganze Kraft dem arabischen Altertum gewidmet war. Aber das ist nur ein kleiner Teil der in diesen Artikeln verarbeiteten Materialien. Die historischen Bemerkungen zu vielen Namen auf jeder Seite des über 500 Quartseiten umfassenden Registers gehen in die Tausende und bilden eine unerschöpfliche Quelle der Belehrung. In ihnen ist auch wenigstens ein Teil des nicht rein genealogischen Textes Ibn al-Kalbī's gerettet worden. Zu den Artikeln des Registers kommen noch die historischen Konsequenzen allgemeiner Art, die sich Caskel bei der Ausarbeitung des Buches ergeben haben und die in den Prolegomena des 1. und den Erläuterungen zu den Tafeln des 2. Bandes niedergelegt sind. Am bedeutsamsten ist wohl die endgültige Bestätigung der schon von Goldziher, *Muh. St.* I, 91 ausgesprochenen Zweifel an der Altertümlichkeit des nord-südarabischen Gegensatzes, der laut Caskel (I, 69) „erst seit 63/683 deutlich geworden (ist) und . . . nie die Stärke erreicht (hat), die ihm spätere Geschichtschreiber verliehen haben."

Die ungeheure Vielfalt von Eigennamen, die die alten Araber gekannt und ihren

Kindern gegeben haben, tritt in diesem Register erst recht in Erscheinung. Dass unter den selteneren zahlreiche sind, die erst hier in richtiger Form erscheinen, während sie in den bisher bekannten Texten falsch punktiert waren (z.B. Yarfā, bei Wüstenfeld Barqā genannt und unter dieser Form leider nicht im Register erscheinend, sondern nur im Apparat zu Yarfā), ist ein weiterer Gewinn. Erst jetzt ist eine solide Grundlage für die Untersuchung der Etymologien der arabischen Eigennamen geschaffen; und ich bin froh, dass ich als junger Mann nicht der Anregung Eugen Mittwochs gefolgt bin, über dieses Thema zu arbeiten. Caskel muss viel Material dazu gehabt haben, hat es aber nicht in diesem, Ibn al-Kalbī und der Genealogie gewidmeten Buch publiziert (II, 99).

Die ausgezeichnete drucktechnische Leistung und die bei den vielen Zahlen besonders schwierige, überaus sorgfältige Korrektur sei gebührend hervorgehoben.

Der reiche Inhalt dieses epochemachenden Werkes des letzten unmittelbaren Schülers August Fischer's konnte hier nicht annähernd beschrieben werden. Manche Äusserlichkeiten schriftstellerischer Art, die die Prolegomena zu einer etwas komplizierten Lektüre machen, verschlagen nichts gegenüber der Dankbarkeit, die die Arabistik Caskel schuldet, und die ich ihm leider nur übers Grab nachrufen kann.

The uninterrupted transmission of genealogy from the times of the Jāhiliyya was conditioned by the socio-political situation of the Arab Empire in the period of the conquests and during the rule of the Umayyads. The revolutionary change in the ʿAbbāsid period is reflected in an utterance attributed to al-Maʾmūn: "Rank is the genealogical affinity connecting people; thus a noble Arab is closer to a noble Persian than he is to a low-class Arab; a noble Persian is nearer to a noble Arab than he is to a low-class Persian, because noble men form a (separate) class and plebeians form a (separate) class".[1] This view is further explained by the following saying of al-Maʾmūn: "People of the market are men of the lowest class, workmen are despised people, merchants are avaricious, while secretaries are kings over the people".[2] This of course mirrors the opinion of the ʿAbbāsid period when tribal organizations had lost their hold, while foreign nobility was gaining in importance and position and the class of secretaries was coming to be among the most respected. But even in this period genealogy did not cease to be recorded, learnt and transmitted as an essential part of the Arabic cultural tradition.

In the first period of Islam knowledge of *nasab* was made necessary by the administrative needs of the *dīwān*. It was further required in connection with the need to affiliate new converts to Islam in accordance

---

[1] Ibn Ḥamdūn, *Tadhkira*, Ms. Br. Mus., Or. 3179, I, 82a: *qāla l-maʾmūnu: al-rutbatu nasabun tajmaʿu ahlahā, fa-sharīfu l-ʿarabi aulā bi-sharīfi l-ʿajami min sharīfi l-ʿarabi bi-waḍīʿi l-ʿarabi; wa-sharīfu l-ʿajami aulā bi-sharīfi l-ʿarabi min sharīfi l-ʿajami bi-waḍīʿi l-ʿajami; fa-ashrāfu l-nāsi ṭabaqatun, kamā anna auḍāʿahum ṭabaqatun.*

[2] *Ib. . . . wa-qāla marratan: ahlu l-sūqi sifalun, wa-l-ṣunnāʿu andhālun, wa-l-tujjāru bukhalāʾu, wa-l-kuttābu mulūkun ʿalā l-nāsi.*

with the various tribal groups. *Nasab* turned to be a considerable factor in differentiating between the upper class of the conquerors and the population of the conquered countries; for the Arabs it was a means of self-identification: to be aware of Arab descent, to have a pure Arab pedigree as confronted with the *mawālī*, the *ʿajam*. It is clear that the compilation of the *Nasab al-ʿArab* was only later counteracted by the compilation of *Nasab al-ʿAjam*.[3]

The fact that the science of genealogy acquired Muslim character and respectability and the tendency to emphasize the superiority of the Arabs led to the invention of a great number of traditions on this subject: they were of course told on the authority of the Prophet. "If the Arabs become weak Islam will become weak"—the Prophet is reported to have said.[4] "May God break the teeth of the man who prefers the *ʿajam*".[5] "Love the Arabs for three reasons: because I am an Arab, because the Qur'ān is Arabic and because the people of Paradise speak Arabic".[6] "Hatred of the Arabs is unbelief, love for the Arabs is belief".[7] The bulk of these traditions bears evidence to the tendency of emphasizing the merits and qualities by which they surpass other nations within Islam.

Closely connected with these traditions were the traditions about Quraysh. Maʿmar b. Rāshid, one of the earliest compilers of *ḥadīth*, records in his *Jāmiʿ* [8] a number of these traditions in the chapter *Faḍā'il Quraysh*. The Prophet said: "People follow Quraysh in this matter—he meant by this: authority—; Muslims follow Muslims of Quraysh and

---

[3] See quotations from Abū ʿUbayda's *Ansāb al-ʿajam* in Mughulṭāy's *al-Zahr al-bāsim fī sīrat abī l-qāsim*, Ms. Leiden Or. 370, ff. 41b, 136a, 152a.

[4] Ibn Abī Ḥātim, *ʿIlal*, Ms. Chester Beatty 3516, f. 287a; al-Muttaqī l-Hindī, *Kanz al-ʿummāl*, Hyderabad 1385/1965, XIII, 37, no. 230; al-Haythamī, *Majmaʿ al-zawā'id*, Beirut 1967, X, 53; ʿAbd al-Raḥīm al-ʿIrāqī, *al-Qurab fi maḥabbati l-ʿarab*, ed. Ibrāhīm Ḥilmī al-Qādirī, Alexandria 1381/1961, p. 99; al-Jarrāḥī, *Kashf al-khafā'*, Beirut 1351, I, 89, no. 232; cf. al-Zajjājī, *Majālis al-ʿulamā'*, ed. ʿAbd al-Salām Hārūn, al-Kuwayt 1962, p. 240: *lā yazālu l-dīnu dhalīlan mā ʿazzat al-ʿarab*.

[5] Al-Jazarī, *Maulid al-nabī*, Ms. Br. Mus., Or. 3608, f. 5a.

[6] ʿAbd al-Raḥīm al-ʿIrāqī, *op. cit.*, p. 96; Ibn Abī Ḥātim, *op. cit.*, f. 287a; al-Muttaqī l-Hindī, *op. cit.*, XIII, 37, no. 229; al-Suyūṭī, *al-Jāmiʿ al-ṣaghīr*, Cairo 1330, I, 10; al-Haythamī, *op. cit.*, X, 52; al-Jarrāḥī, *op. cit.*, I, 54, no. 133.

[7] Al-Jazarī, *op. cit.*, f. 5a; al-Muttaqī l-Hindī, *op. cit.*, XIII, 37, no. 231 (and see no. 232); and see Ibn Abī Ḥātim, *op. cit.*, f. 384a: *kathratu l-ʿarabi qurratu ʿaynin lī* (cf. al-Muttaqī l-Hindī, *op. cit.*, XIII, 39, no. 239); and see a tradition in praise of the Arabs with an addition against Thaqīf: al-Muttaqī al-Hindī, *op. cit.*, XIII, 39: "A believer will not hate the Arabs and will not love Thaqīf." (but see *ib.*, an interesting version of this *ḥadīth* in favour of Thaqīf; the addition of "*illā*" changes the meaning: *lā yubghiḍu l-ʿaraba mu'minun wa-lā yuḥibbu thaqīfan illā mu'minun.*); ʿAbd al-Raḥīm al-ʿIrāqī, *op. cit.*, pp. 94, 107.

[8] Ms. Feyzullah 541, ff. 121a-122a.

unbelievers follow their unbelievers".[9] "God will despise the man who despises Quraysh".[10] "God will hate the man who hates Quraysh".[11] "Sovereignty belongs to Quraysh"—said the Prophet.[12] These traditions about the qualities of Quraysh [13] were followed by traditions about the qualities and merits of the Anṣār, of the tribes of Yemen and of the Northern tribes.

The legal authority of the rule of Quraysh is plainly attested in the utterances of the Prophet. The secondary position of the Anṣār was foretold in the same manner. The people of Yemen are described as "dispersed in the world, repelled from the gates of the rulers"; [14] they will of course enter Paradise with the Prophet. "Azd, the Prophet says, are the lions of God on earth; people want to debase them, but God will extol them; there will come a time when a man will say: 'Would that my father or my mother were from Azd'." [15] These traditions included utterances about groups of tribes like Tamīm, Quḍāʿa, Hawāzin, Ghaṭafān, Muḍar and smaller tribal units [16] like Lakhm, Judhām, Juhayna, Muzayna, ʿUṣayya etc. The tendency of these traditions, the struggle of some tribes for higher position and authority, can be gauged from an utterance like: "Islam will become debased when Rabīʿa will

---

[9] *Ib.*, f. 121a; Ibn Abī Ḥātim, *op. cit.*, f. 384b-385a; ʿAbd al-Raḥīm al-ʿIrāqī, *op. cit.*, p. 126.

[10] Maʿmar b. Rāshid, *op. cit.*, f. 122a; al-Muttaqī l-Hindī, *op. cit.*, XIII, 17, no. 100; al-Haythamī, *op.cit.*, X, 27 (and see the *ḥadīthes* in favour of Quraysh *ib.*, X, 23-28); and see ʿAbd al-Raḥīm al-ʿIrāqī, *op. cit.*, pp. 126-144 (*Faḍāʾil quraysh*).

[11] Ibn Abī Ḥātim, *op. cit.*, f. 382b.

[12] Al-Muttaqī l-Hindī, *op. cit.*, XIII, 20, no. 118; Ibn Abī Ḥātim, *op. cit.*, f. 383a.

[13] Abū Nuʿaym al-Iṣbahānī, *Ḥilyat al-auliyāʾ*, Cairo 1357/1938, IX, 64-66 (see esp. p. 65: *amānu ahli l-arḍi min al-ikhtilāfi l-muwālātu li-qurayshin, qurayshun ahlu llāhi .... fa-idhā khālafahā qabīlatun min al-ʿarabi ṣārū ḥizba iblīsa*; and see this tradition al-Shaukānī, *al-Fawāʾid al-majmūʿa*, ed. ʿAbd al-Wahhāb ʿAbd al-Laṭīf, Cairo 1960, p. 462; al-Muttaqī l-Hindī, *op. cit.*, XIII, 17-32; Ibn Burhān al-Dīn, *al-Sīra al-ḥalabiyya*, Cairo 1351/1932, I, 29-30; al-Haythamī, *op. cit.*, X, 23-28; al-Ṭabarsī, *al-Iḥtijāj*, al-Najaf 1386/1966, I, 211; Ibn ʿAbd al-Barr, *al-Istīʿāb*, ed. ʿAlī Muḥ. al-Bijāwī, Cairo n.d., II, 792, no. 1330.

[14] Al-Muttaqī l-Hindī, *op. cit.*, XIII, 42, no. 260.

[15] Ibn Saʿīd, *Nashwat al-ṭarab*, Ms. Tübingen 1, f. 55r; al-Muttaqī l-Hindī, *op. cit.*, XIII, 49, no. 284; ʿAbd al-Raḥīm al-ʿIrāqī, *op. cit.*, p. 151.

[16] Cf. al-Suyūṭī, *al-Jāmiʿ al-kabīr*, Ms. al-Jazzār, Acre, p. 236: *alā ukhbirukum bi-khayri qabāʾili l-ʿarabi: al-sakūn sakūn kinda, wa-l-umlūk umlūk radmān, wa-l-sakāsik wa-firaq min al-ashʿariyyīn wa-firaq min khaulān;* and see al-Muttaqī l-Hindī, *op. cit.*, XIII, 47, no. 276, (the curse of Tamīm and Bakr b. Wāʾil, the curse of Muqāʿis and Mulādis of Tamīm); and see *ib.*, no. 277 (the blessing of Ghifār and Aslam); ʿAbd al-Raḥīm al-ʿIrāqī, *op. cit.*, p. 156 (qualities of Tamīm), 157-158 (of Juhayna), 159 (ʿUdhra), 160-161 (Qays and Yemen), 162 (Madhḥij), 164 (qualities of Murra b. ʿUbayd of Tamīm) ..... etc.; and see al-Haythamī, *op. cit.*, X, 42-46 (*mā jāʾa fī qabāʾil al-ʿarab*), 46-48 (Tamīm) .... etc.

be powerful; God will grant power to Islam and diminish polytheism and its people as long as Muḍar and Yemen stay strong and powerful".[17]

It was only natural when pious circles of people entertaining universalist ideas about Islam took to discarding traditions of this kind stressing the exclusiveness or superiority of the Arabs. When somebody expressed his surprise that the Prophet allowed Bilāl, Ṣuhayb and Salmān to sit in a circle (scil. in the mosque of the Prophet—K) he said: "God is one, the religion is one and the Ancestor (i.e. Adam—K) is one. Lo, Arabic is not our father, or mother; it is merely a language; he who speaks Arabic is an Arab".[18] "At the Day of Judgment", says a tradition which gained currency in the pious circles, "God will abolish the *nasab* (of the noble tribes—K) and will establish His *nasab*. The most honoured will be a God-fearing man".[19]

A significant story, said to have been told by al-Kalbī himself, mirrors quite well the attitude of the pious orthodox circles towards *nasab* and *nasab* compilations. In Ibn Qutayba's manuscript *Taʿbīr al-ruʾyā* [20], al-Kalbī recounts a dream of his. He saw himself at the Day of Judgment being brought into the Presence of God, Who said: "You are compiling genealogies which you do not know and you speak about (things) you do not know". He ordered to lead al-Kalbī to Hell. While being led to Hell al-Kalbī noticed the Prophet sitting in a circle of men and asked him to intercede for him with God. But the Prophet said: "How can I intercede for you when you compile genealogies which you do not know". Al-Kalbī said: "O Messenger of God, I also compiled a commentary on the Qurʾān". Then the Prophet ordered one of the people of his circle to examine al-Kalbī; the man was ʿAlī b. Abī Ṭālib. He interrogated al-Kalbī on some four or five religious problems. Al-Kalbī answered the questions well, ʿAlī reported this to the Prophet, and the latter interceded, and al-Kalbī was let free. He sat down with the Prophet and asked him when Umayyad rule was going to terminate. The Prophet mentioned the time of the fall of the Umayyads, which in fact occurred at the fixed date. Later al-Kalbī wrote only the genealogy of known tribes, whose pedigree is not in doubt.

The story reveals clearly the tendency of the pious scholars. It is a blameworthy act to compile books of genealogy containing pedigrees of

---

[17] Al-Muttaqī l-Hindī, *op. cit.*, XIII, 48, no. 279.

[18] Baḥshal, *Taʾrīkh Wāsiṭ*, ed. Gurguis ʿAwwād, Baghdād 1967, p. 252; al-Muttaqī l-Hindī, *op. cit.*, XIII, 39, no. 243.

[19] Asad b. Mūsā, *Kit. al-zuhd*, ed. R. Leszynsky, Kirchhain 1909, pp. xxx-xxxi; al-Ṭabarānī, *al-Muʿjam al-ṣaghīr*, ed. ʿAbd al-Raḥmān Muḥ. ʿUthmān, Cairo 1388/1968, I, 230.

[20] Ms. Hebrew University, Coll. Yahuda, Ar. 196, ff. 10b-11a.

tribes of doubtful origin; to record well-established genealogies seems however to have been regarded lawful. Knowledge of the *sharīʿa* and of Qurʾān saves from pains of Hell. Finally: the intercession of ʿAlī points apparently to the Shīʿī sympathies of al-Kalbī.

A story recorded by Maʿmar b. Rāshid [21] reflects the clash between the old *nasab* of the Jāhiliyya type and that of the Muslim period. Al-Shaʿbī passed by a Qaysī man while the latter was annoying an Asadī with questions about his *nasab*. Al-Shaʿbī sat down with the two men and asked the Qaysī about the first banner raised in Islam, about the first spoils granted in Islam, about the man declared by the Prophet to be in Paradise . . . etc.; all these virtues were in the tribe of Asad, not in Qays. The Qaysī went away, leaving the Asadī alone.

This attitude was however not the prevailing one. *Nasab* was diligently studied and gained orthodox approval.[22] The tradition that *nasab* is "a knowledge by which none profits; ignorance of it does not harm" [23] was confronted by tradition favoring the study of *nasab* and stressing its merits. Muslim scholars said that God singled out this people (i.e. the Muslims—K) granting them the *iʿrāb*, the *isnād* and the *nasab*.[24]

I

In the first period of Islam genealogy had to play a special role. Tribal rivalry, changes in alliances of clans and tribes, divisions in tribes, pressure of the government on some factions of tribes—all these were factors which shaped the development of genealogy in the Umayyad period.[25]

The tendency of some weak tribal units to attach themselves to strong and influential tribes is reflected in a passage of al-Jāḥiẓ in which he records the qualities of Quraysh. No Qurashī, al-Jāḥiẓ states, claimed to be a descendant from another tribe, while members of noble tribes claim "until now" the descent from Quraysh. Noble persons from Murra b. ʿAuf,[26] Sulaym, Khuzāʿa and others, says al-Jāḥiẓ, alleged that they

---

[21] *Al-Jāmiʿ*, ff. 119b-120a; Abū Nuʿaym, *Ḥilyat al-auliyāʾ*, IV, 315-316.

[22] See J. Obermann, *Early Islam*, (in R. C. Dentan—ed.—The Idea of History in Ancient Near East, Yale University Press, 1955, pp. 239-310).

[23] Al-Samʿānī, *Ansāb*, ed. ʿAbd al-Raḥmān al-Muʿallamī, Hyderabad 1382/1962, I, 9.

[24] Al-Zurqānī, *Sharḥ al-mawāhib al-ladunniyya*, Cairo 1326, V, 394-395.

[25] See I. Goldziher, *Muh. Studien*, Halle 1890, I, 97-98, 177 seq.; Caskel, *op. cit.*, I, 25-35.

[26] See Caskel, *op. cit.*, II, 433 (and see *Mufaḍḍaliyyāt*, ed. Lyall, 101-103); Ibn Kathīr, *al-Sīra al-nabawiyya*, ed. Muṣṭafā ʿAbd al-Wāḥid, Cairo 1384/1964, I, 91-93.

were Qurashites.[27] The case of Khuzāʿa is well known; their origin is obscure, but some of them indeed claimed to be Qurashites.[28] Al-Kalbī stated that al-Ṣalt b. Naḍr b. Kināna died childless; thus Khuzāʿa could not be his son.[29] Ibn al-Kalbī records them as descendants of Azd from Saba'.[30] Some claimed that they were descendants of Qamaʿa b. Khindif (i.e. al-Yās, their father—K); this was affirmed by an alleged utterance of the Prophet in which ʿAmr b. Luḥayy, the ancestor of Khuzāʿa was mentioned as ʿAmr b. Luḥayy b. Qamaʿa.[31] The discussions about the pedigree of Khuzāʿa, the political reasons for the attachment of Khuzāʿa with Kināna, the instigations of ʿAbd al-Malik and the activity of Kuthayyir ʿAzza are touched upon by Caskel.[32]

The origin of the Khulj is also obscure.[33] They are included in the *Jamhara* in the *nasab* of al-Ḥārith b. Fihr, but Ibn al-Kalbī adds his reservation that they are descendants of the ʿAmālīq.[34] In his *Nawāqil Muḍar* [35] and in his *Kitāb al-buldān* (as quoted by Mughulṭāy) Ibn al-Kalbī states: "*al-khulj min ʿād*". It is in accordance with the answer of ʿUmar when asked to attach the Khulj to Quraysh: "Am I going to attach ʿĀd to Quraysh?" [36] ʿAlī defined more harshly the relation between the Khulj and Quraysh: *mā bayna jaḥfalati l-ḥimāri ilā khurṭūmi l-khinzīri.*[37]

[27] Al-Jāḥiẓ, *Mukhtārāt fuṣūl* . . . ., Ms. Br. Mus., Or. 3183, f. 202b.

[28] See Mughulṭāy, *op. cit.*, f. 48b: *wa-kāna abū aḥnash al-nassāba l-khuzāʿiyyu idhā qīla lahu: mimman anta, qāla: min qurayshin, fa-idhā qīla lahu: min ayyi qurayshin, qāla: min khuzāʿata; wa-kāna yazʿumu anna khuzāʿata min wuldi l-ṣalti (i.e. al-ṣalt b. al-naḍr b. kināna*—K).

[29] *Ib.*

[30] Al-Fāsī, *Shifā' al-gharām*, Cairo 1956, II, 45.

[31] Muṣʿab, *Nasab Quraysh*, ed. Lévi-Provençal, Cairo 1953, pp. 7 ult.-8 sup.; al-Fāsī, *op. cit.*, II, 44.

[32] Caskel, *op. cit.*, II, 39-40; and see Mughulṭāy, *op. cit.*, ff. 48b-49a, 174a-b; al-Fāsī, *op. cit.*, II, 44-47; al-Kalāʿī, *al-Iktifā*, ed. H. Massé, Paris 1931, I, 128-129; al-Wazīr al-Maghribī, *Adab al-khawāṣṣ*, Ms. Brussa, Husayn Çelebi 85b, ff. 85b-87a; Ibn Saʿīd, *op. cit.*, f. 61r; Ibn ʿAbd al-Barr, *al-Inbāh*, al-Najaf 1966, pp. 96-100; al-Nuwayrī, *Nihāyat al-arab*, Cairo n.d., II, 317-318, 343; al-Suhaylī, *al-Rauḍ al-unuf*, ed. ʿAbd al-Raḥmān al-Wakīl, Cairo 1378/1967, I, 102; Goldziher, *op. cit.*, I, 189.

[33] Al-Nuwayrī, *op. cit.*, II, 353; Goldziher, *op. cit.*, I, 181.

[34] The text of *Jamhara*, Ms. Br. Mus., f. 33a: *wa-qaysu bnu l-ḥārithi wa-huwa l-khulju min baqiyyati l-ʿamālīqi* . . . . Mughulṭāy, *op. cit.*, f. 138a says, refuting the statement of Suhaylī, that the Khulj are a group of Quraysh: . . . . *wa-huwa qaulun mardūdun; qāla l-kalbiyyu fī l-jamharati: yuqālu innahum adʿiyā'u min baqiyyati l-ʿamālīqi.*

[35] In text نوامل مصر. On *nawāqil* see Caskel, *op. cit.*, I, 59; and see *ib.*, p. 80, no. 21 in the list of Ibn al-Kalbī's works; and see Ibn al-Kalbī, *Kit. al-aṣnām*, ed. Ahmad Zaki Pacha, Cairo 1924, p. 69, nos. 21-24; and cf. below note 58.

[36] Mughulṭāy, *op. cit.*, 138a.

[37] *Ib.*

The obscure genealogies of Sāma b. Lu'ayy,[38] Sa'd b. Lu'ayy (Bunāna) who were accepted into the *nasab* of Quraysh by 'Uthmān,[39] and al-Ḥārith b. Lu'ayy[40] were also disputed. The Khuzayma b. Lu'ayy (*'Ā'idhat Quraysh*)[41] were affiliated to Quraysh by Mu'āwiya who wanted to strengthen his power by them.[42] In this case the reasons for the affiliation are quite clear.

The opinions of the genealogists about the origin of Quḍā'a are contradictory. Some of them assert that they were descendants of Ma'add, according to others they were from Ḥimyar.[43] The North-Arabian tradition insisted that Quḍā'a was the son of Ma'add. This fact is attested by an alleged utterance of the Prophet; in this utterance the Prophet stated that the *kunya* of Ma'add was Abū Quḍā'a.[44] The South-Arabian tradition claims Quḍā'a as a descendant of Ḥimyar.[45] The alleged utterance of the Prophet plainly attributes Quḍā'a's descent to Ḥimyar.[46] Ibn al-Kalbī records a harmonizing version: Mu'āna,[47] the mother of Quḍā'a was the wife of Mālik b. 'Amr b. Murra b. Mālik b. Ḥimyar; later she got married to Ma'add and brought Quḍā'a b. Mālik with her. Quḍā'a, because of her second marriage, was later called Quḍā'a b. Ma'add.[48] Another tradition states that Mu'āna was the wife of Ma'add

---

[38] See Ibn Ḥamdūn, *Tadhkira*, Ms. Br. Mus., Or. 3180, II, 63b-64a; al-Suhaylī, *op. cit.*, I, 406-407; al-Balādhurī, *Ansāb al-ashrāf*, ed. Muḥ. Ḥamīdullah, Cairo 1959, I, 46-47; al-Mubarrad, *Nasab 'Adnān wa-Qaḥṭān*, ed. al-Maymanī, Cairo 1354/1936, p. 4; Mughulṭāy, *op. cit.*, ff. 49a-50a; Ibn Kathīr, *Sīra*, I, 90-91; al-Nuwayrī, *op. cit.*, II, 354; al-Zajjājī, *Amālī*, ed. 'Abd al-Salām Hārūn, Cairo 1382, pp. 48-50; Goldziher, *op. cit.*, I, 188-189.

[39] Al-Balādhurī, *op. cit.*, I, 44-45; Mughulṭāy, *op. cit.*, f. 49b (quoted from the *Mathālib* of Abū 'Ubayda); al-Suhaylī, *op. cit.*, I, 402-403.

[40] See Caskel, *op. cit.*, s.v. al-Ḥāriṯ b. Lu'aiy.

[41] See Caskel, *op. cit.*, I, 4, 148.

[42] Al-Nuwayrī, *op. cit.*, II, 355: .... *wa-hum qaumun takaththara bihim mu'āwiyatu fa-adkhalahum fī qurayshin;* al-Suhaylī, *op. cit.*, I, 405.

[43] See al-Balādhurī, *op. cit.*, I, 15-16; al-Nuwayrī, *op. cit.*, II, 283, 295; al-Suhaylī, *op. cit.*, I, 117-124.

[44] Al-Hamdānī, *al-Iklīl*, ed. Muḥ. al-Akwa' al-Ḥiwālī, Cairo 1383/1963, I, 170; Mughulṭāy, *op. cit.*, f. 7b-8a (with a discussion of the problem of Quḍā'a); Ibn 'Abd al-Barr, *al-Inbāh*, p. 59; al-Sam'ānī, *op. cit.*, I, 25; al-Balādhurī, *op. cit.*, I, 16; Abū l-Baqā': *al-Manāqib al-mazyadiyya fī akhbār al-mulūk al-asadiyya*, Ms. Br. Mus., Add. 23,296, f. 89a-89b.

[45] Al-Hamdānī, *op. cit.*, I, 154-181; al-Mubarrad, *op. cit.*, p. 23.

[46] Ibn Wahb, *Jāmi'*, ed. J. David-Weill, Cairo 1939, p. 3, ll. 7-9; al-Hamdānī, *op. cit.*, I, 164, 167; Ibn 'Abd al-Barr, *al-Inbāh*, p. 61 sup.; al-Muttaqī al-Hindī, *op. cit.*, XIII, 57, nos. 331-333; Khalīfa b. Khayyāṭ, *al-Ṭabaqāt*, ed. Akram Ḍiyā' al-'Umarī, Baghdād 1387/1967, p. 120.

[47] The name of the mother of Quḍā'a is also recorded as *'Anna, Nā'ima* (on the authority of al-Mazrū'), *'Ukbara*—al-Balādhurī, *op. cit.*, I, 15-16; *Quḍā'a*—al-Nuwayrī, *op. cit.*, II, 283.

[48] See Suhaylī, *op. cit.*, I, 121; al-Balādhurī, *op. cit.*, I, 15; Abū l-Baqā', *op. cit.*, 90a.

and gave birth to his son Quḍā'a; she subsequently married Mālik b. 'Amr from Ḥimyar who adopted her son Quḍā'a; therefore Quḍā'a was called: Quḍā'a b. Mālik al-Ḥimyarī.[49] Ibn Sa'īd reports that Quḍā'a became Ma'addite when they moved into the Ḥijāz.[50] Ibn al-Kalbī states that the first who attached Quḍā'a to the Yemenite Ḥimyar was 'Amr b. Murra al-Juhanī.[51]

The account of Naṣr b. Mazrū' al-Kalbī[52] concerning the factors which brought about the changes in the *nasab* of Quḍā'a, the period of the changes and the persons involved is of some interest. Up to a point in Mu'āwiya's rule as caliph the tribes of Quḍā'a had been and remained descendants of Ma'add. At that time 'Amr b. Murra, a respected man from Juhayna and a Companion of the Prophet, urged the people to join the Yemenites. In the period of Ibn al-Zubayr, Marwān and 'Abd al-Malik, during the raids of 'Umayr b. Ḥubāb al-Sulamī against the Kalb (i.e. Quḍā'a—K) and those of Ḥumayd b. Ḥurayth al-Kalbī against Qays 'Aylan,[53] Kalb allied themselves with the Yemenī tribes. They were aided by Khālid b. Yazīd b. Mu'āwiya, who opposed the Merwanids and intended to weaken their power and to drive the people of Syria away from them.[54] The alliance between Kalb and the Yemenī tribes became permanent at the time of the expedition of Maslama b. 'Abd al-Malik against Constantinople. He treated Kalb wrongly and favoured Qays. Then Kalb finally joined Yemen. Subsequently Khālid b. 'Abdallah al-Qasrī as governor of 'Iraq bribed leaders of Quḍā'a and Bajīla so as to forge their *nasab*. Naṣr b. Mazrū' remarks that pious and righteous people of Quḍā'a refuse to disclaim descent from Ma'add.[55] Similar reports are given on the authority of Sharqī b. al-Quṭāmī and Ibn Ḥabīb.[56] These passages in the works of early historians help us to

---

[49] Al-Balādhurī, *op. cit.*, I, 15; Abū l-Baqā', *op. cit.*, ib.; al-Nuwayrī, *op. cit.*, II, 283.

[50] *Nashwat al-ṭarab*, f. 51r.

[51] Al-Balādhurī, *op. cit.*, I, 15 (and see p. 16: the report of Muḥ. b. Ḥabīb); al-Mauṣilī, *Ghāyat al-wasā'il ilā ma'rifati l-awā'il*, Ms. Cambridge Qq 33 (10), f. 34a; and see the utterance of the Prophet: *antum .... min ḥimyar* in the biography of 'Amr b. Murra in Ibn Ḥajar's *al-Iṣāba*, Cairo 1325/1907, V, 16, ll. 11-12.

[52] See a tradition reported by him above, note 47; and see al-Jāḥiẓ, *Ḥayawān*, ed. 'Abd al-Salām Hārūn, Cairo 1945, VII, 256.

[53] See al-Balādhurī, *Ansāb al-ashrāf*, vol. V, ed. S. D. Goitein, Jerusalem 1936, index s.v. 'Umayr b. al-Ḥubāb and Ḥumayd b. Ḥurayth.

[54] .... *wa-māla'ahum 'alayhi khālidu bnu yazīda bni mu'āwiyata khilāfan li-banī marwāna wa-qaṣdan li-tauhīni mulkihim wa-tafrīqi jamā'ati ahli l-shāmi 'anhum.*

[55] Abū l-Baqā', *op. cit.*, f. 89b-90a; on Khālid b. 'Abdallah al-Qasrī see Muṣ'ab, *op. cit.*, p. 9, ll. 11-12.

[56] Ibn 'Abd al-Barr, *al-Inbāh*, pp. 60-61.

understand the factors behind the far-reaching change of *nasab* of the Quḍāʿa tribes in Syria.[57]

The opinions of genealogists about the *nasab* of Kinda were not unanimous. Some of them stated that Kinda were descendants of Maʿadd.[58] This pedigree was transmitted by Ibn al-Kalbī.[59] Some genealogists claimed that Kinda were descendants of Rabīʿa.[60] In some traditions it is stressed that in the time of the Jāhiliyya Kinda and Rabīʿa shared common dwellings and common places for the performance of rituals during the pilgrimage to Mecca.[61] It is noteworthy that the delegation of Kinda attempted to attach the Prophet to their *nasab* proposing the following *nasab*: Banū ʿAbd Manāf > Banū Ākil al-Murār. The Prophet, however, rejected this pedigree, stressing that he is a

---

[57] See Caskel, *op. cit.*, II, 73-74; see *ib.*, I, 32; and see Hamdānī, *op. cit.*, I, 154-163.

[58] See *Kitāb siyar al-mulūk*, Ms. Br. Mus., Add. 23,298, f. 133b: .... *wa-arāda bi-dhālika mā yaqūlu baʿḍu l-nussāb inna kindata min al-nāqilati* (see above note 35) *lladhīna ntaqalū min aulādi maʿaddin fa-ntasabū ilā qaḥṭāna.*

[59] Al-Wazīr al-Maghribī, *op. cit.*, f. 93b-94a: *qāla hishāmun al-kalbiyyu: dhakara baʿḍu l-nussābi anna kindata bna thauri bni ʿufayri bni muʿāwiyata bni ḥaydata bni maʿaddi bni ʿadnana.* The evidence for the soundness of the tradition was "attested" by the verse of Imru' l-Qays:

ta-llāhi la yadhhabu shaykhī baṭilā:
khayru maʿaddin nasaban wa-nāʾilā.

The contradictory tradition, attaching Kinda to the South Arabians quotes the second hemistich differently:

yā khayra shaykhin ḥasaban wa-nāʾilā.

[60] Al-Wazir al-Maghribī, *op. cit.*, f. 100a: .... *wa-kāna l-nāsu fī l-zamani l-awwali yaqūlūna: kindatu min rabīʿata ...*; and see *ib.*, f. 93b-94a: .... *wa-qāla ākharūna inna kindata min wuldi ʿāmiri bni rabīʿata bni nizāri bni maʿaddin.* And see Mughulṭāy, *op. cit.*, f. 109a-b (quoting *Adab al-khawāṣṣ*).

[61] *Siyar al-mulūk*, f. 134a: .... *wa-yuqālu, bal arāda mā kāna yalī* (? perhaps: "*bayna*"—K) *kindata wa-rabīʿata min al-taʿāqudi, wa-kānat dāruhum wāḥidatan fī dhālika l-zamāni; yaqūlu l-shāʿiru:*

wa-kindatu idh tarmī l-jimāra ʿashiyyatan ..... etc.; al-Wazīr al-Maghribī, *op. cit.*, 94a: .... *wa-li-dhālika kānat maḥallatu kindata wa-rabīʿata wa-dāruhumā fī l-jāhiliyyati l-jahlāʾi wāḥidatan wa-munākhuhum fī l-mawāsimi maʿan, wa-kānū mutaḥālifīna mutaʿāqidīna; wa-mimmā yuḥaqqiqu hādhā ʿindahum qaulu abī ṭālibi bni ʿabdi l-muṭṭalibi:*

wa-kindatu idh tarmī l-jimāra ʿashiyyatan:
yujawwizuhā ḥujjāju bakri bni wāʾili
ḥalīfāni shaddā ʿaqda mā ḥtalafā lahu:
wa-raddā ʿalayhi ʿāṭifāti l-wasāʾili

The Wazīr explains *ʿāṭifāti l-wasāʾil* as "*al-arḥām*"; Abū l-Baqāʾ, *op. cit.*, f. 84a: ... *wa-kānat rabīʿatu bnu nizārin taqifu ʿinda l-maḍīqi ʿinda l-ʿaqabati fa-tujīzu kindata li-annahum kānū ḥulafāʾahum fa-taqūlu l-nāsu* (perhaps:—*li-l-nāsi*—K) *aqīmū ḥattā tajūza l-amlāku min kindata; wa-fī dhālika yaqūlu abū ṭālibin:*

wa-kindatu .... etc.; and see Caskel, *op. cit.*, I, 33.

descendant of Naḍr b. Kināna.[62] 'Abbās and Abū Sufyān, the Prophet remarked, used to claim their descent from Kinda while on their journeys in Yemen.[63] According to the Prophet all the marriages of his ancestors were according to the rules of Islam, pure and unstained.

There was, however, in connection with this utterance the serious problem of Barra bint Murr (the sister of Tamīm b. Murr) who married Kināna b. Khuzayma b. Mudrika and gave birth to al-Naḍr b. Kināna, the ancestor of the Prophet. It was this Barra of whom Jarīr boasted that "Tamīm begot Quraysh": Tamīm were the maternal uncles of Quraysh.[64] Barra, according to some traditions was the wife of Khuzayma, bore him children and was married by his son Kināna after his death, according to the usual custom of the Jāhiliyya, the *nikāḥ al-maqt*. Al-Balādhurī and Muṣ'ab b. 'Abdallāh record this fact plainly.[65] Ibn al-Kalbī mentions the marriage of Barra with Khuzayma (*Jamhara* f. 4b) and with Kināna (f. 5a); she bore thirteen children of Kināna.

Al-Nuwayrī and Mughulṭāy devote lengthy chapters to the elucidation of this problem. Some scholars tried to find the justification for the two marriages of Barra, arguing that they were permissible in the Jāhiliyya, as the *āya* of the Qur'ān (IV, 22) has an explicit reservation: *illā mā qad salafa*.[66] This argument could however hardly be accepted. The problem was solved by al-Jāḥiẓ in his *Kit. al-aṣnām*. Kināna married in fact, according to al-Jāḥiẓ, Barra bint Udd, the wife of his father after his death; she however bore him no child. Then he married Barra bint Murr b. Udd, who gave birth to al-Naḍr, the ancestor of Quraysh, and other children.[67] This proves, of course, the unstained pedigree of the Prophet and removes any suspicion of *nikāḥ al-maqt* among the ancestors of the Prophet. Al-Damīrī, who quotes the passage of al-Jāḥiẓ, wishes al-Jāḥiẓ to be forgiven for what he wrote in his other books as a reward for this information about Barra.[68] Although Ibn al-Kalbī did not quote the tradition of Barra according to the report of al-Jāḥiẓ he nevertheless stated: "I recorded five hundred ancestresses of the Prophet and I did

---

[62] Ibn Sa'd, *Ṭabaqāt*, Beirut 1380/1960, I, 22-33; Ibn Kathīr, *al-Bidāya wa-l-nihāya*, Beirut-Riyāḍ, 1966, II, 200-201; Ibn 'Abd al-Barr, *al-Inbāh*, p. 67; al-Sam'ānī, *op. cit.*, I, 14, 17.

[63] Ibn Sa'd, *op. cit.*, *ib.*; al-Ṭabarī, *Ta'rīkh*, Cairo 1357/1939, II, 394 (here 'Abbās and Rabī'a b. al-Ḥārith).

[64] Ibn Kathīr, *al-Bidāya*, II, 201; Jarīr, *Dīwān*, ed. al-Ṣāwī, Cairo 1353, p. 508.

[65] Muṣ'ab, *op. cit.*, pp. 8, 10; al-Balādhurī, *op. cit.*, I, 35, 37 ult.

[66] See e.g. al-Fakhr al-Rāzī, *al-Tafsīr al-kabīr*, Cairo 1357/1938, X, 23.

[67] Al-Nuwayrī, *op. cit.*, XVI, 13-15; Mughulṭāy, *op. cit.*, ff. 46b, 107a; 'Abd al-Raḥīm al-'Irāqī, *op. cit.*, pp. 103-105.

[68] Al-Zurqānī, *Sharḥ al-mawāhib al-ladunniyya*, Cairo 1325, I, 77 (quoting Mughulṭāy as well).

not find (in these marriages) anything (which belongs to the vices) of the Jāhiliyya".[69]

The obscure origin of Thaqīf gave rise to many contradictory traditions, influenced by the situation in the Umayyad Empire and the role played by some Thaqafite leaders and governors. Ibn al-Kalbī records Thaqīf in the *Jamhara* as a group of Hawāzin.[70] They were however said to be a group of Iyād,[71] or descendants of Thamūd.[72] According to the tradition attaching them to Iyād the Thaqīf in Ṭā'if were allies (*ḥulafā'*) of Qays. As the mother of Qasiyy b. Munabbih (the ancestor of Thaqīf) was the daughter of ʿĀmir b. al-Ẓarib[73] the Thaqīf joined them as allies[74] and adopted the *nasab* of Qays.[75] The traditions concerning the Iyādī or Thamūdī origin of Thaqīf were wholly rejected by al-Ḥajjāj. It is of interest that Ibn al-Kalbī, who records the tradition of the Qaysī origin of Thaqīf, transmits at the same time the tradition about their Iyādī origin.

The tradition about the Thamūdī origin of Thaqīf is, as usual, attested in an alleged utterance of the Prophet. This was certainly not in favour of Thaqīf. It is thus not surprising to find a harmonizing tradition attributed to the Prophet. The Prophet stated that Thaqīf were descendants of Iyād; Iyād were descendants of Thamūd. When the two men from Thaqīf with whom the Prophet talked showed signs of grief the Prophet stated that they were from the righteous group of Thamūd.[76]

Some of the traditions about the Thamūdī descent of Thaqīf linked the person of their ancestor Qasiyy = Thaqif with Abū Righāl. Thaqīf, says one of the traditions, was a man from Thamūd who escaped the disaster of his people and became a slave of Abū Righāl. Another tradition states that Thaqīf was a slave of the prophet Ṣāliḥ; he took flight and lived in the *ḥaram* (of Mecca). ʿAlī b. Abī Ṭālib, who transmitted

---

[69] Al-Nuwayrī, *op. cit.*, XVI, 13; and see a more explicit version *ib.*, p. 5 inf.: .... *katabtu li-l-nabiyyi khamsa mi'ati ummin, fa-mā wajadtu fīhinna sifāḥan wa-lā shay'an mimma kāna min amri l-jāhiliyyati.*

[70] See Caskel, *op. cit.*, II, 16; al-Nuwayrī, *op. cit.*, II, 335; al-Mubarrad, *op. cit.*, p. 13.

[71] Al-Balādhurī, *op. cit.*, I, 25.

[72] Mughulṭāy, *op. cit.*, f. 12a; al-Hamdānī, *op. cit.*, II, 201; Ibn Wahb, *op. cit.*, p. 5, ll. 2-4; al-Samʿānī, *op. cit.*, I, 20; Ibn ʿAbd al-Barr, *al-Inbāh*, p. 96.

[73] *Jamhara*, f. 154a records, however, Zaynab bint ʿĀmir al-ʿAdwānī as the *wife* of Thaqīf (i.e. Qasiyy).

[74] Ibn ʿAbd al-Barr, *al-Inbāh*, p. 93.

[75] Al-Balādhurī, *op. cit.*, I, 25.

[76] Maʿmar b. Rāshid, *op. cit.*, f. 123b: .... *fa-lammā ra'ā rasūlu llāhi (ṣ) anna dhālika shaqqa ʿalayhimā qāla: mā yashuqqu ʿalaykumā; innamā yuḥyi llāhu min thamūda ṣāliḥan wa-lladhīna āmanū maʿahu, fa-antum min dhurriyyati qaumin ṣāliḥīna.*

this tradition argued that the Prophet (Muḥammad) was closer to the prophet Ṣāliḥ (scil. than anyone else; thus he deserves to inherit the patronage of Thaqīf); therefore he decreed that Thaqīf be considered as slaves.[77] South-Arabian tradition however says that he was a slave of Ṣāliḥ b. al-Humaysaʿ b. dhī Maʾdhin.[78] Another tradition says that the slave of the prophet Ṣāliḥ was Abū Righāl; he was sent as tax-collector, treated the people wrongfully and was therefore killed by Thaqīf.[79] According to a tradition reported by al-Zuhrī Abū Righāl was the ancestor of Thaqīf.[80]

Similar cases with regard to the genealogy of tribes and clans could be easily adduced. But the few cases discussed above bear evidence to the complicated and confused character of the *nasab* literature. The information contained in the traditions about pedigrees, alliances between clans and tribes, affiliations of tribal units and detachments—all this has to be closely studied and re-examined.

II

The admirable work of W. Caskel, a comprehensive and detailed study on Ibn al-Kalbī's *Jamharat al-nasab*, is an indispensable book for students of Arabic genealogy, history of the Jāhiliyya and of early Islam. Its detailed and carefully thought out articles about persons, clans and tribes in the Jāhiliyya and early Islam are a treasure of reliable information collected from many early sources and evaluated with great care and deep insight.

The material of the sources of Ibn al-Kalbī has been cautiously and carefully examined by Caskel.[81] A few passages in later compilations

---

[77] Mughulṭāy, *op. cit.*, f. 11b; another version says that Thaqīf was a slave of al-Hayjumāna, the wife of Ṣāliḥ; she gave him the slave as gift.

[78] Al-Hamdānī, *op. cit.*, II, 354; Mughulṭāy, *op. cit.*, f. 11b.

[79] Ibn Ẓuhayra, *al-Jāmiʿ al-laṭīf*, Cairo 1357/1938, p. 170; cf. al-Ḥākim, *al-Mustadrak*, Hyderabad 1342, I, 398 (Thaqīf mentioned as the man who killed Abū Righāl).

[80] Cf. Mughulṭāy, *op. cit.*, f. 11b inf.; Ibn ʿAbd al-Barr, *al-Inbāh*, p. 95; al-Fākihī, *Taʾrīkh Makka*, Ms. Leiden Or. 463, f. 436b, ult.; *al-Fawāʾid al-muntaqāt min ḥadīth Abī l-Ḥasan ʿAlī .... ʿan Yaḥyā b. Maʿīn*, Ms. Chester Beatty 3495, f. 16a; Ibn Kathīr, *Sīra*, I, 32 harmonizes the contradictory traditions: there were two Abū Righāl; one of them was the ancestor of Thaqīf, the other one was the guide of Abraha. And see the stories about Abū Righāl: Ibn Saʿīd, *op. cit.*, f. 141r; Mughulṭāy, *op. cit.*, 11b (a tax collector of the prophet Shuʿayb; Menaḥem Kister draws my attention to the similarity between the word "*Righāl*" and "*Rʿūel*" (one of the names of Shuʿayb = Yethro); al-Balādhurī, *op. cit.*, I, 25 (a slave of Shuʿayb b. dhī Mahdam al-Ḥimyarī). And see EI², s.v. *Abū Righāl* (S. A. Bonebakker).

[81] Caskel, *op. cit.*, I, 72-81.

and scanty quotations in manuscripts not yet published may elucidate some disputed or obscure points about the literary activity of Ibn al-Kalbī.

Yāqūt copies the list of Ibn al-Kalbī's works from Ibn al-Nadīm's *Fihrist* and adds: "Hishām (i.e. Ibn al-Kalbī) has also *al-Farīd fī l-ansāb*, which he wrote for al-Ma'mūn, *al-Mulūkī fī l-ansāb* which he wrote for Ja'far b. Yaḥyā al-Barmakī, *al-Mūjaz fī l-nasab* and other works.[82] Caskel doubted the truth of this information.[83] The book of Ibn al-Kalbī *al-Munzal* recorded by Yāqūt [84] with the remark "*wa-huwa kitābu l-nasabi l-kabīru*" was considered by Caskel as spurious; he proposed to read instead of *al-Munzal*: "*al-Jamharatu wa-huwa kitābu l-nasabi l-kabīru*".[85]

A passage in Ḥamza al-Iṣfahānī's "*al-Tanbīh 'alā ḥudūth al-taṣḥīf*" [86] sheds some light on the disputed problem of the genealogical compilations of Ibn al-Kalbī mentioned by Yāqūt. Ḥamza considers it fortunate that the Arab Empire was granted the two outstanding scholars: al-Khalīl and Hishām b. al-Kalbī (*fa-l-iqbālu sāqa ilā daulati l-'arabi* . . .) who exerted himself by establishing their genealogies (*'uniya lahum bi-ḍabṭi l-ansābi*). He compiled five books on this subject: *al-Munzal, al-Jamhara, al-Mūjaz, al-Farīd, al-Mulūkī.*

Al-Munzal, says Ḥamza, is his largest compilation on *nasab* (*akbaru kitābin lahu fī l-nasabi*). In this book he established the (genealogical) positions of the Arabs (i.e. the Arab tribes—K; *yunzilu l-'araba fīhi manāzilahum*); [87] in some cases he skipped over some clans (*takhaṭṭāhum*) if he found them debased in number or nobility.[88] Ḥamza quotes some clans which Ibn al-Kalbī omitted.[89]

---

[82] *Mu'jam al-udabā'*, ed. Aḥmad Farīd Rifā'ī, Cairo n.d., XIX, 292: . . . . *hādhā ma dhakarahu bnu l-nadīmi min taṣānīfihi; wa-li-hishāmin ayḍan: al-farīdu fī l-ansābi, ṣannafahu li-l-ma'mūni, wa-l-mulūkiyyu fī l-ansābi ayḍan ṣannafahu li-ja'fari bni yaḥyā l-barmakiyyi, wa-l-mūjazu fī l-nasabi ayḍan, wa-ghayru dhālika.*

[83] Caskel, *op. cit.*, I, 79, note 4: "Es ist zweifelhaft ob Yaq.'s Angaben . . . . *al-Farīd fī l-ansāb* sei für al-Ma'mūn, ... *al-Mulūkī fi l-ansāb* für den Barmakiden Ǧa'far b. Yaḥyā verfasst, zutreffen; schon wegen der Prunktitel die I. al-Kalbī bis auf einen Fall meidet: no. 88 = *K. ad-Dībāǧ fī aḫbār aš-šu'arā'*".

[84] Yāqūt, *op. cit.*, XIX, 291.

[85] Caskel, *op. cit.*, I, 97, note 2.

[86] Ed. Muḥ. Ḥasan Yāsīn, Baghdād 1967, pp. 192-194.

[87] The reading "*al-munzil*" seems to be preferable.

[88] The text of the Ms. seems to be corrupted; the reading is doubtful.

[89] The editor did not succeed to decipher the names of these debased clans; the text in the Ms. seems to be unclear. The idea to omit the mean or debased from compilations of *nasab* is indicated in Hamdānī's *al-Iklīl*, II, 386: . . . . *wa-qāla abū muḥammadin: wa-min sharā'iṭi l-nasabi an lā yudhkara min aulādi l-rajuli illā l-nabīhu l-ashharu wa-yulghā l-ghabiyyu; wa-lau-lā dhāka lam yasa' ansāba l-nāsi sijillun wa-lam yaḍbuṭhā kātib* . . .

The *Jamhara* is his middle-sized book and contains some stories (*akhbār*) about the persons recorded, accounts about the mothers of the nobles (of the clans) and the ancestresses of the tribes, (explaining) how they originated from tribes to form their clans. He counted their horsemen, their poets and their illustrious men.[90]

The *Mūjaz*, Ḥamza says, contains material which no student of *adab* and *nasab* can ignore. He recorded in it the genealogical lists of smaller and greater tribal units, the nobles of every group, their poets, leaders and eminent persons.[91]

The *Farīd*, Ḥamza continues, is a book on tribes. Ibn al-Kalbī assigned in this book for every small tribal unit its genealogies the stories of its wars and its poetry; he recorded this material and furnished it with *isnāds* and names of the transmitters. He offered this book to al-Ma'mūn.

Al-Mulūkī contains a great number of known *akhbār* and information not found in his other books; it contains material included in the *Farīd*, although it is smaller in size than the former; this book he offered to Ja'far b. Yaḥyā al-Barmakī.[92]

The details given by Ḥamza seem to be trustworthy. Ḥamza is in fact the earliest authority on the genealogical compilations of Ibn al-Kalbī. The precise details of the description indicate that he had a close acquaintance with these compilations.

It is noteworthy that the *Farīd* presented to al-Ma'mūn was provided with *isnāds* and names of the transmitters; this detail is pointed out by Ḥamza in particular. One may venture to assume that Ibn al-Kalbī added here the *isnāds* in order to adapt himself to the new conditions of Muslim scholarship and requirements of the experts of *ḥadīth*.[93] The other genealogical compilations of Ibn al-Kalbī seem to have had no *isnād*.

---

[90] p. 193: . . . *fīhi ba'ḍu l-akhbāri wa-ta'dādu ummahāti l-ashrāfi wa-l-qabā'ili ilā ḥaythu yaftariqūna 'an qabīlatihim wa-yatajāwazūna ilā buṭūnihim, wa-dhikru fursānihim wa-shu'arā'ihim wa-dhawī nabāhatihim ḥattā* . . . (two words could not be deciphered by the editor).

[91] p. 193: . . . . *wa-ammā l-mūjazu fa-fīhi mā lā yuḥsinu bi-mubtaghī l-adabi wa-l-nāẓiri fī l-nasabi jahluhu, fa-dhakara fīhi man yunsabu ilā baṭnin wa-qabīlin, wa-sharīfa kulli qaumin wa-shā'irahum wa-man ḥtalla l-siṭata minhum wa-stawā 'alā l-ri'āsati fīhim.* (About *baṭn* see EI², J. Lecerf, *Baṭn*).

[92] *Ib.*, . . . *wa-ammā l-farīdu fa-huwa kitābu l-qabā'ili, afrada fīhi li-kulli baṭnin nasabahu mufradan, wa-ayyāmahu, wa-shi'rahu, fa-dhakara kulla dhālika bi-l-asānīdi wa-l-ruwāti, wa-huwa lladhī atḥafa bihi l-ma'mūna; wa-ammā l-mulūkiyyu fa-fīhi akhbārun ghazīratun ma'rūfatun wa-ma'rifatun kathīratun lā taqa'u fī ghayrihi min kutubihi, wa-fīhi mā yaqa'u fī l-farīdi wa-in lam yablugh madāhu, wa-huwa lladhī atḥafa bihi ja'fara bna yaḥyā l-barmakiyya.*

[93] See Caskel, *op. cit.*, I, 78.

We came across a quotation from the *Munzal* in Mughulṭāy's *al-Zahr al-bāsim*[94]. This passage deals with the story of Naṣr b. Ḥajjāj and his beloved nicknamed *al-Mutamanniya*; Ibn al-Kalbī reports that her name was al-Fāriʿa bint Hammām b. ʿUrwa b. Masʿūd from Thaqīf and that she was the mother of al-Ḥajjāj b. Yūsuf (the hated Umayyad governor of ʿIrāq). The *Jamhara* mentions only that Naṣr was nicknamed al-Jamīl.[95]

Mughulṭāy refers to Ibn al-Kalbī in his work about two hundred times, quoting his opinion about particular points of genealogy.[96] The *Jamhara* is quoted about twenty times.[97] Mughulṭāy quotes two additional works of genealogy compiled by Ibn al-Kalbī: *al-Jāmiʿ* (or *al-Jāmiʿ li-ansābi l-ʿarabi*) [98] and *Jamharat al-jamhara*.[99]

A scrutiny of the quotations from *al-Zahr al-bāsim* and an examination of the material found in hitherto unpublished manuscripts may help us to gain a better knowledge of the contents of the genealogical compilations of Ibn al-Kalbī.

The list of compilations of Ibn al-Kalbī contains a book with the title *Mathālib al-ʿarab*.[100] The few extant passages from this compilation are recorded in Shīʿī sources. The odious story of the pedigree of Muʿāwiya sheds some light on the character of this genre of literature and points out some of the ways in which tendencious insertions or deletions were made. Hind, the mother of Muʿāwiya, used to have sexual intercourse

[94] F. 306b.; see al-ʿAskarī, *Jamharat al-amthāl*, ed. Muḥ. Abū l-Faḍl Ibrāhīm - ʿAbd al-Majīd Qūṭāmish, Cairo 1384/1964, I, 588, no. 1110; al-Maydānī, *Majmaʿ ʿal-amthāl*, Cairo 1352, I, 427-428; Abū Nuʿaym, *Ḥilyat al-auliyāʾ*, IV, 322-323.

[95] Caskel, *op. cit.*, II, 446.

[96] See ff. 2a, 3a, 3b, 4b, 5b, 6a, 7a, 7b, 8a, 8b, 9a, 9b, 10a, 14a, 14b, 15b, 17b, 18a, 23a, 23b, 38a, 38b, 40a, 40b, 42a, 43a, 43b, 44a, 45a, 45b, 46b, 48b, 49a, 49b, 50b, 54b, 55a, 56b, 60a, 60b, 62a, 69b, 87a, 93a, 95a, 97b, 109a, 110a, 121a, 121b, 123a, 123b, 131a, 132b, 133a, 133b, 134b, 144b, 150b, 155b, 156b, 200a, 202a, 203b, 207a, 209a, 209b, 210a, 210b, 212b, 214b, 224b, 225b, 226b, 231b, 232b, 233a, 234a, 234b, 235a, 236a, 236b, 237a, 240b, 241a, 247b, 259b, 266a, 277a, 279b, 282b, 285a, 286b, 287b, 295b, 298b, 300a, 310b, 311a, 311b, 312b, 319a, 321a, 322b, 325b, 328a, 330b, 333b, 335b, 336a, 336b, 337a, 339a. (On some pages Ibn al-Kalbī is mentioned two or three times).

[97] Cf. e.g. Mughulṭāy f. 22b = *Jamhara* f. 156a Ḥuṭayṭ; 11b = 244a Umayma bint Saʿd b. Hudhayl; 23a = Caskel, s.v. Munabbih b. Rabīʿa; 52b = 169b Hāshim b. Ḥarmala; 86a = Caskel, *op. cit.*, s.v. A. al-Ğabr (2, 251); 99a = 124b Yazīd b. ʿAmr b. Khuwaylid; 237b = Caskel, s.v. Ḫalīfa b. ʿAdī; 247a = 255b ʿUbād b. Bishr; 287b = Caskel, s.v. Uhbān b. al-Akwaʿ = Uhbān b. Ṣayfī (al-Suhaylī), Uhbān b. Aus al-Aslamī (al-Tirmidhī, al-Bukhārī, Abū Nuʿaym, Ibn Manda), Uhbān b. ʿAbbād (Ibn Durayd, Ibn al-Kalbī, al-Balādhurī) etc. ....; 337b = 173b, Umm Qirfa and her sons; Dubaiyya b. Ḥaramī = 162a.

[98] Mentioned ten times: ff. 36b, 40a, 60a, 67b, 70b, 102b, 142a, 237b, 213a, 238a.

[99] Quoted two times: ff. 102b, 162b.

[100] See Sezgin, GAS, I, 270, no. 4.

with four Qurashites, according to the slanderous tradition of the *Mathālib*. The four shared, of course, the fatherhood of Muʿāwiya. Three of them are named: ʿUmāra b. al-Walīd, Musāfir b. ʿAmr, Abū Sufyān; the name of the fourth is not given and it is only remarked in the report that Ibn al-Kalbī mentioned his name.[101] The name of the fourth person is however explicitly given by Sibṭ b. al-Jauzī: al-ʿAbbās b. ʿAbd al-Muṭṭalib.[102] Muʿāwiya admits in a talk with his son Yazīd that some Qurashites are of the opinion that he is the son of ʿAbbās b. ʿAbd al-Muṭṭalib.[103] One may assume that the name of ʿAbbās was erased from the list of the four adulterers in the period of the ʿAbbāsid rule; it was re-inserted after the fall of the dynasty.

The abominable story of the pedigree of ʿUmar is also quoted from Ibn al-Kalbī's *Mathālib*. It is noteworthy that the shameful story of the complicated bastardy[104] is preceded by a peculiar remark in the Shīʿī compilation of al-Majlisī: ... *wa-rawā l-kalbiyyu, wa-huwa min rijāli ahli l-sunnati, fī kitābi l-mathālibi, qāla: kānat Ṣuhāku* ....[105] This remark aims, of course, to enhance the impartiality and reliability of Ibn al-Kalbī's information and to emphasize the soundness of the tradition.

The story about the father of ʿUthmān, as recorded in Ibn al-Kalbī's *Mathālib*, is not less disgusting than the two preceding cases.[106] The mildest vilification was directed against the father of Abū Bakr: he was the servant of ʿAbdallāh b. Judʿān and called the poor of Mecca to have their charity-meals at the table of ʿAbdallāh. He got, of course, a paltry reward for this "duty".[107]

The story of the illegitimate son of Umayya b. ʿAbd Shams, Dhakwān (his *kunya* was Abū ʿAmr) whose mother Turnā was a slave-woman from Ṣafūriyya (Palestine) is reported by Ibn al-Kalbī; it fits in well with the setting of his *Mathālib* and is probably derived from this com-

---

101 Ibn Ṭāwūs, *Ṭarāʾif ʿAbd al-Maḥmūd*, n.p., n.d., p. 156; Muḥ. Ḥasan al-Muẓaffar, *Dalāʾil al-ṣidq*, III, 1, 215-219; comp. a similar slanderous report from *Mathālib banī umayya* by Ismāʿīl b. ʿAlī al-Sammān al-Ḥanafī, *ib.*, p. 235; and comp. on the fatherhood of ʿAmr b. al-ʿĀṣ shared by five persons (... *wa-la-qad iddaʿāka khamsatun min qurayshin kulluhum yazʿumu annaka bnuhu*) *ib.*, p. 237.

102 *Tadhkirat al-khawāṣṣ*, al-Najaf 1383/1964, p. 202 inf.

103 *Ib.*, p. 203.

104 ... *kāna al-khaṭṭābu aban wa-jaddan wa-khālan li-ʿumara.*

105 *Biḥār al-anwār*, VIII, 311 (lithogr. ed.); and see this story al-Majlisī, *op. cit.*, XXII, 269-271 (new ed., Tehran 1385); Ibn Ṭāwūs, *op. cit.*, p. 144; Muḥ. Ḥasan al-Muẓaffar, *op. cit.*, III, 2, 84.

106 See Ibn Ṭāwūs, *op. cit.*, p. 155.

107 Ibn Ṭāwūs, *op. cit.*, p. 123.

pilation.[108] Abū ʿUbayda seems to have used the same method of slander in his *Mathālib*. Yāqūt quotes in his *Muʿjam al-buldān*[109] from Abū ʿUbayda's *Mathālib* that Hāshim b. ʿAbd Manāf bought a black girl, Ḥayya, at the market of Ḥubāsha. She bore him two sons: Ṣayfī and Abū Ṣayfī. But Muṣʿab gives in his *Nasab*[110] a rather different version: the mother of Ṣayfī and Abū Ṣayfī was Hind bint Thaʿlaba from Khazraj. This *nasab* is recorded by Ibn al-Kalbī (Jamhara, 7b, inf.). The slanderous traditions about the pedigree of al-Ashʿath b. Qays, al-Muhallab b. Abī Ṣufra, Khālid b. Ṣafwān, al-Jahm b. Badr, Abu Dulaf and Khālid b. ʿAbdallāh al-Qasrī seem to have been recorded from the *Mathālib* of Abū ʿUbayda.[111] Ibn al-Kalbī and Abū ʿUbayda both apply the same style of slander directed at the ancestresses, involving accusations of immoral conduct and adultery. The *mathālib* can thus be seen to be in fact nothing but a collection of defamatory genealogical gossip. They are different from *nasab* and serve a different purpose.

The following works of Ibn al-Kalbī seem to be related in subject-matter to his *nasab* compilations: *Kitāb al-alqāb*,[112] mentioned three times in Mughulṭāy's *Zahr*,[113] *Kitāb nawāqil muḍar*,[114] *Kitāb al-buldān*,[115] *Kitāb al-dafāʾin*[116] and *Kitāb man qāla shiʿran fa-nusiba ilayhi*.[117] Al-ʿIṣāmī mentions a list of Qurashī judges from Ibn al-Kalbī's *Ḥukkām Quraysh*.[118]

Of special interest is a compilation of Ibn al-Kalbī not recorded in the

---

[108] *Taʾrīkh al-khulafāʾ*, ed. Piotrowski-Graznewych, Moskwa 1967, f. 4a; Abū l-Baqāʾ, *op. cit.*, f. 12a (Abū l-Baqāʾ records as well the other version, which is the accepted one: the mother of Abū ʿAmr was Umāma bint Ḥimyarī b. al-Ḥārith of Lakhm; see Muṣʿab, *op. cit.*, p. 100).

[109] S.v. *Ḥubāsha*.

[110] *Nasab Quraysh*, p. 4, ll. 12-14.

[111] Ibn Rustah, *al-Aʿlāq al-nafīsa*, ed. M. J. de Goeje, Leiden 1892, pp. 205-207.

[112] See Sezgin, *op. cit.*, I, 271, no. 19.

[113] F. 87a (why ʿAuf was nicknamed Thumāla); f. 102b (explanation of the nickname Janb; cf. Caskel, *op. cit.*, II, 257); f. 207a (the nickname al-Akhṭal).

[114] F. 138a (and see Abū l-Baqāʾ, *op. cit.*, f. 36a where a compilation of *Kit. al-nawāqil* by Abū l-Ḥasan Muḥ. b. Muḥ. al-ʿAlawī is mentioned); and see above note 35.

[115] Ff. 8b, 9b, 19b, 43a, 45a, 47a, 57a-b, 117b, 196b, 306b, 325a.

[116] F. 33b (the correct reading is *Dafāʾin*, not *Daqāʾiq* as given by Sezgin, *op. cit.*, I, 270, no. 13; see al-Karājakī, *Kanz al-fawāʾid*, n.p., 1322, p. 178: *faṣl fīmā ruwiya fī l-qubūr wa-l-dafāʾin*; Aḥmad b. Ḥanbal, *Kit. al-waraʿ*, Cairo 1340, p. 47: *Kit. al-dafāʾin*).

[117] F. 145a, inf.; see Ibn al-Kalbī, *al-Aṣnām*, no. 87.

[118] *Simṭ al-nujūm al-ʿawālī*, Cairo 1380, I, 213: . . . *ʿan al-kalbī fī l-ḥukkām min quraysh qāla* . . .; cf. Muḥ. b. Ḥabīb, *al-Muḥabbar*, ed. I. Lichtenstaedter, Hyderabad 1361/1942, p. 132; idem, *al-Munammaq*, ed. Khurshīd Aḥmad Fāriq, Hyderabad 1384/1964, p. 459; and see *al-Aṣnām*, no. 64: *Aḥkām al-ʿArab* (the correct reading is *ḥukkām* as in note 3 *ib.*).

list of his works. It is mentioned by Mughulṭāy in the following passage: . . . *wa-qāla l-miqdādu bnu l-aswadi l-kindiyyu yamdaḥu ʿaliyyan fīmā dhakarahu l-kalbiyyu fī kitābi l-shūrā, taʾlīfihi*:

kabbara li-llāhi wa-ṣallā wa-mā:
ṣallā dhawū l-ʿaybi wa-mā kabbarū [119]

This short passage of Ibn al-Kalbī's *Kit. al-shūrā* provides us with a clue for the assessment of his religious and political sympathies. The person of Miqdād, the famous champion of the cause of ʿAlī, the content of the verse and the occasion on which it was uttered—all this bears evidence that the compilation was of a Shīʿī character. The Shīʿī sympathies of al-Kalbī [120] and of Ibn al-Kalbī are well known.[121] It is therefore not surprising to find in the *Jamhara* an inserted passage concerning the punishment inflicted on Anas b. Mālik for having denied having heard an utterance of the Prophet in favour of ʿAlī.[122] It is a well-known Shīʿī story.[123]

In spite of his Shīʿī sympathies Ibn al-Kalbī recorded also traditions which were not always in favour of ʿAlī and the Shīʿa.[124] He was a

---

[119] *Al-Zahr*, f. 117b.

[120] Although Ibn Rustah, *op. cit.*, p. 220, l. 4 mentions Muḥ. b. al-Sāʾib as one of the *murjiʾa*.

[121] Caskel, *op. cit.*, I, 73; and see the story told by Muḥ. b. al-Sāʾib: . . . *mariḍtu marḍatan fa-nasītu mā kuntu aḥfaẓu fa-ataytu āla muḥammadin* (ṣ) *fa-nafathū fī fiyya fa-ḥafiẓtu mā kuntu nasītu*—Ibn Abī Ḥātim al-Rāzī, *Kit. al-jarḥ wa-l-taʿdīl*, Hyderabad 1953, III, 2, 270; Ibn Ḥajar, *Tahdhīb al-tahdhīb*, IX, 179 (no. 266). And see the tradition transmitted by him that the angel Gabriel used to transmit the Revelation to ʿAlī in the absence of the Prophet: Ibn Ḥajar, *op. cit.*, ib.; al-Ṣafadī, *al-Wāfī bi-l-wafayāt*, ed. H. Ritter, Wiesbaden 1381/1961, III, 83; and see the story about the killing of Saʿd b. ʿUbāda (cf. al-Ḥusaynī, *al-Darajāt al-rafīʿa*, al-Najaf 1382/1962, p. 334) reported by al-Kalbī in *Yawāqīt al-siyar*, Ms. Br. Mus., Or. 3771, f. 132a, penult.; al-Dhahabī, *Mīzān al-iʿtidāl*, ed. ʿAlī Muḥ. al-Bijāwī, Cairo 1382/1963, III, 557-558; and see *ib.*, IV, 304, ult. on Hishām b. Muḥ. b. al-Sāʾib: *wa-qāla ibn ʿasākir : rāfiḍī, laysa bi-thiqatin* (quoted by the editor of *al-Qurab*, p. 148).

[122] Caskel, *op. cit.*, I, 109: "Ein sonderbarer Einschub . . .".

[123] See al-Majlisī, *op. cit.*, XXXVII, 197-200 (new ed.); Ibn Shahrāshūb, *Manāqib āl Abī Ṭālib*, al-Najaf 1376/1956, II, 13; Ibn Rustah, *op. cit.*, p. 221. There was however an earlier case which caused a grudge of ʿAlī against Anas; see al-Majlisī, *op. cit.*, LX, 301 (new ed.).

[124] See e.g. the tradition that Khālid b. Saʿīd b. al-ʿĀṣ embraced Islam before ʿAlī: Mughulṭāy, *op. cit.*, f. 117a-b (see on Khālid b. Saʿīd: Muṣʿab, *op. cit.*, p. 174, l. 15). Al-Kalbī reports the following saying of Khālid: "I feared my father (therefore I did not announce my Islam publicly—K), but ʿAlī did not fear Abū Ṭālib." And see the favourable tradition about Jarīr b. ʿAbdallāh al-Bajalī (*yaṭlaʿu ʿalaykum min hādhā l-fajji khayru dhī yamanin ʿalayhi masḥatu malikin fa-ṭalaʿa jarīru bnu ʿabdi llāhi l-bajaliyyu*)—al-Khaṭīb al-Baghdādī, *Mūḍiḥ auhām al-jamʿ wa-l-tafrīq*, Hyderabad 1379/1960, II, 355. And see the tradition transmitted by Ibn al-Kalbī (with the *isnād*: Ibn al-Kalbī > his father > Abū Ṣāliḥ > Ibn ʿAbbās) that the Prophet informed secretly Ḥafṣa that her father (i.e. ʿUmar) will be the

transmitter of *nasab* and *akhbār*, and he carried out this vocation with the utmost responsibility. Besides the *Mathālib* he compiled books in which a significant portion of Arab cultural tradition was recorded, thus providing valuable information about social life, beliefs, poetry, genealogy, wars and alliances of tribes. His compilations on genealogy, among them the *Jamhara*, constitute a solid and masterly monument of Arab learning.

We owe a debt of gratitude to the late W. Caskel for making this magnificent book available to modern scholarship.

Caliph after Abū Bakr; Ḥafṣa revealed the secret to ʿĀʾisha—al-Dhahabī, *Mīzān al-iʿtidāl*, IV, 305 (see Ibn Kathīr, *Tafsīr*, Beirut 1385/1966, VII, 57; the tradition is recorded with a different *isnād*. And see al-Ṭabarsī, *Majmaʿ al-bayān*, Beirut 1380/1961, XXVIII, 120 inf.; the tradition is recorded without *isnād*. The tradition is not found in al-Wāḥidī's *Asbāb al-nuzūl* and in Suyūṭī's *Lubāb al-nuqūl*—in the chapter of *Sūrat al-taḥrīm*).

IV

A WORK OF IBN AL-KALBĪ ON THE ARAB PENINSULA

The list of the works of Ibn al-Kalbī recorded by Aḥmad Zakī Pasha (Ibn al-Kalbī, *Kitāb al-aṣnām*, Cairo, 1924, p. 73, no. 57) contains a work *Kitāb Ghuzayya* (correctly: *Kitāb Ghaziyya*; see Yāqūt, *Mu'jam al-udabā'*, ed. Aḥmad Farīd Rifā'ī, Cairo, n.d., XIX, 290, l. 1); Aḥmad Zakī remarks that Ghuzayya is a well-known tribe. The title of the work seems to indicate that it deals with the tradition and stories about the tribe.

The name of the book was, however, transmitted erroneously and it seems that the error crept very early into the copied book of Ibn Nadīm's *Fihrist*. The correct name of the book is recorded in the MS of al-Ḥusayn b. 'Alī b. al-Ḥasan al-Kātib, known as al-Wazīr al-Maghribī (see *GAL*, Suppl., I, 600–1), *Adab al-khawāṣṣ* (MS Brussa, Ḥusayn Çelebi, 85b) in a significant passage in which one of the meanings of the root ' '*arb* ' is discussed (fols. 38b–39b). Al-Wazīr al-Maghribī quotes an opinion that '*arba* denotes the Arab peninsula and records a passage from Ibn al-Kalbī's book '*Arba* (so vowelled) confirming this opinion:

> *fa-min al-shāhidi 'alā anna 'arbata ismu jazīrati 'l-'arabi mā anshadahu hishāmun al-kalbiyyu fī kitābihi 'l-musammā 'arbata li-abī ṭālibin 'ammi 'l-nabiyyi ṣallā 'llāhu 'alayhi wa-'alā ālihi. . . .*[1]
>
> *wa-'arbatu arḍun lā yuḥillu ḥarāmahā: min al-nāsi ghayru 'l-shautariyyi 'l-qunābili.*[2]

Al-Wazīr al-Maghribī gives the explanation of the meanings of *shautarī* and *qunābil*[3] and differs with the opinion of Ibn al-Kalbī that '*arba*—according to the quoted verse—denotes the Arab peninsula. In his opinion '*arba* in the verse quoted by Ibn al-Kalbī denotes Mecca. ' But Hishām (i.e. Ibn al-Kalbī) knows better '[4] remarks al-Wazīr al-Maghribī respectfully at the end of the passage.

Al-Wazīr al-Maghribī may indeed be trusted in his information about genealogy and about the works of Ibn al-Kalbī. He had a profound knowledge of *nasab* which is attested by his book *al-Īnās bi-'ilmi 'l-ansāb* (British Museum,

[1] The author gives a detailed pedigree of Abū Ṭālib: . . . *wa-ismuhu 'Abd Manāf b. 'Abd al-Muṭṭalib (wa-ismuhu Shayba) b. Hāshim (wa-ismuhu 'Amr) b. 'Abd Manāf (wa-ismuhu 'l-Mughīra) b. Quṣayy (wa-ismuhu Zayd) b. Kilāb b. Murra b. Ka'b b. Lu'ayy b. Ghālib b. Fihr b. Mālik b. al-Naḍr (wa-huwa jimā'u Quraysh, man laysa min wuldi 'l-Naḍr fa-laysa min Quraysh) b. Kināna b. Khuzayma b. Mudrika (wa-ismuhu 'Amr) b. al-Yās b. Muḍar b. Nizār b. Ma'add b. 'Adnān.*

[2] See the verse in Yāqūt's *Mu'jam al-buldān*, s.v. '*araba* with the hemistich:

min al-nāsi illā 'l-laudha'iyyu 'l-ḥulāḥilu

and see *L'A*, s.v. '*arb* with the hemistich as in Yāqūt's *Mu'jam*; but *L'A*, s.v. *qnbl*, the hemistich is recorded as in *Adab al-khawāṣṣ*.

[3] A *rajaz* verse of Abū Ghālib al-'Ijlī is quoted:

Banī Kulaybin sāqakum jaddun shaqiyy:
Ḥattā ramākum 'inda āṣāli 'l-'ashiyy:
Bi-muṭrahammin fī 'l-shabābi shautariyy.

[4] . . . *wa-anā arā anna hādhā 'l-bayta yadullu 'alā ghayri mā 'stashhada bihi 'alayhi Hishāmun li-annahu yadullu 'alā Makkata faqaṭ, wa-Hishāmun a'rafu.*

MS Or. 3620).[5] His quotations, glosses, and remarks prove that he had a vast erudition in Jāhiliyya tradition and that he was a connoisseur of Jāhilī poetry. His immense knowledge of *nasab* is evident in his detailed pedigrees given in the recorded stories of *Adab al-khawāṣṣ*. His esteem for Ibn al-Kalbī and his keen interest in his works is attested by the comments and notes recorded on his authority in the margin of the MS of *Kitāb al-aṣnām*.[6]

It is evident that the work of Ibn al-Kalbī referred to by Ibn al-Nadīm in his *Fihrist* is *Kitāb ʿArba* not *Kitāb Ghaziyya*. The cause of the error is obvious: the slight graphical difference between غزية and عرْبة which led to the clerical error. The quotations recorded on the authority of Ibn al-Kalbī in Yāqūt's *Muʿjam al-buldān*[7] are with all probability derived from his *Kitāb ʿArba*, a book obviously dealing with the Arab peninsula.

[5] The note of the editor Aḥmad Farīd Rifāʿī in Ibn Khallikan's *Wafayāt* (v, 39, n. 3): *huwa kitābun fī 'l-muḥāḍarāt wa 'l-adab* is erroneous.

[6] See *al-Aṣnām*, 26–7.

[7] s.v. *ʿAraba* Beirut, 1957, IV, 97a, 97b; see the verses of Ibn Munqidh, and Abū Sufyān al-Aklubī (pp. 97, 98) in *Adab al-khawāṣṣ*, fol. 39b f. (On Abū Sufyān al-Aklubī see al-Samʿānī, *al-Ansāb*, ed. al-Muʿallimī, Hyderabad, 1962, I, p. 337, n. 1.)

V

ON THE WIFE OF THE GOLDSMITH FROM FADAK AND HER PROGENY

A STUDY IN JĀHILĪ GENEALOGICAL TRADITIONS

The section in Ibn al-Kalbī's *Jamhara* concerning the pedigree of Ḥiṣn b. Ḍamḍam and of his clan of Kalb [1] may shed some light on the relations between the different groups of the population in the North of the Arabian peninsula in the second half of the sixth century AD; some additional data from other sources enable us to get a better perception of the events. The passage of Ibn al-Kalbī, summarized by W. Caskel [2], deserves a closer examination.

* * *

Al-Ḥārith, the son of Ḥiṣn b. Ḍamḍam, nicknamed al-Ḥarshā, was the chief of his people. When Fadak was conquered by Kalb in the period of the Jāhiliyya his share of the booty consisted of the captives (*wa-lahu ṣāra sabyu fadaka ḥīna ftataḥahā kalbun fī l-jāhiliyyati*). The very concise report about the conquest of Fadak given by Ibn al-Kalbī is amplified by an account recorded by Abū l-Baqā': al-Ḥārith b. Ḥiṣn b. Ḍamḍam b. ʿAdī b. Janāb al-Kalbī, known as al-Ḥarshā, had the right to the pay (*jaʿāla*) imposed on the people of Fadak; when they refused to pay, he raided them [3]. Among the captured women was Shaqīqa, the wife of the goldsmith. Wā'il b. ʿAṭiyya b. al-ʿUdays (or ʿUdas); al-Ḥārith took her to him and she bore him his son Suwayd. Ibn al-Kalbī points out that Shaqīqa was a Jewess and records her ancestors in a long pedigree which goes back to Abraham [4]. Abū l-Baqā' is more precise: the Jewish goldsmith Wā'il was captured together with his Jewish wife Shaqīqa [5]. Ibn al-Kalbī's

[1] Ibn al-Kalbī, *Jamhara*, Ms. Br. Mus. (Esc.) Add. 11, 376, fol. 74a.

[2] See W. Caskel, *Ǧamharat an-Nasan, das genealogische Werk des Hišām ibn Muḥammad al-Kalbī*, Leiden 1966, II, 307 (al-Ḥāriṯ b. Ḥiṣn al-Ḥaršā'), 520 (Suwaid b. al-Ḥāriṯ), (Ḥiṣn b. Ḍamḍam).

[3] Abū l-Baqā', *al-Manāqib al-mazyadiyya fī akhbāri l-mulūki l-asadiyya*, Ms. Br. Mus., Add. 23, 296, fol. 72b inf. — 73b sup.

[4] Ibn al-Kalbī, *Jamhara* (Esc.), fol. 74a.

[5] Abū l-Baqā', *op. cit.*, fol. 72b.

account seems to contain a vague indication of the time of this event: the mother of al-Ḥārith b. Ḥiṣn was Hirr the daughter of Salāma of ʿUlaym, to whom Imru l-Qays referred in amatory language in his poems[6]. Imru l-Qays died about 550 AD[7], and Hirr should have been a young woman at that time. Other chronological indications may be derived from the additional sources.

Both Ibn al-Kalbī and Abū l-Baqā' report about the four daughters of the couple Wā'il and Shaqīqa; they differ, however, as to their names. Ibn al-Kalbī records Salmā, al-Rābiʿa, (?) al-Shamūs and Hind; Abū al-Baqā' records: Māwiya, Najwa, ʿAfāt (? perhaps ʿUqāb – K) and Salmā[8]; thus only one name is common to both lists: Ṡalmā. The couple had also two sons: Maʿbad and ʿUbayd. The progeny of Maʿbad joined the Banū Suwayd b. al-Ḥārith (i.e. the clan of his uterine brother – K); a family of them attached themselves to an Anṣārī tribal unit, falsely claiming Anṣārī descent. ʿUbayd settled as a tribal unit in Syria[9].

The status of the four daughters can be deduced from Abū l-Baqā's account: they remained with al-Ḥārith, at his abode (... *fa-aṣāba wā'ila bna ʿaṭiyyata l-yahūdiyya l-ṣā'igha wa-maʿahu mra'atahu l-shaqīqata, wa-kānat yahūdiyyatan, wa-arbaʿa banātin lahu... fa-kunna ʿindahu*); the daughters of the Jewish couple married members of various Arab tribes, while Salmā married the king of al-Ḥīra, al-Mundhir b. al-Mundhir, and gave birth to their son al-Nuʿmān b. al-Mundhir b. al-Mundhir, the last king of the Persian-protected vassal state of al-Ḥīra. Later (i.e. after his death) she married Rūmānis b. Muʿaqqil of the ʿAmr b. ʿAbd Wudd of Kalb and bore him a son, Wabara. Al-Nuʿmān and Wabara were thus uterine brothers and this is why al-Nuʿmān granted Wabara the two settlements: Baradān and Laʿlaʿ[10]. Yāqūt records the details about the

[6] Ibn al-Kalbī, *op. cit.*, (Esc.), fol. 74a.

[7] EI² s.v. Imru' al-Ḳays (S. Boustany).

[8] Ibn al-Kalbī, *Jamhara* (Esc.), fol. 74a; Abū l-Baqā', *op. cit.*, 72b.

[9] Ibn al-Kalbī, *Jamhara* (Esc.), fol. 74a.

[10] Ibn al-Kalbī, *Jamhara* (Esc.), fol. 74a; cf. Ḥamza al-Iṣfahānī, *Ta'rīkh sinī mulūki l-arḍi wa-l-anbiyā'*, Beirut 1961, p. 95 (al-Nuʿmān is the son of Salmā, the daughter of Wā'il, the goldsmith from Fadak); al-Ṭabarī, *Ta'rīkh*, ed. Muḥammad Abū l-Faḍl Ibrāhīm, Cairo 1961, II, 194 (Nuʿmān's mother is Salmā, the daughter of Wā'il, the goldsmith from Fadak); al-Yaʿqūbī, *Ta'rīkh*, Najaf 1384/1964, I, 185 (al-Nuʿmān's mother is Salmā, a captive *said to be* from Kalb); al-Masʿūdī, *Murūj al-dhahab*, ed. Ch. Pellat, Beirut 1966, II, 224, no. 1061 (the mother of al-Nuʿmān is Salmā, the daughter of Wā'il b. ʿAṭiyya from Kalb); al-Jāḥiẓ, *al-Bayān wa-l-tabyin*, ed. Ḥasan al-Sandūbī, Cairo 1351/1932, III, 156 (Salmā, the daughter of ʿUqāb, is the mother of al-Nuʿmān); cf. G. Rothstein, *Die Dynastie der Laḥmiden in al-Ḥīra*,

kinship relations between al-Nuʿmān and Wabara and reports that Wabara died in Baradān and was buried there[11].

The story of the marriage of Salmā with al-Mundhir b. al-Mundhir (= al-Mundhir *al-aṣghar*) is presented by Abū l-Baqā' in dramatic terms: al-Mundhir alighted on his way back from one of his raids against Syria in the abode of al-Ḥārith, who welcomed his guest, accomodated him in a tent of hides, slaughtered for him a camel and sent Salmā (i.e. the daughter of the Jewish couple captured in Fadak – K) to anoint his hair. When she entered al-Mundhir seized her and raped her. She returned to al-Ḥārith weeping, complaining that his guest dishonoured her. Al-Ḥārith hurried in rage to the tent of al-Mundhir with his sword drawn, and accused al-Mundhir of having put him to shame amongst Kalb. But al-Mundhir answered asking al-Ḥārith: «Did I bring shame upon you by marrying your maid»? Thus he married Salmā and set out with her to al-Ḥīra. There she bore him his son al-Nuʿmān, who became later king of al-Ḥīra. After the death of al-Mundhir Salmā returned to Kalb and married Rūmānis b. Muʿaqqil of the branch of ʿAbd Wudd of Kalb. She bore him Wabara, who was thus the uterine brother of al-Nuʿmān. Al-Nuʿmān was satirized as the heir of the goldsmith, the coward[12].

According to a tradition recorded by Abū Hilāl al-ʿAskarī, Salmā (the mother of al-Nuʿmān) was a maid servant of ʿAmr b. Thaʿlaba al-Kalbī[13]. During a raid launched by Ḍirār b. ʿAmr al-Ḍabbī[14] against Kalb he captured Salmā with her mother and two of her sisters. ʿAmr asked him to return them, but Ḍirār, who became impressed by Salmā, only agreed to return her mother and sisters. ʿAmr appealed to his generosity by saying: «Let the horse (granted as a gift – K) be followed by the bridle», that is: as you have already

Berlin 1899 (repr.), pp. 108-109; Jawād ʿAlī, *al-Mufaṣṣal fī taʾrīkhi l-ʿarab qabla l-islām*, Beirut 1969, III, 261-2.

[11] See Yāqūt, *Muʿjam al-buldān*, s.v. Baradān; cf. Abū Tammām, *al-Waḥshiyyāt*, ed. al-Maymanī, Cairo 1963, p. 133, no. 212.

[12] Abū l-Baqā', *op. cit.*, fol. 73a (with 8 verses), 31a-b (1 verse); the verses are attributed to al-Nābigha, ʿAbd al-Qays b. Khufāf al-Burjumī and Murra b. Rabīʿa b. Quraʿ al-Saʿdī; cf. W. Ahlwardt, *The Dīwans of the six ancient Arabic poets*, Paris 1913, p. 173 (4 verses); al-Nābigha, *Dīwān*, ed. ʿAbd al-Raḥmān Salām. Beirut 1347/1929, pp. 80-90 (9 verses); Ibn Qutayba, *al-Shiʿr wa-l-shuʿarāʾ*, ed. M.J. de Goeje, Leiden 1904, pp. 73 (1 verse; the mother of al-Nuʿmān is recorded as Salmā, the daughter of ʿAṭiyya, the goldsmith), 76 (3 verses; about the alleged authorship of the verses as in Abū l-Baqā''s Manāqib); al-Jāḥiẓ, *al-Ḥayawān*, ed. ʿAbd al-Salām Hārūn, Cairo 1385/1966, IV, 377, 379.

[13] See on him Caskel, *op. cit.*, II, 185 (ʿAmr b. Thaʿlaba b. al-Ḥārith).

[14] See on him Caskel, *op. cit.*, II, 242.

returned the majority of the captured family, give back the remainder too. Thereupon Ḍirār returned Salmā[15].

The version recorded by Abū l-Baqā' differs in some essential details: when al-Mundhir left the abode of al-Ḥārith b. Ḥiṣn b. Ḍamḍam with Salmā, the daughter of the Jewish goldsmith, given him as a gift by al-Ḥārith, and set out (for al-Ḥīra – K), he was attacked by al-Ḍirār al-Ḍabbī, who was at the head of a very strong troop. Ḍirār robbed him of everything he possessed, including Salmā. Al-Mundhir returned to al-Ḥārith and complained of Ḍirār's action. Al-Ḥārith (who was a friend of Ḍirār) intervened, and Ḍirār returned Salmā to al-Mundhir together with the other booty. Then al-Mundhir said to al-Ḥārith: «Place the bridle on the horse» (he obviously asked an additional gift); al-Ḥārith then gave him as an additional gift («the bridle» – K) a sister of Salmā, and al-Mundhir set out with both of them to al-Ḥīra[16].

The son of Salmā from her second marriage, Wabara (according to some reports Ḥassān b. Wabara) played an important role in the battle of al-Qurnatayn, in which Ḍirār b. ʿAmr al-Ḍabbī fought courageously with his sons on the side of Wabara (or Ḥassān b. Wabara) against the ʿĀmir b. Ṣaʿṣaʿa who attacked both Tamīm and Ḍabba. According to the account of al-Mufaḍḍal al-Ḍabbī, al-Nuʿmān appointed his brother Wabara as governor (*ʿammalahu*) on the Ribāb and he headed the forces of Ḍabba in the battle[17]. He was captured by Yazīd b. al-Ṣaʿiq and released on the payment of a very high ransom[18].

Another tradition, also recorded by al-Balādhurī, gives a quite different account. The attack against the ʿĀmir b. Ṣaʿṣaʿa was well planned and prepared by the king al-Nuʿmān and his brother. Al-Nuʿmān levied a strong force «from the Maʿadd tribes and others» under the command of his uterine brother Wabara. Then he sent to Ḍirār b. ʿAmr and summoned him to join his forces. Ḍirār responded and came with nine of his sons (eighteen according to another account)[19]. Al-Nuʿmān sent a caravan to Mecca and ordered the (warriors escorting the – K) caravan to launch an attack (scil. suddenly

[15] Abū Hilāl al-ʿAskarī, *Jamharat al-amthāl*, ed. Muḥammad Abū l-Faḍl Ibrāhīm, Cairo 1384/1964, I, 92, no. 78.

[16] Abū l-Baqā', *op. cit.*, fols. 128b, inf. — 129a, sup.

[17] Al-Balādhurī, *Ansāb al-ashrāf*, Ms. fol. 956b (= 1016b).

[18] See e.g. *Arabica*, XV (1968), 156-7; Ibn al-Kalbī, *Jamhara* (Esc.), fol. 82a inf. — 82b sup.; idem, *Jamhara*, Ms. Br. Mus., Add. 23, 297, fol. 123b-124a; al-Marzubānī, *Muʿjam al-shuʿarā'*, ed. F. Krenkow, Cairo 1354, p. 394 (al-Nuʿmān's brother captured by Yazīd b. al-Ṣaʿiq is Ru'ba b. Rūmānis, apparently a scribal error for Wabara b. Rūmānis); and see al-Nuwayrī, *Nihāyat al-arab*, Cairo 1368/1949, XV, 375-77.

[19] Al-Balādhurī, *Ansāb*, Ms. fol. 949a (= 1009a).

and treacherously – K) on the 'Āmir b. Ṣa'ṣa'a on the way back, after the arrangements (of buying and selling – K) were accomplished and Quraysh would have come back to Mecca from 'Ukāẓ. The men (escorting the caravan – K) acted according to the plan; but the 'Āmir b. Ṣa'ṣa'a had been warned by 'Abdallah b. Jud'ān and succeeded to defeat the joint forces of Ḍabba and the troops levied by the king and put under the command of Wabara. Ḍirār managed to escape, aided by his sons; Wabara was captured by Yazīd b. al-Ṣa'iq and had to pay a very high ransom: a thousand camels, two singing girls and granting Yazīd the right to a share in his possessions[20].

Some details about the descendants of one of the warriors who fought in the battle give us a hint as to the time in which the battle took place. Al-Mundhir b. Ḥassān b. Ḍirār, the grandson of Ḍirār, was one of the notables of al-Kūfa and gave his daughter in marriage to 'Abd al-Raḥmān b. al-Ḥakam al-Thaqafī[21]. Another grandson of Ḍirār, Harthama, embraced Islam and settled in Baṣra[22]. The daughter of Ḍirār, Mu'ādha, married the Tamīnī leader Ma'bad b. Zurāra and bore him a son, al-Qa'qā', who converted later to Islam[23].

The grandsons and granddaughters of other persons connected with the account of the battle can be traced in the period of the Prophet and of the first Caliphs[24]. It is significant that these persons emigrated to Mecca or Medina and their fate was closely connected with some of the Companions of the Prophet. 'Abd al-Raḥmān b. 'Auf, one of the richest Companions of the Prophet, married Tumāḍir, the daughter of al-Aṣbagh b. 'Amr b. Tha'laba b. al-Ḥārith b. Ḥiṣn b. Ḍamḍam from Kalb. It is evident that she was the direct descendant of al-Ḥārith b. Ḥiṣn, the man who conquered Fadak and captured the family of the Jewish goldsmith Wā'il b. 'Aṭiyya. Tumāḍir was the first Kalbī woman married by a Qurashite, says the report. Muṣ'ab reports further that Tumāḍir's mother was «Juwayriyya the daughter of Wabara b. Rūmānis, who was the brother of al-Nu'mān b. al-Mundhir»[25]. The

[20] Al-Balādhurī, *Ansāb*, Ms. fol. 948b-949a (= 1008b-1009a).

[21] Al-Balādhurī, *Ansāb*, Ms. fol. 949a (= 1009a); and see on him Ibn Ḥajar, *al-Iṣāba fī tamyīz al-ṣaḥāba*, ed. 'Alī Muḥammad al-Bijāwī, Cairo 1292/1972, VI, 314, no. 8470.

[22] Al-Balādhurī, *Ansāb*, Ms. fol. 949a (= 1009a), penult.

[23] Al-Balādhurī, *Ansāb*, Ms. fols. 948b (= 1008b), 965a (= 1025a); and see on him: Ibn Ḥajar, *al-Iṣāba*, V, 452, no. 7133.

[24] See e.g. Ibn Ḥajar, *al-Iṣāba*, VI, 703 (Yazīd b. Qays b. Yazīd b. al-Ṣa'iq), 301, no. 8437 (Mu'ādh b. Yazīd b. al-Ṣa'iq).

[25] Muṣ'ab b. 'Abdallah, *Nasab quraysh*, ed. E. Levi Provençal, Cairo 1953, p. 267; and see al-Zubayr b. Bakkār, *Jamharat nasab quraysh*, Ms. Bodley, Marsh. 384, fol. 95b; Ibn al-Kalbī, *Jamhara* (Esc.), fol. 95b.

honourable position inherited by the descendants of al-Ḥārith b. Ḥiṣn and Wabara can be seen from the account that the Prophet sent ʿAbd al-Raḥmān b. ʿAuf to Kalb and advised him to marry «the daughter of their king» if they would embrace Islam. As Kalb responded, ʿAbd al-Raḥmān married Tumāḍir; her father, al-Aṣbagh, was indeed «the king» (i.e. the chief – K) of Kalb[26]. Another report lists three tribal groups tracing their origin to Juwayriyya, the daughter of Wabara b. Rūmānis[27]. The marriage of the Caliph ʿUthmān with another Kalbī woman, Nā'ila also reflects the position of the family of the conqueror of Fadak: her father was al-Furāfiṣa b. al-Aḥwaṣ b. ʿAmr b. Thaʿlaba b. al-Ḥārith b. Ḥiṣn b. Ḍamḍam b. ʿAdiyy b. Jandal[28].

* * *

It may be of some interest to trace the pedigree and vicissitudes of a Tamīmī woman, who emigrated to Mecca and married a distinguished man from the aristocratic clan of Makhzūm. Her progeny played an important role in the struggle between the Prophet and Quraysh. Asmā', the daughter of Mukharriba[29] from the tribal group of Nahshal b. Dārim of Tamīm, married Hishām b. al-Mughīra from the clan of Makhzūm and bore him two sons: Abū Jahl (= ʿAmr) and al-Ḥārith; after her divorce from Hishām, she married his brother, Abū Rabīʿa b. al-Mughīra, and bore him two sons: ʿAbdallah and ʿAyyāsh[30]. The high status of Asmā' can be inferred from the report that she was entrusted with the keeping of the document of the boycott

[26] Ibn Saʿd, *Ṭabaqāt*, Beirut 1377/1958, VIII, 298.

[27] Ibn al-Kalbī, *Jamhara* (Esc.), fol. 74a.

[28] Ibn Ḥazm, *Jamharat ansāb al-ʿarab*, ed. ʿAbd al-Salām Hārūn, Cairo 1962, p. 456 inf.

[29] On the reading «Mukharriba» and «Mukharrima» see e.g. the note of the Editor of Jumaḥī's *Ṭabaqāt fuḥūl al-shuʿarā'*, p. 123, note 2.

[30] Al-Jumaḥī, *Ṭabaqāt fuḥūl al-shuʿarā'*, ed. Maḥmūd Muḥammad Shākir, Cairo 1952, p. 123, no. 142; *Naqā'iḍ Jarīr wa-l-Farazdaq*, ed. Bevan, Leiden 1908, p. 607; Ibn al-Kalbī, *Jamhara*, fol. 36a inf. — 36b sup. (Hishām is said to have been the first Qurashite to divorce his wife Asmā' by the *ẓihār* formula; it was his father al-Mughīra, who chose for Asmā' her husband after her divorce: his son Abū Rabīʿa b. al-Mughīra), 67b; Muṣʿab b. ʿAbdallah, *op. cit.*, p. 318; al-Zubayr b. Bakkār, *op. cit.*, fol. 135a inf. (she was also the mother of Umm Ḥujayr, the daughter of Abū Rabīʿa), 140b (and see the two verses of Hishām b. al-Mughīra, in which he expresses his regret at divorcing Asmā', the daughter of Mukharriba, *ib.*, fol. 141a, sup.); Ibn Saʿd, *op. cit.*, VIII, 300 (she married Abū Rabīʿa *after the death* of her husband Hishām), V, 443-4, IV, 129 sup.; Ibn ʿAbd al-Barr, *al-Istīʿāb fī maʿrifati l-aṣḥāb*, ed. ʿAlī al-Bijāwī, Cairo 1380/1960, p. 1230, no. 2009, p. 961, no. 1628, p. 301, no. 440; Anonymous, *al-Taʾrīkh al-muḥkam fīman intasaba ilā l-nabiyyi ṣallā llāhu ʿalayhi wa-sallam*, Ms. Br. Mus., Or. 8653, fol. 148a, 1.4.

of the Prophet and his family. Another version says that al-Julās, the daughter of Mukharriba, her sister, kept the document[31]. The marriages of the daughters of this Dārimī (Tamīmī) family with Qurashites are remarkable. Asmā', the daughter of Salāma b. Mukharriba b. Jandal of Nahshal (Dārim, Tamīm), married 'Ayyāsh b. Abī Rabī'a b. al-Mughīra. She joined her husband when he set out for his *hijra* to Abyssinia and there she gave birth to his son 'Abdallah[32]. Asmā', the daughter of Salāma b. Mukharriba, was for a period the wife of 'Abd al-Raḥmān b. 'Auf; his son, 'Abd al-Raḥmān b. 'Abd al-Raḥmān b. 'Auf was born from her[33]. 'Abdallah b. 'Ayyāsh married Hind, the daughter of Muṭarrif b. Salāma b. Mukharriba; she bore him his son al-Ḥārith b. 'Abdallah b. 'Ayyāsh[34]. Al-Ḥārith b. 'Abdallah begot 'Abdallah b. al-Ḥārith b. 'Abdallah; the latter married Umm Abān, the daughter of ['Abbād b.] Muṭarrif b. Salāma b. Mukharriba and she bore him his son 'Abd al-'Azīz[35]. Also to be noted are the marriages of the members of this branch of Makhzūm (descendants of al-Mughīra) with the family of Zurāra (Tamīm). Abū Jahl married the daughter of 'Umayr b. Ma'bad b. Zurāra and she bore him his sons Abū 'Alqama, Zurāra and Abū Ḥājib, Tamīm[36]. 'Abd al-Raḥmān b. 'Abdallah b. Abī Rabī'a, nicknamed al-Aḥwal, was the son of Laylā, the daughter of 'Uṭārid b. Ḥājib b. Zurāra[37]. Umm Ḥujayr, the daughter of Abū Rabī'a[38] married a Tamīmī from another family: Abū Ihāb b. 'Azīz[39].

* * *

[31] Al-Balādhurī, *Ansāb*, I (ed. Muḥammad Ḥamīdullah), 235 sup.

[32] Khalīfa b. Khayyāṭ, *Ṭabaqāt*, ed. Akram Ḍiyā' al-'Umarī, Baghdād 1387/1967, p. 234; Ibn Sa'd, *op. cit.*, VIII, 301; Muṣ'ab b. 'Abdallah, *op. cit.*, p. 319; al-Fāsī, *al-'Iqd al-thamīn*, ed. al-Ṭanāḥi, Cairo 1388/1969, VIII, 180, no. 3300; Ibn Ḥajar, *al-Iṣāba*, VII, 484, no. 10795 (and see *ib.*, p. 492, the elucidation of the relationship between Asmā' bint Mukharriba and Asmā' bint Salāma b. Mukharriba); Ibn 'Abd al-Barr, *op. cit.*, p. 1783; Ibn Ḥazm, *Jamhara*, p. 230; Ibn Hishām, *al-Sīra al-nabawiyya*, ed. al-Saqā, al-Abyārī, Shalabī, Cairo 1355/1936, I, 273.

[33] Ibn Sa'd, *op. cit.*, III, 128; Anonymous, *al-Ta'rīkh al-muḥkam*, Ms. fol. 113a, inf.; Muṣ'ab v. 'Abdallah, *op. cit.*, p. 267 ('Abdallah b. 'Ayyāsh b. Abī Rabī'a was thus the uterine brother of 'Abd al-Raḥmān b. 'Abd al-Raḥmān b. 'Auf, adds Muṣ'ab).

[34] Muṣ'ab b. 'Abdallah, *op. cit.*, p. 319; Ibn Sa'd, *op. cit.*, V, 28; al-Zubayr b. Bakkār, *op. cit.*, fol. 141b.

[35] Muṣ'ab b. 'Abdallah, *op. cit.*, p. 319; al-Zubayr b. Bakkār, *op. cit.*, fol. 142a, sup.

[36] Muṣ'ab, *op. cit.*, p. 312 sup.; al-Zubayr, *op. cit.*, fol. 135b inf.

[37] Al-Zubayr, *op. cit.*, fol. 141a sup.

[38] See above note 30.

[39] Al-Zubayr, *op. cit.*, fol. 135b, 1.1.

The peculiar verses in the *Dīwān* of Ḥassān b. Thābit link the person of Asmā' (the mother of Abū Jahl and al-Ḥārith, the sons of Hāshim b. al-Mughīra al-Makhzūmī) with that of al-Furāfiṣa, the father of Nā'ila, the wife of ʿUthmān:

«Had you been a scion of a noble woman you would prove it for her by a noble deed:
but you are a descendant of the daughter of ʿUqāb»[40].

The verse is directed against al-Ḥārith b. Hishām who fled shamefully from the battlefield of Badr. ʿUqāb is recorded in the commentaries as a slave of the Taghlib. Some daughters of ʿUqāb ended up by chance (*fa-waqaʿa baʿḍuhunna*) at al-Furāfiṣa b. al-Aḥwaṣ where they stayed on as slaves. One of these maids was married by a man from Taghlib and bore him a daughter. This daughter was later married by Mukharriba b. Ubayr (scil. from Nahshal, Tamīm)[41]. The commentary gives insufficient details of the slave and the maids. One has thus to consult the other poem in which ʿUqāb and the maidslaves are mentioned. The *qaṣīda* CLXXVIII is headed by an explanatory note: «He (i.e. Ḥassān) said satirizing al-Ḥārith b. al-Mughīra (i.e. al-Ḥārith b. Hishām b. al-Mughīra – K); his mother, a Nahshalī woman (a descendant of one – K) of the daughters of ʿUqāb, a female slave staying with the Banū Taghlib; she (married and) had daughters who bore children in Kalb, Quraysh and in other tribes». The third verse of the *qaṣīda* runs as follows:

«Lo, al-Furāfiṣa b. al-Aḥwaṣ is vexed:
because of your mother [one] of the daughters of ʿUqāb»[42].

The commentary[43] does not add much for the understanding of the hints included in the two verses. It is therefore fortunate that Ibn al-Kalbī supplies some additional data about Furāfiṣa. It was Furāfiṣa who obtained the heritage of the goldsmith from Fadak and therefore Ḥassān uttered the verses against him. Ibn al-Kalbī mentions the other daughters of the goldsmith: al-Rābiʿa married ʿAmr b. Kulayb b. ʿAdiyy b. Janāb and gave birth to daughters who got married with men from Kalb. The other daughter, al-Shamūs, married

[40] Ḥassān b. Thābit, *Dīwān*, ed. Arafat, London 1971, I, 298 (CXLIX 7):
Lau kunta ḍinʾa karimatin ablaytahā:
ḥusnā, wa-lākin ḍinʾa binti ʿuqābi.

[41] Ḥassān b. Thābit, *op. cit.*, II, 220.

[42] Ḥassān, *op. cit.*, I, 343 (CLXXVIII, 3):
Inna l-furāfiṣata bna l-aḥwaṣi ʿindahu:
shajanun li-ummika min banāti ʿuqābi.

[43] Ḥassān, *op. cit.*, II, 246; and see *ib.*, II, 220: ʿUqāb was a slave (not a slave-maid).

al-Jānn from Taghlib and became the mother of 'Anāq. 'Anāq married Mukharriba b. Ubayr from Nahshal; she gave birth to Julās, the daughter of Mukharriba (usually recorded as Umm Julās Asmā' the daughter of Mukharriba). Umm Julās bore the two sons of Hishām b. al-Mughīra: Abū Jahl and al-Ḥārith[44]. This very pedigree is recorded by al-Balādhurī on the authority of Abū 'Ubayda: Asmā' was the daughter of Mukharriba (or 'Amr b. Mukharriba) and 'Anāq; 'Anāq was the daughter of al-Jānn from Taghlib b. Wā'il, and his wife al-Shamūs, the daughter of Wā'il b. 'Aṭiyya from Fadak[45]. Abū 'Ubayda gives some additional details about the marriage of Asmā' with Hishām. Hishām met Asmā' in Najrān; she was a widow and Hishām married her and moved with her to Mecca. There she gave birth to his two sons. After his death she married his brother, Abū Rabī'a; she bore him two sons too[46]. This has already been mentioned above.

A similar tradition about the marriage of Hishām with Asmā' is recorded by al-Zubayr b. Bakkār on the authority of Ma'mar b. Rāshid; it contains some more details, such as those relating to the talk of Hishām with Asmā', her cleverness and beauty[47]. The date of the death of Asmā' is disputed: some put it at the time of the Prophet, others at the time of 'Umar[48].

A quite different tradition is recorded in Ps. Aṣma'ī's *Nihāyat al-arab*. 'Adiyy b. Zayd introduced al-Nu'mān to the Persian Emperor, telling him that his mother was the daughter of the goldsmith 'Atiyya, who was a Persian. He came by chance to Taymā' and settled there. He married there. The daughter of the goldsmith, Salmā, bore al-Nu'mān[49].

Finally an early tradition identifies the first husband of Salmā as Suwayd b. Rabī'a, the well known Dārimī tribesman who killed the relative of the king of al-Ḥīra and caused thereby the slaughter of the Tamīmīs on the Day of Uwāra[50]. On his flight from the king of al-Ḥīra Suwayd reached Mecca and became an ally (*ḥalīf*) of the

[44] Ibn al-Kalbī, *Jamhara* (Esc.), fol. 74a inf.

[45] Al-Balādhurī, *Ansāb*, I, 209.

[46] Al-Balādhurī, *Ansāb*, I, 208-209.

[47] Al-Zubayr b. Bakkār, *op. cit.*, fol. 135b, sup.

[48] See e.g. Ibn Ḥajar, *al-Iṣāba*, VII, 491, no. 10807; al-Balādhurī, *Ansāb*, I, 209.

[49] Ms. Br. Mus., Add. 23, 298, fol. 237b inf. — 238a.

[50] See e.g. on the Day of Uwāra: al-Balādhurī, *Ansāb*, fols. 966b (= 1026b), 968b (= 1028a); among his descendants was Abū Ihāb b. 'Azīz who was one of the thieves of the «Gazelle of the Ka'ba»; al-Balādhurī (Ms. fol. 342b) records his pedigree as follows: Abū Ihāb b. 'Azīz b. Qays b. Suwayd b. Rabī'a b. 'Abdallah b. Dārim... the *ḥalīf* of the Banū Naufal b. 'Abd Manāf.

Banū Naufal; Asmā' reached al-Yaman; she later married Hishām b. al-Mughīra. When she bore him his first son she named him 'Amr (later nicknamed by the Prophet «Abū Jahl» – K) after her father (as the real name of Mukharriba was 'Amr)[51]. This account closes the chain of stories in which the fates of the descendants of the goldsmith's daughters are related.

* * *

Some comments on the few passages quoted above may be useful. It is instructive that the Jewish settlement, Fadak, had to pay some tribute to the tribal group of Kalb. The account seems to indicate that the power of the Jewish agricultural settlements in that period, the end of the third quarter of the sixth century, began to decrease; the weakness of the rulers of al-Ḥīra, the sudden changes in the Persian Empire, the rise of the strength of the Arab tribes, the emergence of Mecca as an influential centre in the Arabian peninsula — all these factors explain the successful raid of al-Ḥārith b. Ḥiṣn against Fadak and its conquest; it is indeed conspicuous that the account uses the expression: *iftataḥahā kalbun* denoting the conquest of a village or a city. It is noteworthy for the understanding of the event that about the same period the Jewish representative of Persia in Medina was replaced by the Khazrajī 'Amr b. al-Iṭnāba[52], and the dominant position of the Jews in this city declined.

The role which Mecca began to play in that period can be deduced from the reports about the migration of membres of different tribes to Mecca. The marriages between Qurashites and members of the tribal immigrants reflect the evolution of a flourishing mixed population, dominated by a well developed Meccan tradition and custom; the immigrants became integrated into the Meccan order and absorbed into the Meccan society. It was a peculiar blend of Jewish, Christian, Kalbī, Taghlibī, Tamīmī and Qurashī elements, which produced devoted believers like 'Ayyāsh, malicious infidels like Abū Jahl and gifted poets like 'Umar b. Abī Rabī'a.

[51] Al-Balādhurī, *Ansāb*, fol. 986b (= 1046b).
[52] See *Arabica* XV (1968) 146-8.

VI

ON AN EARLY FRAGMENT OF THE QUR'ĀN

Papyrus No. 28 of the *"Arabic papyri from Ḫirbet el-Mird,"* edited by Adolf Grohmann (Louvain-Leuven 1963, Bibliothèque du *Muséon*, vol. 52, pp. 30–32, Pl. XIV), is described by Grohmann as a "fragment of an official letter probably referring to the embola." His reading, translation and comments are reproduced here.

Mird A 31 a 1 (M.A.B.). 22 × 8,5 cm. IInd century A.H. (VIIIth century A.D.).

On the recto 16 lines are written in black ink in a cursive, inelegant hand at right-angles to the horizontal fibres. The verso (A 31b) bears fragments and vestiges of 13 lines written in black ink in a regular, skilled hand, parallel to the vertical fibres.

The fragment, coming from the middle of the letter, is very poorly preserved. Of the lines 12-16 only a small strip of papyrus, 1,7 cm wide, has survived. On the right side a piece, 3,5 cm high and 8,3 cm wide, has detached itself from the upper layer of the papyrus. The verso is so badly damaged that it is impossible to recover much more than some fragments of words, the translation of which is impossible.

Prototype : original.

١ [بســـــــــــــ]م الله الرحمن [الرحيم]

٢ [من فلان بن فلان ا]لى س[لي]من بن حرث[ ]

٣ [امّا بعد فإنى] احمد ا[لي]ك الله [الذى]

٤ [لا اله ا]لّا هو [ ]

٥ [ ] و..؟ فانظ[ر]

[ ] نعمان الكيّال [ف]امنع [ ]

[ ]ن نفانه ولا تمؤر ال[ ]

[ ] واعتصموا [ ]

[ ] . ولا نفر فو[ا]

[ ] بنعمة الله [ ]

[ ] ا[ ].....[ ]

[ ]بوح[ ]

[ ]...[ ]

[ ]...[ ]

[ ]...[ ]

[ ]...[ ]

1. [*In the nam*]*e of God, the Compassionate,* [*the Merciful*].
2. [*From So and So, Son of So and So, t*]*o Su*[*lai*]*mān ibn Ḥāriṯ*.
3. [*Thereafter. Verily, I*] *praise un*[*t*]*o you God,* [*besides*]
4. [*whom there is*] *no god.*
5. [ ] *and . . . . So inspe*[*ct*]
6. [ ] *Nu'mān, the corn-measurer. Therefore, prevent* [ ]
7. [ ] . . . . [ ]
8. [ ] *and they have had recourse* [*to*]
9. [ ] . . . *and no single person* . . . . [ ]
10. [ ] *with God's favour* [ ]
11. [ ] . . . . [ ]
12. [ ] . . . . [ ]
13. [ ] . . . . [ ]
14. [ ] . . . . [ ]
15. [ ] . . . . [ ]
16. [ ] . . . . [ ]

6. For the « corn-measurer » cf. APG nº 18, *3* and p. 66. He is presumably a successor of the *μεσίτης* of the Byzantine and early Arabic period, a trustee in the public barns in the province, who had to make the repartition of the impost in kind among the individual tax-payers. Cf. H. GERSTINGER, *Neue byzantinische Vertragsurkunden aus der Sammlung « Papyri Erzherzog Rainer » in Wien, The Journal of Juristic Papyrology,* XIII (1961), p. 57 (n° 3, VIth cent. A.D.).

However, Grohmann's reading does not correspond to what can be seen quite clearly in the papyrus. Consequently, his rendering and comments are not correct.

The correct reading of the papyrus is as follows:

٤. [لا اله ا] لا هو

٥. [......] قال في كتابه

٦. [......] يا [يه]ا الذي[ن] امنو[ا]

٧. [اتقوا الله حق] تقاته ولا تموت[ن]

٨. [الا وانتم مسلمون] واعتصموا

٩. [بحبل الله جميعا] ولا تفرقوا

١٠. [واذكروا] نعمة الله

The rendering of these lines is as follows:

4. [*there is no god*] *but He*
5. [. . . . .] *said in His Book*
6. [. . . . .] *O ye who believe*
7. [*Observe your duty to Allah*] *with right, observance and do not die*
8. [*save as those who have surrendered unto Him*]. *And hold fast*
9. [*all of you together to the cable of Allah*] *and do not separate*
10. [*and remember*] *Allah's favor* . . . . . .

It is evident that the papyrus is not a "fragment of an official letter" but a fragment (lines 6–10) of the Qur'ān, containing Sūra III, verses 102–103.

There is no doubt whatsoever that this is the correct reading of the text; it seems to be of some importance that we have here one of the earliest specimens of the text of the Qur'ān, written in the second century of the Hijra.*

* I would like to express my sincere gratitude to Mr. A. Etan, Mrs. I. Pomeranz and Mrs. A. Sussmann of the Department of Antiquities and Museums, Ministry of Education and Culture, Jerusalem, Israel, who kindly prepared the photograph of the papyrus for me.

VII

O GOD, TIGHTEN THY GRIP ON MUḌAR...

*Some socio-economic and religious aspects of an early ḥadīth**

To Professor S. D. Goitein
a humble tribute.

The widely current utterances attributed to the Prophet concerning his eponymous ancestor Muḍar and his progeny are usually couched in very favourable terms. Tradition stresses that the angel Jibrīl himself told the Prophet of his descendance from Muḍar [1]); the Prophet, recording his pedigree, thus stated explicitly that he was of Muḍar [2]). Muḍar is obviously counted in Muslim tradition among the highly praised ancestors of the Prophet, chosen by God from amongst the whole of mankind and singled out by Him from among the Arabs [3]). The very early traditions emphasized that Quraysh preserved and kept the monotheistic tradition of Ismāʿīl and Ibrāhīm and that the guardians and champions of this belief were the eponymous ancestors of the Prophet; widely current is the utterance attributed to the Prophet according to which Muḍar was a Muslim and it is not lawful to curse him [4]). The ancestors of the Prophet are said to have stuck to their

---

* A summary of this paper was read in a meeting of the Israel Academy of Sciences and Humanities in Jerusalem on December 2, 1975.

1) Al-Muttaqī l-Hindī, *Kanz al-ʿummāl*, Hyderabad 1385/1965, XIII, 51, no. 297; cf. Muḥammad Anwar al-Kashmīrī al-Dīwabandī *Fayḍ al-bārī ʿalā ṣaḥīḥi l-bukhārī*, Cairo 1357/1938, IV, 121 inf.:...*innamā kāna banū tamīmin min qaumi l-nabiyyi li-anna l-nabiyya kāna min muḍara wa-hāʾulāʾi ayḍan muḍariyyūn*...

2) Al-Wāqidī, *Maghāzī*, ed. M. Jones, London 1966, p. 1011; al-Shāfiʿī, *al-Umm*, Cairo (Būlāq) 1321 (reprint), VI, 215.

3) See e.g. al-Muttaqī l-Hindī, *op. cit.*, XIII, 36-38, nos. 225, 233-234.

4) Al-Balādhurī, *Ansāb al-ashrāf*, ed. Muḥammad Ḥamīdullah, Cairo 1959, I, 31; al-Muttaqī l-Hindī, *op. cit.*, XIII, 51, no. 294; and see *ib.* the version that both Rabīʿa and Muḍar embraced Islām; and see this version: al-Shiblī, *Maḥāsin al-wasāʾil fī*

Arab faith, without converting to Judaism, Zoroastrianism or Christianity [5]). In line with this notion the Prophet is said to have enjoined to follow (the descendants of—K) Muḍar whenever there was a dissension among the believers, as Muḍar would always be on the right path and act justly [6]). Muḍar were indeed granted prophethood and caliphate, Islam gained power and strength through Muḍar and great conquests were made after Muḍar embraced Islam, says Ibn Saʿīd in his *Nashwat al-ṭarab* [7]). The favourable traditions about Muḍar are confronted by a few unpropitious utterances also attributed to the Prophet; these unfavourable sayings refer, however, either to the coarse Bedouin traits of character of Muḍar or are cast in the form of prophecies concerning the wicked role of Muḍar as an oppressive element in the government of the Muslim Empire which persecutes and harms the believers [8]).

Of some importance seems to be a peculiar tradition according to which the Prophet invoked God asking Him to afflict Muḍar with years of drought like those at the time of Joseph. "O God, tighten Thy grip on Muḍar", the Prophet invoked, "Turn barren years upon

---

maʿrifati l-awāʾil, Ms.Br.Mus., Or. 1530, fol. 54a; and see another version of this tradition: al-Naysābūrī, *Gharāʾib al-qurʾān wa-raghāʾib al-furqān*, ed. Ibrāhīm ʿAṭwa ʿIwaḍ, Cairo 1386/1967, XVIII, 31; and see I. Goldziher, *Muslim Studies*, ed. S. M. Stern, London 1967, I, 83-84, note 5.

5) Cf. al-Jāḥiẓ, *Thalāthu rasāʾil* (*al-radd ʿalā l-naṣārā*), ed. J. Finkel. Cairo 1344, p. 15: ...*wa-ukhrā wa-hiya anna l-ʿaraba kānat al-naṣrāniyyatu fīhā fāshiyatan wa-ʿalayhā ghālibatan, illā muḍara, fa-lam taghlib ʿalayhā yahūdiyyatun wa-lā mājūsiyyatun, wa-lam tafshu fīhā l-naṣrāniyyatu... wa-lam taʿrif muḍaru illā dīna l-ʿarabi, thumma l-islāma.*

6) Ibn Abī l-Dunyā, *al- Ishrāf fī manāzil al-ashrāf*, Ms. Chester Beatty 4427, fol. 69b; al-Muttaqī l-Hindī, *op. cit.*, XIII, 51, no. 295-296; Goldziher, *op. cit.*, I, 84, note 5.

7) Ms. Tübingen 1, fol. 94: ...*ilayhā* (i.e. *al-muḍariyya*—K) *ntahā l-sharafu wa-l-ʿiddatu awwalan wa-ākhiran wa-khaṣṣahā llāhu bi-l-nubuwwati wa-l-khilāfati wa-bihā ʿazza l-islāmu wa-ʿaẓumat futūḥuhu lammā dakhalat fīhi afwājan...*

8) See al-Ḥākim, *al-Mustadrak*, Hyderabad 1342, IV, 470; Baḥshal, *Taʾrīkh Wāsiṭ*, ed. Gurguis ʿAwwad, Baghdād 1386/1967, p. 262; al-Ṭaḥāwī, *Mushkil al-āthār*, Hyderabad 1333, I, 435-436; Yūsuf b. Mūsā al-Ḥanafī, *al-Muʿtaṣar min al-mukhtaṣar min mushkil al-āthār*, Hyderabad 1362, II, 385; al-Muttaqī l-Hindī, *op cit.*, XIII, 51, no. 298; and see *ib.*, p. 42, no. 259: *wa-muḍaru ʿinda uṣūli adhnābi l-ibili ḥaythu yaṭlaʿu qarnu l-shayṭān...*; and see *ib.*, no. 263:... *wa-l-jafāʾu fī hādhayni l-ḥayyayni rabīʿata wa-muḍara...*; Ibn al-Athīr, *al-Nihāya fī gharīb al-ḥadīth*, ed. al-Ṭanāḥī, Cairo s.v. m ḍ r: ... ...*wa-dhakara khurūja ʿāʾishata fa-qāla*: *tuqātilu maʿahā muḍaru, maḍḍarahā llāhu fī l-nāri.*

them like the famine years of Joseph" [9]). There are divergent and even contradictory opinions of *ḥadīth* scholars, Qur'ān commentators and biographers of the Prophet about the circumstances in which the Prophet uttered this invocation. The period during which the Prophet pronounced the invocation is disputed and so are also the prayers in the course of which the invocation was performed, the curses and blessings linked with the invocation, whether the invocation was continuous, whether it was abrogated and consequently whether it is, or is not permissible to use invocations during prayers.

A closer examination of these diverse traditions about the Muḍar invocation and a scrutiny of some traditions referring to other events of that period may grant us a clue for a better understanding of the Prophet's attitude towards the different tribal groups and towards the various factions in Mecca, to elucidate some of the economic and political decisions which he took during his struggle with the hostile tribal divisions and during negotiations with his enemies. The analysis of these traditions may help us to get a more adequate assessment of the changes which took place in the perception of invocations and supplications during the prayers and to form a better evaluation of the political situation in Mecca and Medina in the decisive period preceding the conquest of Mecca.

---

9) Ibn Saʿīd, *op.cit.*, fol. 94r., inf.; cf. Ibn Fūrak, *Mushkil al-ḥadīth*, Hyderabad 1362, p. 97; al-Marzūqī, *al-Azmina wa-l-amkina*, Hyderabad 1332, II, 33; al-Mubarrad, *al-Kāmil*, ed. Muḥammad Abū l-Faḍl Ibrāhīm, Cairo; Ibn Saʿd, *al-Ṭabaqāt*, Beirut 1376/1957, II, 53; al-Dāraquṭnī, *Sunan*, ed. ʿAbdallah Hāshim Yamānī, al-Madīna al-munawwara, 1386/1966, II, 38, no. 7; Maḥmūd Muḥammad Khaṭṭāb, *al-Manhal al-ʿadhb al-maurūd sharḥ sunan al-imāmi abī dāwūd*, Cairo 1394, VIII, 80; Abū l-Layth al-Samarqandī, *Tanbīh al-ghāfilīn*, Cairo 1347, p. 197 inf.; Ibn Mājah, *Sunan al-muṣṭafā*, Cairo 1349, I, 375; al-Bayhaqī, *al-Sunan al-kubrā*, Hyderabad 1346, II, 197-198, 200, 210; Ibn Shahrāshūb, *Manāqib āl abī ṭālib*, Najaf 1376/1956, I, 72 (the Prophet invoked against Muḍar according to the request of Khabbāb b. al-Aratt), 189; Shahridār b. Shīrawayh al-Daylamī, *Musnad al-firdaus*, Ms. Chester Beatty 4139, fol. 136b; al-Thaʿālibī, *Thimār al-qulūb*, ed. Muḥammad Abū l-Faḍl Ibrāhīm, Cairo 1384/1956, p. 49, no. 57. Ibn Ḥajar al-ʿAsqalānī, *al-Arbaʿuna l-mutabāyinatu l-asānīdi wa-l-mutūn*, Ms. Hebrew Univ. Yahuda Ar. 20, I, fol. 17a-b (the persons against whom the Prophet invoked were: Abū Jahl, ʿUtba b. Rabīa, Shayba b. Rabīʿa, al-Walīd b. ʿUtba, ʿUqba b. abī Muʿayṭ, Umayya b. Khalaf and a man whose name is not disclosed).

I

According to a tradition recorded by ʿAbd al-Razzāq on the authority of his teacher Maʿmar b. Rāshid (d. 150 H), the Prophet responded to a request by a man of Muḍar to pray for them for rain, after the man had described to the Prophet the grave situation of his tribe as a result of a drought; after the prayer of the Prophet a great deal of rain poured down [10]). Two other traditions indicate that the drought had been caused by a previous invocation of the Prophet [11]). The reason for the Prophet's invocation against Muḍar was, according to a tradition, their stubborn refusal to embrace Islam, their disobedience, arrogance and unbelief [12]). Some Muslim scholars explained that the Prophet's invocation was merely addressed against the evil-doers of Muḍar, not against the whole of this tribal confederation [13]), others however pointed out that the curse afflicted not only the evil-doers of Muḍar, since the Prophet and his Companions were also hit by the famine [14]). Al-Ḥākim records [15]) the name of the man of Muḍar who asked the Prophet to pray for rain: Kaʿb b. Murra al-Bahzī (scil. from the Muḍarī tribe of Sulaym—K) [16]).

The extent of the drought by which the Muḍar tribes were affected

---

10) ʿAbd al-Razzāq, *al-Muṣannaf*, ed. Ḥabību l-Raḥmān al-Aʿẓamī, Beirut 1390/1971, III, 90, no. 4908.

11) ʿAbd al-Razzāq, *op. cit.*, III, nos. 4907, 4909.

12) See e.g. Ibn Saʿīd, *op. cit.*, fol. 94 r., inf.: . . .*wa-qad kāna rasūlu llāhi* (*ṣ*) *yashkū ilā rabbihi min ʿiṣyānihim wa-ʿuluwwihim ḥattā qāla llāhumma shdud*. . .

13) See e.g. Yūsuf b. Mūsā al-Ḥanafī, *op. cit.*, II, 320: . . .*wa-shdud waṭʾataka ʿalā muḍara*, *ay*: *ʿalā man lam yuʾmin minhum*. . .; *ib.*, p. 385: . . . *wa-minhu qauluhu ṣallā llāhu ʿalayhi wa-sallam fī qunūtihi*: *wa-shdud*. . .*wa-huwa wa-kathīrun min al-ṣaḥāba min muḍara*, *wa-l-murādu*: *man kāna minhum ʿalā khilāfi l-ṭarīqati l-mustaqīma*. . .; and see al-Ṭaḥāwī, *Mushkil al-āthār*, I, 436.

14) Ibn Qutayba, *Taʾwīl mukhtalif al-ḥadīth*, Cairo 1326, p. 318: . . . *wa-qad daʿā rasūlu llāhi* (*ṣ*) *ʿalā muḍara*, *fa-qāla*: *llāhumma shdud waṭʾataka ʿalā muḍara*. . .*fa-nāla dhālika l-jadbu rasūla llāhi wa-aṣḥābahu wa-bi-duʿāʾihi ʿūqibū ḥattā shadda l-muslimūna ʿalā buṭūnihim al-ḥijārata min al-jūʿi*.

15) Al-Ḥākim *op. cit.*, I,328.

16) See on him Ibn Ḥajar, *al-Iṣāba*, ed. ʿAlī Muḥammad al-Bijāwī, Cairo 1392/1972, V, 612, no. 1439 (Kaʿb b. Murra merely saw the man who asked the Prophet to invoke for rain).

can be gauged from a report recorded by al-Jāḥiẓ [17]) and quoted by al-Bayhaqī [18]); as a result of the curse rain stopped, trees died, flocks and cattle perished, pastures diminished and people were compelled to eat *ʿilhiz*, a mixfure of blood and hair and hides.

Then Ḥājib b. Zurāra [19]) set out to Kisrā, complaining of the hardship and asking the king to grant his tribe permission to graze their flocks in the region of Sawād al-ʿIrāq; he left his bow as a pledge that his people would not harass the subjects of the Persian ruler. When the suffering of Muḍar reached its point of culmination, and divine proof reached its predestined conclusion (*balaghat al-ḥujja mablaghahā*) the Prophet made a new invocation interceding for them and rain poured down. The reason for the Prophet's invocation against Muḍar, as given in this report, was the allegation raised by Quraysh and the Arab tribes that the Prophet was a liar, causing him harm and the fact that they decided to expend their wealth in order to fight him [20]). The two Muḍar tribes mentioned in this report are Quraysh and Tamīm [21]). It is evident from the reports that when the Prophet cursed Muḍar he cursed the Muḍar tribes; when he prayed for rain he asked for rain and fertility for these Muḍar tribes (Tamīm and Sulaym) on which their flocks were dependent and on which the supply of their vital needs of grain depended. It is obvious that the supply of grain and meat by the allied tribes for the Meccan Qurashites was vital for the very existence of Mecca. The link between the curse of the Prophet and Quraysh is apparent in the comment by al-Baṭalyūsī [22]) on the nickname *sakhīna*

---

17) Ms. Br. Mus., Or. 3138 (*Mukhtārāt fuṣūl al-Jāḥiẓ*) fol. 112b.

18) Ibrāhīm b. Muḥammad al-Bayhaqī, *al-Maḥāsin wa-l-masāwī*, ed. Muḥammad Abū l-Faḍl Ibrāhīm, Cairo 1380/1961, I, 24-25; and see ʿAbd al-Jabbār, *Tathbīt dalāʾil al-nubuwwa*, ed. ʿAbd al-Karīm ʿUthmān, Beirut 1386/1966, I, 80 inf.-81 sup.

19) See on him: EI² s.v. Ḥādjib b. Zurāra.

20) Ibrāhīm b. Muḥammad al-Bayhaqī, *op. cit.*, I, 24: . . . *thumma duʿāʾuhu l-mustajābu lladhī lā taʾkhīra fīhi, wa-dhālika anna l-nabiyya (ṣ) lammā laqiya min qurayshin wa-l-ʿarabi min shiddati adhāhum lahu wa-takdhībihim iyyāhu wa-stiʿānatihim ʿalayhi bi-l-amwāli daʿā an tajdiba bilāduhum*. . .

21) See a slightly different version: Ibn ʿAbd Rabbihi, *al-ʿIqd al-farīd*, ed. Aḥmad Amīn, Aḥmad al-Zayn, Ibrāhīm al-Abyārī, Cairo 1375/1956, II, 20-21.

22) Ibn al-Sīd al-Baṭalyūsī, *al-Iqtiḍāb fī sharḥ adab al-kuttāb*, Beirut 1973 (re-

applied to Quraysh: when Quraysh refused to embrace Islam, though summoned by the Prophet, the Prophet invoked God against them: *allāhumma shdud waṭ'ataka wa-j'alhā 'alayhim sinīna ka-sinī yūsufa*. They suffered from drought for seven years during which time they nourished on *'ilhiz* and on a thin gruel of coarse flour called *sakhīna* [23]). In some cases, indeed, only Quraysh (or the people of Mecca) are mentioned [24]). The course of events connected with the Prophet's curse is the usual one: Quraysh refused to embrace Islam; the Prophet invoked God against them and they were afflicted by hardship and famine; they repented and were relieved, but lapsed into unbelief and were punished on the Day of Badr. This sequence of events is indicated in the verse: ..."upon the day when We shall assault most mightily, then we shall take Our vengeance" [25]). Another version seems to point to the direct and indirect objects of the curse: the curse was directed against Quraysh, but the invocation of the Prophet to lift the curse and his prayer for rain were performed on the request of men from Muḍar and for the benefit of their tribes [26]). Numerous traditions indicate clearly that the stubborn refusal of Quraysh to follow the Prophet, the curse of the Prophet, the drought and hunger, the Prophet's prayer for them, God's help and the reversion of Quraysh to unbelief—all these happened before the *hijra*; Quraysh were punished by God and they suffered defeat on the Day of Badr (AH 2).

Some versions of this tradition state that it was Abū Sufyān who

---

print), p. 46; al-Baghdādī, *Khizānat al-adab*, ed. 'Abd al-Salām Hārūn, Cairo 1397/1977, VI, 527-528 (from *al-Iqtiḍāb*).

23) Cf. *L 'A*, s.v. s kh n.

24) Cf. Ibn Nāqiyā *al-Jumān fī tashbīhāt al-qur'ān*, ed. Aḥmad al-Maṭlūb, Khadīja al-Ḥadīthī, Baghdād 1387/1968, p. 347; and see al-Naysābūrī, *op. cit.*, XXX, 188.

25) Cf. Muqātil, Tafsīr, Ms. Ahmet III, no. 74/2, fol. 84b-85a; al-Bayhaqī, *Dalā'il al-nubuwwa*, ed. 'Abd al-Raḥmān Muḥammad 'Uthmān, Cairo 1389/1969, II, 87 inf.—88 sup.; al-Suyūṭī, *al-Khaṣā'iṣ al-kubrā*, ed. Muḥammad Khalīl Harrās, Cairo 1386/1967, I, 369 inf.—370 sup.; al-Qurṭubī, *Tafsīr* (= *al-Jāmi' li-aḥkām al-qur'ān*) Cairo 1387/1967, XII, 135, XVI, 131; al-Khāzin, *Tafsīr* (= *Lubāb al-ta'wīl*), Cairo 1381/repr.) V, 33; al-Baghawī, *Tafsīr* (=*Ma'ālim al-tanzīl*, on margin of al-Khāzin's *Tafsīr*), V, 33; Abū Ḥayyān, *Tafsīru l-baḥri l-muḥīṭ*, Cairo 1328. VIII. 34.

26) See e.g. al-Suyūṭī, *al-Durr al-manthūr*, Cairo 1314, VI, 28; Ibn Kathīr, *Tafsīr*, Beirut 1385/1966, VI, 246.

came to the Prophet and recounted the plight of Quraysh (scil. asking him to pray for them—K) [27]). In some versions of this tradition it is mentioned that certain Qurashites joined Abū Sufyān when he was on his way to the Prophet. Muqātil records the names of the members of the Qurashite delegation to the Prophet led by Abū Sufyān: ʿUtba b. Rabīʿa, al-ʿĀṣ b. Wāʾil, Muṭʿim b. ʿAdī, Suhayl b. ʿAmr and Shayba b. Rabīʿa [28]). The members of the delegation were indeed the leaders of the Meccan opposition against the Prophet; they were captured or killed in the battle of Badr. Some traditions explicitly say that the delegation headed by Abū Sufyān came to the Prophet when he was still in Mecca, before he left on his *hijra* to Medina [29]). These traditions, possessing as they do fine narrative structure, belong to the type of miracle-traditions which encompasses a well-known cycle of edifying stories: the Prophet calls to a group of people to embrace the true religion, his call is harshly rejected, God punished them in answer to the Prophet's request, then the Prophet's invocation rescues the unvelievers who, after a short period of repentance, soon revert to unbelief and are severely punished. But though they are vague and imprecise, these traditions seem to contain some historical details which may be elucidated from other versions of this event.

It is the Muslim scholars themselves, aware of the incongruity of these traditions, who transmitted diverse reports about the circumstances of the curse of Muḍar, some of them more tallying with the historical events and more reliable.

---

27) Al-Ḥākim, *al-Mustadrak*, II, 394; al-Suyūṭī, *al-Khaṣāʾiṣ al-kubrā*, I, 370; idem, *al-Durr al-manthūr*, VI, 28; al-Khāzin, *op.cit.*, V, 34; al-Baghawī, *op.cit.*, V. 34; al-Bayhaqī *Dalāʾil al-nubuwwa*, II, 89, 90 inf.; Abū Nuʿaym al-Iṣfahānī, *Dalāʾil al-nubuwwa*, Hyderabad 1369/1950, pp. 382-383; al-ʿAynī, *ʿUmdat al-qārī*, Cairo 1348, VII, 27-28, 45-46; and see Ibn Kathīr, *Tafsīr*, V, 31 inf.—32 sup.; Ibn Junghul, *Taʾrīkh*, Ms. Br. Mus., Or. 5912, I, fol. 192b; al-Naysābūrī, *op. cit.*, XXV, 66.

28) Muqātil, *op. cit.*, Ms. 74/II, fol. 146a-b.

29) Al-ʿAynī, *op. cit.*, VII, 28, 1.9: ... *wa-dalla hādhā ʿalā anna l-qiṣṣata kānat qabla l-hijrati* ...; al-Jamal, *al-Futūḥāt al-ilāhiyya*, Cairo n.d., IV, 103, 1.2 (and see *ib.*, p. 102) and see the comments of al-ʿAynī, *op. cit.*, VII, 45: ...*wa-kāna majīʾuhu qabla l-hijrati* ... *wa-lam yunqal anna abā sufyāna qadima l-madīnata qabla badrin* (commenting on the interpretation that *al-baṭsha l-kubrā* refers to the Muslim victory at Badr).

II

Al-Bayhaqī refers to a tradition according to which Abū Sufyān came to the Prophet in Medina asking him to pray for the Qurashites afflicted by famine as a result of the Prophet's curse and remarks with some reservation that he came to him twice: once when the Prophet stayed in Mecca and the other time in Medina [30]). Al-Jamal. commenting on the interpretations of al-Jalālayn on Sūra XXIII, states that this verse and the two following ones were revealed to the Prophet in Medina and that Quraysh were afflicted by the Prophet's curse when he emigrated to Medina; hence Abū Sufyān came to the Prophet to Medina. Al-Jamal records a version of the talk of Abū Sufyān with the Prophet as reported by al-Bayḍāwī: Abū Sufyān reproaches the Prophet by reminding him of his claim to have been sent as a mercy for the people of the world, while he has killed the fathers (scil. from among Quraysh—K) by the sword and the children by famine [31]). The tradition affirms the assumption of al-Jamal and indicates clearly that Abū Sufyān set out to Medina to intercede on behalf of his people after a military encounter between the forces of the Prophet and those of Quraysh brought about the defeat of the Qurashites and caused a number of them to be killed; at the same time children in Mecca were dying of hunger caused by some actions of the Prophet which are however not specified in the tradition.

The clash between the forces of the Prophet and those of Mecca, the results of the military and economic actions of the Prophet against Mecca and her tribal allies are fairly reflected in a commentary of Sūra XVI, 112: Ibn 'Abbās, Mujāhid and Qatāda are quoted as stating that the verse refers to the seven years of famine to which the Meccans were exposed; they also were in fear of the Prophet and his Companions who were attacking their caravans; these events took place when the Prophet uttered his invocation: "O God, tighten Thy grip on Mu-

---

30) Al-Bayhaqī, *Dalā'il*, II, 91, 11. 1-2.
31) Al-Jamal, *op. cit.*, III, 198 inf.—199.

ḍar..." [32]), More detailed and concrete is the version recorded by al-Thaʿlabī in his *Tafsīr*: the Qurashites suffered hunger for seven years and the Arab tribes cut off their food-supplies according to the order of the Prophet (... *ibtalāhā bi-l-jūʿi sabʿa sinīna wa-qaṭaʿa l-ʿarabu ʿanhumu l-mīrata bi-amri l-nabiyyi*). The Meccan delegation, including Abū Sufyān, described the sufferings of the people and the unjustified pain of the children; they asked the Prophet to invoke God for them, which the Prophet indeed did. Then the Prophet permitted to carry food to them (i.e. to Mecca), while they (i.e. the people of Mecca—K) were still unbelievers (... *fa-daʿā lahum rasūlu llāhi wa-adhina li-l-nāsi bi-ḥamli l-ṭaʿāmi ilayhim wa-hum baʿdu mushrikūn*) [33]). This report is quite explicit about the situation in Mecca: a tribal group obedient to the Prophet cut off the food supply of Mecca on the order of the Prophet and the population of Mecca were afflicted by hunger. The Prophet's permission to resume food supplies to Mecca for the unbelievers of Quraysh is forcefully formulated in this account. Similar reports are recorded in the commentaries of al-Rāzī [34]). al-Baghawī [35]) and al-Jāwī [36]). Ṭabarī records in his commentary (Sūra XVI, 113-115) a slightly divergent tradition referring to the story of the curse and the hunger; he records however an additional comment on the phrase: ...*fa-kulū mimmā razaqakumu llāhu*..., according to which the phrase refers to the provisions which the Prophet sent, out of mercy, for the unbelievers of Mecca when they were afflicted by drought and hunger [37]). The detail about the dispatching of food to Mecca by the Prophet out of mercy is indicated in the report recorded in the *Tafsīr* of al-Jiyānī: the Prophet sent to them alms for the poor and goods (...*fa-baʿatha ilayhim bi-ṣadaqatin wa-mālin*) [38]). The very early commentary of al-Farrā' (d. 207 AH) describes the hunger suffered by

32) Al-Ṭabarsī, *Majmaʿ al-bayān*, Beirut 1380/1961, XIV, 132.
33) Al-Thaʿlabī, Ms. Vatican, Ar. 1394, fol. 8a.
34) Al-Rāzī, *Mafātīḥ al-ghayb*, Cairo 1357/1938, XX, 128-130.
35) Al-Baghawī, *op. cit.*, IV, 98-99; al-Khāzin, *op. cit.*, IV, 98-99.
36) Al-Jāwī, *Marāḥ labīd*, Cairo n.d., I, 467.
37) Al-Ṭabarī, *Tafsīr* (Bulāq) XIV, 125-126.
38) Abū Ḥayyān, *op. cit.*, VIII, 34.

Quraysh, their fear of the raids of the Prophet's troops and states that the Prophet sent to them food out of mercy, while they remained unbelievers [39]). Another account mentions the messenger who carried the Prophet's gifts to Mecca; it was ʿAmr b. Umayya al-Ḍamrī [40]), a well-known Companion of the Prophet, whom the Prophet happened to entrust with some special missions [41]). Al-Qurṭubī records explicitly the invocation against Muḍar and quotes fragments of the different versions mentioning the plight of Quraysh, their fear as a result of the raids of the forces of the Prophet, the talk of the Meccan delegation with the Prophet, Abū Sufyān's pledge and the order of the Prophet to carry food to Mecca in order to divide it among them [42]).

The date of the boycott against Mecca is indicated in the commentaries of the Qur'ān, Sūra XXIII, 76: "We already seized them with the chastisement...": the boycott of food supplies was carried out by Thumāma b. Uthāl [43]) who stopped it after some time by an order of the Prophet [44]).

Ibn Kathīr gives a very concise summary of the relations between the Prophet and Quraysh: when they refused to convert to Islam and

---

39) *Maʿānī l-qur'ān*, ed. Muḥammad ʿAlī al-Najjār, Cairo 1972, II, 114: ... *thumma inna l-nabiyya (ṣ) raqqa lahum fa-ḥamala ilayhim al-ṭaʿāma wa-hum mushrikūna.*

40) Al-Balādhurī, *Ansāb*, Ms. fol. 896a: ... *wa-baʿatha rasūlu llāhi ʿamran ilā mushrikī qurayshin bi-ṣilatin wa-qad aqḥaṭū wa-jahadū ḥattā akalū l-rimmata wa-l-'ilhiza.*

41) See e.g. Ibn Ḥajar, *al-Iṣāba*, IV, 602-603, no. 5769; al-Dhahabī, *Siyar aʿlām al-nubalā'*, ed. Asʿad Ṭalas, Cairo 1962, III, 40, 1.12; Ibn al-Athīr, *Usd al-ghāba*, Cairo 1280, IV, 86.

42) Al-Qurṭubī, *op. cit.*, X. 194-195.

43) Al-Ṭabarī, *Tafsīr* (Būlāq) XVIII, 34-35; al-Qurṭubī, *op. cit.*, XII, 143; cf. al-Wāḥidī, *Asbāb al-nuzūl*, Cairo 1388/1968, p. 211; al-Suyūṭī, *al-Durr al-manthūr*, V, 13; and see Ibn Saʿd, *op. cit.*, V. 550: ...*fa-ḍayyaqa ʿalā qurayshin fa-lam yadaʿ ḥabbatan ta'tīhim mina l-yamāmati*; Ibn Ḥajar, *al-Iṣāba*, I, 411: ... *wa-manʿuhu ʿan qurayshin al-mīrata* ...; and see *ib.*, on the Yamāma: ... *wa-kānat rīfa ahli makkata.* and see F. McGraw Donner, Mecca's Food Supplies and Muḥammad's Boycott, *JESHO*, XX, 249-266.

44) Ibn ʿAbd al-Barr, *al-Istīʿāb fī maʿrifati l-aṣḥāb*, ed. ʿAlī al-Bijāwī, Cairo 1380/1960, I, 215: ... *wa-kānat mīratu qurayshin wa-manāfiʿuhhum min al-yamāmati, thumma kharaja fa-ḥabasa ʿanhum mā kāna ya'tīhim min mīratihim wa-manāfiʿihim* ...; according to this narrative the Qurashites sent a letter to the Prophet asking him to order Thumāma to lift the boycott; the Prophet responded to their request; Ibn al-Athīr, *Usd al-ghāba*, I, 247.

recognize the mission of the Prophet they were afflicted by drought and hunger, according to the Prophet's curse; after the *hijra* they suffered from the attacks of the Muslim troops; after their conversion to Islam the situation changed: they became leaders and rulers of the people [45]).

III

The Prophet's invocation against Muḍar is in some traditions linked with the *qunūt*-invocation during the prayer. The one uttered by the Prophet is said to have contained either blessings (scil. for the oppressed believers—K) or curses (against the unbelieving enemies of the Prophet—K) or blessings and curses coming both together [46]). These *qunūt*-invocations which refer to some historical events may be useful for establishing the date when boycott was imposed and of the time when it was lifted, following the appeasement.

ʿAbd al-Razzāq records three names of the persecuted believers in Mecca: ʿAyyāsh b. Abī Rabīʿa [47]), Salama b. Hishām [48]), and al-Wālīd b. al-Walīd b. al-Mughīra [49]), quoting the formula of the Prophet's

---

45) Ibn Kathīr, *Tafsīr*, IV, 230-231.

46) Al-Munāwī, *Fayḍ al-qadīr, sharḥ al-jāmiʿ al-ṣaghīr*, Cairo, 1391/1972, V, 96, no. 6554. (On the efficacy of such an invocation see ʿAbd al-Razzāq, *op. cit.*, II, 446, no. 4030: A dog passed a group of people praying behind the Prophet; one of the people made an invocation against the dog and it immediately fell dead on the ground. The Prophet remarked that had this person made an invocation against a whole people, God would have responded to his invocation (and the people would have perished—K).

47) See on him: Ibn Ḥajar, *al-Iṣāba*, IV, 750, no. 6127; al-Zurqānī, *Sharḥ ʿalā l-mawāhib al-laduniyya*, Cairo 1328, VII, 344.

48) See on him Ibn Saʿd, *op. cit.*, IV, 130-131; Ibn ʿAbd al-Barr, *op. cit.*, p. 643, no. 1032; al-Zurqānī, *op. cit.*, VII, 344; Ibn Ḥajar, *al-Iṣāba*, III, 155-156, no. 3405; *al-ʿIqd ad-thamīn fī akhbār al-balad al-amīn*, ed. Fuʾād Sayyid, Cairo 1384/1965, IV, 599-600, no. 1325; al-Dhahabī, *Taʾrīkh al-Islām*, Cairo 1367, I, 379.

49) See on him: Ibn Ḥajar, *al-Iṣāba*, VI, 619, no. 9157; al-Zurqānī, *op. cit.*, VII, 344; al-Wāqidī, *Maghāzī*, p. 46 records another account: the Prophet made an invocation on behalf of Salama b. Hishām, ʿAyyāsh b. Rabīʿa and other unprotected and oppressed (literally: "weak") believers (scil. in Mecca—K); this happened when the Prophet was on his way to Badr. Al-Wāqidī stresses that another invocation, namely for al-Walīd b. al-Walīd was uttered by the Prophet later, as al-Walīd b. al-Walīd was

invocation for them, which is linked with the invocation against Muḍar [50]). The date of the escape of these three believers from Mecca and their arrival in Medina is given either "after Uḥud" [51]) or after the Battle of the Ditch [52]). Accordingly the date of the Prophet's invocation may be established either after the year 3H (Uḥud) or after the year five (the Battle of the Ditch).

Some traditions link the story of the Prophet's invocation with the revelation of Sūra III, 128:..."no part of the matter is thine, whether He turns towards them again or chastises them, for they are evildoers". As the Prophet made an invocation for the believers and uttered a curse against Muḍar, God revealed the verse mentioned above:..."no part of the matter is thine..." [53]). Other traditions comment on the verse differently: the Prophet used to curse certain persons of the *munāfiqūn* during the morning prayer; then the verse mentioned above was revealed and the Prophet was implicitly bidden to cease to curse these persons [54]). One of the traditions mentions that four persons, whose names are not specified, were cursed by the Prophet [55]). A tradition traced to Ibn ʿUmar gives a list of the three unbelievers against whom the Prophet invoked: Abū Sufyān, al-Ḥārith b. Hishām and Ṣafwān b. Umayya; the verse..."no part of the matter is thine"...

---

captured by the forces of the Prophet at Badr; he was released, embraced Islam and returned to Mecca. There he was put in shackles and imprisoned; cf. al-Dhahabī, *Siyar aʿlām*, I, 228, no. 10.

50) ʿAbd al-Razzāq, *op. cit.*, II, 446-447, nos. 4028, 4031-4032; Nūr al-Dīn al-Haythamī, *Majmaʿ al-zawāʾid wa-manbaʿ al-fawāʾid*, Beirut 1967 (reprint), II, 137 inf.—138.; al-Suyūṭī, *al-Durr al-manthūr*, II, 71; Ibn Abī Shayba, *al-Muṣannaf*, ed. ʿAbd al-Khāliq Afghānī, Hyderabad 1387/1967, II, 316-317; al-Naḥḥās, *al-Nāsikh wa-l-mansūkh*, Cairo 1357/1938, p. 91; Ibn ʿAsākir, *Tahdhīb taʾrīkh dimashq*, Damascus 1349, VI, 234-235.

51) See al-Balādhurī, *Ansāb*, I, 208 penult.

52) See al-Balādhurī, *Ansāb*, I, 208, ll. 4-5; and cf., *ib.*, pp. 209-211; al-Dhahabī, *Siyar aʿlām*, I, 228, no. 10.

53) Al-Ṭabarī, *Tafsīr*, ed. Shākir, VII, 201, no. 7820 (and see *ib.*, the references of the Editors).

54) Al-Naḥḥās, *op. cit.*, p. 91 sup.; al-Wāhidī, *op. cit.*, pp. 80-81; ʿAbdallah b. al-Mubārak, *Kit. al-jihād*, ed. Nazīh Ḥammād, Beirut 1391/1971, p. 58, no. 58; Ibn ʿAsākir, *op. cit.*, VI, 429.

55) Al-Ṭabarī, *Tafsīr*, ed. Shākir, VII, 199, no. 7818.

was revealed in connection with this invocation (and the Prophet ceased to curse them—K) [56]). In the list given by ʿAbdallah b. al-Mubārak the names of the three persons are different: Ṣafwān b. Umayya, Suhayl b. ʿAmr and al-Ḥārith b. Hishām; the name of Abū Sufyān is missing [57]). Al-Suyūṭī mentions Ṣafwān b. Umayya, al-Ḥārith b. Hishām, Abū Sufyān and the fourth man against whom the Prophet invoked (at the Day of Uḥud) Suhayl b. ʿAmr [58]). Noteworthy is the additional phrase in al-Suyūṭī's tradition: God accepted their repentance (*fa-tība ʿalayhim kullihim*), and, as one may deduce, He forgave them their sins [59]). These persons were indeed the leaders of Quraysh; they remained among the leading personalities of the community after they had embraced Islam and they participated im some of the decisive events in Islam. The utterance of the Prophet about their repentance being accepted made their conversion easier and enabled them to keep their high positions in society, their former enmity to the Prophet being forgotten.

The traditions in which the curse of Muḍar is linked to the Battle of Uḥud are contradicted by a report according to which the Prophet wounded in the battle and stained with blood made an invocation only against those who attacked and wounded him. God, however, did not respond to his invocation and forbade to curse the wicked people [60]). Peculiar is a tradition which states that the Prophet intended to curse the people who fled from the battle-field at Uḥud. He was prevented from doing it by the revelation of the verse: ..."no part of the matter is thine" [61]). The tendency of this tradition is evident

---

56) Al-Ṭabarī, *Tafsīr*, ed. Shākir, VII, no. 7819 (and see the references given by the Editors); Ibn ʿAsākir, *op. cit.*, VI, 429; cf. Shahridār al-Daylamī, *op. cit.*, Ms Chester Beatty 4139, fol. 136b, ll 1-2.

57) ʿAbdallah b. al-Mubārak, *op. cit.*, p. 58, no. 57; al-Fāsī, *al-ʿIqd al-thamīn*, IV, 35-36; Ibn ʿAsākir, *op. cit.*, VI, 429.

58) See on him Ibn Ḥajar, *al-Iṣāba*, III, 213 sup., no. 3575.

59) Al-Suyūṭī, *al-Durr al-manthūr*, II, 71.

60) See e.g. al-Ṭabarī, *Tafsīr*, ed. Shākir, VII, 194-199, nos. 7805-7817; al-Zurqānī, *op. cit.*, VII, 343 ult.—344, ll. 1-3; Ibn Ḥajar, *Fatḥ al-bārī*, Cairo 1301 (reprint) VII, 281.

61) Al-ʿAynī, *op. cit.*, XVII, 155, l. 14.

from the phrase which it contains, according to which one of the people who forsook the Prophet in this battle was 'Uthmān b. 'Affān. The majority of scholars are said to have been of the opinion that the verse "no part of the matter is thine" was revealed after the battle of Uḥud [62]).

IV

The invocation against Muḍar can hardly be related either to the Meccan period, or to the battle of Uḥud. In the Meccan period the Prophet and his Companions suffered from the persecutions of the Qurashites and only in some rare cases were the Qurashites compelled to act in agreement with their tribal allies [63]); in the battle of Uḥud the Qurashites were those who fought the Muslim forces and wounded the Prophet, while the Muḍar alliance is not mentioned as an active factor in the preparations for that battle. The invocation of the Prophet could only be uttered in the period when the tribes of the Muḍar federation, the allies of Mecca, acted in cooperation with Quraysh against the Muslim community harasshing, attacking, damaging and killing. Such was the case with the expedition of Bi'r Ma'ūna. In some traditions the curse of Muḍar is actually reported to have taken place after the massacre of the Companions by the tribal groups of Sulaym and 'Āmir b. Ṣa'ṣa'a which were allied with Mecca and acted in close cooperation with the Qurashite enemies of the Prophet. According to these traditions the curse was linked with the invocation for the three Companions oppressed in Mecca by the unbelievers [64]). In some of

62) Al-Zurqānī, *op. cit.*, VII, 344, 11. 9-10: ... *wa-l-ṣawāb annahā nazalat bi-sababi qiṣṣati uḥud ... wa-qāla ṣāḥibu "l-lubābi"; ttafaqa aktharu l-'ulamā'i 'alā nuzūlihā fī qiṣṣati uḥud.*

63) See e.g. Ibn Ḥazm, *Ḥajjat al-wadā'*, ed. Maḥmūd Ḥaqqī, Beirut 1966, p. 148; Muḥibb al-Dīn al-Ṭabarī, *al-Qirā li-qāṣidi ummi l-qurā*, ed. Muṣṭafā l-Saqā, Cairo 1390/1970, p. 547; 'Alī b. Burhān al-Dīn, *al-Sīra al-ḥalabiyya*, Cairo 1382/1962, III, 198, 1. 3 from bottom; and see JESHO, 1972, p. 64, note 3.

64) See e.g. al-Ṭahāwī, *Sharḥ ma'ānī l-āthār*, ed. Muḥammad Zuhrī l-Najjār, Cairo 1388/1966, I, 241-244; al-Zurqānī, *op. cit.*, VII, 344-345; al-Wāḥidī, *op. cit.*, p. 81; Ibn Abī Shayba, *op. cit.*, II, 316 inf.—317 sup.; al-Dāraquṭnī, *Sunan*, II, 38, no. 7; al-Ṭabarī, *Tafsīr*, VII, 202, no. 7821 (and see the references of the Editors); cf. Ibn Sa'd, *op. cit.*, II, 53; cf. al-Shāfi'ī, *Musnad*, Ārah 1306/1889, p. 108.

the Prophet's invocations the curse is directed against the wicked tribal groups without any mention of Muḍar at all [65]). The account of Muqātil links the verse Sūra III, 128:..."no part of the matter is thine"... with Sūra XCIV (*a-lam nashraḥ*). According to this comment both the passages refer to the massacre of Bi'r Ma'ūna. The story recorded by Muqātil differs in many details from the current reports: there were four hundred Companions known as *ahl al-ṣuffa* who lived on the alms given to them; they gave the surplus of these alms to other poor persons. They had no relatives in Medina. They went out as a military force (*mujayyashīn*) and fought the Banū Sulaym (who were unbelievers—K). Seventy warriors of this group (i.e. the *ahl al-ṣuffa*) were killed. The Prophet made an invocation against the evildoers (scil. of Sulaym) praying to God to punish them. But God revealed to him the verse: ... "no part of the matter is thine" and, since it was obviously predestined that they would embrace Islam, the text of Sūra XCIV, 1 seq. was revealed [66]). In some cases the invocation against the wicked tribal groups goes together with a blessing bestowed on Ghifār and Aslam [67]), the two tribal groups which supported the Prophet at a

---

65) See e.g. ʿAbd al-Razzāq, *op. cit.*, II, 446, no 4029; al-Zurqānī, *op. cit.*, II, 78; Ibn Ḥajar, *Fatḥ al-bārī*, VII, 282 sup.; al-Bayhaqī, *al-Sunan*, II, 199, 206; ʿAlī b. Burhān al-Dīn, *op. cit.*, III, 196-197; Nūr al-Dīn al-Haythamī, *op. cit.*, VI, 125; al-Shaukānī, *Nayl al-auṭār*, Cairo 1372/1953, II, 390, no. 8; al-Suyūṭī, *al-Durr al-manthūr*, II, 71; Ibn Sayyid al-Nās, *ʿUyūn al-athar*, Cairo 1356, II, 47, 1. 24; Ibn Abī Shayba, *op. cit.*, II, 310; Abū Nuʿaym al-Iṣfahānī, *Ḥilyat al-auliyāʾ*, Cairo 1387/1967, III, 113 inf.; (and see the peculiar invocation against ʿUṣayya: ... *samiʿtu rasūla llāhi yaqūlu fī qunūtihi*: *yā umma mildam ʿalayki bi-banī ʿuṣayyata, fa-innahum ʿaṣau llāha wa-rasūlahu*, al-Khaṭīb al-Baghdādī, *Mūḍiḥ auhām al-jamʿ wa-l-tafrīq*, Hyderabad 1379/1960, II, 2); cf. al-Majlisī, *Biḥār al-anwār*, Tehran 1386, LX, 232 (the curse here is uttered inter alia against Riʿl, Dhakwān, ʿAḍl, Liḥyān, those from among Asad and Ghaṭafān inflicted by elephantiasis, Abū Sufyān b. Ḥarb, Suhayl ["the man with the teeth"; in the text "Shahbal" instead of "Suhayl"], the two sons of Mulayka b. Jizyam, Marwān [evidently: b. al-Ḥakam,—K], Haudha and Hauna. The tradition is quoted from *al-Kāfī*]).

66) Muqātil, *op. cit.*, 74/II, fol. 243a-b; and see al-ʿAynī, *op. cit.*, XVII, 155, 1. 15; . *wa-qāla inna aṣḥāba l-ṣuffati kharajū ilā qabīlatayni min banī sulaymin ʿuṣayyata wa-dhakwāna fa-qutilū fa-daʿā ʿalayhim arbaʿīna ṣabāḥan* ....

67) Al-Ṭaḥawī, *Sharḥ maʿānī l-āthār*, I, 243 sup., 267 sup; Nūr al-Dīn al-Haythamī, *op. cit.*, II, 138; al-Daylamī, *Firdaus*, Ms. Chester Beatty 3037, fol. 108a; Ibn Abī Shayba, *op. cit.*, II, 317 inf.; al-Wāqidī, *op. cit.*, pp. 349 inf.—350.

very early period[68]). Al-Ṭaḥāwī analyses the divergent traditions, emphasizes the contradictory interpretations concerning the period in which the Prophet's utterance was given and surveys its circumstances, but does not reach a decisive conclusion[69]). The statement that the invocation against the evildoers who had committed the massacre at Bi'r Ma'ūna was the first time that the Prophet uttered a *qunūt*-invocation during prayer[70]) is of some importance for establishing the circumstances of this invocation and its date.

It is in character with the custom of *ḥadīth* scholars that they tried to bridge between the various versions of the tradition about the curse of Muḍar. Some of them were of the opinion that the period of drought and hunger did not last seven years, but only a year or even less. Thus, for instance, the formula: ... *ij'alhā 'alayhim sinīna ka-sinī yūsufa* was interpreted as referring either to the harshness of the chastisement or to the period of drought: days, weeks, months or years[71]).

The most reliable report about the Prophet's curse of Muḍar appears to be the one stating that the Prophet uttered if after the massacre of Bi'r Ma'ūna. The close relations between Quraysh and their Muḍar allies can be gauged from a significant passage of the report about this expedition: when the Muslim warrior 'Amr b. Umayya al-Ḍamrī was captured by 'Āmir b. al-Ṭufayl, the man who planned and carried out the massacre of Bi'r Ma'ūna, he was asked about his pedigree. When he stated that he was from Muḍar, 'Āmir b. al-Ṭufayl freed him and let him go, saying that he would not like to harm a man from Muḍar[72]). 'Āmir's decision was, of course, in line with the ideas

68) Ibn 'Abd al-Ḥakam, *Futūḥ Miṣr*, ed. C. Torrey, Leiden—New Haven, 1920-22, p. 303 sup.; Ibn Ḥajar, *Fatḥ al-bārī*, II, 410, 11. 16-23.

69) Al-Ṭaḥāwī, *Mushkil al-āthār*, I, 236-238.

70) Al-Zurqānī, *op. cit.*, II, 78, 1. 17; al-Ḥākım, *op. cit.*, I, 226 sup.

71) Al-Zurqānī, *op. cit.*, VII, 344, 11. 21-22: *waṭ'ataka... 'alā [kuffār qurayshin, aulādi] muḍara... allāhumma j'alhā ay al-waṭ'ata au al-sinīna au al-ayyām...*; Ibn Ḥajar, *Fatḥ al-bārī*, II, 410, 11. 12-14: ... *wa-ahlu l-mashriqi yauma'idhin min muḍara mukhālifūna lahu...*

72) See e.g. Ibn al-Kalbī, *Jamharat al-nasab*, Ms. Br. Mus., Add. 23297, fol. 46a, 1.1: ... *fa-lam yuflit aḥadun ghayruhu khallā sabīlahu 'āmiru bnu l-ṭufayli ḥīna qāla lahu*

of tribal loyalty according to which he was expected to refrain from killing a member of the Muḍar federation even though the latter might participate in an expedition of a hostile troop. On the other hand, the individuals and groups who joined the Muslim community cut their bonds with their tribes, keeping their loyalty and solidarity exclusively for their religious leaders and the community of the faithful.

V

Abū Sufyān was one of the prominent leaders of Quraysh, a stubborn opponent of the Prophet during his stay at Mecca and the head of the active struggle against him after he moved to Medina. Abū Sufyān played a considerable role in three decisive encounters between Quraysh and the Muslim forces: in the Battle of Badr (anno 2 H), in the Battle of Uḥud (anno 3H) and in the Battle of the Ditch (anno 5H). Tradition does not mention any meeting during the Prophet's Medinan period between the Prophet and Abū Sufyān for negotaitions except the latter's visit to the Prophet as a single delegate of Quraysh a short time before the Prophet set out on his expedition to conquer Mecca (anno 8H). There are, however, a few reports which indicate contacts between the Prophet and Abū Sufyān during a relatively long period before the conquest of Mecca by the Prophet.

According to a tradition recorded by Muqātil, the leading hypocrites of Medina, ʿAbdallah b. Ubayy [73]), ʿAbdallah b. Saʿd b. Abī Sarḥ [74]) and Ṭuʿma b. Ubayriq [75]) cunningly arranged a meeting between the Prophet and the leaders of the unbelievers of Mecca: Abū Sufyān, ʿIkrima b. Abī Jahl and Abū l-Aʿwar al-Sulamī [76]). The Prophet refused

---

innī min muḍar; about the position of the chiefs of the Muḍarī tribes see Ibn Kathīr, *Tafsīr*, V, 488: ... *fa-dakhala ʿuyaynatu bnu ḥiṣnin al-fazāriyyu ʿalā l-nabiyyi (ṣ) wa-ʿindahu ʿāʾishatu fa-dakhala bi-ghayri idhnin, fa-qāla lahu rasūlu llāhi*: *fa-ayna l-istiʾdhān*? *fa-qāla*: *yā rasūla llāhi mā staʾdhantu ʿalā rajulin min muḍara mundhu adraktu*...

73) See on him EI², s.v. ʿAbd Allāh b. Ubayy b. Salūl (W. Montgomery Watt).

74) See on him EI², s.v. ʿAbd Allāh b. Saʿd (C. H. Becker).

75) See on him Ibn Ḥajar, *al-Iṣāba*, III, 518, no. 4249; Ibn al-Athīr, *Usd al-ghāba*, III, 52-53.

76) See on him Ibn Ḥajar, *al-Iṣāba*, IV, 641, no. 5855 (ʿAmr b. Sufyān); Ibn ʿAbd al-Barr, *op. cit.*, p. 1600, no. 2849; Khalīfa b. Khayyāṭ, *Ṭabaqāt*, ed. Akram

to accept the requests of the mixed Hypocrite-Qurashī delegation that he should acknowledge the power of the idols to grant intercession (*shafāʿa*, scil. with God for the unbelievers—K). He pacified the enraged ʿUmar who was about to kill the members of the arrogant delegation and granted them a letter of safe-conduct, enabling them to return safely to their homes [77]). This event is said to have been hinted at in Sūra XXXIII, 1-3: "O Prophet, fear God and obey not the unbelievers and the hypocrites. God is All-knowing, All-wise. And follow what is revealed to thee from thy Lord"... (Translation of A. J. Arberry).

Ḍiyāʾ al-Dīn, Baghdād 1387/1967, p. 51; Naṣr b. Muzāḥim al-Minqarī, *Waqʿat Ṣiffīn*, ed. ʿAbd al-Salām Hārūn, Cairo 1382/1962, index (Sufyān b. ʿAmr al-Sulamī). Abū l-Aʿwar was a *ḥalīf* of Abū Sufyān. Abū l-Aʿwar's grandmother was Arwā bint Umayya b. ʿAbdshams. And see on him EI², s.v. Abū l-Aʿwar (H. Lammens).

77) Muqātil, *op. cit.*, Ahmet III, 74/II, fols. 85b-86a; and see a shorter version: al-Wāḥidī, *op. cit.*, p. 236 with an explicit statement that the event took place after the battle of Uḥud; and see al-Baghawī, *op. cit.*, V, 189; al-Khāzin, *op. cit.*, V, 189-190; al-Nasafī, *Tafsīr*, Cairo n.d., III, 292. The earliest version recorded by al-Farrāʾ, Maʿānī l-Qurʾān II, 334 states that the Prophet forbade to kill the Meccan members of the delegation, as there was a peace-treaty (*muwādaʿa*) between them. Al-Samarqandī gives the report of Muqātil, but also records the account of Ibn al-Kalbī, according to which the Meccan delegates alighted in the courts of ʿAbdallah b. Ubayy, Muʿattib b. Qushayr (see on him Ibn Ḥajar, *al-Iṣāba*, VI, 175, no. 8125) and Jadd b. Qays (see on him Ibn Ḥajar, *al-Iṣāba*, I, 468, no. 1112). According to this version it was the Prophet himself who intended to (order to—K) kill the arrogant Meccan delegates; but God forbade him to violate the pact (...*wa-ʿaraḍū ʿalayhi ashyāʾa fa-karihahā minhum, fa-hamma bihim rasūlu llāhi* (*ṣ*) *an yaqtulūhum* (!) *fa-nazala*: *yā ayyuhā l-nabiyyu ttaqi llāha wa-lā tanquḍi l-ʿahda lladhī baynaka wa-baynahum ilā l-muddati wa-lā tuṭiʿ al-kāfirīna min ahli makkata*). Another account says that the Muslims intended to kill the Meccan delegates, but the verses of Sūra XXXIII, revealed at that time, prevented them from carrying out of their plan (al-Samarqandī, *Tafsīr*, Ms. Chester Beatty 3668, vol. II, 129a). There is a curious tradition recorded by al-Suyūṭī, *Lubāb al-nuqūl fī asbābi l-nuzūl*, Cairo 1374/1954, p. 174: it makes no mention of the delegation, but speaks of the stipulations made by the Prophet's enemies (also mentioned in other sources—K): the Jews and the Hypocrites in Medina threaten to kill the Prophet if he does not abandon his ideas, while the Meccans promise to grant the Prophet half of their property if he retracts. The tradition, traced back to al-Ḍaḥḥāk, mentions among the persons who summoned the Prophet to relinquish his call al-Walīd b. al-Mughīra and Shayba b. Rabīʿa. The latter was killed in the battle of Badr; consequently the event has to go back, according to this tradition, to the period of the first two years after the *hijra*. And see this tradition: al-Suyūṭī, *al-Durr al-manthūr*, V, 180, 11. 25-27.

The reports do not specify the date of the arrival of the Meccan delegation in Medina; the only indication as to its time is the remark that it took place after Uḥud. The style of the narrative and the circumstances of the visit, viz. the stratagem by which the Medinan hypocrites got the Prophet's consent to meet the delegation, the demand of the delegation and ʿUmar's sharp reaction, all this seems to indicate that the delegation came to Medina after the Battle of the Ditch. The battle itself was a defeat for the Qurashites and some of them probably realized that the Meccans would not be able to destroy the Muslim community in Medina and that they should set up a relationship with Medina based on the new balance of power. Some of the Qurashite leaders perceived that they were unable to resume their commercial activities without securing their trade routes from the attacks of the Muslim forces, and that it was necessary to gain a recognition by the Prophet of the pagan deities of the Kaʿba in order to preserve the authority of Quraysh as keepers of the House and to secure an uninterrupted flow of pagan pilgrims to Mecca. The Qurashites were exhausted by the heavy war-expenditures and weakened by the lack of loyalty of some allied tribal groups who joined Muḥammad. The boycott of Thumāma b. Uthāl, who at the Prophet's order cut off food-supplies from the Yamāma was causing the population of Mecca serious hardship [78]). The situation was aggravated by a severe drought in the same year, anno 6H [79]). It is precisely the drought often mentioned in the sources. Lack of economic stability seems to have prevailed until anno 8H, when people complained of high prices (of food—K) and asked the Prophet to fix the prices and control them, a request which the Prophet refused [80]). In this situation the Qurashites were compelled

---

78) See e.g. al-Balādhurī, *Ansāb*, I, 367; al-Zurqānī, *op. cit.*, II, 144-146; al-Diyārbakrī, *Ta'rīkh al-khamīs*, Cairo 1283, II, 2-3; ʿAlī b. Burhān al-Dīn, *op. cit.*, III, 197-199.

79) ʿAbd al-Malik b. Ḥabīb, *Ta'rīkh*, Ms. Bodley, Marsh 288, p. 88: ... *wa-fī hādhihi l-sanati* (i.e. anno 6th H.) *ajdaba l-nāsu jadban shadīdan fa-stasqā lahum rasūlu llāhi* (ṣ) *fī ramaḍāna*...; al-ʿAynī, *op. cit.*, VII, 34, 1.11: ... *wa-dhakara bnu ḥibbāna: kāna khurūjuhu* (ṣ) *ilā l-muṣallā li-l-istisqā' fī shahri ramaḍāna sanata sittin min al-hijrati.*

80) ʿAbd al-Malik b. Ḥabīb, *op. cit.*, p. 90: ... *wa-fī hādhihi l-sanati* (i.e. anno 8th—

to come to the Prophet and ask for some recognition of the idols, their aim being to try and save their position and authority among the tribes. The Prophet could not accept their request. His call to his Companions was to believe in the one God and any concession made to Quraysh would mean that he was willing to associate idols with the one God. His decision was intransigent, given out of a position of strength; he refused to discuss the requests of the delegation. He could wisely foresee that a moderate and more flexible faction would arise in Mecca, which might strive for a peace with the Muslim community in Medina and its leader, the Prophet. As a result, Mecca might be torn by discussion and the position of Quraysh would be weakend. It is clear that the Prophet tried to win over the leaders of this moderate group in order to assert his influence in Mecca and prepare for the conquest of the town.

The tradition about the exchange of gifts between the Prophet and Abū Sufyān is recorded by Abū ʿUbayd on the authority of ʿIkrima: The Prophet sent to Abū Sufyān in Mecca *ʿajwa*-dates and asked him to send in return as gift hides. Abū Sufyān carried out the request. Abū ʿUbayd analyses the tradition concluding that the exchange of gifts happened at the time of the armistice between the Prophet and the people of Mecca, before Mecca was conquered by the Prophet [81]). A precise date is attached to the event recorded by Abū ʿUbayd: after the pact of al-Ḥudaybiyya. The Meccans were at that period unbelievers, but this did not prevent the Prophet from exchanging gifts with his former enemy, Abū Sufyān. Abū ʿUbayd is right in deducing from this incident the general law that the Prophet accepted gifts from unbelievers when they were not in war with the Muslims.

Another version of this story, also traced back to ʿIkrima, gives a slightly different construction to the events, records some additional

---

K) *ghalā l-siʿru jiddan*. Cf. al-ʿAynī, *op. cit.*, VII, 36, l. 10 from bottom: *wa-qāla l-wāqidī: wa-lammā qadima wafdu salāmāna sanata ʿashrin fa-shakau ilayhi l-jadba fa-qāla rasūlu llāhi (ṣ) bi-yadayhi*...

81) Abū ʿUbayd, *al-Amwāl*, ed. Muḥammad Ḥāmid al-Fiqī, Cairo 1353, pp. 257-258, no. 631; Ibn Zanjawayh, *al-Amwāl*, Ms. Burdur 183, fol. 96a; Ibn Ḥajar, *al-Iṣāba*, III, 413, no. 4050 (the messenger was ʿAmr b. Umayya al-Ḍamrī); on *ʿajwa*-dates see G. Jacob, *Altarabisches Beduinenleben*, Berlin 1897 (reprint), p. 229.

details and sheds some light on the split within Quraysh as a result of the policy of the Prophet. The Prophet, says the tradition, sent some goods (*ba'atha bi-shay'in*) to Abū Sufyān, and to some of the Qurashī unbelievers in Mecca. Some of them accepted, some of them returned (the things sent by the Prophet—K). Abū Sufyān said: "I shall accept it and shall not send it back". Then he sent to the Prophet weapons and other things which the Prophet accepted. Then the Prophet sent him *'ajwa*-dates and Abū Sufyān sent him in return hides [82]).

It is evident that this tradition about the exchange of goods between the Prophet and Abū Sufyān is quite different from that of Abū 'Ubayd: it was not dates which were sent in exchange for hides for private usage; the weapons sent to the Prophet were obviously intended for the use of the Muslim forces and Medinan dates were quite as obviously sent for the unbelieving Qurashites. This conspicous exchange of weapons for food could only have happened when Abū Sufyān had lost his hope of Mecca's victory over the Medinan community and it was most probably preceded by negotiations between the Prophet and Abū Sufyān. A report related on the authority of Abū Hurayra adds more details about the first steps of the appeasement and how the relations between the Prophet and Abū Sufyān were resumed. The Prophet sent to Quraysh a man with money to be distributed among them; they were at that time unbelievers, adds the report. Abū Sufyān, with a group of Quraysh, asked the messenger to hand them over the money which Quraysh refused to accept. The messenger returned to the Prophet asking for instructions. The Prophet's reply was clear: "Why didn't you hand over (the money—K) to those of them who agreed to accept it" [83])? Another tradition, this one too recorded by al-Fākihī, mentions the name of the messenger who carried the money: 'Amr b. al-Faghwā' al-Khuzā'ī. The Prophet warned the messenger of 'Amr b. Umayya al-Ḍamrī who tried, as foretold by the Prophet, to attack 'Amr b. al-Faghwā' and rob him of the money. The messenger escaped and

82) Ibn 'Asākir, *Tahdhīb Ta'rīkh*, VI, 395.
83) Al-Fākihi, *op. cit.*, fol. 397a.

succeeded to reach Mecca and to hand over the money to Abū Sufyān [84]).

A tradition traced back to 'Abdallah, the son of 'Alqama b. al-Faghwā' (the brother of 'Amr b. al-Faghwā') states that it was his father (not his uncle—K) who was dispatched by the Prophet with money to be distributed to the poor among the unbelievers of Quraysh in order to gain their sympathy (scil. for the Prophet and Islam, *yata'allafuhum*—K). As in the former tradition, 'Amr b. Umayya al-Ḍamrī joins the messenger and tries to rob him of his money, but ʿAlqama succeeds in escaping. Abū Sufyān remarks (scil. after receiving of the money—K): "I have not seen anyone more pious (*abarr*) and more generous towards the kindred (*auṣal*) than this man (i.e. the Prophet). We fight him and try to shed his blood, while he beneficently sends us gifts" [85]).

Abū Sufyān's remark about the Prophet reflects in a true manner the attitude of the unbelievers towards the generosity displayed by the Prophet with regard to his opponents. Some utterances of the non-believer Qurashites, expressing admiration for the clemency of the Prophet and his generosity are recorded in the reports about the conquest of Mecca; they are indeed similar to the utterance of Abū Sufyān mentioned above. The report names the social group which refused to accept the money sent by the Prophet and thus objected to collaboration, or even contact, with him: they were the *ashrāf*, the notables, whose attitude of deep devotion to the ancestral rites, and their firm adherence to the accepted mould of relations between tribes, based as it was on the loyalty and allegiance to the Kaʿba and its pagan rites, are reflected in their staunch opposition to any peaceful contact

---

84) Al-Fākihī. *op. cit.*, fol. 397a (reported on the authority of the son of the messenger, ʿAbdallah b. ʿAmr b. al-Faghwā); but see the version saying that the Prophet sent the gifts after the conquest of Mecca: Ibn Saʿd, *op. cit.*, IV, 296; Ibn al-Athīr, *Jāmiʿ al-uṣūl*, ed. Muḥammad Ḥāmid al-Fiqī, Cairo 1374/1955, XII, 361, no. 9435; al-Kharqūshī, *Sharaf al-muṣṭafā*, Ms. Br. Mus., Or. 3014, fol. 72a.

85) See Ibn Ḥajar, *al-Iṣāba*, IV, 559, no. 5680; al-Dhahabī, *Siyar aʿlām*, III, 120; al-Muttaqī l-Hindī, *op. cit.*, IX, 104, no. 943; and cf. Ibn Ḥajar, *Tahdhīb al-tahdhīb*, V, 340. no. 580.

with the Muslim body politic headed by the Prophet. They were confronted by a group of Quraysh under the leadership of Abū Sufyān who made a shrewd assessment of the situation of Quraysh after the defeat of the Battle of the Ditch and the extermination of the Banū Qurayẓa. As already pointed out above, he knew that establishing relations and creating economic contacts with Muḥammad and his community was unavoidable. He believed that Mecca could no more face the Prophet in war and therefore did not hesitate to send weapons to the Prophet. As a result, there is a dramatic change in the attitude of the Prophet towards Abū Sufyān, and it is admirably reflected in the narrative reviewed above: after the bloody events of al-Rajīʿ and Biʾr Maʿūna the Prophet sent ʿAmr b. Umayya al-Ḍamrī ordering him to kill Abū Sufyān [86]) in retaliation for Abū Sufyān's attempt to kill the Prophet by an assassin. Now, after the Battle of the Ditch, the Prophet strived to gain the co-operation of the leader of Quraysh, Abū Sufyān. The man who accompanied the Prophet's messenger to Abū Sufyān was the very man whom the Prophet had sent two years before to kill him: ʿAmr b. Umayya al-Ḍamrī.

Other reports about the actions of Abū Sufyān seem to confirm the reports about the contacts between the Prophet and Abū Sufyān during that period. The Prophet married Umm Ḥabība (Ramla), the daughter of Abū Sufyān anno 6H, the year of the peace of Ḥudaybiyya; Abū Sufyān is said, according to some reports, to have given his approval. Other accounts say that the permission to marry her was granted the Prophet by Khālid b. Saʿīd b. al-ʿĀṣ or by ʿUthmān b. ʿAffān [87]). A tradition recorded by Muslim states that Abū Sufyān put

---

86) See e.g. al-Diyārbakrī, *op. cit.*, I, 459; al-Zurqānī, *op. cit.*, II, 177-179; al-Ṭabarī, *Taʾrīkh*, ed. Abū l-Faḍl Ibrāhīm, Cairo 1969, II, 542-545.

87) See e.g. the various reports about the marriage: al-Ḥākim, *op. cit.*, IV, 20-23; Muṣʿab al-Zubayrī, *Nasab Quraysh*, ed. Levi-Provençal, Cairo 1953, p. 122; al-Maqrīzī, *Imtāʿ al-asmāʿ*, ed. Maḥmūd Maḥammad Shākir, Cairo 1941, I, 325, 358 inf.—359 sup.; al-Ṭabarī, *Taʾrīkh*, II, 653-654, III, 165; al-Balādhurī, *Ansāb*, I, 438-439; Ibn Kathīr, *al-Sīra al-nabawiyya*, ed. Muṣṭafā ʿAbd al-Wāḥid, Cairo 1385/1966, IV, 273, 275 ult.-276; Ibn Sayyid al-Nās, *ʿUyūn al-athar*, II, 306-307;o;Yāsīn b. Khayrallah, *Muhadhdhab al-rauḍa al-fayḥāʾ fī tawārīkh al-nisāʾ*, ed. Rajāʾ Maḥmūd al-Sāmarrāʾī, Baghdād 1386/1966, pp. 117-120.

forth three requests in his talk with the Prophet: to let him marry his daughter, Umm Ḥabība bint Abī Sufyān, to appoint his son Muʿāwiya as a scribe of the Prophet, and that the Prophet should appoint him to fight the unbelievers with the same zeal as he had when fighting the Muslims [88]). Orthodox scholars discussed at length the tradition according to which it was Abū Sufyān who gave his daughter in marriage to the Prophet. It is evident that they found it hard to accept the tradition as sound, although it was recorded by Muslim, since according to Muslim law an unbeliever has no authority over the legal acts of any of his family who has converted to Islam. Consequently the unbeliever Abū Sufyān could not either permit or prohibit the marriage of his believing daughter. The scholars had therefore recourse to harmonizing interpretations, attaching to the marriage request a quite different meaning: Abū Sufyān's intention was not to grant permission to the Prophet's marriage with his daughter, but rather, as the setting of the tradition was placed at the conquest of Mecca, when Abū Sufyān had converted to Islam, the tradition was interpreted as meaning that Abū Sufyān gave confirmation and legitimacy to the marriage [89]). One is inclied to assume that during the negotiations between the Prophet and Abū Sufyān, which preceded the exchange of goods between them, some decisions about the position of Abū Sufyān and of his family had been reached, including an agreement concerning the Prophet's marriage with Umm Ḥabība. The Prophet indeed appointed Muʿāwiya as his scribe and Abū Sufyān, formerly the violent opponent of Islam, was entrusted with responsible tasks, and put in charge of the collection of taxes in certain districts [90]). The co-operation between the Prophet and Abū Sufyān in the period of the Ḥudaybiyya agreement can be gauged from some traditions saying that Muʿāwiya went out from Mecca in the company of ʿAbd al-Raḥmān b. Abī Bakr and other

---

88) Ibn Sayyid al-Nās, *op. cir.*, II, 307.; cf. Ibn ʿAsākir, *op. cit.*, VI, 399, 404 inf.

89) See e.g. Ibn Qayyim al-Jauziyya, *Jalāʾu l-afhām fī l-ṣalāti wa-l-salām ʿalā khayri l-anām* ed. Ṭāhā Yūsuf Yāsīn, Kuwayt-Beirut 1977, pp. 128-135.

90) See e.g. al-Balādhurī, *Ansāb al-ashrāf*, ed. M. Schloessinger, IVA, p. 6 (and see the references supplied by the Editor); Ibn ʿAsākir, *op. cit.*, VI, 404 inf.—405 sup.

Qurashī youths before the conquest of Mecca in order to meet the Prophet and convert to Islam[91]). There is no mention of Abū Sufyān's activity during the negotiations over the pact of al-Ḥudaybiyya, nor after the pact was signed. The change in his attitude towards the Prophet was, however, fully reflected in his censure of the aggressive action of some Qurashī leaders against Khuzāʿa, the allies of the Prophet[92]). It is plausible that no else than Abū Sufyān was the person sent to the Prophet in Medina in order to prevent the Prophet's expedition against Mecca and to reaffirm the pact of al-Ḥudaybiyya in spite of the violation of one of its paragraphs through the attack against Khuzāʿa. Abū Sufyān could not prevent the expedition against Mecca and its conquest by the Muslims, but he contributed much to the peaceful surrender of the city. He was in reward given a great privilege by the Prophet: to anyone being in his court when the Muslim troops occupy Mecca was to be granted safety. The feelings of anger and contempt at his role in the Muslim conquest of Mecca were clearly expressed by his wife Hind bint ʿUtba: "Kill this fat greasy bladder of lard!"—she cried when Abū Sufyān announced on behalf of the Prophet safety for those who would enter his court. "What a rotten protector of the people"[93])! The kindness of the Prophet towards Abū Sufyān, the favours granted him, the appointment of Muʿāwiya as secretary of the Prophet, and the appointment of Yazīd as tax collector[94]) were important factors in creating a favourable Muslim attitude towards Abū Sufyān and his family. The caliphs who succeeded the Prophet continued to employ members of Abū Sufyān's family in high posts.

To this crucial period in the relations between Abū Sufyān and the Prophet seems to refer the utterance attributed to the Prophet: "The faith (scil. Islam—K) has been continually aided by Abū Sufyān

---

91) Al-Zubayr b. Bakkār, *Jamharat nasab quraysh*, Ms. Bodley Marsh. 384, fol. 111a, penult.; al-Fāsī, *al-ʿIqd al-thamīn*, V, 371; Ibn Ḥajar, *al-Iṣāba*, IV, 326, 11. 1-4.

92) See e.g. al-Wāqidī, *op. cit.*, pp. 785-788.

93) A. Guillaume, *The Life of Muhammad*, Oxford 1955 (reprint), p. 548; al-Fāsī, *Shifāʾ al-gharām*, Cairo 1956, II, 216.

94) See e.g. Ibn Ḥajar, *al-Iṣāba*, VI, 658 inf., no. 9271.

both before and after his conversion to Islam" [95]). The affection and sympathy of the Prophet is exposed in a prediction attributed to the Prophet about the events of the Day of Judgment: Abū Sufyān will expect the Prophet when he will return from the Presence of Allah and serve him with a drink from a glass of red sapphire saying: Drink, my friend [96]).

VI

The *qunūt*-invocation during prayer was the subject of heated discussions among the orthodox scholars. Some of them considered the *qunūt*-invocation abrogated by the verse of Sūra III, 128: ... "no part of the matter is thine"...; the Prophet used to curse some persons during the morning prayer and this practice is said to have been abrogated by this verse. Other scholars argued that the verse did not abrogate the *qunūt*-invocation; it merely stressed God's exclusive authority to decree on the fate of man [97]). A divergent tradition says that the Prophet merely intended to curse some wicked persons from among the unbelievers; after the revelation of the verse; ... "no part..." the Prophet invoked God in the style of (the invocations of) one of the prophets (i.e. Jesus—K): "God, forgive my people, because they do not know" (what they do—K) [98]). Some scholars tried to detach invocation from prayer by arguing that anything not grounded in the Qur'ān cannot be considered as part of the prayer [99]); it is not surprising to find some scholars who used to read certain chapters of the Qur'ān coupling the reading with supplications (...*kāna yaqnutu bi-arbaʿi āyātin*... or: *kāna yaqnutu bi-hātayni l-sūratayni*...) [100]).

The transition from the *qunūt* as practised by the Prophet after the massacre of the Muslim troop at Bi'r Maʿūna to one which was supplicatory in its form and content is vividly depicted in a tradition

95) Ibn ʿAsākir, *op. cit.*, VI, 405 ult.
96) Ibn ʿAsākir, *op. cit.*, VI, 406 sup.
97) Al-Naḥḥās, *op. cit.*, p. 91 sup.; al-Qurṭubī, *op. cit.*, IV, 200.
98) Al-Qurṭubī, *op. cit.*, IV, 199-200.
99) Al-Naḥḥās, *op. cit.*, p. 91.
100) See e.g. ʿAbd al-Razzāq, *op. cit.*, III, 114, no. 4978 and 116, no. 4983.

traced back to Khālid b. abī ʿImrān [101]). While the Prophet was making an invocation against Muḍar, the angel Jibrīl descended, bidding him be silent, ordered him to cease to curse Muḍar. The angel then taught him another *qunūt*, which contains elements of prayer, praise of God, supplication and expressions of submission to God [102]). It is in connection with this change in the meaning of *qunūt* that al-Suyūṭī found himself unable to answer the question whether the Prophet's invocation against some people during thirty days followed or preceded the (new--K) *qunūt* formula: *allāhumma hdinā*. . . [103]). Al-Ṭaḥāwī draws a clear line between *duʿā* and *qunūt*, commenting on the report that Abū Hurayra used to practise *qunūt* during the morning prayer. He argues that this account indicates that Abū Hurayra considered as abrogated the invocation (*duʿā*) against persons whom the Prophet cursed (*innamā kāna huwa l-duʿāʾa ʿalā man daʿā ʿalayhi rasūlu llāhi ṣallā llāhu ʿalayhi wa-sallam*), but considered as valid and obliging the *qunūt* linked with it [104]); *qunūt* is thus conceived here as supplication and this supplication, indeed, remained valid.

Some scholars stated by analogy with the *qunūt* that the invocation for a sneezing person during prayer is permissible; the blessing of a sneezer belongs to the type of blessing or curse practised by the Prophet during prayer and is therefore permissible [105])'

Certain reports seem to consider *qunūt* as an invocation against enemies, which the Prophet practised only for a number of days [106]), for

---

101) See on him Ibn Ḥajar, Tahdhīb al-tahdhīb, III, 110, no. 205.

102) Al-Qurṭubī, *op. cit.*, IV, 201; al-Bayhaqī, *al-Sunan*, II, 210 inf.; ... *baynā rasūlu llāhi* (*ṣ*) *yadʿū ʿalā muḍara idh jāʾahu jibrīlu fa-aumaʾa ilayhi an uskut fa-sakata, fa-qāla yā muḥammadu inna llāha lam yabʿathka sabbāban wa-lā laʿānan wa-innamā baʿathaka raḥmatan wa-lam yabʿathka ʿadhāban, laysa laka min al-amri shayʾun ... thumma ʿallamahu hādhā l-qunūta: allāhumma innā nastaʿīnuka wa-nastaghfiruka wa-nuʾminu bika wa-nakhḍaʿu laka wa-nakhlaʿu wa-natruku man yakfuruka, allāhumma iyyāka naʿbudu wa-laka nuṣallī*...

103) Al-Suyūṭī, *al-Ḥāwī li-l-fatāwī*, ed. Muḥammad Muḥyī l-Dīn ʿAbd al-Ḥamīd, Cairo 1959, I, 532 sup.

104) Al-Ṭaḥāwī, *Sharh maʿānī l-āthār*, I, 248.

105) Abū ʿĀṣim al-ʿAbbādī. *Ṭabaqāt al-fuqahāʾ al-shāfiʿiyya*, ed. G. Vitestam, Leiden 1964, p. 43.

106) ʿAbd al-Razzāq, *op. cit.*, III, 105, no. 4945.

twenty days[107]), directed against the rebelling tribes and which he later ceased to practise.[108]) Consequently traditions of this kind emphasize that the Caliphs who succeeded the Prophet did not utter the *qunūt* in their prayers[109]). But certain traditions in conflict with the former ones said that the Prophet continued to practise *qunūt* until he died[110]); these accounts should be interpreted as using *qunūt* in the sense of supplications, and not as invocations directed agaisnt specific people or as blessings addressed to specific individuals. A peculiar reason for the prohibition of *qunūt* as practised by the Prophet in the first period, when it was used to curse or bless individuals or groups is indicated in certain reports: it was considered odious to specify persons or groups in *qunūt* as done initially by the Prophet[111]). Another reason mentioned why the invocation in favour of the oppressed believers was discontinued was the fact that the oppressed believers manage to escape and reach Medina. During fifteen days (i.e. from the 15th of Ramaḍān until the Yaum al-Fiṭr) the Prophet made invocations for them[112]); after their arrival in Medina there was no more reason to do this[113]). Another interpretation says that the *qunūt*-invocation which

107) Al-Ṭaḥāwī, *Sharḥ maʿānī*, I, 244, 1.18, 247, 1.3 from bottom.

108) Al-Ṭaḥāwī, *Sharḥ maʿānī*, I, 244-245, 248; and see al-Dhahabī, *Mīzān al-iʿtidāl*, ed. ʿAlī Muḥammad al-Bijāwī, Cairo 1382/1963, II, 653, no. 5196 (the tradition *innamā qanata rasūlu llahi (ṣ) thalāthīna laylatan yadʿū ʿalā l-nāsi sammāhum* is marked as a *manākīr* tradition).

109) See e.g. ʿAbd al-Razzāq, *op. cit.*, III, 105-106, nos. 4946-4952; al-Ṭaḥāwī *Sharḥ maʿānī*, I, 246.

110) See e.g. al-Ṭaḥāwī, *Sharḥ maʿānī*, I, 243, 11. 15-17; al-Qurṭubī, *op. cit.*, IV, 201, 11. 14-15.

111) See e.g. ʿAbd al--Razzāq, *op. cit.*, II, 447 no. 4032, 454, no. 4058; al-Shaukāni, *Nayl* II, 389, 1.9; Maḥmūd Muḥammad Khaṭṭāb, *op. cit.*, VIII, 82, 11. 20-22; Ibn Abī Shayba, *op. cit.*, II, 317, 1.7; and see *ib.*, 441-442: *fī tasmiyati l-rajuli fī l-duʿā* (Abū l-Dardāʾ performed invocations for seventy of his brethren while prostrating in prayer; ʿAlī used to name the persons for whom he invoked after the prayer; al-Shaʿbī and al-Ḥasan were of the opinion that the invocation is left to the discretion of the believer in his prayer).

112) See Ibn Abī Shayba, *op. cit.*, II, 305-306; al-Ṭurṭūshī, *al-Ḥawādith wa-l-bidaʿ*, ed. M. Talbi, Tunis 1959, p. 56, 11. 4-6.

113) See al-Ṭaḥāwī, *Sharḥ al-maʿānī*, I, 242, 1.3; Maḥmūd Muḥammad Khaṭṭāb *op. cit.*, VIII, 82, 11. 14-15; cf. ʿAbd al-Razzāq, *op. cit.*, III, 121, no. 4996; and see

contained both curses and blessings became redundant when the oppressed believers managed to come to Medina while the unbelievers repented and embraced Islam [114]). The opinion that *qunūt* was abrogated in all the prayers of the day though retained in the morning prayer led to an unrestrained attack on al-Shāfiʿī, who championed it [115]). Some scholars considered *qunūt* in the morning prayer a *bidʿa* [116]) and we have lively discussions of the problem whether *qunūt* was to be practised after performing the prescribed *rakʿas* or before [117]), and whether the invocation was practised before and after the *rakʿas* [118]). According to some traditions the believers used to practise *qunūt* during the night-prayer of the 15th of Ramaḍān [119]). Some scholars recommend the qunūt during the whole year [120]).

Orthodox scholars tried to bridge between the two conflicting sets of traditions, the one reporting that the Prophet was followed by the Guided Caliphs, who used to practise *qunūt* until the day of their death, and the other, denying this practise to both the Prophet and the Guided Caliphs. The harmonizing interpretation said that the Prophet and the Guided Caliphs continued to practise the kind of *qunūt* which was a personal prayer in which they asked God for guidance and grace [121]). Several invocations traced back to the Prophet, Ubayy b. Kaʿb, ʿUmar and al-Ḥasan are moulded in this style [122]).

The early formulae of *qunūt* were revived again during the bloody

---

al-Ṭurṭūshī, *op. cit.*, p. 56, 11. 7-10 and p.57, 11. 8-15 (about the *qunūt* in the second half of Ramaḍān).

114) See e.g. al-Zurqānī, *op. cit.*, VII, 345, 11.g -20; al-Shaukānī, *Nayl*, II, 387: ... *thumma tarakahu lammā qadima man daʿā lahum wa-khaluṣū min al-asri wa-aslama man daʿā ʿalayhim wa-jāʾū tāʾibīna...*

115) Al-ʿAynī, *op. cit.*, VII, 22; cf. al-Ṭurṭūshī, *op. cit.*, p. 57, 11.2-3; and see al-Shāfiʿī, *op. cit.*, VII, 235, 285.

116) Al-ʿAynī, *op. cit.*, VII, 22, 1.3. from bottom, 23 ult.; cf. Abū Yūsuf, *Ikhtilāf Abī Ḥanīfa wa-Bni Abī Laylā*, ed. Abū l-Wafāʾ l-Afghānī, Cairo 1357, p. 111 ult.

117) Al-Ṭaḥāwī, *Sharḥ maʿānī*, I, 248; Abū Nuʿaym, *op. cit.*, IX, 19, 21.

118) See e.g. Abū Nuʿaym, *op. cit.*, IX, 33.

119) See al-Ṭurṭūshī, *op. cit.*, p. 56 ult.

120) See ʿAbd al-Razzāq, *op. cit.*, III, 121, 11. 2-3; al-Ṭurṭūshī, *op. cit.*, p. 57. 11. 1-2.

121) See e.g. al-Shaukānī, *op. cit.*, II, 387, 11. 15-20.

struggle between ʿAlī and Muʿāwiya. The two early scholars, ʿAlqama and al-Aswad [123]) stated that the Prophet used to practise *qunūt* only when he fought, and then he did so in all his prayers; Abū Bakr, ʿUmar and ʿUthmān did not practise *qunūt* until their death; ʿAlī started to practise invocation only when he fought Muʿāwiya and then he did so in all the prayers. The same thing was done by Muʿāwiya and they cursed each other (scil. in every prayer—K) [124]). ʿAlī's adherents probably disapproved of his invocation against Muʿāwiya, considering it perhaps as *bidʿa*; ʿAlī, trying to justify it, explains his *qunūt* as being merely an invocation for God's help against the enemy [125]). ʿAlī, says a report, did not practise *qunūt* as long as he stayed in the Arab peninsula; he started to practise it when he moved to ʿIrāq [126]). ʿAlī is said to have invoked against Muʿāwiya cursing him for forty days; he did it in imitation of the *qunūt* of the Prophet [127]). Another account, recorded on the authority of Abū Mikhnaf, specifies the names of the persons against whom ʿAlī invoked: Muʿāwiya, ʿAmr (b. al-ʿĀṣ), Abū l-Aʿwar al-Sulamī, Ḥabib b. Maslama, ʿAbd al-Raḥmān b. Khālid (b. al-Walīd) and al-Walīd b. ʿUqba; Muʿāwiya retaliated cursing in his *qunūt* ʿAlī, Ḥasan, Ḥusayn, Ibn ʿAbbās and al-Ashtar [128]). The question whether it is permissible to curse the

122) See e.g. ʿAbd al-Razzāq, *op. cit.*, III, 108, no. 4957, 110, no. 4968-4969, 114, no. 4978, 116, nos. 4982-4983.

123) See on them Ibn Ḥajar, *Tahdhīb al-tahdhīb*, VII, 276, no. 484, I, 342, no. 6251.

124) ʿAbd al-Razzāq, *op. cit.*, III, 107, n . 4953; Muḥmūd Muḥammad Khaṭṭāb, *op. cit.*, VIII, 85, 11. 4-8; Abū Yūsuf, *Kitāb al-āthār*, ed. Abū l-Wafā, Cairo 1355, p. 71, no. 352; idem, *Ikhtilāf*, pp. 111 inf—112, 1.1.

125) Ibn Abī Shayba, *op. cit.*, II, 310, 11, 6-8.

126) Al-Shaukānī, *op. cit.*, II, 385; Ibn Abī Shayba, *op. cit.*, II, 311.

127) Ibn ʿAsākir, *Taʾrīkh*, Ms. Ẓāhiriyya, IX, fol. 128a (for the invocation during fourty days cf. Abū Yūsuf, *Ikhtilāf*, p. 112, note 1, 1.7).

128) Ibn Junghul, *op. cit.*, II, fol. 185b: ... *wa-dhakara abū mikhnafin anna ʿaliyyan lammā balaghahu mā faʿala ʿamrun kāna yalʿanu fī qunūtihi muʿāwiyata wa-ʿamran wa-abā aʿwara l-sulamiyya wa-ḥabība bna maslamata wa-ʿabda l-raḥmāni bna khālidin wa-l-walīda bna ʿuqbata, fa-lammā balagha dhālika muʿāwiyata kāna ayḍan yalʿanu fī qunūtihi ʿaliyyan wa-ḥusaynan wa-bna ʿabbāsin wa-l-ashtara*; and see another Shīʿī *qunūt*: al-Majlisī, *op. cit.*, XXII, 128, no. 101; and see e.g. the formula of Muʿāwiya's invocation against ʿAlī: Muḥammad b. ʿAqīl al-ʿAlawī l-Ḥusaynī, *al-Naṣāʾiḥ al-kāfiya li-man yatawallā muʿāwiya*, Najaf 1386/1966, pp. 86 inf.—87, 95-97.

Companions of the Prophet became subject of extensive discussions in Shīʿī compilations [129]).

In the second half of the second century there were still heated discussions as to whether the *qunūt*-invocation is permitted during prayer, in which part of the prayer it may be uttered and during which of the prayers the invocation may be performed [130]). In some circles the *qunūt* was even considered as a kind of a voluntary private invocation and a scholar could remark that he disliked *qunūt* as an established formula of invocation [131]). The legitimacy of the *qunūt* as a private invocation during the formal prayer is seen in a tradition reported on the authority of ʿĀʾisha. The Prophet, making an invocation in the morning prayer before performing of the *rakʿa*, said: "I merely invoke in front of you in order that you invoke (your) God and ask Him to grant you your needs" [132]). The *qunūt* in fact changed during the following centuries to become a supplication during calamities and disasters and a private invocation of the believer in which he implored God to fulfil his wishes and to give success to himself and his kindred.

The scrutiny of the traditions about the invocation against Muḍar has helped us to lineate the changes which the perception of this invocation underwent in the Muslim community against the background of the Prophet's struggle with the unbelievers of Quraysh and of the later discussions between the factions of the nascent Muslim Empire at the time of ʿAlī and Muʿāwiya. In later centuries it turned into a private supplication for guidance and success.

The scrutiny of this material gives us a clue for a better assessment

---

129) Cf. e.g. Ṣadr al-Dīn ʿAlī Khān -al-Shīrāzī, *al-Darajāt al-rafīʿa fī ṭabaqāt al-shīʿa*, Najaf 1381/1962, pp. 11-20.

130) See e.g. ʿAbd al-Razzāq, *op. cit.*, II, 448-449, nos. 4033-4035, 4039-4041

131) Abū Yūsuf, *al-Āthār*, p. 70, no. 348: *akrahu an ajʿala fī l-qunūti duʿāʾan maʿlūman.*

132) Hishām b. ʿUrwa, *Juzʾ fīhi min ʿawālī ḥadīthi hishāmi bni ʿurwata*, Ms. Ẓāhiriyya, majmūʾa 61, fol. 188a: ... *innamā aqnutu bikum li-tadʿū rabbakum wa-tasʾalūhu ḥawāʾijakum.*

of the economic pressure carried out on the Prophet's order against the unbelievers of Mecca by cutting off their food supplies from the Yāmama and by the raids on the Muḍar tribal groups allied with Mecca. Under this pressure Abū Sufyān, convinced that Mecca could not stand against the growing forces of the Prophet, decided to enter into peaceful co-operation with the Prophet and to initiate a commercial exchange of goods. Abū Sufyān's change of attitude towards the Prophet explains why he accepted the money sent by the Prophet, why he refrained from aiding the Qurashī attack against Khuzāʿa (the allies of the Prophet), why he consented to the marriage of his daughter to the Prophet and why he went out to Medina to intercede with the Prophet on behalf of Quraysh. Only in the light of these events does one get an insight into the privileges and concessions granted him and his family by the Prophet: safety for all who entered his court on the day of the conquest of Mecca, the missions and offices with which he was entrusted by the Prophet and the appointment of Muʿāwiya as the secretary of the Prophet. It is significant that the Muslim community accepted the decisions of the Prophet without reservation and Abū Sufyān regained his leading position in the Muslim society. His sons were appointed by Abū Bakr, ʿUmar and ʿUthmān and hold high positions in the Muslim state. Muʿāwiya, the son of the leader of the Muḍar alliance, became the founder of the Umayyad dynasty which held sway over the Muslim Empire for a very long time.

VIII

THE MASSACRE OF THE BANŪ QURAYẒA
A re-examination of a tradition

The story of the massacre of the Banū Qurayẓa (April 627 A.D./Dhū l-Qaᶜda 5 A.H.),[1] as recorded in various compilations of the *Sīra*-literature, is concerned with the final blow which the prophet Muḥammad struck at the last Jewish tribal group in Medina.

According to the widely current tradition, transmitted by the early Muslim scholars of *ḥadīth*, biographers of the Prophet, jurists and historians, Qurayẓa are said to have concluded a pact with the Prophet in which they committed themselves not to help the enemies of the Prophet. But when the enemies of the Prophet (i.e. the Confederates, Quraysh and their Allies, the Aḥzāb – K.) besieged Medina the Banū Qurayẓa are alleged to have aided the forces of the Prophet's enemies, the Aḥzāb. Ḥuyayy b. Akhṭab, a former leader of the exiled Jewish tribe of the Banū Naḍīr is blamed for having instigated Kaᶜb b. Asad, the leader of Qurayẓa, to violate the agreement with the Prophet and for having pressed him to negotiate with the leaders of the Aḥzāb. The Prophet succeeded by stratagem to undermine the mutual confidence between Qurayẓa and the Aḥzāb and to spoil their strategic plans against him and against the Muslim community at Medina. The failure of the siege of Medina by the Aḥzāb and their disordered and hasty retreat marked a manifest victory for the Prophet and left Qurayẓa in a precarious position, facing the forces of the Prophet in isolation.

Immediately after the withdrawal of the Aḥzāb the Prophet was actually summoned by the angel Jibrīl to march out against the Banū Qurayẓa. The siege laid by the forces of the Prophet on the stronghold of Qurayẓa brought about a deterioration of the situation of the besieged shortly afterwards. Their leader, Kaᶜb b. Asad put forward three proposals as solution: (*a*) that they should convert to Islam, (*b*) that they should kill the women and children and march out from the stronghold to fight courageously the besieging force of the Muslims, or (*c*) that they should

[1] See J.M.B. Jones, The Chronology of the Maghāzī, *BSOAS* XIX, 1957, pp. 274, 251.

surprise Muḥammad and his troops by a speedy and unexpected attack on the eve of Saturday. All the proposals were, however, rejected by the Banū Qurayẓa.

When the situation deteriorated Qurayẓa sent their messenger to negotiate with the Prophet the terms of their surrender. They proposed to surrender and depart leaving behind their land and property and taking with them movable property only, the load of a camel per person. When this proposal was rejected, the messenger returned asking that Qurayẓa be permitted to depart without any property, taking with them only their families; but this proposal too was rejected and the Prophet insisted that they surrender unconditionally and subject themselves to his judgment. Qurayẓa asked for Abū Lubāba, a Companion of the Prophet whom they trusted, to be sent to them in order to have his advice. Abū Lubāba indiscreetly pointed with his hand to his throat, a movement which clearly conveyed slaughter; he regretted his treason towards God and the Prophet, repented and the Prophet was glad to convey to him the joyous tiding of God's forgiveness, as it was revealed to him.

The Banū Qurayẓa, compelled to surrender, descended from their stronghold and were led to Medina. The men, their hands pinioned behind their backs, were put in a court (*dār*) in Medina; the women and children are said to have been put in another one. When the Prophet was asked by people of Aus, who were allies of Qurayẓa, to show leniency towards their allies the Qurayẓa, he proposed to appoint as arbiter a man from Aus, Saᶜd b. Muᶜādh. Qurayẓa consented and so did the attending Muslims; among the Muslims were, of course, the Aus who in turn began to intercede with Saᶜd for Qurayẓa; Saᶜd's harsh answer was a bad omen for the fate of Qurayẓa. When all the parties agreed to abide by the judgment of Saᶜd he gave his concise verdict: the men shall be put to death, the women and children sold into slavery, the spoils divided among the Muslims. The Prophet ratified the judgment and stated that Saᶜd's decree had been issued as a decree of God pronounced from above the Seven Heavens. Accordingly some 400 (or 600, or 700, or 800, or even 900) men from Qurayẓa were led on the order of the Prophet to the market of Medina; trenches were dug in the place, the men were executed and buried in the trenches. The Prophet attended the executions, which were carried out by ᶜAlī and al-Zubayr. Youths who had not reached maturity were spared. Women and children were sold into slavery; a number of them were distributed as gifts among the Companions.

The story of the massacre of Qurayẓa, of which a short summary has been given above, was thoroughly studied and analysed by several western scholars, who severely criticized the Prophet for it.[2] Although not unanimous in their assessment of certain details of the story, the scholars are in agreement concerning the cruelty of the judgment of Saᶜd b. Muᶜādh. Some Muslim scholars didn't deny the merciless character of Saᶜd's judgment, but justified it pointing out that the Banū Qurayẓa had yielded to the treacherous activities of Ḥuyayy b. Akhṭab and had committed deeds of treason. Saᶜd's decree, although severe and harsh, was a vital necessity as he regarded the fate of the Jews as a question of life and death for the Muslim community. The responsibility for the killing of Qurayẓa should be placed on Ḥuyayy b. Akhṭab who instigated the war-activities against the Prophet.[3]

[2] See e.g. Martin Hartmann, *Der Islam*, Leipzig 1909, p. 16: "Ein ewiges Schandmal bleibt die Ruchlosigkeit mit der Muhammed gegen den Stamm Quraiẓa verfuhr: 600 Männer erlitten den Tod durch Henkershand, die Weiber und Kinder wurden verkauft." W. Muir, *Mahomet and Islam*, London 1895, p. 151: "The massacre of Banu Coreitza was a barbarous deed which cannot be justified by any reason of political necessity..." "But the indiscriminate slaughter of the whole tribe cannot be recognized otherwise than as an act of monstrous cruelty, which casts an indelible blot upon the Prophet's name..." J. Andrae, *Mohammed, Sein Leben und sein Glaube*, Göttingen 1932, p. 126: "Es war der letzte Jundenstamm in Medina, Banū Kuraiza, den er nun exemplarisch zu strafen beschloss wegen der Unzuverlässigkeit, die er während der Belagerung gezeigt hatte. Bei dieser Gelegenheit zeigte er wieder den Mangel an Ehrlichkeit und moralischem Mut, der einen weniger sympathischen Zug seines Charakters bildete..." F. Buhl, *Das Leben Muhammeds*, Transl. H.H. Schaeder, Heidelberg 1955, p. 275: "... Diesmal war Muhammad jedoch zu erbittert um Schonung zu gewähren: aber die Art wie er seinen Willen durschsetzte, hatte etwas in hohem Grade Raffiniertes und zeigt wieder seinen Charakter in einem sehr abstossenden Licht..." M. Gaudefroy-Demombynes, *Mahomet*, Paris 1969, p. 145: "L'incident des B. Qoraïza est une vilaine page de l'histoire de Mohammed, mais c'est un acte qui fut tres profitable à la gloire d'Allah et de son prophète..." W. Montgomery Watt, *Muḥammad at Medina*, Oxford, 1956, p. 214: "Some European writers have criticized this sentence for what they call its savage and inhuman character..." Maxime Rodinson, *Mohammed*, New York 1974, p. 213: "It is not easy to judge the massacre of the Qurayẓa. It must be remembered that the customs of the time were extremely primitive..." F. Gabrieli, *Muhammad and the Conquest of Islam*, London 1968, p. 73: "This dark episode, which Muslim tradition, it must be said, takes quite calmly, has provoked lively discussion among western biographers of Muḥammed, with caustic accusations on the one hand and legalistic excuses on the other... In this case he was ruthless, with the approval of his conscience and of his God, for the two were one; we can only record the fact, while reaffirming our consciousness as Christians and civilised men, that this God or at least this aspect of Him, is not ours."

[3] Muḥammad Ḥusayn Haykal, *Ḥayāt Muḥammad*, Cairo 1358, p. 321. And see e.g. Ḥāfiẓ Ghulām Sarwar, *Muḥammad the Holy Prophet*, Lahore 1967, p. 247: "No one can dispute the justice of the sentence on the Quraiẓa... Traitors are always executed unless they ask pardon and circumstances justify the pardon being granted... Muḥammad was absolutely

I

Odd assumptions appear in W.N. Arafat's article on this subject.[4] Arafat tries to prove the unreliability of the account of the events of the massacre of Qurayẓa as recorded by Ibn Isḥāq (d. 151 A.H.) and transmitted by later Muslim scholars, historians and biographers of the Prophet. The later historians "draw, and in most cases depend on Ibn Isḥāq", states Arafat and comments: "But Ibn Isḥāq died in 151 A.H., i.e., 145 years after the event in question".[5] Arafat's severe criticism refers first of all to the way in which Ibn Isḥāq collected his information: his sources were untrustworthy, uncertain and late; his account is in Arafat's opinion "a sum-total of the collective reports, pieced together". Arafat quotes thrice the opinion of Mālik b. Anas (from Ibn Sayyid al-Nās, *ᶜUyūn al-athar*) about Muḥammad b. Isḥāq: "he was a liar", "an impostor" who "transmits his stories from the Jews"[6] and stresses twice that "against the late and uncertain sources on the one hand, and the condemning authorities on the other must be set the only contemporary and entirely authentic source, The Qur'ān." (Sūra XXXIII, 26: "He caused those of the People of the Book who helped them (i.e. the Quraysh) to come out of their forts. Some you killed, some you took prisoner." [as quoted by Arafat]).[7] If 600 or 700 people were killed there would have been a clearer reference to it in the Qur'ān; as only the guilty leaders were executed the reference in the Qur'ān is very brief – argues Arafat. He rejects without hesitation the widely circulated story about the massacre of the Banū Qurayẓa and reiterates his argument: the verse of the Qur'ān indicates clearly that only those men of Qurayẓa who were actually fighting were

free from blame. The real culprit in this tragedy, for it was a most horrible tragedy... was Ḥuyayy b. Akhṭab..." Ameer Alī, *A short history of the Saracens*, London 1961, p. 13: "It was considered unsafe to leave the traitorous Banū Koraiza so near the city, as their treachery might at any moment lead to the destruction of Medina... This was a severe punishment according to our ideas, but it was customary according to the rules of war then prevalent." Muḥammad Ḥamidullāh, *Muslim Conduct of State*, Lahore 1961, §443: "...The females and children of the Jewish tribe of Banū Quraiẓah were, by the decision of the arbitrator nominated by themselves, enslaved and distributed as booty. This arbitral award was in conformity with the Jewish personal law..."; §497: "...In the case of the Banū Quraiẓah, it was the arbitrator of their own choice who awarded exactly what Deuteronomy provided..."

[4] W.N. Arafat, "New Light on the Story of Banū Qurayza and the Jews of Medina," *JRAS* (1976), 100-107.

[5] Arafat, *op. cit.*, pp. 101, ll. 1-2.

[6] Arafat, *op. cit.*, pp. 101, l. 8, 102 ult. -103 l.1, 106 ll. 2-3.

[7] Arafat, *op. cit.*, pp. 101 l. 20, 103 ll. 11-15.

executed; according to the rule of Islam only those responsible for the sedition were punished. Killing a large number of people is opposed to the Islamic sense of justice and the Qur'ānic rule regarding prisoners, argues Arafat. Why should the Qurayẓa have been slaughtered, asks Arafat, while other Jewish groups which surrendered both before and after the Banū Qurayẓa were treated leniently and were allowed to go. If so many hundreds of people were indeed put to death in the market-place and trenches were dug for the operation, why, asks Arafat, is there no trace of all that and no sign or word to point to the place? "Had this slaughter actually happened", contends Arafat, "the jurists would have adopted it as a precedent"; "in fact exactly the opposite had been the case" – asserts Arafat. Arafat stresses further that the details of the story imply inside knowledge, i.e. from the Jews themselves. Both the descendants of the Banū Qurayẓa and the descendants of the Medinan Muslims were eager to glorify their ancestors; it was one of the descendants of Saᶜd b. Muᶜādh who transmitted the judgment of Saᶜd and the saying of the Prophet to Saᶜd: "You have pronounced God's judgment upon them [as inspired] through Seven Veils".[8] Finally Arafat raises some additional questions: how could many hundreds of persons be incarcerated in a house belonging to a woman of the Banū l-Najjār, and how can one explain the fact that some Jews are mentioned as remaining in Medina after the alleged expulsion of all the Jewish tribes?

Arafat draws a comparison between the story of Masada as recorded by Josephus Flavius and the story of the Banū Qurayẓa. Arafat's conclusions are surprising: the descendants of the Jews who fled to Arabia after the Jewish wars superimposed details of the siege of Masada on the story of the siege of the Banū Qurayẓa. According to Arafat, the mixture provided the basis for Ibn Isḥāq's story.

Arafat's article was followed by another one by a certain Zaid. In his article entitled "The Masada Legend in Jewish and Islamic Tradition"[9] the author reiterates Arafat's arguments, arrives at the same con-

[8] Arafat's rendering of this sentence is erroneous: *min fauqi sabᶜati arqiᶜatin* does not mean "Seven Veils". Guillaume translates: "You have given the judgment of Allah above the seven heavens." Montgomery Watt, "The Condemnation of the Jews of Banu Qurayẓah", *MW* 42 (1952), p. 163: "You have judged their case with the judgment of God from above seven heavens."

[9] *IQ*, vols. XX-XXII (1978), 94-103.

clusions and does not add any genuine opinion of his own. It seems thus that this article does not deserve any comment.

The daring assumptions put forth by Arafat and summarized above ought to be investigated. Data about the events surrounding the massacre of Banū Qurayẓa should be re-examined and certain traditions analysed and re-assessed.

II

Four of Arafat's twelve arguments are of particular importance and have in fact a common denominator: the data of the story of Qurayẓa stand, according to Arafat, in contradiction to Muslim rules, Muslim law, Muslim justice and Qur'ānic principles. The rule in Islam, says Arafat, is to punish only those who are responsible for sedition (argument no. 2); killing such a large number of people is diametrically opposed to the Islamic sense of justice and to the basic principles laid down in the Qur'ān (argument no. 3); the slaughter of prisoners is against the Qur'ānic rule which orders that they either be granted their freedom or else be allowed to be ransomed (argument no. 4); had this slaughter actually happened, maintains Arafat, jurists would have adopted it as a precedent; in fact exactly the opposite has happened (argument no. 7). In order to strengthen arguments nos. 3 and 7, Arafat quotes Qur'ān XXXV, 18: *"No soul shall bear another's burden."* If these four arguments put forward by Arafat are valid and sound – they would prove convincingly that the reports about Saᶜd b. Muᶜādh's judgment, its approval by the Prophet and the cruel massacre of the Banū Qurayẓa are all ficticious. If Arafat's arguments are true, then indeed no Muslim jurist could have based his judgment on an account totally alien to the spirit of Muslim law and contrary to Muslim justice and Muslim ethics.

Arafat's arguments are however unfounded, his conclusions incorrect and his opinion about *Sīra* tradition is misappreciative. Muslim jurists were well acquainted with the story of the Banū Qurayẓa and based themselves in their judgments and decrees on the account of the massacre. It was in fact al-Shāfiᶜī (d. 204 A.H.) who with deep insight analysed the case of Banū Qurayẓa, defined the nature of their mischievous actions, assessed the character of the transgression committed by them and elucidated the problem of individual and collective punishment. In a passage entitled "Violation of an agreement" (*naqḍu l-ᶜahdi*) Shāfiᶜī says:

If the Imām concludes with a people an agreement of non-agression (*wādaᶜa* – K.) for a (certain) period or he receives from a people *jizya* and the person or persons who concluded the agreement of *muwādaᶜa* or of the *jizya* on behalf of the people belong to that people we shall not oblige them (i.e. those who concluded the agreement, scil. to carry out the stipulations of the agreement – K.) until we know that those who remained (i.e. the people who stayed in their abode while their leaders concluded the agreement – K.) approved of it and were satisfied with it (*ḥattā naᶜlama anna man baqiya minhum qad aqarra bi-dhālika wa-raḍiyahu*). If this is so, no one from among the Muslims is permitted to take from them (anything – K.) of their property or [harm them in their] body (literally: *wa-daman*, "of their blood"); if a Muslim commits it (a mischievous deed of this kind – K.) he has to be indicted for what he spent (from the property which he took unjustly) as long as the people (who concluded the agreement – K.) remain upright. If those who concluded the agreement violate it, or if a group from among them violate it and the people (who concluded the treaty – K.) do not oppose the violators by an open action or word (*wa-lam yukhālifū al-nāqiḍ bi-qaulin au fiᶜlin ẓāhirin*) before they (i.e. the righteous - K.) come to the Imām or leave the territory (in which the violators stay - K.) and inform the Imām that they are continuing to adhere to the agreement (*innā ᶜalā ṣulḥinā*); or if the violators go out to fight the Muslims or to fight the people under their protection (i.e. under the protection of the Muslims, *ahl dhimmat li-l-muslimīn*) and aid thus the fighting men (i.e. of the enemy - K.) or help (the forces - K.) fighting them (i.e. those who fight the Muslims - K.) then the Imām is entitled to raid them. If he does it and there is nobody of the people (who opposed the violators - K.) who would (leave their abode - K.) and come out to the Imām - it is up to the Imām to (order to - K.) kill their fighting men (*qatlu muqātilatihim*), to enslave their progeny and to take their property as booty, whether they be in the *dār al-islām* or in the territory of of the enemy. So the Prophet acted in the case of the Banū Qurayẓa: he concluded with their leader an agreement of reconciliation on the basis of a truce (*al-ṣulḥ bi-l-muhādana*) and (their leader) violated it; but they did not abandon him (*wa-lam yufāriqūhu*). The Prophet then went out to fight them in their own abode which was in the extreme part of Medina (*wa-hiya maᶜahu bi-ṭarafi l-madīna*) and killed their fighting men (*fa-qatala muqātilatahum*) and captured their property as booty; and (that while - K.) not all of them took part in aiding (scil. the Aḥzāb - K.) against the Prophet and his Companions, but all of them remained in their stronghold and did not abandon the treacherous people from among them, except a small party (*nafar*) and this (action) saved their lives and kept their possessions in their hands.[10]

[10] Al-Shāfiᶜī, *al-Umm*, n.p. 1321 (repr. Kitāb al-shaᶜb 1388 (1968) IV, 107).

It is evident that according to the judgment of al-Shāfiʿī the Muslim law enjoins punishing people who were not responsible for breaking the agreement, but who merely remained passive in the territory occupied by the transgressors; this rule contradicts Arafat's argument no. 2. It is obvious that people who do not revolt against their iniquitous leaders and join the righteous party (i.e. the Muslim community – K.) may be put to death by order of the Imām; this is in fact contrary to Arafat's argument no. 3. It is apparent that the Banū Qurayẓa who surrendered did not enjoy the status of prisoners of war; this is, of course, contrary to Arafat's argument no. 4. Al-Shāfiʿī considered the report about the slaughter of the Banū Qurayẓa reliable and sound and he based his judgment on it; this contradicts Arafat's argument no. 7.

In order to reinforce his argument that Muslim jurists did not adopt the case of Banū Qurayẓa as a precedent and championed ideas totally opposed to those reflected in the story of the slaughter of the Banū Qurayẓa, Arafat quotes a judgment of al-Auzāʿī as recorded in Abū ʿUbayd's *Amwāl*. But Arafat seems to have been unaware of the fact that it was the selfsame Abū ʿUbayd al-Qāsim b. Sallām (d. 224 A.H.) who in his *Amwāl* recorded carefully the traditions about the "Day of Qurayẓa" with their *isnāds* and attached his own valuable legal comments. Abū ʿUbayd records the tradition about the execution of Ḥuyayy b. Akhṭab: Ḥuyayy concluded a treaty (*ʿāhada*) with the Prophet committing himself not to aid anybody against the Prophet. On the "Day of the Banū Qurayẓa" he was captured and brought into the presence of the Prophet. The Prophet ordered that he and his son be killed. Abū ʿUbayd comments:

> The Prophet declared the shedding of the blood of Qurayẓa lawful because they extended their help against him (*li-muẓāharatihim*) to the Aḥzāb, after they had concluded a treaty with him. The Prophet considered it a violation of their treaty (*fa-ra'ā dhālika nakthan li-ʿahdihim*) although they did not kill anyone of his Companions (*wa-in kānū lam yaqtulū min aṣḥābihi aḥadan*). A verse concerning this was revealed in *Sūrat al-Aḥzāb (wa-nazala bi-dhālika l-qur'ān fī sūrati 'l-aḥzāb)*.[11]

Arafat did not realize that the widely circulated traditions about the massacre of the Banū Qurayẓa (the report about the appearance of Ji-

[11] Abū ʿUbayd, *Kitāb al-amwāl*, ed. Muḥammad Ḥāmid al-Fiqī, Cairo.

brīl, the siege, the judgment of Saᶜd b. Muᶜādh and details about the numbers of the killed) were recorded by Abū ᶜUbayd;[12] it is precisely the material discussed by Arafat in his article and it clearly contradicts his assumptions; the contents of the reports are almost identical with those of the *Sīra* of Ibn Isḥāq, the *isnāds* are different and Abū ᶜUbayd, the great Muslim jurist, records those traditions as precedents as regards Muslim jurisdiction.

Another eminent Muslim jurist, al-Māwardī (d. 450 A.H.), elucidates the slaughter of the Banū Qurayẓa from a quite different aspect: it was a religious duty incumbent on the Prophet to order the slaughter of the Banū Qurayẓa. Al-Māwardī emphasizes, among the other virtues of the Prophet, his leniency, kindness and his disposition to forgive his enemies their sins. He then continues as follows:[13]

> If it is argued: "He struck the heads of the Banū Qurayẓa deliberately during one day (*fa-in qīla: fa-qad ḍaraba riqāba banī qurayẓata ṣabran fī yaumin wāḥidin*), their number being about seven hundred, so where is his disposition to forgive and pardon? After all he retaliated like a man who was not inclined towards them by mercy, nor had in his soul softness for them", the answer would be: " He merely did it in order to carry out the rules of God (incumbent upon him) (. . . *qīla: innamā faᶜala dhālika fī ḥuqūqi llāhi taᶜālā*). The Banū Qurayẓa had consented to Saᶜd b. Muᶜādh's arbitration in their case and he judged that those on whom the razors passed (i.e. those who reached puberty – K.)[14] should be killed; those on whom the razors did not pass should be enslaved". Then the Prophet said: "This is God's judgment (issued – K.) from above the seven heavens". Therefore it was not permitted (the Prophet – K.) to forgive (in a case of) God's injunction incumbent upon them; he could merely forgive (transgressions, offences etc. – K.) in matters concerning his own person (*fa-lam yajuz an yaᶜfuwa ᶜan ḥaqqin wajaba llāhu taᶜālā ᶜalayhim, wa-innamā yakhtaṣṣu ᶜafwuhu bi-ḥaqqi nafsihi*).

It is thus obvious that the slaughter of the Banū Qurayẓa and the execution of those among them who had reached puberty was carried out ac-

[12] *Al-Amwāl*, pp. 129-130 (nos. 346-350), 167 (nos. 460-463).

[13] Al-Māwardī, *Aᶜlām al-nubuwwa*, Cairo 1319, pp. 146-147.

[14] See the different versions: Barakat Ahmad, *Muḥammad and the Jews*, New Delhi 1979, pp. 81-82.

cording to the order of God revealed to the Prophet. Al-Māwardī's opinion apparently reflects the current Sunnī view about the slaughter of the Banū Qurayẓa.

The report about the presence of the Prophet at the execution of the captives of Qurayẓa is fully confirmed by the great Muslim scholar Ibn Ḥazm (d. 456 A.H.):[14a] "It is impossible (to assume – K.) that people could have been killed in the presence of the Prophet, while he would not know whether the execution was right or not. A Muslim can never assume this, as the Qurayẓa people were killed in his presence and at his order. (*Qāla abū muḥammadin: wa-mina l-muḥāli l-mumtaniᶜi an tuqtala l-nāsu bi-ḥaḍrati l-nabiyyi ṣallā llāhu ᶜalayhi wa-sallama, wa-huwa lā yaᶜlamu a-bi-ḥaqqin am bi-bāṭilin; hādhā mā lā yaẓunnuhu muslimunu l-battata. wa-qatlā qurayẓata qutilū bi-ḥaḍrati l-nabiyyi (ṣ) wa-bi-amrihi.)*

One of Arafat's arguments for the rejection of the story of the Banū Qurayẓa (argument no. 5) is that "it is unlikely that the Banū Qurayẓa should be slaughtered when the other Jewish groups who surrendered *before* Banū Qurayẓa and *after* them were treated leniently and allowed to go." The answer is plainly given by Ibn Qayyim al-Jauziyya. He mentions the expulsion of the Qaynuqāᶜ and the Naḍīr, and the confiscation of their possessions and states:

> As to Qurayẓa, they were the strongest among the Jews in their hatred of the Prophet and the most persistent in their unbelief; therefore their fate differed from that of their brethren. (*wa-ammā qurayẓatu fa-kānat ashadda l-yahūdi ᶜadāwatan li-rasūli llāhi (ṣ) wa-aghlaẓahum kufran wa-li-dhālika jarā ᶜalayhim mā lam yajri ᶜalā ikhwānihim.*)[15]

Since Arafat quotes in his article this compilation of Ibn Qayyim al-Jauziyya, it is odd indeed that he should have overlooked this passage.

In order to strengthen his argument that the Prophet was lenient towards Jewish tribes, groups and clans Arafat mentions the case of the clan of Abū l-Ḥuqayq: when the Prophet conquered Khaybar he promised the Jews of this locality safety (*amān*) on condition that they handed him over everything (of value – K.) in the stronghold. The utterance

[14a] Ibn Ḥazm, *al-Iḥkām fī uṣūli l-aḥkām*, ed. Muḥammad Aḥmad ᶜAbd al-ᶜAzīz, Cairo 1398/1978, V-VIII, 897 inf.

[15] Ibn Qayyim al-Jauziyya, *Zād al-maᶜād fī hadyi khayri l-ᶜibād*, Beirut n.d., II , 72, ll. 6-7.

of the Prophet quoted by Arafat [16] indicates that in spite of the hostility of the clan of Abū l-Ḥuqayq he would grant them safety, as he had granted their brethren, if they would hand him over all their property. In fact a treasure belonging to the Banū l-Ḥuqayq was detected. The Prophet then ordered to torture one of the sons of Abū l-Ḥuqayq and to kill the others. The women and children of the executed sons of Abū l-Ḥuqayq were enslaved, and their property confiscated.[17] The attitude of the Prophet towards the clan of Abū l-Ḥuqayq can hardly be described as lenient although the Prophet's order can formally be justified: as one of the sons of Abū l-Ḥuqayq did not disclose the place of the family's treasure he thereby violated the terms of the surrender; this was considered a violation of an agreement and the Prophet was entitled to have him put to death.[18] It may be worthwhile to remark that Kināna b. Abī l-Ḥuqayq, whom the Prophet ordered to torture and who was executed after the torture by al-Zubayr, was the husband of the captured woman Ṣafiyya whom the Prophet married on the night of her husband's execution. Ḥuyayy b. Akhṭab, killed by order of the Prophet during the massacre of the Banū Qurayẓa, was Ṣafiyya's father.[19]

The legal basis for the torture, the execution and the confiscation of the property of the Banū l-Ḥuqayq is plainly outlined in one of the earliest compilations of Muslim law, the *Siyar* of al-Shaybānī (d. 189 A.H.).[20] The case of the clan of Abū l-Ḥuqayq is related in a special chapter entitled: "Safety (granted) on condition" (*al-amān ᶜalā l-sharṭ*). Al-Shaybānī concludes that if the enemy is conditionally granted safety by the Muslims and then acts treacherously or conceals from them the object (scil. which was to be handed over under the terms of the agreement – K.) the *imām* is permitted to kill the enemy.[21] Al-Sarakhsī

[16] Arafat, *op. cit.*, p. 104, argument no. 5.

[17] See Abū ᶜUbayd, *op. cit.*, pp. 165-166 (nos. 457-459); Ibn Qayyim al-Jauziyya, *op. cit.*, II, 76-77; al-Ṭabarī, *Ta'rīkh*, ed. Muḥammad Abū l-Faḍl Ibrāhīm, Cairo 1969, III, 14; al-Balādhurī, *Futūḥ al-buldān*, ed. ᶜAbdallah and ᶜUmar al-Ṭabbāᶜ, Beirut 1377/1957, 34-35; al-Wāqidī, *al-Maghāzī*, ed. Marsden Jones, London 1966, pp. 672-673.

[18] Abū ᶜUbayd, *op. cit.*, p. 168, no. 463: "...*fa-hādhā mā kāna min nakthi banī qurayẓata wa-bihi staḥalla rasūlu llāhi (ṣ) dimā'ahum; wa-kadhālika ālu abī l-ḥuqayqi, ra'ā kitmānahum iyyāhu mā sharaṭū lahu an lā yaktumūhu nakthan.*"

[19] See e.g. Ibn Ḥajar, *al-Iṣāba fī tamyīzi l-ṣaḥāba*, ed. ᶜAlī Muḥammad al-Bijāwī, Cairo 1392/1972, VII, 738-742, no. 11401.

[20] Muḥammad b. al-Ḥasan al-Shaybānī, *Kitāb al-siyar al-kabīr*, ed. Ṣalāḥ al-Dīn al-Munajjid, Cairo 1957, I, 278-282.

[21] Al-Shaybānī, *op. cit.*, I, 278.

raises in his comment the question whether the Prophet issued this order of torture before or after he had uttered the prohibition of torture.[22]

The killing of the captured fighting men of the enemy is explicitly permitted. Al-Shaybānī records the case of the Banū Qurayẓa as a convincing precedent: they were put to death on the order of the Prophet after they had been captured and after hostilities had ceased.[23] The problem discussed concerns the permissiblity of killing the captured enemy while his hands are tied. Al-Shaybānī decrees that it is preferable to execute the captured enemy with his hands free; but if there is a danger that he may escape or kill a Muslim, he has to be executed with his hands tied.[24] al-Shaybānī emphasizes that the suffering of the captured ought to be alleviated by providing them with food and water; here, too, al-Shaybānī has recourse to the precedent of the Banū Qurayẓa: the Prophet ordered that the Quraẓī captives be provided with dates,[25] be allowed to rest at mid-day and that their execution be delayed so as not to coincide with the hottest part of the day.[26] The alleviation of the captives' suffering is also recorded in the chapter dealing with the judgment of a Muslim to whom the fate of the captive *ahl al-ḥarb* had been entrusted on the basis of their consent to his arbitration.[27] The chapter deals in fact with the judgment of Saᶜd b. Muᶜādh and the Prophet's approval of his decree. One of the problems touched upon is the age at which the fighting men of the enemy forces may be subjected to the death penalty. According to the decree of Saᶜd b. Muᶜādh (fighting) persons of Qurayẓa had to be put to death if they reached the age of puberty.[28] Al-Shaybānī's opinion is different: he points out that there are differences in the age of puberty between various peoples (for instance between Turks and Indians). But in the case of Banū Qurayẓa the

[22] Al-Shaybānī, *op. cit.*, I, 280.

[23] Al-Shaybānī, *op. cit.*, III, 1024-1025 (*wa-dalīlunā ᶜalā jawāzi l-qatli baᶜda l-asri qiṣṣatu banī qurayẓata, fa-qad qatalahum rasūlu llāhi (ṣ) baᶜda l-asri wa-baᶜda mā waḍaᶜati l-ḥarbu auzārahā*). This rejects the argument (no. 4) of Arafat about the prohibition to kill prisoners of war.

[24] Al-Shaybānī, *op. cit.*, III, 1026, no. 1991.

[25] Al-Shaybānī, *op. cit.*, III, 1029, ult.: *wa-qad kāna amara rasūlu llāhi (ṣ) bi-aḥmāli l-tamri fa-nuthirat bayna aydīhim, fa-kānū yakdumūnahā kadma l-ḥumuri*. Al-Wāqidī (p. 513) has the same expression: *fa-bātū yakdumūnahā kadma l-ḥumur*. It probably refers to the fact that their hands were tied and they were compelled to grasp the dates with their lips.

[26] Al-Shaybānī, *op. cit.*, III, 1029.

[27] Al-Shaybānī, *op. cit.*, II, 587-592.

[28] Al-Shaybānī, *op. cit.*, II, 590.

Prophet disclosed to Saᶜd b. Muᶜādh (on the basis of a revelation) that their age of puberty was the limit of their penal responsiblity as fighting persons.[29] ᶜUmar is said to have ordered the commanders of the (Muslim) troops to kill (as in the case of Qurayẓa – K.) every person on whom the razor had passed and to refrain from capturing anyone of the unbelievers.[30] Al-Sarakhsī quotes a passage from the *maghāzī*-compilations (... *wa-fī l-maghāzī*...) according to which ᶜAlī and al-Zubayr carried out the execution of the captured Quraẓīs. He records two different versions concerning the number of those killed (700 men were executed; according to Muqātil: 450 were killed, 650 were enslaved) and mentions the place where the Quraẓīs were put to death: at the *dār abī l-jahm*; their blood flowed until it reached *aḥjār al-zayt*.[31] This in fact is the place which is mentioned by al-Wāqidī[32] and al-Samhūdī.[33] It is worthwhile to point out that al-Samhūdī quotes the report of Mūsā b. ᶜUqba who stated that the execution of the Banū Qurayẓa was carried out at the *dār abī l-jahm* (it was close to the *balāṭ*; but – al-Samhūdī says – the *balāṭ* did not exist at that time): "some people claimed that their blood flowed and reached the *aḥjār al-zayt* (the olive trees) which were in the market."[34]

The references quoted above from the compilations of al-Shaybānī, al-Shāfiᶜī, Abū ᶜUbayd and al-Māwardī show that the early scholars of Muslim law and jurisprudence were well acquainted with the literature of the *sīra* and *maghāzī*. The early jurists availed themselves of the traditions of the *maghāzī*; having examined some of the chapters of the compilation of al-Shaybānī referring to the story of the Banū Qurayẓa we could see how every detail was closely studied and analysed. The events of this expedition served as precedents, conclusions were duly drawn and

29 Al-Shaybānī, *op. cit.*, II, 591.

30 Al-Shaybānī, *op. cit.*, II, 592: *wa-dhukira ᶜan ᶜumara (r) annahu kataba ilā umarā'i al-ajnādi an: uqtulū man jarat ᶜalayhi l-mūsā wa-lā tasbū ilaynā mina l-ᶜulūji aḥadan.*

31 Al-Shaybānī, *op. cit.*, II, 592, sup.

32 Al-Wāqidī, *op. cit.*, p. 513, ll. 6-7.

33 See al-Samhūdī, *Wafā'u l-wafā bi-akhbāri dāri l-muṣṭafā*, ed. Muḥammad Muḥyī l-Dīn ᶜAbd al-Ḥamīd, Cairo 1374/1955, pp. 744 inf. - 745, 1121-1123; and see Abū l-Baqā Muḥammad Bahā' l-Dīn b. al-Ḍiyā' al-Makkī al-Qurashī l-ᶜUmarī l-ᶜAdawī, *Aḥwāl Makka wa-l-madīna*, MS. Br. Mus. Or. 11865, fol. 172a: *wa-nazala rasūlu llāhi (ṣ) ᶜalā kulthūm b. al-hidmi; wa-fī hādhihi l-ḥarrati qiṭᶜatun tusammā aḥjāra l-zayti, summiyat bihi li-sawādi aḥjārihā ka-annahā ṭuliyat bi-l-zayti, wa-huwa mauḍiᶜun kāna yastaqirru fīhi rasūlu llāhi (ṣ); wa-baᶜḍuhum yaqūlu: aḥjāru l-bayt, wa-dhālika khaṭa'un.*

34 Al-Samhūdī, *op. cit.*, p. 745 sup.

rules of the Muslim law of war were moulded according to these precedents. Al-Shaybānī was in fact a student of Abū Ḥanīfa, al-Awzāᶜī, Abū Yūsuf and Mālik b. Anas. He was a scholar of immense knowledge, penetrating mind and deep isight; yet in his *Siyar* he did not hesitate to base himself completely on the compilations of the *maghāzī*.

The close links between *fiqh* and *maghāzī* can be gauged from the fact that the famous *qāḍī* Abū Yūsuf (d. 182 A.H.) attended the council (*majlis*) of Muḥammad b. Isḥāq and heard from him the *maghāzī*.[35] The report about the Banū Qurayẓa and Saᶜd b. Muᶜādh's judgment is given by Abū Yūsuf on the authority of Ibn Isḥāq and is followed by a detailed discussion of the various possibilities of the decree of the arbiter.[36] Mālik b. Anas had an interest in *maghāzī*-literature and recommended the *maghāzī* of Mūsā b. ᶜUqba (d. 141 A.H.) whom he considered a reliable transmitter.[37] *Fiqh* and *maghāzī* were even subjects of competition among Muslim jurists. In a *mudhākara*-competition between Mālik and al-Auzāᶜī in Medina, Mālik b. Anas beat Auzāᶜī on the subject of *fiqh*, but Auzāᶜī had the upper hand on the subject of *maghāzī*.[38]

*

Arafat also raises some minor questions [39] and dwells at length upon Ibn Isḥāq's transmission of the *maghāzī* tradition. As already mentioned Ibn Isḥāq is accused of transmitting dubious traditions derived from unreliable authorities.

[35] Al-Muᶜāfā b. Zakariyā, *al-Jalīs al-ṣāliḥ al-kāfī wa-l-anīs al-nāṣiḥ al-shāfī*, Topkapi Saray, MS. Ahmet III, 2321, fol. 134a.

[36] Abū Yūsuf, *Kitāb al-kharāj*, Cairo 1382, pp. 201-204.

[37] Ibn Abī Ḥātim, *al-Jarḥ wa-l-taᶜdīl*, Hyderabad 1371/1952, Taqdima p. 22; vol. VIII, 154.

[38] Ibn Kathīr, *al-Bidāya wa-l-nihāya*, Beirut - al-Riyāḍ, 1966, X, 116.

[39] How could so many hundreds of persons (scil. of the Banū Qurayẓa) be incarcerated in the house belonging to a woman of Banū l-Najjār - asks Arafat (*op. cit.*, p. 105, argument no. 11). But *dār* does not only denote "a house"; it often denotes a compound building, sometimes of considerable dimensions, containing in certain cases stores, workshops, magazines and even markets. (See M.J. Kister, "Some Reports Concerning Mecca," *JESHO* XV (1972), 85-86 [about the *dūr* <translated "courts"> bought by Muᶜāwiya]; and see *ib.* p. 86, no. 1; and see e.g. Ibn Ḥajar, *al-Iṣāba,* V, 744, sup.: the court (*dār*) known as *dār banī naṣr* in Damascus was a church (*kanīsat al-naṣārā*); Mālik b. ᶜAuf alighted there at the beginning of the Muslim conquest of Damascus; therefore the court was known as *dār banī naṣr*.) It is quite possible that some hundreds of people could be incarcerated in such a *dār*. (See about the *dār bint al-ḥārith*: al-Suhaylī, *al-Rauḍ al-unuf*, ed. ᶜAbd al-Raḥmān al-Wakīl, Cairo 1390/1970, VI, 333-334).

In the case of the Banū Qurayẓa both the descendants of Saᶜd b. Muᶜādh and the descendants of the Jews who converted to Islam are accused by Arafat of inventing tendentious traditions transmitted and recorded by Ibn Isḥāq.[40]

Concerning the judgment of Saᶜd b. Muᶜādh one may remark that Ibn Isḥāq was certainly not the only scholar who transmitted this tradition. Montgomery Watt's important article "The Condemnation of the Jews of Banū Qurayẓah"[41] contains rich material about the transmitters of this tradition. A glance at the article shows convincingly that there existed not just one tradition, namely the one transmitted by Ibn Isḥāq; there were in fact many. Moreover, the tradition is recorded in the very early compilations, some of them contemporary with that of Ibn Isḥāq, in Qur'ān commentaries, in later compilations in which early sources were quoted, in compendia of *fiqh* and in *ḥadīth* collections.[42] It is obvious that there were many sources for the tradition about the Banū Qurayẓa. In his instructive article "The Materials used by Ibn Isḥāq" Montgomery Watt rightly points out that "the criticism of Ibn Isḥāq that he took material from Jews and Christians reflects the later attitude of suspicion towards such sources and the tendency to avoid them (at least in theory)."[43] The utterance of Mālik b. Anas about Ibn Isḥāq as it is recorded by Arafat from Ibn Sayyid al-Nās is in fact a combined saying blended together in a later period. The story about the enmity between Mālik b. Anas and Ibn Isḥāq has it that Ibn Isḥāq spoke with disdain about Mālik's compilation and said: "Lay the knowledge of Mālik before me, I will handle it as a surgeon". Thereupon Mālik said: "Look at this *dajjāl* of the *dajājila*, are my books to be in front of him?"[44] Mālik's

[40] Arafat, *op. cit.*, p. 105, argument no. 10.

[41] *MW* 42 (1952), 160-171.

[42] See e.g. ᶜAbd al-Razzāq, *al-Muṣannaf*, ed. Ḥabīburraḥmān al-Aᶜẓamī, Beirut 1392/1972, V, 360, no. 9733; 367-372 no. 9737; VI, 54, no. 9988; Ibn Saᶜd, *Ṭabaqāt*, Beirut 1380/1960, II, 74-77, III, 420-436; al-Ṭabarī, *Tafsīr*, ed. Shākir, Cairo 1958, XIV, 21-26, 35-36, 44; XXI (Būlāq), 95-97; al-Wāqidī, *op. cit.*, 496-531.

[43] B. Lewis and S.M. Holt (ed.) *Historians of the Middle East*, London 1964, p. 33.

[44] Al-Fasawī, *al-Maᶜrifa wa-l-ta'rīkh*, ed. Akram Ḍiyā' al-ᶜUmarī, Beirut 1401/1981, III, 32; Ibn ᶜAdiyy, *al-Kāmil fī ḍuᶜafā'i l-rijāl*, MS. Ahmet III, 2943/3, fol. 25b, 26b, 27a; Ibn Abī Ḥātim, *Taqdimat al-jarḥ*, p. 20; Yāqūt, *Muᶜjam al-udabā'*, ed. A.F. Rifāᶜī, Cairo 1358/1938, XVIII, 7 inf. - 8 sup.; J. Horovitz, "The Earliest Biographies of the Prophet and their Authors", *IC* (1928), p. 171; al-Khaṭīb, *Ta'rīkh Baghdād*, Cairo 1349/1931, I, 224 sup.; al-Dhahabī, *Tadhkirat al-ḥuffāẓ*, Hyderabad 1375/1955, I, 173.

answer indicates his contempt of Ibn Isḥāq and his lack of respect for Ibn Isḥāq's knowledge. According to another version Mālik was informed that Ibn Isḥāq prided himself on being the surgeon of the *maghāzī*; Mālik commented: "He told you that he was a surgeon of it? We expelled him from Medina."[45] In this utterance Mālik points to Ibn Isḥāq's ignorance, his lies, his lack of belief and other vices which caused the scholars of Medina to expel him from the city. Ibn Isḥāq was indeed accused of many faults like: *shīʿī* leanings, *qadarī* beliefs, transmission of *ṣifāt* traditions,[46] playing with cocks,[47] *tadlīs* in transmission,[48] and of course transmission of unreliable traditions, especially traditions of the descendants of Jews who had embraced Islam. The only version in which the utterance of Mālik about Ibn Isḥāq as an impostor (*dajjāl min al-dajājila*) is coupled with the accusation that he transmitted traditions of the descendants of Jewish converts to Islam is the version recorded by Ibn Sayyid al-Nās,[49] and quoted by Arafat.

The assumption that the enmity between Mālik and Ibn Isḥāq was caused mainly (or even solely) by the fact that Ibn Isḥāq disseminated traditions of Jewish converts to Islam seems an oversimplification. The main cause for the antagonism is indicated in the report of Ibn Sayyid

[45] Ibn Abī Ḥātim, *Taqdima*, p. 19 inf.; al-Khaṭīb, *op. cit*., I, 223; Ibn Abī Ḥātim, *al-Jarḥ wa-l-taʿdīl*, vol. III 2 (= vol. 7 repr.) p. 192 inf., no. 1087; Ibn Khallikān, *Wafayāt al-aʿyān*, ed. Iḥsān ʿAbbās, Beirut 1971, IV, 277, 612; and see H.R. Idrīs, "Reflexions sur Ibn Isḥāq", *Studia Islamica* XVII (1962), 29-30.

[46] See e.g. al-Dhahabī, *al-ʿUluww li-l-ʿaliyyi l-ghaffār*, ed. ʿAbd al-Raḥmān Muḥammad ʿUthmān, Cairo 1388/1968, pp. 108-109 (and see pp. 70-72); cf. al-Bayhaqī, *al-Asmāʾ wa-l-ṣifāt*, ed. Muḥammad Zāhid al-Kautharī, Cairo 1358, pp. 397-398; cf. al-Dhahabī, *Siyar aʿlām al-nubalāʾ*, ed. Salāḥ al-Dīn al-Munajjid, Cairo n.d. I, 205, 206, 212-215 (see esp. p. 215 inf.); al-ʿAynī, *Umdat al-qārī*, Cairo 1348, XVI, 268; al-Fasawī, *op. cit.*, I, 137 (Makkī b. Ibrāhīm disliked the traditions of Ibn Isḥāq about the *ṣifa*).

[47] See al-Dhahabī, *Tadhkirat al-ḥuffāẓ*, I, 173.

[48] Ibn Abī Ḥātim, *al-Jarḥ*, VII, 194, l. 1.

[49] Ibn Sayyid al-Nās, *ʿUyūn al-athar fī funūn al-maghāzī wa-l-siyar*, Cairo 1356, I, 16 inf.-17 sup. (*dajjālun mina l-dajājila yarwī ʿani l-yahūd*); Ibn Sayyid al-Nās stresses that Mālik did not find fault with Ibn Isḥāq's activity of transmission of *ḥadīth*, but he criticized severely his transmission of reports about the raids and expeditions against the Jewish tribes, based on the accounts of the "Children of the Jews" who converted to Islam. According to Yāqūt (*op. cit.*, XVIII, 8) Ibn Isḥāq used to transmit on the authority of Jews and Christians and used to refer to them in his compilations as *"ahlu l-ʿilmi l-awwal"*. A witty anecdote is recorded by Ibn ʿAdiyy: Ibn Isḥāq said: "the reliable transmitter told me" (*haddathanī l-thiqa*). When asked about who was the transmitter he answered: "The Jew Yaʿqūb" (Ibn ʿAdiyy, *op. cit.*, III, 26b, sup.).

al-Nās: Ibn Isḥāq surpassed every scholar in the Ḥijāz in his knowledge of the tribal strifes and tribal genealogy. He claimed that Mālik had to be counted as a *maulā* of the Dhū Aṣbaḥ; Mālik stated that he was a genuine descendant of this clan. When Mālik completed the compilation of the *Muwaṭṭa'* Ibn Isḥāq asked for it to be brought to him for examination, since he had said that he would be its surgeon. Mālik responded with the contemptuous comment quoted above.[50] The genealogical discussion seems to have been heated, as it touched upon the status of Mālik and humiliated his ancestors: Ibn Isḥāq claimed that these ancestors had come to Medina as a group of clients of Taym (*mawālī*), not as their allies (*ḥulafā'*).[51]

Ibn Isḥāq was, however, not the first scholar who questioned the truth of Mālik's pedigree. He was preceded in this matter by the highly respected traditionist Sa^c^d b. Ibrāhīm (d. ca 125 A.H.),[52] the grandson of ^c^Abd al-Raḥmān b. ^c^Auf, the distinguished companion of the Prophet. Sa^c^d's criticism of Mālik's pedigree brought about a clash between the two scholars. This fact can be deduced from a peculiar conversation with Aḥmad b. Ḥanbal in which he said that Mālik did not transmit traditions reported by Sa^c^d b. Ibrāhīm because "there was a story between them" (*kāna lahu ma^c^a sa^c^din qiṣṣatun*); then Aḥmad said: "Sa^c^d did not care that Mālik did not transmit his reports."[53] More details about the reasons for the enmity between the two scholars can be gleaned from the answer given by Yaḥyā (b. Ma^c^īn – K.) who questioned whether the reason of Mālik's reluctance to transmit Sa^c^d's *ḥadīth*s was not that Sa^c^d was suspect of being a believer in *qadar*. Yaḥyā explained: Sa^c^d did not believe in *qadar*; Mālik merely refrained from transmitting on his authority because he criticized the reliability of his *nasab* (*li-annahu ta-*

50 Ibn Sayyid al-Nās, *op. cit.*, I, 16, inf.; H.R. Idrīs, *op. cit.*, p. 29-30.

51 See the lengthy passage on the problem: al-Qāḍī ^c^Iyāḍ, *Tartīb al-madārik wa-taqrīb al-masālik li-ma^c^rifati a^c^lām madhhab mālik*, ed. Aḥmad Bakīr Maḥmūd, Beirut 1388/1968, I, 102-107; and see the references in F. Sezgin, *GAS* I, 458.

52 See e.g. the opinions of Aḥmad b. Ḥanbal about Sa^c^d: Aḥmad b. Ḥanbal, *al-^c^Ilal wa-ma^c^rifatu l-rijāl*, ed. Ṭal^c^at Koçyigit and Ismā^c^īl Çerrahoğlu, Ankara 1963, I, 278 sup.: *sa^c^du bnu ibrāhīma athbatu min ^c^umara bni salamata khamsīna marratan*; and see about him Ibn ^c^Asākir, *Ta'rīkh (Tahdhīb)*, ed. ^c^Abd al-Qādir Badrān, Damascus 1399/1979, VI, 83; al-Bukhārī, *al-Ta'rīkh al-kabīr*, Hyderabad 1384/1964, IV, 51, no. 1928; Wakī^c^, *Akhbār al-quḍāt*, ed. ^c^Abd al-^c^Azīz Muṣṭafā al-Marāghī, Cairo 1366/1947, I, 150-167.

53 Al-Fasawī, *al-Ma^c^rifa wa-l-ta'rīkh*, ed. Akram Ḍiyā' al-^c^Umarī, Beirut 1401/1981, I, 411; and see Ibn Ḥajar, *Tahdhīb al-tahdhīb*, III, 465.

kallama fī nasabi mālik); it is therefore that Mālik did not transmit on his authority.[54] It is evident that Ibn Isḥāq did not invent the suspicions against Mālik's pedigree, but merely quoted earlier reports which had already gained currency in Medina.

The accounts saying that the only reason for the enmity between Mālik b. Anas and Muḥammad b. Isḥāq was the problem of Mālik's pedigree are verified by a report transmitted by the well-known scholar of *ḥadīth*, Baqiyy b. Makhlad (d. 276 A.H.)[54a] and recorded in the compilation of Abū l-ᶜArab (d. 333 A.H.) "*Kitāb al-miḥan*".[54b] Baqiyy relates a question of Yaᶜqūb b. Ibrāhīm b. Saᶜd (d. 208 A.H.)[54c] addressed to his father Ibrāhīm b. Saᶜd b. Ibrāhīm (d. 183 A.H.).[54d] He inquired whether Ibn Isḥāq was indeed affected by the vices and faults of which he was accused by the people of Medina. Ibrāhīm denied it; Ibn Isḥāq had the misfortune to abide in Medina with its people. They charged him with foul deeds because he knew the pedigrees (of the people of Medina – K.); thus there was no clan in Medina the pedigree of which Ibn Isḥāq did not impeach. Therefore the people of Medina were hostile towards him. He (i.e. the governor of Medina) therefore seized him and ordered to flog him 100 times. (*qāla: wa-ḥaddathanī yaḥyā ᶜan baqiyyi bni makhladin ᶜan yaᶜqūba bni ibrāhīma bni saᶜdin qāla: sa'altu abī hal kāna fi muḥammadi bni isḥāqa mimmā yuḥaddithu bihi ᶜanhu ahlu l-madīnati; qāla: lā, wa-lākinnahu buliya bi-ahli l-madīnati, kānū yushanniᶜūna ᶜalayhi wa-kāna rajulan* [text: *rajul*] *yaᶜrifu l-ansāb, fa-lam yakun fi ahli l-madīnati baytun illā wa-qad adkhala ᶜalayhim fi ansābihim shay'an, faᶜādāhu ahlu l-madīnati fa-akhadhahu* (sic!) *wa-ḍarabahu mi'ata sauṭ*)

The report of Ibrāhīm b. Saᶜd is credible. He was a student of Ibn Isḥāq and he recorded 17,000 legal traditions on the authority of Ibn Isḥāq in addition to traditions of *maghāzī*.[54e]

It is quite natural, on this background, for Qāḍī ᶜIyāḍ to provide a list of several scholars denying the suspicions about the pedigree of Mālik, asserting that he was a genuine scion of the genuine tribe of the Yemenite Dhū Aṣbaḥ and adding that his clan was not a client of the

[54] Ibn Ḥajar, *Tahdhīb al-tahdhīb*, III, 465.

[54a] See on him F. Sezgin, *GAS*, I, 152, no. 97.

[54b] MS. Cambridge Or. Qq. 235(8), fol. 142b.

[54c] See on him: Ibn Ḥajar, *Tahdhīb al-tahdhīb*, XI, 380, no. 741.

[54d] See on him F. Sezgin, *GAS*, I, 95, no. 14.

[54e] Al-Khaṭīb al-Baghdādī, *Ta'rīkh baghdād*, VI, 83.

Taym b. Murra.[55] In the same vein, some distinguished members of Taym are said to have testified that the clan of Dhū Aṣbaḥ, the ancestors of Mālik had an alliance with, and were no clients of, Taym.[56]

It may be well to note that Mālik seems to have referred in his contemptuous comment merely to the faults of Ibn Isḥāq's *Sīra* compilation. This attitude on the part of a great scholar of Muslim law towards *Sīra* compilations in general and towards that of Ibn Isḥāq in particular is by no means surprising. Ibn ᶜAdiyy (d. 360 A.H.) emphasized that it was Ibn Isḥāq's virtue and merit to have engaged the kings in reading the *maghāzī*, the stories of the beginning of Creation and the beginning of the Prophecy (of Muḥammad – K.), thus distracting them from reading books of no import (*lā yaḥṣulu minhā shay'un*). In this he outdid other scholars who fell short of his accomplishment. Ibn ᶜAdiyy states in his concluding sentence that the many traditions transmitted by Ibn Isḥāq became widely current (*wa-qad fashat aḥādīthuhu l-kathīratu*); he (i.e. Ibn ᶜAdiyy – K.) could however find in his traditions nothing which might be characterized as "weak" (*fa-lam ajid fī aḥādīthihi mā yatahaya'u an yuqtaᶜa ᶜalayhi bi-l-ḍaᶜfi*).[57] Ibn Duḥaym, a *maulā* of Mālik admitted that Mālik called Ibn Isḥāq *dajjāl* merely because of the suspicion of his belief in *qadar*, not because of his transmissions of *ḥadīth* (*qāla abū zurᶜa al-dimashqiyyu: dhākartu duḥayman maulā mālikin fa-ra'ā anna dhālika laysa li-l-ḥadīth, innamā huwa li-annahu ttahamahu bi-l-qadari*).[58] Ibn Isḥāq may have erred or been mistaken like others, states Ibn ᶜAdiyy; but reliable and distinguished transmitters of *ḥadīth* did not refrain from reporting his traditions. The mark granted him by Ibn ᶜAdiyy is *"la ba'sa bihi"*.[59]

Rigorous Muslim scholars of jurisprudence and *ḥadīth*, who usually display a highly critical attitude, had indeed a very high opinion of Ibn Isḥāq. Ibn Taymiyya (d. 728 A.H.), quoting a *Sīra* tradition recorded by Ibn Isḥāq, marks him as a man possessing knowledge and a perceptive

[55] See al-Qāḍī ᶜIyāḍ, *op. cit.*, I, 104-105 (the readings *Tamīm b. Murra* are erroneous: read correctly *Taym b. Murra*).

[56] Ibid., p. 105.

[57] Ibn ᶜAdiyy, *op. cit.*, III, 30b.

[58] Al-ᶜIrāqī, *Ṭarḥ al-tathrīb fī sharḥi l-taqrīb*, Ḥalab n.d., I, 98.

[59] Ibn ᶜAdiyy, *op. cit.*, III, 30b: *wa-rubbamā akhṭa'a au wahima fī l-shay'i baᶜda l-shay'i kamā yukhṭi'u ghayruhu, wa-lam yatakhallaf ᶜanhu fī l-riwāyati ᶜanhu l-thiqātu wa-l-a'immatu, wa-huwa lā ba'sa bihi*.

mind in this matter (*wa-huwa dhū ᶜilmin wa-baṣīratin bi-hādhā l-sha'ni*), a man who kept in his mind more (knowledge – K.) than anyone else.[60] Ibn Ḥajar, in arguing against Ibn al-Jauzī who qualified Ibn Isḥāq as *majrūḥ* (in connection with his transmission of a tradition with a clear Shīᶜī tendency about the death of Fāṭima) states that Ibn al-Jauzī's attack lacks substance; the leading scholars (of *ḥadīth* – K.), according to Ibn Ḥajar, accepted Ibn Isḥāq's transmission and he was accused of nothing worse than that he had transmitted on the authority of some unknown persons (*majhūlīn*) and that he was a *mudallis*. Ibn Isḥāq himself was a truthful person and an authority in the field of *maghāzī* (*hujjatun fī l-maghāzī*) in the opinion of the people (scil. of *ḥadīth*, *ᶜinda l-jumhūr*).[61]

One can hardly agree with Arafat as to the "glorification" of their ancestors by the descendants of Qurayẓa. They are described in the reports as wavering, undecided even in the most dangerous moments of their existence, stubborn and disobeying their leaders. Barakat Ahmad discussed the problem thoroughly in a lengthy passage in his book *Muhammad and the Jews* and concluded: "One might, however, ask in parenthesis if Mālik b. Anas' charge was fair. It shows a latter-day prejudice against the Jewish converts. Why should they be less reliable than the sons of the pagan Arab converts?" etc.[62] Watt is right indeed in his assessment of the reports about Qurayẓa: "About the primary matters, the broad outlines of events, there is practically no doubt. The Banū Qurayẓa were besieged and eventually surrendered; their fate was decided by Saᶜd: nearly all the men were executed; Muḥammad did not disapprove."[63]

III

A closer examination of the various reports about the expedition against Qurayẓa and their massacre may provide us with a clue to a better understanding of some of the events and a deeper insight into the circum-

[60] Ibn Taymiyya, *al-Jawāb al-ṣaḥīḥ li-man baddala dīna l-masīḥ*, ed. ᶜAlī al-Sayyid Ṣubḥ al-Madanī, Cairo 1383/1964, I, 92 ult.-93 l.1.

[61] Ibn Ḥajar, *al-Qaulu l-musaddad fī l-dhabbi ᶜani l-musnad li-l-imāmi aḥmad*, Hyderabad 1386/1967, p. 62.

[62] Barakat Ahmad, *op. cit.*, p. 12; Montgomery Watt, The Materials, *Historians*, p. 33.

[63] Montgomery Watt, *The condemnation*, p. 171.

stances and causes which brought about the calamity of the Banū Qurayẓa.

Usually the Banū Qurayẓa are accused of having violated their treaty with the Prophet. This accusation is stated clearly in the commentary to Sūra VIII (al-Anfāl), 55 – 58:

> Surely the worst beasts in God's sight are the unbelievers, who will not believe, those of them with whom thou hast made compact, then they break their compact every time, not being godfearing. So, if thou comest upon them anywhere in the war, deal with them with such wise as to scatter the ones behind them; haply they will remember. And if thou fearest treachery any way at the hands of a people, dissolve it with them equally; surely God loves not the treacherous.
>
> (A.J. Arberry's translation)

Al-Ṭabarī comments on "those of them with whom thou hast made compact, then they break their compact every time": "You, Muḥammad, took from them their bonds (*mawāthīqahum*) and compacts (*ᶜuhūdahum*) that they would not fight you nor aid anyone who fights you (*wa-lā yuẓāhirū ᶜalayka muḥāriban laka*), like Qurayẓa and (people) like them, who had compacts (*ᶜahd*) and treaties (*ᶜaqd*)"; "then they break"... is glossed: "they fight you (*ḥārabūka*) and aid (*ẓāharū*) (your enemy – K.) against you".[64] The denunciation is defined more precisely by Mujāhid: the verse refers to Qurayẓa; they aided (*māla'ū*) the enemies of the Prophet on the "Day of the Ditch" against him.[65] The expression *"fa-sharrid bihim man khalfahum"* ("to scatter through them those who are behind them"; or "... as to strike fear"... or "... punish them an exemplary punishment, so as to spread fear...", or "to deter") refers consequently to Qurayẓa.[66] Verse 58 is also alleged to refer to Qurayẓa. The phrase: "And if thou fearest treachery then throw back to them (their treaty) fairly"... has to be re-interpreted according to the commentaries. "If somebody should say" argues al-Ṭabarī, "how is it permissible to violate a pact on the ground of (mere – K.) fear of treachery, while fear is (just – K.) a conjecture, not a certainty (... *wa-l-khaufu ẓannun lā yaqīnun*), he may be answered: "the opposite of what

[64] Al-Ṭabarī, *Tafsīr*, ed. Shākir XIV, 21-22.

[65] Al-Ṭabarī, *op. cit.*, XIV, 22, no. 16210; and see Mujāhid, *Tafsīr*, ed. ᶜAbd al-Raḥmān al-Sūratī, Islāmābād n.d., I, 266-267.

[66] Al-Ṭabarī, *Tafsīr*, XIV, 22-23.

you assumed is true: if the signs of the enemy's treachery become apparent, and you fear that you may be affected by it, then throw back to them the keys of peace (treaties – K.) and announce war to them" (*wa-ādhinhum bi-l-ḥarbi*).[67] Al-Ṭabarī argues that this was the case of Qurayẓa: they responded to the summons of Abū Sufyān and the unbelievers to help them against the Prophet and to fight on their side. This response followed the conclusion of a treaty with the Prophet based on peaceful relations (*ᶜalā musālama*) and (the promise) not to fight the Prophet. When the signs of their treachery became manifest the Prophet had the right to declare war against them, concluded al-Ṭabarī.[68] The same method of explanation is followed by Ibn al-ᶜArabī,[69] al-Qurṭubī[70], and al-Suyūṭī.[71]

The treaty itself between the Prophet and Qurayẓa is usually referred to as *ᶜahd*,[72] *walthu ᶜahdin*,[73] the already mentioned *musālama* and *muwādaᶜa* and the verbs[74] *ᶜāhada* and *ᶜāqada*. In fact the expressions *ᶜaqd* and *ᶜahd* do not define clearly the nature of the treaty and its contents. A more precise term is the *muwādaᶜa*, usually concluded with the unbelievers; it denotes a treaty of non-aggression, of renunciation of violence. A compact of this kind would mean that Qurayẓa and the forces of the Prophet would both refrain from any hostile action and would not aid any attacking force acting against either of these two parties. *Muwādaᶜa* is thus a treaty of peaceful co-existence. It is interesting to note the expression *walthu ᶜahdin* used by Ibn Saᶜd: a precarious, crude, incomplete agreement.[75] How this kind of agreement was concluded can be learned from a report recorded by ᶜAbd al-Razzāq on the authority of Mūsā b. ᶜUqba:[76] The Naḍīr and Qurayẓa fought the Prophet; the Prophet expelled the Naḍīr but agreed that Qurayẓa should stay. Later

[67] Al-Ṭabarī, *Tafsīr*, XIV, 25.

[68] Al-Ṭabarī, *Tafsīr*, XIV, 26.

[69] *Aḥkām al-qur'ān*, ed. Alī Muḥammad al-Bijāwī, Cairo, 1378/1967, p. 860.

[70] *Tafsīr* (= *al-Jāmiᶜ li-aḥkāmi l-qur'ān*) Cairo 1387/1967, VIII, 31–32.

[71] *Al-durr al-manthūr*, Cairo 1314, III, 191.

[72] See Ibn Saᶜd, *op. cit.*, II, 71; al-Qurṭubī, *Tafsīr*, XIV, 139; Muqātil, *Tafsīr*, Topkapi Saray, Ahmet III, 74/I 147a; Ibn Kathīr, *Tafsīr*, Beirut 1385/1966, V, 442.

[73] Ibn Saᶜd, *op. cit.*, II, 77.

[74] See e.g. al-Qurṭubī, *Tafsīr*, XIV, 132.

[75] See Ibn al-Athīr, *al-Nihāya fi gharībi l-ḥadīth*, s.v. *wlth;* al-Zamakhsharī, *al-Fā'iq*, s.v. *wlth; LᶜA*, s.v. *wlth*.

[76] *al-Muṣannaf* VI, 54 ult.-55, no. 9988 (the *isnād* recorded is: ᶜAbd al-Razzāq – Ibn Jurayj – Mūsā b. ᶜUqba – Nāfiᶜ – Ibn ᶜUmar).

Qurayẓa fought the Prophet. They were defeated, the men were executed, the women, children and property were divided among the Muslims. Some of the Jews received the *amān* (safety) of the Prophet and converted to Islam. This account is corroborated and elucidated by a report traced back to al-Zuhrī: the Prophet, informed about the treacherous intentions of the Naḍīr, marched out against them with troops (*bi-l-katā'ib*) and besieged them. He demanded that they conclude a compact with him; if they refused, he in turn would refuse to grant them an assurance of safety (*...innakum lā ta'manūna ᶜindī illā bi-ᶜahdin tuᶜāhidūnī ᶜalayhi*). They refused and the forces of the Prophet fought them (i.e. the Naḍīr) throughout the day. Next day the Prophet left the Naḍīr, went out with horsemen and troops against Qurayẓa and summoned them to conclude an agreement; they consented and concluded a treaty and the Prophet left them. He returned with his troops to the Naḍīr and fought them until they surrendered on condition that they would be expelled.[77] The agreement between Qurayẓa and the Prophet was thus, as it is called by Ibn Saᶜd, *walthu ᶜahdin*, a crude, not elaborated agreement of peaceful co-existence. It was probably of the *muwādaᶜa* kind granting assurances of mutual safety.[78]

An interesting case of *muwādaᶜa* is recorded in some of the commentaries of *Sūrat al-nisā'* 87–89: *fa-mā lakum fī l-munāfiqīna fi'atayn...* Surāqa b. Mālik is said to have received information that the Prophet intended to send (after the battles of Badr and Uḥud and after the conversion of the people of these localities to Islam) Khālid b. al-Walīd to the Banū Mudlij (scil. to attack them – K.). He went to the Prophet and said: "I heard that you intend to send to my people, but I would like you to conclude with them a *muwādaᶜa* (... *wa-ana urīdu an tuwādiᶜahum*); so if your people (i.e. Quraysh – K.) convert to Islam they (i.e. the Mudlij – K.) would embrace Islam; if they (i.e. Quraysh) would not convert to Islam they would not be harsh towards them (i.e. towards Mudlij – K.). The Prophet ordered Khālid to act according to Surāqa's request; Khālid indeed concluded with them an agreement on the basis that they would not give (anyone) aid against the Prophet of God (*an lā yuᶜīnū ᶜalā rasūli llāhi*) and they would embrace Islam after

[77] ᶜAbd al-Razzāq, *op. cit.*, V, 360, no. 9733.

[78] Comp. *EI*², s.v. Ḳuḍāᶜa (vol. V, 316 sup.): *fa-authiq lanā ḥattā na'manaka wa-ta'mananā*.

the conversion of Quraysh.[79] One of the versions recorded by al-Suyūṭī contains an additional clause according to which people who would join Mudlij will join the *muwādaᶜa* of Mudlij (*wa-man waṣala ilayhim min al-nāsi kāna ᶜalā mithli ᶜahdihim*).[80] It is thus an interesting case of a treaty concluded with unbelievers granting them security and allowing other people to join them on the basis of that treaty.[81]

According to other traditions the verses of the Qur'ān refer to another *muwādaᶜa:* a group of Meccans, claiming to be *muhājirūn*, came to the Prophet; however, having renounced Islam, they asked the Prophet's permission to go to Mecca in order to bring their merchandise. Some believers, who had received information about the treacherous plans of the group, wanted to kill them. Then the group declared that they were proceeding to Hilāl b. ᶜUwaymir al-Aslami who had concluded a treaty of alliance (*ḥilf* or *ᶜahd*) with the Prophet; this kept them from the attack of the believers and they hoped to get security from both parties (*wa-yurīdūna bi-dhālika an ya'manū hāhunā wa-hāhunā*). It is noteworthy that people "whose hearts were restricted" (*ḥaṣirat ṣudūruhum*), who were reluctant to fight their own people and who consequently did not have the courage to join the Muslim force, were not forced at that early period to join the Muslim force.[82]

The concise report recorded by al-Thaᶜlabī is of some interest: the Prophet concluded a *muwādaᶜa* with Hilāl b. ᶜUwaymir al-Aslamī when he left Mecca. According to this *muwādaᶜa* Hilāl made a promise to aid neither the Prophet nor his adversary against him (*an lā yuᶜīnahu wa-lā yuᶜīna ᶜalayhi*).[83] The following stipulation established that anyone of his tribe or others who joined his court or asked shelter could be granted

[79] Ibn Kathīr, *Tafsīr*, Beirut 1385/1966, II, 353.

[80] Al-Suyūṭī, *al-Durr al-manthūr*, II, 191.

[81] See the discussion of this treaty and the problem of its abolition: al-Naḥḥās, *al-Nāsikh wa-l-mansūkh fi l-qur'āni l-karīm*, Cairo 1357/1938, pp. 110-112; cf. al-Shaukānī, *Fatḥ al-qadīr al-jāmiᶜ bayna fannayi l-riwāya wa-l-dirāya min ᶜilmi l-tafsīr*, Beirut (reprint) n.d., I, 497; about the intent of the treaty see Ibn ᶜArabi, *Aḥkām al-qur'ān*, Cairo 1387/1967, I, 470; and see the judicial analysis in Jaṣṣāṣ, *Aḥkām al-qur'ān*, Qusṭanṭiniyya, 1338 (reprint Beirut), II, 219-221.

[82] Mujāhid, *Tafsīr*, I, 168-169; and see al-Ṭabarī, *Tafsīr*, IX, 9-10 (from Mujāhid); al-Suyūṭī, *al-Durr al-manthūr*, II, 190 inf. (from Mujāhid).

[83] The clause following this stipulation: *ḥattā yarā wa-yurā* (so vowelled in text) is slightly enigmatic; it probably means: until he would consider (the matter) and things would be considered.

the same protection (*jiwār*) as given to Hilāl (*wa-man waṣala ilā hilālin min qaumihi wa-ghayrihim wa-laja'a ilayhim fa-lahum min al-jiwāri mithlu lladhī li-hilālin*).[84]

Al Jaṣṣāṣ gives a concise comment on the legal status of Qurayẓa: both Naḍīr and Qurayẓa had no protection (of the Prophet and of the Muslim community – K.) at all; the Prophet expelled the Naḍīr and ordered to have Qurayẓa killed. If they had had protection he would not have expelled them nor killed them. Between them and the Prophet there was merely a treaty and a truce which they violated. (*wa-maᶜlūmun anna banī qurayẓata wa-l-naḍīra lam takun lahum dhimmatun qaṭṭu, wa-qad ajlā l-nabiyyu (ṣ) banī l-naḍīri wa-qatala banī qurayẓata; wa-lau kāna lahum dhimmatun lamā ajlāhum wa-lā qatalahum; wa-innamā kāna baynahu wa-baynahum ᶜahdun wa-hudnatun fa-naqaḍūhā...*)[85] This corresponds exactly to what al-Shāfiᶜī described as *al-ṣulḥ bi-l-muhādana*.[86] It is evident that a person or a tribal group, or a community could conclude a treaty of *muwādaᶜa* (or *muhādana*) with two conflicting parties. Qurayẓa seem to have been in such a situation when Quraysh and their Confederates arrived: they had a favourable attitude towards the Prophet and the Muslims (who were their neighbours) and were not happy when the Aḥzāb started the siege on Medina. Their attitude is described as follows by al-Wāqidī: "... they were at that time peacefully inclined towards the Prophet and disliked the arrival of Quraysh (... *wa-hum yauma'idhin silmun li-l-nabiyyi yakrahūna qudūma qurayshin*).[87] In fact, according to the report of al-Wāqidī, Qurayẓa lent the besieged Muslims many tools for digging the ditch (for the defence of Medina – K.) like shovels, baskets and axes.[88] The fact that they adhered to the concluded treaty (the *muwādaᶜa* or *muhādana*) is clearly reflected in a passage from the speech of Ḥuyayy b. Akhṭab in which he tried to convince Qurayẓa to abandon their neutrality and begin cooperating with the besieging Quraysh: You are not with Muḥammad nor are you with Quraysh (*fa-lā antum maᶜa rasūli llāhi wa-lā maᶜa quray-*

[84] Al-Thaᶜlabī, *Tafsīr*, MS. Br. Mus. Add 19,926, p. 227.

[85] Al-Jaṣṣaṣ, *Aḥkām al-qur'ān*, Istanbul 1338, II, 435.

[86] Al-Shāfiᶜī, *al-Umm*, IV, 107.

[87] Al-Wāqidī, *op. cit.*, p. 445.

[88] Al-Wāqidī, *op. cit.*, p. 445; and see al-Samhūdī, *op. cit.*, p. 1207, l.1: *wa-staᶜārū min banī qurayẓata mithla l-maᶜāwili wa-l-fu'ūs wa-ghayri dhālika*.

shin).[89] The lending of the tools to the forces of the Prophet in order to enable them to dig the ditch was certainly a display of the goodwill of Qurayẓa towards the Prophet and his force. There is no report whatsoever about military actions of Qurayẓa against the force of the Prophet. The expedition against Qurayẓa and the severe punishment inflicted on them are justified in the Muslim sources by reference to the clandestine negotiations said to have been arranged between Qurayẓa and Quraysh, and the secret plan to attack the forces of the Prophet, a plan which failed however due to a stratagem of the Prophet carried out by Nuᶜaym b. Masᶜūd.[90] As these negotiations were clandestine, the reliability of reports concerning them cannot be established.

What may however be assumed is that Qurayẓa had some commercial relations with the besieging Aḥzāb. This can be deduced from a story about a clash between a group from among the besieged Muslims and a caravan of the besieging Aḥzāb. According to the report, a group of the Banū ᶜAmr b. ᶜAuf who dwelt in Qubā' asked the Prophet's permission to arrange a funeral for one of their relatives. When they went out to the plain in order to bury the dead man they met Ḍirār b. al-Khaṭṭāb with a group of unbelievers on camels loaded with wheat, barley, straw and dates. This group had been sent by Abū Sufyān on his camels to the Banū Qurayẓa in order to purchase provisions from them. They were on their way back to the camp of the besieging Aḥzāb. In the encounter which ensued between the Muslims and the caravan of the unbelievers Ḍirār was wounded, the camel riders managed to escape and the camels loaded with the provisions were led to the Prophet's camp; the booty proved a relief for the besieged, helping them in their expenditure.[91] A more detailed version is recorded by Daḥlān. A group of the Anṣār, who went out to bury their deceased relative, met a caravan of twenty camels with loads of straw, barley and dates. The caravan, which

[89] Hāshim b. Sulaymān al-Baḥrānī al-Taubalī al-Katakānī, *al-Burhān fi tafsīri l-qur'ān*, Qumm 1393, III, 299.

[90] See e.g. al-Wāqidī, *op. cit.*, 480 seq.; but see the report recorded by al-Majlisī, *Biḥār al-Anwār*, Tehran 1392, XX, 246, no. 11: The Prophet got information that Qurayẓa sent to Abū Sufyān and promised him to aid Quraysh in the case of an encounter between Quraysh and the Prophet. Then the Prophet stood up and addressed the Believers. He said: "Qurayẓa sent to us and promised us their aid and succour in the case of an encounter between us and Abū Sufyān." When Abū Sufyān was informed about the speech of the Prophet he said: "The Jews betrayed (us)." And he departed from them.

[91] Al-Samhūdī, *op. cit.*, p. 304.

had been sent as succour and assistance (*madadan wa-taqwiyatan*) to Quraysh, was led by Ḥuyayy b. Akhṭab. The Anṣār seized the caravan and brought it to the Prophet; it was a relief for the Muslims.[92] We can probably gauge from this report that Qurayẓa had large warehouses with provisions which they could sell. This confirms the soundness of the data about the huge quantities of food, cattle, utensils, weapons and coats of mail seized in the stronghold of Qurayẓa after their surrender. The comparison of these data with those of the numbers of the fighting troops and the data about the executed Quraẓīs and the enslaved women and children can help us to assess the details of the first stages of the clash and to evaluate properly the reports about the decisive period of the events. According to a widely current tradition the angel Jibrīl came to the Prophet, urged him to march out against Qurayẓa and promised him to crush their stronghold.[93] The stronghold seems to have been fortified. According to a tradition recorded by al-Suyūṭī, the Prophet, urged by Jibrīl to raid Qurayẓa, asked him: "How can I conquer their fortress" (*kayfa lī bi-ḥiṣnihim*); Jibrīl assured him of his help in destroying their force.[94] The aim of the raid is indicated in another tradition: Jibrīl ordered the Prophet to march out against Qurayẓa to kill the fighting men and to enslave their offspring, promising him that they would be a means of subsistence for him (*fa-inna llāha ᶜazza wa-jalla qad adhina laka fī dhālika, fa-hum laka ṭuᶜmatun*).[95] *Ṭuᶜma* was a well known politico-

[92] Daḥlān, *al-Sīra al-nabawiyya*, Cairo 1310, II, 8.

[93] See e.g. al-ᶜAyni, *op. cit.*, XVII, 189; al-Katakānī, *op. cit.*, III, 304; al-Balādhurī, *Ansāb al-ashrāf*, ed. Muḥammad Ḥamīdullāh, Cairo 1959, I, 347 inf.; Ibn Kathīr, *al-Bidāya wa-l-nihāya*, Beirut - Riyāḍ 1966, IV, 116-118; Ibn Sayyid al-Nās, *op. cit.*, II, 68; ᶜAlī b. Burhān al-Dīn, *Insān al-ᶜuyūn fī sīrat al-amīn al-ma'mūn*, (= *al-Sīra al-ḥalabiyya*), Cairo 1382/1962, II, 354; al-Diyārbakrī, *Ta'rīkh al-khamīs*, Cairo 1283, I, 493; Ibn Kathīr, *Tafsīr*, V, 443; Ibn Hishām, *al-Sīra al-nabawiyya*, ed. al-Saqqā, al-Abyārī, Shalabī, Cairo 1355/1936, III, 244; al-Samarqandī, *Tafsīr al-qur'ān*, MS. Chester Beatty 3668, II, 134b; al-Qurṭubī, *op. cit.*, XIV, 138-139; Ibn Saᶜd, *op. cit.*, II, 74; ᶜAbd al-Razzāq, *op. cit.*, V, 369; Abū ᶜAwāna, *Musnad*, Hyderabad 1385/1965, IV, 167 seq.; al-Haythamī, *Majmaᶜ al-zawā'id*, Beirut 1967 (repr.) VI, 137; al-Kalāᶜī, *al-Iktifā' fī maghāzī rasūli llāhi wa-l-thalāthati l-khulafā'*, ed. Muṣṭafā ᶜAbd al-Wāḥid, Cairo 1389/1970, II, 176; Ibn Ḥibbān al-Bustī, *al-Thiqāt*, Hyderabad 1393/1973, I, 274; Ibn Abī Shayba, Ta'rīkh, MS. Berlin 9409 (Sprenger 104), fol. 49a; al-ᶜIṣāmī, *Simṭ al-nujūm al-ᶜawālī*, Cairo 1380, II, 135; al-Suyūṭī, *al-Khaṣā'is al-kubrā*, ed. Muḥammad Khalīl Harrās, Cairo 1386/1967, II, 9; al-Maqrīzī, *Imtāᶜu l-asmāᶜ bimā li-l-rasūli min al-anbā'i wa-l-amwāli wa-l-ḥafadati wa-l-matāᶜ*, ed. Maḥmūd Muḥammad Shākir, Cairo 1941, I, 241; al-Wāqidī, *op. cit.*, p. 497.

[94] *Al-Durr al-manthūr*, III, 178.

[95] Muqātil, *Tafsīr*, II, 90b.

economic term in the period of the Jāhiliyya and in the period of the Prophet.

The firm economic position of Qurayẓa enabled them to invite the so-called "hypocrites", the Medinan *munāfiqūn*, during the siege of Medina to seek refuge in their stronghold.[96] The *munāfiqūn* were in fact a group of Medinans who had outwardly converted to Islam, but who had remained loyal to their former allies, faithful to their Jāhilī ideals and their tribal relations; they cooperated with Qurayẓa and knew that they could rely on their help in times of need. They were reluctant to be involved in the conflicts of the Prophet with Quraysh or with other tribal groups. This attitude of the group of *munāfiqūn* can be gauged from a passage recorded by Ibn al-ᶜArabī:

> The *munāfiqūn* used to aid the Jews of Qurayẓa and the Christians of Najrān because they (i.e. the Jews and the Christians – K.) were people of cultivated land and used to supply them with provisions and lend them money. Therefore they said: "How are we to sever the bonds of friendship with a people who make our dwellings spacious when we are afflicted by a year of drought and are in need of them".[97]

The close relations between Qurayẓa and the Aus, which had deep roots in the Jāhiliyya period, brought about the peculiar situation that several members of the Muslim Aus interceded with Saᶜd b. Muᶜādh, asking him to be lenient in his judgment of Qurayẓa. They were, of course, aware of being faithful believers, but they could not free themselves from the feeling that they should remain faithful to their Quraẓī allies in accordance with their obligations from the period of the Jāhiliyya. This group is often referred to as *"al-munāfiqūn"*.

The extent of the raid against Qurayẓa and its results can be judged by the number of the Muslim warriors who participated in the siege of the stronghold. Widely current reports give their number as three thou-

[96] Muqātil, *Tafsīr*, II, 89a: *wa-dhālika anna l-yahūda arsalū ilā-l-munāfiqīna yauma l-khandaqi fa-qālū mādhā yaḥmilukum ᶜalā an taqtulū anfusakum bi-aydī abī sufyāna wa-man maᶜahu...innā la-nushfiqu ᶜalaykum, innamā antum ikhwānunā wa-naḥnu jīrānukum, fa-halumma ilaynā...*; and see al-Qurṭubī, *op. cit.*, XIV, 152 sup.

[97] Ibn al-ᶜArabī, *Aḥkām al-qur'ān*, II, 629: *...kāna l-munāfiqūna yuwāzirūna yahūda qurayẓata wa-naṣārā najrāna li-annahum kānū ahla rīfin wa-kānū yamīrūnahum wa-yuqriḍūnahum, fa-qālū: kayfa naqṭaᶜu mawaddata qaumin idhā aṣābatnā sanatun fa-ḥtajnā ilayhim wassaᶜū ᶜalaynā l-manāzila...*; and cf. al-Wāqidī, *op. cit.*, p. 704: *fa-innī ᶜārifun bi-khaybara, hiya rīfu l-ḥijāzi ajmaᶜa.*

sand warriors and thirty-six horsemen.[98] The data about the length of the siege[99] and the number of the executed Quraẓī men and enslaved women and children are divergent.[100] The large force which marched out against Qurayẓa seems to indicate that the Prophet was aware of the strength of Qurayẓa. The Prophet could draw some conclusions from the "Campaign of the Ditch": he mobilized a great number of his troops. They could surround the stronghold of Qurayẓa and wait patiently until the besieged surrendered. There was some shooting,[101] but there were no serious encounters and the number of killed from both parties was very small.[102] The besieged Qurayẓa, forsaken by their allies, could not expect

[98] See Ibn Saᶜd, *op. cit.*, II, 74; al-Maqrīzī, *op. cit.*, I, 250; al-ᶜAynī, *op. cit.*, XVII, 188; ᶜAlī b. Burhān al-Dīn, *op. cit.*, II, 355: Ibn Sayyid al-Nās, *op. cit.*, II, 68; al-Wāqidī, *op. cit.*, 522.

[99] See e.g. al-Qurṭubī, *op. cit.*, XIV, 139 (20 nights); al-Samarqandī, *op. cit.*, II, 134b (15 nights); Muqātil, *op. cit.*, II, 90b, I, 143b (21 nights); Ibn Saᶜd, *op. cit.*, II, 74 (14 nights); Ibn ᶜAbd al-Barr al-Qurṭubī, *al-Durar fī khtiṣāri l-maghāzī wa-l-siyar*, ed. Shauqī Ḍayf, Cairo 1386/1966, p. 189 (more than 20 nights); Ibn Kathīr, *Tafsīr*, V, 443 (25 nights); al-Diyārbakrī, *op. cit.*, I, 493 (10, 15, 21, 25 nights); ᶜAlī b. Burhān al-Dīn, *op. cit.*, II, 357 (15 days, 25 nights, a month); Ibn Kathīr, *al-Bidāya*, IV, 124 (25 nights); al-ᶜAynī, *op. cit.*, XVII, 188 (more than 20, 15, 25 nights); al-Maqrīzī, *op. cit.*, I, 241 (25 nights, 15 days, a month); al-ᶜIṣāmī, *op. cit.*, II, 136 (15 nights, 25 nights, more than 10 nights); al-Balādhurī, *Futūḥ al-buldān*, ed. ᶜAbdallah and ᶜUmar al-Ṭabbāᶜ, Beirut 1377/1957, p. 32 (15 nights); al-Kalāᶜī, *op. cit.*, II, 177 (25 nights); Ibn Ḥibbān, *op. cit.*, I, 274 (25 nights); and see Barakat Ahmad, *op. cit.*, p. 73 (notes 7-8).

[100] See e.g. Muqātil, *op. cit.*, II, 90b (450 men killed, 750 enslaved); al-Wāqidī, *op. cit.*, 517-518 (600-700 executed); Mughulṭāy, *al-Zahr al-bāsim fī sīrat abī l-qāsim*, MS Leiden, or. 370, fol. 278a (400 men executed); al-Suyūṭī, *al-Durr al-manthūr*, V, 193 (on the authority of Qatāda: 400 fighting men executed, 700 women and children enslaved); Abū ᶜUbayd, *al-Amwāl*, p. 130, no. 348 (400 men killed); Ibn Junghul, *Ta'rīkh*, MS. Br. Mus. Or. 5912, fol. 287a (600-700 men, 800-900 men; on the authority of al-Layth b. Saᶜd: 400 men); al-Dhahabī, *Siyar aᶜlām al-nubalā'*, ed. Ṣalāḥ al-Dīn al-Munajjid, Cairo 1956, I, 205 (400 men executed); Ibn Saᶜd, *op. cit.*, II, 74 (600-700 men killed); al-Maqrīzī, *op. cit.*, II, 138 (400, 800-900 killed); Ibn Ḥibbān al-Bustī, *op. cit.*, I, 278 (600-900 executed); al-ᶜAynī, *op. cit.*, XVII, 192 (400, 600, 700, 900 beheaded); Ibn Kathīr, *al-Bidāya*, IV, 122, (400, 600-700, 800-900 executed); Ibn Sayyid al-Nās, *op. cit.*, II, 73 (600, 700, 800-900 killed); Ibn al-Athīr, *Jāmiᶜ al-uṣūl*, ed. Muḥammad Ḥāmid al-Fiqī, Cairo 1371/1952, IX, 202, no. 6088 (400 men executed); ᶜAlī b. Burhān al-Dīn, *op. cit.*, II, 360 (400, 600, 700, 750, 800 killed); al-Zurqānī, *Sharḥ al-mawāhib al-laduniyya*, Cairo 1325, II, 137 (600, 700, 800-900, 400 men executed); Ibn Kathīr, *Tafsīr*, V, 444 (700-800); al-Nasafī, *Tafsīr*, Cairo n.d. II, 300 (800-900 fighting men killed, or 600; 700 enslaved women and children); al-Diyārbakrī, *op. cit.*, I, 497 (400, 700, 700-800); al-Yaᶜqubī, *Ta'rīkh*, ed. Muḥammad Ṣādiq Baḥr al-ᶜUlūm, Najaf 4384/1964, II, 43 (750 fighting men executed); al-Majlisī, *op. cit.*, XX, 212 (600 fighting men executed; or 450 men killed; 750 enslaved); al-Maqdisī, *al-Bad' wa-l-ta'rīkh*, ed. Huart, Paris 1899, IV, 220 (700 killed); Ibn ᶜAbd al-Barr, *al-Istīᶜāb*, ed. ᶜAlī Muḥammad al-Bijāwī, Cairo 1380/1960, p. 603 (400 men killed).

[101] See e.g. al-Wāqidī, *op. cit.*, p. 500.

[102] See e.g. al-Wāqidī, *op. cit.*, p. 529.

any success if they launched an attack against the besieging force. They could probably attack suddenly and cause some losses to the besieging force, but they could not save themselves. The speech of Ka^c^b b. Asad with his three proposals which were rejected by Qurayẓa [103] is probably an invention, but it reflects the grave situation of Qurayẓa, their despair and the few alternatives left to them. The stronghold of Qurayẓa was not far from Medina; al-Katakānī reports that the abode of Qurayẓa was 2 miles from Medina; the place was called Bi'r ^c^Abd al-Muṭṭalib.[104] The besieging force received their supplies from Medina; Sa^c^d b. ^c^Ubāda supplied them with dates.[105] As mentioned above, there is no reference to serious war activities; but there was a lively movement of Quraẓī delegates who went down in order to negotiate with the Prophet the terms of their surrender. Finally they were compelled to surrender unconditionally. They probably still fostered some hopes that they would be expelled, losing all their possessions. There were in fact some of the Aus who dared to intercede with the Prophet, asking him to be lenient with Qurayẓa. The Prophet preferred to transfer the authority of arbitration and judgment to Sa^c^d b. Mu^c^ādh, a member of the Aus, who were the allies of Qurayẓa. The Prophet could indeed trust Sa^c^d b. Mu^c^ādh and rely on his decision: after all, he had been entrusted with arranging the murder of Ka^c^b b. al-Ashraf; it was Sa^c^d b. Mu^c^ādh who sent Muḥammad b. Maslama to Ka^c^b b. al-Ashraf to slay him.[106] As arbiter, *ḥakam*, Sa^c^d had to obtain in advance approval for his verdict from all the parties involved.[107] Only then could he issue his judgment concerning Qurayẓa. The Prophet granted it his approval stating that it had been revealed from heaven.[108]

[103] See Barakat Ahmad, *op. cit.*, p. 72 seq. and his analysis of Ka^c^b's speech. And see al-Majlisī, *op. cit.*, XX, 210-211.

[104] Al-Katakānī, *op. cit.*, III, 296; al-Majlisī, *op. cit.*, XX, 217; but see al-Samhūdī, *op. cit.*, p. 1141 (Bi'r Muṭṭalib 5 miles from Medina).

[105] See e.g. al-Wāqidī, *op. cit.*, p. 500; ^c^Alī b. Burhān al-Dīn, *op. cit.*, II, 357.

[106] See al-Bayhaqī, *al-Sunan al-kubrā*, Hyderabad 1344, IX, 183: *fa-lammā abā ka^c^b b. al-ashraf an yanzi^c^a ^c^an adhā rasūli llāhi (ṣ) wa-adhā l-muslimīn amara rasūlu llāhi (ṣ) sa^c^da bna mu^c^ādhin (r) an yab^c^atha rahṭan li-yaqtulūhu; fa-ba^c^atha ilayhi sa^c^du bnu mu^c^ādhin muḥammada bna maslamata l-anṣāriyya...*; Ibn al-Dayba^c^, *Taysīr al-wuṣūl ilā jāmi^c^ l-uṣūl*, Cairo 1388/1968, I, 285.

[107] See Barakat Ahmad, *op. cit.*, pp. 77-78 (nos. VI-X) and the discussion pp. 79-82.

[108] See Watt, *The Condemnation*; and cf. al-Dhahabī, *al-^c^Uluww*, p. 32; Ibn ^c^Abd al-Barr, *al-Istī^c^āb*, p. 603-604; and see al-Suyūṭī, *al-Durr*, III, 178: the decree conveyed to the Prophet in the morning by an angel (*...fa-ḥakama* [i.e. Sa^c^d] *fīhim an tuqtala muqātilatuhum wa-tusbā*

The order of the Prophet to stand up in honour of Saᶜd, their *sayyid*, and the remark of ᶜUmar: "the *sayyid* is God"[109] seem to combine two elements: the injunction to honour an eminent person of the community (or of the tribe – K.) by standing up, and the permissibility of naming this person *sayyid*; ᶜUmar had the courage to differ and to state that "*sayyid*", Lord, could only refer to God. The order of the Prophet to stand up in honour of Saᶜd contradicts utterances attributed to the Prophet in which he is said to have forbidden standing up in honour of important persons and to have prohibited notables from asking their people to stand up in front of them,[110] as it is a practice of the *aᶜājim*.[111]

dhrarīhim fa-qāla rasūlu llāhi (ṣ): bi-dhālika ṭaraqanī l-malaku saḥaran); and see al-Zurqānī, *Sharḥ al-mawāhib* II, 135-136 (different versions of the judgment, the explanation of *bi-dhālika ṭaraqanī al-malak saḥaran*, the discussion whether the *imām* is permitted to transfer his authority to the arbiter); and see Muqātil, *Tafsīr*, ed. ᶜAbdallah Maḥmūd Shaḥāta, Cairo 1969, I, 61 (commenting on *faᶜfū wa-ṣfaḥū* Muqātil renders *faᶜfū* by: *utrukūhum wa-ṣfaḥū, yaqūlu: wa-aᶜriḍū ᶜani l-yahūdi; ḥattā ya'tiya llāhu bi-amrihi* Muqātil explains: *fa-atā llāhu ᶜazza wa-jalla bi-amrihi fī ahli qurayẓata: al-qatlu wa-l-sabyu*...; and see *ib.* p. 303: *fa-kāna amru llāhi fīhim al-qatla wa-l-sabya*. The fate of Qurayẓa was thus predestined by God).

[109] See Watt, *The Condemnation*, p. 161; Barakat Aḥmad, *op. cit.*, p. 92.

[110] See e.g. al-Sakhāwī, *al-Maqāṣid al-ḥasana*, ed. ᶜAbdallah Muḥammad al-Ṣadīq, Beirut 1399/1979, p. 393, no. 1043 (but the permissibility recorded according to the precedent of Saᶜd b. Muᶜādh); Ibn Ḥamza l-Ḥusaynī, *al-Bayān wa-l-taᶜrīf fī asbāb wurūdi l-hadīthi l-sharīf*, Beirut 1400/1980, III, 194, no. 1508; al-Muᶜāfa b. ᶜImrān, *Kitāb al-zuhd*, MS. Ẓāhiriyya ḥadīth 359, fol. 246b (*man aḥabba an yamthula*...); Ibn Kathīr, *al-Bidāya*, VII, 126 (*man aḥabba*...); Ibn ᶜAbd al-Barr, *Bahjat al-majālis wa-uns al-mujālis*, ed. Muḥammad Mursī al-Khūlī and ᶜAbd al-Qādir al-Quṭṭ, Cairo, I, 274 (*man sarrahu*...; and: *qūmū ilā sayyidikum*); al-Shaᶜrānī, *Lawāqiḥ al-anwār*, Cairo 1381/1961, p. 834 inf. (*man aḥabba an yatamaththala*...); al-Bayhaqī, *Shuᶜab al-īmān*, MS Reisülküttab 219, fol. 149, sup. (*man aḥabba an yatamaththala*...); ᶜAlī b. Muḥammad al-Muᶜaddil, *Juz'*, MS. Ẓāhiriyya 18, fol. 274a (*man aḥabba an taqūma lahu*...); Ṣalāḥ al-Dīn al-Munajjid (ed.), *Rasā'il wa-nuṣūṣ* III, Ibn Taymiyya, *Fatwā fī l-nuhūḍ wa-l-alqāb*, Beirut 1963, p. 11 (*man sarrahu*...).

[111] See e.g. al-Zajjājī, *Amālī*, ed. ᶜAbd al-Salām Hārūn, Cairo 1382/1963, p. 68 (*lā taqūmū kamā taqūmu l-aᶜājim*); al-Muᶜāfā b. Imrān, *op. cit.*, fol. 246b (*lā-taqūmū kamā tuᶜaẓẓimu (!) l-aᶜājimu baᶜḍuhum baᶜḍan; laᶜana llāhu man qāmat lahu l-ᶜabīdu ṣufūfan qiyāman*; and see esp. *ult.*: *lā yuqāmu lī, innamā yuqāmu li-llāhi*); al-Bayhaqī, *Shuᶜab*, fol. 148b inf. (*ᶜan anas: mā kāna shakhṣun aḥabba ilayhim min rasūli llāhi (ṣ) wa-kānū idhā raᶜauhu lam yataḥarrakū li-mā ᶜarafū min karāhiyyatihi li-dhālika*); *ib.*: *lā taqūmū kamā taqūmu l-aᶜājim*...; al-Shaᶜrānī, *Lawāqiḥ*, p. 834 (*lā-taqūmū ᶜalā ru'ūsi a'immatikum kamā taqūmu l-aᶜājimu ᶜalā ru'ūsi mulūkihā*; and p. 835: *lā taqūmū kamā taqūmu l-aᶜājimu*); ᶜAlī b. Muḥammad al-Muᶜaddil, *al-Juz' al-awwal, al-Fawā'id al-ḥisān*, MS. Ẓāhiriyya 18, fol. 274a (*ᶜan anas: mā kāna shakhṣun aḥabba ilayhim*...; *qūmū ilā sayyidikum*...); Ibn ᶜAdiyy, *al-Kāmil fī ḍuᶜafā'i l-rijāl*, MS. Ahmet III, 2943/I. fol. 127b.(*innamā halaka man kāna qablakum bi-an ᶜaẓẓamū mulūkahum bi-an qāmū wa-qaᶜadū*...); Ṣalāḥ al-Dīn al-Munajjid, ed., *Rasā'il*, p. 10 (*lam yakun shakhṣun*...).

The utterance *qūmū ilā sayyidikum* was commented in various ways in order to evade unnecessary polemics. *Qūmū* was in some of the commentaries interpreted as a summons to the people to stand up and aid the wounded Saᶜd to alight.[112] The word *sayyid* was explained as pointing to the idea of *siyāda* inherent in his authority as appointed arbiter.[113] According to some traditions, however, reflecting the ideas of conservative-ascetic circles in Islam, the Prophet himself forbade addressing people by the title *sayyid*: When ᶜAbdallah b. al-Shikhkhīr came to the Prophet and addressed him by *"sayyidunā"* the Prophet said: "The *sayyid* is God."[114] It was a plausible solution to record another version, which did not cause polemics: *qūmū ilā khayrikum.*[115] The phrase *qūmū ilā sayyidikum,* which was in fact an expression of esteem and respect, seems to have been current in the period of the Prophet and became in later times a subject of politico-theological polemics.

The number of the besieging forces: 36 horsemen and 3000 foot-soldiers and the period of the siege generally given as lasting between 15 – 25 days indicates that the stronghold was fortified and that the population was numerous. The number of 400 Quraẓī men able to fight, which is the smaller number recorded in all the versions about the surrender, seems to be plausible; nowhere in all the sources available is a smaller number mentioned. The different reports of Saᶜd's decree vary in their wording as to those who were to be put to death: "men", "those over whom the razors had passed", "fighting men", "adults".[116] The meaning of all the reports is the same: the men able to fight have to be beheaded; in many compendia of *fiqh* this is identified with the age of puberty or adolescence.

The details about the place of execution and its duration are divergent or even contradictory. The commentators claim that Saᶜd issued his

[112] See e.g. al-Munāwī, *Fayḍ al-qadīr*, Beirut 1391/1972, IV, 530, no. 6164: ...*wa-qīla maᶜnāhu qūmū li-iᶜānatihi fi-l-nuzūli ᶜani l-dābbati li-mā bihi min al-jarḥ...*

[113] See e.g. al-ᶜAynī *op. cit.*, XVI, 269: ...*wa-immā bi-an yurāda bihi al-siyādatu l-khāṣṣatu, ay min jihati taḥkīmihi fi-ḥādhihi l-qaḍiyya...* and see the comment of Suhaylī, *al-Rauḍ al-unuf*, VI, 368.

[114] Mughulṭāy, *op. cit.*, fol. 282a; Ibn Saᶜd, *op. cit.*, I, 311, l.5; Ibn al-Athīr, *Usd al-ghāba,* III, 182-183.

[115] See e.g. al-ᶜAynī, *op. cit.*, XVI, 269, XVII, 191; Ibn Ḥamza al-Ḥusaynī, *op. cit.*, III, 70, no. 1286; Yūsuf b. Mūsā l-Ḥanafī, *al-Muᶜtaṣar min al-mukhtaṣar min mushkili l-āthār*, Hyderabad 1362, II, 387; al-Bayhaqī, *Shuᶜab*, fol. 148a; Ibn al-Athīr, *Jāmiᶜ al uṣūl min aḥādīthi l-rasūl*, IX, 203, no. 6089.

[116] See Barakat Ahmad, *op. cit.*, 81-82.

judgment in the mosque erected on the territory of Qurayẓa.[117] Some other sources state that he uttered it in the mosque of Medina. All the reports agree, however, that the Qurayẓa were led to Medina and executed there.

There are diverse traditions concerning the exact place of execution. Several reports say that the Quraẓīs were beheaded in the market of Medina and buried there;[118] some Shīʿī sources report that the ditches were dug in Baqīʿ, and the corpses of the executed Quraẓīs were buried there.[119] The Baqīʿ, according to some reports, was adjacent to the market of Medina ; some reports mention it as forming part of the market.[120] According to Shīʿī sources the executions were carried out in the cool periods of the day: in the morning and in the evening, over a period of three days.[121] This was in compliance with an explicit order of the Prophet not to increase the sufferings of the Quraẓīs by executing them in the hottest hours of the day; the Prophet also ordered that they be provided with sweet water and good food and that proper conditions for their captivity be maintained.[122] Other reports say that the executions were carried out during one day and lasted until the evening when they were carried out at the light of firebrands.[123] Shīʿī reports say that ʿAlī beheaded twenty Quraẓī captives; each Companion beheaded one or two captives.[124] Certain reports tell an interesting story about how the Aus, who had criticized the execution of the Quraẓīs, became involved in the operation: some captives were divided among the different clans of the Aus and each clan had to put to death their captives.[125] Several accounts stress that ʿAlī and al-Zubayr carried out the executions in the market of Medina.[126]

The number of women and children which is given in some sources is 1000. This seems to be trustworthy when it is compared with the num-

[117] Ibn Ḥajar, *Fatḥ al-bārī*, VII, 317; al-ʿAynī, *op. cit.*, XVI, 269; Barakat Ahmad, *op. cit.*, pp. 90-91.

[118] See above, and notes 31-34.

[119] Al-Katakānī, *op. cit.*, III, 305; al-Majlisī, *op. cit.*, XX, 23b.

[120] See M. Lecker, *The Markets of Medina*, note 57.

[121] Al-Katakānī, *op. cit.*, III, 305; al-Majlisī, *op. cit.*, XX, 237 inf.-238.

[122] See e.g. al-Majlisī, *op. cit.*, XX, 238, ll.1-2.

[123] See e.g. al-Wāqidī, *op. cit.*, p. 517; ʿAlī b. Burhān al-Dīn, *op. cit.*, II, 365.

[124] al-Katakānī, *op. cit.*, III, 306.

[125] See Barakat Ahmad, *op. cit.*, p. 91; M. Watt, *Muḥammad at Medina*, 215 inf.-216; al-Zurqānī, *Sharḥ al-mawāhib*, II, 137.

[126] See e.g. Barakat Ahmad, *op. cit.*, pp. 83, 85; M. Watt, *Muḥammad at Medina*, p. 216.

ber of executed men, which is said to have been 400. The women and children were sent to Syria and Najd and sold there in exchange for horses and weapons.[127] Some of them were bought by the Jews of Khaybar, Wādī l-Qurā, Taymā, and by a Jew of Medina;[128] others were bought by ᶜAbd al-Raḥmān b. ᶜAuf and ᶜUthmān; these two are said to have made a profit; it was especially ᶜUthmān who was successful in this commercial enterprise.[129] Several women were divided among the believers in Medina; some accounts say that this was done in accordance with one of the injunctions of Saᶜd b. Muᶜādh: to kill the men and spare the women "in order that the believers might be aided by them" (i.e. by the women – K.).[130]

The list of the booty of Qurayẓa which was collected by the believers after the surrender is of importance: 1500 swords, 300 coats of mail, 200 spears, 1500 shields; in addition to the weapons there were household goods, utensils, camels and cattle. The wine was, of course, poured out.[131] The large quantities of weapons are disproportionate relative to the number of fighting men (i.e. men who reached puberty – K.): 1500 swords, 1500 shields and 2000 spears exceed the military needs of 400 men able to fight. The only possible conjecture is that Qurayẓa used to sell (or lend) some of the weapons kept in the storehouses in their stronghold. The title *"ahlu l-ḥalqa"* "the people of the weapons" by which Quraysh in their letter addressed the Jews is to be explained by reference to these storehouses, in which weapons were accumulated and stored.[132] These weapons seem to have strengthened their position and prestige in the tribal society.

The suspicions that Qurayẓa attempted to plot with Quraysh against the Prophet would probably not justify the cruel punishment of execu-

[127] See al-Wāqidī, *op. cit.*, p. 523.

[128] See Barakat Ahmad, *op. cit.*, p. 88.

[129] See e.g. al-Wāqidī, *op. cit.*, p. 523; ᶜAlī b. Burhān al-Dīn, *op. cit.*, II, 379; al-Maqrīzī, *Imtāᶜ*, I, 251.

[130] Abū ᶜUbayd, *op. cit.*, p. 130, no. 348; Ibn al-Athīr, *Jāmiᶜ al-uṣūl*, IX, 202, no. 6088.

[131] See e.g. al-Wāqidī, *op. cit.*, 509-510; al-Zurqānī, *Sharḥ al-mawāhib*, II, 137 (500 shields); al-Maqrīzī, *op. cit.*, I, 245; ᶜAlī b. Burhān al-Dīn, *op. cit.*, II, 363 ult. (500 shields); Ibn Sayyid al-Nās, *op. cit.*, II, 74 (500 shields); al-Diyārbakrī, *op. cit.*, I, 496 inf. (500 shields); Ibn Saᶜd, *op. cit.*, II, 75; Muḥammad b. Yaḥyā Bahrān, *Ibtisām al-barq, sharḥ manẓūmat al-qaṣaṣ al-ḥaqq fī sīrat khayri l-khalq*, ed. Yaḥyā b. ᶜAbd al-Karīm al-Fuḍayl, Beirut 1394/1974, p. 178 (100 spears).

[132] See e.g. ᶜAbd al-Razzāq, *op. cit.*, V, 359.

tion of the fighting men and the sale of the women and children; Qurayẓa repented of their deeds, the people of Aus beseeched the Prophet, asking him to pardon Qurayẓa.[133] One might have expected the Prophet to pardon them. There must have been an additional reason for the hostility of the Prophet against Qurayẓa, not disclosed in the vague accounts about the violation of the treaty. This can be gauged from the passage in the commentary of Muqātil on *Sūrat al-Anfāl*, verse 57: "The Jews violated the compact between them and the Prophet and aided the unbelievers of Mecca by providing them with weapons with which to fight the Prophet and his Companions."[134]

Qurayẓa were, as mentioned, ready to depart with their families leaving the huge quantities of weapons as booty for the Prophet. The Prophet's approval of the cruel judgment of Saᶜd cannot be explained in this case. Never before had the Prophet inflicted such a punishment on any tribal group.

Current reports say that the land and booty of Qurayẓa were divided among the 3000 warriors and 36 horsemen; the *khums* was taken out of the booty.[135] A different account reports that Saᶜd b. Muᶜādh ordered in his decree that the property of Qurayẓa be divided among the Muhājirūn only, not among the Anṣār.[136] According to another report it was the Prophet who allotted land and immovable property to the Muhājirūn, emphasizing in his address to the Anṣār that they were living in their abode (and consequently did not need additional land – K.).[137] There seems to have been some feeling of discontent amont the Anṣār in connection with the division of the land of Qurayẓa. This is reflected in a report stating that Saᶜd b. Muᶜādh decreed that the land of Qurayẓa be allotted to the Muhājirūn (*wa-takūna l-diyāru li-l-muhājirīn*); the Anṣār

133 Al-Wāqidī, *op. cit.*, p. 510.

134 Muqātil, *op. cit.*, I, 147a: ...*wa-dhālika anna l-yahūda naqaḍū l-ᶜahda lladhī kāna baynahum wa-bayna l-nabiyyi (ṣ) wa-aᶜānū mushrikī makkata bi-l-silāḥi ᶜalā qitāli l-nabiyyi (ṣ) wa-aṣḥābihi thumma yaqūlūna nasīnā wa-akhṭa'nā, thumma yuᶜāhiduhum al-thāniyata fa-yanquḍūna l-ᶜahda.*

135 See e.g. al-Wāqidī, *op. cit.*, p. 521-525; Ibn Hishām, *Sīra*, III, 256; al-Balādhurī, *Futūḥ*, p. 33; al-Maqrīzī, *op. cit.*, I, 250; Ibn Ḥibbān, *op. cit.*, I, 278; al-Kalāᶜī, *al-Iktifā'*, II, 186; Ibn ᶜAbd al-Barr, *al-Durar*, p. 193; al-Qurṭubī, *op. cit.*, XIV, 142; and see Barakat Ahmad, *op. cit.*, p. 89.

136 Al-Yaᶜqūbī, *op. cit.*, II, 43; al-Katakānī, *op. cit.*, III, 306.

137 Al-Nasafī, *Tafsīr*, III, 301: *ruwiya anna rasūla llāhi jaᶜala ᶜaqārahum li-l-muhājirīna dūna l-anṣāri wa-qāla lahum innakum fī manāzilikum.*

objected, arguing that they had property shared with the Muhājirūn. Saᶜd replied: "I wanted them (i.e. the Muhājirūn – K.) to become self-sufficient, and not need your aid".[138] More details about the division of the palm trees of Qurayẓa are given by Ibn Ḥajar: the Anṣār helped the Muhājirūn by granting them palm trees for their use. After the conquest of the lands of Naḍīr and Qurayẓa the Muhājirūn were granted land and palm trees and could thus return the trees which the Anṣār had given them.[139]

The division of the land and property improved the status of the Muhājirūn at Medina and helped them to gain their economic independence. The military strength of the Muslim community of Medina grew due to the weapons taken as booty; the sale of the captured women and children as slaves for horses and weapons enabled to enlarge the Muslim military force for further conquests.

The Jewish tribe of Qurayẓa ceased to exist.

[138] ᶜAlī b. Burhān al-Dīn, *op. cit.*, II, 362 (*innī aḥbabtu an yastaghnū ᶜankum*); and cf. al-Majlisī, *op. cit.*, XX, 212 sup.: *innakum dhawū ᶜaqārin wa-laysa li-l-muhājirīna ᶜaqār*.

[139] *Fatḥ al-bārī*, VII, 316.

IX

...*ILLĀ BI-ḤAQQIHI*...
A STUDY OF AN EARLY *ḤADĪTH*

In memory of my friend Dov ʿĪron

The revolt of the tribes in the Arabian peninsula after the death of the prophet Muḥammad, the so-called *ridda*, endangered the very existence of the Muslim community in Medina and the survival of the nascent commonwealth set up by the Prophet. The rebellious tribes, aware of the weakness of the new leadership of the Medinan community, strove to sever their ties with the new authority in Medina, broke their allegiance to the newly elected Caliph, Abū Bakr, and declared that the agreements they had concluded with the Prophet were null and void. They sought to regain their separate tribal existence, and to rid themselves of the authority of Medina. Thus, returning to the type of relations with Mecca which were in effect during the Jāhiliyya, they were willing to negotiate over agreements with the Medinan leadership which would be based on the principle of non-aggression. Some chiefs of tribes proposed to defend Medina, and to protect the city against attacks by other tribes, in return for certain payments they would get. Abū Bakr refused to negotiate with the chiefs of the tribes and decided to fight the hostile forces in the vicinity of Medina. The Muslim troops dispatched by Abū Bakr succeeded in crushing the revolt and in bringing the tribes of the peninsula under the authority of Medina. Abū Bakr thus assured the survival and the perpetuation of the commonwealth of Medina. Having brought the tribal forces under the control of Medina and having laid a solid foundation for their unity and loyalty, he sent tribal troops under Medinan command towards the northern and the eastern borders of the Arab peninsula, thus initiating the powerful Muslim conquests in the Persian and Byzantine empires.

An examination of some data incorporated in the reports about the *ridda* may help in elucidating certain economic aspects of the revolt. The scrutiny of a *ḥadīth* which is often quoted in the story of the *ridda* may enable us to get a glimpse into the ideas held by certain groups of Muslim scholars concerning the conditions imposed on those willing to embrace Islam after the death of the Prophet, the status of the *ridda* people, and the question whether it was right to make war on them.

The term *ridda*, apostasy, applied in the sources to the rebellious movement of the tribes, was questioned by Western scholars who pointed out the political and social aspects of the revolt.[1] The economic factors leading to the rebellion were clearly expounded by Shaban,[2] who emphasized the struggle which the tribes, whether allied to Medina or not, carried against the Medinan hegemony and the commercial interests which played a major part in intertribal relations.

The economic effect of conversion to Islam can indeed be noticed in some early traditions. Al-Shāfi'ī carries a report that (members of -K) Quraysh used to travel to Syria and Iraq with their merchandise. Upon their conversion to Islam they spoke to the Prophet of their fear that their income might suffer as a result of their break with unbelief and of their having become Muslims, a step which might displease the rulers of Syria and Iraq. The Prophet allayed their anxiety by predicting that the end of Persian and Byzantine rule was near.[3] The unrest in Mecca after the death of the Prophet, the feeling of uncertainty and the fear of losing their means of sustenance if they remained loyal to Islam and kept their obligations seem to have cast a shadow over the city;[4] the inhabitants wavered in face of the tribal revolt and were reluctant to pay their taxes. Suhayl b. 'Amr[5]

1 See e.g. A.J. Wensinck, *The Muslim Creed*, London 1965 (repr.); pp. 11-12; J. Wellhausen, *Das Arabische Reich und Sein Sturz*, Berlin 1960 (repr.), pp. 14-15; C. Brockelmann, *History of the Islamic Peoples*, New York 1947, pp. 45-6 (..."In this religious motives played scarcely any role at all; there was simply a desire to be rid of the troublesome rule of the Muslims in Medina."); W. Montgomery Watt, *Muḥammad at Medina*, Oxford 1956, pp. 79-80, 147-150.

2 M.A. Shaban, *Islamic History, A new interpretation*, Cambridge 1971, pp. 19-23.

3 Al-Shāfi'ī, *al-Umm*, Cairo 1321 (repr. 1388/1968), IV, 94; al-Ṭaḥāwī, *Mushkil al-āthār*, Hyderabad 1333, I, 214 (from al-Shāfi'ī); and see the *ḥadīth: idhā halaka kisrā...:* al-Ṭaḥāwī, *Mushkil*, I, 212-217; al-Suyūṭī, *al-Khaṣā'iṣ al-kubrā*, ed. Khalīl Harrās, Cairo 1387/1967, II, 412; Ibn Kathīr, *Nihāyat al-bidāya wa-l-nihāya*, ed. Muḥammad Fahīm Abū 'Ubayya, Riyāḍ 1968, I, 9-10; idem, *Shamā'il al-rasūl*, ed. Muṣṭafā 'Abd al-Wāḥid, Cairo 1386/1967, p. 352; idem *al-Bidāya wa-l-nihāya*, Beirut 1966, VI, 194; Abū l-Maḥāsin Yūsuf b. Mūsā al-Ḥanafī, *al-Mu'taṣar min al-mukhtaṣar*, Hyderabad 1362, I, 248-249.

4 Several reports stress however that Mecca was not affected by the *ridda* movement; see e.g. al-Ṭabarī, *Ta'rīkh*, Cairo 1357/1939, II, 475; al-Maqdisī, *al-Bad' wa-l-ta'rīkh*, ed. Huart, Paris 1899, V, 151 inf.; al-Shawkānī, *Nayl al-auṭār*, IV, 135; al-'Aynī, *'Umdat al-qārī*, VIII, 244, l. 11 from bottom.

5 See on him e.g. al-Zubayr b. Bakkār, *Jamharat nasab quraysh wa-akhbārihā*, Ms. Bodley, Marsh 384, fols. 189a-190a; Muṣ'ab b. 'Abdallāh, *Nasab quraysh*, ed. Lévi-Provençal, Cairo 1953, pp. 417-418; Anonymous, *al-Ta'rīkh al-muḥkam fīman intasaba ilā l-nabiyyi ṣallā llāhu 'alayhi wa-sallam*, Ms. Br. Mus. Or. 8653, fols. 196a-197a; al-Dhahabī, *Siyar a'lām al-nubalā'*, ed. As'ad Ṭalas, Cairo 1962, III, 32, I, 141-142; idem, *Ta'rīkh al-islām*, Cairo 1367, II, 15; Ibn Ḥajar, *al-Iṣāba*, ed. 'Alī Muḥammad al-Bijāwī, Cairo 1392/1972, III, 212, no. 3575; Ibn 'Abd al-Barr, *al-Istī'āb*, ed. Muḥammad al-Bijāwī, Cairo 1380/1960, pp. 669-672, no. 1106; Ibn al-Athīr, *Usd al-ghāba*, Cairo 1280, II, 371-373; al-Ḥākim, *al-Mustadrak*, Hyderabad 1342, III, 281-282; Ibn al-'Arabī, *Aḥkām al-qur'ān*, ed. 'Alī al-Bijāwī, Cairo 1387/1967, II, 951 inf. = 952.

ascended the *minbar* and addressed Quraysh; stressing the extent of his wealth he urged them to hand over their *zakāt* to the governor and promised to compensate them for any *zakāt* payment should the regime of Medina collapse.[6] Al-Jārūd, the leader of 'Abd al-Qays, promised his people to repay double the losses they would incur if they remained faithful to Islam.[7] The tribes' unwillingness to pay the tax, the *zakāt*, is plainly reflected in the recorded speeches of the tribal leaders and in the verses of their poets. It is noteworthy indeed that when the leaders of the rebellious tribes were captured and brought before Abū Bakr accused of apostasy, they defended themselves by saying that they had not become unbelievers, but were merely stingy with their wealth (i.e. they were reluctant to pay the *zakāt* from it — K).[8]

Another aspect of the secession movement was the tribal leaders' contention that their allegiance was confined to the Prophet; they had concluded their agreements with him, had accepted his authority and had given him the oath of allegiance; they had no commitment to Abū Bakr.[9] The arguments of the secessionist tribes, who stressed the incompetence of the successor of the Prophet and claimed that they were exempted from paying the *zakāt*, are recorded in some commentaries of the Qur'ān. They are said to have based themselves on Sūra IX, 103: "...Take alms of their wealth to purify them and to cleanse them thereby and pray for them, thy prayers are a comfort for them...". It is the Prophet who is addressed in this verse and ordered to collect the tax; and it was the Prophet who was authorized to purify and cleanse them and to pray for them in return for

6 Muḥammad b. Ḥabīb, *al-Munammaq*, ed. Khurshīd Aḥmad Fāriq, Hyderabad 1384/1964, pp. 260-261; al-Balādhurī, *Ansāb al-ashrāf*, ed. Muḥammad Ḥamīdullāh, Cairo 1959, p. 304: *...wa-anā ḍāminun, in lam yatimma l-amru, an aruddahā ilaykum...* Cf. Ibn al-Athīr, *Usd*, II, 371 penult: *anna rasūla llāhi lammā tuwuffiya irtajjat makkatu limā ra'at qurayshun min irtidādi l-'arabi wa-khtafā 'attābu bnu asīdin al-umawiyyu, amīru makkata li-l-nabiyyi(ṣ) fa-qāma suhaylu bnu 'amrin khaṭīban...*; and see Ibn Hishām, *al-Sīra al-nabawiyya*, ed. Muṣṭafā l-Saqā, Ibrāhīm al-Abyārī, 'Abd al-Ḥāfiẓ al-Shalabī, Cairo 1355/1936, IV, 316: *...anna akthara ahli makkata, lammā tuwuffiya rasūlu llāhi(ṣ) hammū bi-l-rujū'i 'an al-islāmi wa-arādū dhālika ḥattā khāfahum 'attābu bnu asīdin fa-tawārā, fa-qāma suhaylun...*; 'Abd al-Jabbār, *Tathbīt dalā'il al-nubuwwa*, ed. 'Abd al-Karīm 'Uthmān, Beirut 1386/1966, p. 317; and cf. pp. 227-228.

7 Ibn Abī l-Ḥadīd, *Sharḥ nahj al-balāgha*, ed. Muḥammad Abū l-Faḍl Ibrāhīm, Cairo 1964, XVIII, 57.

8 Al-Shāfi'ī, *op. cit.*, IV, 134: *...wa-qālū li-abī bakrin ba'da l-isāri: mā kafarnā ba'da īmāninā wa-lākin shaḥaḥnā 'alā amwālinā...*; al-Bayhaqī, *al-Sunan al-kubrā*, Hyderabad 1355, VIII, 178; al-Kalā'ī, *Ta'rīkh al-ridda*, ed. Khurshīd Aḥmad Fāriq, New Delhi 1970, p. 42; cf. *ib.* pp. 149, 170.

9 See e.g. al-Shāfi'ī, *op. cit.*, IV, 134; al-Ṭabarī, *Ta'rīkh*, II, 417: *aṭa'nā rasūla llāhi mā kāna wasṭanā: fa-yā 'ajaban mā bālu mulki abī bakri*; Ibn al-'Arabī, *op. cit.*, II, 994; Ibn Kathīr, *al-Bidāya*, VI, 313; al-Khaṭṭābī, *Ma'ālim al-sunan*, Ḥalab 1933, II, 4; al-Bayhaqī, *al-Sunan al-kubrā*, VIII, 178.

their payment. Consequently they considered themselves dispensed from their obligations towards the Prophet, as his successor had not the ability to grant them the compensation mentioned in the Qur'ān.[10] It is rather doubtful whether the leaders of the seceding tribes indeed used arguments based on the interpretation of Qur'ānic verses when they debated with the Muslim leaders; the recorded interpretation reflects however the idea held by the seceding tribal leaders that their obligations and allegiance were only binding towards the Prophet, not towards his successor.

It is noteworthy that the Muslim tradition which emphasizes the religious aspects of the *ridda* secession also provides a clue to a better evaluation of the intentions of the rebellious tribes. Certain late compilations of *ḥadīth* and of *fiqh* are of importance for the elucidation of a number of terms occurring in the traditions. Wensinck quotes the commentary of al-Nawawī (d. 676 H) on Muslim's (d. 261 H) *Ṣaḥīḥ* in which it is said that there were three kinds of resistance in Arabia: there were two groups of unbelievers (viz. the followers of the false prophets and people who gave up religion altogether — K) and a group who did not renounce Islam, but refused to pay the *zakāt*. Wensinck puts forward a very similar division: "those who followed religious or political adventurers and therefore turned their backs on Medina and Islam and those who cut the links with Medina without associating themselves with any new religious leader. This latter group did not, in all probability, reject Islam; for their attachment to religion must have been too insignificant a fact. What they rejected was *zakāt*."[11]

The division, as recorded by al-Nawawī, can however be traced back to a period some four and half centuries earlier. Al-Shāfi'ī (d. 204 H) gives a similar division of the seceding groups, drawing a clear line between those who fell into unbelief like the followers of Musaylima, Ṭulayḥa and al-Aswad al-'Ansī and those who refused to pay the *zakāt*, while remaining faithful to Islam.[12] It is significant that al-Shāfi'ī, in analyzing the problem whether it is permitted to fight and kill members of these groups, raises doubts whether the term *ahl-al-ridda*, "people of apostasy", can be applied to both of them. He finally justifies it by referring to them common usage of Arabic, in which *irtadda* denotes retreat from former tenets; this

[10] Ibn al-'Arabī, *op. cit.*, II, 994; al-Qasṭallānī, *Irshād al-sārī li-sharḥ ṣaḥīḥi l-bukhārī*, Cairo 1327, III, 6; al-Qurṭubī, *Tafsīr* (= *al-Jāmi' li-aḥkāmi l-qur'ān*), Cairo 1386/1967, VIII, 244-245; Ibn Kathīr, *al-Bidāya*, VI, 311.

[11] Wensinck, *op. cit.*, p. 13.

[12] Al-Shāfi'ī, *op. cit.*, IV, 134.

includes, of course, both: falling into unbelief and the refusal to pay the taxes.[13]

When al-Shāfi'ī analyzes the status of the second group, he remarks that in their refusal to pay the *zakāt* they acted as if they were interpreting the verse Sūra IX, 103 in the way mentioned above. Shāfi'ī is concerned with the problem of the false interpretation of the verse (*al-muta'awwilūn al-mumtani'ūn*) and seeks to establish that fighting this group and killing its members is lawful, by comparing it to the group of Muslims rebelling unjustly against a just ruler (*al-bāghūn*). He ultimately justifies without reserve the war-action taken by Abū Bakr against the group which refused to pay the *zakāt*.[14]

The status of this group is discussed at length by al-Khaṭṭābī (d. 384 H) who states that they were in fact unjust rebels (*wa-hā'ulā'i 'alā l-ḥaqīqati ahlu baghyin*) although they were not given this name at the time; this name became current at the time of 'Alī.[15] He remarks that among this group there were some factions who were ready to pay the tax, but who were prevented from doing so by their leaders. He further stresses that they were indeed not unbelievers (*kuffār*); they shared the name *ahl al-ridda* with the unbelievers because like them they refused to carry out certain duties and prescriptions of the faith.[16] The argument of this group in connection with the verse Sūra IX, 103 is here recorded in a peculiar context, revealing some details of later polemic over religious and political issues in connection with the decision of Abū Bakr to fight those who refused to pay the *zakāt*. Al-Khaṭṭābī identifies explicitly the people who passed sharp criticism on Abū Bakr's action; those were certain people from among the Shī'ī *rawāfiḍ*, who stated that the tribes refusing to pay the *zakāt* merely held a different interpretation for the verse mentioned above (Sūra IX, 103): it was the Prophet who was addressed in the verse and only the Prophet could purify them and pray for them.[17] As a consequence it was not right to fight them and Abū Bakr's military action was oppressive and unjust. A certain Shī'ī faction argued indeed that the group which had refused the *zakāt* payment suspected Abū Bakr and considered him unworthy of being entrusted with their property (scil. of having it handed over to him as tax — K). Al-Khaṭṭābī refutes these arguments and marks them as lies and

13 Al-Shāfi'ī, *op. cit., ib. (...fā-in qāla qā'ilun: mā dalla 'alā dhālika wa-l-'āmmatu taqūlu lahum ahlu l-ridda...).*

14 Al-Shāfi'ī, *op. cit.*, IV, 134.

15 Al-Khaṭṭābī, *op. cit.*, II, 4; and see p. 6: *...fa-ammā māni'ū l-zakāti minhum l-muqīmūna 'alā aṣli l-dīni fa-innahum ahlu baghyin...*; cf. al-Shawkānī, *Nayl al-auṭār*, Cairo 1372/1953, IV, 135-137 (quoting al-Khaṭṭābī).

16 Al-Khaṭṭābī, *op. cit.*, II, 6.

17 Cf. above, note 10; and see al-Shawkānī, *Nayl*, IV, 136.

calumnies. Al-Khaṭṭābī argues that the verse was actually addressed to the Prophet, but that it put an obligation on all the believers and that it is incumbent upon all the believers at all times. Cleansing and purification will be granted to the believer who hands over the *zakāt* and it is recommended that the *imām* and the collector of taxes invoke God's blessing for the payer of the tax. Further al-Khaṭṭābī strengthens his argument by a *ḥadīth* of the Prophet. According to this tradition the last words of the Prophet were: "Prayer and what your right hands possess." This *ḥadīth* is usually interpreted as a bid to observe the prayer and to take care of one's dependents; but al-Khaṭṭābī's interpretation is different; according to him "*mā malakat aymānukum*", "what your right hands possess" refers to property and possessions and has to be understood as an injunction to pay the *zakāt* tax.[18] According to this interpretation *zakāt* goes together with prayer. Consequently al-Khaṭṭābī deduces that *zakāt* is as obligatory as prayer and that he who is in charge of prayer is also in charge of the collection of *zakāt*. This was one of the considerations which induced Abū Bakr not to permit that prayer be separated from tax and to set out to fight the group loyal to Islam, but refusing to pay the *zakāt*. Finally al-Khaṭṭābī compares Abū Bakr's attitude towards this group and the rules which would apply nowadays should such a group, or a similar one arise. In the period of Abū Bakr the aim was merely to compel the rebels to pay the tax; they were not killed. The leniency shown towards them took into consideration their ignorance since they had been in Islam only for a short period. But a group who would deny *zakāt* nowadays would be considered as falling into unbelief and apostasy and the apostate would have to be killed.[19]

The discussions concerning the lawfulness of Abū Bakr's decision to fight this group can thus be understood as a later debate with the aim of a positive evaluation of Abū Bakr's action against the rebellious tribes, and providing convincing proof that his action was in accordance with the prescriptions and injunctions of the Qur'ān and with the *sunna* of the Prophet. The precedent of Abū Bakr had to serve as an example for dealing with similar cases of revolt in the contemporary Muslim Empire.

The Sunnī assessment of Abū Bakr's action is put forward in an utterance attributed to al-Ḥasan al-Baṣrī and recorded by Abū Sukayn (d. 251

18 See both interpretations in Ibn al-Athīr's *al-Nihāya* s.v. mlk; *L'A* s.v. mlk; and cf. e.g. Ibn Sa'd, *Ṭabaqāt*, Beirut 1376/1957, II, 253-254; 'Abd al-Razzāq, *al-Muṣannaf*, ed. Ḥabīb al-Raḥmān al-A'ẓamī, Beirut 1392/1972, V 436 (*ittaqū llāha fī l-nisā'i wa-mā malakat aymānukum*); Nūr al-Dīn al-Haythamī, *Majma' al-zawā'id*, Beirut 1967 (reprint) IV, 237.

19 Al-Khaṭṭābī, *op. cit.*, II, 6-9; cf. Ibn Kathīr, *Tafsīr al-qur'ān*, Beirut 1385/1966, III, 488.

H)[20] in his *Juz'*.[21] Al-Ḥasan evaluates the crucial events in the history of the Muslim community according to the actions of the men who shaped the destiny of the community for ever. Four men set aright the Muslim community. al-Ḥasan says, and two men impaired and spoilt it. 'Umar b. al-Khaṭṭāb set it aright on the Day of the Hall of the Banū Sā'ida, answering the arguments of the Anṣār who demanded an equal share in authority with Quraysh. He reminded the assembled that the Prophet ordered Abū Bakr to pray in front of the people (thus establishing his right to rule the people — K) and that the Prophet uttered the bidding saying: "The leaders are from Quraysh" (*al-a'immatu min quraysh*). The Anṣār convinced by the arguments of 'Umar dropped their claim for a Qurashī-Anṣāri duumvirate of two amīrs. But for 'Umar people would litigate upon the rights of the Caliphate until the Day of Resurrection. Abū Bakr set aright the Muslim community during the *ridda*. He asked the advice of the people (i.e. the Companions of the Prophet — K) and all of them advised him to accept from the rebelling tribes their commitment of prayer and give up their *zakāt*. But Abū Bakr insisted and swore that if they withheld even one string which they had been in the habit of paying to the Messenger of Allah he would fight them. But for Abū Bakr, says al-Ḥasan, people would stray away from the right path until the Day of Resurrection. 'Uthmān saved the community like 'Umar and Abū Bakr by the introduction of the single reading of the Qur'ān. But for 'Uthmān people would go astray on the Qur'ān until the Day of Resurrection. Finally 'Alī like his predecessors set aright the community by refusing to divide the captives and spoils of his defeated enemies after the Battle of the Camel, thus establishing the rules which apply in a case when factions of the believers (*ahl al-qibla*) fight each other. In contradistinction to these four righteous Caliphs two men corrupted the Muslim community: 'Amr b. al-'Āṣ by the advice he gave to Mu'āwiya to lift the Qur'āns (at Ṣiffīn — K) which caused the *khawārij* and their *taḥkīm* to appear; this (fateful split of the community — K) will last until the Day of Resurrection. The other wicked man is al-Mughīra b. Shu'ba, who advised Mu'āwiya to appoint his son (Yazīd) as Caliph, thus establishing a hereditary rule. But for al-Mughīra the *shūrā* principle of election would have persisted until the Day of Ressurection.

The utterance of al-Ḥasan al-Baṣrī expounds clearly the Sunnī view about the role of the four Guided Caliphs in Muslim historiography. It is an adequate response to the Shī'ī accusations directed against the three

20 Zakariyā b. Yaḥyā al-Kūfī; see on him Ibn Ḥajar, *Tahdhīb al-tahdhīb*, III, no. 627; al-Khaṭīb al-Baghdādī, *Ta'rīkh baghdād*, VIII, 456, no. 4569.

21 Ms. Leiden Or. 2428, fols. 4b-5a (not recorded by Sezgin); cf. Abū l-Maḥāsin Yūsuf b. Mūsā, *op. cit.*, I, 222.

first Caliphs. The credit given to Abū Bakr in establishing the *zakāt* as a binding prescription lasting until the Day of Resurrection is ignored in the Shī'ī commentaries of the Qur'ān: it is true that *zakāt* is a fundamental injunction imposed on every believer; but the prerogative of the Prophet mentioned in Sura IX, 103 (purification and cleansing) was transferred to the *imām* (i.e. the Shī'ī *imām* — K). Accordingly people need the *imām* to accept their alms in order to gain purification; the *imām*, however, does not need their property (handed over to him — K); any one who claims that the *imām* is in need of the wealth of the people is a *kāfir*.[22]

In support of the notion that Abū Bakr's decision to fight the people of the *ridda* was right, Sunnī tradition states that the revolt and Abū Bakr's steps are foretold in the revelation of the Qur'ān (Sura V, 54): "O believers, whosoever of you turns from his religion God will assuredly bring a people He loves and who love Him"... The people whom God loves and who love God refers to Abū Bakr and the men who aided him in the struggle against the *ridda* revolt.[23]

Shī'ī traditions maintain that the verse refers to 'Alī and his adherents, to whom the description of people loving God and loved by God is applied. 'Alī and his adherents were thus ordered to fight the people who had

22 Al-Baḥrānī al-Taubalī al-Katakānī, *al-Burhān fī tafsīri l-qur'ān*, Qumm 1393, II, 156: al-'Ayyāshī, *al-Tafsīr*, ed. Hāshim al-Rasūlī al-Maḥallātī, Qumm 1371, II, 106, no. 111; and see about the case of payment of the *ṣadaqa* to the governors of Mu'āwiya during the struggle between him and 'Alī: al Majlisī, *Biḥār al-anwār*, Tehran 1388, XCVI, 69-70, no. 45 (*...laysa lahu an yanzila bilādanā wa-yu'addiya ṣadaqata mālihi ilā 'aduwwinā*); cf. *ib.* p. 68, no. 41 (*al-mutaṣaddiqu 'alā a'dā'inā ka-l-sāriqi fī ḥarami llāhi*); and see the argument establishing that it is lawful for the Shī'ī *imāms* to receive the *zakāt*, because they were deprived of the *khums*: *ib.*, p. 69 no. 44. Comp. Ibn Bābūyah al-Qummī *'Ilal al-sharā'i*, Najaf 1385/1966 p. 378 (about receiving of the *khums* by the Shī'ī *imām*: *...innī la-ākhudhu min aḥadikum l-dirhama wa-innī lamin akthari ahli l-madīnati mālan, mā urīdu bi-dhālika illā an tuṭṭaharū*).

23 Al-Ṭabarī, *Tafsīr*, ed. Shākir, Cairo 1957, X, 411-414 (nos. 12177-12187), 418 (no. 12201), 419-420; al-Qurṭubī, *op. cit.*, VI, 220; 'Abd al-Jabbār, *Tathbīt dalā'il al-nubuwwa*, ed. 'Abd al-Karīm 'Uthmān, Beirut 1386/1966, pp. 417 inf. -418, 424 (and see 'Abd al-Jabbār's refutation of the claim of the *zanādiqa* that Abū Bakr was an apostate, p. 418); Abū l-Layth al-Samarqandī, *Tafsīr*, Ms. Chester Beatty 3668, I, 165a; al-Tha'labī, *Tafsīr*, Ms. Br. Mus. Add. 19926, p. 389; al-Naysābūrī, *Gharā'ib al-qur'ān wa-raghā'ib al-furqān*, Cairo 1381/1962, VI, 114; al-Khāzin, *Lubāb al-ta'wīl*, Cairo 1381, II, 54 (see *ib.*: *wa-qāla abū bakr b. 'ayyāsh: sami'tu abā ḥusayn yaqūlu: mā wulida ba'da l-nabiyyi afḍalu min abī bakrin l-ṣiddīqi; laqad qāma maqāma nabiyyin min al-anbiyā fī qitāli ahli l-ridda*; al-Baghawī, *Ma'ālim al-tanzīl* (on margin of al-Khāzin's *Lubāb*) II, 53-54; Abū Ḥayyān, *al-Baḥr al-muḥīṭ*, Cairo 1328, III, 511; al-Suyūṭī, *al-Durr al-manthūr*, Cairo, II, 292-293; Ibn Kathīr, *Tafsīr*, II, 595. According to other traditions the verse refers to some tribal groups of al-Yaman (Kinda, Ash'ar, Tujīb, Sakūn), to the Anṣār, to the people who fought at Qadisiyya, to the Persians who will embrace Islam. And see Ibn Kathīr, *al-Bidāya*, VI, 312; Ibn Ḥajar al-Haytamī, *al-Ṣawā'iq al-muḥriqa*, ed. 'Abd al-Wahhāb 'Abd al-Laṭīf, Cairo 1375, pp. 14-15.

broken their vow of allegiance (*al-nākithīn* — i.e. Ṭalḥa and al-Zubayr), the people who strayed away from the true faith (*al-māriqīn* — i.e. the *khawārij*) and the unjust (*al-qāsiṭīn* — i.e. Mu'āwiya and his adherents).[24]

The various interpretations recorded in the Qur'ān commentaries expound the diverse views about the *ridda* revolt, evaluate the decision of Abū Bakr to fight the rebellious tribes and try to establish the legal base of his fight, emphasizing his sound judgment, his courage and devotion to the faith of Islam.

*

The widely current tradition about Abū Bakr's decision to fight the rebellious tribes is connected with the interpretation of an utterance of the Prophet concerning the creed of Islam and the conditions of conversion. Abū Bakr is said to have discussed the intent of the utterance with 'Umar and to have succeeded in convincing 'Umar that his interpretation was the right one. Consequently 'Umar and the Companions joined Abū Bakr who declared war on the tribes who, though claiming allegiance to Islam, refused to pay the prescribed tax of *zakāt*. This crucial report is rendered by Wensinck as follows:

> When the Apostle of Allah had departed this world and Abū Bakr had been appointed his vicegerent, and some of the Beduins had forsaken Islam, 'Umar ibn al-Khaṭṭāb said to Abū Bakr: How is it possible for thee to make war on these people, since the Apostle of Allah has said: I am ordered to make war on people till they say: There is no God but Allah? And whoever says: There is no God but Allah has thereby rendered inviolable his possessions and his person, apart from the duties which he has to pay. And it belongs to Allah to call him to account. Thereupon Abū Bakr answered: By Allah, I shall make war on whomsoever makes a distinction between the *ṣalāt* and the *zakāt*. For the *zakāt* is the duty that must be paid from possessions. By Allah, if they should withhold from me a string which they used to pay to the Apostle of Allah, I would make war on them on account of their refusal. Thereupon 'Umar said: By Allah, only because I saw that Allah had given Abū Bakr the conviction that he must wage war, did I recognize that he was right.[25]

This report with its different versions, was the subject of thorough analysis and discussion by Muslim scholars. The significant feature of this tradition is the single *shahāda*: "There is no deity except Allah." Acting

[24] Al-Baḥrānī, *op. cit.*, I, 478-479; al-Naysābūrī, *op. cit.*, VI, 114 inf. -115; al-Ṭabarsī, *Tafsīr* (= *Majma' al-bayān fī tafsīri l-qur'ān*) Beirut 1380/1961, VI, 122-124 (quoting *sunnī* traditions as well).

[25] Wensinck, *op. cit.*, pp. 13-14.

according to the *ḥadīth* cast in this way would indicate that the single *shahāda* declaring the oneness of God, without complementing it with the *shahāda* of the prophethood of Muḥammad, is sufficient as a declaration of faith, preventing any Muslim to attack or harm the person uttering it and protecting that person and his possessions from any injury and damage. There are indeed some traditions in which it is prohibited to fight people uttering the *shahāda* of belief: *lā ilāha illā llāh.* "If one of you draws the spear against a man and the spearhead reaches already the pit of his throat, he has to withdraw it if the man utters the *shahāda* of *lā ilāha illā llāh.*"[26] This injunction is supplemented by a decision of the Prophet in a hypothetical case brought before him by al-Miqdād b. 'Amr. "If an unbeliever fighting me would cut off my hand, then he would utter *lā ilāha illā llāh*, shall I spare him or kill him"? — asked Miqdād. "You should spare him", answered the Prophet. "After he had cut off my hand?" — interpellated al-Miqdād. The Prophet said confirming his prior utterance: "Yes. And if you were to kill him (scil. after he had uttered the single *shahāda* — K) you would be in his position before his utterance (i.e. you would become an unbeliever — K)."[27] Another case is recorded in connection with the Prophet himself: a man talked secretly with the Prophet. Then the Prophet gave the order to kill him. When he turned back the Prophet called him and asked him: "Do you attest that there is no deity except Allah"? "Yes", answered the man. The Prophet then ordered to release him and said: "I have been merely ordered to make war on people until they say *lā ilāha illā llāh*: when they do their blood and possessions are inviolable by me."[28] It is noteworthy that the phrase of exception *illā bi-ḥaqqihā* is not recorded in this version. It is however recorded by al-Ṭaḥāwī[29] and by Ibn Mājah himself in two other traditions recorded by him.[30]

This tradition according to which the mere utterance of the oneness of God was sufficient as proof of conversion to Islam and granted inviolability of person and property was of paramount importance to scholars of Muslim jurisprudence in establishing the terms of conversion. It is obvious that these scholars could hardly agree with the formula of one *shahāda* as a condition of conversion.[31] Some of the commentators of this tradition

26 See e.g. al-Muttaqī al-Hindī, *Kanz al-'ummāl*, Hyderabad 1364, I, 76, no. 369 (and cf. e.g. *ib.*, pp. 38-41, nos. 111, 112, 118, 119, 120, 123, 124, 126, 127, 130-132, 136...).

27 Al-Ṭaḥāwī, *Sharḥ ma'ānī l-āthār*, ed. Muḥammad Zuhrī l-Najjār, Cairo 1388/1968, III, 213; Abū l-Maḥāsin Yūsuf b. Mūsā, *op. cit.*, I, 215-217; al-Bayhaqī, *al-Sunan al-kubrā*, VIII, 195.

28 Ibn Mājah, *Sunan al-muṣṭafā*, Cairo 1349, II, 458.

29 Al-Ṭaḥāwī, *Sharḥ ma'ānī l-āthār*, III, 213.

30 Ibn Mājah, *op. cit.*, II, 457; al-Muttaqī l-Hindī, *op. cit.*, I, 77, no. 373.

31 In a similar story recorded by Ibn Ḥajar, *al-Iṣāba*, VI, 419, Nūr al-Dīn al-Haythamī, *op. cit.*, VI, 262. The man who apostatized three times and finally converted to Islam

tried to attach to the *shahāda* of the oneness of God the implied sense of the *shahāda* of the prophethood of Muḥammad; the *ḥadīth* in the recorded version is merely an allusion (*kināya*) to the open announcement of conversion to Islam (*iẓhār shi'ār al-islām*) and includes in fact the *shahāda* about the prophethood of Muḥammad and the acceptance of the tenets of his faith.[32] Some scholars regarded those who uttered the *shahāda* of the oneness of God as Muslims who shared the rights and obligations of other Muslims.[33] Other scholars maintained that the utterance of the *shahāda* itself did not indicate conversion to Islam; it merely indicated a renunciation of the former belief. It could however not be concluded that they had embraced Islam; they might have joined another monotheistic faith which, though attesting the oneness of God, is yet considered unbelief (*kufr*). As a result it was necessary to suspend fight against such people until it was made clear that there was an obligation to make war on them. It could thus be deduced that this tradition refers to polytheists, who had to utter the *shahāda*.[34] It is evident that the injunction of the *ḥadīth* does not apply to Jews, who are monotheists and who uphold the oneness of God as a tenet of their faith. Hence when the Prophet handed over the banner to 'Alī and bade him fight the Jews of Khaybar, he enjoined him to fight them until they utter both *shahādas*: of the oneness of God and of the prophethood of Muḥammad.[35] But the utterance of both *shahādas* by the Jews is not sufficient in the opinion of al-Ṭaḥāwī, as it does not confirm beyond doubt the Jews' conversion to Islam. It is, namely, possible that they attest the prophethood of Muḥammad besides the oneness of God while they believe that Muḥammad was sent as Messenger to the Arabs only.[36] The utterance of the two *shahādas* by Jews denotes that they have renounced their faith; but it does not necessarily mean that they have embraced Islam. The Muslims fighting them are therefore obliged to cease fighting until they ascertain what is the real intention of the Jews, exactly as in the case of the polytheists uttering the sole *shahāda* of the oneness of God. In both cases there is no evidence that the people making the declaration have joined Islam; conversion to Islam cannot be affected without the renunciation of the former faith of the convert; in the case of the Jews an additional

uttered, however, the double *shahāda*: of the oneness of God and of the prophethood of Muḥammad.

32 Al-Sindī, *Ḥāshiya* (= al-Nasā'ī, *Sunan*, Cairo 1348/1930) V, 15; idem, *Ḥāshiya* (= Ibn Mājah, *op. cit.*, II, 457).

33 Al-Ṭaḥāwī, *Sharḥ ma'ānī*, III, 213, penult: *qāla abū ja'far: fa-qad dhahaba qaumun ilā anna man qāla lā ilāha illā llāhu faqad ṣāra bihā musliman, lahu mā li-l-muslimīna wa-'alayhi mā 'alā l-muslimīna wa-ḥtajjū bi-hādhihi l-āthāri.*

34 Al-Ṭahāwī, *Sharḥ ma'ānī*, III, 214.

35 Muslim, *op. cit.*, VII, 121.

36 Al-Ṭaḥāwī, *Sharḥ ma'ānī*, III, 214.

stipulation was added: to ascertain that they have fully accepted the tenets of Islam without reservations. A peculiar case of this kind is reported in a tradition about two Jews who uttered the two *shahādas*, but were reluctant to follow the Prophet because the Jews believe that Dāwūd prayed to God asking that prophethood remain among his descendants; had those two Jews joined the Prophet the other Jews would have killed them.[37] The confession of the two Jews and their declaration of the prophethood of Muḥammad was insufficient to make them Muslims and they remained Jews. The Prophet did not order to fight them so as to force them to commit themselves to all the injunctions and tenets of Islam, as stated by al-Ṭaḥāwī.[38]

In harmony with the idea that conversion to Islam implied the convert's renunciation of the former faith was a tradition attributed to the Prophet according to which one who utters the *shahāda* of oneness of God and renounces the gods which he had worshipped before — God will make inviolable his person and property (literally: *ḥarrama llāhu damahu wa-mālahu*) and it is up to God to call him to account.[39] It was, of course, essential to establish in which period the Prophet uttered *ḥadīths* of this type in which the condition of conversion to Islam was confined to the *shahāda* of the oneness of God and to assess their validity. Sufyān b. 'Uyayna maintained that this utterance was announced at the beginning of Islam, before the prescriptions of prayer, *zakāt*, fasting and *hijra* were revealed.[40] One can easily understand why some Muslim scholars tried to establish the early date of this tradition and state that as a result it must have been abrogated after the imposition of the above mentioned injunctions. This can be deduced from the comment of Sufyān b. 'Uyayna. Ibn Rajab tries to undermine the validity of the *ḥadīth* and also of Ibn 'Uyayna's comment. The transmitters of the *ḥadīth*, says Ibn Rajab, were the Companions of the Prophet in Medina (i.e. not in the first period of Islam, in Mecca — K); some of the persons on whose authority the *ḥadīth* is reported converted to Islam in the late period (scil. of the life of the Prophet — K); therefore the soundness of the tradition as traced back to Sufyān is a moot question (*wa-fī ṣiḥḥatihi 'an sufyāna naẓar*) and his opinion has to be

[37] See e.g. al-Dhahabī, *Ta'rīkh,* Cairo 1367, I, 223; Ibn Kathīr, *Shamā'il al-rasūl wa-dalā'il nubuwwatihi...* ed. Muṣṭafā 'Abd al-Wāḥid, Cairo 1386/1967, p. 333; Ibn al-Athīr, *Jāmi' al-uṣūl min aḥādīthi l-rasūl,* ed. Muḥammad Ḥāmid al-Fiqī, Cairo 1374/1955, XII, 96, no. 8899; Ibn Abī Shayba, *Ta'rīkh,* Ms. Berlin 9409 (Sprenger 104), fol. 5a-6a; al-Ṭaḥāwī, *Sharḥ ma'ānī,* III, 215.

[38] Al-Ṭaḥāwī, *Sharḥ ma'ānī,* III, 215.

[39] Muslim, *op. cit.,* I, 40 sup.; Ibn Rajab, *Jāmi' al-'ulūm wa-l-ḥikam*, ed. Muḥammad al-Aḥmadī Abū l-Nūr, Cairo 1389/1970, I, 180.

[40] Ibn Rajab, *Jāmi'*, *ib.*

considered weak. Ibn Rajab examines further the phrase *'aṣamū minnī dimā'ahum wa-amwālahum* (they will cause their blood and property to be inviolable by me) in the tradition, arguing that this phrase indicates that the Prophet had already been ordered to make war on those who refused to convert to Islam; this injunction was revealed to the Prophet after his *hijra* to Medina.[41] According to the arguments of Ibn Rajab the Prophet uttered this *ḥadīth* after his *hijra* to Medina.

Ibn Rajab puts forward a different assumption about the persistent validity of the tradition, and explains its origin on the background of the Prophet's custom and conduct with regard to conversion to Islam. The Prophet used to be satisfied with the mere recitation of the two *shahādas* by a convert to Islam; he would then grant the convert the right of inviolability for his person and regard him as Muslim. He even rebuked Usāma b. Zayd for killing a man who uttered only the *shahāda* of the oneness of God. The Prophet, argues Ibn Rajab, did not stipulate with converts prayer and the payment of *zakāt*. There is even a tradition according to which he accepted the conversion of a group who asked to be dispensed from paying the *zakāt*. Further, Ibn Rajab quotes from Aḥmad b. Ḥanbal's *Musnad* the *ḥadīth* (recorded on the authoity of Jābir b. 'Abdallāh) reporting that the delegation of Thaqīf stipulated (in their negotiations with the Prophet — K)[42] that they would not pay the *ṣadaqa* nor would they participate in the expeditions of the holy war, *jihād*; the Prophet (agreed and — K) said: "They will (in the future — K) pay the *ṣadaqa* and will fight."[43]

Another tradition recorded by Ibn Ḥanbal and quoted by Ibn Rajab states that the Prophet accepted the conversion of a man who stipulated that he would pray only two prayers (instead of five, during the day — K). Ibn Ḥanbal also records a tradition reporting that Ḥakīm b. Ḥizām gave the Prophet the oath of conversion on the condition that he would not perform the *rak'a* during prostration.[44] Basing himself on these traditions Aḥmad b. Ḥanbal concluded that conversion to Islam may be accomplished despite a faulty stipulation; subsequently, the convert will be obliged to carry out the prescriptions of the law of Islam.[45]

41 Ibn Rajab, *Jāmi'*, *ib.;* cf. idem, *Kalimat al-ikhlāṣ*, ed. al-Shawīsh and al-Albānī, Beirut 1397, pp. 19-21.

42 Cf. *JSAI* (= Jerusalem Studies in Arabic and Islam) I (1979), 1-18, "Some Reports Concerning al-Ṭā'if."

43 Ibn Rajab, *Jāmi'*, I, 180; the version quoted is in some traditions followed by the phrase: *idhā aslamū.*

44 Ibn Rajab, *Jāmi'*, I, 180-181.

45 Ibn Rajab, *Jāmi'*, I, 181: *...wa-akhadha l-imāmu aḥmadu bi-hādhihi l-aḥādīthi wa-qāla: yaṣiḥḥu l-islāmu 'alā l-sharṭi l-fāsidi; thumma yulzamu bi-sharā'i'i l-islāmi.*

Ibn Rajab joins Ibn Ḥanbal in his opinion and sums up the subject as follows: The utterance of the two *shahāda*s by itself forms the conversion and is sufficient to turn the convert inviolable; when he enters Islam he has to carry out the obligatory prescriptions of the Muslim law including, of course, prayer and *zakāt*. If he performs them, he shares in the rights and duties of the Muslim community. If a group of converts does not carry out any of these fundamental obligations, they should be fought and compelled to carry them out.[46]

It may be assumed that the utterance of the Prophet promising inviolability to the person and property of converts who utter the *shahāda* of the oneness of God, as quoted by 'Umar in his discussion with Abū Bakr, was contrasted by traditions according to which the convert had to utter the *shahāda*s of oneness of God, and of the prophethood of Muḥammad and renounce the tenets of his former faith. There was a clear tendency to bridge over the divergent traditions. The question of 'Umar as to how Abū Bakr could fight the people (*al-nās*) since the Prophet had stated that he would make war on them only until they utter the single *shahāda* of the oneness of God was explained as a misunderstanding. 'Umar referred in his question to the unbelievers, as *al-nās* denoted in his perception idol worshippers; the utterance of the Prophet referred, of course, to these people. But Abū Bakr intended to fight also people who refused to pay *zakāt*, but did not renounce Islam; thus the word *al-nās* included in his opinion this category of people as well. Both Abū Bakr and 'Umar did not remember during their talk the *ḥadīth* transmitted by 'Abdallāh, the son of 'Umar, in which conversion to Islam was explicitly said to depend upon the utterance of both *shahāda*s, the performance of prayers and the payment of *zakāt*.[47] Abū Bakr based himself on the last phrase of this utterance and replied: "By God I shall make war on those who make a distinction between prayer and the *zakāt*-tax, as the *zakāt* is a duty imposed on property"; 'Umar seems not to have noticed the phrase of exception: *illā bi-ḥaqqihi* at the end of the utterance. This phrase was rendered by the commentators: *illā bi-ḥaqqi l-islāmi* and explicated as referring to murder, refusal to perform the prayer, refusal to pay the *zakāt* by false interpretation (of the verses of the Qur'ān — K) and other things (i.e. either the committing of crimes or negligence to carry out the prescriptions of the Muslim law — K). Abū Bakr thus explained to 'Umar that the person uttering the *shahāda* of the oneness of God is in fact granted the inviolability of body and property and should not be fought except on the ground of

[46] Ibn Rajab, *Jāmi'*, I, 181-182,

[47] See the tradition e.g. Ibn Rajab, *Kalimat al-Ikhlāṣ*.

the Islamic law, which makes it necessary to fight people committing crimes or grave religious sins. As there was unanimity among the Companions that the non-performance of prayer was a grave sin, it was the duty of a Muslim ruler to make war on groups refusing to carry out this prescription. Abū Bakr, stating that he will make war on people who would separate prayer from *zakāt*, based himself on the principle of *qiyās*, analogy, putting *zakāt* on a par with prayer, *ṣalāt*.[48]

Some other aspects in connection with the legitimacy of the war against the *ridda* people are pointed out by al-Jaṣṣāṣ. Abū Bakr decided to fight the people of the *ridda* not because they did not pray, or because they did not pay *zakāt*; the decision to fight people for not paying the *zakāt* cannot be taken in the period of the year when people are not expected to pay; and people cannot be fought because they do not pray, as there are special times for prayer. The right reason for Abū Bakr's decision to make war on the people of the *ridda* was the fact that they refused to commit themselves to pay the *zakāt*; by this refusal they renounced (*kafarū*) a verse of the Qur'ān (scil. a prescription of the Qur'ān) which was in fact a renunciation of the whole Qur'ān. This was the basis for the decision of Abū Bakr to fight them, since they turned apostates by this renunciation.[49]

Another problem discussed by al-Jaṣṣāṣ is the person authorized to levy the tax. Some of the tribal leaders were ready to collect the tax and accept the injunction of the Qur'ān as obligatory; they were however reluctant to hand over the tax to the Caliph or his officials. But Abū Bakr adhered to the precedent of the Prophet, demanded that the *zakāt* be delivered to the Caliph and considered war against people who refused to deliver it as justified.[50] This argument was, of course, closely connected with the practice which was followed in the Muslim empire towards rebellious groups who refused to hand over the collected tax to the official of the Caliph.

Some Muslim scholars drew weighty conclusions from the story about the discussion between Abū Bakr and 'Umar about the way in which utterances of the Prophet circulated during that early period. These scholars assume that Abū Bakr and 'Umar were not familiar with the utterance of the Prophet in which prayer and the *zakāt* were explicitly mentioned as necessary concomitants of conversion. It is presumed that Ibn 'Umar who transmitted this tradition (i.e. in which prayer and *zakāt* were mentioned as fundamental conditions for conversion to Islam — K) did not attend their conversation. It can further be deduced, according to some scholars, that even great men among the *ṣaḥāba* could have been ignorant of a *sunna*,

48 Cf. Ibn Rajab, *Jāmi'*, I, 184 inf. -185.

49 Al-Jaṣṣāṣ, *Aḥkām al-qur'ān*, Qusṭanṭīniyya 1338, III, 82-83.

50 Al-Jaṣṣāṣ, *op. cit.*, III, 82 inf. -83 sup.

while others might have known it. Hence one should not lend weight to personal opinions of men if they may contradict a reliable tradition about a *sunna*. The word *uqātil* served as argument for some scholars, who concluded that people refusing to pay the *zakāt* should be fought until the *zakāt* is collected from them; there is no permission to kill them; others maintained that it is lawful to kill.[51]

The interpretation of the crucial expression *illā bi-ḥaqqihi* (or: *bi-ḥaqqihā*) seems to have been closely connected with the commentaries on Sūra VI, 151: *wa-lā taqtulū l-nafsa llatī ḥarrama llāhu illā bi-l-ḥaqqi* "and that you slay not the soul God has forbidden, except for right". Al-Qurṭubī states that the verse constitutes a prohibition to kill a person whose killing is forbidden, whether a believer or an ally (*mu'minatan kānat* [i.e. *al-nafs*] *aw mu'āhidātan*) except on the basis of (a prescription of) Muslim law, which bids to kill him.[52] Al-Qurṭubī, basing himself on Qur'ān verses and on *ḥadīths*, enumerates the cases in which the execution of sinners is mandatory: murderers, fornicators, rebels, usurpers and homosexuals; the list includes people refusing to perform the prescribed prayers and to pay the *zakāt*; the *ḥadīth*: *umirtu...illā bi-ḥaqqihi* is quoted as reference for the indication of *illā bi-ḥaqqihi*.[53]

Slightly different is the explanation given to the expression *illā bi-ḥaqqihā*, appearing in another version of this *ḥadīth*.[54] The personal suffix *hā* in this version refers to *dimā'uhum wa-amwāluhum*, "Their blood and property" (literally: *their blood and properties*) and is explained by saying that their blood and possessions are inviolable except when they are convicted of crimes or sins or unfulfilled religious prescriptions (like abandonment of prayer, or the non-payment of *zakāt* — K); "*bi-ḥaqqihā*" indicates

[51] See the discussion: Ibn Ḥajar, *Fatḥ al-bārī, sharḥ ṣaḥīḥ al-bukhārī*, Būlāq 1300, I, 71-72; al-'Aynī, *'Umdat al-qārī, sharḥ ṣaḥīḥ al-bukhārī*, n. p. 1348 (repr. Beirut), I, 110 inf., 179-183, VIII, 235-236, 244-277; al-Qasṭallānī, *Irshad al-sārī*, III, 6-7; cf. Maḥmūd Muḥammad Khaṭṭāb al-Subkī, *al-Manhal al-'adhb al-maurūd sharḥ sunan abī dāwūd*, Cairo 1390, IX, 114-123; Ibn Rajab, *Jāmi'*, I, 185-188; al-Qurṭubī, *Tafsīr*, Cairo 1387/1967, VII, 331-332.

[52] Al-Qurṭubī, *Tafsīr*, VII, 133... *au mu'āhidatan illā bi-l-ḥaqqi lladhī yūjibu qatlahā*. Cf. al-Ṭabarī, *Tafsīr* (ed. Shakir) XII, 220: *...bi-l-ḥaqqi, yu'nā bi-mā abāḥa qatlahā bihi* (murder, fornication of a married woman and apostasy are mentioned); al-Naysābūrī, *Gharā'ib al-qur'ān*, VIII, 56 inf; al-Suyūṭī, *al-Durr al-manthūr*, III, 54-55.

[53] Al-Qurṭubī, *op. cit.*, VIII, 133.

[54] See e.g. al-Nasā'ī, *Sunan*, ed. Ḥasan Muḥammad al-Mas'ūdī, Cairo 1348/1930 (repr. Beirut) VI, 6;- Aḥmad b. 'Alī al-Marwazī, *Musnad abī bakr al-ṣiddīq*, ed. Shu'ayb al-Arnā'ūṭ, Beirut 1390/1970, pp. 145-146, no. 77 (comp. another version: pp. 208-209, no. 140); al-Muttaqī l-Hindī, *op. cit.*, I, 78, no. 375 (and see *ib.*, pp. 76-79, nos. 265-285), VI, 294-295, nos. 2256-2259; al-Qurṭubī, *Tafsīr*, VIII, 74-75; al-Bayhaqī, *al-Sunan al-kubrā*, VIII, 19, 176-177, 196, 202; Nūr al-Dīn al-Haythamī, *op. cit.*, I, 24-26; Ps. Ibn Qutayba, *al-Imāma wa-l-siyāsa*, ed. Ṭāhā Muḥammad al-Zaynī, Cairo 1387/1967, I, 22 inf. -23 (2 different versions of Abū Bakr's answer).

the obligations and duties imposed on the person and property of the believer. The preposition "*bi*" (in *bi-ḥaqqihā*) is explained as equal to *'an* or *min*, "on the ground", "on the base", "on account."[55] Another explanation states that "*bi-ḥaqqihā*" refers to the declaration of the oneness of God; consequently, *illā bi-ḥaqqihā* has to be rendered except on the grounds of the (unfulfilled) duties incumbent on the person and on the property, according to this declaration.[56]

*

It is noteworthy that the authenticity of the tradition in which the *shahāda* of the oneness of God is maintained as sufficient and which has caused some difficulties of interpretation[57] was not questioned by scholars, whereas the one which speaks of two *shahāda*s and which mentions the obligations of the Muslim was subject to suspicion, its reliability being put to doubt.[58] Al-Jāḥiẓ rightly states that both Shī'ī and Murji'ī scholars accepted the report about the conversation between Abū Bakr and the Companions in which they quoted the *ḥadīth* of the Prophet with the *shahāda* of the oneness of God, and about Abū Bakr's decision to wage war against the tribal dissidents basing himself on the final phrase of the *ḥadīth*. Only the extremist *rawāfiḍ* denied this report.[59] According to a report recorded by al-Jāḥiẓ both the Anṣār and the Muhājirūn urged Abū Bakr to concede to the demands of the *ahl al-ridda* and proposed to exempt them for some time from paying the *zakāt*.[60] The other report recorded by al-Jāḥiẓ says that it was the Anṣār who tried to convince Abū Bakr to concede to the demands of the *ridda* people.[61] The first report says the Abū Bakr reminded the people who came to him of the final phrase: *illā bi-ḥaqqihā*; in the other report the people themselves quoted the utterance with the final sentence and Abū Bakr merely stated that the *zakāt* is part of the *ḥaqq* (obligation, duty) imposed on it. The tendency of recording both traditions can be seen in the comments and conclusions drawn by al-Jāḥiẓ:

55 Al-Munāwī, *Fayḍ al-qadīr*, Cairo 1391/1972, II, 188-189, no. 1630 (*illā bi-ḥaqqihā, ay al-dimā' wa-l-amwal, ya'nī hiya ma'sūmatun illā 'an ḥaqqin yajibu fīhā ka-qawadin wa-riddatin wa-ḥaddin wa-tarki ṣalātin wa-ẓakātin bi-ta'wīlin bāṭilin wa-ḥaqqin ādamiyyin).*

56 Al-Munāwī, *op. cit.*, II, 189.

57 See e.g. Ibn Ḥajar, *Fatḥ al-bārī*, I, 71 sup.; al-'Aynī, *'Umdat al-qārī*, I, 183; Ibn Abī Ḥātim, *'Ilal al-ḥadīth*, Cairo 1343, II, 147 (no. 1937), 152 (no. 1952); and comp. *ib.*, II, 159 (no. 1971); al-Jarrāḥī, *Kashf al-khafā wa-muzīl al-ilbās*, Cairo 1351, I, 194, no. 586; al-Maqdisī, *al-Bad' wa-l-ta'rīkh*, V, 153; 'Abd al-Razzāq, *al-Muṣannaf*, VI, 66-67, nos. 10020-10022; Abū l-Maḥāsin Yūsuf b. Mūsā l-Ḥanafī, *al-Mu'taṣar*, I, 130 ult. -132.

58 See e.g. al-'Aynī, *op. cit.*, I, 183, 11. 6-8: *...qultu: wa-min hādhā qāla ba'ḍuhum: fī ṣiḥḥati ḥadīthi bni 'umara l-madhkūri naẓarun...*; and see Ibn Rajab, *Jāmi'*, I, 184 inf. -185 sup.

59 Al-Jāḥiẓ, *al-'Uthmāniyya*, ed. 'Abd al-Salām Hārūn, Cairo 1374/1955, pp. 81-82.

60 Al-Jāḥiẓ, *op. cit.*, p. 81; Ibn 'Abd al-Barr, *Jāmi' bayān al-'ilm*, al-Madīna al-munawwara, n.d. (reprint), II, 85, 102; 'Abd al-Jabbār, *Tathbīt*, pp. 227-228.

61 Al-Jāḥiẓ, *op. cit.*, p. 82.

Abū Bakr, who knew things which others (of the Companions) did not know, interpreted the utterance of the Prophet in the proper way and got the approval of it by all the people of the *ṣaḥāba*. The two reports of al-Jāḥiẓ are certainly a sufficient answer for the slanders circulated by the *rawāfiḍ*.

Moreover: according to a tradition it was 'Alī who encouraged Abū Bakr to take his decision concerning the *ahl al-ridda*, stating that if Abū Bakr gave up anything collected by the Prophet from them he would have acted contrary to the *sunna*.[62] It is obvious that this tradition serves as an argument against the *rawāfiḍ*,[63] emphasizing as it does the friendly relations between Abū Bakr and 'Alī, 'Alī's participation in the decisions of Abū Bakr and 'Alī's full approval of Abū Bakr's action against *ahl al-ridda*.

Sunnī scholars tried to extend the ideological basis of Abū Bakr's utterance. He had recourse, they said, not only to *qiyās* (analogy); he based himself also on an explicit injunction (*naṣṣ*) of the Qur'ān (Sūra IX, 11: "Yet if they repent and perform the prayer and pay the alms, then they are your brothers in religion...") and on inference (*dilāla*). When Abū Bakr decided to fight the *ahl al-ridda* he acted in accordance with the injunction given in this verse; hence 'Umar could say: *mā huwa illā an sharaḥa llāhu ṣadra abī bakrin li-l-qitāli wa-'araftu annahu l-ḥaqq*.[64] But the utterance of 'Umar and his approval of Abū Bakr's decision seems to have been criticized, probably by some Shī'ī circles, and designated as *taqlīd*. This was firmly denied by Sunnī scholars.[65] The link between the revealed verse: Sūra IX, 11 and the decision of Abū Bakr is sharply pointed out in the Muslim tradition: this verse was one of the latest verses revealed to the Prophet before his death.[66]

A trenchant reply to the *rāfiḍī* scholars was made by Ibn al-'Arabī: Had Abū Bakr been compliant with the demands of refusal of *zakāt*, their force would have become stronger, their wicked innovations would have gained

[62] Al-Muḥibb al-Ṭabarī, *al-Riyāḍ al-naḍira fī manāqib al-'ashara*, ed. Muḥammad Badr al-Dīn al-Na'sānī al-Ḥalabī, Cairo n.d., I, 98; cf. 'Abd al-Jabbār, *op. cit.*, p. 418.

[63] About their arguments see e.g. Ibn 'Arabī, *op. cit.*, p. 995: *...wa-bi-hādhā 'taraḍat al-rāfiḍatu 'alā l-ṣiddīqi, fa-qālū: 'ajila fī amrihi wa-nabadha l-siyāsata warā'a ẓahrihi wa-arāqa l-dimā'a*.

[64] See al-'Aynī, *op. cit.*, VIII, 246: *...bi-l-dalīl lladhī aqāmahu l-ṣiddīq naṣṣan wa-dilālatan wa-qiyāsan...*; cf. Ibn al-'Arabī, *Ahkam al-qur'ān*, p. 995; and see al-Ṭabarī, *Tafsīr*, XIV, 153, no. 16518.

[65] Al-Bayhaqī, *al-Sunan al-kubrā*, VIII, 177, ll. 8-12; al-'Aynī, *op. cit.*, VIII, 246: *...fa-lā yuqālu lahu innahu qallada abā bakrin li-anna l-mujtahida la yajūzu lahu an yuqallida l-mujtahida... wa-fīhi dilālātun 'alā anna 'umara lam yarji' ilā qauli abī bakrin taqlīdan*.

[66] See e.g. al-Ṭabarī, *Tafsīr* (ed. Shakir) XIV, 135, no. 16475: *...wa-taṣdīqu dhālika fī kitābi llāhi fī ākhiri mā anzala llāhu; qāla llāhu: fa-in tābū...*; al-'Atā'iqī, *al-Nāsikh wa-l-mansūkh*, ed. 'Abd al-Hādī l-Faḍlī, Najaf 1390/1970, pp. 52-53; cf. al-'Aynī, *op. cit.*, I, 178; Hibatullah b. Salāmah, *al-Nāsikh wa-l-mansūkh*, Cairo 1387/1967, p. 51.

hold in the hearts of people and it would have been difficult to turn them to obedience; Abū Bakr decided therefore to act quickly and resolutely in order to prevent it. It is certainly better to shed blood in order to strengthen the foundations of Islam than in order to gain the Caliphate, Ibn al-'Arabī observed.[67] A significant report corroborating this view is recorded by al-Jāḥiẓ: Abū Bakr is said to have stated that any concession granted to one of the tribes would bring about demands from other tribes, as a consequence of which the strength of Islam would ultimately be shattered.[68]

The refusal to pay the *zakāt* was prompted by feelings of tribal independence opposed to the control and authority of Medina. The Medinan community being the only body politic which represented the legacy of the Prophet, it was bound to serve as the target for the struggle of the seceding tribes. The problem was not one of theological formulations seeking to establish who is a believer. We may not suppose Abū Bakr to have discussed the meaning of Qur'ānic verses with tribal leaders. A few years later, when knowledge of Qur'ān was set up as a criterion for the division of booty, the Muslim warriors demonstrated a rather poor knowledge of the Qur'ān; well-known warriors could only quote the *basmala*.[69] The concise confession of the oneness of God: *lā ilāha illā llāhu* seems to have from the very beginning served as a token of adherence to the Muslim community; the testimony of the prophethood of Muḥammad was probably very shortly afterwards added to it. It is mentioned in the very early compilations of the *sīra* and in the biographies of the Companions[70] and it was supplemented by the addition of various stipulations and injunctions during the first century of Islam. The fact that there were in circulation numerous traditions which were more detailed and more elaborate, and in which the various obligations of conversion were enumerated and that these nevertheless could not undo the short formula of the *shahāda* of the oneness of God, seems to be a convincing evidence that this tradition is one of the very earliest *ḥadīths*. The efforts of the commentators to establish the time of this utterance, its contents and circumstances indicate that it was a rather difficult task to harmonize between the tradition and later practice,

67 Ibn al-'Arabī, *op. cit.*, p. 995.

68 Al-Jāḥiẓ, *al-'Uthmāniyya*, p. 83.

69 Abū l-Faraj al-Iṣfahānī, *Aghānī*, XIV, 39.

70 See e.g. Ibn Sa'd, *op. cit.*, I, 279; Muḥammad Ḥamīdullah, *Majmū'at al-wathā'iq al-siyāsiyya*, Cairo 1376/1956, p. 245, no. 233; cf. *ib.*, p. 90, no. 67; *ib.*, p. 159 no. 120; Ibn Ḥajar, *al-Iṣāba*, VII, 211, no. 10114; Ibn al-Athīr, *Usd al-ghāba* V, 225; Nūr al-Dīn al-Haythamī, *Majma' al-zawā'id*, I, 29, III, 64; Muḥammad Ḥamidūllah, *op. cit.*, p. 98, no. 77 (and cf. on Abū Shaddād: Ibn Abī Ḥātim, *al-Jarḥ wa-l-ta'dīl*, VII, no. 1830 (= IX, 389); al-Sam'ānī, *Ansāb*, V, 373, no. 1616; Yāqūt, *al-Buldān*, s.v. al-Damā); but see the opinion of Wensinck, *op. cit.*, pp. 11-12.

and it seems to have been difficult to explain its validity for the time of the *ridda*.

The socio-economic factors behind the *ridda* movement can be glimpsed between the lines of those reports which relate how certain tribal leaders refused to levy the prescribed *zakāt*[71] while others had collected the *zakāt* but were requested to return it to their people after the death of the Prophet.[72] The obligation to pay the collected *zakāt*-tax to the rulers said to have been imposed on the *ridda*-people, seems to have been questioned as late as the end of the second century of the *hijra*; certain scholars had the courage to recommend not to hand it over to the rulers (who were considered vicious and unjust and liable to squander the tax on unworthy causes) or to their officials, but to distribute it among the poor of the community.[73]

The concise *shahāda*s of the oneness of God and of the message of Muhammad enabled the masses of the conquered peoples to join Islam. These *shahāda*s could even be rendered easier and more concise for the convenience of aliens converting to Islam.[74] The vague expression *illā bi-ḥaqqihā*[75] secured that the converts would faithfully carry out the prescriptions of Islam.

[71] See e.g. al-Muḥibb al-Ṭabarī, *op. cit.*, I, 67: *...irtaddati l-'arabu wa-qālū: lā nu'addī zakātan...*; *ib.*, I, 98; al-Muttaqī l-Hindī, *op. cit.*, VI, 295, no. 22588... *irtadda man irtadda min al-'arabi wa-qālū: nuṣallī wa-lā-nuzakkī...*

[72] Ps. Wāqidī, *Akhbār ahli l-ridda*, Ms. Bankipore XV, 108-110, no. 1042, fol. 9a: *...fa-qāla lahu rajulun min qaumihi: yā hādhā, naḥnu wa-llāhi aulā bi-ṣadaqātinā min abī bakrin, wa-qad jama'nāhā ilayka wa-dafa'nāhā li-tamḍī bihā ilā muḥammadin (ṣ) fa-rudda ṣadaqātinā, fa-ghaḍiba l-zibriqān...*; al-Kalā'ī, *op. cit.*, p. 51-52, 161.

[73] See e.g. 'Abd al-Razzāq, *op. cit.*, IV, 46, no. 6923: *...'an ibn ṭāwūs 'an abīhi qāla: lā yudfa'u ilayhim idhā lam yaḍa'ūhā mawāḍi'ahā...*; p. 48, no. 6931: *'an makḥūlin sami'tuhu yaqūlu: lā tadfa'hā ilayhim, ya'nī l-umarā'a...*; no. 6932: *...kāna ibnu 'abbāsin wa-bnu l-musayyibi wa-l-ḥasanu bnu abī l-ḥasani wa-ibrāhīmu l-nakha'īyyu wa-muḥammadu bnu 'aliyyin wa-ḥammādu bnu abī sulaymāna yaqūlūna: lā tu'addū l-zakāta ilā man yajūru fīhā...*; Ibn Abī Shayba, *Muṣannaf*, ed. 'Abd al-Khāliq al-Afghānī, Hyderabad 1387/1968, III, 156: *...qāla bnu 'umara: dfa'ū zakāta amwālikum ilā man wallāhu llāhu amrakum, fa-man barra fa-li-nafsihi wa-man athima fa-'alayha... ib., idfā'ha ilayhim wa-in akalū bihā luḥūma l-kilāb...*; p. 158: *...'an ṭāwūs qāla: ḍa'hā fī l-fuqarā...* Ibn 'Umar: *lā tadfa'hā ilayhim fa-innahum qad aḍā'ū l-ṣalāt...*

[74] See e.g. al-Shabrakhītī, *Sharḥ alā l-arba'īna l-nawawiyya*, Beirut, Dār al-fikr, n.d., p. 126: *...wa-'lam annahu lā yushtaraṭu fī ṣiḥḥati l-īmāni al-talaffuẓu bi-l-shahādatayni wa-lā l-nafyu wa-l-ithbātu, bal yakfī an yaqūla: llāhu wāḥidun wa-muḥammadun rasūlu llāhi...*

[75] See e.g. al-Jaṣṣaṣ, *op. cit.*, III, 197 ult. -198 sup. (commenting on *wa-āti dhā l-qurbā ḥaqqahu...*): *qāla abū bakrin* [i.e. al-Jaṣṣāṣ]: *al-ḥaqqu l-madhkūru fī hādhihi l-āya mujmalun muftaqarun ilā l-bayāni wa-huwa mithlu qaulihi ta'ālā: wa-fī amwālihim ḥaqqun... wa-qauli l-nabiyyi (ṣ) umirtu an uqātila... illā llāhu fa-idhā qāluhā 'aṣamū... illā bi-ḥaqqihā fa-hādhā l-ḥaqqu ghayru ẓahiri l-ma'nā fī l-āyati, bal huwa mauqūfun 'alā l-bayāni...*

X

Pare Your Nails: A Study of an Early Tradition

The Islamic injunction that one should pare one's nails is usually given in the sources as belonging to the set of practices observed by the prophets before Muḥammad, enjoined by them for their people and thus known as one of the practices of the *fiṭra*.[1] These practices were followed by the Prophet and prescribed for his community. A widely current tradition, reported on the authority of the Prophet, recommended paring the nails by stressing that the Devil takes up his abode in the dirt originating between the nail and the flesh.[2] It is evident that the believer has to be alert to the dangers associated with the presence of the Devil; negligence or heedlessness in paring one's

---

1 See, e.g., al-Bayhaqī, *al-Sunan al-kubrā*, (Hyderabad 1344), I, 149; idem, *Maʿrifat al-sunan wa-l-āthār*, ed. Aḥmad Ṣaqr (Cairo 1390/1970), I, 390–91; al-Shaukānī, *Nayl al-auṭār* (Cairo 1372/1953), I, 130–33; al-Muttaqī l-Hindī, *Kanz al-ʿummāl* (Hyderabad 1377/1958), VI, 371–74, nos. 2648–52, 2654, 2672–75; al-ʿAynī, *ʿUmdat al-qārī*, (Cairo reprint), XXII, 44–46 (and see the definition of the *fiṭra* on p. 45: *al-fiṭra khamsun, ay khamsatu ashyāʾa, wa-arāda bi-l-fiṭrati al-sunnata l-qadīma llatī khtārahā l-anbiyāʾu ʿalayhim al-salām wa-ttafaqat ʿalayhi l-sharāʾiʿu fa-ka-annahā amrun jaliyyun fuṭirū ʿalayhi);* Ibn Ḥajar, *Fatḥ al-bārī* (Cairo 1301), X, 282–85; Faḍlullah al-Jīlānī, *Faḍlu llāhi l-ṣamad li-tauḍīḥi l-adabi l-mufrad,* (Ḥimṣ, 1388), II, 680, no. 1257; Abū Ṭālib al-Makkī, *Qūt al-qulūb* (Cairo 1351/1932), IV, 8–9; al-Shaʿrānī, *Minaḥ al-minna fī l-tamassuk bi-l-sharīʿa wa-l-sunna* (Cairo, n.d.), 21; Taqī l-Dīn ʿAbd al-Malik b. Abī l-Munā, *Nuzhat al-nāẓirīn* (Cairo 1373/1954), 59; al-Suyūṭī, *al-Ẓafar bi-qalmi l-ẓufr,* Ms. Bodley, Walker 8, fol. 368a; idem, *al-Isfār ʿan qalmi l-aẓfār,* Ms. Hebrew Univ., Yahuda Ar. 749/4, fols. lb–2a; al-Munāwī, *Fayḍ al-qadīr* (Beirut 1391/1972), III, 455, no. 2953. Cf. a different argument exposed by al-Waṣṣābī, *al-Baraka fī faḍli l-saʿyi wa-l-ḥaraka* (Cairo, 1354), 214–15: cleanliness is one of the conditions of faith (*wa-qāla ṣallā llāhu ʿalayhi wa-sallam: buniya l-dīnu ʿalā l-naẓāfa*); one of the requirements of cleanliness is to pare one's nails. These injunctions, including paring of nails, are recorded in the commentaries of the Qurʾān as related to Sūra II, 124: ". . .and when his Lord tested Abraham with certain words"; see, e.g., al-Ṭabarī, *Tafsīr*, ed. Shākir (Cairo, n.d.), II, 9–10, nos. 1910–14; al-Suyūṭī, *al-Durr al-manthūr* (Cairo, 1314), I, 111–12; al-Qurṭubī, *Tafsīr (=al-Jāmiʿ li-aḥkāmi l-qurʾān)* (Cairo 1387/1967), II, 98; al-Jaṣṣāṣ, *Aḥkām al-qurʾān* (Istanbul, 1335), I, 66; al-Diyārbakrī, *Taʾrīkh al-khamīs* (Cairo, 1283), I, 208; al-Dāraquṭnī, *Sunan,* ed. ʿAbdallāh Hāshim Yamānī (al-Madīna, 1386/1966), I, 94–95; al-Khaṭīb al-Baghdādī, *Mūḍiḥ auhām* (Hyderabad, 1379/1960), II, 199, l. 14; *Juzʾ fīhi aḥādīth abī muḥammad sufyān b. ʿuyayna,* Ms. Ẓāhiriyya, ḥad. 18, fol. 264b; cf. Ibn Bābūyah, *al-Khiṣāl,* ed. ʿAlī Akbar al-Ghaffārī (Tehran, 1389), 271, no. 11; al-Muttaqī l-Hindī, *Kanz al-ʿummāl,* IX, 170, no. 1375; Muḥammad al-Safārīnī, *Ghidhāʾu l-albāb li-sharḥi manẓūmati l-ādāb (Cairo 1324), I, 381.*

2 See the various versions: al-Daylamī, *Firdaus al-akhbār,* Ms. Chester Beatty 3037, fol. 116b, infra (*qallim aẓfāraka fa-inna l-shayṭāna yaqʿudu ʿalā mā ṭāla minhā*); Murtaḍā l-Zabīdī, *Itḥāfu l-sāda l-*

nails may turn out to be harmful not only to the careless person, but also to other members of the Muslim community, and may even impede the continuous dispensation of God's grace or hamper the faithful from carrying out their religious duties.

A peculiar case in which the Prophet is said to have uttered his opinion about the detrimental effects of dirty nails is exposed in a tradition reported by al-Zuhrī and recorded in a papyrus edited by Nabia Abbott, who read the text as follows:[3]

10. [قال و] حدثني الليث قال حدثني عقيل عن ابن شهاب قال بلغنا ان رسول الله عليه السلام.

11. كان يسال عن الرويا فيجبه الرجل فاذا ابوا يسالهم مرارا فلم يخبره احد منهم بشي.

12. فرا أظفارهم قد طالت ودخلها وسخ فقال تر[و]ن وتر[و]ن هذا في أظفارهم.

Professor Abbott did not translate the document. In her comments[4] she merely states that "the tradition has no parallel in the standard collections" and adduces a considerable number of references to demonstrate the preoccupation of the Prophet and of his contemporaries with dreams and their interpretation. Professor Abbott is indeed right in stating that this tradition has no parallel in the *standard* collections. Furthermore, because of the damaged state of the papyrus, serious difficulties have been incurred in deciphering the text of this tradition; some minor misreadings made a correct reading almost impossible to achieve and blurred the meaning of the tradition.

It is evident from the text as it was read that the tradition is based on an implied contrast between dirty nails and dreams. The thread can be grasped in a tradition recorded by Ibn Abī Ḥātim al-Rāzī:

...عن النبي صلى الله عليه وسلم أنه قال: كيف تصدق رؤياكم وأظفاركم مملوءة وسخا.

Abū Ḥātim marks this tradition as *munkar,*[5] the reason for this being that al-Faḍl b. al-

---

muttaqīn bi-sharḥi asrāri iḥyāʾi ʿulūmi l-dīn (Cairo, 1311), II, 410 infra (*al-shayṭān* of the tradition is glossed by *iblīs*; another version of the tradition is recorded as well: *quṣṣū aẓāfīrakum fa-inna l-shayṭāna yajrī mā bayna l-laḥmi wa--ẓufri, ib.,* 410 ult.); al-Suyūṭī, *al-Ẓafar,* fol. 368 a; idem, *al-Durr al-manthūr,* I, 113, supra; al-Baḥrānī, *al-Ḥadāʾiq al-nāḍira* (Najaf, 1384), V, 570 (*ʿan abī jaʿfarin ʿalayhi l-salām, qāla: innamā quṣṣū l-aẓfāra li-annahā maqīlu l-shayṭān, wa-minhu l-nisyān, ...; . . . . . ʿan abī ʿabdi llāh ʿalayhi l-salām, qāla: inna astara wa-akhfā mā yusalliṭu l-shayṭāna min ibni ādama in ṣāra yaskunu taḥta l-aẓāfiri. . .*); cf. Raḍī l-Dīn al Ṭabarsī, *Makārim al-akhlāq* (Cairo, 1347), 25, ult.

3 Nabia Abbott, *Studies in Arabic Literary Papyri, II: Qurʾanic Commentary and Tradition* (Chicago, 1967), p. 166, Document 6, no. 6, ll. 10–12.

4 Ibid., p. 168.

5 Ibn Abī Ḥātim, *ʿIlal al-ḥadīth* (reprint: Cairo, 1343), II, 282, no. 2349.

Mukhtār, the transmitter of the tradition, is considered *majhūl*.[6] The intent of the tradition is clear: people with dirty nails are unable to have *true* dreams (*ṣādiqa*); it may be concluded that they can have only false dreams (*bāṭila, aḍghāth al-aḥlām*).[7]

Identical in content with the tradition of the papyrus, but differently shaped, is the report given by Khargūshī:

فقد روى عن رسول الله (ص) أنه كان يسأل أصحابه كل يوم هل رأى أحد منكم رؤيا فيقصون عليه رؤياهم فيعبرها لهم، ثم سألهم أياما فلم يقص أحد منهم رؤيا، فقال لهم: كيف ترون و[8] في أظفاركم الرفغ [9] وذلك أن أظفارهم قد طالت وتقليمها من الفطرة.[10]

This is indeed the version recorded in the compilation of Ps. Ibn Sīrīn.[11]

In the light of these traditions the few errors in Miss Abbott's reading of the text of the papyrus can be rectified and the precise sense of al-Zuhrī's tradition provided:

10. [قال و] حدثني الليث قال حدثني عقيل عن بن شهاب قال بلغنا أن رسول الله عليه السلام

11. [كان يسأل] عن الرويا فيجيبه الرجل [ث]م [انه]م أتو [او] سألهم مرارا فلم يخبره أحد منهم بشي

12. فرا أظفارهم قد طالت ودخلها وسخ فقال تر[و]ن وتر[و]ن وهذا في أظفاركم.

The Prophet used to ask [his Companions] about their dreams, and they would respond. Then [when] they [once] came[12] he asked them several times but none of them gave him any information (about his dreams - K.); then the Prophet noticed that their nails had lengthened and that dirt had penetrated them. "How will you see (dreams - K.) or be shown (dreams -K.)[13] while[14] this (i.e., the dirt) is underneath your nails," asked the Prophet.

6 See the negative opinions on him: Ibn Abī Ḥātim, *al-Jarḥ wa-l-taʿdīl* (Hyderabad, 1361), III/II, 69, no. 391 (*aḥādīthuhu munkara, yuḥaddithu bi-l-abāṭīl*); al-Dhahabī, *Mīzān al-iʿtidāl*, ed. ʿAlī Muḥammad al-Bijāwī (Cairo, 1382/1963), III, 358–59, no. 6750; Ibn Ḥajar, *Lisān al-mīzān* (Hyderabad, 1330), IV, 449, no. 1374.

7 On the distinction between true and false dreams, see, e.g., ʿAbd al-Ghanī al-Nābulusī, *Taʿṭīr al-anām fī taʿbīri l-manām* (Cairo, 1384), I, 3–4.

8 The "و" missing in text.

9 In text: الرفع

10 Al-Kharqūshī, *al-Bishāra wa-l-nidhāra*, Ms. Br. Mus., Or. 6262, fol. 6a.

11 Ps. Ibn Sīrīn, *Tafsīru l-aḥlāmi l-kabīr* (Cairo, 1382/1963), 23.

12 Miss Abbott's reading أبوا, "they refused", seems to be unbased.

13 Cf. this expression about dreams: al-Suyūṭī, *al-Durr al-manthūr*, III, 311–12 (*yarāhā l-muʾminau turā lahu*); al-Rāghib al-Iṣfahānī, *Muḥāḍarāt al-udabāʾ* (Beirut, 1961), I, 149 (*yarāhā l-rajul au turā lahu*); al-Zurqānī, *Sharḥ al-mawāhib al-ladunniyya* (Cairo, 1328), VII, 163.

14 This "و" omitted in the reading of Miss Abbott blurred, of course, the meaning of the tradition.

The intent of the tradition is obvious: believers with long nails[15] are barred from seeing true, veridical dreams.

The dirt under the nails of the believers was even more harmful for the religious practices of the Prophet himself, as pointed out in another tradition. The Prophet was once heedless and committed an error in his prayer; he explained his error by the fact that some people attending the prayer had not cleaned their nails.[16]

Another serious event, which might have endangered the continuity of the prophetic revelation, is connected, according to one tradition, with the injunction to pare one's nails. When the angel Jibrīl had ceased for a period to convey the revelation to the Prophet, he explained to his worried believers that this was a result of the fact that they were not careful in paring their nails, trimming their moustaches, and cleaning their finger-joints.[17]

This, however, is a fragmentary tradition in which no details about the time of the event and its circumstances are given. The current reports concerning the pause in the revelation usually refer to Sūra XVIII, 24–25: "And do not say, regarding anything, 'I am going to do that tomorrow', but only 'If God will'; and mention thy Lord when thou forgettest. . ."; or to *Sūra* XCIII, 3: "Thy Lord has neither forsaken thee nor hates thee. . ."; and differ in their setting and details. The reason for the suspension of the revelation was, according to one of the reports, an illness of the Prophet lasting two or three nights. A woman then came and derided him by saying that God had forsaken him. Some traditions name the woman: she was Umm Jamīl, the wife of Abū Lahab. A version of this tradition links the story of Umm Jamīl and the verses of Sūra CXI about her (. . ."and his wife, the carrier of the firewood. . .") with the verses of Sūra XCIII: the revelation was delayed after a short time after her talk with the Prophet, in which the latter asserted that the verses about her were revealed by God. When the revelation was suspended, she came to the Prophet and mocked him, stating that his Devil had left him. Then the verses of Sūra XCIII were revealed. Another tradition presents an opposing point of view: when the pause in the revelation occurred, it was Khadīja who

---

15 Some Shīʿī compendia draw a clear line between men and women: while men were enjoined to pare their nails, women were ordered to let their nails grow because "it is nicer for them." See al-Baḥrānī, *al-Ḥadāʾiq al-nāḍira*, V, 571 ult.–572, l. 1: *qāla rasūlu llāhi* (*ṣ*) *li-l-rijāli: quṣṣū aẓfārakum, wa-li-l-nisāʾi: trukna, fa-innahu azyanu lakunna*; al-Ṭabarsī, *Makārim al-akhlāq*, 26, l. 1 (but curiously: *wa-qāla li-l-nisāʾi: lā tatrukna min aẓāfīrikunna,* which seems to be an error).

16 See Thābit b. Abī Thābit, *Khalqu l-insān*, ed. ʿAbd al-Sattār *Farrāj*, (Kuwayt, 1965), 229; al-Ḥākīm al-Tirmidhī, *Nawādir al-uṣūl* (Istanbul, 1293), 45 (. . .*annahu sahā fī ṣalātihi fa-qāla: mā lī lā ūhimu wa-rufghu aḥadikum bayna ẓufrihi wa-anmulatihi*. . .); al-Zamakhsharī, *al-Fāʾiq*, ed. Muḥammad Abū l-Faḍl Ibrāhīm, ʿAlī Muḥammad al-Bijāwī (Cairo, 1971), IV, 83 (*fa-auhama fī ṣalātihi*. . .*wa-kayfa lā ūhimu*. . .; *auhama* is glossed by: *auhama fī kalāmihi wa-kitābihi idhā asqaṭa minhu shayʾan*); al-Muttaqī l-Hindī, *Kanz al-ʿUmmāl*, VI, 375, nos. 2682–83; Nūr al-Dīn al-Haythamī, *Majmaʿ al-zawāʾid* (Beirut, 1967), I, 238; Ibn Ḥajar, *Fatḥ al-bārī*, X, 291; al-Suyūṭī, *al-Durr al-manthūr*, I, 113; *LʿA*, s.v. *r-f-gh*, *w-h-m* (see the variants recorded: *lā ahimu, lā ayhamu, lā ūhimu*); Ibn al-Athīr, *al-Nihāya fī gharībi l-ḥadīth*, s.v. *w-h-m, r-f-gh*; al-Qurṭubī, *Tafsīr*, II, 102; al-Jaṣṣāṣ, *Aḥkam al-qurʾān*, I, 66 infra.

17 Al-Suyūṭī, *al-Durr al-manthūr*, I, 112; Murtaḍā l-Zabīdī, *Itḥāfu*, II, 399; al-Zamakhsharī, *al-Fāʾiq*, IV, 83; al-Baḥrānī, *al-Hadāʾiq*, V, 569; al-Muttaqī l-Hindī, *Kanz al-ʿUmmāl*, VI, 375, no. 2681; ʿAlī b. Rabban al-Ṭabarī, *Kitāb al-dīn wa-l-daula*, ed. ʿĀdil Nuwayhiḍ, (Beirut, 1393/1973), 62; al-Ṭabarsī, *Makārim al-akhlāq*, 25 infra.

worried about it and asked the Prophet whether God had forsaken him; the verses of Sūra XCIII came as an authoritative answer. Another tradition links the verses of Sūra XCIII with Sūra XVIII, 24–25, recording a different report: the Jews, consulted by the unbelievers of Mecca, advised them to ask the Prophet certain questions in order to test whether he was a true Prophet. Having come and put these questions to him, the Prophet promised to give an answer the next day without adding the clause *in shā'a llāhu.* Then the revelation was suspended, only to resume after a time. A peculiar tradition says that the Prophet, hit by a stone, his finger bleeding, recited the well known verse: *hal anti illā iṣba'un damīti. . .*; then God withheld the revelation. After being mocked by a woman about that, the Prophet uttered the revealed verses. Finally, there is a tradition according to which Jibrīl could not enter the Prophet's abode and deliver the revelation to him because there was a dead whelp under his bed. The period of the delay is given, according to contradictory reports, as two or three days, twelve days, fifteen days or forty days.[18]

The tradition recorded by Muqātil in his *Tafsīr*, giving the reason for the revelation of the verses in Sūra XCIII, is different. It is, in fact, the tradition mentioned above (see note 17) with some additional details. The Prophet missed Jibrīl, who used to convey to him the revelation, for forty days (or three days, according to another report). The unbelievers in Mecca claimed that Muḥammad's revelation was not from God and that Muḥammad had his revelation withheld, proving that God had abandoned him and hated him. When the Muslims (in Mecca - K.) asked the Prophet, he replied that the revelation had stopped because some of them did not clean the joints of their fingers and did not pare their nails.[19]

It is evident that this tradition, recorded in a commentary of the second century and echoed in some later commentaries,[20] shows the importance attached to the paring of nails in the early period of Islam; negligence on the part of the believers could endanger the continuity of the revelation granted to the Prophet by God.

Mujāhid (d. 104 H) comments on Sūra XIX, 64: "We come not down save at the commandment of thy Lord" that the revelation was suspended and that it was Jibrīl who explained to the Prophet that the reason was that the believers were careless in paring their nails, trimming their moustaches, cleansing their teeth (with a *siwāk*) and cleaning their finger-joints.[21]

---

18 See al-Ṭabarī, *Tafsīr* (Būlāq) XXX, 148; al-Qurṭubī, *Tafsīr*, XX, 92–93; Ibn Kathīr, *Tafsīr* (Beirut, 1385/1966), IV, 365–66, VII, 313; al-Wāḥidī, *Asbāb al-nuzūl* (Cairo, 1388/1968), 301–2; al-Suyūṭī, *Lubāb al-nuqūl fī asbābi l-nuzūl* (Cairo, 1373/1954), 144–45, 237–38; idem, *al-Durr al-manthūr*, VI, 360–61; Ibn Ḥajar, *al-Kāfī l-shāf fī takhrīji aḥādīthi l-kashshāf*, (Cairo, 1354), 102, no. 306; 185, nos. 325–26; al-Samarqandī, *Tafsīr*, Ms. Chester Beatty 3668, II, 326a; al-Khāzin, *Tafsīr* (*Lubāb al-taʾwīl fī maʿānī l-tanzīl*) (Cairo 1381), VII, 214–15; al-Rāzī, *al-Tafsīr al-kabīr* (= *Mafātīḥ al-ghayb*) (Cairo, 1357/1938), XXXI, 210–11; al-Naysābūrī, *Gharāʾib al-qurʾān*, ed. Ibrāhīm ʿAṭwa ʿAwaḍ (Cairo, 1390/1970), XXX, 115–16.

19 Muqātil, *Tafsīr*, Ms. Ahmet III, 74/II, fol. 242b.

20 See al-Qurṭubī, *Tafsīr*, XX, 93 infra; al-Rāzī, *al-Tafsīr al-kabīr*, XXXI, 211; al-Naysābūrī, *Gharāʾib al-qurʾān*, XXX, 115 infra.

21 See al-Wāḥidī, *Asbāb al-nuzūl*, 203; al-Qurṭubī, *Tafsīr*, XI, 127; al-Suyūṭī, *al-Durr al-manthūr*, IV, 279, ll. 9–14.

Muslim scholars, of course regarded it as necessary to classify the practice of paring one's nails, establishing its rank and position in relation to other practices bearing on cleanliness and purity, like trimming one's moustache, plucking out the hair of the armpits, and shaving the privates. It was necessary to decide whether the practice is obligatory and forms part of the *sunna.* The mandatory character of the practice was derived from a tradition quoted from the compilation of Aḥmad b. Ḥanbal and attributed to the Prophet: "He who does not shave his privates, pare his nails, and trim his moustache is not of us."[22] This tradition was, however, sharply criticized. Scholars pointed out that one of the transmitters, Ibn Lahīᶜa,[23] was considered unreliable and that another version of this tradition, recorded by al-Tirmidhī,[24] does not include the paring of nails (it only mentions the trimming of the moustache). Even granted that the *ḥadīth* is trustworthy, the expression *fa-laysa minnā* 'he is not one of us' merely denotes that the man does not follow the *sunna* of the Prophet. Al-Munāwī concludes that the tradition does not establish the mandatory character of the practice. It is a commendable practice (*mandūbun nadban mu'akkadan*), and failure to carry out the injunction of the *ḥadīth* can only be considered as neglect of the *sunna.*[25]

However, there was a problem in connection with the paring of nails which caused division of opinions among the scholars: if the water of ablution (*wuḍūᶜ*) does not reach the place blocked by the dirt, should one repeat the ablution or not.[26] Al-Shāfiᶜī gives an unequivocal decision concerning one specific question: if someone performs the ablution and subsequently trims his beard and pares his nails, does he have to repeat the ablution? According to al-Shāfiᶜī the answer is negative.[27]

Scholars were not unanimous about the period prescribed by the Prophet for performing the practices of the *fiṭra* (trimming the moustache, shaving the privates, paring the nails, and pulling out the hairs of the armpits). According to a current tradition it is enjoined every forty days.[28] The problem under discussion was whether this was the prescribed period or whether it was a maximum which one should not exceed but which can be shortened according to need.[29] The tradition recorded by al-Bukhārī states that Ibn 'Umar used to pare his nails every two weeks,[30] implying that the Prophet himself practiced it in this way. Another report says that the Prophet used to trim his moustache and pare his nails on Friday before going out to perform the Friday prayer.[31] The latter tradition is contradicted by an opinion recorded in the

---

22 Murtaḍā l-Zabīdī, *Itḥāfu*, II, 411, 413; al-Munāwī, *Fayḍ al-qadīr*, VI, 223, no. 9021: *man lam yaḥliq ᶜānatahu wa-yuqallim aẓfārahu wa-yajuzza shāribahu fa-laysa minnā.*

23 See on him *EI*[2], s.v. Ibn Lahīᶜa (F. Rosenthal).

24 See al-Munāwī, *Fayḍ al-qadīr*, VI, 222, no. 9016.

25 See the commentary of al-Munāwī, *Fayḍ al-qadīr*, VI, 223; Murtaḍā l-Zabīdī, *Itḥāfu*, 411, 413.

26 See Ibn Ḥajar, *Fatḥ al-bārī*, X, 291; Murtaḍā l-Zabīdī, *Itḥāfu*, II, 411 sup.; Faḍlullāh al-Jīlānī *Faḍlu. . .*, II, 685.

27 Al-Shāfiᶜī, *al-Umm* (reprint: Cairo, 1388/1968), I, 18.

28 See e.g. al-Suyūṭī, *al-Durr al-manthūr*, I, 112; idem, *al-Isfār*, fol. 2a; al-Bayhaqī, *al-Sunan al-kubrā*, I, 150; Ibn Qayyim al-Jauziyya, *Zād al-maᶜād* (reprint: Beirut, n.d.) I, 45; Murtaḍā l-Zabīdī, *Itḥāfu*, II, 399 supra.

29 Al-Shaukānī, *Nayl al-auṭār*, I, 131–32; Ibn Ḥajar, *Fatḥ al-bārī*, X, 292.

30 Faḍlullāh al-Jīlānī, *Faḍlu. . .*, II, 685, no. 1258.

31 See Ibn al-Jauzī, *al-Wafā bi-aḥwāli l-muṣṭafā*, ed. Muṣṭafā ᶜAbd al-Wāḥid (Cairo, 1386/1966), 591;

Fatāwī Tātārkhāniyya, which disapproves of paring the nails before the morning prayer on Friday. The argument of this statement is of some interest: prayer partakes of the idea of *ḥajj.* As shaving the hair and paring the nails are forbidden during the *ḥajj* and only permitted afterwards, these practices must also be considered unlawful before prayer. This opinion is further corroborated by a tradition saying that he who pares his nails *after* the Friday prayer has merit equal to that of one who, having performed the pilgrimage and the *ᶜumra*, shaves his hair and pares his nails.[32]

As against the tradition which sets a period of forty days between one performance of these practices and the next, we have a more elaborate tradition attributed to the Prophet. He is said to have established the following periods: shaving the privates every forty days, pulling out the hairs of the armpits whenever hair is seen, trimming the moustache as it grows long, paring the nails every Friday, and cleaning of the finger-joints at every *wuḍūᶜ*.[33]

The widely circulated tradition of the paring on Friday was contradicted by traditions which recommend paring the nails on Thursday.[34] The Prophet is said to have pronounced that whoever wants to escape from poverty, disease of the eyes, leprosy and madness should pare his nails on Thursday afternoon.[35] An explicit opinion against paring the nails on Friday is recorded on the authority of Abū Ḥanīfa: he disapproved of Friday as the day of paring; the moustache has to be trimmed and the nails pared only when needed.[36] The tradition assuring rewards to those who pare their nails on Friday is somewhat more generous, though its fulfillment is slightly delayed. "He who picks his teeth, trims his moustache, pares his nails, pulls out the hair of his armpit, and washes (the prescribed *ghusl*) on Friday, deserves Paradise," says a tradition attributed to the Prophet.[37] More reserved was a tradition promising those who pare their nails on Friday that God will banish disease from them and instill in them remedy.[38] A harmonizing tradition attributed to the Prophet states that nails should be pared on Thursday and Friday as this assures one of wealth.[39] Reconciling as well seems to be the tradition that enjoins paring the nails, trimming the moustache, pulling out the hair

---

al-Suyūṭī, *al-Ẓafar,* fol. 368b ult.–369a, l.l; idem, *al-Durr al-manthūr,* I, 112 ult.; al-Jaṣṣāṣ, *Aḥkam al-qurʾān,* I, 66 ult.; al-Diyārbakrī, *Taʾrīkh,* I, 208; al-Munāwī, *Fayḍ al-qadīr,* V, 238, no. 7131 (and see the contradictory traditions in the commentary); cf. Abbott, *Studies,* II, 200, no. 9 (and see the notes of the Editor, 203–04).

32 See Anonymous, Ms. Univ. of Istanbul, 6258, fol. 9b–10a (quoted from *Risālat aḥkām al-fiṭra l-islāmiyya*).

33 Murtaḍā l-Zabīdī, *Itḥāfu,* II, 399, 413 supra; Ibn Ḥajar, *Fatḥ al-bārī,* X, 292 infra; al-Suyūṭī, *al-Durr al-manthūr,* I, 113, ll. 1–2; idem, *al-Isfār,* fol. 2a (and cf. ibid, fol. 3b, another schedule for the performance of these practices); al-Dhahabī, *Mīzān al-iᶜtidāl,* I, 33, no. 95.

34 See, e. g., Murtaḍā l-Zabīdī, *Itḥāfu,* II, 413–14; al-Suyūṭī, *al-Ẓafar,* fol. 370a–b.

35 Al-Waṣṣābī, *al-Baraka,* 216; al-Suyūṭī, *al-Ẓafar,* fol. 369b supra.

36 Anonymous, Ms. Univ. of Istanbul 6258, fol. 9b.

37 Al-Suyūṭī, *al-Ẓafar,* fol. 369a; al-Tabarsī, *Makārim al-akhlāq,* 25.

38 Ibn Abī Shayba, *Muṣannaf,* ed. ᶜAbd al-Khāliq Afghānī (Hyderabad, 1387/1967), II, 159; Abū Ṭālib al-Makkī, *Qūt al-qulūb,* I, 98; al-Jīlānī, *al-Ghunya* (Cairo, 1322), I, 17; al-Suyūṭī, *al-Ẓafar,* fol. 369b. But this very reward was promised the Saturday nail-parers; al-ᶜAynī, *ᶜUmdat al-qārī,* XXII, 46 supra.

39 Al-Waṣṣābī, *al-Baraka,* 216.

of the armpit, and shaving the privates on Thursday; on Friday the believer has to wash (*ghusl*) his body, to perfume himself, and to wear nice clothes.[40]

The most liberal tradition is reported on the authority of Abū Hurayra. The Prophet gives a detailed account of the rewards which will be granted the believers who pare their nails on any day of the week; no special day for paring is singled out.[41]

Special importance is attached to the order of paring the nails.[42] Scholars of *ḥadīth* stress that there is no sound tradition concerning the order of paring the nails,[43] but there exist certain utterances of early scholars and some verse compositions serving as mnemonic devices for knowing the right order.[44]

There are scholarly disputes over the problem of how to dispose of the parings. The accepted opinion is that, according to the utterances of the Prophet, the parings should be buried. While there is nothing wrong in discarding them, to dispose of them in the privy or in the wash-house is reprehensible.[45] The reason for the injunction to bury the parings was that it would not allow sorcerers to play with them. Ibn Ḥajar records another reason for burying: they are a part of the human body and have to be buried like the body itself.[46] The verses of Sūra LXXVII, 26–27 (*a-lam najʿali l-arḍa kifātan aḥyāʾan wa-amwātan*) "made we not the earth to be a housing for the living and for the dead?" refer to nail-parings and hair, according to one of the commentaries.[47] Al-Ḥakīm al-Tirmidhī records a tradition on the authority of ʿĀʾisha, stating that the Prophet ordered the burial of seven things from the human body: hair, parings, blood, menstruation. . . ., (fallen) teeth, prepuce, and placenta. The reverence for the body of the believer should be extended to the elements extracted from it.[48]

Though the paring of nails is commonly accepted as a commendable *sunna* it must be performed privately; the paring of nails in mosques is condemned.[49]

Abraham is said to have been the first person in humanity who pared his nails.[50] This practice, one of the usages which belong to the observances of the *fiṭra,* is carefully observed by believers until today.

---

40 Murtaḍā l-Zabīdī, *Itḥāfu,* II, 414.

41 Al-ʿAynī, *ʿUmdat al-qārī*, XXII, 46 supra; al-Suyūṭī, *al-Ẓafar,* fol. 370b–71a; idem, *al-Isfār*, fol. 3a; al-Shaukānī, *al-Fawāʾid al-majmūʿa fī l-aḥādīth al-mauḍūʿa,* ed. ʿAbd al-Raḥmān al-Muʿallamī l-Yamānī (repr.: Beirut,1392), 197, no. 569 (marked as forged, *mauḍūʿ*); Ibn al-Jauzī, *al-Mauḍūʿāt,* ed. ʿAbd al-Raḥmān Muḥammad ʿUthmān (Cairo, 1386/1966), III, 53 (marked as *mauḍūʿ*); cf. al-Ṭabarsī, *Makārim al-akhlāq*, 25: . . .*khudhhā in shiʾta fī l-jumuʿati wa-in shiʾta fī sāʾiri l-ayyāmi.*

42. Al-Waṣṣābī, *al-Baraka* 216; al-Jīlānī, *al-Ghunya,* 17; al-Ṭabarsī, *Makārim al-akhlāq*, 25.

43 See, e.g., Murtaḍā l-Zabīdī, *Ith«āfu,* II, 411.

44 See, e.g., al-Waṣṣābī, *al-Baraka*, 216.

45 Faḍlullāh al-Jīlānī, *Faḍlu. . .,* II, 685; cf. al-Tabarsī, *Makārim al-akhlāq,* 26 supra; al-Baḥrānī, *al-Ḥadāʾiq,* V, 573.

46 Ibn Ḥajar, *Fatḥ al-bārī*, X, 292 ult.–293, ll. 1–3.

47 Sulaymān b. Ismāʿīl al-Baḥrānī al-Taubalī al-Katakānī, *al-Burhān fī tafsīri l-qurʾān,* Qumm IV, 417; al-Baḥrānī, *al-Ḥadāʾiq,* V, 573.

48 Al-Ḥakīm al-Tirmidhī, *Nawādir al-uṣūl*, 45; al-Qurṭubī, *Tafsīr*, II, 102 (quoting *Nawādir al-uṣūl*).

49 ʿAbd al-Razzāq, *al-Muṣannaf,* ed. Ḥabīburraḥmān al-Aʿẓamī, (Beirut, 1390/1970), I, 439, no. 1718; and see Ibn al-Ḥajj, *al-Madkhal* (Beirut, 1972), II, 240.

50 Al-Suyūṭī, *al-Ẓafar*, fol. 368a.

XI

"SHA'BĀN IS MY MONTH..."

A STUDY OF AN EARLY TRADITION

"Sha'bān is my month": this utterance attributed to the Prophet is widely current and usually coupled with his statement about the status of Rajab and Ramaḍān.[1] A corroborative utterance, linking the month of Sha'bān with the person of the Prophet, evaluates the status of Sha'bān in relation to other months as follows: "The superiority of Sha'bān over other months is like my superiority over other prophets".[2] Peculiar is the commentary of Sūra 28:69: "Thy Lord creates whatsoever He will and He chooses...", stating that this verse refers to the month of Sha'bān: "God adorns everything by something and He embellished the months by the month of Sha'bān".[3] In numerous utterances attributed to the

1 Al-Munāwī, *Fayḍ al-qadīr, sharḥ al-jāmi' al-ṣāghīr*, Cairo 1391/1972, IV, p. 162, no. 4889; al-'Azīzī, *al-Sirāj al-munīr*, Cairo 1377/1957, II, p. 369; 'Abd al-Qādir al-Jīlānī, *al-Ghunya li-ṭālibī ṭarīqi l-ḥaqq 'azza wa-jalla*, Cairo 1322 A.H., I, p. 211; al-Suyūṭī, *al-La'ālī al-maṣnū'a*, Cairo n.d., II, p. 114; al-Majlisī, *Biḥār al-anwār*, Tehran 1388 A.H., XCVII, pp. 68–69, 71, 75–77, 181–183; al-Ṣaffūrī, *Nuzhat al-majālis*, Beirut n.d., pp. 190, 195 ult.; Ibn Dayba', *Tamyīz al-ṭayyib min al-khabīth*, Cairo 1382/1963, p. 81 (and see ibid., p. 91, l. 1); Ibn Bābūyah, *Thawāb al-a'māl*, Tehran 1375 A.H., p. 60; Id., *Amālī*, Najaf 1389/1970, p. 17; al-Zandawaysitī, *Rauḍat al-'ulamā'*, Ms. BM, Add. 7258, fol. 255b; and see Kister, *IOS*, 1 (1971), p. 198 note 50.

2 Al-Daylamī, *Firdaus al-akhbār*, Ms. Chester Beatty 3037, fol. 109b, penult.; al-Zandawaysitī, op. cit., fol. 255b; cf. al-Suyūṭī, *al-Durr al-manthūr*, Cairo 1314 A.H., III, p. 236: ... *sha'bānu shahrī fa-man 'aẓẓama shahra sha'bāna fa-qad 'aẓẓama amrī wa-man 'aẓẓama amrī kuntu lahu farṭan wa-dhukhran yauma l-qiyāmati* ... (the *ḥadīth* is marked as *munkar*); and see Aḥmad b. Ḥijāzī, *Tuḥfat al-ikhwān fī faḍā'il rajab wa-sha'bān wa-ramaḍān*, Cairo 1308 A.H., p. 41: ... *kāna rasūlu llāhi (ṣ) yaqūlu idhā dakhala sha'bānu: ṭahhirū anfusakum li-sha'bāna wa-aḥsinū niyyatakum fīhi, fa-inna llāha 'azza wa-jalla faḍḍala sha'bāna 'alā sā'iri l-shuhūri ka-faḍlī 'alaykum* ...; and see *IOS*, 1, p. 199, note 55.

3 Al-Zandawaysitī, op. cit., fol. 255b: *qāla fī tafsīri hādhihi l-āyati: wa-rabbuka yakhluqu mā yashā'u wa-yakhtāru mā kāna lahumu l-khiyaratu, inna llāha ta'ālā zayyana kulla shay'in* (on marjin: *bi-shay'in*) *wa-zayyana l-shuhūra bi-sha'bāna; fa-kamā zayyana bihi l-shuhūra ka-dhālika yatazayyanu l-'abdu bi-l-ṭā'ati fīhi li-l-ghufrāni* ...

Prophet, he is said to have recommended the devotional practice of fasting, prayer, vigil and supplication during this month, especially on the eve of the 15th of Sha'bān (= the night of the 15th of Sha'bān).

Practices of the night of the 15th of Sha'bān, closely resembling those of *laylat al-qadr*, were scrutinized by A.J. Wensinck, who regarded these two nights as determining a New Year's period of six weeks to two months. This was challenged by K. Wagtendonk, who considered the 15th of Sha'bān to be "a starting day of a voluntary fast, which arose out of the ascetic tendency of extending the fast of Ramaḍān".[4]

A survey of the traditions on the virtues of the month of Sha'bān may clarify some of the controversies in reports of practices performed during this month, explain diverse tenets of certain circles of Muslim scholars and aid in gaining insight into the ideas of the virtuousness of Sha'bān.

I

The traditions on the Prophet's fast during the month of Sha'bān are controversial. It is not clear whether the Prophet would fast throughout the entire month of Sha'bān, or whether he would fast only part of the month. The reports on this subject are often vague; some say merely that he used to fast during this month (... *kāna yaṣūmu sha'bāna*); others, ambiguous in style and cast, assert that he would fast most of the month, or the entire month (... *kāna yaṣūmuhu kullahu illā qalīlan, bal kāna yaṣūmuhu kullahu* ...). Still others, unequivocal but contradictory, relate that he fasted the entire month of Sha'bān or, on the contrary, that he never completed an entire month's fasting except in Ramaḍān (... *kāna yaṣūmu sha'bāna kullahu* ... confronted by: ... *wa-lā ṣāma shahran kāmilan qaṭṭu ghayra ramaḍāna* ...).[5]

4 *EI*2 Sha'bān (A.J. Wensinck); A.J. Wensinck, Arabic New Year and the Feast of Tabernacles, VKAW, Afd. Let., N.R. XXV, 2, Amsterdam 1925; K. Wagtendonk, *Fasting in the Koran*, Leiden 1968, pp. 100–105; S.D. Goitein, *Studies in Islamic History*, Leiden 1968, pp. 90–110: Ramaḍān the Muslim Month of Fasting.

5 Al-Nasā'ī, *Sunan*, Beirut n.d. (reprint) IV, pp. 151–153, 199–201 (and see e.g. other versions ibid., *in ṣāma shahran ma'lūman siwā ramaḍāna ḥattā maḍā li-wajhihi* ...; ... *wa-lam yaṣum shahran tāmman mundhu atā l-madīnata illā an yakūna ramaḍānu* ... etc.); al-Ṭaḥāwī, *Sharḥ ma'ānī l-āthār* (ed. Muḥammad Zuhrī l-Najjār), Cairo 1388/1968, II, pp. 82–83; al-Tirmidhī, *Ṣaḥīḥ*, Cairo 1350/1931, III, p. 273; Ibn Abī Shayba, *al-Muṣannaf* (ed. 'Abd al-Khāliq al-Afghānī), Hyderabad 1388/1968, III, p. 103 (and see ibid., another version: ... *kāna yaṣūmu sha'bāna illā qalīlan*); Abū Dāwūd, *Ṣaḥīḥ sunan al-muṣṭafā*, Cairo 1348 A.H., I, p. 381 inf. –382 sup.; al-Ṣaffūrī, *op. cit.*, p. 198; al-Qasṭallānī, *Irshād al-sārī*, Cairo 1323 A.H., III, pp. 401–403; 'Abd al-Razzāq, *al-Muṣannaf* (ed. Ḥabīb al-Raḥmān al-A'ẓamī), Beirut 1392 A.H., IV,

Debate turned on the word *kullahu* in the tradition relating that the Prophet fasted the entire month of Sha'bān. Muslim scholars tended to limit the connotation of "wholeness" in the word, making it mean a major part. This was the explanation of 'Abdallah b. al-Mubārak (d. 181) as recorded by al-Tirmidhī.[6] The phrase that the Prophet fasted the entire month (*kullahu*) conveys in fact that he would fast for the major part of the month (*akthara l-shahri*), argues Ibn al-Mubārak, basing himself on the Arab manner of speech: when a man says that he spent the whole night in vigil, he means in fact to say that the major part of the night was spent in vigil. This interpretation indeed clears away the contradiction inherent in the two traditions: the one that the Prophet would fast the entire month (*kullahu*), and the other that 'Ā'isha never saw him completing an entire month's fast (. . . *istakmala ṣiyāma shahrin* . . .) save Ramaḍān.[7] The contradiction can thus be removed on the basis of Ibn al-Mubārak's interpretation: the only complete month during which the Prophet would fast was Ramaḍān; he also fasted for the major part of Sha'bān. Al-Qasṭallānī could rightly remark that the Prophet did not complete an entire month's fasting during Sha'bān, so as to dismiss any thought that the fast of Sha'bān was obligatory.[8]

This interpretation of *kull* cannot, however, be applied to other traditions in which the Prophet's Sha'bān fast was coupled with that of Ramaḍān, and in which the account was preceded by a verb or noun denoting wholeness and referring to both months. Certain *ḥadīths* relate

pp. 292–293, nos. 7858–7861; Ibn Ḥajar, *Fatḥ al-bārī*, Cairo 1301 A.H., IV, pp. 186–188; Ibn Rajab, *Laṭā'if al-ma'ārif*, Cairo 1343 A.H., pp. 127–142; Nūr al-Dīn al-Haythamī, *Majma' al-zawā'id*, Beirut 1967, III, p. 192; al-Mundhirī, *al-Targhīb wa-l-tarhīb* (ed. Muḥammad Muḥyī al-Dīn 'Abd al-Ḥamīd), Cairo 1379/1960, II, pp. 241–243, nos. 1481–1486; al-Ḥākim, *al-Mustadrak*, Hyderabad 1342 A.H., I, p. 434; al-Muttaqī l-Hindī, *Kanz l-'ummāl*, Hyderabad 1380/1960, VIII, p. 409, no. 2969; al-Zurqānī, *Sharḥ al-mawāhib al-laduniyya*, Cairo 1328 A.H., VIII, pp. 124–126; al-Bayhaqī, *al-Sunan al-kubrā*, Hyderabad 1352 A.H., II, p. 210; al-Shaukānī, *Nayl al-auṭār*, Cairo 1372/1953, IV, pp. 274–277; al-Zurqānī, *Sharḥ muwaṭṭa'i mālik*, Cairo 1381/1961, pp. 451–460; al-Khaṭīb al-Baghdādī, *Ta'rīkh*, Cairo 1349/1931, IV, p. 437; Ibn Wahb, *Juz'*. Ms. Chester Beatty 3497, fol. 37a, inf. (. . . *wa-kāna ṣiyāmuhu fī sha'bān*); Aḥmad b. Ḥijāzī, op. cit., p. 42; al-Ghazālī, *Mukāshafat al-qulūb*, Cairo n.d., p. 249; Maḥmūd Muḥammad Khaṭṭāb al-Subkī, *al-Manhal al-'adhb al-maurūd, sharḥ sunan abī dawūd* (ed. Amīn Maḥmūd Khaṭṭāb), Cairo 1394 A.H., X, p. 55.

6 Al-Tirmidhī, op. cit., III, p. 273.

7 'Abd al-Razzāq, op. cit., IV, p. 293, no. 7861; al-Qasṭallānī, *op. cit.*, III, pp. 401–403; al-'Aynī, '*Umdat al-qārī*, Cairo 1348 A.H., XI, pp. 82–85; Ibn Ḥajar, *Fatḥ*, IV, p. 187.

8 Al-Qasṭallānī, op. cit., III, p. 401 (. . . *li'allā yuẓanna wujūbuhu*).

that the Prophet did not fast an entire month (*shahran kāmilan*) except Sha'bān, which he concatenated with (the fast of) Ramaḍān;[9] other *ḥadīths*, on the authority of 'Ā'isha, say: "I did not see the Prophet fasting two consecutive months except Sha'bān and Ramaḍān".[10] As it was out of the question that the Prophet would fast for only the major part of Ramaḍān, the interpretation of *kull* or *kāmil* as "a greater part" (scil. of the month) had to be abandoned. Scholars accepted the explanation of *kull* as "entire", but found another way to reconcile the contradictory traditions: the Prophet would sometimes fast the entire month of Sha'bān, and sometimes only a part of it. Another explanation tending to soften the contradiction was that the Prophet would fast during different periods of the month of Sha'bān, sometimes at the beginning, sometimes in the middle and sometimes at the end.[11] It is evident that scholars sought to draw a clear line between the obligatory fast of the entire month of Ramaḍān and the voluntary fast of Sha'bān, adjusting the controversial traditions to the orthodox view, which approved of fasting for only a part of Sha'bān.

Certain reports give the reasons for the Prophet's fast during Sha'bān. The Prophet, says one tradition, would fast during Sha'bān to replace the days of voluntary fast which he had missed over the course of the year.[12] Another tradition held that, as a person's fate is decided in Sha'bān, the Prophet said he would prefer the decision of his fate to be made while he was fasting.[13] Slightly different is the utterance of the Prophet in which he defined Sha'bān as a month straddled by the two significant months of Rajab and Ramaḍān, and remarked that people were heedless of the virtues of this month. It is in Sha'bān that the deeds of men are brought before the Presence of God, and the Prophet said he would prefer his

9 Abū Dāwūd, op. cit., I, p. 368; al-Dārimī, *Sunan* (ed. 'Abdallah Hāshim Yamānī), Medina 1386/1966, I, p. 350: . . . Umm Salama: *mā ra'aytu rasūla llāhi* (*ṣ*) *ṣāma shahran tāmman illā sha'bāna, fa-innahu kāna yaṣiluhu bi-ramaḍāna li-yakūnā shahrayni mutatābi'ayni wa-kāna yaṣūmu min al-shahri ḥattā naqūl* . . .; Murtaḍā l-Zabīdī, *Itḥāf al-sādati l-muttaqīn bi-sharḥi asrāri iḥyā'i 'ulūmi l-dīn*, Cairo 1311 A.H., IV, p. 257, ll. 1–2; al-Muttaqī l-Hindī, op. cit., VIII, p. 410, no. 2972; Maḥmūd Khaṭṭāb al-Subkī, ibid.

10 Al-Tirmidhī, op. cit., III, p. 272; Ibn Mājah, *Sunan al-muṣṭafā*, Cairo 1349 A.H., I, pp. 505–506: . . . *kāna yaṣūmu sha'bāna kullahu ḥattā yaṣilahu bi-ramaḍāna.*

11 Al-'Aynī, op. cit., XI, p. 83; al-Qasṭallānī, op. cit., III, pp. 401–402.

12 Ibn Rajab, op. cit., p. 141; al-Zurqānī, *Sharḥ al-mawāhib*, VIII, p. 125;

13 Al-Khaṭīb al-Baghdādī, op. cit., IV, p. 437; Ibn Abī Ḥātim, *'Ilal al-ḥadīth*, Cairo 1343 A.H., I, p. 250, no. 737 (the *ḥadīth* is marked as *munkar*); Ibn Rajab, op. cit., p. 140; al-Zurqānī, *Sharḥ al-mawāhib*, VIII, p. 126; al-Suyūṭī, *Sharḥ al-ṣudūr bi-sharḥ ḥāli l-mautā wa-l-qubūr*, Cairo n.d., p. 22.

deeds to be brought before God while he was fasting.[14] The month of Sha'bān, says one story, complained before God that He had placed it between the significant months of Rajab and Ramaḍān; God consoled Sha'bān, ordering the reading of the Qur'ān during that month. Sha'bān was indeed called "The Month of the Qur'ān Readers" (*shahr al-qurrā'*); during it pious scholars would redouble their efforts in reading the Qur'ān.[15]

As is usual in the "literature of virtues" (*al-faḍā'il*), the qualities and merits of deeds, places, times and devotional practices are measured and assessed, and a scale of merit is established. In an utterance attributed to the Prophet, the voluntary fast of Sha'bān is unequivocally set over the fast of Rajab. When he heard of persons fasting in Rajab, the Prophet said: "How far are they from those who fast in the month of Sha'bān" (scil. in reward)![16] This, however, faced a reported statement of the Prophet that the most meritorious fast (apart from Ramaḍān) was that during Muḥarram. Scholars explained that the Prophet received knowledge of the superiority of the fast of Muḥarram only in the last period of his life; and though he expressed the preference, there was no time to put fasting in Muḥarram into practice, or he may have been held up by current affairs.[17]

The virtue of fasting during Sha'bān was closely linked with the

14 Al-Shaukānī, *Nayl*, IV, p. 276; al-Muttaqī l-Hindī, op. cit., VIII, p. 410, no. 2973; al-Mukhalliṣ, *Majālis*, Ms. Ẓāhiriyya, majmū'a 60, fol. 108a; Ibn Qayyim al-Jauziyya, *I'lām al-muwaqqi'īn* (ed. Ṭāhā 'Abd al-Ra'ūf Sa'd), Beirut 1973, IV, p. 297; Ibn Rajab, op. cit., pp. 127 inf., 136 ult. — 137 sup.; al-Zurqānī, *Sharḥ al-mawāhib*, VIII, p. 126 sup.; al-Ghazālī, *Mukāshafa*, p. 249; al-Zandawaysitī, op. cit., fol. 255b; Abū Nu'aym, *Ḥilyat al-auliyā'*, Beirut 1387/1967 (reprint), IX, p. 18; Maḥmūd Khaṭṭāb al-Subkī, ibid.

15 Ibn Rajab, op. cit., pp. 141 inf. — 142 sup.; cf. al-Zandawaysitī, op. cit., fol. 256a (. . . *'an anas b. mālik (r) annahu qāla: kāna aṣḥābu rasūli llāhi (ṣ) idhā naẓarū ilā hilāli sha'bāna nkabbū 'alā l-maṣāḥifi yaqra'ūnahā wa-akhraja l-muslimūna zakāta amwālihim li-yataqawwā bihā l-ḍa'īfu wa-l-miskīnu 'alā ṣiyāmi ramaḍāna wa-da'ā l-wulātu ahla l-sujūni fa-man kāna 'alayhi ḥaddun aqāmū 'alayhi, wa-illā khallau sabīlahu wa-nṭalaqa l-tujjāru* (above the line: *al-sujjān*) *fa-qaḍau mā 'alayhim wa-qtaḍau mā lahum*.

16 'Abd al-Razzāq, op. cit., IV, p. 292, no. 7858; al-Shaukānī, *Nayl*, IV, p. 277; al-Zurqānī, *Sharḥ muwaṭṭa' mālik*, II, p. 458; Id., *Sharḥ al-mawāhib*, VIII, p. 126; Ibn Abī Shayba, op. cit., III, p. 102; Ibn Bābūyah, *Thawāb*, p. 59; al-Majlisī, op. cit., XCVII, p. 77; and see *IOS*, 1, p. 206, note 96.

17 Al-Qasṭallānī, op. cit., III, p. 402; Al-'Aynī, op. cit., XI, p. 84; al-Zurqānī, *Sharḥ al-muwaṭṭa'*, II, p. 458; Ibn Ḥajar, *Fatḥ*, IV, p. 187 inf.; cf. Ibn Rajab, op. cit., p. 29; al-Shaukānī, *Nayl*, IV, 271 sup.; Nūr al-Dīn al-Haythamī, op. cit., III, pp. 190–191; al-Tirmidhī, op. cit., III, pp. 276–277; Ibn Abī Shayba, op. cit., III, p. 103.

veneration of Ramaḍān: to fast in Sha'bān was held to be a means of honouring Ramaḍān.[18] All the traditions but one,[19] stress the superiority of Ramaḍān — the month of obligatory fast — over the other months. Consequently a clear line had to be drawn between Ramaḍān and the virtuous months of voluntary fast, and a distinction made between Sha'bān and Ramaḍān. The Prophet indeed is said to have prohibited fasting on the day or two days preceding Ramaḍān. In other traditions this concept was defined slightly differently: the Prophet is said to have forbidden fasting to be carried over uninterruptedly from Sha'bān to Ramaḍān; accordingly, a pause in fasting (*faṣl*) between these two months was to be observed.[20] Some sources record an utterance of the Prophet in which the period forbidden for fasting, between Sha'bān and Ramaḍān was extended considerably: fasting in Sha'bān was to be suspended from the 15th of the month until the 1st of Ramaḍān.[21] The interdiction against fasting on the days immediately preceding Ramaḍān was, however, affected by the dispensation (*rukhṣa*) for those who were continuing a fast begun earlier in Sha'bān.[22]

18 Al-Shaukānī, *Nayl*, IV, p. 275 inf.: . . . *su'ila rasūlu llāhi* (*ṣ*) *ayyu l-ṣaumi afḍalu ba'da ramaḍāna, fa-qāla*: *sha'bānu li-ta'ẓīmi ramaḍāna*; al-Daylamī, op. cit., Ms. Chester Beatty 4139, fol. 93b; al-Zurqānī, *Sharḥ al-muwaṭṭa'*, II, p. 458; Ibn Abī Shayba, op. cit., III, p. 103; al-Jīlānī, op. cit., I, p. 210; al-Munāwī, op. cit., II, p. 42, no. 1277; al-Muttaqī l-Hindī, op. cit., VIII, p. 348, no. 2535; al-Mukhalliṣ, *Majālis*, Ms. Ẓāhiriyya, majmū'a 60, fol. 110b; Ibn Bābūyah, *Thawāb*, p. 59; al-Majlisī, op. cit., XCVII, p. 77; al-Ṭaḥāwī, *Sharḥ ma'ānī*, II, 83 inf.; cf. al-Daylamī, op. cit., Ms. Chester Beatty 4139, fol. 130a: *allāhumma bārik lanā fī rajab wa-sha'bān wa-ballighnā ramaḍān* . . .

19 Al-Jīlānī, op. cit., I, p. 211: . . . *wa-khtāra min al-shuhūri arba'atan*: *rajaba wa-sha'bāna wa-ramaḍāna wa-l-muḥarrama, wa-khtāra minhā sha'bāna wa-ja'alahu shahra l-nabiyyi* (*ṣ*): *fa-kamā anna l-nabiyya* (*ṣ*) *afḍalu l-anbiyā'i ka-dhālika shahruhu afḍalu l-shuhūri.*

20 'Abd al-Razzāq, op. cit., IV, pp. 158–160; Ibn Abī Shayba, op. cit., III, pp. 21–22; Nūr al-Dīn al-Haythamī, op. cit., III, p. 148; al-Bayhaqī, *al-Sunan*, IV, pp. 207–208; al-Muttaqī l-Hindī, op. cit., VIII, p. 310, nos. 2140–2141, 2144; cf. Ibn Qayyim al-Jauziyya, *Badā'i' al-fawā'id*, Beirut n.d. (reprint), III, p. 96.

21 Ibn Abī Shayba, op. cit., III, p. 21; 'Abd al-Razzāq, op. cit., IV, p. 161, no. 7325; al-Sakhāwī, *al-Maqāṣid al-ḥasana* (ed. 'Abdallah Muḥammad al-Ṣiddīqī), Cairo 1375/1956, p. 35, no. 55; al-Dārimī, op. cit., I, p. 350; al-Murtaḍā l-Zabīdī, op. cit., IV, p. 256; al-Suyūṭī, *Jam' al-jawāmi'*, Cairo 1391/1971, I, p. 430, nos. 489–490, 445 no. 540, 745–746, nos. 1517–1519, 760, no. 1566; al-Munāwī, op. cit., I, p. 304, no. 494; al-Tirmidhī, op. cit., III, p. 274; Abū Dāwūd, op. cit., I, p. 368; al-Ṣaffūrī, op. cit., p. 198; al-Shaukānī, *Nayl*, IV, pp. 290–292; al-Bayhaqī, *al-Sunan*, IV, p. 209; Maḥmūd Khaṭṭāb al-Subkī, op. cit., X, p. 56.

22 Al-Dāraquṭnī, *Sunan* (ed. 'Abdallah Hāshim Yamānī), Medina 1386/1966, II, p. 191, no. 57; Ibn Abī Shayba, op. cit., III, p. 23; al-Dārimī, op. cit., I, p. 336; Abū

The traditions explicitly recommending fasting in the final days of Sha'bān were controversial.[23] The Prophet is said to have made the following utterance: "He who fasts on the last Monday of Sha'bān, God will forgive him for his sins".[24] Another tradition of the Prophet promises those who fast on the first and last Thursdays of Sha'bān entrance into Paradise.[25] God will protect from hellfire the body of a believer who fasts even a single day of Sha'bān and he will be granted the company of Yūsuf in Paradise and given the reward of Dāwūd and Ayyūb. If he completes the entire month in fasting, God will ease the pangs of his death, remove the darkness of his grave and hide his shame on the Day of Resurrection.[26]

Especially stressed were the virtues of devotional observance of the first night of Sha'bān. "He who performs on the first night of Sha'bān 12 prostrations (*rak'a*), reading during the first of them the *fātiḥa* and repeating five times *qul huwa aḥad*, God will grant him the reward of 12,000 martyrs and he will be absolved of his sins, as on the day his mother bore him, and no sin will be reckoned against him for eighty days",[27] says a tradition attributed to the Prophet.

The month of Sha'bān was considered by the Prophet as protection from the fires of Hell; he enjoined those who sought to meet him in Paradise to fast at least three days in Sha'bān.[28]

Dāwūd, op. cit., I, p. 368; al-Shaukānī, *Nayl*, IV, pp. 290–292; al-Bayhaqī, *al-Sunan*, IV, p. 210; al-Muttaqī l-Hindī, op. cit., VIII, p. 310, nos. 2142–2143; Ibn Mājah, op. cit., I, p. 506; al-Ṭaḥāwī, *Sharḥ ma'ānī*, II, p. 84; Aḥmad b. Ḥanbal, *Musnad* (ed. Aḥmad Muḥammad Shākir), Cairo 1373/1953, XII, p. 188, no. 7199, XIV, 192, no. 7766; Maḥmūd Khaṭṭāb al-Subkī, op. cit., X, p. 54.

23 See al-Bahyaqī, *Sunan*, IV, pp. 210–211; al-Shaukānī, op. cit., IV, p. 291; al-Zamakhsharī, *al-Fa'iq* (ed. 'Alī Muḥammad al-Bijāwī, Muḥammad Abū l-Faḍl Ibrāhīm), Cairo 1971, II, p. 171. And see Ibn Rajab, op. cit., pp. 149 inf. — 150 (*. . . wa-kharraja abū dāwūd fī bābi taqaddumi ramaḍāna min ḥadīthi mu'āwiyata annahu qāla: innī mutaqaddimun al-shahra fa-man shā'a fa-l-yataqaddam: fa-su'ila 'an dhālika fa-qāla: sami'tu l-nabiyya (ṣ) yaqūlu: ṣūmū l-shahra wa-sirrahu . . . fa-yakūnu l-ma'nā: ṣūmū awwala l-shahri wa-ākhirahu, fa-li-dhālika amara mu'āwiyatu bi-ṣiyāmi ākhiri l-shahri . . .*); Maḥmūd Khaṭṭāb al-Subkī, op. cit., X, pp. 45–49; see *Lisān al-'Arab*, s.v. srr.

24 Al-Daylamī, op. cit., Ms. Chester Beatty 3037, fol. 143a; al-Jīlānī, op. cit., I, p. 210 (Al-Jīlānī adds the reservation that this utterance does not apply when this Monday coincides with the last days of Sha'bān during which fasting is forbidden).

25 Al-Ṣaffūrī, op. cit., p. 195.

26 Ibid., p. 196.

27 Ibid., p. 195; cf. al-Nāzilī, *Khazīnat al-asrār al-kubrā*, Cairo 1349 A.H. (reprint), p. 43 inf.

28 Al-Ṣaffūrī, op. cit., p. 195.

Shī'ī tradition does not differ from Sunnī in content; it is, however, richer in *faḍā'il* — lore and its stories are of course marked by specific Shī'ī features. A lengthy report on a victory of a Muslim expedition against unbelievers during Sha'bān contains an account of a miracle wrought for the leaders of the expedition — Zayd b. Ḥāritha, 'Abdallah b. Rawāḥa and Qays b. 'Āṣim al-Minqarī — on account of their pious deeds at the beginning of Sha'bān. The Prophet, who welcomed the victorious expedition on its return, expounded to the people the virtues of pious deeds on the first day of Sha'bān: alms-giving, reading the Qur'ān, visiting the sick, reconciling husbands and wives, parents and children, praying and fasting and performing other deeds of piety and devotion. Such deeds would afford a hold on a branch of the Paradise-tree of *Ṭūbā*, to appear on the first day of Sha'bān. Those who perpetrate evil deeds on that day will grasp the branches of the Hell-tree of *Zaqūm*, which will emerge from Hell. On the first day of Sha'bān God dispatches His angels to guide the people and summon them to perform good deeds, while Iblīs sends his accomplices to lead them astray. The faithful are to be alert and to revere the month of Sha'bān in order to gain happiness.[29] Detailed lists of rewards for fasting each day of this month, compiled after the pattern of the lists of rewards for fasting in Rajab, record the graces and rewards to be granted to the pious who exert themselves in the Sha'bān fast.[30] Even serious crimes will be forgiven those who fast during Sha'bān.[31] The two months of fasting prescribed in cases of incidental killing (Sūra 4:92) were interpreted as synonymous with the two consecutive months of Sha'bān and Ramaḍān.[32]

The idea of intercession linked with the rewards of fasting during this month is remarkable. According to tradition, the Prophet will intercede on the Day of Resurrection for him who fasts even one day of Sha'bān.[33] The month itself is called "The Month of Intercession", for the Prophet is to intercede for those who utter the prayer of blessing for the Prophet during this month.[34]

29 Al-Majlisī, op. cit., XCVII, pp. 55–65 (from the *Tafsīr* of the Imām al-'Askarī).

30 Al-Majlisī, op. cit., XCVII, p. 65 ult. — 70; Ibn Bābūyah, *Thawāb*, pp. 60–61; Id., *Amālī*, pp. 20–22.

31 Al-Majlisī, op. cit., XCVII, p. 74.

32 Al-'Ayyāshī, *Tafsīr* (ed. Hāshim al-Rasūli l-Maḥallātī), Qumm 1380 A.H., I, p. 266, nos. 232, 235; Ibn Bābūyah, *Thawāb*, pp. 57–58.

33 Al-Majlisī, op. cit., XCVII, p. 81, no. 49; Ibn Bābūyah, *Amālī*, pp. 17, 486.

34 Al-Majlisī, op. cit., XCVII, p. 78: . . . *wa-summiya shahru sha'bāna shahra l-shafā'ati li-anna rasūlakum yashfa'u likulli man yuṣallī 'alayhi fīhi.*

Like Sunnī scholars, Shī'ī scholars were concerned with the permissibility of uninterrupted fasting over the two consecutive months of Sha'bān and Ramaḍān. And as in Sunnī sources, the traditions in the Shī'ī sources are contradictory or divergent. According to one Shī'ī report, the Prophet would fast over the two months without pause (*faṣl*) between them; however he forbade believers to do this.[35] A means of breaking the fast, thus discontinuing a fast of two consecutive months, was provided by advice given by the Imām, to desist from fasting for a single day after the 15th of Sha'bān, and then to continue fasting uninterruptedly.[36] Some Shī'ī traditions recommended fasting the last three days of Sha'bān, continuing uninterruptedly into the fast of Ramaḍān;[37] others report that the Prophet would fast three days at the beginning of Sha'bān, three days mid-month, and three days at the end.[38] Later Shī'ī scholars quoted early traditions concerning Sha'bān, traced back to the Shī'ī Imāms, in an attempt to reconcile the controversial reports and to establish fixed patterns for the observances and devotions of this month.[39]

Both Shī'ī and Sunnī traditions are imbued with sincere reverence for Sha'bān and its devotional observances and recommend almost without exception[40] fasting during the month and performance of pious deeds. The only controversy was over the period of fasting during the month and the pause separating the voluntary fast of Sha'bān from the obligatory month of fasting of Ramaḍān.

II

The eve of the 15th of Sha'bān is the holiest time of the month and it is recommended to spend the night in vigil prayer and supplication, and the

35 Ibn Bābūyah, *Thawāb*, p. 58; al-Majlisī, op. cit., XCVII, p. 76 (from Ibn Bābūyah).

36 Al-Majlisī, op. cit., XCVII, p. 72, no. 13: . . . *mā taqūlu fī ṣaumi shahri sha'bāna? qāla*: *ṣumhu. qultu*: *fa-l-faṣlu? qāla*: *yaumun ba'da l-niṣfi, thumma ṣil.*

37 Al-Majlisī, op. cit., XCVII, p. 72, no. 16; p. 80, no. 47.

38 Ibn Bābūyah, *'Uyūn akhbār al-Riḍā*, Najaf 1390/1970, II, p. 70, no. 330; al-Majlisī, op. cit., XCVII, p. 73, no. 18.

39 See e.g. al-Baḥrānī, *al-Ḥadā'iq al-nāḍira fī aḥkām al-'itra l-ṭāhira* (ed. Muḥammad Taqiyy al-Ayrawānī), Najaf 1384 A.H., XIII, pp. 382–386.

40 But see al-Baḥrānī, op. cit., XIII, p. 383 (quoted from Kulīnī's *al-Wasā'il*): . . . *annahu su'ila* [*'alayhi l-salām*] *'anhu fa-qāla*: *mā ṣāmahu* [*i.e. Sha'bān* — K] *rasūlu llāhi* (*ṣ*) *wa-lā aḥadun min ābā'ī* . . .; and see the interpretation given by al-Kulīnī, ibid.; and see the contradictory traditions, al-Majlisī, op. cit., XCVII, p. 76, nos. 32–33; p. 82, no. 51.

morrow in fasting.[41] At sunset, says a tradition, God would descend to the lowest heaven, grant His forgiveness to those seeking it, food to those begging for it and health to the sick, and would respond to those imploring His aid for other needs until the break of day.[42] A version (recorded in the early compilation of 'Abd al-Razzāq) holds that on the night of mid-Sha'bān God would look upon His servants and grant forgiveness to all people on earth save unbelievers and those bearing a grudge against others. Other versions include drunkards, wizards, prostitutes and sinners of other varieties in the list of those denied forgiveness.[43]

The prayers and supplications on the night of mid-Sha'bān are connected with the idea that this is the night when the life and death of all creatures in the world are decided. Some commentators on the Qur'ān took verses 2–4 of *Sūrat al-Dukhān* (44): "We have sent it down in a blessed night . . . therein every wise bidding determined as a bidding from Us . . ." to refer to the night of the 15th of Sha'bān. They consequently interpreted the pronominal suffix in *anzalnāhu*, "We have sent it down", as relating to "the bidding", "the order", "the decree". This

41 But see the *ḥadīth*, reported on the authority of Abū Hurayra, forbidding fasting on the 15th of Sha'bān, al-Suyūṭī, *Jam' al-jawāmi'*, I, p. 760, no. 1566.

42 Ibn Mājah, op. cit., I, p. 421; Ibn Khuzayma, *Kitāb al-tauḥīd* (ed. Muḥammad Khalīl Harrās), Cairo 1387/1968, p. 136; al-Suyūṭī, *Jam' al-jawāmi'*, I, p. 761, no. 1568 (cf. ibid., no. 1567); Id., *al-Durr al-manthūr*, VI, p. 26 inf.; Aḥmad b. Ḥijāzī, op. cit., p. 51; Ibn Rajab, op. cit., pp. 143, 145; al-Zurqānī, *Sharḥ al-mawāhib*, VII, pp. 412–413; al-Jamal, *al-Futūḥāt al-ilāhiyya*, Cairo n.d., IV, p. 100; al-Fākihī, *Ta'rīkh Makka*, Ms. Leiden Or. 463, fol. 418b; al-Khāzin, *Tafsīr*, Cairo 1381 A.H., VI, p. 120; al-Baghawī, *Tafsīr*, VI, p. 119 (on margin of al-Khāzin's *Tafsīr*); al-Mundhirī, op. cit., II, p. 244, no. 1491; al-Muttaqī l-Hindī, op. cit., XVII, p. 143, no. 467; al-Majlisī, op. cit., XCVIII, p. 415; al-Ṭurṭūshī, *al-Ḥawādith wa-l-bida'* (ed. Muḥammad al-Ṭalbī), Tunis 1959, p. 118; al-Sha'rānī, *Lawāqiḥ al-anwār al-qudsiyya*, Cairo 1381/1961, p. 185; cf. al-Malaṭī, *al-Tanbīh wa-l-radd 'alā ahli l-ahwā'i wa-l-bida'* (ed. Muḥammad Zāhid al-Kautharī), n.p. 1388/1968, p. 113; Abū Shāma, *al-Bā'ith 'alā inkāri l-bida'i wa-l-ḥawādith* (ed. Muḥammad Fu'ād Minqāra), Cairo 1374/1955, p. 26.

43 'Abd al-Razzāq, op. cit., IV, p. 316, ult., no. 7923; Ibn Mājah, op. cit., I, p. 422; cf. al-Suyūṭī, *Jam' al-jawāmi'*, I, p. 761, no. 1659; al-Mundhirī, op. cit., V, p. 123, no. 4007 (and see nos. 4009–4010); Ibn Rajab, op. cit., p. 143 (and see p. 144: the list of sinners, and p. 146: the explanation of the grave sins); Aḥmad b. Ḥijāzī, op. cit., p. 50; cf. al-Munāwī, op. cit., II, p. 316, no. 1942; IV, p. 459, no. 5963; al-Zurqānī, *Sharḥ al-mawāhib*, VII, p. 410 ult. — 411 sup.; Ibn Ḥajar, *al-Kāfī l-shāf fī takhrīji aḥādīthi l-kashshāf*, Cairo 1354 A.H., p. 148, nos. 380–381; al-Sha'rānī, op. cit., p. 185; al-Naysābūrī, *Gharā'ib al-Qur'ān* (ed. Ibrāhīm 'Aṭwa 'Awaḍ), Cairo 1393/1973, XXV, p. 65; al-Rāzī, *Tafsīr*, Cairo 1357/1938, XXVII, p. 238; al-Muttaqī l-Hindī, op. cit., XVII, p. 143, no. 467; XIII, pp. 269–270, nos. 1481–1482, 1485, 1489, 1491.

interpretation was vehemently rejected by commentators asserting that the verses refer to the "*laylat al-qadr*" and the pronominal suffix to the Qur'ān, sent down in Ramaḍān.[44]

But the widespread popular belief was indeed that the night of the 15th of Sha'bān was the night of decrees concerning life and death. Those destined to die would plant trees, set out on pilgrimage, beget children, not knowing that they were to die in the course of the year.[45] On this night God would order the Angel of Death to seize the souls of those upon whose death during the following year He had decided.[46] As the Angel of Death is thus occupied in receiving the decrees of death from God, no one dies between sunset and nightfall of this eve.[47] This night is indeed called *laylat al-ḥayāt, laylat al-qisma wa-l-taqdīr, laylat al-raḥma,*

44 See Aḥmad b. Ḥijāzī, op. cit., p. 47 inf. — 48; cf. al-Zurqānī, *Sharḥ al-mawāhib,* VII, p. 414; al-Qurṭubī, *Tafsīr,* Cairo 1387/1967, XVI, pp. 126–127; Ḥasan al-Madābighī, *Risāla fīmā yata'allaqu bi-laylati l-niṣfi min sha'bān,* Ms. Hebrew University, AP Ar. 8⁰ 439, fol. 9b–10a; al-Luddī, *Fayḍu l-ḥannān fī faḍli laylati l-niṣfi min sha'bān,* Ms. Hebrew University, AP Ar. 8⁰ 479, fol. 4a: . . . *fa-l-hā' fī anzalnā ḍamīru l-amri, ay innā anzalnā amran min 'indinā fī hādhihi l-laylati, qaḍaynāhu wa-qaddarnāhu min al-ājāli wa-l-arzāqi . . .* And see contradictory explanations Ibn al-'Arabī, *Aḥkām al-Qur'ān* (ed. 'Alī Muḥammad al-Bijāwī), Cairo 1388/1968, p. 1678: . . . *fī laylatin mubārakatin . . . ya'nī anna llāha anzala l-qur'āna bi-l-layli . . . wa-jumhūru l-'ulamā'i 'alā annahā laylatu l-qadri, wa-minhum man qāla innahā laylatu l-niṣfi min sha'bāna, wa-huwa bāṭilun . . .*; Ibn Kathīr, *Tafsīr,* Beirut 1385/1966, VI, p. 245; al-Ṭurṭūshī, op. cit., pp. 118–121; cf. al-Rāzī, op. cit., XXVII, p. 238.

45 'Abd al-Razzāq, op. cit., IV, p. 317, nos. 7925–7926; cf. al-Ṭabarī, *Tafsīr* (Būlāq), XXV, p. 65; al-Muttaqī l-Hindī, op. cit., XVII, p. 143, no. 468; al-Madābighī, op. cit., fol. 15a–b.

46 Al-Munāwī, op. cit., IV, p. 459, no. 5964; Ibn Rajab, op. cit., p. 148, ll. 1–2; al-Suyūṭī, *al-Durr al-manthūr,* VI, p. 26; al-Muttaqī l-Hindī, op. cit., XIII, p. 269, no. 1483. The story of the tree in Paradise (see G.E. von Grunebaum, *Muhammadan Festivals,* New York 1951, pp. 53–54, quoted from Lane's *Manners and Customs of the Modern Egyptians*) is recorded by al-Luddī, op. cit., fol. 5b: The tree at the side of the Throne (*al-'arsh*), resembling a pomegranate-tree, has as many leaves as there are human beings in the world. On each leaf is written the name of a person. The Angel of Death watches the leaves; when a leaf yellows he perceives that the date of the death of the person is imminent and he dispatches his helpers; when the leaf falls the Angel of Death catches his soul. According to a version of this tradition, when the leaf falls on its back, it denotes a positive decree for the person (*ḥusn al-khātima*); if it falls on its underside, it denotes an unfortunate decree. Al-Suyūṭī records the tradition on this tree on the authority of Muḥammad b. Juḥāda in *al-Durr al-manthūr,* III, p. 15 (commenting on Sūra 6:60) and in his compilation *Sharḥ al-ṣudūr,* p. 22.

47 Aḥmad b. Ḥijāzī, op. cit., p. 48 inf.; al-Luddī, op. cit., fol. 5b inf. — 6a sup.; al-Madābighī, op. cit., fol. 17a.

laylat al-ijāba, laylat al-takfīr.[48] In reference to the forgiving of sins, the current popular name of this night is *laylat al-sukūk* or *laylat al-barā'a*, "the night of acquittance".[49] It is the "feast of the angels" (*'īd al-malā'ika*)[50] and the "night of intercession" (*laylat al-shafā'a*); on the 13th of Sha'bān the Prophet pleaded for intercession for a third of his people and this was granted; on the 14th he was granted intercession for a second third and on the 15th of Sha'bān he was granted intercession for his entire people.[51] An exceptional night, indeed, distinguished by peculiar virtues.[52]

A lengthy report, recorded on the authority of 'Ā'isha, gives us details of the origin of the devotions of this night. 'Ā'isha missed the Prophet in her bedchamber that night and sought him eagerly; she found him prostrated in supplication, praying a most moving prayer. The Prophet explained to 'Ā'isha the importance of this night, conveying to her the good tidings that God would grant His forgiveness to a countless multitude of believers, as many as the hairs of the flocks of the tribe of Kalb.[53]

48 See al-Jamal, op. cit., IV, p. 100; Aḥmad b. Ḥijāzī, op. cit., pp. 48–49; al-Ghazālī, *Mukāshafa*, pp. 249–250; al-Luddī, op. cit., fol. 5b–6a.

49 For the expression *barā'a* as "acquittance", "discharge of sins", see the story about the letter sent by God and found on the breast of 'Umar b. 'Abd al-'Azīz during his burial: Ps. Ibn Qutayba, *al-Imāma wa-l-siyāsa* (ed. Ṭāhā Muḥammad al-Zaynī), Cairo 1378/1967, II, p. 102: *bi-smi llāhi l-raḥmāni l-raḥīm, kitābun bi-l-qalami l-jalīl, min allāhi l-'azīzi l-'alīm, barā'atun li-'umara bni 'abdi l-'azīz min al-'adhābi l-alīm.* And see al-Madābighī, op. cit., fol. 17b: ...*fa-fī laylati l-barā'ati mithlu dhālika yu'ṭā l-wāḥidu barā'atan, fa-yuqālu aufayta l-ḥaqqa wa-qumta bi-sharā'iṭi l-'ubūdiyyati fa-khudh barā'atan min al-nāri; wa-yuqālu li-wāḥidin istakhfafta bi-ḥaqqī wa-lam taqum bi-sharā'iṭi l-'ubūdiyyati, fa-khudh barā'ataka min al-jināni.*

50 Al-Jīlānī, op. cit., I, p. 216; al-Luddī, op. cit., fol. 6a; Aḥmad b. Ḥijāzī, op. cit., p. 48 inf.; al-Ghazālī, *Mukāshafa*, p. 249; al-Madābighī, op. cit., fol. 17a–b.

51 Al-Jamal, op. cit., IV, pp. 100; Aḥmad b. Ḥijāzī, op. cit., p. 49; al-Ghazālī, *Mukāshafa*, p. 250; al-Naysābūrī, op. cit., XXV, p. 65; al-Rāzī, op. cit., XXVII, p. 238.

52 'Abd al-Razzāq, op. cit., IV, p. 317, no. 7927; Ibn 'Asākir, *Tahdhīb ta'rīkh* (ed. 'Abd al-Qādir Badrān), Damascus 1330 A.H., I, p. 47; III, p. 296; Ibn Rajab, op. cit., p. 144 inf.; al-Suyūṭī, *al-Durr al-manthūr*, VI, p. 26; al-Zandawaysitī, op. cit., fol. 259a; al-Jīlānī, op. cit., I, p. 215; Aḥmad b. Ḥijāzī, op. cit., pp. 48, 51; Ibn Ḥajar, *al-Kāfī l-shāf*, p. 148, no. 382; al-Waṣṣābī, *al-Baraka fī faḍli l-sa'yi wa-l-ḥaraka*, Cairo n.d., p. 78; al-Madābighī, op. cit., fol. 17a.

53 See Ibn Mājah, op. cit., I, pp. 421–422; al-Mundhirī, op. cit., II, p. 243, nos. 1488, 1490; V, p. 124, no. 4008, 126, no. 4012; al-Suyūṭī, *al-Durr al-manthūr*, VI, pp. 26–27; al-Jīlānī, op. cit., I, pp. 213–215; Ibn Rajab, op. cit., p. 143; Aḥmad b. Ḥijāzī, op. cit., p. 49; al-Zurqānī, *Sharḥ al-mawāhib*, VII, pp. 410–411; al-Majlisī, op. cit., XCVII, pp. 88–89 (no. 16); XCVIII, pp. 416–419 (and see XCVII, p. 86, no. 8); al-

Special prayers and supplications were recommended and precious rewards promised to those who would exert themselves in devotion and prayer during this night. Among the numerous rewards were forgiveness of sins and entry into Paradise. Orthodox scholars sharply criticized these *ḥadīths*, often branding them as weak or forged.[54]

Shī'ī sources outdo the Sunnī in propagating the virtues of the night of the 15th of Sha'bān; they emphasize that the Imāms were singled out by the blessings of this night. God granted the Prophet *laylat al-qadr*, while He granted the Imāms (*ahl al-bayt*) the night of the 15th of Sha'bān, according to a report transmitted on the authority of al-Bāqir.[55] A tradition attributed to the Prophet says that the position of 'Alī within the family of the Prophet (*ālu muḥammadin*) is like that of the best of the days and nights of Sha'bān, i.e. the night of the 15th of Sha'bān.[56] Noteworthy is the tradition recommending a visit to the grave of Ḥusayn on this night; forgiveness of sins will be the assured reward.[57]

Orthodox Muslim scholars emphasized the superiority of *laylat al-qadr* over the night of the 15th of Sha'bān, *laylat al-barā'a*. Although some scholars opined that there is no fixed date for *laylat al-qadr* and that it

Dhahabī, *Mīzān al-i'tidāl* (ed. 'Alī Muḥammad al-Bijāwī), Cairo 1382/1963, IV, p. 262, no. 9081; al-Zandawaysitī, op. cit., fol. 259b–260b; al-Rāzī, op. cit., XXVII, p. 238; al-Madābighī, op. cit., fols. 18a–20b; al-Muttaqī l-Hindī, op. cit., XIII, p. 270, nos. 1486–1488, 1491.

54 Al-Suyūṭī, *al-Durr al-manthūr*, VI, p. 27 inf. — 28 sup.; Abū Ṭālib al-Makkī, *Qūt al-qulūb*, Cairo 1351/1932, I, p. 93; al-Muttaqī l-Hindī, op. cit., XVII, p. 144, no. 469; Aḥmad b. Ḥijāzī, op. cit., p. 52 inf. — 53; al-Jīlānī, op. cit., I, p. 216; al-Shaukānī, *al-Fawā'id al-majmū'a fī l-aḥādīthi l-mauḍū'a* (ed. 'Abd al-Raḥmān al-Mu'allamī l-Yamānī), Cairo 1380/1960, pp. 50–51, no. 106; Id., *Tuḥfat al-dhākirīn bi-'uddati l-ḥiṣn al-ḥaṣīn min kalāmi sayyid al-mursalīn* (ed. Muḥammad Zabāra al-Ḥasanī al-Ṣan'ānī), Cairo 1393/1973, pp. 182–183; al-Ṣaffūrī, op. cit., p. 197; al-Jamal, op. cit., IV, p. 100; al-Majlisī, op. cit., XCVII, pp. 85–86 (nos. 5, 7), 87 (no. 13), 89 (no. 17); XCVIII, pp. 408–418; Ibn Bābūyah, *'Uyūn akhbār al-Riḍā*, I, p. 228; Id., *Amālī*, p. 24; al-Ṭūsī, *Amālī*, Najaf 1384/1964, I, p. 303; Ibn al-Jauzī, *al-Mauḍū'āt* (ed. 'Abd al-Raḥmān Muḥammad 'Uthmān), Medina 1386/1966, II, pp. 127–130; al-Suyūṭī, *al-La'ālī al-maṣnū'a fī l-aḥādīthi l-mauḍū'a*, Cairo n.d., II, pp. 57–60; Ibn Ḥajar, *al-Kāfī al-shāf*, p. 148, no. 379; al-Waṣṣābī, op. cit., pp. 76–78; Mā' al-'Aynayn, *Na't al-bidāyāt wa-tauṣīf al-nihāyāt*, Fās(?) 1312 A.H., pp. 184–185; al-Nāzilī, op. cit., pp. 43–44; al-Rāzī, op. cit., XXVII, p. 238.

55 Al-Ṭūsī, *Amālī*, I, p. 303; al-Majlisī, op. cit., XCVII, p. 85, no. 5 (from the *Amālī*).

56 Al-Majlisī, op. cit., XCVII, p. 87, no. 9 (from the *Tafsīr* of al-Imām al-'Askarī).

57 Al-Majlisī, op. cit., XCVII, p. 85, no. 4, p. 87, nos. 10–11.

can occur on any night throughout the entire year,[58] the majority held that *laylat al-qadr* is a night of Ramaḍān, thus inherently excelling any night of the inferior month of Sha'bān. The early scholar and judge Ibn Abī Mulayka[59] is reported to have sharply rebuked those scholars who held that the reward for observance of the night of the 15th of Sha'bān equals that of *laylat al-qadr*.[60] This report indicates that orthodox scholars were reconciled to the veneration of the night of the 15th of Sha'bān, and merely stressed the inferiority of this night (*laylat al-barā'a*) in comparison with *laylat al-qadr*. Legitimization of *laylat al-barā'a* was linked with the elaboration of the idea of its virtues and merits as compared with those of *laylat al-qadr*. Scholars stressed the difference between the two nights, as well as their relationship: the date of *laylat al-barā'a* was announced and fixed, but that of *laylat al-qadr* (referring to that during Ramaḍān — K) is not revealed, for *laylat al-barā'a* is the night of judgement and decree, while *laylat al-qadr* is the night of mercy. Were the date of *laylat al-qadr* divulged and precisely determined, people would abstain from every exertion and rely upon the mercy of God.[61] A report, recorded on the authority of Ibn 'Abbās, defines the mutual, complementary functions of the two nights: God issues His decrees on *laylat al-barā'a*, but delivers them for execution on *laylat al-qadr*.[62] In another, more detailed version, the copying from the Preserved Tablet commences on *laylat al-barā'a* and is completed on *laylat al-qadr*, when the list of sustenances is handed over to the angel Mīkā'īl, the list of earthquakes, lightning and wars to Jibrīl, and the list of deeds (*a'māl*) to the angel Ismā'īl who is in charge of lower Heaven and is an angel of very high rank.[63]

58 See al-Ṭaḥāwī, *Sharḥ ma'ānī*, II, p. 92: . . . *anna bna mas'ūdin qāla*: *man qāma l-sanata kullahā aṣāba laylata l-qadri* . . . (see the contradictory opinion of Ubayy b. Ka'b, ibid.); Ibn 'Asākir, op. cit., II, p. 324; al-'Āmilī, *al-Kashkūl* (ed. Ṭāhir Aḥmad al-Zāwī), Cairo 1380/1961, I, p. 405: . . . *wa-minhum man qāla*: *hiya fī majmū'i l-sanati, lā yakhtaṣṣu bihā shahru ramaḍāna wa-lā ghayruhu*; *ruwiya dhālika 'ani bni mas'ūdin, qāla*: *man yaqumi l-ḥaula yuṣibhā*.

59 See on him Ibn Ḥajar, *Tahdhīb al-tahdhīb*, V, p. 306, no. 523; Ibn Sa'd, *Ṭabaqāt*, Beirut 1377/1957, V, p. 472; al-Fāsī, *al-'Iqd al-thamīn* (ed. Fu'ād Sayyid), Cairo 1385/1966, V, p. 204, no. 1570; al-Dhahabī, *Tadhkirat al-ḥuffāẓ*, Hyderabad, I, p. 101; Wakī', *Akhbār al-quḍāt* (ed. 'Abd al-'Azīz al-Marāghī), Cairo 1366/1947, I, p. 261.

60 'Abd al-Razzāq, op. cit., IV, p. 317, no. 7928; al-Ṭurṭūshī, op. cit., p. 119.

61 Al-Jīlānī, op. cit., I, p. 216; al-Ṣaffūrī, op. cit., p. 198; cf. al-Zandawaysitī, op. cit., fol. 273b.

62 Al-Baghawī, *Tafsīr*, VI, p. 120, l. 7; al-Jamal, op. cit , IV, p. 100, ll. 25–26; al-Majlisī, op. cit., XCVIII, p. 414.

63 Al-Jamal, op. cit., IV, p. 100 inf.; Aḥmad b. Ḥijāzī, op. cit., p. 48 sup.; al-Luddī, op. cit., fol 5b; al-Naysābūrī, op. cit., XXV, p. 65; al-Madābighī, op. cit., fol. 10b.

The beginnings of the devotional observance of *laylat al-barā'a* seem to go back a long way. A legendary report of an expedition sent by Abū 'Ubayda, during his conquest of Syria, contains an interesting passage on *laylat al-barā'a*. The commander of the expedition, appointed by Abū 'Ubayda, was 'Abdallah b. Ja'far, son of the uncle of the Prophet, the famous martyr Ja'far al-Ṭayyār. Among the warriors of his troop was the pious Wāthila b. al-Asqa'.[64] When the troop was about to set out, 'Abdallah noticed the brightness of the moon. Wāthila declared that it was the night of the 15th of Sha'bān, the blessed night of great virtue. On that night, he said, sustenances and decrees concerning life and death are set down, sins and wrong deeds are forgiven. Wāthila stressed that, regardless of his desire to spend the night in vigil (*wa-kuntu aradtu an aqūmahā*, scil. in devotional observance — K), setting out to fight for God's sake was preferable. Consequently the troop indeed marched out.[65] Some reports relate that certain *tābi'ūn* in Syria would perform the devotional practices of this night, mentioning specifically Makḥūl[66] Luqmān b. 'Āmir[67] and Khālid b. Ma'dān.[68] The well-known scholar Isḥāq b. Rāhawayh[69] adopted their view and was favourable toward the observance of *laylat al-barā'a*. 'Aṭā' b. Abī Rabāḥ,[70] Ibn Abī Mulayka[71] and the majority of the scholars of al-Ḥijāz opposed these practices; Mālikī and Shāfi'ī scholars followed in their path, severely criticizing the obser-

64 See on him Ibn Ḥajar, *Tahdhīb*, XI, p. 101, no. 174; Abū Nu'aym, op. cit., II p. 21, no. 120; Ibn Ḥajar, *al-Iṣāba* (ed. 'Alī Muḥammad al-Bijāwī), Cairo 1392/1972, VI, p. 591, no. 9093; Ibn 'Abd al-Barr, *al-Istī'āb* (ed. 'Alī Muḥammad al-Bijāwī), Cairo 1380/1960, p. 1563, no. 2738.

65 Ps. Wāqidī, *Futūḥ al-Shām*, Cairo 1348, I, p. 57.

66 See on him Sezgin, *GAS*, I, p. 404, no. 5; Ṣafiyy al-Dīn al-Khazrajī, *Tadhhīb tahdhīb al-kamāl* (ed. Maḥmūd 'Abd al-Wahhāb Fāyid), Cairo 1391/1971, III, p. 54, no. 7178.

67 See on him Ibn Ḥibbān al-Bustī, *Kitāb al-thiqāt* (ed. 'Abd al-Khāliq al-Afghānī, Hyderabad 1388/1968, p. 229; Ṣafiyy al-Dīn al-Khazrajī, op. cit., II, p. 372, no. 6005.

68 See on him Ibn Ḥibbān al-Bustī, op. cit., p. 55; Ibn Ḥajar, *Tahdhīb*, III, p. 118, no. 222; al-Bukhārī, *Ta'rīkh*, III, no. 601; Ṣafiyy al-Dīn al-Khazrajī, op. cit., I, p. 284, no. 1802.

69 See on him al-Dhahabī, *Tadhkirat al-ḥuffāẓ*, p. 433; Ibn Ḥajar, *Tahdhīb*, I, p. 216, no. 408; Ibn Abī Ḥātim, *al-Jarḥ wa-l-ta'dīl*, Hyderabad 1371/1952, II, p. 209, no. 714; al-Dhahabī, *Mīzān al-i'tidāl*, I, p. 182, no. 733; *al*-Ṣafadī, *al-Wāfī bi-l-wafayāt* (ed. Muḥammad Yūsuf Najm), Wiesbaden 1391/1971, VIII, p. 386, no. 3825 (and see the references of the editor); al-Subkī, *Ṭabaqāt al-shāfi'iyya* (ed. al-Ḥulw — al-Ṭanāḥī), Cairo 1383/1964, II, p. 83, no. 19.

70 See on him Sezgin, *GAS*, I, p. 31; al-Fāsī, *al-'Iqd al-thamīn*, VI, pp. 84–93.

71 See on him above, note 59.

vances, branding them as *bid'a*. Amongst the Syrian scholars advocating the devotions there were certain differences of opinion concerning the forms of observance: some of them would wear fine garments, scent themselves with incense, anoint their eyes with collyrium and spend the night in the mosque praying and supplicating publicly. Others preferred solitary prayer and devotion in the privacy of their homes. Some persons, says the tradition, refrained from observing this night when they learned that the shcolars and pious men who advocated such veneration based their belief of *Isrā'īliyyāt* traditions.[72]

There were some extremist opinions, which totally denied the basis of the traditions on the virtues of *laylat al-barā'a* and branded the reports as forged.[73] But generally orthodox circles merely reproved the manner of these devotions. A late report vividly describes them as practiced in the seventh century of the Hijra. Mosques were lavishly lit and the governor would come to the courtyard of the mosque; firebrands were kindled and the seated governor would act as judge. People would submit complaints against the unjust and wicked, and those convicted were punished on the spot. The adversaries shouting their arguments, the cries of the punished, the barking of the guards (*janādira*) and the noise of the crowd turned the mosque into a police-station (*dāru shurṭa*), as noted by Ibn al-Ḥājj.[74] The latter especially denounced processions to cemeteries, performed on this night by mixed crowds of men and women. Some women sang, some beat tambourines; a sort of cupola-shaped canopy (*ka-l-qubba 'alā 'amūd*), surrounded by lamps (*qanādīl*) was carried in the crowd and so the people arrived at the cemetery. Wooden posts were set up on the graves and hung with the clothes of the dead. Relatives sat down on the graves and talked to the dead about their troubles and sorrows, or complained at the graves of scholars and the righteous. Ibn al-Ḥājj stresses that some of these practices resemble those of the Christians, who would dress their statues and pray before their images.[75]

A rather late date for the introduction of the prayer of the night of the

72 Al-Zurqānī, *Sharḥ al-mawāhib*, VII, p. 413; Ibn Rajab, op. cit., p. 144; Aḥmad b Ḥijāzī, op. cit., p. 52; 'Alī Maḥfūẓ, *al-Ibdā' fī maḍārr al-ibtidā'*, Cairo 1388/1968, p. 295.

73 See e.g. Ibn 'Arabī, op. cit., IV, p. 1678: . . . *wa-laysa fī laylati l-niṣfi min sha'bāna ḥadīthun yu'awwalu 'alayhi, lā fī faḍlihā wa-lā fī naskhi l-ājāli fīhā, fa-lā taltafitū ilayhā.* And see note 44 above.

74 Ibn al-Ḥājj, *al-Madkhal*, Beirut 1972, I, pp. 302–303.

75 Ibid., pp. 304–307.

15th of Sha'bān in Jerusalem is recorded by al-Ṭurṭūshī. According to his report, a man from Nābulus came to Jerusalem in 448 A.H. and performed this prayer in the mosque of al-Aqṣā. From then onward the prayer became current and was held in al-Aqṣā and in homes, coming to be considered a *sunna.*[76]

III

The reports on the early origin of the observance of *laylat al-barā'a* seem to be trustworthy. The favourable attitude of the Syrian *tābi'ūn* (in the second half of the first century of the Hijra) towards these practices probably points to an earlier tradition, to be traced back to some of the Companions, such as Wāthila b. al-Asqa'; indeed Makḥūl, who championed the observance of *laylat al-barā'a,* was a student of Wāthila and transmitted *ḥadīth* on his authority.[77] These practices were, as we have said, attributed to the Prophet himself.

The observance of the night of the 15th of Sha'bān was not confined to Syria; so much can be deduced from the utterance of Ibn Abī Mulayka, quoted above. Ibn Abī Mulayka was a Qurashite appointed by 'Abdallah b. al-Zubayr as judge in Ṭā'if and in Mecca. It is implausible that his utterance (in which he vigorously opposed the idea of granting *laylat al-barā'a* equal rank with *laylat al-qadr*) was directed solely against the people of Syria; more probably it was aimed at the people of Mecca and Ṭā'if. Furthermore, the transmitter of this report is Ayyūb (al-Sakhtiyānī)[78] who lived in Baṣra and may have been interested in knowing the opinion of his teacher on a practice observed in his town, or country, al-'Irāq. It is to be remarked that the utterance of Ibn Abī Mulayka was directed against a *qāṣṣ*;[79] it is well known that the *quṣṣās* were obliged to edify and encourage people to exert themselves in devotional practices such as *laylat al-barā'a.* Finally, a short passage in the biography of Ibn

76 Al-Ṭurṭūshī, op. cit., p. 121; Abū Shāma, op. cit., p. 24 (from al-Ṭurṭūshī); 'Alī Maḥfūẓ, op. cit., pp. 296–297 (from al-Ṭurṭūshī); Jamāl al-Dīn al-Qāsimī, *Iṣlāḥ al-masājid min al-bida'i wa-l-'awā'id,* Cairo 1341 A.H., p. 106 (from al-Ṭurṭūshī).

77 Al-Dhahabī, *Tadhkirat al-ḥuffāẓ,* I, p. 108, no. 96.

78 See on him Sezgin, *GAS,* I, p. 87, no. 12.

79 'Abd al-Razzāq, op. cit., IV, 317, no. 7928: . . . *'an ma'mar, 'an ayyūb qāla: qīla li-bni abī mulaykata inna ziyādan al-minqariyya* (probably: *al-namariyya*; see al-Suyūṭī, *Taḥdhīr al-khawāṣṣ* (ed. Muḥammad al-Ṣabbāgh), n.p. 1392/1972, p. 179; al-Dhahabī, *Mīzān al-i'tidāl,* II, p. 90, no. 2945), *wa-kāna qāṣṣan, yaqūlu inna ajra laylati l-niṣfi min sha'bāna mithlu ajri laylati l-qadri, fa-qāla: lau sami'tuhu yaqūlu dhālika, wa-fī yadī 'aṣan, la-ḍarabtuhu bihā*; Abū Shāma, op. cit., p. 25 sup.

Abī Mulayka, recorded by Ibn Sa'd, may serve to illuminate his disapproval of putting *laylat al-barā'a* on a par with *laylat al-qadr*: Ibn Abī Mulayka used to lead the prayers of the people in Mecca during Ramaḍān.[80] It is thus clear why he would stress the superiority of *laylat al-qadr*, celebrated during Ramaḍān, over the night of the 15th of Sha'bān.

The charge that the celebration of the night of the 15th of Sha'bān was based on *Isrā'īliyyāt*[81] should be taken with reserve; it was not uncommon for scholars to discredit their opponents by ascribing *bid'a* ideas to them, or accusing them of adopting *Isrā'īliyyāt* traditions. In the same category was the accusation that the lavish lighting of mosques on the night of the 15th of Sha'bān was an innovation of the Barmakids, who were thus actually advocating fire-worship.[82]

The data stating that the majority of Ḥijāzī scholars objected to the observance of the night of the 15th of Sha'bān seem to be inaccurate, at least as far as the third century of the Hijra is concerned. The account given by al-Fākihī is a detailed and vivid description of the devotional practices performed at Mecca on that night. The entire population of Mecca, says al-Fākihī, would go out to the mosque and spend the night reading the Qur'ān, so as to finish the recitation of the entire Qur'ān and perform the *ṭawāf*; some of them would perform a hundred *rak'a*, reciting *Sūrat al-Ḥamd* (i.e. the *Fātiḥa* — K) and *qul huwa llāhu aḥadun* (i.e. *Sūrat al-Ikhlāṣ* — K) at every prostration. They would drink the waters of Zamzam, wash (their faces — K) in it and take a supply of the water home to heal their ills through the blessings of this night (combined, of course, with those of the waters themselves — K).[83] We have here, indeed, the first reliable information on the prayers of the night of the 15th of Sha'bān, as recorded in the sources,[84] and as performed in

80 Ibn Sa'd, op. cit., V, p. 473 sup.

81 Al-Zurqānī, *Sharḥ al-mawāhib*, VII, p. 413: . . . *wa-'anhum akhadha l-nāsu ta'ẓīmahā, wa-yuqālu innahum balaghahum fī dhālika āthārun isrā'īliyyatun, fa-lammā shtahara dhālika 'anhumu khtalafa l-nāsu fīhi, fa-minhum man qabilahu minhum, wa-minhum man abāhu* . . .

82 Abū Shāma, op. cit., p. 25 inf.

83 Al-Fākihī, op. cit., fol 418b: *dhikru 'amali ahli makkata laylata l-niṣfi min sha'bāna wa-jtihādihim fīhā li-faḍlihā. wa ahlu makkata fīmā maḍā ilā l-yaumi, idhā kānat laylatu l-niṣfi min sha'bāna kharaja 'āmmatu l-rijāli wa-l-nisā'i ilā l-masjidi fa-ṣallau wa-ṭāfū wa-aḥyau laylatahum ḥattā l-ṣabāḥi bi-l-qirā'ati fī l-masjidi l-ḥarāmi ḥattā yakhtimū l-qur'āna kullahu wa-yuṣallū, au man ṣallā minhum tilka l-laylata mi'ata rak'atin, yaqra'u fī kulli rak'atin bi-l-ḥamdi wa-qul huwa llāhu aḥad 'ashra marrātin, wa-akhadhū min mā'i zamzama tilka l-laylata fa-sharibūhu wa-ghtasalū bihi wa-khaba'ūhu 'indahum li-l-marḍā yabtaghūna bi-dhālika l-barakata fī hādhihi l-laylati.*

84 See above note 54; and see Abū Shāma, op. cit., pp. 27, 29.

the *ḥaram* in the third century A.H. The prayer mentioned here is one of the prayers recommended for the night of the 15th of Sha'bān, recorded by Ibn al-Jauzī and branded by him as forged. Needless to say, the *ṭawāf* and drinking of Zamzam water are features peculiar to certain devotional practices and feasts in Mecca.

A tradition of the "reward promise" type, recorded by al-Fākihī, belongs to the lore of current traditions on this subject and is reported by Ibn al-Jauzī; He who recites a thousand times within a hundred *rak'a*: *qul huwa llāhu aḥad*, on the night of the 15th of Sha'bān, will not die before God sends him a hundred angels: thirty to bring him good tidings that God is to introduce him into Paradise; thirty to shield him from God's chastisement; thirty to deter him from sin, and ten to aid him against his enemies.[85] This indicates how widespread the traditions concerning the virtues of the night of the 15th of Sha'bān were in Mecca — and Mecca scholars were considered orthodox and were said to be opposed to public observance of this night.

The continuity of the observance of the night of the 15th of Sha'bān can be traced from the second half of the first century A.H. It is attested in the second century in the traditions recorded by 'Abd al-Razzāq. The passage in al-Fākihī's *Ta'rīkh Makka* gives a description of the celebration in Mecca in the third century. Al-Zandawaysitī records the virtues of this night in the fourth century. Al-Ṭurṭūshī's account refers to the practices witnessed in the fifth century, and Ibn al-Ḥājj's description depicts the observance at the end of the seventh century. A rich polemical literature concerning this night was produced over the centuries, and numerous *faḍā'il* treatises were compiled. The night of the 15th of Sha'bān is revered even today, and modern compilations still attack the popular observance, branding it as *bid'a* and quoting, as usual, early sources.

The continuity of custom and usage during these celebrations can be illustrated by example. At the end of the seventh century A.H. Ibn al-Ḥājj mentions the sittings of the governor in the courtyard of the mosque on the night of the 15th of Sha'bān, at which he would judge and punish the guilty. In the fourth century al-Zandawaysitī includes among the laudable deeds of the various classes during Sha'bān the sessions of the rulers, who would summon the imprisoned, punish the guilty and free the innocent.[86] This practice seems to reflect the idea of God's judgment

85 Al-Fākihī, op. cit , fol. 418b; Ibn al-Jauzī, *al-Mauḍū'āt*, II, p. 128; al-Naysābūrī' op. cit., XXV, p. 65; al-Rāzī, op. cit., XXVII, p. 238.

86 See above note 15.

in this month or during this night. The custom of visiting cemeteries on this night (Shīʿī sources promoted visits to the tomb of Ḥusayn) may be related to the *ḥadīth* according to which ʿĀʾisha found the Prophet praying in the cemetery of Baqīʿ al-Gharqad on this night; it was at this spot that he explained to her the virtues of the night of the 15th of Shaʿbān.

The observances and celebrations of the night of the 15th of Shaʿbān seem to be rooted in Jāhiliyya belief and ritual, as rightly assumed by Wensinck.[87] When the month of Ramaḍān became the month of the obligatory fast, however, the night of the 15th of Shaʿbān apparently lost its primacy: *laylat al-qadr* was fixed by the majority of Muslim scholars within Ramaḍān (usually as the night of the 27th of Ramaḍān[88]) and became one of the most venerated nights of the Muslim community. But esteem of the night of the 15th of Shaʿbān survived and, lacking the support of official scholars, it became a favoured occasion for devotional practices in pious and ascetic circles, as well as a night of popular celebration (including practices disapproved of by zealous conservative scholars). Moderate orthodox scholars strove to reconcile the traditions of the two nights, granting legitimacy to the devotions of *laylat al-barāʾa* but establishing the superiority of *laylat al-qadr*. Also conciliatory was the idea of a division of functions between the two nights: *laylat al-barāʾa* was considered as the night of decrees, *laylat al-qadr* as the night in which God's biddings (or His mercy) were carried out. All this is, of course, a later development; hence Wensinck's theory of two genuine New Year's nights seems to be untenable.

Orthodox Muslim scholars, though disapproving of the public celebrations, agreed to private devotional observances on the night of the 15th of Shaʿbān.[89] On these conditions *laylat al-barāʾa* could gain their approval and became a recommended night of devotional exertion.

The fasting of the Prophet over the two consecutive months of Rajab and Shaʿbān may be linked with the *taḥannuth*, which he was wont to

87 See Wensinck, op. cit., p. 6 ("This belief is already recorded by Ṭabarī; it is probably pre-Islamic").

88 See Wagtendonk, op. cit., pp. 106, 112, note 5.

89 See the *fatwā* of Abū ʿAmr b. Ṣalāḥ, as recorded by Abū Shāma, op. cit., p. 32, 1.5: . . . *wa-ammā laylatu l-niṣfi min shaʿbāna fa-lahā faḍīlatun wa-iḥyāʾuhā bi-l-ʿibādati mustaḥabbun, wa-lākin ʿalā l-infirādi min ghayri jamāʿatin; wa-ttikhādhu l-nāsi lahā wa-laylata l-raghāʾibi mausiman wa-shiʿ āran bidʿatun munkaratun.*

observe in the following month of Ramaḍān.[90] The *taḥannuth* is said to have been initiated by the Prophet's grandfather, 'Abd al-Muṭṭalib,[91] and was observed by some people of Quraysh.[92] This socio-religious observance combined the element of charitable deeds with a practice of veneration toward the *ḥaram* of Mecca. It was observed on Mount Ḥirā' and is sometimes referred to as *i'tikaf* or *jiwār* in the story of the first revelation of the Prophet. Some reports say that the Prophet sojourned on Mount Ḥirā' in solitude, but others explicitly state that he stayed there in the company of his wife Khadīja.[93] Some details on the *jiwār* of the people of Mecca and its purpose are given by al-Azraqī: the Qurashites would leave Shi'b al-Ṣufiyy and sojourn on Jabal al-Rāḥa "out of veneration of the *ḥaram*". This practice was followed in summer.[94] The place of the *jiwār* of 'Ā'isha[95] and its duration are indicated in a report recorded by al-Fākihī. 'Ā'isha sojourned for two months at a spot between Mount Ḥirā' and Thabīr. People would visit her there and converse with her. In the absence of 'Abdallah b. 'Abd al-Raḥmān b. Abī Bakr the prayer was headed by her servant, Dhakwān.[96] The two

90 See Goitein, op. cit., p. 93 sup.; Wagtendonk, op. cit., pp. 32–35.

91 See *BSOAS*, 31 (1968), pp. 232–233.

92 See al-Balādhurī, *Ansāb* I, p. 105, no. 192: *kānat qurayshun idhā dakhala ramaḍānu kharaja man yurīdu l-taḥannutha minhā ilā ḥirā'a.*

93 See *BSOAS* 31 (1968), p. 225, note 15; p. 227, notes 26–27; and see al-Muṭṭawi'ī, *Man ṣabara ẓafira*, Ms. Cambridge, Or. 1473(10), fol. 43b: . . . *ḥattā idhā kāna l-shahru lladhī arāda llāhu fīhi bihi mā arāda min karāmatihi wa-raḥmatihi l-'ibāda min al-sanati llati ba'athahu llāhu tabāraka wa-ta'ālā fīhā, wa-dhālika l-shahru ramaḍānu, kharaja rasūlu llāhi (ṣ) ilā ḥirā'a kamā kāna yakhruju li-jiwārihi wa-ma'ahu ahluhu khadījatu* . . . A significant version is recorded by al-Fākihī, op. cit., fol. 499b, ult. — 500a, ll. 1–2; the Prophet sojourned on Ḥirā'. Khadīja used to come to him from Mecca in the evening. The Prophet descended from the mountain and stayed with her in (the place in which later) the mosque of Shi'b Qunfudh (was erected. — K). In the morning they used to depart. (. . . *anna l-nabiyya (ṣ) kāna yakūnu fī ḥirā'a bi-l-nahāri fa-idhā* (the verb is missing; perhaps: *atā, jā'a* or another similar verb has to be supplied) *l-laylu nazala min ḥirā'a fa-atā l-masjida lladhī fī l-shi'bi lladhī khalfa dāri abī 'ubaydata yu'rafu bi-l-khalafiyyīn wa-ta'tīhi khadījatu (r) min makkata fa-yaltaqiyāni fī l-masjidi lladhī fī l-shi'bi, fa-idhā qaruba l-ṣabāḥu ftaraqā, au naḥwahu*). About the place, Shi'b āl Qunfudh, see al-Azraqī, *Akhbār Makka* (ed. F. Wüstenfeld), p. 491 penult. — 492.

94 Al-Azraqī, op. cit., p. 482 inf.: . . . *li-anna qurayshan kānat fī l-jāhiliyyati takhruju min shi'bi l-ṣufiyyi fa-tabītu fīhi* (the suffix *hi* refers to *al-rāḥa* — K) *fī l-ṣayfi ta'ẓīman li-l-masjidi l-ḥarāmi, thumma yakhrujūna fa-yajlisūna fa-yastarīḥūna fī l-jabali* . . .

95 See Wagtendonk, op. cit., p. 35.

96 Al-Fākihī, op. cit., fol. 486b: . . . *'ani bni abī mulaykata qāla: inna 'ā'ishata (r) jāwarat bayna ḥirā'a wa-thabīrin shahrayni, fa-kunnā na'tīhā wa-ya'tīhā nāsun min*

reports may help us in the evaluation of the *jiwār* of the Prophet (apparently identical with *taḥannuth*): the Prophet, like the people of Shi'b al-Ṣufiyy, used to leave his home in summer and sojourn on Mount Ḥirā'. Like them he did it "out of veneration of the *ḥaram* of Mecca"; like 'Ā'isha he sojourned there for some fixed time. None of the reports mentions fasting explicitly.

The duration of the Prophet's fast during Rajab and Sha'bān was not fixed; it was sporadic and the Prophet broke fast arbitrarily. The *ḥadīths* reporting this manner of the Prophet's fasting[97] seem to be trustworthy. The reports of his fasting during the month of Sha'bān recorded in early sources are not questioned anywhere, nor doubted by any authority; they are certainly as reliable as the reports of his fasting during Rajab.[98] It may be stressed that there were no rules of fasting, nor any regulations; the Prophet's fast was a voluntary, pious observance, the duration of which he fixed at his own discretion.

In Medina, after his *hijra*, the Prophet was faced with the task of establishing a code of law and ritual. One of the injunctions of this code was to fast. The verses of the Qur'ān imposing the fast of Ramaḍān upon the emerging Muslim community were revealed against the background of the confrontation with the Jewish community,[99] the encounter with the hostile Meccan unbelievers and their allies and the victory won on the battlefield of Badr. Even if affected by Jewish, Christian or other influences, these rules formed a genuine independent trend in the nascent body of law for the Muslim community.[100]

The injunction of the fast of Ramaḍān did not, however, abolish voluntary fasting during Rajab or Sha'bān. Some of the controversial traditions concerning the change in the Prophet's fast during Sha'bān after his arrival in Medina may facilitate a better insight into the persistence of this voluntary fast. Some scholars asserted that the Prophet, while in Mecca, fasted only some parts of the month of Sha'bān; after his arrival in Medina, however, he fasted the entire month. Al-Qasṭallānī refutes this report, basing himself on the *ḥadīth* of 'Ā'isha, who stated

qurayshin yataḥaddathūna ilayhā, fa-idhā lam yakun thamma 'abdu llāhi bnu 'abdi l-raḥmāni bni abī bakrin (r) ṣallā bihā ghulāmuhā dhakwānu abū 'amrin (r); Ibn Sa'd, op. cit., V, pp. 295–296.

97 See e.g. al-Nasā'ī, op. cit., IV, pp. 150–151: . . . *kāna rasūlu llāhi (ṣ) yaṣūmu ḥattā naqūlu lā yufṭiru, wa-yufṭiru ḥattā naqūlu lā yaṣūmu . . .*

98 See Goitein, op. cit., pp. 93–94.

99 See ibid., pp. 95–102.

100 See Wagtendonk, op. cit., p. 144 inf.

that the Prophet, after his arrival in Medina, never fasted any full month, except Ramaḍān.[101] This tradition transmitted on the authority of 'Ā'isha deserves our trust. The phrase in this *ḥadīth* of 'Ā'isha "*mundhu qadima l-madīnata*" gives us a clue in assessing the change at Medina. 'Ā'isha is indeed a reliable witness of the Prophet's life in Medina, and her *ḥadīth* with the quoted phrase, limiting it to Medina, is apparently sound. The voluntary fast of Sha'bān was now transfigured into an obligatory fast, that of Ramaḍān, the month of the Prophet's own devotional exertions, the month of his *taḥannuth* in Mecca. This fast became a distinctive mark of the Muslim community and one of the pillars of Islam.

The importance of the fast during Sha'bān consequently declined, but it never lost its virtuous position as a recommended voluntary fast, observed over the ages and revered especially by pious and devout Muslims; the night of the 15th of Sha'bān became the culmination of the month's devotions. The observances of Sha'bān were finally approved of and legitimized by moderate orthodox scholars. The high esteem of Sha'bān was clearly expressed in the utterance attributed to the Prophet: "Rajab is the month of God, Sha'bān is my month, Ramaḍān is the month of my community".

101 Al-Zurqānī, *Sharḥ al-mawāhib*, VIII, p. 125.

XII

"CALL YOURSELVES BY GRACEFUL NAMES..."

The transition from Jāhiliyya to Islam was acompanied by considerable changes in the ideas and perceptions of the traditional tribal society of the Arabs. Some concepts of the Jāhiliyya did, however, survive among the Arab tribes who conquered the territories of the Persian and Byzantine empires. The struggle between the new ideas of Islam, often enriched by the adoption of the cultural values of the conquered peoples, with the persistence of concepts of the old Arab tradition left its traces in the prolific literature of the *Ḥadīth*. The hard contest between these diverse ideas and trends is reflected by the conflicting utterances attributed to the Prophet or to his Companions. One of the topics for discussion was the problem of personal names. The contradictory traditions on this theme reflect the divergent attitudes of different groups in Muslim society. Goldziher dealt with some aspects of this problem in his "Gesetzliche Bestimmungen űber Kunja-Namen im Islam,"[1] Bräu scrutinized the cultic personal names in his detailed study: "Die altnordarabischen kultischen Personennamen"[2] and Barbara Stowasser-Freyer touched upon it in her Ph. D. thesis, "Formen des geselligen Umgangs und Eigentűmlichkeiten des Sprachgebrauchs in der frűhislamischen städtischen Gesellschaft Arabiens" (Nach Ibn Sa'd and Bukhārī).[3] The perusal of some additional data about proper names may help us to elucidate certain aspects of this problem.

The Muslim concept of names is defined in an utterance of the Prophet recorded by Abū Dāwūd:[4] "You will be called on the Day

1 *ZDMG* 51 (1897), 256–266.

2 *WZKM* 32 (1925), 31–59, 85–115.

3 *Der Islam* 42 (1965), 26–40.

4 *Ṣaḥīḥ sunan al-Muṣṭafā,* Cairo 1348, II, 307; al-Bayhaqī, *al-Sunan al-kubrā,* Hyderabad 1355, IX, 306; al-Mundhirī, *al-Targhīb wa-l-tarhīb,* ed. Muḥammad Muḥyī l-Dīn 'Abd al-Ḥamīd, Cairo 1381/1962, IV, 139, No. 2890; al-'Aynī, *'Umdat al-qārī,* [Istanbul 1308-11] x, 451; Ibn Ḥajar, *Fatḥ al-bārī,* Cairo 1325, x, 438.

of Resurrection by your names and the names of your fathers, therefore call yourselves by graceful names." The same emphasis on graceful names is apparent in two other traditions: "When you send to me a messenger, send a man with a pleasant face and a beautiful name," [5] and "He whom God granted a pretty face and a graceful name and put him in a place which is not disgraceful, he is the choicest man of God among His creature." [6] As is to be expected, tradition credited the Prophet with the changing of ugly and unpleasant names into pleasant ones. "The Prophet, when he heard an odious name, used to change it into a pretty one," [7] says a tradition reported on the authority of 'Urwa.

The collections of *ḥadīth* and the *Ṭabaqāt* compilations record a good deal of the changes of names performed by the Prophet. The first to be changed, as one would expect, were the names indicating worship of idols. 'Abd al-'Uzzā was changed by the Prophet to 'Abd al-Raḥmān [8] or 'Abd Rabbihi [9] or 'Abdallah [10] or 'Abd al-'Azīz.[11] 'Abd

5 Ibn Abī Ḥātim, *'Ilal al-ḥadīth*, Cairo 1343, II, 329, No. 2508; al-Munāwī, *Fayḍ al-qadīr, sharḥ al-jāmi' al-ṣaghīr*, Cairo 1391/1972, I, 311, No. 511; 'Alī al-Qārī, *al-Asrār al-marfū'a fī l-akhbār al-mauḍū'a*, ed. Muḥammad al-Ṣabbāgh, Beirut 1391/1971, 437; al-Samarqandī, *Bustān al-'ārifīn* (on margin of *Tanbīh al-ghāfilīn*), Cairo 1347, 155 inf.; 'Alī b. Burhān al-Dīn, *Insān al-'uyūn* (= *al-Sīra al-ḥalabiyya*), Cairo 1351/1932, I, 94; al-Muttaqī l-Hindī, *Kanz al-'ummāl*, Hyderabad 1377/1958, VI, 22–3, Nos. 196–7; al-Suyūṭī, *al-La'ālī al-maṣnū'a fī l-aḥādīth al-mauḍū'a*, Cairo n. d., I, 112–3; al-Nawawī, *Kit. al-adhkār al-muntakhab min kalām sayyid al-abrār*, Cairo 1323, 127.

6 Al-Shaukānī, *al-Fawā'id al-majmū'a*, ed. 'Abd al-Raḥmān al-Mu'allamī al-Yamānī, Cairo 1380/1960, 221; :Alī l-Qārī, *op. cit.*, 437; al-Rāghib al-Iṣfahānī, *Muḥāḍarāt al-udabā'*, Beirut 1961, III, 336.

7 Al-'Aynī, *op. cit.*, X, 451; al-Munāwī, *op. cit.*, V, 144, No. 6727; al-Mundhirī, *op. cit.*, IV, 140, No. 2895.

8 Ibn Sa'd, *Ṭabaqāt*, Beirut 1377/1957, III, 474; al-Balādhurī, *Futūḥ al-buldān*, ed. 'Abdallah Anīs al-Ṭabbā' and 'Umar al-Ṭabbā', Beirut 1377/1957, 125; al-Fāsī, *al-'Iqd al-thamīn*, ed. Fu'ād Sayyid, Cairo 1385/1966, V, 371, line 1; Ibn 'Abd al-Barr, *al-Istī'āb*, ed. 'Alī Muḥammad al-Bijāwī, Cairo 1380/1960, p. 832, No. 1408 and 838, No. 1432; Nūr al-Dīn al-Haythamī, *Majma' al-zawā'id*, Beirut 1967, VIII, 50, 54; Ibn Qudāma al-Maqdisī, *al-Istibṣār fī nasabi l-ṣaḥāba min al-anṣār*, ed. 'Alī Nuwayhiḍ, Beirut 1392/1972, 319.

9 Ibn Ḥajar, *al-Iṣāba*, Cairo 1328, II, 388, No. 5074.

Shams was changed by the Prophet to 'Abdallah.[12] 'Abd Kulāl was changed to 'Abd al-Raḥmān,[13] 'Abd al-Jānn to 'Abdallah.[14] 'Abd al-Ka'ba to 'Abd al-Raḥmān [15] or 'Abdallah.[16] The Banū 'Abd Manāf were renamed by the Prophet and called Banū 'Abdallah.[17] 'Abd al-Ḥajar (or al-Ḥijr) was altered to 'Abdallah,[18] 'Abd 'Amr into 'Abd al-Raḥmān.[19] The substitution of 'Abdallah for Bujayr [20] as recorded

10 Abū Nu'aym al-Iṣfahānī, *Ḥilyat al-auliyā'*, Beirut 1387/1967 (reprint), I, 365; Ibn 'Abd al-Barr, *op. cit.*, 871, No. 1480; Anonymous, *History of the prophets* (Ar.), Ms.Br.Mus., Or. 1510, fol. 234a; Ibn Ḥajar, *al-Iṣāba,* II, 280, No. 4557.

11 Ibn 'Abd al-Barr, *op. cit.*, 1006, No. 1700; Ibn Ḥajar, *al-Iṣāba,* II, 428, Nos. 5240–41.

12 Ibn 'Abd al-Barr, *op. cit.*, 884, No. 1496; Ibn Ḥajar, *al-Iṣāba,* II, 292, No. 4602 and 293, No. 4606.

13 Nūr al-Dīn al-Haythamī, *op. cit.*, VIII, 55; Ibn Qutayba, *al-Ma'ārif,* ed. al-Ṣāwī, Cairo 1390/1970 (reprint), 132.

14 Al-Zubayr b. Bakkār, *Jamharat nasab quraysh,* Ms. Bodley, Marsh. 384, fol. 106b; Mughulṭāy, *al-Zahr al-bāsim fī sīrat Abī l-Qāsim,* Ms. Leiden, Or. 370, fol. 145a; Anonymous, *al-Ta'rīkh al-muḥkam fī man intasaba ilā l-nabiyyi ṣallā llāhu 'alayhi wa-sallam,* Ms.Br.Mus., Or. 8653, fols. 115b, ult.–116a sup.; Ibn Ḥajar, *al-Iṣāba,* II, 325, No. 4753; Ibn al-Kalbī, *Jamhara,* Ms.Br.Mus., Add. 23297, fol. 27b inf

15 Ibn 'Abd al-Barr, *op. cit.*, p. 844, Nos. 1446–7 and 824, No. 1394; Anonymous, *al-Ta'rīkh al-muḥkam,* Ms., fol. 112b; Muṣ'ab b. 'Abdallah al-Zubayrī, *Nasab Quraysh,* ed. Levi-Provençal, Cairo 1953, 265, line 17 (his name was 'Abd 'Amr); 'Alī b. Burhān al-Dīn, *op. cit.*, I, 312 ('Abd 'Amr, or 'Abd al-Ka'ba, or 'Abd al-Ḥārith).

16 Al-Fāsī, *op. cit.*, V, 208; Ibn Qutayba, *al-Ma'ārif,* 73; al-Majlisī, *Biḥār al-anwār* (lithogr. ed.) VIII, 272, line 5.

17 Nūr al-Dīn al-Haythamī, *op. cit.*, VIII, 53; comp. Ibn Ḥajar, *al-Iṣāba,* II, 431, No. 5263 ('Abd Manāf changed into 'Abdallah).

18 Faḍlullah l-Jīlānī (= al-Jīlānī), *Faḍlu llāhi l-ṣamad fī tauḍīḥ al-adab al-mufrad,* Ḥimṣ 1388/1969, II, 283, No. 811; Ibn 'Abd al-Barr, *op. cit.*, 943, No. 1596, and 895, No. 1524.

19 Nūr al-Dīn al-Haythamī, *op. cit.*, VIII, 53; al-Mu'āfā b. Zakariyā, *al-Jalīs al-ṣāliḥ al-kāfī wa-l-anis al-nāṣiḥ al-shāfī,* Ms. Ahmet III, No. 2321, fol. 113a; al-Fasawī, *al-Ma'rifa wa-l-ta'rīkh,* Ms. Esad Ef. 2391, fol. 134b, sup.; al-Wāqidī, *al-Maghāzī,* ed. Marsden Jones, London 1966, I, 82 (he was however addressed 'Abd al-Ilāh, because the name of Musaylima was al-Raḥmān).

20 See Goldziher, *Gesetzliche Bestimmungen,* 257, line 7.

by al-Balādhurī[21] may have been connected with the odious name of the idol Bājir.[22]

It was deemed equally desirable to change the names of persons and tribes in which mention of devils or demons could be found. The name of the Banū Shayṭān was changed to Banū 'Abdallah;[23] Shayṭān b. Qurṭ was altered to 'Abdallah b. Qurṭ.[24] 'Umar changed the name of Masrūq b. al-Ajda' to Masrūq b. 'Abd al-Raḥmān; al-Ajda', he said, is the name of the Devil.[25] Another man was called Ḥubāb; the Prophet changed his name to 'Abdallah, stating that Ḥubāb is the name of the Devil.[26] It apparently denotes an idol, as assumed by Wellhausen.[27] A rather humorous story narrates another version by which the name Ḥubāb was changed unintentionally: A man called Ḥubāb negotiated with a bedouin for the purchase of two camels; he succeeded in getting the camels and set off with them. When he was later brought into the presence of the Prophet, the Prophet addressed him as "Surraq," "the thief." The man refused to change this name, because it was the Prophet who granted it to him.[28] The name of 'Abd al-Ḥārith

21 *Ansāb al-ashrāf*, ed. Muḥammad Ḥamīdullah, Cairo 1959, I, 233; al-Ṭabarī, *Dhayl al-mudhayyal*, Cairo 1358/1939, 59.

22 See *L'A*, s. v. *bjr;* and see Ibn al-Kalbī, *al-Aṣnām*, ed. Aḥmad Zakī Pasha, Cairo 1343/1924, 63.

23 Ibn Wahb, *Jāmi'*, ed. J. David-Weill, Cairo 1939, 11, lines 4–6.

24 Nūr al-Dīn al-Haythamī, *op. cit.*, VIII, 51 sup.; Ibn Ḥajar, *al-Iṣāba*, II, 358, No. 4890.

25 Ibn Ḥanbal, *'Ilal*, ed. Talat Koçiğit and Ismail Cerrahoğlu, Ankara 1963, I, 9, No. 31; Ibn Mājah, *Sunan*, Cairo 1349, II, 405; *L'A*, s. v. *jd';* Ibn Ḥajar, *al-Iṣāba*, III, 492, No. 8406; Ibn Sa'd, *op. cit.*, V, 76.

26 Al-Balādhurī, *Futūḥ*, 125; Nūr al-Dīn al-Haythamī, *op. cit.*, VIII, 50; Ibn Wahb, *op. cit.*, 6, lines 12–14; 7, lines 5–7; 9, lines 11–13, 16–19; 10, lines 1–2; al-Fasawī, *op. cit.*, fol. 134b sup.; Ma'mar b. Rāshid, *Jāmi'* (attached to 'Abd al-Razzāq, *al-Muṣannaf*, ed. Ḥabību l-Raḥmān al-A'ẓamī, Beirut 1392/1972), XI, 40, No .19849; Anonymous, *History*, Ms.Br.Mus., Or. 1510, fol. 233a; *L'A*, s. v. *ḥbb;* and see al-Suyūṭī, *al-Durr al-manthūr fī l-tafsīr bi-l-ma'thūr*, Cairo 1314, I, 48 (the name of Iblīs at the time when God created Adam was Ḥubāb), 50 (the name of Iblīs was al-Ḥārith; in other traditions his name was 'Azāzīl).

27 J. Wellhausen, *Reste Arabischen Heidentums*, Berlin 1887, 171, n. 2.

28 Ibn 'Abd al-Barr, *op. cit.*, 683, No. 1132; Ibn Ḥajar, *al-Iṣāba*, II, 20, No. 3122.

was changed by the Prophet to 'Abdallah;[29] the name of Iblīs in Heaven was al-Ḥārith.[30] He frightened Ḥawwā' when she became pregnant by telling her that she would give birth to a beast and promised that she would have a normal human baby if she gave it his name; he lied, claiming that his name was 'Abd al-Ḥārith (not al-Ḥārith). The baby born was indeed normal, was named 'Abd al-Ḥārith, but died as a child.[31] It is of interest that this very name, al-Ḥārith, the name of Iblīs and apparently the name of an idol, survived in the period of the Prophet and was even recommended by the Prophet, according to one tradition.[32] It subsequently became one of the names with the widest circulation.

It was not only the name of the Devil which was prohibited. His *kunya,* Abū Murra,[33] was also considered disagreeable and was changed by the Prophet to Abū Ḥulwa.[34] Murra is the name most disliked by God,[35] stated the Prophet. The name of a *jinnī* who embraced Islam,

29 Ibn Ḥajar, *al-Iṣāba,* II, 374, No. 4983; 388, No. 5068; and see *ibid,* 387–8.

30 Al-Majlisī, *Biḥār al-anwār,* Tehran 1390, LXIII, 241, 247; Anonymous, *History,* Ms.Br.Mus., Or. 1510, fol. 4b; al-Shiblī, *Ākām al-marjān fī gharā'ibi l-akhbār wa-aḥkām al-jānn,* ed. 'Abdallah Muḥammad al-Ṣadīq, Cairo 1376, 156; al-'Iṣāmī, *Simṭ al-nujūm al-'awālī,* Cairo 1380, I, 35; Bräu, *op. cit.,* 56.

31 Muqātil, *Tafsīr,* Ms. Ahmet III, 741, fol. 140a; and see al-Ḥākim, *al-Mustadrak,* Hyderabad 1342, II, 545; Ibn 'Asākir, *Ta'rīkh (Tahdhīb),* Damascus 1349, VI, 353; al-Suyūṭī, *al-Durr,* III, 151–2 (in one of the reports, 151 ult., the Devil advised Ḥawwā' to name the baby 'Abd Shams); al-Nuwayrī, *Nihāyat al-arab,* Cairo n.d., XIII, 30; al-Shāṭibī, *al-Jumān* Ms. Br.Mus., Or. 1555, fol. 8b (Adam tries in vain to convince Ḥawwā' to name the child 'Abdallah); Ibn Kathīr, *al-Bidāya wa-l-nihāya,* Beirut—al-Riyāḍ 1966, I, 96; al-Ṭabarī, *Tafsīr,* ed. Maḥmūd and Aḥmad Shākir, Cairo 1958, XIII, 306–314, Nos. 15510–15525; Ibn 'Asākir, *op. cit.,* VI, 353; Muḥammad Nāṣir al-Dīn al-Albānī, *Silsilat al-aḥādīth al-ḍa'īfa wa-l-mauḍū'a,* Damascus 1384, No. 342.

32 Ibn Ḥajar, *al-Iṣāba,* II, 288, No. 4588; Ibn Wahb, *op. cit.,* page 6, lines 16–17; al-Munāwī, *op. cit.,* I, 169, No. 207; Abū Dāwūd, *op. cit.,* II, 307; al-Jīlānī, *op. cit.,* II, 286, No. 814 . . .; etc.

33 See Ibn al-Athīr, *al-Muraṣṣa'* ed. C. F. Seybold, Weimar 1896, 97: . . . *abū murrata huwa ashharu kunā iblīs . . .;* and see al- Majlisī, *op. cit.,* LXIII, 226; al-Zamakhsharī, *Rabī' al-abrār,* Ms.Br.Mus., Or. 6511, fol. 104a, sup.

34 Ibn Wahb, *op. cit.,* 8 ,line 10.

35 Al-Jīlānī, *op. cit.,* II, 286, No. 814; Ibn Wahb, *op. cit.,* page 6, line 17; 8, line 18; 9, line 1, 4–7.

Samhaj, (a mare thin in the belly) was changed by the Prophet to 'Abdallah.[36] Ḍurays is mentioned as a name of the Devil,[37] but this is not recorded in any other source; the name must have been felt to be odious: The Prophet bought a horse named al-Ḍaris and changed its name to al-Sakb.[38] The ominous name Ghaylān, which is reminiscent of the demons, was changed to 'Abdallah; [39] 'Abd Sharr was changed to 'Abd Khayr,[40] Ḥarām was altered into Ḥalāl.[41]

In the overwhelming majority of the cases quoted above the odious name was changed to 'Abd al-Raḥmān or 'Abdallah. These two names, belonging to the type of *ta'bīd* names, in which the word "'*abd*" is attached to one of the names of God, were a clear indication of the new Islamic spirit of obedience and submission to Allah. This trend was given expression in the utterance of the Prophet: "In naming (your children — K.) use the expression '*abd*" (*idhā sammaytum fa-'abbidū*).[42] Among this group of names 'Abdallah and 'Abd al-Raḥmān were considered the best. "The names most liked by God are 'Abdallah and 'Abd al-Raḥmān," says an utterance of the Prophet.[43] This idea brought about changes in the names which served in Islam as attributes of Allah. Jabbār was changed to 'Abd al-Jabbār,[44] al-Qayyūm to 'Abd al-Qayyūm,[45] 'Azīz to 'Abd al-'Azīz [46] and to 'Abd al-Raḥmān.[47] An

36 Ibn Nāṣir al-Dīn, *Jāmi' al-āthār,* Ms. Cambridge, Or. 913, fol. 358b; al-Damīrī, *Ḥayāt al-ḥayawān,* Cairo 1383/1963, I, 208.

37 *Rijāl al-Kashshī,* Karbalā' n.d., 156 inf.

38 *L'A,* s.v. *ḍrs.*

39 Nūr al-Dīn al-Haythamī, *op. cit.*, VIII, 54.

40 Ibn Ḥajar, *al-Iṣāba,* II, 388, No. 5072.

41 Nūr al-Dīn al-Haythamī, *op. cit.*, VIII, 51.

42 Nūr al-Dīn al-Haythamī, *op. cit.*, VIII, 50.

43 Al-Bayhaqī, *al-Sunan,* IX, 306; Ibn 'Abd al-Barr, *op. cit.*, 834, No. 1419; Nūr al-Dīn al-Haythamī, *op. cit.*, VIII, 49–50; al-Mundhirī, *op. cit.*, IV, 139, No. 2891; Ibn Wahb, *op. cit.*, 9, line 3–4; al-Munāwī, *op. cit.*, I, 168, No. 206; Ibn Mājah, *op. cit.*, II, 404; Ibn Ḥajar, *al-Iṣāba,* II, 288, No. 4588.

44 Ibn Ḥajar, *al-Iṣāba,* II, 387, No. 5063.

45 Nūr al-Dīn al-Haythamī, *op. cit.*, VIII, 54.

46 Ibn Ḥajar, *al-Iṣāba,* II, 428, No. 5242.

47 Ibn 'Abd al-Barr, *op. cit.*, 834, No. 1419; Nūr al-Dīn l-Haythamī, *op. cit.*, VIII, 49–50; Ibn Sa'd, *op. cit.*, VI, 50.

utterance of the Prophet gives explicitly the reason why the name al-Ḥakam and the *kunya* Abū l-Ḥakam are prohibited. "Do not name (your children) al-Ḥakam, nor Abū l-Ḥakam, as God is the *ḥakam*."[48] Consequently, the name of al-Ḥakam b. Sa'īd was changed to 'Abdallah b. Sa'īd;[49] the *kunya* of Hāni', Abū l-Ḥakam, was changed to Abū Shurayḥ.[50]

The abhorrence which the pious felt with regard to using names denoting the attributes of Allah gave rise to an early tradition, recorded by Ma'mar b. Rāshid and attributed to the Prophet: "The names most detested by God are Khālid and Mālik."[51] Kingdom and eternal existence are, of course, attributes of God and man is not permitted to apply them in his name. It is of interest that another version of this tradition states: "The most deceiving names are Khālid and Mālik" (*akdhabu l-asmā'i khālidun wa-mālikun*).[52] The *kunya* Abū Mālik is listed among the four *kunyas* prohibited by the Prophet: Abū 'Īsā, Abū l-Ḥakam, Abū Mālik and Abū l-Qāsim; the last one in the case when the child is named Muḥammad.[53]

Contrary to the Bedouin custom to call their slaves by nice names and to call their own children by disagreeable names,[54] the Muslims

48 Ma'mar b. Rāshid, *op. cit.*, XI, 42, No. 19859; al-Majlisī, *op. cit.*, LXXVI, 175; al-'Aynī, *op. cit.*, X, 457 inf.

49 Anonymous, *al-Ta'rīkh l-muḥkam*, Ms.Br.Mus., Or. 8653, fol. 67b, inf.; Nūr al-Dīn al-Haythamī, *op. cit.*, VIII, 53; Ibn 'Abd al-Barr, *op. cit.*, 355, No. 523; Ibn al-Kalbī, *Jamhara*, fol. 14a.

50 Al-Jīlānī, *op. cit.*, II, 283, No. 811; Ibn al-Athīr, *al-Nihāya*, s.v. *ḥkm;* Ibn 'Abd al-Barr, *op. cit.*, 1688, No. 3031; 'Alī b. Balabān, *al-Iḥsān fī taqrīb ṣaḥīḥ Ibn Ḥibbān*, Ms.Br.Mus., Add. 27519, fol. 117b; Ibn al-Ḥājj, *al-Madkhal*, Beirut 1972, I, 120; Ibn Sa'd, *op. cit.*, VI, 49; al-Nawawī, *op. cit.*, 129 sup.

51 Ma'mar b. Rāshid, *op. cit.*, XI, 42, No. 19860; al-'Aynī, *op. cit.*, X, 457 ult. –8.

52 Ibn Abī Ḥātim, *op. cit.*, No. 2525.

53 Al-'Aynī, *op. cit.*, X, 450; about the use of the *kunya* Abū l-Qāsim see e.g. Ma'mar b. Rāshid, *op. cit.*, XI, 44, No. 19867; Abū Dāwūd, *op. cit.*, II, 309–310; al-'Aynī, *op. cit.*, X, 449; al-Ṭaḥāwī, *Sharḥ ma'ānī l-āthār*, ed. Muḥammad Zuhrī l-Najjār, Cairo 1388/1968, IV, 335–341.

54 Al-Rāghib al-Iṣfahānī, *op. cit.*, III, 339; al-Ṣāliḥī, *Subul al-hudā wa-l-rashād fī sīrat khayri l-'ibād* (= *al-Sīra al-shāmiyya*), ed. Muṣṭafā 'Abd al-Wāḥid,

were required to give their children graceful names. The Prophet stated that the obligation of a father towards his child is to give him a graceful name and a good education.[55] The Prophet used to ask about the name of a man whom he met and was glad to hear that his name was a nice one.[56] One should be careful to select a beautiful name, as an angel and a devil attend the birth of a child; the angel advises to give him a graceful name, the devil recommends a disagreeable one.[57] The name of the child constitutes a proof for the intelligence of his father.[58] There is a very close relationship between the meaning of the name and the character of the child who is given it. The name chosen by the father thus has considerable bearing on the fate and life of the child.[59] A name fits the character of the person named, by decree of God. The Prophet was given names which were precisely fitting: Muḥammad and Aḥmad. The name and the person named, says Ibn Qayyim, were in this case as closely connected to each other as the body is to the soul.[60] The name Muḥammad, for instance is derived from the name of God as attested by the verse of Ḥassān:

> *wa-shaqqa lahū min ismihī li-yujillahū:*
> *fa-dhū l-'arshi maḥmūdun wa-hādhā muḥammadū*
> And He derived (a name) from His name in order to honour him: thus the Owner of the Throne is Maḥmūd (Praised) and this one is Muḥammad.[61]

Cairo 1392/1972, I, 326; Ibn Durayd, *al-Ishtiqāq*, ed. 'Abd al-Salām Hārūn, Cairo 1378/1958, 4.

55 Nūr al-Dīn al-Haythamī, *op. cit.*, VIII, 47.

56 Nūr al-Dīn al-Haythamī, *op. cit.*, VIII, 47; al-'Aynī, *op. cit.*, X, 197.

57 Al-Rāghib al-Iṣfahānī, *op. cit.*, III, 336.

58 Al-Rāghib al-Iṣfahānī, *op. cit.*, III, 336.

59 Ibn Qayyim al-Jauziyya, *Zād al-ma'ād fī hadyi khayri l-'ibād*, Beirut n.d. II, 5; Majd al-Dīn al-Fayrūzābādī, *Sifr al-sa'āda*, Cairo 1382/1962, 88.

60 Ibn Qayyim, *op. cit.*, II, 5.

61 See A. Fischer, *Muḥammad and Aḥmad, die Namen des arabischen Propheten*, Leipzig 1932, 20; al-Suyūṭī, *al-Khaṣā'iṣ al-kubrā*, ed. Muḥammad Khalīl Harrās, Cairo 1386/1967, I, 194–5; al-Bayhaqī *Dalā'il al-nubuwwa*, ed. 'Abd al-Raḥmān Muḥammad 'Uthmān, al-Madīna al-munawwara 1389/1969, I, 93, 122; Ḥassān b. Thābit, *Dīwān*, ed. W. N. 'Arafāt, London 1971, I, 306.

The name of Muḥammad was given to the Prophet as a good omen.[62] The name Uḥud was given to the mountain by God, pointing to the people who believed in the unity of God and to the Prophet who summoned people to this faith.[63]

*

The *fa'l,* the omen, either good or bad, become the leading principle in the choice of names. It had, of course, to be distinguished from *ṭiyara,* which was interdicted by Islam as a practice of the Jāhiliyya. The Prophet is said to have disliked augury, but was pleased by the use of good omens.[64] "There is no *ṭiyara,* augury, and the best of it is the *fa'l,* the good omen." The Prophet was asked about the *fa'l* and he defined it as "a good (*ṣāliḥ*) word heard by one of you." [65] Ibn Ḥajar devotes a lengthy and detailed discussion to the problem of the relation between *ṭiyara* and *fa'l,* stressing that the meaning of *ṭiyara* is negative and undesirable while that of *fa'l* is acceptable.[66] "The truest (kind of) augury is the omen," says the Prophet.[67] The favourable attitude of the Prophet towards omens of names is mirrored in a tradition about the milking of a camel. Three men volunteered to milk the camel. The Prophet disapproved of the first because of his name Murra, and of the second because of his name Ḥarb; he ordered the third to milk because of his name: Ya'īsh.[68] Another version of

62 Fischer, *op. cit.,* 18.

63 Majd al-Dīn al-Fayrūzābādī, *al-Maghānim al-muṭāba fī ma'ālim Ṭāba,* ed. Ḥamad al-Jāsir, al-Riyāḍ 1389/1969, 10.

64 Al-Munāwī, *op. cit.,* v, 231, No. 7101; Ibn Ḥajar, *Fatḥ al-bārī,* x, 167, lines 3–4.

65 Ibn Ḥajar, *Fatḥ,* x, 166–7; al-'Aynī, *op. cit.,* x, 197.

66 Ibn Ḥajar, *Fatḥ,* x, 167–8; cf. al-Munāwī, *op. cit.,* i, 312, line 10 seq.

67 Ibn Wahb, *op. cit.,* 93, line 16 (*aṣdaqu l-ṭiyarati l-fa'lu*); Ma'mar b. Rāshid, *op. cit.,* x, 406, No. 19512 (the same version); Ibn 'Abd al-Barr, *op. cit.,* 280, No. 379 (*aṣdaqu l-ṭayri l-fa'lu*). This tradition was misread by T. Fahd in *EI*², s.v. *fa'l* (*aṣdaqa l-ṭayru l-fa'la*) and consequently misinterpreted.

68 Ibn Wahb, *op. cit.,* 96, line 10–14; Ma'mar b. Rāshid, *op. cit.,* xi, 41, No. 19854; Nūr al-Dīn al-Haythamī, *op. cit.,* viii, 47; 'Alī b. Burhān al-Dīn, *op. cit.,* i, 94; Ibn Qayyim, *op. cit.,* ii, 5; Majd al-Dīn al-Fayrūzābādī, *Sifr al-sa'āda,* 88; al-Suyūṭī, *Tanwīr al-ḥawālik, sharḥ 'alā Muwaṭṭa' Mālik,* Cairo n.d. iii, 140–1; al-Samarqandī, *op. cit.,* 157; Ibn 'Abd al-Barr, *op.*

this story reflects the tendency of separation of augury, *ṭiyara*, which should be rejected, from *fa'l*, acting according to the principle of "omen nomen", which should be permitted. Two persons volunteered to milk a she-camel: al-Musāwir and Khaddāsh. Both were disqualified by the Prophet. Then 'Umar asked the Prophet: "Shall I speak or remain silent?" The Prophet said: "Remain silent and I shall tell you what you wanted (to say)" 'Umar said: "Then tell me, O Messenger of God." The Prophet said: "You thought that is was augury." He (i.e. the Prophet — K.) said: "There is no bird except His bird, there is no good except His good; but I like the good omen."[69] The evident intention of this tradition is to reject augury and to legitimize the practice of *fa'l*. It may be mentioned that the names Ḥarb and Murra mentioned above as a bad *fa'l* are included in the list of the names disliked by the Prophet: Ḥarb, Murra, Jamra, Ḥanẓala,[70] Kalb and Kulayb.[71] In another case the Prophet preferred a man called Nājiya to two other men (evidently with unpleasant names) and let him lead his camel.[72] The Prophet chose the way of "Marḥab" for reasons of good omen when on his way to attack Khaybar in preference to all other ways proposed to him (al-Ḥazn, Shās, Ḥāṭib).[73] When the Prophet went out on his *hijra* to Medina he met Burayda al-Aslamī with a group of seventy riders of the clan of Sahm. The Prophet drew the omens from these names: Burayda — *barada amrunā wa-ṣaluḥa,* firm and just is our affair; *Aslam* — we are safe; *sahm* — our arrow came

cit., 459, No. 694; 1588, No. 2820; Ibn Ḥajar, *al-Iṣāba*, III, 669; cf. Anonymous, *al-Dhakhīra wa-kashfu l-tauqī' li-ahli l-baṣīra*, Ms.Br.Mus., Or. 3922, fol. 52b: ... *al-asmā'u l-dāllatu 'alā l-nuḥūsi fa-mithlu ḥarbin wa-fahdin wa-kalbin wa-namirin wa-ḥimārin wa-abī lahabin wa-abī l-ḥārithi wa-abī murrata wa-abī shihābin wa-mā ashbahahā* . . .

69 Ibn Wahb, *op. cit.*, 97, lines 1–7; cf. 'Alī b. Burhān al-Dīn, *op. cit.*, I, 94.

70 Ibn al-Ḥājj, *op. cit.*, I, 122.

71 Al-Munāwī, *op. cit.*, VI, 342, No. 9523.

72 Al-Jīlānī, *op. cit.*, II, 284, No. 812; Nūr al-Dīn al-Haythamī, *op. cit.*, VIII, 47; and see about the name Dhakwān changed into Nājiya: Ibn 'Abd al-Barr, *op. cit.*, IV, 1522, No. 2650; Ibn Ḥajar, *al-Iṣāba*, III, 541, No. 8642.

73 Majd al-Dīn al-Fayrūzābādī, *al-Maghānim*, 376.

out.[74] When the Prophet entered Medina he heard a man shouting: "Yā Ghānim"; the Prophet drew the following omen from the name: "We have earned without effort." [75] When Suhayl came to the Prophet at Ḥudaybiyya to negotiate peace, the Prophet drew from his name the following omen: "Suhayl has come to you, your affair has become easy." [76] When the Prophet heard a man in his army addressing someone: "Yā Ḥasan", he said: "From your mouth we have taken the good omen." [77] When the Prophet once went out for some of his needs he was pleased to hear (incidentally) someone addressing another person: "Yā Nājiḥ, yā Rāshid." [78]

Disagreeable names caused, of course, misfortune and had to be altered. When a man came to 'Umar and told him that his name was Jamra (= burning coal), the son of Shihāb (= bright blaze), from the tribal group of Ḥurqa (= fire), staying in Ḥarrat al-nār (= the stony tract of fire), in the part of it called Dhāt al-laẓā (= that of the fiery

74 Al-Samhūdī, *Wafā'u l-wafā*, ed. Muḥammad Muḥyī l-Dīn 'Abd al-Ḥamīd, Cairo 1374/1955, I, 243; Ibn 'Abd al-Barr, *op. cit.*, 185, No. 217; al-Kāzarūnī, *Sirat al-nabi*, Ms.Br.Mus., Add. 18499, fol. 139a (noteworthy is the formulation of the phrase: *kāna lā yataṭayyaru, wa-kāna yatafā'alu*); al-Zandawaysitī, *Rauḍat al-'ulamā'*, Ms.Br.Mus., Add. 7258, fol. 277a.

75 Al-Rāghib al-Iṣfahānī, *op. cit.*, I, 144.

76 Ibn 'Abd al-Barr, *op. cit.*, 670 No. 1106; al-Rāghib al-Iṣfahānī, *op. cit.*, I, 144; al-Shaukānī, *Nayl al-auṭār, sharḥ muntaqā l-akhbar*, Cairo 1380/1961, VIII 47; cf. al-Ṭabarī, *Dhayl al-mudhayyal*, 17: *nabbilū sahlan fa-innahu sahlun.*

77 Ibn Abī l-Dunyā, *al-Ishrāf fi manāzil al-ashrāf*, Ms. Chester Beatty 4427, fol. 74b; al-Rāghib al-Iṣfahānī, *op. cit.*, I, 144; al-Sakhāwī, *al-Maqāṣid al-ḥasana*, ed. 'Abdallah Muḥammad al-Ṣadīq, Cairo 1375/1956, 27, No. 40; al-Munāwī, *op. cit.*, I, 212, No. 290 (see *ibid*, inf. the additional stories about omens drawn by the Prophet: when he went out against Khaybar he heard 'Alī exclaiming "*yā khuḍra*"; he said: "we took the omen from your mouth, let us go out against Khuḍra" [= Khaybar]. No sword was drawn [by the Muslims] in this expedition. And see the opinion of al-Zamakhsharī about the difference between *ṭiyara* and *fa'l*); al-Muttaqī l-Hindī, *op. cit.*, X, 66, No. 511; al-Shaukānī, *Nayl*, VII, 194.

78 Al-Munāwī, *op. cit.*, V, 229, No. 7089; Yūsuf b. Mūsā l-Ḥanafī, *al-Mu'taṣar min al-mukhtaṣar min mushkil al-āthār*, Cairo 1362, II, 206; and see al-Jīlānī, *op. cit.*, II, 285; Ibn al-Jauzī *al-Wafā bi-aḥwāli l-muṣṭafā*, ed. Muṣṭafā 'Abd al-Wāḥid, Cairo 1386/1966, II, 465.

blaze), 'Umar ordered him to return to his family because they were caught by fire. It happened as 'Umar foretold.[79] The Prophet indeed changed the name Shihāb to Hishām.[80]

The rough Jāhilī character of names is emphasized in a dubious tradition about the conversion of Abū Ṣufra to Islam. He came clad in a yellow robe and presented himself as Ẓālim (= the oppressing) b. Sāriq (= the thief) b. Shihāb (= the blazing fire) . . . the scion of Julandā who used to snatch the passing ships. "I am a king," said Abū Ṣufra. The Prophet advised him gently to "leave the thief and the oppressor" and named him Abū Ṣufra (= the man of the yellow suit). Thereupon Abū Ṣufra decided to name his new born female-baby Ṣufra.[81] Anti-Muhallabid traditions wholly refute this story, stating that he did not meet the Prophet at all, that he was captured during he ridda, etc.; one of the traditions claims that he was uncircumcised and did not even know the meaning of circumcision.

A man with the name Ḥazn (= hard, rugged ground) was told by the Prophet to change it to Sahl (plain, easy ground). His answer reflects the Jāhiliyya spirit: "The plain is trodden and despised" (or in another version: "I am not going to change a name given to me by my father").[82]

*

79 Al-Suyūṭī, *Tanwīr al-ḥawālik*, III, 141; Ibn Qayyim, *op. cit.*, II, 5; al-Samarqandī, *op. cit.*, 157; Ibn Ḥajar, *al-Iṣāba*, I, 275; No. 1294; Ma'mar b. Rāshid, *op. cit.*, XI, 43, No. 19864; Ibn Wahb, *op. cit.*, 10, lines 2–5; al-Rāghib al-Iṣfahānī, *op. cit.*, III, 340; Ibn al-Jauzī, *Sīrat 'Umar b. al-Khaṭṭāb*, Cairo 1342/1924, 63; Ibn Abī l-Ḥadīd, *Sharḥ nahj al-balāgha*, ed. Muḥammad Abū l-Faḍl Ibrāhīm, Cairo 1961, XII, 103; al-Nuwayrī, *op. cit.*, III, 144; *al-Manāsik wa-amākin ṭuruqi l-ḥajj*. ed. Ḥamad al-Jāsir, al-Riyāḍ 1389/1969, 518; al-Bakrī, *Mu'jam mā sta'jam*, ed. Muṣṭafā al-Saqā, Cairo 1364/1945, I, 436–7.

80 Abū Dāwūd, *op. cit.*, II, 308; al-Mundhirī, *op. cit.*, IV, 141; al-Jīlānī, *op. cit.*, II, 298, No. 825; Nūr al-Dīn al-Haythamī, *op. cit.*, VIII, 51; Ibn 'Abd al-Barr, *op. cit.*, 1541, No. 2685; al-Bayhaqī, *al-Sunan*, IX, 308.

81 Al-Samarqandī, *op. cit.*, 156; Ibn Ḥajar, *al-Iṣāba*, III, 500, No. 8454, 535, No. 8633; IV, 108, No. 652; Ibn Sa'd, *op. cit.*, ff)), 101.

82 Al-Jīlānī, *op. cit.*, II, 309, No. 841; Ma'mar b. Rāshid, *op. cit.*, XI, 41, No. 19851; Ibn 'Abd al-Barr, *op. cit.*, 401, No. 560; Ibn Wahb, *op. cit.*, 8, line

Some names changed by the Prophet are connected with the Meccan aristocracy in the period of the Jāhiliyya. The disagreeable name Ḥarb (= war) was changed into Silm.[83] 'Alī intended to name his sons Ḥarb; the Prophet himself named them Ḥasan, Ḥusayn, Muḥassin; these names correspond to the names of Aharon's sons: Shubbar, Shubbayr, Mushabbir. As the position of 'Alī in relation to the Prophet corresponds in Shī'a faith to the position of Aharon to Moses, it is plausible to consider this tradition as a Shī'ī one.[84] According to one tradition the Prophet disapproved of the name Ḥarb and described it as one of the worst names.[85] As one of the ancestors of the Umayyads was Ḥarb, this tradition might have been rather unpleasant for the ruling dynasty.

One of the Jāhilī names changed by the Prophet was al-Walīd. This name was a common one among the Banū Makhzūm and the Prophet remarked that the Banū Makhzūm nearly turned al-Walīd into a deity (*mā kādat banū makhzūmin illā an taj'ala l-walīda rabban;* in another version: *ḥanānan*). The Prophet changed the name of al-Walīd b. abī Umayya to al-Muhājir b. abī Umayya,[86] the name of al-Walīd b. al-Wālid b. al-Walīd b. al-Mughīra into 'Abdallah b. al-Walīd.[87] The

10; Abū Dāwūd, *op. cit.*, II, 308; al-'Aynī, *op. cit.*, X, 450, 452; al-Bayhaqī, *al-Sunan,* IX, 307; al-Muttaqī l-Hindī, *op. cit.*, XV, 319, No. 898; Muṣ'ab b. 'Abdallah, *op. cit.*, 345; al-Nawawī, *op .cit.*, 128 inf.; al-Qasṭallānī, *Irshād al-sārī*, Cairo 1326, IX, 111; Muḥammad Ḥasan al-Muẓaffar, *Dalā'il al-ṣidq*, n.p., 1373, III, II 29 inf.

83 Al-Bayhaqī, *al-Sunan,* IX, 308; al-Mundhirī, *op. cit.*, IV, 141; al-Sha'rānī, *Lawāqiḥ al-anwār,* Cairo 1381/1961, 756, line 2.

84 Al-Jīlānī, *op. cit.*, II, 296, No. 823; al-Samarqandī, *op. cit.*, 155 inf.; Anonymous, *al-Ta'rīkh al-muḥkam,* fol. 41a sup.; Ibn 'Abd al-Barr, *op. cit.*, 384, No. 555; Nūr al-Dīn al-Haythamī, *op. cit.*, VIII, 52; al-Munāwī, *op. cit.*, IV, 111, No. 4710; and see Israel Oriental Studies 2 (1972), 223, n. 37.

85 See e.g. al-Bayhaqī, *al-Sunan,* IX, 306; Ibn Wahb, *op. cit.*, 8, line 18–9; ... *wa-sharruhū ḥarbun wa-murra;* al-Jīlānī, *op. cit.*, 755.

86 Al-Zubayr b. Bakkār, *op. cit.*, fol. 138b; al-Fāsī, *op. cit.*, VII, 291–2; Ibn Ḥajar, *al-Iṣāba,* III, 465, No. 8253; III, 636, No. 9142; cf. about the name 'Amr changed into Muhājir: Ibn 'Abd al-Barr, *op. cit.*, 1454, No. 2506; Ibn Ḥajar, *al-Iṣāba,* III, 466, No. 8256.

87 Al-Zubayr b. Bakkār, *op. cit.*, fol. 146a; Ibn 'Asākir, *op. cit.*, VI, 230; Ibn

interdiction of the Prophet was often associated with the statement that al-Walīd was a name of one of the tyrannical Pharaohs and with a prophecy that there will come a ruler with the name al-Walīd, who will be worse for the community than Pharaoh.[88] The question as to which one of the Umayyad rulers was meant by the Prophet and the problem of the character of the Prophet's interdiction to use the name al-Walīd were extensively discussed by scholars of ḥadīth.[89]

The disagreeable name al-ʿĀṣ (close in association to al-ʿĀṣī) was changed into al-Muṭīʿ [90] and ʿAbdallah.[91] ʿĀṣiya was changed into Jamīla.[92] It is noteworthy that the names of al-ʿĀṣ were common among the ʿAbd Shams, the tribal group of the Umayyads; al-ʿĀṣ, Abū l-ʿĀṣ, al-ʿĪṣ, and Abū l-ʿĪṣ were the sons of Umayya and were called al-Aʿyāṣ.[93] It is sufficient to mention al-Ḥakam b. al-ʿĀṣ, the stubborn enemy of the Prophet, to understand what the change of the name al-ʿĀṣ could mean for the ruling descendants of Marwān b. al-Ḥakam b. al-ʿĀṣ.

*

Ḥajar, *al-Iṣāba,* II, 380, No. 5024; III, 640, No. 9151; Anonymous, *al-Taʾrīkh al-muḥkam,* fol. 136a.

88 See al-Muttaqī l-Hindī, *op. cit.*, XI, 237, No. 1074; Maʿmar b. Rāshid, *op. cit.*, XI, 43, No. 19861; al-Suyūṭī, *al-Laʾālī al-maṣnūʿa,* I, 107–111; al-Qasṭallānī, *op. cit.*, IX, 115; Ibn al-Athīr, *al-Nihāya,* s.v. *ḥnn.*

89 See al-ʿAynī, *op. cit.*, X, 454; and see al-Ṭabarsī, *Iʿlām al-warā bi-aʿlām al-hudā,* ed. Akbar al-Ghaffārī, Tehran 1389, 45; al-Suyūṭī, *al-Laʾālī al-maṣnūʿa,* I, 107–110.

90 Al-Zubayr b. Bakkār, *op. cit.*, fol. 174b inf.–175a sup.; al-Bayhaqī, *al-Sunan,* IX, 308; al-Jīlānī, *op. cit.*, II, 298, No. 826; Ibn Wahb, *op. cit.*, 9, line 15 (and see 8, line 10); al-Fāsī, *op. cit.*, VII, 224, No. 2473; Ibn Saʿd, *op. cit.*, V, 450; Muʾarrij al-Sadūsī, *Ḥadhf min nasab quraysh,* ed. Ṣalāḥ al-Dīn al-Munajjid, Cairo 1960, 83, line 2.

91 Nūr ʾal-Dīn al-Haythamī, *op. cit.*, VIII, 53; al-Dhahabī, *Siyar aʿlām al-nubalāʾ*, ed. Asʿad Ṭalas, Cairo 1962, III, 138; Ibn Ḥajar, *al-Iṣāba,* II, 291, No. 4598.

92 Ibn Saʿd, *op. cit.*, III, 266; Ibn Wahb, *op. cit.*, 9, lines 13–14; al-Jīlānī, *op. cit.*, II, 294, No. 820; al-Bayhaqī, *al-Sunan,* IX, 307; Ibn ʿAbd al-Barr, *op. cit.*, 1803, No. 3277; Ibn Mājah, *op. cit.*, II, 405; al-Mundhirī, *op. cit.*, IV, 140, No. 2896; Ibn ʿAsākir, *op. cit.*, VII, 366; Ibn al-Jauzī, *al-Wafā,* II, 465–6; al-Nawawī, *op. cit.*, 128 inf.

93 Ibn Durayd, *op. cit.*, 54, 73, 166.

Further changes of names may be mentioned. Aswad (= black) was changed to Abyaḍ (= white),[94] Akbar (= the greatest) to Bashīr (= the messenger of good tidings),[95] Jaththāma (= the sleepy) to Ḥassāna,[96] Dhū l-shimalayn to Dhū l-yadayn,[97] Aṣram (= waterless desert) to Zur'a (= seed),[98] al-Ṣarm to Sa'īd,[99] 'Atala (= clod of earth; or iron rod for lifting stones) to 'Utba,[100] Qirḍāb (= the thief) to Rāshid,[101] Ghāfil (= the heedless, the neglectful) to 'Āqil,[102] Ẓālim to Rāshid,[103] Qalīl to Kathīr,[104] Ghurāb (= the crow) to Muslim,[105] Dhu'ayb (= the little wolf) to 'Abdallah,[106] Kalāḥ (= a barren year) to Dhu'ayb (= a forelock; he had namely a long forelock),[107] Muhān (= despised) to

94 Ibn 'Abd al-Barr, *op. cit.*, 138, No. 143; Ibn Wahb, *op. cit.*, 11, lines 1–2; Nūr al-Dīn al-Haythamī, *op. cit.*, VIII, 55.

95 Ibn 'Abd al-Barr, *op. cit.*, 177, No. 209; Goldziher, *Gesetzliche Bestimmungen*, 257.

96 Ibn Nāṣir al-Dīn, *op. cit.*, fol. 266a; Ibn 'Abd al-Barr, *op. cit.*, 1810, No. 3295; al-Jarrāḥī, *Kashf al-khafā'i wa-muzīlu l-ilbās* (reprint, Beirut), I, 360, No. 1146.

97 Ibn 'Abd al-Barr, *op. cit.*, 478; Ibn Rustah, *al-A'lāq al-nafīsa*, ed. de Goeje, Leiden 1892, 214; al-Mubarrad, *al-Kāmil*, ed. Abū l-Faḍl Ibrāhīm, Cairo 1376/1956, IV, 101.

98 Abū Dāwūd, *op. cit.*, II, 308; Nūr al-Dīn al-Haythamī, *op. cit.*, VIII, 54; al-Bayhaqī, *al-Sunan*, IX, 308; Ibn 'Abd al-Barr, *op. cit.*, 519, No. 816 (and see 141, No. 153).

99 Al-Ṣafadī, *Nakt al-himyān*, Cairo 1911, 159–160; al-Jīlānī, *op. cit.*, II, 290, No. 822; Ibn 'Abd al-Barr, *op. cit.*, 627, No. 993 (and see 835, No. 1421); Nūr al-Dīn al-Haythamī, *op. cit.*, VIII, 52 inf.–53 sup.; Ibn Ḥajar, *al-Iṣāba*, II, 51. No. 3291.

100 Nūr al-Dīn al-Haythamī, *op. cit.*, VIII, 53; L'A, s.v. *'atl;* Ibn Ḥajar, *Iṣāba*, II, 454, No. 5407.

101 Ibn al-Kalbī, *al-Jamhara*, fol. 245b; Ibn Ḥajar, *al-Iṣāba*, I, 495, No. 2516.

102 Al-Mauṣilī, *Ghāyat al-wasā'il ilā ma'rifati l-awā'il*, Ms. Cambridge Qq 33(10), fol. 26a; al-Fāsī, *op. cit.*, V, 81, No. 1453; Ibn Ḥajar, *al-Iṣāba*, II, 247, No. 3461; Ibn Rustah, *op. cit.*, 228.

103 Ibn Ḥajar, *al-Iṣāba*, I, 494, No. 2514.

104 Ibn Wahb, *op. cit.*, 9, lines 14–15; Ibn 'Abd al-Barr, *op. cit.*, 296, No. 419; 3308, No. 2176.

105 Al-Fāsī, *op. cit.*, VII, 194, No. 2454; al-Jīlānī, *op. cit.*, II, 297, No. 824; Nūr al-Dīn al-Haythamī, *op. cit.*, VIII, 52 inf.

106 Ibn 'Abd al-Barr, *op. cit.*, 464, No. 707; Ibn Ḥajar, *al-Iṣāba*, I, 493, No. 2506.

107 Ibn 'Abd al-Barr, *op. cit.*, 465, No. 709; Ibn Ḥajar, *al-Iṣāba*, I, 490, No. 2490 (his name: al-Kilābī — an error).

Mukram.[108] Kusayr was changed to Jubayr,[109] Khālifa to Rāshida,[110] al-Muḍṭaji' to al-Munba'ith,[111] Abū Maghwiyya to Abū Rāshid,[112] Banū l-Ghawiyy to Banū l-Rashad,[113] Banū Ghayyān to Banū Rashdān,[114] Banū l-Ṣammā' to Banū l-Samī'a,[115] Zaḥm to Bashīr,[116] and Muqsim to Muslim.[117] The Prophet changed the name of al-Sā'ib (= the freely flowing) to 'Abdallah; his people, however, continued to call him al-Sā'ib and he became mad.[118] To 'Abdallah were changed the names of the famous Jewish convert al-Ḥuṣayn (= the small fortress) b. Salām [119] as well as those of Dīnār [120] and Nu'm.[121]

The Prophet gave some names in connection with certain events and occasions. A Persian slave (of whose name some 21 versions are recorded), on whom the Companions of the Prophet loaded their garments when on a walk on a hot day, was granted the name Safīna (= the ship).[122] A girl, born when Sūrat Maryam was revealed, was

108 Al-Muttaqī l-Hindī, *op. cit.*, xv, 264, No. 766; Ibn Ḥajar, *al-Iṣāba*, iii, 456, No. 8194.
109 Anonymous, *al-Dhakhīra wa-kashf al-tauqī'*, fol. 52a.
110 Ibn Wahb, *op. cit.*, 11, lines 4–6.
111 Ibn Ḥajar, *al-Iṣāba*, iii, 457–8, Nos. 8103–4.
112 Ma'mar b. Rāshid, *op. cit.*, xi, 43, No. 19862; al-Muttaqī l-Hindī, *op. cit.*, xv, 290, No. 819.
113 Ibn al-Kalbī, *al-Jamhara*, fol. 48b.
114 *Ibid*, fol. 166b.
115 Ibn Qudāma al-Maqdisī, *al-Istibṣār*, 326.
116 Ibn 'Abd al-Barr, *op. cit.*, 173, No. 196; Nūr al-Dīn al-Haythamī, *op. cit.*, viii, 51; al-Jīlānī, *op. cit.*, ii, 302–3, Nos. 829–30; Ibn Sa'd, *op. cit.*, vi, 50; al-Muttaqī l-Hindī, *op. cit.*, xv, 272, No. 782; Ibn Ḥajar, *al-Iṣāba*, i, 159, No. 704.
117 Ibn Ḥajar, *al-Iṣāba*, iii, 415, No. 7966; Nūr al-Dīn al-Haythamī, *op. cit.*, viii, 54.
118 Ibn Wahb, *op. cit.*, 6, lines 5–8; 10, lines 14–17; Ibn Ḥajar, *al-Iṣāba*, ii, 385, No. 5047.
119 Anonymous, *History of prophets*, Ms.Br.Mus., Or. 1510, fol. 181b; Ibn 'Abd al-Barr, *op. cit.*, 921, No. 1561; Ibn Ḥajar, *al-Iṣāba*, ii, 320, No. 4725; al-Fasawī, *op. cit.*, fol. 134a inf.; Ibn 'Asākir, *op. cit.*, vii, 443.
120 Ibn Ḥajar, *al-Iṣāba*, ii, 370, No. 4957.
121 Al-Ḥākim, *Ma'rifat 'ulūm al-ḥadīth*, ed. Mu'aẓẓam Ḥusayn, Cairo 1937, 101; Nūr al-Dīn al-Haythamī, *op. cit.*, viii, 53.
122 Ibn 'Abd al-Barr, *op. cit.*, 685; Ibn Ḥajar, *al-Iṣāba*, ii, 58, No. 3335.

named by the Prophet Maryam.[123] The slave Fatḥ was granted the name Sirāj, because he made light in the mosque of the Prophet.[124] A baby born on the day of a battle fought by the Prophet was called by him Sinān (= spear head).[125]

Scholars of *ḥadīth* discuss vigorously a special group of names given to slaves and servants. The Prophet is said to have forbidden, or intended to forbid, the names of Rabāḥ, Yasār, Najīḥ, Aflaḥ, Nāfi', al-'Alā', Ya'lā and the female names Baraka and Barra.[126] The reason given for it is that if a person asks about a servant whose name denotes success, good luck or blessing and the servant is not there, he may have a feeling of disappointment and failure.

Recommended names were Yazīd, al-Ḥārith and Hammām. These names might be called "neutral ones". In the explanation given for these names the traditions point out that everybody increases (*yazīdu*) in good or bad (deeds), that everybody tills (*yaḥruthu*) for his affairs in this world and in the next one and that everybody cares (*yahtammu*) for his affairs in this world and in the next one.[127] Al-Ḥārith and Hammām are called by the Prophet "*aṣdaqu l-asmā',*" "names most truthful." A recommended name was Ḥamza.[128] The Prophet granted

123 Nūr al-Dīn al-Haythamī, *op. cit.*, VIII, 55.

124 Ibn 'Abd al-Barr, *op. cit.*, 683, No. 1131; Ibn Ḥajar, *al-Iṣāba,* II, 18, No. 3103.

125 Ibn 'Abd al-Barr, *op. cit.*, 657, No. 1071.

126 Nūr al-Dīn al-Haythamī, *op. cit.*, VIII, 50; Ibn Mājah, *op. cit.*, I, 405; Abū Dāwūd, *op. cit.*, II, 308; al-Jīlānī, *op. cit.*, II, 305, No. 834; al-Bayhaqī, *al-Sunan*, IX, 306 ('Umar also intended to forbid, but later refrained); al-Samarqandī, *op. cit.*, 157; al-Munāwī, *op. cit.*, VI, 349, No. 9562; 402, No. 9799; Yūsuf b. Mūsā al-Ḥanafī, *op. cit.*, II, 206; al-Mundhirī, *op. cit.*, IV, 140, No. 2893; al-Sha'rānī, *op. cit.*, 755. On Barra changed into Zaynab or Juwayriya see: Ibn 'Abd al-Barr, *op. cit.*, 1805, No. 3282; 1849, No. 3355; 1855, No. 3361; 1915–6, No. 4099 (changed into Maymūna); Ibn Wahb, *op. cit.*, 8, lines 6–7; al-Jīlānī, *op. cit.*, II, 294, No. 821; 303, No. 831; al-Qasṭallānī, *op. cit.*, IX, 112; al-'Aynī, *op. cit.*, X, 452; Abū Dāwūd, *op. cit.*, II, 307; al-Bayhaqī, *al-Sunan*, IX, 307; al-Mundhirī, *op. cit.*, IV, 141, Nos. 2897–8; al-Nawawī, *op. cit*, 127 inf.

127 Ibn Wahb, *op. cit.*, 7, lines 7–9.

128 Al-Munāwī, *op. cit.*, IV, 111, No. 4712; Ibn Wahb, *op. cit.*, 10, lines 9–11.

a baby the name al-Mundhir (= the warner); [129] a slave was given by him the name 'Āṣim.[130]

*

The close relation between Muḥammad and the former prophets, the idea that Muḥammad continued the mission of the preceding messengers found the expression in the domain of names in the utterances attributed to the Prophet: "Call yourselves by the names of the prophets" (*tasammau bi-asmā'i l-anbiyā'i*) and "the names most liked by God are the names of prophets." [131] Ibn al-Ḥājj stresses that names conforming to the prescriptions of Islam (*al-asmā'u l-shar'iyya*) contain the name of Allah, or (are — K.) the names of prophets or Companions; he points out the blessing (*baraka*) which such names impart.[132] "There is no family, said the Prophet, in which the name of a prophet is carried by one of its members to which God, the Exalted and Blessed, does not send an angel in the morning and in the evening to bless them." [133] The Prophet himself gave his child, born from his female-servant Māriya, the name Ibrāhīm.[134] The same name was given by the Prophet to the child born to Abū Mūsā al-Ash'arī.[135] The Prophet changed the name of Yasār b. Ṣurad to Sulaymān b. Ṣurad,[136] and gave the son of 'Abdallah b. Salām the name Yūsuf.[137] Giving the son of Khallād b. Rāfi' the name Yaḥyā, the Prophet remarked: "I shall

129 Al-Jīlānī, *op. cit.*, II, 288, No. 816; al-Bayhaqī, *al-Sunan*, IX, 306; al-Qasṭallānī, *op. cit.*, IX, 111.

130 Nūr al-Dīn al-Haythamī, *op. cit.*, VIII, 54.

131 Al-Jīlānī, *op. cit.*, II, 286, No. 814; Abū Dāwūd, *op. cit.*, II, 307; Ibn Abī Ḥātim, *op. cit.*, II, 312, No. 2451; al-Qasṭallānī, *op. cit.*, IX, 114; al-Nawawī, *op. cit.*, 127.

132 Ibn al-Ḥājj, *op. cit.*, I, 123.

133 Al-Suyūṭī, *al-La'ālī l-maṣnū'a*, I, 100; Ibn al-Ḥājj, *op. cit.*, I, 123.

134 Ibn 'Abd al-Barr, *op. cit.*, 54–61.

135 Al-Jīlānī, *op. cit.*, II, 308, No. 840; al-Qasṭallānī, *op. cit.*, IX, 114 (see the arguments that Abū Mūsā was his *kunya* before his first-born was named Ibrāhīm); al-'Aynī, *op. cit.*, IX, 711; X, 454.

136 Ibn 'Abd al-Barr, *op. cit.*, 650, No. 1056; al-Ṭabarī, *Dhayl al-mudhayyal*, 26, line 12; 73, line 6.

give him a name, by which none was called after Yaḥya b. Zakariyā'." [138]

There were, however, differences in opinion as to whether it is permissible to use name of angels. In a combined tradition the Prophet recommended to give children the names of prophets, but forbade to give them names of angels (*sammū bi-asmā'i l-anbiyā' wa-lā tusammū bi-asmā'i l-malā'ikati*).[139] This opinion was not commonly accepted. Mālik disliked naming children by the names of angels,[140] but Ḥammād b. abī Sulaymān [141] stated that there is nothing objectionable in naming a person Jibrīl or Mīkā'īl.[142]

It is most highly recommended indeed to name the child Muḥammad. He who names his child Muḥammad hoping for blessing by this, both he and the one who got the name will gain Paradise, says an utterance attributed to the Prophet.[143] On the Day of Resurrection the believer bearing the name Aḥmad or Muḥammad will stand up in the Presence of God and God will rebuke him for his sins committed even though he was named by the name of His beloved Muḥammad. The believer will confess his sins and God will order Jibrīl to introduce him to Paradise, as God is ashamed to chastise with the fire of Hell a believer bearing the name Muḥammad.[144] It is highly recommended to name

137 Al-Jīlānī, *op. cit.*, II, 307, No. 838; Ibn Ḥajar, *al-Iṣāba*, III, 671, No. 9375; Ibn 'Abd al-Barr, *op. cit.*, 1590, No. 2827 (the Prophet gave him the *kunya* Abū Ya'qūb).

138 Ibn Ḥajar, *al-Iṣāba*, III, 671, No. 9380; Ibn 'Abd al-Barr, *op. cit.*, 1569, No. 2750.

139 Al-Munāwī, *op. cit.*, IV, 113, No. 4717.

140 Al-Qasṭallānī, *op. cit.*, IX, 111 sup.; and see Ibn al-Ḥājj, *op. cit.*, I, 122 (... mālik: *lā yanbaghī an yusammā l-rajulu bi-yāsīn wa-lā jibrīl wa-lā mahdī*).

141 See on him Ibn Ḥajar, *Tahdhīb al-tahdhīb*, II, 16, No. 15.

142 Ma'mar b. Rāshid, *op. cit.*, XI, 40, No. 19850.

143 Al-Ṣāliḥī, *op. cit.*, I, 509; al-Jarrāḥī, *op. cit.*, II, 284, No. 2644; Ibn Qayyim al-Jauziyya, *al-Manār al-munīf fī l-ṣaḥīḥ wa-l-ḍa'īf*, ed. 'Abd al-Fattāḥ Ghudda, Ḥalab 1390/1970, 61, No. 94; and see *ibid*, No. 93.

144 Ibn al-Ḥājj, *op. cit.*, I, 123.

one of the children in the family Muḥammad and to treat the child named by this name with due respect.[145]

Goldziher quotes in his article, *"Gesetzliche Bestimmungen..."* a phrase from Ibn Qutayba's *al-Maʿārif*, according to which ʿUmar intended to change the names of all the Muslims to those of prophets. If this were true, it would mean that we have here a continuation and a deepening of the Muslim trend expounded in the saying of the Prophet when he named his child Ibrāhīm: "I named him with the name of my father (i.e. ancestor) Ibrāhīm." The passage referred to (as quoted by Goldziher) runs as follows: *arāda* (i.e. ʿUmar) *an yughayyira asmāʾa l-muslimīna bi-asmāʾi l-anbiyāʾi.*[146] The reading of Wüstenfeld was, however, erroneous and Goldziher was misled by this reading. The correct reading is: *arāda an yughayyira asmāʾa l-musammayna bi-asmāʾi l-anbiyāʾi* "He wanted to alter the names of these who were called by the names of prophets."

ʿUmar tried indeed to carry out his plan. Ibrāhīm b. al-Ḥārith b. Hishām entered the court of ʿUmar "at the time when he wanted to alter the names of those who were called by the names of the prophets" and he changed his name to ʿAbd al-Raḥmān b. al-Ḥārith.[147] ʿUmar changed the name of Mūsā b. Saʿīd to ʿAbd al-Raḥmān b. Saʿīd.[148] When ʿUmar heard how the son of his nephew, Muḥammad b. ʿAbd al-Raḥmān b. Zayd b. al-Khaṭṭāb was slandered by a person, who repeatedly abused his name Muḥammad, he vowed not to have the Prophet Muḥammad being abused through the name of the son of his nephew anymore; he thereupon changed his name to ʿAbd al-Raḥmān.[149]

The action of ʿUmar seems to have been wider in scope than the

145 Al-Munāwī, *op. cit.*, I, 385, Nos. 705–6; VI, 237, No. 9084; and see Ibn Abī Ḥātim, *op. cit.*, II, 299, No. 2410.

146 Goldziher, *Gesetzliche Bestimmungen*, 256.

147 Ibn Saʿd, *op. cit.*, V, 6; Ibn Ḥajar, *al-Iṣāba*, III, 66, No. 6199; see Stowasser-Freyer, *op. cit.*, *Der Islam*, 42(1965), 29.

148 Ibn Saʿd, *op. cit.*, V, 51.

149 See Ibn Ḥajar, *al-Iṣāba*, III, 69, No. 6211; Ibn Saʿd, *op. cit.*, V, 50; al-ʿAynī, *op. cit.*, VII, 143; Ibn Ḥajar, *Fatḥ al-bārī*, X, 435.

mere changing of some names of persons called by the names of prophets. 'Umar is reported to have written to the people of al-Kūfa and ordered them not to name their children by the names of prophets; he also ordered "a group of people" at Medina to change the names of their children called Muḥammad. They argued that the Prophet permitted them to call their children by this name, and 'Umar let them. Al-'Aynī argues that the reason for 'Umar's action was the case of abusing Muḥammad, the bearer of the name of the Prophet; he states that the consensus of the community has been established, that it is permitted to give children names of prophets.[150] Who was "the group" who were called by the names of prophets, can be gauged from a very short report, recorded by Ibn Ḥajar about the attempt of 'Umar to change names of prophets and the name of Muḥammad as well. He summoned the sons of Ṭalḥa, ordering them to change their names. Muḥammad b. Ṭalḥa, the first born, answered that is was the Prophet who had named him Muḥammad; 'Umar had to admit that he could not do anything against him. Ibn Ḥajar concludes that 'Umar withdrew from his plan.[151] The names of the sons of Ṭalḥa bear clear evidence for the tendency to name children by names of prophets in the earliest period of Islam. Ṭalḥa had nine children and he gave them the following names: Muḥammad, 'Imrān, Mūsā, Ya'qūb, Ismā'īl, Isḥāq, 'Īsā, Zakariyyā', Yaḥyā.[152] It is not surprising to read in a remarkable story how Ṭalḥa in a talk with al-Zubayr prided himself with the names of his sons. "The names of my sons are names of prophets," he said; "the names of your sons are names of martyrs." "I hope that my sons will become martyrs," said al-Zubayr, "while you don't have hopes that your sons will become prophets." [153] This anecdote points

150 Al-'Aynī, *op. cit.*, VII, 143; X, 449 inf.; cf. Ibn Ḥajar, *Fatḥ al-bārī*, X, 435, 440; al-Qasṭallānī, *op. cit.*, IX, 110 inf.–111 sup.

151 Ibn Ḥajar, *Fatḥ al-bārī*, X, 435, lines 21–2.

152 See Muṣ'ab b. 'Abdallah, *op. cit.*, 281 seq.; Ibn Ḥazm, *Jamharat ansāb al-'arab*, ed. Levi-Provençal, Cairo 1948, 129 (and see the list of the sons of Ibrāhīm b. Muḥammad b. Ṭalḥa: Ya'qūb, Ṣāliḥ, Sulaymān, Yūnus, Dāwūd, al-Yasa', Shu'ayb, Hārūn — Muṣ'ab, *op. cit.*, 285; Ibn Ḥazm, *op. cit.*, 129).

153 Ibn Ḥajar, *Fatḥ al-bārī*, X, 440.

clearly to the importance which was attached to the names in early Islam and to the diverging opinions about this subject.

The alleged intervention of 'Umar is justified by 'Umar's care in respecting these names and preventing them from being tarnished. The real reason seems, however, to be quite different. We gain a deeper insight into the motives of 'Umar from a significant passage recorded by Ibn Wahb. A female servant (*muwallada*) came to 'Umar asking for a garment for herself. When asked who her *maulā* was, she said: Abū 'Īsā, the son of 'Umar. 'Umar ordered to bring his son, beat him and said: "Do you know what the names of Arabs are? They are: 'Āmir, 'Uwaymir, Mālik, Ṣurma, Muwaylik, Sidra and Murra." He repeated this three times and finally said: "Leave 'Īsā! By God, we do not know of 'Īsā having a father." [154] The parallel passage, recorded by Ibn Abī l-Ḥadīd gives the name of 'Umar's son: 'Ubaydullah b. 'Umar. 'Umar counts, beating him, the *kunyas* of the Arabs: Abū Salama, Abū Ḥanẓala, Abū 'Urfuṭa and Abū Murra.[155]

Needless to recall that the list of names recommended by 'Umar contains names disapproved of by the Prophet, like Murra, Ṣurma, Ḥanẓala and Mālik. It is evident that this story ascribed to 'Umar reflects a reaction against the naming of children by the foreign names of prophets. The story affords an insight into the struggle between the effort of introducing Biblical elements already present in the Qur'ān, and later developed in the *ḥadīth*, into the sphere of name-giving in Muslim society against the opposition of conservative groups among the Arabs, who persevered in their resistance to this new pietistic trend. It is not surprising that this idea is expressed as coming from the mouth of 'Umar, the representative of Arab conservatism, as is evident from his famous saying: *ikhshaushinū wa-tama'dadū*.[156]

*

154 Ibn Wahb, *op. cit.*, 7, lines 15 — 8, line 5.

155 Ibn Abī l-Ḥadīd, *op. cit.*, XII, 44.

156 Al-Ṭabarī, *Dhayl al-mudhayyal*, 78 (attributed to the Prophet); Ibn Durayd, *op. cit.*, 31 (traced back to 'Umar); al-Sakhāwī, *al-Maqāṣid*, 163, No. 348; Ibn 'Asākir, *op. cit.*, VII, 349; al-Ṣāliḥī, *op. cit.*, I, 346.

The old ways of naming children and the Jāhilī names themselves persisted in Bedouin society. The statement of J. J. Hess that names containing the name of Allah and these of specific Islamic nature like Aḥmad, Ṭāhā etc. were almost wholly missing in the material examined by him, is instructive.[157] Unpleasant names were, like in the Jāhiliyya, reserved for children of free Bedouin, while pretty names were given to slaves.[158] It is noteworthy that the explanation for this practice given by the shaykh of the 'Oneze ("The names of our slaves are for us, our names are for our enemies") corresponds exactly to the answer given by al-'Utbī to Abū Ḥātim al-Sijistānī.[159] Accordingly one can find in the list of names supplied by Hess, slaves named Yāqūt, Mabrūk, Mubashshir, Sa'īd, and names like Ghurāb, Barghūth, Juway'il, Juraydhī, Jukhaydib, Juḥaysh, Jarbū', Shubaytha, Qurāda, Hijris borne by free Bedouin. The names disliked in Islam, like Murra, Kalb, Mālik and Ḥarb, are recorded in the list of Hess as names of free Bedouin. Names given according to the place, time or conditions of birth of the children[160] are reminiscent of similar cases in the Jāhiliyya.[161] As in the Jāhiliyya, children are called Julaymid, Fihrān, Fahra and Ḥajar,[162] and sometimes several children are called by their father by names derived from the same root.[163]

These vestiges of the Jāhiliyya, which can be traced in Bedouin society, clearly underline the considerable changes and developments which took place in Muslim society.

157 J. J. Hess, *Beduinennamen aus Zentralarabien*, Sitzungsberichte der Heidelberger Akademie der Wissenschaften, Philosophisch-historische Klasse, Heidelberg 1912 (III, 19), 4.
158 Hess, *op. cit.*, 7 ("6").
159 Hess, *op. cit.*, 7; Ibn Durayd, *op. cit.*, 4 (and see n. 54 above).
160 Hess, *op. cit.*, 6–7.
161 See e.g. Ibn al-Kalbī, *Jamhara*, fol. 95a; Ibn Durayd, *op. cit.*, 6–7.
162 See e.g. Ibn Durayd, *op. cit.*, 5, penult.
163 Hess, *op. cit.*, 7 ("8"); cf. e.g. Ibn al-Kalbī, *Jamhara*, fol. 175b, line 1 (Khushayn, Khashin, Mukhāshin, Khashshān); fol. 154a, (Mu'attib, 'Attāb, 'Itbān); fol. 107b (Hāshim, Hishām, Hushaym, Muhashshim); Ibn Durayd, *op. cit.*, 166 (al-'Āṣ, Abū l-'Āṣ, al-'Īṣ, Abū l-'Īṣ, 'Uwayṣ — the sons of Umayya, called al-A'yāṣ).

ADDITIONAL NOTES

ad note 4: Abū Nu'aym, *Ḥilyat al-auliyā' wa-ṭabaqāt al-aṣfiyā', Beirut 1387/1967, IX, 58 ult.-59 l.1 ; and see Aḥmad b. Muḥammad al-'Allāmī al-Ḥanafī, Kitāb al-karāhiya*, MS. Hebrew Univ., Yah. Ar. 335, fol. 16 a, inf.

ad note 6: al-Māwardī, *al-Amthāl wa-l-ḥikam*, MS. Leiden Or. 655 (2), fol. 68b.

ad note 8: al-Zubayr b. Bakkār, *Jamharat nasabi quraysh wa-akhbārihā*, MS. Bodleiana, Marsh 384, fol. 111a ; Ibn Ḥajar, *al-Iṣāba*, ed. 'Alī Muḥammad al-Bijāwī, Cairo 1392/1972, IV, 325, no. 5154.

ad note 12: Ibn Ḥajar, *al-Iṣāba*, IV, 50, no. 4609 ; *Ibid.*, IV, 373, no. 5238, s. v. 'Abd Ruḍā [and see the comment of Ibn Ḥajar: *qultu anā: fa-astab'idu an yakūna l-nabiyyu* [ṣallā llāhu 'alayhi wa-sallam] *lam yughayyir ismahu l-madhkūr*. And see *Ibid.*, IV, 374, no. 5241, s. v. 'Abd Shams: *wa-anā astab'idu an yakūna l-nabiyyu* [ṣallā llāhu 'alayhi wa-sallam] *lam yughayyir ismahu kamā ghayyara sma samiyyihi, wa-huwa abū ẓabyān al-a'raj...* ; al-Shabrakhītī, *Sharḥ 'alā l-arba'īna ḥadīth* [!] *al-nawawiyya*, Beirut n. d., p. 131 ['Abd Shams changed into 'Abd al-Raḥmān] ; al-Bukhārī, *al-Ta'rīkh al-kabīr*, Hyderabad 1378/1959, VI [=III/2], 133, no. 1938.

ad note 14: Muṣ'ab b. 'Abdallah al-Zubayrī, *Nasab quraysh*, ed. Levi-Provencal, Cairo 1953, p. 274.

ad note 15: al-Ṭabarānī, *al-Mu'jam al-kabīr*, ed. Ḥamdī 'Abd al-Majīd al-Silafī, n. p. 1397, I, 126, no. 253 ; Ibn Ḥajar, *al-Iṣāba*, IV, 326, no. 5155.

ad note 17: al-Ṭabarānī, *al-Mu'jam al-kabīr*, II, 275, no. 2155 ad note 18: Ibn Ḥajar, *al-Iṣāba*, IV, 160, no. 4803 ; Ibn Qayyim al-Jauziyya, *Tuḥfat al-maudūd bi-ahkāmi l-maulūd*, Beirut n. d., p. 90.

ad note 19: al-Ṭabarānī, *al-Mu'jam al-kabīr*, I, 26, no. 254 ; Muṣ'ab, *Nasab quraysh*, p. 265.

ad note 20: al-Zubayr b. Bakkār, *Jamhara*, MS. Bodleiana, fol. 140 b.

ad note 22: Muṣ'ab b. 'Abdallah, *Nasab quraysh*, p. 317 ; Anonymous, *al-Ta'rīkh al-muḥkam fī man intasaba ilā l-nabiyyi ṣallā llāhu 'alayhi wa-sallam*, MS. Br. Library, Or. 8653, fol. 148 a, ult. ; Ibn Ḥajar, *al-Iṣāba*, I, 303, no. 671 [Baḥīrā changed into Bashīr].

ad note 24: al-Suyūṭī, *Jam' al-jawāmi'*, Cairo 1978, II, 531.

ad note 25: Ibn Qayyim al-Jauziyya, *Tuḥfat al-maudūd*, p. 93 ; and see *ib.* names of other *shayāṭīn*: Ḥubāb, Khinzib, al-Walhān, al-A'war and al-Ajda'.

ad note 26: al-Munāwī, *Fayḍ al-qadīr*, III, 402, no. 3779 ; al-Ṭabarī, *Tafsīr*, ed. Shākir, XIV, 392, no. 17029 ; and see note 25.

ad note 28: al-Naḥḥās, *al-Nāsikh wa-l-mansūkh*, Cairo 1357/1938, pp. 82 inf.-83 ; al-Dāraquṭnī, *Sunan*, al-Madīna al-munawwara, 1386/1966, III, 62, no. 236 [and see no. 235] ; Ibn 'Adiyy, *al-Kāmil fī ḍu'afā'i l-rijāl*, Beirut 1405/1985, IV, 1608 ; Ibn Ḥajar, *al-Iṣāba*, III, 44, no. 3124.

ad note 31: 'Abd al-Malik b. Ḥabīb, *al-Ta'rīkh*, MS. Bodleiana, Marsh 288, pp. 22-23 ; al-Shiblī, *Ākām al-marjān fī gharā'ibi l-akhbār wa-aḥkāmi l-jānn*, Cairo 1376, 205-206 ; al-Ṭabarī, *Ta'rīkh al-rusul wa-l-mulūk*, ed. Abū l-Faḍl Ibrāhīm, Cairo 1387/1967, I, 149 ; Isḥāq b. Bishr, *Mubtada' al-dunyā wa-qiṣaṣ al-anbiyā'*, MS. Bodleiana, Huntingdon 388, fols. 69b-72b ; al-Qurṭubī, *Tafsīr*, Cairo 1387/1967, VII, 338 ; Mujāhid, *Tafsīr*, ed. 'Abd al-Raḥmān al-Sūratī, Beirut n. d., I, 252-253.

ad note 34: Ibn Ḥajar, *al-Iṣāba*, VII, 93, no. 9778.

ad note 35: al-Munāwī, *Fayḍ al-qadīr*, VI, 349, no. 9562.

ad note 36: al-Fākihī, *Ta'rīkh makka*, MS. Leiden Or. 463, fol. 471 b.

ad note 38: See Ḥammād b. Isḥāq b. Ismā'īl, *Tarkat al-nabiyyi* [ṣ], ed. Akram Ḍiyā' al-'Umarī, Beirut 1404/1984, p. 96.

ad note 42: al-Munāwī, *Fayḍu l-qadīr*, I, 169, no. 207: *aḥabbu l-asmā'i ilā llāhi mā tu'ubbida lahu wa-aṣdaqu l-asmā'i hammām wa-ḥārith* ; al-Ṭabarānī, *al-Mu'jam al-kabīr*, X, 89, no. 9992.

ad note 43: al-Ābī, *Nathr al-durr*, ed. Muḥammad 'Alī Qarna and 'Alī Muḥammad al-Bijāwī, Cairo 1980, I, 212: *sammū aulādakum asmā'a l-anbiyā'i, wa-aḥsanu l-asmā'i 'abdu llāhi wa-'abdu l-raḥmān wa-aṣdaquhā al-ḥārith wa-hammām wa-aqbaḥuhā ḥarbun wa-murra.* And see a slightly different version in Daylamī's *Firdaus*, MS Chester Beatty 4139, fol. 97a: *aḥabbu l- asmā'i ilā llāhi 'azza wa-jalla 'abdu llāhi wa-'abdu l-raḥmāni wa-aṣdaquhā ḥārith wa-hammām wa-aqbaḥuhā ḥarb wa-murra wa-akdhabuhā khālid wa-mālik* ; Ibn 'Adiyy, *al-Kāmil*, I, 282 ; cf. Aḥmad b. Muḥammad al-'Allāmī, *Kitāb al-karāhiya*, MS. Hebrew Univ., Yah. Ar. 335, fol. 16 a, ult.-16 b. l. 1 ; Ibn Qayyim al-Jauziyya, *Tuḥfat al-maudūd*, p. 89. And see a list of the disagreeable names prohibited by the Prophet: Ibn 'Adiyy, *al-Kāmil*, I, 325. 'Alūn, Ḥamdūn, Ya'mūsh were stated by the Prophet to be names of Satans ; he forbade also to call children by names including the diphthong *awh* or *way*. The Prophet enjoined as well in this utterance not to use diminutives of names like *musayjid* or *muṣayḥif*.

ad note 47: al-Mu'āfā, *al-Jalīsu l-ṣāliḥ*, MS. fol. 58a, inf.

ad note 48: al-Bayhaqī, *al-Sunan al-kubrā*, X, 145 ; Ibn Ḥajar, *al-Iṣāba*, III, 116 ; al-Daylamī, *Firdaus*, MS. Chester Beatty 3037, fol. 186 b, inf. ; Ibn Qayyim al-Jauziyya, *Tuḥfat al-maudūd*, p. 99 ; Aḥmad b. Muḥammad al-'Allāmī, *Kit. al-karāhiya*, MS. Yah. 335, fol. 16 b. sup.

ad note 50: Ibn Qayyim al-Jauziyya, *Tuḥfat al-maudūd*, p. 99.

ad note 53: Aḥmad b. Muḥammad al-'Allāmī, *Kit. al-karāhiya*, MS. Yah. Ar. 335, fol. 16 b. [Abū 'Isā forbidden]

4

ad note 54: Ibn Sa'd, *Ṭabaqāt*, V, 287 [Ibn 'Abbās used to call his slaves, *'abīd*, by Arab names: 'Ikrima, Sumay', Kurayb] ; al-Diyārbakrī, *Ta'rīkh al-khamīs*, Cairo 1283, I, 153 ; Daḥlān, *al-Sīra al-nabawiyya*, Cairo 1310, I, 8 sup.

ad note 55: al-Daylamī, *Firdaus*, MS. Chester Beatty 4139, fol. 11b. ; and see the complaint of Shu'ayb b. 'Abd al-Raḥmān in Ibn 'Asākir, *Tahdhīb ta'rīkh*, Beirut 1399/1979, VI, 325: "... my father did for me nothing of this kind ; he gave me the name Shu'ayb and handed me over to a tanner [evidently as an apprentice-k] and lodged me in the quarter of the Jews"

ad note 64: Nūr al-Dīn al-Haythamī, *Mawārid al-ẓam'ān ilā zawā'idi bni ḥibbān*, ed. Muḥammad 'Abd al-Razzāq Ḥamza, Cairo n. d., p. 346, no. 1429.

ad note 68: See Ibn Qayyim, *Tuḥfat al-maudūd*, p. 94.

ad note 70: al-Munāwī, *Fayḍ*, VI, 349, no. 9562 [The Prophet forbade to call men by the names of Ḥarb, Walīd, Murra, al-Ḥakam, Abū l-Ḥakam, Aflaḥ, Najīḥ and Yasār ; but see note 78].

ad note 74: al-Diyārbakrī, *Ta'rīkh al-khamīs*, I, 335 ; Ibn Qayyim, *Tuḥfat al-maudūd*, p. 95.

ad note 79: Ibn al-Kalbī, *al-Nasab al-kabīr*, MS. Escorial 1698, p. 523 ult.-524 ; Ibn Ḥazm, *Jamharat ansābi l-'arab*, ed. 'Abd al-Salām Hārūn, Cairo 1382/1962, p. 446 ; Ibn Qayyim, *Tuḥfat al-maudūd*, p. 96.

ad note 80: Ibrāhīm b. Muḥammad al-Ḥusaynī al-Ḥanafī al-Dimashqī, *al-Bayān wa-l-ta'rīf fī asbāb wurūdi l-ḥadīthi l-sharīf*, Beirut 1400/1980, II, 56, no. 629 ; Muḥammad b. al-Qāsim b. Ma'rūf b. Ḥabīb, *Juz' min fawā'id...*, MS. Chester Beatty 3495, fol. 111 b.

ad note 82: Anonymous, *al-Ta'rīkh al-muḥkam*, MS. Br. Mus. Or. 8653, fol. 156 b. ; al-Zamakhsharī, *Rabī'u l-abrār*, II, 336 inf. -337 sup. ; al-'Aynī, *'Umdat al-qārī*, XVI, 290 ; 'Abd al-Mu'min b. Xalaf ad-Dimyāṭī'nin bir Muhācirūn Listesi, ed. Albert Dietrich, *Sarkiyat Mecmuasi*, III, (1959) 143 ; Anonymous, *al-Bilādu llatī sumi'a bihā l-ḥadīth*(?), MS. al-Ẓāhiriyya, majmūʿa 18, fol. 42 a ; Muḥammad b. al-Qāsim, *Juzʾ min fawāʾid...*, MS. Chester Beatty 3495, fol. 111 b. ; Ibn Qayyim, *Tuḥfat al-maudūd*, pp. 95, 102.

ad note 83: Muḥammad b. al-Qāsim b. Maʿrūf, *Juzʿ min fawāʾid...*, MS. Chester Beatty 3495, fol. 111 b.

ad note 84: al-Balādhurī, *Ansāb al-ashrāf*, I, 404 ; al-Majlisī, *Biḥār al-anwār*, CIV, 111 ; al-Daylamī, *Firdaus*, MS. Chester Beatty 3037, fol. 92 a ; Abū Nuʿaym al-Iṣfahānī, *Ḥilyat al-auliyāʾ*, Beirut 1387/1967, II, 275 ; Abū ʿAlī Muḥammad b. al-Qāsim b. Maʿrūf b. Ḥabīb, *Juzʾ*, MS. Chester Beatty 3495, fol. 112 a, inf. ; al-Ṣaffūrī, *Nuzhatu l-majālis wa-muntakhabu l-nafāʾis*, Beirut n. d., p. 477 ; Ibn Bābūyah al-Qummī, *ʿUyūn akhbāri l-riḍā*, Najaf 1390/1970, II, 24-25 ; Muḥammad b. al-Ḥasan b. ʿAlī b. al-Ḥusayn al-Ḥurr al-ʿĀmilī, *al-Jawāhiru l-saniyya fī l-aḥādīthi l-qudsiyya*, Najaf 1384/1964, pp. 238, 243-244, 266 ; Abū Yaʿlā, *Musnad*, ed. Ḥusayn Salīm Asad, Damascus 1409/1988, I, 384 ; Ibn Qayyim al-Jauziyya, *Tuḥfat al-maudūd*, pp. 103-104.

ad note 86: Ibn Ḥajar, *al-Iṣāba*, VI, 228, no. 8259.

ad note 90: Anonymous, *al-Taʾrīkh al-muḥkam*, MS. Br. Mus., fol. 176 b.

ad note 91: read correctly: Ibn Ḥajar, *al-Iṣāba*, IV, 192-193, no. 4850 ; Ibn Qayyim, *Tuḥfat al-maudūd*, p. 103.

ad note 92: Ibn Ḥajar, *al-Iṣāba*, VII, 558-559, no. 1098.

ad note 94: Ibn ʿAbd al-Ḥakam, *Futūḥ miṣr wa-akhbāruhā*, ed. Ch. Torrey, New Haven 1922, p. 275.

ad note 98: Ibn Saʿd, *al-Ṭabaqāt al-kubrā*, VII, 78-79 ; Ibn Qayyim, *Tuḥfat al-maudūd*, p. 102 inf. ; Aḥmad b. Muḥammad al-ʿAllāmī, *Kit. al-karāhiya*, MS. Yah. Ar. 335, fol. 16 b. l.2.

ad note 99: al-Dāraquṭnī, *Sunan*, II, 301, no. 293 ; Anonymous, *al-Ta'rīkh al-muḥkam*, MS. Br. Mus., fol. 158 b, ult.

ad note 106: Cf. Ibn ʿAsakir, *Ta'rīkh (tahdhīb)*, ed. Beirut 1399/1979, III, 270 [Rakham changed into Bashīr]

ad note 111: Aḥmad b. Muḥammad al-ʿAllāmī, *Kit. al-karāhiya*, MS. Yah. Ar. 335, fol. 16 b., l. 2.

ad note 119: al-Dhahabī, *Siyar a'lāmi l-nubalā'*, ed. Ibrāhīm al-Abyārī, II, Cairo 1957, p. 297 l.1

ad note 121: al-Ṭabarānī, *al-Muʿjam al-kabīr*, II, 25, no. 1173.

ad note 122: Mughulṭāy, *al-Zahr al-bāsim*, MS. Leiden, Or. 370, fol. 224 a.

ad note 126: See the various traditions about the changes which the Prophet planned to introduce in the names: Ibn Qayyim al-Jauziyya, *Tuḥfat al-maudūd*, pp. 91-93: the names mentioned are: Yasār, Rabāḥ, Najāḥ, Aflaḥ, Nāfiʿ, Yaʿlā, Baraka, Najīḥ and Barra. All these names were given mainly to slaves and clients. And see the comprehensive discussion of this subject and the arguments of the scholars in Ṭabarī's *Tahdhīb al-āthār*, ed. Maḥmūd Muḥammad Shākir, Cairo 1403/1982, I-2, [Musnad ʿumar b. al-khaṭṭāb] pp. 274-288, nos. 441-457 ; al-Suyūṭī, *Jamʿ al-jawāmiʿ*, I, 637, 892 [the names discussed are: Rabāḥ, Yasār, Aflaḥ, Nāfiʿ, Najīḥ] and I, 1266 [Nāfiʿ Baraka and Yasār] ; Ibn Abī Shayba, *al-Muṣannaf*, VIII, 478, no. 5957 ; al-Ṭaḥāwī, *Mushkil al-āthār*, II, 302-305 [Rabāḥ, Aflaḥ, Yasār, Yusr, ʿAlā', Nāfiʿ, Baraka] ; al-Daylami, *Firdaus*, MS. Chester Beatty 3037, fol. 189 [Aflaḥ, Najīḥ, Yasār]. Aḥmad b. Muḥammad al-ʿAllāmī, *Kit. al-karāhiya*, MS. Yah. Ar. 335, fol. 16 b., ll. 3-4 ; Sulaymān b. Dāwūd al-Saqsīnī, *Zahrat al-riyāḍ wa-nuzhat al-qulūb al-mirāḍ*, MS. Hebrew Univ., Yah. Ar. 571, p. 46 [against naming of servants Khayr, Bishr and Muqbil]

Ibn Qayyim a-Jauziyya records in his *Aḥkām ahli l-dhimma* [ed. Ṣubḥī al-Ṣāliḥ, Damascus 1381/1961, II, 768-769] a list of names by which it is forbidden to call the *ahl al-dhimma*, like: Muḥammad, Aḥmad, Abū Bakr, ʿUthmān, ʿAlī, Ṭalḥa and al-Zubayr ; they are permitted to call themsevels Jirjis, Buṭrus, Yuḥannā, Mattā and the like, while Muslims are prohibited to call themselves by these names in order not to assimilate themselves to the *ahl al-dhimma* ; names shared by Muslims and the *ahl al-dhimm*a are: Yaḥyā, ʿIsā, Ayyūb, Dāwūd, Sulaymān, Zayd, ʿUmar {?}, ʿAbdallah, ʿAṭiyya, Mauhūb, Salām and the like.

ad note 128: See the answer of the Prophet when consulted about the nicest name for a newborn baby as recorded by Ibn ʿAsākir in his *Ta'rikh* [*tahdhīb*], VII, 327, inf.: ...*inna khayra asmāʾikum al-ḥārith wa-hammām wa-niʿma l-ismu ʿabdu llāh wa-ʿabd al-raḥmān wa-sammū bi-asmāʾi l-malāʾikati. qāla: wa-bi-ismika ? qāla: wa-bi-smī, wa-lā tukannu bi-kunyatī.*

ad note 140: A humourous story reports that ʿUmar heard a man addressing a person by "Dhū Qarnayn" and said: Have you gone through all the names of the prophets so that you can ascend to those of angels? [*a-faraghtum min asmāʾi l-anbiyāʾi fa-rtafaʿtum ilā asmāʾi l-malāʾikati* ?] See: al-Maqrīzī, *Dhikru mā warada fī bunyāni l-kaʿbati l-muʿaẓẓama*, MS. Leiden, Or. 560, fol. 171 a, inf.

ad note 143: Muḥammad Nāṣir al-Dīn al-Albānī, *Silsilat al-aḥādīthi l-ḍaʿīfa wa-l-mauḍūʿa*, Beirut 1405/1985, I, 207–208, no. 171: *man wulida lahu maulūdun fa-sammāhu muḥammadan tabarrukan bihi kāna huwa wa-maulūduhu fī l-janna.* The utterance is marked by al-Albānī as *mauḍūʿ* ; and see Ibn Himmāt al-Dimashqī Shams al-Dīn Abū ʿAbdallah Muḥammad b. Ḥasan, *al-Tankīt wa-l-ifāda fī takhrīj aḥādīth khātimat sifr al-saʿāda*, ed. Aḥmad al-Bazra, Damascus 1407/1987, pp. 21–22: *bāb faḍli l-tasmiyati bi-muḥammad wa-aḥmad: lam yaṣiḥḥa fīhi shayʾun.* Taqiyy al-Dīn al-Ḥarrānī regards all the traditions concerning the virtues of naming the children by these names as *mauḍūʿ* ; and see *ibid.* the discussion of the quoted utterance and the references of the editor.

ad note 144: See the traditions about the virtues of naming the children by the name of Muḥammad: Ibn ʿAdiyy, *al-Kāmil*, I, 172 inf., III, 890, VI, 2107 ; Muḥammad Nāṣir al-Dīn al-Albānī, *Silsilat al-aḥādīth al-ḍaʿīfa wa-l-mauḍūʿa*, I, 435–438, no. 437 [see the references of al-Albānī and the opinions of the quoted scholars] ; al-Thaʿlabī, *al-Kashf wa-l-bayān*, MS. Univ. Tel-Aviv, p. 170 ; Anonymous, *Durr al-waʿiẓīn wa-dhukhr al-ʿābidīn*, MS. Leiden Or. 957, fol. 8 b.: A man devoid of any quality was led to Hell ; God noticed that he bore the name of His beloved,

Muḥammad, and ordered to lead him to Paradise ; and see the opinion of Ibn Himmāt, *al-Tankīt*, pp. 22-24 [and see the references supplied by the editor].

ad note 145: See Ibn Himmāt, *al-Tankīt*, p. 22, sup. [and see the references of the editor].

ad note 149: See Ibn Himmāt, *al-Tankīt*, p. 22 [and see the references of the editor].

ad note 154: See al-Fasawī, *al-Ma'rifa wa-l-ta'rīkh*, I, 460-461. A divergent tradition recorded by al-Balādhurī, *Ansāb al-ashrāf*, MS. fol. 1199 b says that the Prophet granted al-Mughīra b. Shu'ba the *kunya* Abū 'Isā. Mūsā b. Ṭalḥa was also given by the Prophet the *kunya* Abū 'Isā ; see Ibn Ḥajar, *al-Iṣāba*, III, 481, no. 8338.

ad note 156: Nūr al-Dīn al-Haythamī, *Majma' al-zawā'id*, V, 136 ; al-Ṭaḥāwī, *Sharḥ ma'ānī l-āthār*, IV, 275 ; al-Mu'āfā b. 'Imrān, *Kitāb al-zuhd*, MS. Ẓāhiriyya, ḥadīth 359, fol. 259 b ; Aḥmad b.'Abdallah al-Samdī al-Nazwī, *al-Muṣannaf*, ed. 'Abd al-Mun'im 'Āmir and Jādallah Aḥmad, 'Umān 1979, II, 55 ; Ibn al-Jauzī, *Manāqib 'umara bni l-khaṭṭāb*, ed. Zaynab Ibrāhīm al-Qārūṭ, Beirut 1402/1982, p. 128.

XIII

On 'Concessions' and Conduct
A Study in Early *Ḥadīth*

Traditions about early ritual practices and customs reported on the authority of the Prophet, of his Companions (*ṣaḥāba*) or their Successors (*tābiʿūn*) are often divergent and even contradictory. Early compilations of *ḥadīth* occasionally record these traditions in separate chapters with headings which point out their differences; they also enumerate the scholars who held these divergent views. So, for example, the chapter *Man kāna yutimmu l-takbīr* is followed by the chapter *Man kāna lā yutimmu l-takbīr* ; the chapter *Man qāla laysa ʿalā man nāma sājidan wa-qāʿidan wuḍuʾ* is followed by *Man kāna yaqūlu idhā nāma fa-l-yatawaḍḍaʾ*. Traditions arranged under headings *Man kariha* ... followed by *Man rakhkhaṣa fī* ... are of a similar type. It is obvious that these diverse traditions reflect differences in the opinions of various circles of Muslim scholars and indicate that in the early period of Islam many ritual prescriptions were not yet firmly established.

The *rukhaṣ* or "concessions," i.e., the changes in ritual prescriptions designed to soften their harshness, were indeed an efficient tool in adapting the prescriptions to the real conditions of life and its changing circumstances. They established practices that were in keeping with the new ideas of Islam. Yet it is evident that the concession, *rukhṣa*, had to acquire authoritative sanction and legitimacy; this could be achieved only through an utterance of the Prophet. As a matter of fact, the following *ḥadīth* is attributed to the Prophet: "Truly, God desires that His concessions be carried out [just] as He desires His injunctions to be observed" (*inna llāha yuḥibbu an tu'tā rukhaṣuhu kamā yuḥibbu an tu'tā 'azā'imuhu).*[1] This tradition was interpreted in manifold ways. According to one interpretation it implies a whole view of life; al-Shaybānī (died 189/805) states that the believer who restricts himself to the most basic means of subsistence acts according to the prescriptions, whereas pleasant life and delights are for him a concession, a *rukhṣa*.[2] The purchase of the arable *kharāj* land in Iraq by Muslims was approved by 'Umar b. 'Abd al-'Azīz on the ground of a *rukhṣa* interpretation of a Qur'ānic verse; grants of land in the Sawād, given to Muslims, were also based on *rukhṣa* precedents.[3]

---

1 'Abd al-Razzāq, *al-Muṣannaf*, ed. Ḥabīb al-Raḥmān al-A'ẓamī (Beirut: 1392/1972), 11: 291, no. 20569 (=*Jāmi'* Ma'mar b. Rāshid: ... *an yu'mala bi-rukhaṣihi*); Ibn Balbān, *al-Iḥsān fī taqrib ṣaḥīḥi bni Ḥibbān*, MS. Br. Mus., Add. 27519, fol. 90a; al-Suyūṭī, *al-Durr al-manthūr fī l-tafsīr bi-l-ma'thūr* (Cairo: 1314), 1: 193; Abū Nu'aym, *Ḥilyat al-awliyā'* (Beirut: 1387/1967, reprint), 6: 191 inf., 276, 2: 101 inf. (... *an tuqbala rukhaṣuhu*); al-Māwardī, *al-Amthāl wa-l-ḥikam*, MS Leiden, Or. 655, fol. 87b (... *an yu'khadha bi-rukhaṣihi kamā yuḥibbu an yu'khadha bi-farā'iḍihi*), al-Mundhirī, *al-Targhīb wa-l-tarhīb*, ed. Muḥammad Muḥyī l-Dīn 'Abd al-Ḥamīd (Cairo: 1279/1960), 2: 261, no. 1541 (and see ibid. no. 1539: ... *an tu'tā rukhaṣuhu kamā yakrahu an tu'tā ma'ṣiyatuhu* ; another version: ... *kamā yuḥibbu an tutraka ma'ṣiyatuhu*); al-Munāwī, *Fayḍ al-qadīr, sharḥ al-jāmi' al-ṣaghīr* (Beirut: 1391/1972), 2: 292, no. 1879, 293, no. 1881 (... *an tuqbala rukhaṣuhu kamā yuḥibbu l-'abdu maghfirat rabbihi* ; 2: 296, no. 1894: ... *Kamā yakrahu an tu'tā ma'ṣiyatuhu*); al-Daylamī, *Firdaws al-akhbār*, Chester Beatty 4139, fol. 53a; al-Khaṭīb al-Baghdādī, *Mūḍiḥ awhām al-jam' wa-l-tafrīq* (Hyderbad: 1379/1960), 2: 10 (... *an tu'tā mayāsiruhu kamā yuḥibbu an tu'tā 'azā'imuhu*); cf. al-Kulaynī *al-Kāfī*, ed. Najm al-Dīn al-Āmulī (Tehran: 1388), 1: 208–209, no. 4.

2 al-Shaybānī, *al-Iktisāb fī l-rizqi l-mustaṭāb*, Talkhīṣ Muḥammad b. Samā'a, ed. Maḥmud 'Arnūs (Cairo: 1357/1938), p. 81: ... *fa-ṣāra l-ḥāṣilu anna l-iqtiṣāra 'alā adnā mā yakfīhi 'aẓīmatun, wa-mā zāda 'alā dhālika min al-tana''umi wa-l-nayli min al-ladhdhāti rukhṣatun, wa-qāla ṣallā llāhu 'alayhi wa-sallam: inna llāha yuḥibbu an yu'tā bi-rukhaṣihi* ....

3 Abū 'Ubayd, *Kitāb al-amwāl*, ed. Muḥammad Ḥāmid al-Fiqī (Cairo: 1353), pp. 84–85; cf. al-Bayhaqī, *al-Sunan al-kubrā* (Hyderabad: 1356), 9: 140–1: "... *bāb man kariha shirā'a arḍi l-kharāj* ..." And see the traditions against buying of *kharāj* land: Ibn Zanjawayh, *al-Amwāl*, MS. Burdur 183, fols.

The Prophet is said to have denied believers permission to enter baths, but later granted them a *rukhṣa* to enter them, provided they wore loincloths, *ma'āzir*.[4] There were in fact two contradictory attitudes in the matter of baths: the one disapproving[5] and the other

---

29a–32a (and see e.g. ibid., fol. 30a, inf., "... *sami'a l-ḥasana yaqūlu: man khala'a ribqata mu'āhidin fa-ja'alahā fī 'unuqihi fa-qad istaqāla hijratahu wa-wallā l-islāma ẓahrahu wa-man aqarra bi-shay'in min al-jizyati fa-qad aqarra bi-bābin min abwābi l-kufri*").

4 al-Shawkānī, *Nayl al-awṭār, sharḥ muntaqā l-akhbār min aḥādīthi sayyidi l-akhyār* (Cairo: 1372/1953), 1: 299; Ibn Abī Shayba, *al-Muṣannaf*, ed. 'Abd al-Khāliq Khān al-Afghānī (Hyderabad: 1386/1966), 1: 109–110; 'Abd al-Razzāq, 1: 290–296, nos. 1116–1136; al-Fākihī, *Ta'rīkh Makka*, MS. Leiden Or. 463, fol. 412a; al-Mundhirī, 1: 118–122, nos. 267–278; al-Sharīshī, *Sharḥ maqāmāt al-Ḥarīrī*, ed. Muḥammad 'Abd al-Mun'im Khafājī (Cairo: 1372/1952), 3: 74; al-Muttaqī l-Hindī, *Kanz al-'ummāl* (Hyderabad: 1381/1962), 9: 231–234, nos. 1978–2010; cf. al-Ḥākim, *Ma'rifat 'ulūm al-ḥadīth*, ed. Mu'aẓẓam Ḥusayn (Cairo: 1937), p. 98.

5 See e.g. al-Munāwī, 2: 54, no. 1311: "... *uffin li-l-ḥammām* ..." enjoins husbands to forbid their wives to enter baths, stresses the filthiness of their water and confines the entrance of men to those wearing the *ma'āzir* ; cf. al-Ṭayālisī, *Musnad* (Hyderabad: 1321), p. 212, no. 1518: 'Ā'isha reproaches the women from Ḥims for entering baths. And see Nūr al-Dīn al-Haythamī, *Majma' al-zawā'id wa-manba' al-fawā'id* (Beirut: 1967, reprint), 1: 277–278 (the prohibition for women to enter baths; and see ibid., p. 114: the bath is the abode of the Devil); al-Ṭabarī, *Dhayl al-mudhayyal* (Cairo: 1353/1934), 10: 246; al-Dhahabī, *Mīzān al-i'tidāl*, ed. 'Alī Muḥammad al-Bajāwī (Cairo: 1382/1963), 3: 631, no. 7889; al-Daylamī, MS. Chester Beatty 3037, fol. 90b (the prohibition to enter baths by women is preceded by a prediction of the Prophet that the Muslims will conquer the lands of the *'ajam* and will find there "buildings called baths"; a concession at the end of the *ḥadīth* is granted to women who are ill, or after confinement). And see al-Kattānī, *Juz'*, MS. Chester Beatty 4483, fol. 9b ("... *bi'sa l-bayt al-ḥammām*"; the Prophet permitted, however, men to enter the bath wearing the *ma'āzir*, after being told of the importance of the bath for the cleanness of the body and the treatment of the sick). Cf. Aḥmad b. Ḥanbal, *al-'Ilal wa-ma'rifat al-rijāl*, ed. Talât Koçyiğit and Ismail Cerrahoğlu (Ankara: 1963), 1: 266, no. 1716 (the prayer in a bath is disliked), 271, no. 1745 ("*al-arḍu kulluhā masjidun illā l-ḥammām wa-l-maqbara*"). And see the story of Ibn 'Umar who was shocked when he saw the naked men in the bath (Ibn Sa'd,

recommending them.[6] Accordingly scholars are divided in their opinion as to whether the water of the bath can be used for ritual washing, *ghusl*, or whether, on the contrary, *ghusl* has to be performed for cleaning oneself from the very water of the bath.[7]

The knowledge of *rukhaṣ* granted by the Prophet is essential for the proper understanding of the faith and its injunctions. The misinterpretation of the verse: "Those who treasure up gold and

---

Ṭabaqāt (Beirut: 1377/1957), 4: 153–154); and see the various Shīʿī traditions in Yūsuf al-Baḥrānī's *al-Ḥadāʾiq al-nāḍira fī aḥkām al-ʿitra al-ṭāhira*, ed. Muḥammad Taqiyy al-Ayrawānī (Nadjaf: 1378), 5: 528–540.

6 See al-Khaṭīb al-Baghdādī, 2: 311, 11.4–5; Ibn al-Sunnī, *ʿAmal al-yawm wa-l-layla* (Hyderabad: 1358), p. 85: "*niʿma l-bayt al-ḥammām yadkhuluhu l-rajulu l-muslim ...*"; al-Daylamī, MS. Chester Beatty 3037, fol. 174b; al-Waṣṣābī al-Ḥabashī, *al-Baraka fī faḍli l-saʿyi wa-l-ḥaraka* (Cairo: n.d.), p. 268; Nūr al-Dīn al-Haythamī, 1: 279 (a bath was built on the spot approved of by the Prophet). The tradition that the Prophet used to frequent the bath is vehemently refuted by al-Qasṭallānī, as recorded in al-Zurqānī's *Sharḥ al-mawāhib al-laduniyya* (Cairo: 1327), 4: 214. Al-Qasṭallānī, quoting the opinion of Ibn Kathīr, states that there were no baths in the Arabian peninsula in the time of the Prophet. Al-Khaṭīb al-Baghdādī, discussing the tradition of Umm al-Dardāʾ about her entering a bath in Medina (*Mūḍiḥ* 1: 359), states that there were no baths in Medina in the period of the Prophet; in that period baths existed only in Syria and Persia (*Mūḍiḥ* 1: 362–364). Cf. al-Suyūṭī, *al-Ḥāwī li-l-fatāwī*, ed. Muḥammad Muḥyī l-Dīn ʿAbd al-Ḥamīd (Cairo: 1378/1959), 1: 526–528; Ibn ʿAsākir, *Taʾrīkh* (*Tahdhīb*) (Damascus: 1329), 3: 380; Murtaḍā al-Zabīdī, *Itḥāf al-sāda al-muttaqīn bi-sharḥ asrār iḥyāʾ ʿulūm al-dīn* (Cairo: 1311) (reprinted Beirut), 2: 400. On the building of baths in Baṣra in the early period of Islam and the profits gained from them see al-Balādhurī, *Ansāb al-ashrāf*, 1, ed. Muḥammad Ḥamīdullah (Cairo: 1959): 502; al-Thaʿālibī, *Thimār al-qulūb*, ed. Abū l-Faḍl Ibrāhīm (Cairo: 1384/1965), p. 318, no. 476.

7 See Ibn Abī Shayba, 1: 107–108; ʿAbd al-Razzāq, 1: 295–298 (see e.g. the answer of Ibn ʿAbbās, "*innamā jaʿala llāhu l-māʾa yuṭahhiru wa-lā yuṭahharu*," ibid., no. 1142; and see the answer of al-Shaʿbī when asked, on leaving the bath, whether one is obliged to perforn the *ghusl* (to clean oneself) from the water of the bath: "So why did I enter the bath?", ibid., no. 1146); and see the outspoken answer of Ibn ʿAbbās when he entered a bath in the state of *iḥrām*: "*Mā yaʿbaʾu llāhu bi-awsākhinā shayʾan,*" al-Bayhaqī, *al-Sunan al-kubrā*, 5: 63 inf.

silver, and do not expend them in the way of God -- give them good tidings of a painful chastisement ..." (Qur'ān 9:34) by Abū Dharr is explained by the fact that Abū Dharr met the Prophet and heard from him some injunctions of a severe character (*yasma'u min rasūli llāhi* [ṣ] *l-amra fīhi l-shiddatu*); he then left for the desert. The Prophet, in the meantime, alleviated the injunction (*yurakhkhiṣu fīhi*) and people adopted the concession. But Abū Dharr, unaware of this, came back and adhered to the first (scil. severe) injunction.[8] In later periods of Islam the practice of *rukhaṣ* was presented as the attitude of the first generations of Islam. The righteous predecessors (*al-salaf*), argues Abū Ṭālib al-Makkī, were in the habit of alleviating (*yurakhkhiṣūna*) the rules of ritual impurity, but were strict in the matter of earning one's living by proper means alone as well as in the moral aspects of behavior like slander, futile talk, excessive indulgence in rhetoric etc., whereas contemporary scholars, Abū Ṭālib continues, are heedless in problems of moral behavior, but are rigid (*shaddadū*) with regard to ritual impurity.[9] Sufyān al-Thawrī speaks about *rukhṣa* in the following terms: "Knowledge in our opinion is merely [the knowledge of] a *rukhṣa* [reported on the authority] of a reliable scholar; the rigid, rigoristic practice can be observed by everyone."[10] The pious 'Aṭā' al-Sulaymī asked for the traditions of *rukhaṣ* ; they might relieve his grief, he said.[11] The *rukhaṣ*-traditions were of great importance for the strengthening of belief in God's mercy for the believers (*ḥusnu l-ẓanni bi-llāh*).[12] Sulaymān b. Ṭarkhān asked his son to tell him *rukhaṣ*-traditions in order to come to the Presence of God (literally: to meet God) with hope for God's mercy.[13]

---

8 al-Suyūṭī, *al-Durr al-manthūr*, 3: 243.

9 Abū Ṭālib al-Makkī, *Qūt al-qulūb* (Cairo: 1351/1932), 2: 46.

10 Ibn 'Abd al-Barr, *Jāmi' bayān al-'ilm wa-faḍlihi* (al-Madīna al-munawwara: n.d., reprint), 2: 36: *innamā l-'ilmu 'indanā l-rukhṣatu min thiqatin ; fa-ammā l-tashdīdu fa-yuḥsinuhu kullu aḥadin.*

11 Abū Nu'aym, 6: 217.

12 See Ibn Abī l-Dunyā, *Majmū'at al-rasā'il* (Cairo: 1354/1935), pp. 39-72: *kitābu ḥusni l-ẓanni bi-llāh.*

13 Ibid., p. 45, no. 29; Abū Nu'aym, 3: 31.

In a wider sense *rukhaṣ* represent in the opinion of Muslim scholars the characteristic way of Islam as opposed to Judaism and Christianity. The phrase "... and he will relieve them of their burden and the fetters that they used to wear" (Qur'ān 7:157) is interpreted as referring to the Prophet, who removed the burden of excessively harsh practices of worship[14] and of ritual purity.[15] The rigid and excessive practices of worship refer to Jews and Christians alike. The Prophet forbade his believers to follow the harsh and strict way of people who brought upon themselves destruction. The remnants of these people can be found in the cells of monks and in monasteries; this, of course, refers to Christians.[16] These very comments are coupled with the *ḥadīth* about the *rukhaṣ* mentioned earlier: *inna llāha yuḥibbu* ... It is thus not surprising to find this *rukhaṣ* tradition together with an additional phrase: ... *fa-qbalū rukhaṣa llāhi wa-lā takūnū ka-banī isrā'īla ḥīna shaddadū 'alā anfusihim fa-shaddada llāhu 'alayhim.*[17]

The *rukhṣa* tradition is indeed recorded in chapters condemning hardship in the exertion of worship and ritual practices,[18] stressing the benevolence of God for His creatures even if they commit grave sins, reproving cruelty even towards a cat,[19]

---

14 ... *al-tathqīlu lladhī kāna fī dīnihim ... al-tashdīdu fī l-'ibādati ... al-shadā'idu llatī kānat 'alayhim ... tashdīdun shuddida 'alā l-qawmi, fa-jā'a Muḥammadun (ṣ) bi-l-tajāwuzi 'anhum.*

15 al-Suyūṭī, *al-Durr al-manthūr*, 3: 135; al-Ṭabarī, *Tafsīr*, ed. Maḥmūd and Aḥmad Shākir (Cairo: 1958), 13: 167-168; al-Qurṭubī, *Tafsīr*, (Cairo: 1387/1967), 7: 300; Hāshim b. Sulaymān al-Baḥrānī al-Tawbalī al-Katakānī, *al-Burhān fī tafsīri l-qur'ān* (Qumm: 1393), 2: 40, no. 3.

16 al-Suyūṭī, *al-Durr al-manthūr*, 1: 193.

17 al-'Āmilī, *al-Kashkūl*, ed. Ṭāhir Aḥmad al-Zāwī (Cairo: 1380/1960), 1: 221.

18 See Ibn Balbān, fol. 90a-b, the headings: ... *dhikru l-ikhbāri 'ammā yustaḥabbu li-l-mar'i min qubūli mā rukhkhiṣa lahu bi-tarki l-taḥammuli 'alā l-nafsi mā lā tuṭīqu min al-ṭā'ati ... ; al-ikhbāru bi-anna 'alā l-mar'i qubūla rukhṣati llāhi lahu fī ṭā'atihi dūna l-taḥammuli 'alā l-nafsi mā yashuqqu 'alayhā ḥamluhu ... ; ... mā yustaḥabbu li-l-mar'i l-taraffuqu bi-l-ṭā'āti wa-al-amru bi-l-qaṣdi fī l-ṭā'āti dūna an yuḥmala 'alā l-nafsi mā lā tuṭīqu.*

19 See 'Abd al-Razzāq, 11, no. 20549. The authenticity of the story of the woman who was put in Hell because she caused the death of a cat, was

and recommending leniency, moderation and mildness towards the believers. *Rukhṣa* is *rukhṣatu llāh*, God's concession for His community; it imposes on the believers kindness and moderation towards each other. *Rukhṣa* is in this context associated with *rifq*, *yusr*, *samāḥa* and *qaṣd*.[20]

In a different context a concession, *rukhṣa*, is meant to ease the burden of the decreed prescription (*al-ḥukm*) for an excusable reason (*li-'udhrin ḥaṣala*); the acceptance of *rukhṣa* is almost obligatory in such a case (*yakādu yulḥaqu bi-l-wujūb*); the believer must act according to the *rukhṣa*, subduing his pride and haughtiness.[21] Breaking the fast of *ṣawm al-dahr* is such a *rukhṣa* ; continuing the fast is stubborness.[22] Commenting on the *ḥadīth* "The best of my people are those who act according to the *rukhaṣ*," al-Munāwī stresses that the *rukhaṣ* apply to specific times only; otherwise one should follow the incumbent prescription.[23] The *ḥadīth* "He who does not accept the concession of God will bear a sin as heavy as the mountains of 'Arafāt" [24] was quoted in connection with a concession according to which it is recommended

---

questioned by 'Ā'isha. She asserted that the woman was an unbeliever, a *kāfira*. The believer is more respected by God (*akramu 'inda llāhi*) than that He would chastise him because of a cat, she argued. She rebuked Abū Hurayra, the transmitter of the *ḥadīth*, and bade him to transmit the tradition more accurately. See al-Zarkashī, *al-Ijāba li-īrādi mā stadrakat-hu 'Ā'ishatu 'alā l-ṣaḥāba* (Cairo: n.d.), p. 61; Nūr al-Dīn al-Haythamī, 1: 116; and see Ibn 'Abd al-Ḥakam, *Futūḥ miṣr*, ed. C. Torrey (Leiden: 1920), p. 292; Hannād b. al-Sariyy, *Kitāb al-zuhd*, MS. Princeton, Garret 1419, fol. 101a, inf. -101b.

20 See 'Abd al-Razzāq, 11: 282-288, nos. 20546; 20559 (*Bāb al-rukhaṣ wa-l-shadā'id*) and 11: 290-292, nos. 20566-20574 (*Bāb al-rukhaṣ fī l-'amal wa-l-qaṣd*).

21 al-Munāwī, 2: 296-297; and see ibid., pp. 292-293 (see the commentary: the *'azīma*, injunction, order, has an equal standing with the *rukhṣa*. According to the circumstances the ordained *wuḍū'* is as obligatory as the *rukhṣa* of *tayammum*). And see ibid., p. 293: the concessions have to be carried out according to the circumstances for which they were given.

22 Abū Ṭālib al-Makkī, 1: 111.

23 al-Munāwī, 2: 51, no. 1300; al-Daylamī, MS. Chester Beatty 4139, fol. 94b.

24 Ibn 'Abd al-Ḥakam, p. 292; al-Munāwī, 6: 225, no. 9031; al-Daylamī, MS.

to break the fast when on a journey. The core of the discussion was whether the breaking of the fast during a journey is obligatory or merely permitted. Some scholars considered it as a *rukhṣa*.[25] The phrase in Qur'ān 2:187 "... and seek what God had prescribed for you" (*fa-l-āna bāshirūhunna wa-btaghū mā kataba llāhu lakum*) indicates, according to one interpretation, God's concession concerning the nights of Ramaḍān.[26] The phrase in Qur'ān 2:158 ... *fa-lā junāḥa 'alayhi an yaṭṭawwafa bihimā* ... ("... it is no fault in him to circumambulate them ..."), referring to the circumambulation of al-Ṣafā and Marwa, gave rise to the discussion whether it indicated an order or a concession.[27] The bewailing of the dead by hired women, the *niyāḥa*, is forbidden; but the Prophet granted the afflicted relatives the *rukhṣa* to mourn the dead and to weep over a dead person's grave.[28]

Chester Beatty 3037, fol. 158b.

25 al-Suyūṭī, *al-Durr al-manthūr*, 1: 193; Ibn 'Abd al-Ḥakam, p. 265; Aḥmad b. Ḥanbal, *Musnad*, ed. Shākir (Cairo: 1368/1949), 8: 238, no. 5392; al-Dhahabī, 2: 483; Ibn Kathīr, *Tafsīr* (Beirut: 1385/1966), 1: 382; cf. al-Ṭabarī, *Tafsīr* 3: 461-469 (see p. 460: *al-ifṭāru fī l-maraḍi 'azmatun min allāhi wājibatun wa-laysa bi-tarkhīṣ* ; and see p. 464: *al-ifṭāru fī l-safari rukhṣatun min allāhi ta'ālā dhikruhu, rakhkhaṣahā li-'ibādihi wa-l-farḍu l-ṣawmu* ...); Ibn Balbān, fol. 90b, sup.; al-Sha'rānī, *Lawāqiḥ al-anwār* (Cairo: 1381/1961), pp. 716-717; al-Mundhirī, 2: 258-262; Ibn Qutayba, *Ta'wīl mukhtalif al-ḥadīth* (Cairo: 1326), pp. 307-308; al-Zurqānī, *Sharḥ al-muwaṭṭa'* (Cairo: 1381/1961), 2: 415-420.

26 al-Ṭabarī, *Tafsīr*, 3: 500 ult., 508; Ibn Kathīr, *Tafsīr*, 1: 390, line 5 from bottom; al-Suyūṭī, *al-Durr al-manthūr*, 1: 199, line 1.

27 See al-Ṭabarī, *Tafsīr*, 3: 230-246; al-Qurṭubī, 2: 182 (and see ibid., about the reading: *fa-lā junāḥa 'alayhi an lā yaṭṭawwafa*); al-Majlisī, *Biḥār al-anwār* (Tehran: 1388), 99: 235, 237-8, 239 line 2; al-Zarkashī, *al-Ijāba*, pp. 78-9; al-Fākihī, fols. 374b-380a; al-Bayhaqī, *al-Sunan al-kubrā*, 5: 96-8; Amīn Maḥmūd Khaṭṭāb, *Fatḥ al-malik al-ma'būd, takmilat al-manhal al-'adhb al-mawrūd, sharḥ sunan abī dāwūd* (Cairo: 1394/1974), 1: 243-50, 2: 15-16.

28 al-Ḥākim, *al-Mustadrak* (Hyderabad: 1342), 1: 203; al-Khaṭīb al-Baghdādī, *Mūḍiḥ*, 2: 12 sup.; al-Zajjājī, *Amālī*, ed. 'Abd al-Salām Hārūn (Cairo: 1382), p. 181 (... *wa-kadhālika al-naq'u: raf'u l-ṣawti bi-l-bukā'i* ; *wa-hādhā kāna manhiyyan 'anhu fī awwali l-islāmi--a'nī l-bukā'a 'alā l-mayyit, thumma rukhkhiṣa fīhi* ... ; al-Rāghib al-Iṣfahānī, *Muḥāḍarāt al-udabā'* (Beirut: 1961),

In some cases the choice between the prescription and the *rukhṣa* has been left to the believer: such is the case of the ablution of the *junub*. Three traditions about how the Prophet practised *wuḍū'* ablution, when in the state of *janāba* contain contradictory details: two of them state that he, being a *junub*, performed the *wuḍū'* before he went to sleep, while the third one says that he went to sleep without performing *wuḍū'*. Ibn Qutayba, trying to bridge between the contradictory traditions, states that in a state of *janāba* washing before one goes to sleep is the preferred practice (*afḍal*); by not washing the Prophet pointed to the *rukhṣa*.[29] The believer may choose one of the two practices.

In some cases the *rukhṣa* completely reverses a former prohibition. The Prophet forbade the visiting of graves, but later changed his decision and granted a *rukhṣa* to visit them: *nahā rasūlu llāhi* [ṣ] *'an ziyārati l-qubūri thumma rakhkhaṣa fīhā ba'du.*[30]

Cupping during a fast was forbidden by the Prophet; both the cupper and the person whose blood was drawn were considered to have broken their fast. The Prophet, however, changed his decision and granted a *rukhṣa* ; cupping did not stop the fast.[31]

Lengthy chapters contain discussions of the problem as to whether kissing one's wife while fasting is permitted. Some scholars considered kissing or touching the body of the wife as breaking the fast, others considered it permissible. Both parties quote traditions in support of their arguments. The wives of the Prophet, who

---

4: 506; Ibn Abī Shayba, 3: 389–395; al-Ṭabarānī, *al-Mu'jam al-ṣaghīr*, ed. 'Abd al-Raḥmān Muḥammad 'Uthmān (al-Madīna al-munawwara: 1388/1968), 2: 82 (noteworthy is the report of Ibn Abī Shayba 3: 391 about the *faqīh* Abū l-Bakhtarī: ... *kanā rajulan faqīhan wa-kāna yasma'u l-nawḥ*); Maḥmūd Muḥammad Khaṭṭāb al-Subkī, *al-Manhal al-'adhb al-mawrūd*, 8: 281–4; al-Zarkashī, *al-Ijāba*, pp. 34, 50–1.

29 Ibn Qutayba, pp. 305–6.

30 al-Ḥāzimī, *al-I'tibār fī bayāni l-nāsikh wa-l-mansūkh min al-akhbār* (Hyderabad: 1359), pp. 130–1, 228; al-Fākihī, fol. 478b, 479 penult.

31 Ibn Daqīq al-'Īd, *al-Ilmām bi-aḥādīthi l-aḥkām*, ed. Muḥammad Sa'īd al-Mawlawī (Damascus: 1383/1963), p. 244, no. 592; al-Zurqānī, *Sharḥ al-muwaṭṭa'*, 2: 428–30; al-Ḥāzimī, pp. 137–42.

testified as to their experience, were not unanimous about the problem. 'Ā'isha's evidence was in favor of kissing. The statement that old and weak people may kiss their wives, while men may not, is an obvious attempt at harmonization.[32]

A similar problem was whether kissing one's wife imposes *wuḍū'*. Scholars were divided in their opinions. 'A'isha testified that the Prophet used to kiss his wives and set out to pray without performing ablution. Many scholars stated that kissing or touching one's wife does not require *wuḍū'*, but others argued that it does. Some scholars found a compromise: *wuḍū'* is required if the kiss is accompanied by a feeling of lust.[33]

The *rukhaṣ*, apparently, were exploited by scholars attached to rulers and governors. As usual precedents of wicked court-scholars in the period of *banū isrā'īl* were quoted: they frequented the courts of kings, granted them the required *rukhaṣ* and, of course, got rewards for their deeds. They were happy to receive the rewards and to have the kings accept their

---

32 al-Ṭaḥāwī, *Sharḥ ma'ānī l-āthār*, ed. Muḥammad Zuhrī l-Najjār (Cairo: 1388/1968), 2: 88-96; Ibn Abī Shayba, 3: 59-64; al-Bayhaqī, *Ma'rifat al-sunan wa-l-āthār*, ed. Aḥmad Ṣaqr (Cairo: 1969), 1: 21 sup.; Ibn Qutayba, pp. 308-9; al-Dhahabī 2: 398 sup.; Abū Nu'aym, 7: 138; al-Zarkashī, *al-Ijāba*, p. 54; al-Zurqānī, *Sharḥ al-muwaṭṭa'*, 2: 410-15; 'Abd al-Razzāq, 4: 182-94, nos. 8406-8456. See e.g. nos. 8412, 8418; kissing during the fast was considered as *rukhṣa* ; against the rigid prohibition to look at a woman (see e.g. nos. 8452-8453) there are traditions permitting much more than kissing (see e.g. no. 8444 and the extremely permissive tradition no. 8439); and see Abū Nu'aym, 9: 309 (*kullu shay'in laka min ahlika ḥalālun fī l-ṣiyāmi illā mā bayna l-rijlayn*); and see this tradition al-Daylamī, MS. Chester Beatty 3037, fol. 120b, 1.1; al-Muttaqī l-Hindī, 8: 384-5, nos. 2787-2793; Ibn Daqīq al-'Īd, pp. 243-4, nos. 590-1; al-Kattānī, MS. Chester Beatty 4483, fol. 3a; al-Shāfi'ī, *al-Umm* (Cairo: 1321 reprint), 2: 84 sup.; Maḥmūd Muḥammad al-Subkī, *al-Manhal al-'adhb al-mawrūd, sharḥ sunan abī dāwūd* (Cairo: 1390), 10: 109-13, 115-16; Ibn Abī Ḥātim, *'Ilal al-ḥadīth* (Cairo: 1343 reprint), 1: 47, no. 108.

33 Ibn Abī Shayba, 1: 44 (*man qāla: laysa fī l-qubla wuḍū'*), 45 (*man qāla: fīhā l-wuḍū'*); 'Abd al-Razzāq, 1: 132-6, nos. 496-515; al-Ḥākim, *al-Mustadrak*, 1: 135; al-Shawkānī, *Nayl*, 1: 230-3; al-Zurqānī, *Sharḥ al-muwaṭṭa'*, 1: 129-30; Ibn Abī Ḥātim, 1: 48, nos. 109-110, 63 no. 166.

concessions. The verse in Qur'ān 3:189 "Reckon not that those who rejoice in what they have brought, and love to be praised for what they have not done -- do not reckon them secure from chastisement ..." refers, according to one tradition, to these scholars.[34] Orthodox, pious scholars fiercely criticized the Umayyad court-jurists and *muḥaddithūn*.[35] The *fuqahā'* seem to have been liberal in granting *rukhaṣ*, as can be gauged from a remark of the pious Sulaymān b. Ṭarkhān (who himself very much appreciated the granted *rukhaṣ*, see above note 13) that anyone who would adopt every *rukhṣa* of the *fuqahā'* would turn out a libertine.[36] In order to assess the actions of rulers it became quite important to find out to what extent they made use of *rukhaṣ*. 'Umar is said to have asked Muhājirs and Anṣārīs in his council what their opinion would be if he applied *rukhaṣ* in some problems. Those attending remained silent for a time and then Bishr b. Sa'īd said: "We would make you straight as we make straight an arrow." 'Umar then said with approval: "You are as you are" (i.e., you are the proper men).[37] When al-Manṣūr bade Mālik b. Anas to compile the *Muwaṭṭa'* he advised him to stick to the tenets agreed upon the Muslim community and to beware of the rigoristic opinions of Ibn 'Umar, the *rukhaṣ* of Ibn 'Abbās and *shawādhdh* (readings of the Qur'ān) of Ibn Mas'ūd.[38]

---

34 al-Suyūṭī, *al-Durr al-manthūr*, 2: 109 inf.

35 Ibn 'Asākir, 6: 218: ... *fa-ataw l-umarā'a fa-ḥaddathūhum fa-rakhkhaṣū lahum, wa-a'ṭawhum fa-qabilū minhum* ...; al-Qāḍī 'Iyāḍ, *Tartīb al-madārik*, ed. Aḥmad Bakīr Maḥmūd (Beirut: 1387/1967), 1-2, 616 (Saḥnūn): ... *wa-balaghanī annahum yuḥaddithūnahum min al-rukhaṣ mā yuḥibbūna, mimmā laysa 'alayhi l-'amalu* ...; al-Dhahabī, 1: 14 inf.: ... *ilā kam tuḥaddithu l-nāsa bi-l-rukhaṣi*? ...; and see al-Suyūṭī, *al-Durr al-manthūr*, 3, 139.

36 Abū Nu'aym, 3:32; al-Rāghib al-Iṣfahānī, 1: 133: ... *man akhadha bi-rukhṣati kulli faqīhin kharaja minhu fāsiq*. And See Aḥmad b. Ḥanbal, *'Ilal*, 1: 238, no. 1499: Mālik, asked about the *rukhaṣ* of singing granted by some people of Medina, said: "In our place the libertines behave in this way."

37 Muṣ'ab b. 'Abdallāh, *Ḥadīth*, MS. Chester Beatty 3849/4 (*majmū'a*), fol. 44b, inf.-45a (the text: *antum idhan antum*); al-Muttaqī al-Hindī, 5: 405 inf., no. 2414 (the text: *antum idhan antum idhan*).

38 'Abd al-Malik b. Ḥabīb, *Ta'rīkh*, MS. Bodley. Marsh. 288, p. 167: ... *wa-qāla*

Many a *rukhṣa* indeed served to regulate relations between people, establish certain privileges for the weak and disabled, to alleviate some rigorous practices and finally, in some cases, to turn Jāhilī practices into Muslim ones by providing them with a new theoretical basis. Al-Ḥākim al-Naysābūrī[39] says that the Prophet's command to Zayd b. Thābit to learn the writing of the Jews (*kitābat al-yahūd*) in order to be able to answer their letters, serves as the only *rukhṣa* permitting the study of the writings of the People of the Book. Weak and disabled people were given special instructions on how more easily to perform certain practices during the pilgrimage.[40] The Prophet enjoined that the ritual ablution (*wuḍū'*) should start with the right hand; but a *rukhṣa* was granted to start from the left.[41] The cutting of trees and plants was forbidden in the *ḥaram* of Mecca, but the Prophet allowed as a *rukhṣa* the *idhkhir* rush (*schoenantum*) to be cut since it was used in graves and for purification.[42] A special *rukhṣa* was given by the Prophet to take freely the meat of animals sacrificed by him; the *nuhba* (plunder) of sugar and nuts at weddings was also permitted by the Prophet.[43] A *rukhṣa* was issued by the Prophet allowing use of gold and silver for the embellishment of swords, for the repair and fastening of damaged cups and vessels, for a treatment in

---

abū ja'farin al-manṣūru li-māliki bni anasin ḥīna amarahu bi-waḍ'i muwaṭṭa'ihi: yā abā 'abdi llāhi ttaqi shadā'ida bni 'umara wa-rukhaṣa bni 'abbāsin wa-shawādhdha bni mas'ūdin wa-'alayka bi-l-amri l-mujtama'i 'alayhi.

39 al-Ḥākim, *al-Mustadrak*, 1: 75.

40 al-Ṭaḥāwī, *Sharḥ ma'ānī*, 2: 215–218.

41 al-Bayhaqī, *al-Sunan al-kubrā*, 1: 86–87.

42 al-Balādhurī, *Futūḥ al-buldān*, ed. 'Abdallah and 'Umar al-Ṭabbā' (Beirut: 1377/1958), p. 58, 1.3.

43 Abū 'Ubayd, *Gharību l-ḥadīth* (Hyderabad: 1384/1965), 2: 54; al-Ṭaḥāwī, *Sharḥ ma'ānī*, 3: 49–50; al-Zurqānī, *Sharḥ al-mawāhib* ; 4: 325 inf. -326; al-Fasawī, *al-Ma'rifa wa-l-ta'rīkh*, MS. Esad Ef. 2391, fol. 32a, sup. ('*an ibni mas'ūdin annahu kariha nihāba l-sukkar*).

dentistry and for the restitution of a cut nose.[44] The Prophet uttered a *rukhṣa* about the *nabīdh* of jars;[45] the use of jars for *nabīdh* (steeping of dates) was forbidden before that. The muttering of healing incantations, the *ruqya*, a current practice in the Jāhiliyya period, was forbidden by the Prophet. Later he fixed the formulae of these healing incantations for various kinds of illnesses, bites from snakes and scorpions, and the evil eye, giving them an Islamic character.[46] This was, of course, a *rukhṣa* of the Prophet.

It is also a *rukhṣa* to denounce Islam in case of danger to one's life. Two Muslims were captured by a troop of Musaylima and were ordered to attest the prophethood of Musaylima. One of them refused and was killed; the other complied and saved his life. When he came to the Prophet, the Prophet said that he had chosen the way of the *rukhṣa*.[47]

The discussion of a *rukhṣa* could, in certain circumstances, turn into a bitter dispute. ʿUthmān disapproved of the *tamattuʿ* pilgrimage.[48] ʿAlī, who was at the council of ʿUthmān, opposed this opinion fiercely, arguing that *tamattuʿ* was a *sunna* of the Prophet and a *rukhṣa* granted by God to his servants. ʿUthmān

---

44 al-Ṭaḥāwī, *Mushkil al-āthār* (Hyderabad: 1333), 2: 166–179; Nūr al-Dīn al-Haythamī, 5: 147–151; al-Bayhaqī, *al-Sunan al-kubrā*, 1: 28–30.

45 al-Ḥākim, *Maʿrifat ʿulūm*, p. 196 sup.; al-Ḥāzimī, pp. 228–230.

46 Ibn Wahb, *Jāmiʿ*, ed. J. David-Weill (Cairo: 1939), pp. 103–106; al-Ṭaḥāwī, *Sharḥ maʿānī*, 4: 326–329; Nūr al-Dīn al-Haythamī, 5: 109–114; al-Zurqānī, *Sharḥ al-muwaṭṭaʾ*, 6: 348–350; idem, *Sharḥ al-mawāhib*, 7: 68–82; al-Waṣṣābi, *al-Baraka*, pp. 268–270; Ibn Qayyim al-Jawziyya, *al-Ṭibb al-nabawī*, ed. ʿAbd al-Ghanī ʿAbd al-Khāliq, ʿĀdil al-Azharī, Maḥmūd Faraj al-ʿUqda (Cairo: 1377/1957), pp. 127, 131 inf.–147; idem, *Zād al-maʿād* (Beirut: n.d.), 3: 116–125; al-Damīrī, *Ḥayāt al-ḥayawān* (Cairo: 1383/1963), 2: 139–140; al-Thaʿālibī, *Thimār al-qulūb*, pp. 126, no. 672, 431, no. 690.

47 al-Suyūṭī, *al-Durr al-manthūr*, 4: 133.

48 On the *tamattuʿ* pilgrimage see e.g. Ibn Ḥazm, *Ḥajjat al-wadāʿ*, ed. Mamdūḥ Ḥaqqī (Beirut: 1966), pp. 49, 89, 90, 102; Nūr al-Dīn al-Haythamī, 3: 236; al-Bayhaqī, *al-Sunan al-kubrā*, 5: 15–26.

excused himself saying that he had merely expressed his personal opinion which anybody could accept or reject. A man from Syria who attended the council and disliked ʿAlī's argument said that he would be ready to kill ʿAlī, if ordered to do so by the Caliph, ʿUthmān. He was silenced by Ḥabīb b. Maslama[49] who explained to him that the Companions of the Prophet knew better the matter in which they differed.[50] This remark of Ḥabīb b. Maslama is a projection of later discussions and represents the attitude of orthodox circles which recommend refraining from passing judgement on the contradictory arguments of the *ṣaḥāba.* However the passage also reflects the contrasting ways in which the pilgrimage was performed. It is noteworthy that Ibn Qayyim al-Jawziyya wrote lengthy passages in which he examined in a thorough manner the contradictory opinions of the scholars about the *tamattuʿ* pilgrimage.[51]

Close to the concept of *rukhṣa* was the idea of *naskh*, abrogation, total change, referring to *ḥadīth.* Such a case of *naskh* is the practice of *wuḍūʾ* after the consumption of food prepared on fire. The Prophet is said to have uttered a *ḥadith*: *tawaḍḍaʾū mimmā massat al-nār*. A great number of traditions assert that the Prophet later used to eat cooked food and immediately afterwards prayed without performing the *wuḍūʾ*. The traditions concerning this subject are found in some of the compendia arranged in two separate chapters, recording the opinions and deeds of the righteous predecessors who respectively practised *wuḍūʾ* or objected to it.[52]

---

49 See on him al-Fāsī, *al-ʿIqd al-thamīn fī taʾrīkhi l-baladi l-amīn*, ed. Fuʾād Sayyid (Cairo: 1384/1965), 4: 49–52; Naṣr b. Muzāḥim, *Waqʿat Ṣiffīn*, ed. ʿAbd al-Salām Hārūn (Cairo: 1382), index; Ibn Ḥajar, *al-Iṣāba*, ed. ʿAlī Muḥammad al-Bajāwī (Cairo: 1392/1972), 2: 24–26, no. 1602.

50 Ibn ʿAbd al-Barr, *Jāmiʿ bayān*, 2: 30; cf. al-Zurqānī, *Sharḥ al-muwaṭṭaʾ*, 3: 52 (and see pp. 48–51); al-Muttaqī l-Hindī, 5: 83, no. 678, 88, no. 704.

51 *Zād al-maʿād*, 1: 188–191, 203–18.

52 ʿAbd al-Razzāq 1: 163–171 (*man qāla lā yutawaḍḍaʾu mimmā massat al-nār*), pp. 172–174 (*mā jāʾa fīmā massat al-nār min al-shidda*); Ibn Abī Shayba, 1: 46–52 (*man kāna lā yatawaḍḍaʾu mimmā massat al-nār* ; *man kāna yarā l-wuḍūʾa mimmā ghayyarat al-nār*); al-Bayhaqī, *al-Sunan al-kubrā*, 1: 153–158; al-Ḥāzimī, pp. 46–52; Nūr al-Dīn al-Haythamī, 1: 248–249 (*al-wuḍūʾ*

The arguments brought forth by the partisans of both groups and the traditions reported by them may elucidate some aspects of the problem under discussion. According to a tradition, reported by al-Ḥasan b. ʿAlī, the Prophet was invited by Fāṭima and was served the shoulder of a ewe. He ate and immediately afterwards started to pray. Fāṭima asked him why he had not performed the *wuḍūʾ* and the Prophet answered, obviously surprised, "[To wash] after what, o my daughter?" She said, "[To wash] after a meal touched by fire." Then he said, "The purest food is that touched by fire."[53] A similar tradition is recorded on the authority of ʿĀʾisha. When she asked the Prophet why he did not perform the *wuḍūʾ* after eating meat and bread he answered, "Shall I perform the *wuḍūʾ* after the two best things: bread and meat?"[54] There is a tradition on the authority of Umm Ḥabība, the wife of the Prophet, who had ordered the performance of *wuḍūʾ* after having eaten gruel of parched barley (*sawīq*) on the grounds of the *ḥadīth*: *Tawaḍḍaʾū mimmā massat al-nār*,[55] but traditions recorded on the authority of Ṣafiyya, Umm Salama and the Companions of the Prophet affirm that the Prophet prayed after eating cooked food without performing the *wuḍūʾ*.[56] The scholars who deny the obligation of *wuḍūʾ* after the consumption of meals state that the principle established by the Prophet was that *wuḍūʾ* is obligatory

---

mimmā massat al-nār), pp. 251-254 (*tarku l-wuḍūʾ mimmā massat al-nār*); al-Ṭaḥāwī, *Sharḥ maʿānī*, 1: 62-70; Aḥmad b. Ḥanbal, *al-ʿIlal*, 1: 305, nos. 1984-1985, 317, no. 2062, 366, no. 2424; al-Shawkānī, *Nayl*, 1: 245-247, al-Fasawī, fol. 229a; Abū Yūsuf, *Kitāb al-āthār*, ed. Abū l-Wafā (Cairo: 1355), pp. 9-11, nos. 41-50; al-Ḥākim, *Maʿrifat ʿulūm*, pp. 30, 217; al-Bayhaqī, *Maʿrifat al-sunan*, 1: 401; Ibn Saʿd, 7: 158; al-Bukhārī, *al-Taʾrīkh al-kabīr* (reprint), I, 2 no. 1543, III, 2 nos. 2361, 2805; Abū Nuʿaym, 5: 363; Ibn ʿAsākir, 6: 125, 174, 321; al-Khaṭīb al-Baghdādī, *Taʾrīkh Baghdād* (Cairo: 1351/1931), 13: 100; Ibn Ḥajar, *al-Iṣāba*, 3: 263, no. 3701, 8: 248, no. 12125; Ibn Ḥibbān, *Kitāb al-majrūḥīn*, ed. ʿAzīz al-Qādirī (Hyderabad: 1390/1970), 2: 173.

53 Nūr al-Dīn al-Haythamī, 1: 252 inf.-253.

54 al-Dhahabī, 3: 243, no. 6270.

55 Ibn Abī l-Jawṣāʾ, *Ḥadīth*, al-Ẓāhiriyya, Majmūʿa 60, fol. 64b.

56 al-Ṭaḥāwī, *Sharḥ maʿānī*, 1: 65.

after what comes out (of the body) not after food taken in.[57] Ibn 'Abbās, who authoritatively stated that there is no injunction of *wuḍū'* after food prepared on fire, argued that fire is a blessing; fire does not make anything either forbidden or permitted.[58] On the authority of Mu'ādh b. Jabal, a Companion of the Prophet and a very indulgent person in matters of ablutions, who stated that no ablution is needed in case of vomiting, bleeding of the nose or when touching the genitalia, the following philological explanation is given: people had indeed heard from the Prophet the utterance: *tawaḍḍa'ū mimmā massat al-nār*, but they did not understand the Prophet's meaning. In the time of the Prophet people called the washing of hands and mouth *wuḍū'* ; the Prophet's words simply imply the washing of hands and mouth for cleanliness (*li-l-tanẓīf*); this washing is by no means obligatory (*wājib*) in the sense of ritual ablution.[59] There are in fact traditions stating that the Prophet ate meat, then rinsed his mouth, washed his hands and started to pray.[60] Another tradition links the abolition of the Prophet's injunction of this *wuḍū'* with the person of Anas b. Mālik, the servant of the Prophet, and puts the blame for the persistence of *wuḍū'* after the consumption of cooked food on authorities outside Medina. Anas b. Mālik returned from al-Iraq and sat down to have his meal with two men of Medina. After the meal he came forth to perform the *wuḍū'*. His companions blamed him, asking: "Are you

---

57 Nūr al-Dīn al-Haythamī, 1: 252; al-Bayhaqī, *al-Sunan al-kubrā*, 1: 157 inf.; 'Abd al-Razzāq, 1: 170-171, nos. 658, 663; al-Ṭaḥāwī, *Sharḥ ma'ānī*, 1: 69.

58 'Abd al-Razzāq, 1: 168-169, nos. 653, 655-656; al-Bayhaqī, *al-Sunan al-kubrā*, 1: 158, lines 4-5; al-Ṭaḥāwī, *Sharḥ ma'ānī*, 1: 70 sup.

59 al-Bayhaqī, *al-Sunan al-kubrā*, 1: 141; Nūr al-Dīn al-Haythamī, 1: 252 ult.-253, line 1; al-Sharīf al-Murtaḍā, *Amālī*, ed. Muḥammad Abū l-Faḍl Ibrāhīm (Cairo: 1373/1954), 1: 395-396.

60 al-Ṭaḥāwī, *Sharḥ ma'ānī*, 1: 66, 68; al-Bayhaqī, *al-Sunan al-kubrā*, 1: 157; Nūr al-Dīn al-Haythamī, 1: 252, lines 12-15, 254, line 8 and line 18; Muḥammad b. Sinān al-Qazzāz, *Ḥadīth*, al-Ẓāhiriyya, Majmū'a 18, fol. 2a; Muḥammad b. Aḥmad al-Qaṭṭān, *al-Fawā'id*, al-Ẓāhiriyya, Majmū'a 18, fol. 24a inf.

following the Iraqi way?"[61] This story implies that in the practice of Medina no *wuḍū'* was observed after eating cooked meals. The emphasis that Anas's practice was Iraqi is noteworthy. It can hardly be conceived that the Iraqis stuck to the earlier practice of the Prophet which was later abrogated by him. It is more plausible to assume that Anas adopted an Iraqi usage observed there since the Sasanian period. The severe reproach which Anas faced seems to indicate that it was a foreign custom, considered as a reprehensible innovation by the Muslim community.[62]

The lenient character of the abrogation of *wuḍū'* after eating food prepared on fire is exposed in a tradition reporting that the Prophet ate roast meat, performed the *wuḍū'* and prayed; later he turned to eat the meat that was left over, consumed it and set to pray the afternoon prayer without performing *wuḍū'* at all.[63] It is evident that his later action (*ākhiru amrayhi*) is the one to be adopted by the community, as it constitutes an abrogation, *naskh*, of the former tradition, although some scholars consider it as *rukhṣa*.

The problem of *wuḍū' mimmā massat al-nār* was left in fact to the inventiveness of the *fuqahā'* of later centuries; it becomes still more complicated by an additional *ḥadīth* according to which the Prophet enjoined *wuḍū'* after the consumption of the meat of camels, but did not regard *wuḍū'* as necessary after eating the meat of small cattle (*ghanam*).[64] The two chapters in the *Muṣannaf* of Ibn Abī Shayba about *wuḍū'* after consuming meat of

---

61 al-Ṭaḥāwī, *Sharḥ ma'ānī*, 1: 69; al-Bayhaqī, *al-Sunan al-kubrā*, 1: 158 (Anas regrets his mistake and wishes he had not done it: *laytanī lam af'al*); 'Abd al-Razzāq, 1: 170, no. 659; al-Zurqānī, *Sharḥ al-muwaṭṭa'*, 1: 88 inf.-89.

62 See 'Abd al-Razzāq, 1: 170, no. 659: ... *mā hādhihi l-'irāqiyyatu llatī aḥdathtahā* ...?

63 al-Shawkānī, *Nayl*, 1: 247; al-Ḥākim, *Ma'rifat 'ulūm*, p. 85; al-Bayhaqī, *al-Sunan al-kubrā*, 1: 156; al-Ṭaḥāwī, *Sharḥ ma'ānī*, 1: 67; al-Bayhaqī, *Ma'rifat al-sunan*, 1: 395, 401, lines 1-2; Ibn 'Asākir, 6: 321.

64 Ibn Abī Shayba, 1: 46-7; al-Ṭaḥāwī, *Sharḥ ma'ānī*, 1: 70-1; al-Shawkānī, *Nayl*, 1: 237-9; al-Bayhaqī, *al-Sunan al-kubrā*, 1: 158-9; idem, *Ma'rifat al-sunan*, 1: 402-6; Ibn Qayyim al-Jawziyya, *I'lām al-muwaqqi'īn 'an rabbi l-'ālamīn*, ed. Ṭāhā 'Abd al-Ra'ūf Sa'd (Cairo: 1973), 2: 15-16, 106; Nūr al-Dīn al-Haythamī, 1: 250.

camels, contradictory as they are, bear additional evidence to the diversity of practice and usage, and to the divergencies in opinions held by the scholars of *ḥadīth.* No less divergent are the views of the scholars about the *wuḍū'* before the consumption of food,[65] the confinement of *wuḍū'*, as an obligatory act, before prayer only, the question whether ablution before every prayer was obligatory for the Prophet only,[66] and whether the *wuḍū'* may be replaced as a concession by cleaning the mouth with a toothpick.[67]

The great number of diverse traditions, merely hinted at above, clearly indicate that the formation of a normative code of ritual and usage began relatively late.

A survey of some traditions about the *ṭawāf*, the circumambulation of the Ka'ba, and certain practices of the *ḥajj* may shed some light on the peculiar observances and customs followed in the early period and may explain how they were later regulated, transformed or established.

The *ṭawāf* was equated by the Prophet with prayer (*ṣalāt*). In an utterance attributed to him the Prophet said, "The *ṭawāf* is indeed like a prayer; when you circumambulate diminish your talk."[68] In another version of this *ḥadīth* the Prophet, making

---

65 See al-Zurqānī, *Sharḥ al-mawāhib*, 4: 352 (... *barakat al-ṭa'ām al-wuḍū' qablahu* ; and see the interpretation).

66 See al-Zurqānī, *Sharḥ al-mawāhib*, 7: 247, lines 24-30 (... *fa'altuhu yā 'umaru--ya'nī li-bayāni l-jawāzi li-l-nāsi wa-khawfa an yu'taqada wujūbu mā kāna yaf'alu min al-wuḍū'i li-kulli ṣalātin* ; *wa-qīla innahu nāsikhun li-wujūbi dhālika, wa-ta'aqqaba bi-qawli anasin: kāna khāṣṣan bihi dūna ummatihi wa-annahu kāna yaf'aluhu li-l-faḍīla* ...).

67 Ibid., 7: 248, line 1 seq. Concerning the concept of Ṣufī *rukhaṣ* cf. M. Milson, *A Sufi Rule for Novices, Kitāb adab al-murīdīn* (Harvard: 1975), pp. 72-82; and see his discussion on the subject in the Introduction, pp. 19-20.

68 'Abd al-Razzāq, 5: 496; al-Qasṭallānī, *Irshād al-sārī*, (Cairo: 1323), 3: 173-4; al-Nasā'ī, *Sunan*, ed. Ḥasan al-Mas'ūdī (Beirut: n.d.), 5: 222; al-Bayhaqī, *al-Sunan al-kubrā*, 5: 85; Yūsuf b. Mūsā al-Ḥanafī, *al-Mu'taṣar min al-mukhtaṣar* (Hyderabad: 1362), 1: 174; al-Munāwī, 4: 292-3, nos. 5345-5347; al-Muttaqī l-Hindī, 5: 24, nos. 220-222; cf. al-Azraqī, *Akhbār Makka*, ed. F. Wüstenfeld, p. 258; Muḥibb al-Dīn al-Ṭabarī, *al-Qirā li-qāṣidi ummi l-qurā*, ed. Muṣṭafā l-Saqā (Cairo: 1390/1970), pp. 306, 331; al-Ṭaḥāwī, *Sharḥ*

ṭawāf equal to prayer, bade the faithful confine their conversation to good talk. During the *ṭawāf* the Prophet invoked God saying, "Our Lord, give to us in this world and in the world to come and guard us against the chastisement of Fire" (Qur'ān 2:201). This verse was recited as an invocation by some of the Companions.[69] Some of the invocations were extended and included praises of God, assertion of His oneness and omnipotence as they were uttered by the angels, by Adam, Abraham and the Prophet while they went past various parts of the Ka'ba during the *ṭawāf*.[70] The pious Ibn 'Umar and Ibn 'Abbās are said to have performed the *ṭawāf* refraining from talk altogether.[71] Ṭāwūs and Mujāhid circumambulated in solemnity and awe "as if there were birds on their heads."[72] This was, of course, in the spirit of the *imitatio prophetarum* ; Wahb b. Munabbih reported on the authority of Ka'b that three hundred Messengers (the last among whom was Muḥammad) and twelve thousand chosen people (*muṣṭafan*) prayed in the *ḥijr* facing the *maqām*, none of them speaking during the *ṭawāf*, except to mention the name of God.[73] When 'Urwa b. al-Zubayr approached Ibn 'Umar during the *ṭawāf*, asking him to give him his daughter in marriage, Ibn 'Umar did not reply. After some time 'Urwa came to Medina and met 'Abdallāh b. 'Umar. The latter explained that he had not been able to answer him because

---

ma'ānī , 2: 178 inf.

69 al-Azraqī, p. 258; al-Fākihī, fols. 292a, 296a; 'Abd al-Razzāq, 5: 50, 52; al-Muttaqī l-Hindī, 5: 90, nos. 717-719, 722; al-Wāqidī, *Maghāzī*, ed. M. Jones (London: 1966), p. 1098; al-Bayhaqī, *al-Sunan al-kubrā*, 5: 84; Ibn Ẓuhayra, *al-Jāmi' al-laṭīf* (Cairo: 1357/1938), p. 124; Ibn Kathīr, *Tafsīr*, 1: 432-3.

70 See e.g. al-Fākihī, fo. 296a, sup. (The Prophet urges the people to praise God and to extol Him during the *ṭawāf* ; and see ibid., similar reports about some Companions); al-Azraqī, pp. 259 inf.-260; 'Abd al-Razzāq, 5: 51, nos. 8964-8965; al-Qasṭallānī 3: 170; al-Ḥarbī, *al-Manāsik wa-amākin ṭuruqi l-ḥajj*, ed. Ḥamad al-Jāsir (al-Riyāḍ: 1389/1969), pp. 431-3; Muḥibb al-Dīn al-Ṭabarī, pp. 305-6; al-Shawkānī, *Nayl*, 5: 53-4.

71 al-Fākihī, fol. 292a; 'Abd al-Razzāq, 5: 50, no. 8962.

72 al-Fākihī, fol. 292a-b; cf. Muḥibb al-Dīn al-Ṭabarī, p. 271.

73 al-Fākihī, fol. 292a, inf.

he "conceived that he faced God" during the *ṭawāf* (*wa-naḥnu natakhāyalu llāha ʿazza wa-jalla bayna aʿyuninā*). Now he replied and gave him his daughter in marriage.[74] Merriment and joviality were, of course, forbidden and considered as demeaning. Wahb b. al-Ward,[75] while staying in the *ḥijr* of the mosque of Mecca, heard the Kaʿba complain to God and Jibrīl against people who speak frivolous words around it.[76] The Prophet foretold that Abū Hurayra would remain alive until he saw heedless people playing; they would come to circumambulate the Kaʿba, their *ṭawāf* would, however, not be accepted.[77]

The concession in the matter of speech granted during the *ṭawāf* was "good talk."[78] Pious scholars used to give guidance, exhort, edify and recount *ḥadīth*s of the Prophet.[79] Common people made supplications during the *ṭawāf*, asking God to forgive them their sins and to grant them Paradise, children, and wealth. It was, however, forbidden to stand up during the *ṭawāf*, and to raise one's hands while supplicating. "Jews in the synagogues practise it in this way," said ʿAbdallāh b. ʿAmr (b. al-ʿĀṣ) and advised the man who did it to utter his invocation in his council, not to do it during the *ṭawāf*.[80] The fact that large crowds were gathered during the *ṭawāf* was, however, exploited by the political leaders. Ibn al-Zubayr stood up in front of the door of the Kaʿba and recounted before the people the evil deeds of the Umayyads, stressing

---

74 al-Zubayr b. Bakkār, *Jamharat nasab quraysh*, MS. Bodley, Marsh 384, fol. 160b; al-Fākihī, fol. 292b; Muḥibb al-Dīn al-Ṭabarī, p. 270.

75 See on him Abū Nuʿaym, 8: 140-61; al-Fāsī, *al-ʿIqd*, 7: 417, no. 2678.

76 al-Azraqī, p. 259; Abū Nuʿaym, 8: 155 (the *tafakkuh* is explained as talking about women and describing their bodies during the *ṭawāf*); Muḥibb al-Dīn al-Ṭabarī, p. 271.

77 al-Fākihī, fol. 292b.

78 See Muḥibb al-Dīn al-Ṭabarī, p. 271, line 1: ... *wa-anna ḥukmahu ḥukmu l-ṣalāti, illā fīmā waradat fīhi l-rukhṣatu min al-kalām.*

79 See e.g. al-Fākihī, fols. 311a-312a; ʿAbd al-Razzāq, 3: 377, no. 6021.

80 al-Fākihī, fol. 296b; and see al-Azraqī, p. 257; Amīn Maḥmūd Khaṭṭāb, *Fatḥ al-malik al-maʿbūd*, 1: 200-2; Ibn Abī Shayba, 4:96; al-Bayhaqī, *al-Sunan al-kubrā*, 5: 72-3.

especially the fact that they withheld their payment of *fay'*.[81] 'Alī b. al-Ḥusayn cursed al-Mukhtār, after his death, at the door of the Ka'ba.[82]

Some traditions narrate details of the behavior of certain persons in the *ṭawāf* who did not conform to this requirement of awe and solemnity in the holy place. Sa'īd b. Jubayr used to talk during the *ṭawāf* and even to laugh.[83] 'Abd al-Raḥmān b. 'Awf was seen to perform the *ṭawāf* wearing boots and singing *ḥidā'* tunes. When rebuked by 'Umar he replied that he had done the same at the time of the Prophet and so 'Umar let him go.[84] Al-Fākihī records certain frivolous conversations which took place during the *ṭawāf*, which may indeed be considered coarse and were certainly out of place in the sanctuary.[85] But groups of people engaged in idle talk during the *ṭawāf* were reprimanded. 'Abd al-Karīm b. Abī Mukhāriq[86] strongly reproved such talk; al-Muṭṭalib b. Abī Wadā'a[87] was surprised when he came to Mecca after a period of stay in the desert and saw people talk during the *ṭawāf*. "Did you turn the *ṭawāf* into a meeting place," he asked.[88] The "arabization" of the *ṭawāf* is evident from an utterance attributed to the Prophet making it unlawful to talk in Persian during circumambulation. 'Umar gently requested two men who held a conversation in Persian during the *ṭawāf* to turn to Arabic.[89] Reciting verses of the

---

81 al-Fākihī, fol. 296b.

82 al-Fākihī, fol. 296b.

83 al-Azraqī, p. 259; Muḥibb al-Dīn al-Ṭabarī p. 273; al-Fākihī, fol. 293b, sup.

84 Nūr al-Dīn al-Haythamī, 3: 244.

85 See al-Fākihī, fol. 293a (the remark of Ḥusayn b. 'Alī about the buttocks of Mu'āwiya during the *ṭawāf* ; and see fol. 294a: al-Sā'ib b. Ṣayfī and his talk with Mu'āwiya about Hind).

86 See on him Ibn Ḥajar, *Tahdhīb*, 6: 376–378, no. 716; al-Fāsī, *al-'Iqd*, 5: 480, no. 1856.

87 See on him al-Fāsī, *al-'Iqd*, 7: 218, no. 2469.

88 al-Azraqī, p. 260; Muḥibb al-Dīn al-Ṭabarī, p. 278.

89 al-Fākihī fol. 291b (*dhikru karāhiyati l-kalāmi bi-l-fārisiyyati fī l-ṭawāf*); see the tradition about 'Umar: 'Abd al-Razzāq, 5: 496, no. 9793; cf. al-Ṭurṭūshī, *al-Ḥawādith wa-l-bida'*, ed. Muḥammad Ṭalbī (Tunis: 1959), p. 104.

Qur'ān during the *ṭawāf* in a loud voice was disliked and considered a bad innovation (*muḥdath*); the Prophet is said to have asked 'Uthmān to turn to *dhikru llāh* from his *qirā'a.* Nevertheless certain groups of scholars permitted the recitation of verses from the Qur'ān.[90]

The problem of the reciting of poetry during the *ṭawāf* is complicated. The Prophet is said to have told Abū Bakr who recited *rajaz* verses during the circumambulation to utter *allāhu akbar* instead. This injunction of the Prophet seems to have been disregarded. Ibn 'Abbās, Abū Sa'īd al-Khudrī and Jābir b. 'Abdallāh used to talk during the *ṭawāf* and recite verses.[91] A report on the authority of 'Abdallah b. 'Umar says that the Companions used to recite poetry to each other (*yatanāshadūn*) during the circumambulation.[92] The argument in favor of the lawfulness of the recitation of poetry during *ṭawāf* was based on the precedent of 'Abdallah b. Rawāḥa who had recited his verses during the Prophet's *ṭawāf* in the year A.H. 7 (*'umrat al-qaḍā'*): *Khallū banī l-kuffār 'an sabīlih* ...[93] Also during the *ṭawāf* 'Ā'isha discussed with some women of Quraysh the position of Ḥassān b. Thābit and spoke in his favor, mentioning his verses in defense of the Prophet; [94] Ḥassān, some traditions say, was aided by the angel Jibrīl in composing seventy verses in praise of the Prophet.[95] Al-Nābigha al-Ja'dī recited his verses in the mosque of Mecca, praising Ibn al-Zubayr and asking for his help at a time of drought.[96] Ibn al-Zubayr asked, during the *ṭawāf*, a son of Khālid

---

90 Ibn Abī Shayba, 4: 10; Al-Azraqī, p. 258; al-Fākihī, fols. 295b-296a; and see the survey of the different opinions: Ibn Ẓuhayra, pp. 129-30; al-Majlisī, 99: 209, no. 19.

91 al-Fākihī, fol. 307b.

92 al-Fākihī, fol. 307b.

93 al-Wāqidī, p. 736; Nūr al-Dīn al-Haythamī, 8: 130; al-Fākihī, fol. 307a; al-Muttaqī l-Hindī, 5: 95, no. 745.

94 al-Azraqī, p. 257; Ibn 'Abd al-Barr, *al-Istī'āb*, ed. 'Alī al-Bajāwī (Cairo: 1380/1960), 1: 347; al-Fākihī, fol. 307b.

95 al-Fākihī, fol. 307b.

96 Maria Nallino, *Le Poesie di an-Nābigah al-Ǧa'dī* (Rome: 1953), p. 137 (IX) (and see the references of the editor); al-Fākihī, fol. 307b inf. 308a.

b. Ja'far al-Kilābī to recite some verses of his father against Zuhayr (b. Jadhīma al-'Absī). "But I am in a state of *iḥrām*," argued the son of Khālid. "And so am I," said Ibn al-Zubayr and urged him to recite the verses. He responded and quoted the verse: "And if you catch me, kill me ..." (*Fa-immā ta'khudhūnī fa-qtulūnī: wa-in aslam fa-laysa ilā l-khulūdi*). Ibn al-Zubayr sadly remarked that this verse suited his position in relation to the Banū Umayya.[97] Sa'īd b. Jubayr recalled having heard during the *ṭawāf* the verses of a drunkard who prided himself on the fact that he would not refrain from drinking wine even in old age.[98] An old woman recalled verses composed about her beauty in her youth.[99] There are moving verses composed by devoted sons, who carried on their backs their old mothers during the *ṭawāf* and supplications by women asking God to forgive them their sins. Poets had the opportunity to watch women doing their *ṭawāf* and composed verses extolling their beauty.[100] The wearing of a veil by women performing the *ṭawāf* was the subject of a heated discussion among scholars who used as arguments the contradictory utterances attributed to the Prophet and quoted as precedents the *ṭawāf* of his wives.[101] Another important problem was whether men and women could lawfully perform the *ṭawāf* together. According to one tradition women used to perform the *ṭawāf* together with men in the early period. The separation of women from men was first ordered by Khālid b. 'Abdallāh al-Qasrī.[102] Al-Fākihī remarks that this injunction was

---

97 al-Fākihī, fol. 307b; and see a different version of this verse *Aghānī* (Būlāq), 10: 12.

98 al-Fākihī, fol. 308a; and see the verses: Yāqūt, *Mu'jam al-buldān*, s.v. Amaj; and see Ibn Abī l-Dunyā, *Dhamm al-muskir*, al-Ẓāhiriyya, Majmū'a 60, fol. 8a (Sa'īd b. Jubayr changes the text of the verse from *wa-kāna karīman fa-lam yanzi'* into *wa-kāna shaqiyyan fa-lam yanzi'*).

99 al-Fākihī, fol. 308a.

100 al-Fākihī, fols. 307b-310a.

101 al-Shāfi'ī, 2: 127; al-Azraqī, p. 260; al-Fākihī, fols. 296a-297a; Nūr al-Dīn al-Haythamī, 3: 219-20; Ibn Ẓuhayra, pp. 133 ult.-134.

102 al-Azraqī, pp. 265-6; al-Fākihī, fols. 299a ult.-299b; Muḥibb al-Dīn al-Ṭabarī, pp. 319-20; al-Qasṭallānī, 3: 172-3; Ibn Ḥajar, *Fatḥ al-bārī*, 3: 384-5; Ibn Ẓuhayra, p. 127; al-Fāsī, *al-'Iqd*, 4: 273.

received with approval and people conformed to it until al-Fākihī's own time. Two other decrees of al-Qasrī continued to be observed by the people of Mecca: *takbīr* during the ceremony of *ṭawāf* in the month of Ramaḍān and a special arrangement of rows of men around the Kaʿba.[103] The separation between men and women in the mosque of Mecca was carried out by the governor ʿAlī b. al-Ḥasan al-Hāshimī as late as the middle of the third century by drawing ropes between the columns of the mosque; the women sat behind the ropes.[104] At the beginning of the third century (about 209) the governor of Mecca under al-Ma'mūn, ʿUbaydallāh b. al-Ḥasan al-Ṭālibi,[105] ordered a special time to be set apart for the women's *ṭawāf* after the afternoon prayer; men were not allowed to perform the *ṭawāf* at that time. This regulation was implemented again by the governor of Mecca, Ibrāhīm b. Muḥammad about A.H. 260.[106] These changes in the ceremony of the *ṭawāf* seem to point to a considerable fluctuation of ideas and attitudes among the rulers and the orthodox in connection with the sanctuary and the form of the *ṭawāf*.

The new arrangements, which were apparently meant to grant the *ḥaram* more religious dignity and sanctity and to turn the *ṭawāf* into a solemn ceremony with fixed rules, may be compared with some peculiar customs practised in the early *ṭawāf*, as recorded by al-Fākihī. The passage given by al-Fākihī begins with

---

103 al-Fākihī, fol. 432a (and see ibid., fol. 439b, lines 5-7 and fol. 354b: *dhikru idārati l-ṣaffi fī shahri ramaḍāna wa-awwalu man faʿalahu wa-awwalu man aḥdatha l-takbīra bayna l-tarāwīḥi ḥawla l-bayti fī shahri ramaḍāna wa-tafsīru dhālika*); al-Zarkashī, *Iʿlāmu l-sājid bi-aḥkāmi l-masājid*, ed. Abū l-Wafā Muṣṭafā l-Marāghī (Cairo: 1385), p. 98; al-Fāsī, *al-ʿIqd*, 4: 272, 276 sup.; al-Shiblī, *Maḥāsin al-wasāʾil fī maʿrifati l-awāʾil*, MS. Br. Mus., Or. 1530, fols. 38b-39a, 41b-42a.

104 al-Fākihī, fol. 443a; al-Fāsī, *al-ʿIqd*, 6; 151, no. 2050 (quoted from al-Fākihī); idem, *Shifāʾ al-gharām* (Cairo), 2: 188 (quoted from al-Fākihī); Ibn Ẓuhayra, p. 300 inf. (quoted from al-Fākihī).

105 See on him Wakīʿ, *Akhbār al-quḍāt*, ed. ʿAbd al-ʿAzīz Muṣṭafā al-Marāghī (Cairo: 1366/1947), 1: 257-258; Ibn Ẓuhayra, p. 297.

106 al-Fākihī, fol. 443a; al-Fāsī, *al-ʿIqd*, 3: 247-8, no. 720 (quoted from al-Fākihī).

a rather cautious phrase: *wa-qad zaʿama baʿḍu ahli makkata*, which clearly expresses a reservation on the part of the compiler. In the old times (*kānū fīmā maḍā*) when a girl reached the age of womanhood her people used to dress her up in the nicest clothes they could afford, and if they were in possession of jewels they adorned her with them; then they introduced her into the mosque of Mecca, her face uncovered; she circumambulated the Kaʿba while people looked at her and asked about her. They were then told "This is Miss so and so, the daughter of so and so," if she was a free-born person. If she was a *muwallada* they said: "She is a *muwallada* of this or that clan." Al-Fākihī remarks in a parenthetical phrase that people in those times had religious conviction and trustworthiness (*ahlu dīnin wa-amānatin*) unlike people of his day, whose manner of belief is obnoxious (*laysū ʿalā mā hum ʿalayhi min al-madhāhibi l-makrūha*). After the girl had finished her *ṭawāf* she would go out in the same way, while people were watching her. The purpose of this practice was to arouse in the people the desire to marry the girl (if she was free-born) or to buy her (if she was a *muwallada*). Then the girl returned to her home and was locked up in her apartment until she was brought out and led to her husband. They acted in the same way with slave-maidens: they led them in the *ṭawāf* around the Kaʿba clad in precious dresses, but with their faces uncovered. People used to come, look at them and buy them. Al-Awzāʿī asked ʿAṭā' (apparently Ibn Abī Rabāḥ) whether it was lawful to look at maidens who were led in *ṭawāf* around the Kaʿba for sale; ʿAṭā' objected to this practice except for people who wanted to buy slave-girls.[107] This report is corroborated by a story recorded by Ibn Abī Shayba, according to which ʿĀ'isha dressed up a maiden, performed the *ṭawāf* with her and remarked: "We may perhaps succeed in catching (literally: hunting) a youth of Quraysh" (scil. for

---

107 al-Fākihī, fol. 309b.

the girl).[108] 'Umar is said to have encouraged the selling of slave-maidens in this manner.[109] All these reports – al-Fākihī's reference to "people with religious conviction and trustworthiness," al-Awzā'ī's inquiry, 'Aṭā"s answer, 'Ā'isha's story – seem to reflect *ṭawāf* customs prevailing in the early period of Islam, in all likelihood during the first century of the Hijra. The reports indicate a certain informality and ease of manners. All this was bound to change if the *ḥaram* was to acquire an atmosphere of sanctity and veneration.

The early informality and intimacy can be gauged from a number of traditions concerned with the daily behaviour of the faithful in the mosque of Mecca. Ibn al-Zubayr passed by a group of people who were eating their meal in the mosque and invoked upon them his benediction. Abū Nawfal b. Abī 'Aqrab[110] saw Ibn 'Abbās there eating roasted meat with thin bread; the fat dripped from his hands. A broth of crumbled bread used to be brought to Ibn al-Zubayr in the mosque. One day a boy crawled towards it and ate from it; 'Abdallāh b. al-Zubayr ordered the boy to be flogged. The people in the mosque, in their rage, cursed Ibn al-Zubayr.[111]

A similar problem was whether it is lawful to sleep in the mosque of Mecca. Scholars arguing for it quoted the precedent of the Prophet whose *isrā'* took place (according to the report of Anas b. Mālik) from the mosque of Mecca where he had slept.[112] Another

---

108 *al-Muṣannaf*, 4: 410; *Lisān al-'Arab*, s.v. sh-w-f; Ibn al-Athīr, *al-Nihāya*, s.v. sh-w-f.

109 Ibn Abī Shayba, 4: 411 ('Umar remarks, however, that girls should not be compelled to marry ugly [or mean; in text *dhamīm* ; but probably *damīm*] men; "the girls like in this matter what you like," he said); cf. Ibn Ra's Ghanama, *Manāqil al-durar fī manābit al-zahar*, MS. Chester Beatty 4254, fol. 19b: *qāla 'umaru: lā yuzawwijanna l-rajulu bnatahu l-qabīḥa fa-innahunna yarghabna fīmā targhabūn.*

110 See on him Ibn Ḥajar, *Tahdhīb*, 12: 260.

111 al-Fākihī, fol. 355b: *dhikru l-akli fī l- masjidi l-ḥarāmi wa-l-ghadā' fīhi* ; and see al-Ṭurṭūshī, pp. 106–8; al-Zarkashī, *I'lām al-sājid*, pp. 329–30.

112 al-Fākihī, fol. 355b.

argument in favor of sleeping in mosques was mentioned by Sulaymān b. Yasār,[113] when questioned by al-Ḥārith b. ʻAbd al-Raḥmān b. Abī Dhubāb: [114] "How do you ask about it, said Sulaymān, knowing that the *aṣḥāb al-ṣuffa* slept in the mosque of the Prophet and prayed in it." [115] Ibn ʻUmar used to sleep in the mosque (of Medina) in the Prophet's lifetime.[116] When Thābit (al-Bunānī) consulted ʻAbdallāh b. ʻUbayd b. ʻUmayr[117] whether to turn to the *amīr* in the matter of the people sleeping in the mosque of Mecca, ʻAbdallāh bade him not to do that, quoting the opinion of Ibn ʻUmar who considered these people as *ʻākifūn*, people praying in seclusion. The pious Saʻīd b. Jubayr used to sleep in the mosque of Mecca. ʻAṭā' b. Abī Rabāḥ spent forty years in the mosque of Mecca, sleeping there, performing the *ṭawāf*, and praying.[118] In a conversation with his student Ibn Jurayj he expressed a very favourable opinion about sleeping in mosques. When ʻAṭā' and Saʻīd b. Jubayr were asked about people sleeping in the mosque of Mecca who have night-pollutions they nevertheless gave a positive answer and advised them to continue to sleep in the mosque. In the morning, says a tradition, Saʻīd b. Jubayr used to perform the *ṭawāf*, wake up the sleepers in the mosque, and bid them recite the *talbiya*.

These reports quoted from a chapter of al-Fākihī entitled *Dhikru l-nawmi fī l-masjidi l-ḥarāmi wa-man rakhkhaṣa fīhi wa-man karihahu*[119] give some insight into the practices in the

---

113 See on him Ibn Ḥajar, *Tahdhīb*, 4: 228, no. 381.

114 See on him ibid., 2: 147, no. 249; al-Dhahabī, 1: 437, no. 1629.

115 al-Ṭurṭūshī, p. 105.

116 al-Zarkashī, *I'lām al-sājid*, p. 307; al-Ṭurṭūshī, p. 105; al-Marāghī, *Taḥqīq al-nuṣra bi-talkhīṣ ma'ālim dāri l-hijra*, MS. Br. Mus., Or. 3615, fol. 50a.

117 See on him al-Bukhārī, *al-Ta'rīkh al-kabīr*, 31, no. 430; Ibn Ḥajar, *Tahdhīb*, 5: 308, no. 524.

118 Cf. al-Ṭurṭūshī, p. 105.

119 *Ta'rīkh Makka*, fol. 355b-356a; al-Zarkashī, *I'lām al-sājid*, pp. 306-8, 317-18; Muḥibb al Dīn al-Ṭabarī, pp. 659-60, nos. 30-31; al-Majlisī, 99: 240, no. 1; about the odious impurity which causes bad smells see al-Fākihī, fol. 357b, ult.-358a (*dhikru irsāli l-rīḥi fī l-masjidi l-ḥarāmi*); al-Zarkashī, *I'lām al-sājid*, pp. 313-14; cf. about a superstitious belief

mosque of Mecca in the early period of Islam and help us to understand the ideas about ritual and the sanctity of the *ḥaram* current at the time.

Of special interest are some customs of *ṭawāf* and *ḥajj* which include hardships, rigid self-exertion and self-castigation. Tradition tells about people who vowed to perform the *ṭawāf* while crawling,[120] or fastened to each other by a rope,[121] or being led with a rope threaded through a nose-ring.[122] Tradition reports that the Prophet and his Companions unequivocally condemned these practices, prohibited them and prevented the people from performing the *ṭawāf* in this way. It is obvious that these usages reflected the Jāhiliyya ideas of self-imposed harshness, of vows of hardship and severe practices. These went contrary to the spirit of Islam which, while transforming it into an Islamic ritual, aimed to give the *ṭawāf* its own religious values. Ibn Ḥajar is right in tracing back the prohibited forms of *ṭawāf* to their Jāhilī source.[123]

Similar to these vows of self-exertion during the *ṭawāf* are the vows of hardship during the *ḥajj*. The traditions tell about men who vowed to perform the *ḥajj* on foot. Some women vowed to perform the *ḥajj* walking, or with faces uncovered, or wearing coarse garments, or keeping silent.[124] The Prophet passed censure on

---

current among common people in Egypt: ʿAlī Maḥfūz, *al-Ibdāʿ fī maḍārr al-ibtidāʿ* (Cairo: 1388/1968), p. 454.

120 al-Fākihī, fol. 297a; al-Azraqī, p. 261; ʿAbd al-Razzāq, 8: 457, no. 15895.

121 al-Fākihī, fol. 297b; al-Azraqī, p. 261; ʿAbd al-Razzāq, 8: 448, no. 15862; al-Bayhaqī, *al-Sunan al-kubrā*, 5:88; al-Qasṭallānī, 3: 173–4; al-Ḥākim, *al-Mustadrak*, 1: 460; Ibn Ḥajar, *Fatḥ al-bārī*, 3: 386–7; Muḥibb al-Dīn al-Ṭabarī, p. 319, no. 73.

122 al-Fākihī, fol. 297b; ʿAbd al-Razzāq, 8: 448, nos. 15860–15861, 11: 292, no. 20572; *Lisān al-ʿArab*, s.v. z-m-m-, kh-z-m.

123 *Fatḥ al-bārī*, 3: 386.

124 al-Ṭaḥāwī, *Sharḥ maʿānī*, 3: 128–132; Yūsuf b. Mūsā al-Ḥanafī, 1: 260–2; al-Suyūṭī, *al-Durr al-manthūr*, 1: 351–2; idem, *Taʾrīkh al-khulafāʾ*, ed. Muḥammad Muḥyī l-Dīn ʿAbd al-Ḥamīd (Cairo: 1371/1952), p. 99; al-Shāṭibī, *al-Iʿtiṣām* (Cairo: n.d.), 2: 52; Baḥshal, *Taʾrīkh Wāsiṭ*, ed.

these practices, emphasizing that God does not heed (literally: does not need) vows by which people cause harm and suffering to themselves.

These practices recall certain customs observed by the Ḥums which therefore had to be abolished in Islam. It may however be remarked that some early Muslim ascetics or pious men used to perform the *ḥajj* on foot, or vowed not to walk under a shade during their *ḥajj*.[125] It is true that the outer form of these practices recalls the old Jāhiliyya ones; there is however a clear line which has to be drawn between them: the devotional practices of the pious Muslims are different in their content and intention; they are undertaken out of a deep faith and performed for God's sake. These practices of the pious gained the approval of the orthodox circles and were considered virtuous. This attitude is clearly reflected in a *ḥadīth* attributed to the Prophet: "The advantage of the people performing the *ḥajj* walking over those who ride is like the advantage of the full moon over the stars."[126]

Fasting on the Day of ʻArafa gave rise to another important controversy. The contradictory traditions and reports are arranged in Fākihī's compilation in two chapters: the one encouraging the

---

Gurguis ʻAwwād (Baghdād, 1387/1967), p. 231; Ibn Saʻd, 8: 470; al-Bayhaqī, *al-Sunan al-kubrā*, 10: 76; al-Fasawī, fol. 157b; Ibn ʻAbd al-Ḥakam, p. 294; al-Muttaqī l-Hindī, 5: 341, no. 2265, 449, no. 2507; Aḥmad b. Ḥanbal, *Musnad*, 11: 7, no. 6714; al-Ṭayālisī, p. 112, no. 836; al-Ṭaḥāwī, *Mushkil al-āthār*, 3: 37–41; ʻAbd al-Razzāq, 8: 438, no. 15825, 448, no. 15863; al-Fākihī, fols. 315a-b; Ibn Daqīq al-ʻĪd, pp. 310–11, nos. 791–793. (And see al-Fākihī, fol. 511b: the story of the woman who vowed to perform the pilgrimage in silence if God would help to reconcile the fighting factions of her tribe. Abū Bakr, ordering her to discontinue her silence, remarked: *takallamī, fa-inna l-islāma hadama mā kāna qabla dhālika*); al-Ṭūsī, *Amālī* (Najaf: 1384/1964), 1: 369.

125 Ibn Abī l-Dunyā, *al-Tawba*, MS. Chester Beatty 3863, fol. 17b; Baḥshal, p. 167; al-Khuwārizmī, *Mukhtaṣar ithārati l-targhīb wa-l-tashwīq ilā l-masājidi l-thalāthati wa-ilā l-bayti l-ʻatīq*, MS. Br. Mus., Or. 4584, fol. 8a-b.

126 al-Fākihī, fols. 321b-322a (*dhikru l-maṣhyi fī l-ḥajji wa-faḍlihi*); al-Khuwārizmī, fol. 8b: *wa-li-l-māshī faḍlun ʻalā l-rākibi ka-faḍli laylati l-qadri ʻalā sāʼiri l-layālī*.

faithful to fast on this day, the other reporting about Companions who refrained from fasting.[127] According to a tradition of the Prophet the sins of a man who fasts on the Day of 'Arafa will be remitted for a year;[128] another version says two years,[129] a third version a thousand days.[130] The list of persons who did fast includes also 'Ā'isha, who emphasized the merits of fasting on that day. The opponents who forbade fasting on that day based their argument on accounts and evidence that the Prophet had broken the fast on the Day of 'Arafa.[131] 'Umar,[132] his son 'Abdallāh and Ibn 'Abbās prohibited fasting.[133] In another version Ibn 'Umar stressed that he performed the pilgrimage with the Prophet and the three first caliphs; none of them fasted on the Day of 'Arafa. He himself did not fast, but did not explicitly enjoin either eating or fasting.[134] The

---

127 al-Fākihī, fols. 528a-529a (*dhikru ṣawmi yawmi 'arafa wa-faḍli ṣiyāmihi* ; *dhikru man lam yaṣum yawma 'arafa makhāfata l-ḍu'fi 'ani l-du'ā*); Ibn Abī Shayba, 4: 1-3, 21, 3: 104; al-Ṭaḥāwī, *Mushkil*, 4: 111.

128 al-Fākihī, fol. 528a, ult.; al-Mundhirī, 2: 236, no. 1463; Ibn Abī Shayba, 3: 97; al-Ṭaḥāwī, *Sharḥ ma'ānī*, 2: 72; al-Bayhaqī, *al-Sunan al-kubrā*, 4: 283.

129 al-Fākihī, fols. 528a, inf., 528b; al-Ṭabarānī, 1: 255, 2: 71; Baḥshal, p. 276; al-Mundhirī, 2: 236; 7 nos. 1461-1462, 1464-1465, 1467-1468; Muḥibb al-Dīn al-Ṭabarī, p. 403; Ibn Abī Shayba, 3: 96-97; al-Ṭaḥāwī, *Sharḥ ma'ānī*, 2: 72; idem, *Mushkil*, 4: 112; al-Shawkānī, *Nayl*, 4: 267, no. 2; al-Bayhaqī, *al-Sunan al-kubrā*, 4: 283,

130 al-Mundhirī, 2: 237, no. 1466; al-Fākihī, fol. 528b; al-Suyūṭī, *al-Durr al-manthūr*, 1: 231 (another version 1,000 years).

131 Muṣ'ab b. 'Abdallāh, *Ḥadīth*, MS. Chester Beatty 3849/4, fol. 40a; Abū 'Umar, Ghulām Tha'lab, *Juz'*, MS. Chester Beatty 3495, fol. 97a; al-Fākihī, fol. 528b; al-Shawkānī, *Nayl*, 4: 267, no. 4; al-Bayhaqī, *al-Sunan al-kubrā*, 4: 283-4; al-Suyūṭī, *al-Durr al-manthūr*, 1: 231.

132 al-Bukhārī, *al-Ta'rīkh al-kabīr*, 3^2, no. 1600.

133 al-Fākihī, fol. 529a; Aḥmad b. Ḥanbal, *al-'Ilal*, 1: 286, nos. 1849, 1852; al-Khaṭīb al-Baghdādī, *Mūḍiḥ*, 2: 338-9; al-Fasawī, fol. 61a; cf. Abū Nu'aym, 7: 164; Muḥibb al-Dīn al-Ṭabarī, p. 404.

134 Abū 'Ubayd, *Gharīb al-ḥadīth* 3: 4; al-Khaṭīb al-Baghdādī, *Mūḍiḥ*, 1: 434; al-Ṭaḥāwī, *Sharḥ ma'ānī*, 2: 72; Muḥibb al-Dīn al-Ṭabarī, p. 404 (and see ibid., p. 405 inf.); al-Shawkānī, *Nayl*, 4: 268; al-Suyūṭī, *al-Durr al-manthūr*, 1: 231; Ibn Kathīr, *al-Bidāya wa-l-nihāya* (Beirut, al-Riyāḍ: 1966), 5: 174.

conciliatory interpretation assumed that the prohibition of fasting referred to the people attending 'Arafa; but people not present on that Day of 'Arafa may fast, and are even encouraged to fast.[135] The reason given for not fasting on that day in 'Arafa was the care for the pilgrims, who might be weakened by the fast and prevented from properly performing the *du'ā'* and *dhikr*, which are the most important aims of the pilgrims staying at 'Arafa.[136]

The transfer of some rites performed at 'Arafa to the cities conquered by the Muslims is of special interest. This practice was introduced in Baṣra by 'Abdallāh b. 'Abbas[137] and by 'Abd al-'Azīz b. Marwān in Fusṭāṭ.[138] On the Day of 'Arafa people used to gather in the mosques to invoke and to supplicate. When Ibn 'Abbās summoned the people to gather in the mosque he argued that he wished that the supplications of the people may be associated with those attendant at 'Arafa and that God may respond to these supplications; thus they would share God's grace with the attendants

---

135 al-Ṭaḥāwī, *Sharḥ ma'ānī*, 2: 72; idem, *Mushkil* 4: 112; Abū Nu'aym, 3: 347; al-Fasawī, fol. 32b; al-Shawkānī, *Nayl*, 4: 267, no. 3; al-Bayhaqī, *al-Sunan al-kubrā* 4: 289; Yūsuf b. Mūsā al-Ḥanafī, 1: 152; al-Suyūṭī, *al-Durr al-manthūr*, 1: 231.

136 al-Fākihī, fol. 529a; cf. Muḥibb al-Dīn al-Ṭabarī, p. 405, lines 3–7 (fasting on the Day of 'Arafa is not favored for people performing the pilgrimage; it is however encouraged for people not performing the *ḥajj*. See the compromise-recommendations of al-Mundhirī, 2: 238: "... there is nothing wrong in fasting, if it does not weaken him in his *du'ā'* ... for the pilgrims it is preferable to break the fast ..." See the story of Ibn Wahb, who broke the fast at 'Arafa because he was occupied by the thought of breaking the fast: al-Qāḍī 'Iyāḍ, *Tartīb al-madārik*, 1, 430; and see on this subject: al-Shawkānī, *Nayl* 4: 269).

137 See al-Quḍā'ī, *Ta'rīkh*, MS. Bodley, Pococke 270, fol. 67b (quoted from al-Jāḥiẓ's *Naẓm al-qur'ān*); al-Qalqashandī, *Ma'āthir al-ināfa fī ma'ālim al-khilāfa*, ed. 'Abd al-Sattār Aḥmad Farrāj (Kuwait: 1964), 1: 129; Muḥibb al-Dīn al-Ṭabarī, pp. 387 inf.–388 sup.; al-Fasawī, fol. 16a: ... *ḥaddathanā abū 'awāna, qāla: ra'aytu l-ḥasana kharaja yawma 'arafa min al-maqṣūrati ba'da l-'aṣri fa-qa'ada fa-'arrafa* ; al-Bayhaqī, *al-Sunan al-kubrā* 5: 117 inf.; see S.D. Goitein, *Studies in Islamic History and Institutions* (Leiden: 1966), p. 137.

138 al-Kindī, *Wulāt Miṣr*, ed. Ḥusayn Naṣṣār (Beirut: 1379/1959), p. 72.

at ʿArafa.[139] Muṣʿab b. al-Zubayr introduced this innovation in Kūfa.[140] Some pious Muslims participated in these gatherings, others considered them as *bidʿa*.[141] The *taʿrīf* in Jerusalem is linked in some sources with ʿAbd al-Malik, who is accused of having built the Dome of the Rock in Jerusalem in order to divert the pilgrimage from Mecca to Jerusalem, since ʿAbdallāh b. al-Zubayr, the rival caliph in Mecca, forced the pilgrims to give the oath of allegiance. When the Dome of the Rock was built people used to gather there on the Day of ʿArafa and performed there the *wuqūf*.[142] So the *bidʿa* of *wuqūf* in Jerusalem arose. Al-Ṭurṭūshī describes a gathering of the people of Jerusalem and of its villages in the mosque, raising their voices in supplications. They believed that four "standings" (*waqafāt*) in Jerusalem were equal to a pilgrimage to Mecca.[143] Ibn Taymiyya, of course, strongly censured this innovation.[144]

It is evident that the idea behind the *taʿrīf* is that it is possible to transfer sanctity from ʿArafa to another sanctuary where the rites of ʿArafa are being performed on the same day, or that one may share in the blessing of ʿArafa through the performance of certain devotions at the same time as they are done at ʿArafa (as is the case with the supplications in the *taʿrīf* mentioned in note 139 above), or the notion that two sanctities may be combined as indicated in the tradition about Zamzam visiting Sulwān on the night of ʿArafa.[145]

The idea of transfer of sanctity is clearly reflected in a

---

139 al-Mawṣilī, *Ghāyat al-wasāʾil ilā maʿrifati l-awāʾil*, MS. Cambridge Qq 33 (10), fol. 153a.

140 al-Suyūṭī, *al-Durr al-manthūr*, 1: 231 inf.

141 Ibn Kathīr, *al-Bidāya*, 9: 307; al-Ṭurṭūshī, pp. 115-16; al-Suyūṭī, *al-Durr al-manthūr*, 1: 231 inf.

142 al-Quḍāʿī, fol. 67b; al-Qalqashandī, 1: 129.

143 al-Ṭurṭūshī, pp. 116-17.

144 *Majmūʿat al-rasāʾil al-kubrā* (Cairo: 1323), 2: 57; Jamāl a-Dīn al-Qāsimī, *Iṣlāḥ al-masājid min al-bidaʿ wa-l-ʿawāʾid* (Cairo: 1341), p. 215 (from Ibn Taymiyya).

145 al-Muqaddasī, *Aḥsan al-taqāsīm*, ed. M.J. de Goeje (Leiden: 1906), p. 171, line 11.

peculiar Shī'ī tradition in which a Shī'ī adherent asks the *imām* Ja'far al-Ṣādiq whether he may perform the *ta'rīf* on the grave of Ḥusayn if the opportunity to perform the *ḥajj* (scil. to Mecca) escapes him. The *imām* enumerates in his answer the rewards for visiting the grave of al-Ḥusayn on common days and those for visits on feasts, emphasizing that these rewards are multiplied for a visit on the Day of 'Arafa. This visit is equal in rewards with a thousand pious pilgrimages to Mecca and a thousand *'umra* accepted by God and a thousand military campaigns fought on the side of a prophet or a just *imām*. The adherent then asked, how he could get a reward similar to that of the *mawqif* (of 'Arafa). The *imām* looked at him as if roused to anger and said: "The believer who comes to the grave of al-Ḥusayn on the Day of 'Arafa, washes in the Euphrates and directs himself to the grave, he will be rewarded for every step as if he had performed a *ḥajj* with all due rites." The transmitter recalls that the *imām* did say: "and [took part in] a military campaign.[146]

Some changes of ritual were attributed to the Umayyads and sharply criticized by orthodox scholars. A number of innovations of this kind are said to have been introduced by Mu'āwiya. It was he who refrained from the *takbīr* on the Day of 'Arafa, because 'Alī used to practise it.[147] He forbade the loud recitation of the *talbiya* at 'Arafāt, and people obeyed his order; then Ibn 'Abbās ostentatiously came forth and uttered the *talbiya* loudly.[148] It was Mu'āwiya who transformed a place where the Prophet had urinated into a place of prayer,[149] and invented (*aḥdatha*) the *adhān* in the *ṣalāt al-'īdayn*.[150] He changed the order of the ceremony of the *'īd*

---

146 Ibn Bābawayh, *Amālī l-ṣadūq* (Najaf: 1389/1970), pp. 126–7.

147 al-Fākihī, fol. 529a.

148 Muḥibb al-Dīn al-Ṭabarī, p. 403; al-Ḥākim, *al-Mustadrak*, 1: 464 inf.–465; al-Muttaqī al-Hindī, 5: 79, nos. 646, 648.

149 Muḥibb al-Dīn al-Ṭabari, p. 417; Amīn Maḥmūd Khaṭṭāb, *Fatḥ al-malik al-ma'būd*, 2: 59 inf.–60, lines 1–7; al-Fākihī, fol. 531a, sup.

150 al-Suyūṭī, *Ta'rīkh al-khulafā'*, p. 200.

al-aḍḥā and ordered the *khuṭba* to be delivered before the prayer.[151] He was also the one who banned the *tamattuʿ* pilgrimages.[152] Changes of this kind were recorded as wicked innovations of the impious Umayyad rulers.

The inconsistencies of the usages, customs and ritual practices of the early period of Islam are reflected in almost every subject dealt with in the early sources of *ḥadīth*. Opinions divergent and contradictory are expressed about the *sutra* which has to be put in front of the praying Muslim and whether a dog or a donkey or a woman passing by invalidates the prayer.[153] Scholars differ in their opinions as to whether the form of sitting during the prayer called *iqʿāʾ* is permitted,[154] whether the prayer by a believer clad in one garment (*thawb*) is valid,[155] and whether counting of the *tasbīḥ* by pebbles is allowed.[156]

Some of the subjects dealt with in the early *ḥadīth*s lost their actuality and relevance. It is however a special feature of Muslim *ḥadīth* literature and *ḥadīth* criticism that some of these themes reappear and are discussed even in our days. Thus, for instance, the contemporary scholar Nāṣir al-Dīn al-Albānī examines

---

151 al-Shiblī, *Maḥāsin al-wasāʾil*, fol. 120a; al-Suyūṭī, *Taʾrīkh al-khulafāʾ*, p. 200.

152 al-Muttaqī al-Hindī, 5: 88, no. 708; al-Shiblī, *Maḥāsin al-wasāʾil*, fol. 119b (and see above notes 48, 50); and cf. the wicked innovations of al-Ḥajjāj: Abū Ṭālib al-Makkī, 2: 53–4.

153 al-Ḥākim, *al-Mustadrak*, 1: 251–2; Nūr al-Dīn al-Haythamī, 2: 59–62; al-Fākihī, fol. 481a inf.; al-Fasawī, fol. 217b; Ibn Abī Shayba, 1: 276–83; ʿAbd al-Razzāq, 2: 9–38, nos. 2272–2396; al-Ṭaḥāwī, *Sharḥ maʿānī*, 1: 458–64; al-Muttaqī l-Hindī, 8: 132–8, nos. 946–989; al-Zarkashī, *al-Ijāba*, pp. 66, 84.

154 Ibn Abī Shayba, 1: 285; ʿAbd al-Razzāq, 2: 190–7, nos. 3024–3053; and see Ibn al-Athīr, *al-Nihāya*, s.v. q-ʿ-a, ʿ-q-b.

155 al-Ṭaḥāwī, *Sharḥ maʿānī*, 1: 377–83; al-Shawkānī, *Nayl*, 2: 83–4; Ibn Abī Shayba, 1: 310–15.

156 Ibn Abī Shayba, 2: 389–91; Ibn Abī l-Ḥadīd, *Sharḥ nahj al-balāgha*, ed. Muḥammad Abū l-Faḍl Ibrāhīm (Cairo: 1964), 18: 164; and cf. Aḥmad b. Ḥanbal, *al-ʿIlal*, 1: 325, no. 2122; Saʿīd b. Jubayr throws out the pebbles with which a woman counted her circlings during the the *ṭawāf*.

the tradition prohibiting fasting on the Day of 'Arafa for people attending 'Arafa.[157] He carefully analyzes the *isnāds*, finding out their faults; he harshly reprimands al-Ḥākim for his heedlessness in considering the *ḥadīth* sound and states that the *ḥadīth* is in fact weak. He argues that the *ḥadīth* about the forgiveness of sins for a period of two years for him who fasts on the Day of 'Arafa is a sound tradition; but the attached phrase about the rewards for fasting on every day of Muḥarram is a forged one.[158] An exhaustive scrutiny of *ḥadīths* about the counting of *tasbīḥ* by pebbles is included by al-Albānī in the examination of the *ḥadīth* about the rosary (*al-subḥa*).[159]

Of interest are certain traditions in which some social and cultural, as well as religious, trends are exposed. Of this kind are the traditions in which the Prophet predicted that his community would erect sumptuous mosques in the manner of Jewish synagogues and Christian churches, adorn them richly and embellish them with inscriptions. This will be the sign of decline of the Muslim community and portend the End of the Days. Traditions of the very early period of Islam reflect the opposition against arched *miḥrābs*. "Beware these altars" (*ittaqū hādhihi l-madhābiḥ*), followed by an explanatory comment, "he meant the *maḥārīb*" (*ya'nī l-maḥārīb*), says a tradition attributed to the Prophet.[160] "My people will fare well as long as they will not build in their mosques altars

---

157 Nāṣir al-Dīn al-Albānī, *Silsilat al-aḥādīth al-ḍa'īfa wa-l-mawḍū'a* (Damascus: 1384), no. 404.

158 Ibid., no. 412.

159 Ibid., no. 83.

160 al-Daylamī, MS. Chester Beatty 4139, fol. 27a (al-Daylamī adds: *wa-kāna ibrāhīmu l-taymī lā yuṣallī fī ṭāqi l-miḥrāb*); al-Suyūṭī, *al-Khaṣā'iṣ al-kubrā*, 3: 189; al-Munāwī, 1: 144-5, no. 153 reviews the different meanings of the word *miḥrāb*. And see the peculiar story of the Christian youth in the *miḥrāb*: al-Khaṭīb al-Baghdādī, *Ta'rīkh Baghdād*, 9: 45; al-Ṭurṭūshī, p. 94; al-Baḥrānī, 7: 281-5; Maḥmūd Mahdī al-Mūsawī al-Khawansārī, *Tuḥfat al-sājid fī aḥkām al-masājid* (Baghdad: 1376), pp. 111-16. And see R.B. Serjeant, "Miḥrāb," *BSOAS* (1959): pp. 439-53.

like the altars of the Christians," the Prophet foretold.[161] Pious men usually refrained from praying in these *miḥrābs*.[162] Of the same kind were traditions against the adornment of mosques,[163] prayers in the *maqṣūra* of the mosque,[164] and against writing Qur'ān verses on the walls of the mosque, or in the *qibla* of the mosque.[165]

These traditions should, of course, be studied against the background of the reports about the sumptuous buildings which were erected by the impious rulers and their governors and the richly decorated *jāmiʿ* mosques in which delegates of the rulers led the prayer. Many a time a pious Muslim had to ask himself whether he should pray behind them, as can be deduced from the numerous traditions dealing with this subject.

The few traditions reviewed in this paper clearly demonstrate the fluidity of certain religious and socio-political ideas reflected in the early compilations of *ḥadīth*, as already proved by I. Goldziher. The diversity and divergence of traditions expose the different opinions of various groups of Muslim scholars. The divergent traditions are faithfully recorded in the compilations

161 al-Suyūṭī, *al-Khaṣāʾiṣ al-kubrā*, 3: 188–9; Ibn Abī Shayba, 2: 59; and see the careful evaluation of this *ḥadīth* by Albānī, *Silsila*, no. 448.

162 ʿAbd al-Razzāq, 2: 412, no. 3898–3902; the tradition about the altars of the Christians, no. 3903; Ibn Abī Shayba, 2: 59–60 (*al-ṣalāt fī l-ṭāq, man rakhkhaṣa l-ṣalāt fī l-ṭāq*); Aḥmad b. Ḥanbal, *al-ʿIlal*, 1: 64, no. 373.

163 al-Suyūṭī, *al-Khaṣāʾiṣ al-kubrā*, 3: 56–7; Ibn Abī Shayba, 1: 309; al-Suyūṭī, *al-Durr al-manthūr*, 3: 217 inf.; al-Shaybānī, pp. 77–8; Abū ʿUbayd, *Gharīb al-ḥadīth*, 4: 225; al-Shawkānī, *Nayl*, 2: 167–70; idem, *al-Fawāʾid al-majmūʿa*, ed. ʿAbd al-Wahhāb ʿAbd al-Laṭīf (Cairo: 1960), pp. 25–7; Abū Ṭālib al-Makkī, 2: 51 inf.; Ibn Abī Jamra, *Bahjat al-nufūs* (Beirut: 1972 reprint), 1: 183; al-Samarqandī, *Bustān al-ʿārifīn* (on margin of *Tanbīh al-ghāfilīn*) (Cairo: 1347), pp. 127–8; Yūsuf b. ʿAbd al-Hādī, *Thimār al-maqāṣid fī dhikri l-masājid*, ed. Asʿad Ṭalas (Beirut: 1943), pp. 166, 170; al-Baḥrānī, 7: 277; al-Zarkashī, *Iʿlām al-sājid* pp. 335–8; Muḥammad Mahdī al-Mūsawī, pp. 87–92.

164 See ʿAbd al-Razzāq, 2: 414–16, nos. 3907–3913; al-Bayhaqī, *al-Sunan al-kubrā*, 3: 238; Abū Ṭālib al-Makkī, 2: 51 inf.; Ibn Saʿd, 7: 96.

165 Ibn Abī Shayba, 2: 46; al-Ṭurṭūshī, p. 97; al-Zarkashī, *Iʿlām al-sājid*, p. 337; cf. Yūsuf b. ʿAbd al-Hādī, p. 170.

of the second century of the Hijra with no obligatory conclusions imposed and no prescriptions issued.

This activity reflects a sincere effort to establish the true path of the Prophet, the Sunna, which the believer should follow.

ADDITIONAL NOTES

ad note 4: Ibn ʿAbd al-Barr al-Qurṭubī, *Bahjat al-majālis wa-uns al-mujālis*, ed. Muḥammad Mursī l-Khūlī and ʿAbd al-ʿQādir al-Qiṭṭ, Cairo 1969, II, 95: The Prophet predicts that the believers would conquer Syria and find there houses called "baths"; let no woman enter such a house except when ill and let no man enter it except when clad in a loincloth.

al-Mundhirī, *al-Targhīb wa-l-tarhīb mina l-ḥadīthi l-sharīf*, ed. Muḥammad Muḥyī l-Dīn ʿAbd al-Ḥamīd, Cairo 1379/1960, I, 119, no.268.

And see Abū Ṭālib al-Makkī, *Qūt al-qulūb*, Cairo 1351/1952, IV, 180 inf. : ... *wa-ḥarrama rasūlu llāhi ṣallā llāhu ʿalayhi wa-sallam dukhūla l-ḥammami ʿalā l-nisāʾi wa-ḥarramahu ʿalā l-rijāli illā bi-miʾzar. fa-in dakhalati l-marʾatu l-ḥammām ḍarūratan min ʿillatin au ḥayḍin au nifāsin au fī shitāʾin fa-lā baʾsa, wa-qad dakhalat ʿāʾishatu raḍiya llāhu ʿanhā min saqamin kāna bihā* ...

Aḥmad b. Muḥammad b. ʿAlī b. Ḥajar al-Haytamī, *al-Zawājir ʿani qtirāfi l-kabāʾir*, Cairo 1390/ 1970, I, 128, inf.

Baḥshal, *Taʾrīkh wāsiṭ*, ed. Kurkīs ʿAwwād, Baghdād 1387/1967, p.80.

Muḥammad b. al-Fattāl al-Naysābūrī, *Rauḍatu l-wāʿiẓīn*, ed. Muḥammad Mahdī al-Kharsān, Najaf 1386/1966, p. 307, inf., where the invocations to be uttered at the entrance to the different chambers of the bath are also given.

ad note 5: Ibn ʿAbd al-Barr, *Bahjat al-majālis*, II, 95: On the authority of Abū Hurayra: *biʾsa l-baytu l-ḥammām, yakshifu l-ʿaura wa-yudhhibu l-ḥayāʾ*.

This tradition occurs also in ʿAlī b. Burhān al-Dīn's *al-Sīra al-ḥalabiyya [= Insān al-ʿuyūn fī sīrati l-amīn al-maʾmūn]*, Cairo 1382/1962, I, 410.

Abū Manṣūr al-Thaʿālibī, *al-Laṭāʾif wa-l-ẓarāʾif*, [compiled by Abū Naṣr Aḥmad al-Maqdisī], Cairo 1324, pp. 36-37.

Ibn Ḥajar al-Haytamī, *al-Zawājir*, I, 129: in a conversation with ʿĀʾisha the Prophet forbade women to enter baths even if wearing loinclothes; and see *ibid.* other utterances of the Prophet prohibiting women to enter baths.

Comp. Abū Ṭālib al-Makkī, *Qūt al-qulūb*, IV, 179, inf.: *wa-qāla l-nabiyyu ṣallā llāhu ʿalayhi wa-sallam: dukhūlu l-ḥammam ʿalā l-nisāʾi ḥarām wa-ʿalā l-rijāli illā bi-miʾzar.*

About how the prohibition for women to enter baths by ʿUmar b. ʿAbd al-ʿAzīz is to be implemented: ʿAlī b. ʿUmar al-Ḥarbī, *al-Fawāʾid al-muntaqāt wa-l-gharāʾib al-ḥisān*, MS. Chester Beatty 3495 [*majmūʿa*] fol. 19 a.

al-Haytamī, *al-Zawājir*, I, 130: The evidence of witnesses who enter baths not wearing loinclothes should not be accepted.

al-Bayhaqī, *al-Jāmiʿ li-shuʿabi l-īmān*, ed. ʿAbd al-ʿAliyy ʿAbd al-Ḥamīd Ḥāmid, Bombay 1408/1988, V, 569–571, nos. 2394–2396: reading the Qurʾān and mentioning God's name in a bath is forbidden; an isolated opinion of a scholar saying that there is no objection to read [i. e. the Qurʾān-k] in a bath [and see the references of the editor].

Saʿdī Ḥusayn Jabr, *Fiqhu l-imām abī thaur*, Beirut 1403/1983, pp. 200–201 [discussion of the tradition forbidding prayer in cemeteries and baths: *al-arḍu kulluhā masjidun illā l-ḥammāma wa-l-maqbarata*]

See further the *ḥadīth*: *al-arḍ kulluhā masjidun illā l-maqbarata wa-l- ḥammām*: al-ʿAynī, *ʿUmdat al-qārī sharḥ ṣaḥīḥ al-bukhārī*, Cairo 1348, IV, 188; a discussion about whether it is permissibile to pray in baths, *ibid.* p. 190.

A discussion whether the Prophet congratulated Abū Bakr and ʿUmar as they came out from a bath saying *ṭāba ḥammāmukumā*, whether he met Umm Dardāʾ when she left the bath, and whether he happened to see a bath in Syria or in Buṣrā: al-Ḥalabī, *al-Sīra al-ḥalabiyya*, I, 410.

ad note 6: Ibn ʿAbd al-Barr, *Bahjat al-majālis*, II, 95: Abū l-Dardāʾ : *niʿma l-bayt al-ḥammām, yudhhibu l-darana wa-yudhakkiru l-nāra.*

Ibn ʿAdiyy [ʿAbdallah b. ʿAdiyy al-Jurjānī], *al-Kāmil fī ḍuʿafāʾi l-rijāl*, Beirut 1404/1985, I, 283: The first who built a bath was Sulaymān; when he entered the bath and was affected by the heat of the place he was stirred and recalled God's punishment.

This tradition occurs also in al-Shiblī's *Maḥāsin al-wasāʾil fī maʿrifati l-awāʾil*, MS. Brit. Library, Or. 1530, fol. 56 a and Ibn Ḥajar al-Haytamī, *al-Zawājir*, I, 129.

al-Thaʿālibī, *al-Laṭāʾif*, pp. 35–36.

A discussion whether it is permissibile to have a massage in the bath: Abū Ṭālib al-Makkī, *Qūt al-qulūb*, IV, 179. It is noteworthy that ʿUmar and Abū ʿUbayda are said to have forbidden Muslim women to be accompanied by *dhimmī* women in order to be served by them.

ad note 28: See e. g. al-Ṭurṭūshī, *Kitāb al-ḥawādith wa-l-bidaʿ*, pp. 160-161: Some utterances of the Prophet against the bewailing women are formulated in a very stern tone, like: ... *"laʿana llāhu l-nāʾiḥata wa-l-mustamiʿata"*, *"laysa minnā man laṭama l-khudūda wa-shaqqa l-juyūba"*, *"laysa minnā man ḥalaqa wa-man salaqa wa-man kharaqa"*. A calamitous fate awaits the bewailing woman in the hereafter according to an utterance of the Prophet: *tuksā l-nāʾiḥatu yauma l-qiyāma sirbālan min qaṭirān wa-dirʿan min jarabin.*
Noteworthy are the arguments recorded by al-Ṭurṭūshī against bewailing the dead: it is reminiscent of a kind of complaint against God and a supplication for assistance against His decree [... *li-anna dhālika yushbihu l-taẓalluma wa-l-istighāthata ʿalā llāhi* ʿazza wa-jalla *wa-fīhi tashabbuhun bi-l-istiʿdāʾi, wa-mā faʿalahu llāhu* taʿālā *fa-huwa ḥaqqun wa-ʿadlun*].
Further al-Ṭurṭūshī records opinions about whether it is allowed to weep over the dead [p. 161].

ad note 29: See al-Ḥakīm al-Tirmidhī, *al-Manhiyyāt*, ed. Muḥammad al-Saʿid Basyūnī Zaghlūl, Beirut 1405/1985, p. 76: *wa-ammā qauluhu "wa-nahā an yabīta l-rajulu wa-huwa junub ḥattā yatawaḍḍaʾa" fa-hādhā taʾdīb, wa-qad jāʾat rukhṣatun fī dhālika.* And see *ibid.* the tradition recorded on the authority of ʿĀʾisha: *kāna rasūlu llāhi ṣallā llāhu ʿalayhi wa-sallam yajnubu thumma yanāmu wa-lā yamassu māʾan.*

ad note 30: See the tradition *"kuntu nahaytukum ʿan ziyārati l-qubūr fa-zūrū l-qubūr fa-innahā tuzahhidu fī l-dunyā wa-tudhakkiru l-ākhirata"* and the explication of al-Munāwī in his *Fayḍu l-qadīr, sharḥu l-jāmiʿ l-ṣaghīr*, V, 55-56, nos. 6430-6431: the prohibition to visit graves was released in the first period of Islam, when the faith was weak and the believers were still under the influence of the Jāhiliyya. When the belief became firm the prohibition was lifted and the visit of graves was permitted.

ad note 32: al-Suyūṭī, *ʿAynu l-iṣāba fī stidrāki ʿāʾishata ʿalā l-ṣaḥāba*, ed. ʿAbdallah Muḥammad al-Darwīsh, Cairo 1409/1988, p. 34, no. 3. [and the references of the editor *ibid.* p. 35, note 6].
Muḥammad b. Jaʿfar al-Kattānī, *Naẓmu l-mutanāthir mina l-ḥadīthi l-mutawātir*, Cairo 1983, p. 131, no. 124.
Ibn ʿAbd al-Barr al-Qurṭubī, *Tajrīdu l-tamhīd li-mā fī l-muwaṭṭaʾ mina l-maʿānī wa-l-asānīd*, Beirut n. d., p. 49, no. 101.

This tradition is also in al-Shāfiʿī's *Risāla*, ed. Muḥammad Sayyid Kaylāni, Cairo 1403/1983, p. 176, no. 1109.

Ibn al-ʿArabī, *Tafsīr* [= *Aḥkāmu l-qurʾān*], Cairo 1387/1967, I, 94-96.

Ibn ʿAbd al-Ḥakam, *Futūḥ miṣr*, ed. Charles C. Torrey, New Haven 1922 [reprint], p. 265 [the tradition reported on the authority of Ibn ʿUmar].

Ibn ʿAdiyy, *al-Kāmil fī ḍuʿafāʾi l-rijāl*, VI, 2121 [*ʿan ʿāʾishata qālat: ahwā ilayhā rasūlu llāhi* ṣallā llāhu ʿalayhi wa-sallam *fa-qālat: innī ṣāʾimatun, fa-qāla: wa-anā ṣāʾim, thumma qabbalanī*; and see *ibid.* VI, 2205: the tradition transmitted by Muḥammad b. Dīnār al-Ṭāḥī on the authority of ʿĀʾisha: *kāna yuqabbiluhā wa-huwa ṣāʾim wa-yamuṣṣu lisānahā.*

The problem whether one may kiss one's wife during the fast is touched upon by Ibn Khuzayma in his *Ṣaḥīḥ*, III, 242-245, nos. 1997-2000. Further Ibn Khuzayma scrutinizes the problem of the *mubāshara* during the period of the fast. The *rukhṣa* is confined to one kind of *mubāshara*: touching the body of one's wife, or having skin to skin contact with one's wife. This way of *mubāshara* is permitted as a *rukhṣa*. But as the Arabic is the most comprehensive of languages, which no one can encompass in its entirety [*qāla abū bakrin* - i. e. Ibn Khuzayma - *innamā khāṭaba llāhu* jalla thanāʾuhu *nabiyyahu* ṣallā llāhu ʿalayhi wa-sallam *wa-ummatahu bi-lughati l-ʿarabi ausaʿi l-lughāti kullihā llatī lā yuḥīṭu bi-ʿilmi jamīʿihā aḥadun ghayra nabiyyin*], the verb bāshara possesses another meaning as well, namely sexual intercourse. This latter activity is forbidden during day-time in the period of fasting, while *mubāshara* in the sense of skin to skin contact with one's wife is permitted. This way of *mubāshara*, practised by the Prophet during day-time in the period of the fast, was attested by ʿĀʾisha, *ibid.* p. 243.

See further al-Dāraquṭnī, *Sunan*, ed. ʿAbdallah Hāshim Yamānī l-Madanī, al-Madīna al-munawwara, 1386/1966, I, 135-145, II, 180-181

al-Dhahabī, *Siyar aʿlāmi l-nubalāʾ*, ed. Ibrāhīm al-Abyārī, Cairo 1957, II, 121 penult.-122 sup.

Ibn Abī Shayba, *al-Muṣannaf*, III, 59-64.

Some pious believers however considered reprehensible kissing the wife during the period of fast. ʿUmar saw in his dream the Prophet averting his eyes from him, and he inquired angrily about the reason. The Prophet answered asking: "Aren't you the man who kisses [scil. his wife-k] during the period of fast?". ʿUmar promised to refrain from doing so in the future. [Ibn al-Jauzī, *Manāqib amīri l-muʾminīna ʿumara bni l-khaṭṭābi*, ed. Zaynab Ibrāhīm al-Qārūṭ, Beirut 1402/1982, p. 234 inf.]

In another dream a man saw himself eating a jellylike sweet [*khabīṣ*] during prayer. The interpreter of the dream explained to him that he used to kiss his wife in the period of the fast and enjoined him to stop that. [Ibn Abī Shayba, *al-Muṣannaf*, XI, 82, no. 10575].

ad note 33: Muḥammad b. al-Ḥasan al-Shaybānī, *al-Ḥujja ʿalā ahli l-madīnati*, ed. Mahdī Ḥasan al-Kaylānī, Beirut 1403/1983, I, 65–66: the scholars of Medina assumed that *wuḍūʾ* is obligatory after kissing one's wife; but Abū Ḥanīfa refuted this claim. ʿĀʾisha attested that the Prophet used to kiss her after performing of *wuḍūʾ* and used to pray afterwards without repeating the *wuḍūʾ*.
al-Bayhaqī, *al-Sunan al-kubrā*, Hyderabad 1344, I, 123–128 records the various contradictory views concerning the subject.
al-Ṭabarānī, *al-Muʿjam al-kabīr*, X, 316, no. 10604: Ibn ʿAbbās was asked by a young man and an old man whether kissing one's wife during day-time in the period of fasting was permitted. He allowed this to the old and forbade the young man. When asked by the young man why he made this difference, as they were both believers in the same faith, he explained that a young man could be exposed to sinful lust while an old man was in control of his desire.
al-Bayhaqī, *Maʿrifat al-sunan wa-l-āthār*, ed. Aḥmad Ṣaqr, Cairo 1389/1969, I, 309–326.
Ibn Ḥazm, *al-Muḥallā*, ed. Aḥmad Muḥammad Shākir, Cairo n. d., I, 244–249 gives a survey of the different opinions of Muslim lawyers, criticizing the views of Mālik and Abū Ḥanīfa who assumed in their legal decisions that there is no obligation to perform *wuḍūʾ* after kissing and *mulāmasa*.
al-Buṣīrī, *Miṣbāḥu l-zujājah fī zawāʾidi bni mājah*, ed. Mūsā Muḥammad ʿAlī and ʿIzzat ʿAlī ʿAṭiyyah, I, 200–201.
al-Munāwī, *Fayḍu l-qadīr*, Cairo 1391/1972, V, 203, no. 6981.
al-Ṭabarānī, *al-Muʿjam al-kabīr*, IX, 285–286, nos. 9226–9229.
al-Zurqānī, *Sharḥ al-mawāhibi l-laduniyya*, Cairo 1326, V, 226 inf.– 228.

ad note 46: Some traditions come out strongly against the muttering of healing incantations [*ruqya*] and the wearing of charms and amulets. A tradition attributed to the Prophet describes the practices of the *ruqya* and of wearing talismans as sheer idolatry: *al-ruqā wa-l-tamāʾim wa-l-tiwala shirk* [al-Khallāl, *al-Musnad min masāʾil aḥmad*, MS. Br. Mus. Or. 2675, fol. 135 a].
And see this tradition and its explanation: al-Munāwī, *Fayḍ al-qadīr*, II, 342, no. 2002.
The inmates of Paradise are people who did not utter healing incantations, did not watch the evil omina from flying birds and did not cauterise themselves [Muqātil, *Tafsīr*, MS. Ahmet III, 74/2, fol. 19 b: ... *humu lladhīna lā yarqūna wa-lā*

6

yastarqūna wa-lā yaktawūna wa-lā yataṭayyarūna wa-ʿalā rabbihim yatawakkalūna].
The *rukhṣa* to mutter healing incantations was released by the Prophet for special cases of people aflicted by the evil eye, suffering from pricking, itching, bites of scorpions or snakes, or having an incessant flow of blood. [See e.g. Muḥammad Muḥammad Murtaḍā l-Zabīdī, *ʿUqūdu l-jawāhiri l-munīfa*, ed. Wahbī Sulaymān Ghāwujī l-Albānī, Beirut 1406/1985, II, 154].
According to one tradition the Prophet permitted muttering healing invocations on condition that they do not contain idolatrous elements. [Ibn Daybaʿ, *Taysīru l-wuṣūl ilā jāmiʿi l-uṣūl*, Cairo 1390/1970, III, 177, no. 1]
al-Bayhaqī, *al-Sunan al-kubrā*, Hyderabad 1356, IX, 347-352, includes the *ruqya* for facial paralysis [*laqwa*] and special cases where the fastening of *tamāʾim* is permitted.
Ibn Kathīr, *Tafsīr*, Beirut 1385/1966, VII, 92 penult.-98 the different *ruqā* of the Prophet.
Muḥammad b. Aḥmad b.ʿAbd al-Hādī l-Ḥanbalī, *al-Muḥarrar fī l-ḥadīth*, ed. Yūsuf ʿAbd al-Raḥmān al-Marʿashlī, Muḥammad Salīm Ibrāhīm Samāra, Jamāl Ḥamdī l-Dhahabī, Beirut 1405/1985, II, 679, no.1298].
According to a tradition recorded on the authority of Abū Saʿīd al-Khudrī the angel Jibrīl descended from Heaven when the Prophet became ill [*ishtakā*] and taught him the following *ruqya*: *bi-smi llāhi arqīka, min kulli shayʾin yuʾdhīka, min sharri kulli nafsin, au ʿayni ḥāsidin, allāhu yashfīka* [*al-Muḥarrar*, II, 680, no. 1302; and see the references of the editors].
Compare Ibn Kathīr, *Tafsīr*, VII, 420: Anas, the servant of the Prophet, used a similar *ruqya* of the Prophet for healing purposes: *allāhumma rabba l-nasi, mudhhiba l-bāʾsi, ishfi -anta l-shāfī- lā shāfiya illā anta, shifāʾan lā yughādiru saqaman* [*al-Muḥarrar*, p. 680, no. 1301; and see the references of the editors]. A similar *ruqya* used by the Prophet: Nūr al-Dīn al-Haythamī, *Mawārid al-ẓamʾān ilā zawāʾidi bni ḥibbān*, ed. ʿAbd al-Raḥmān Ḥamza, Cairo n. d., p. 342, no. 1415-1420, 1423.
Another form of *ruqya* was blowing upon a sick person [*nafath*], rubbing his body with the hand [*masḥ*] and reciting the *muʿawwidhdhāt*. When the Prophet was in his mortal illness ʿĀʾisha treated him in the very same manner: she blew on his body and rubbed it; however she rubbed him with his hand rather than with hers, because his hand was more beneficent [*kānat aʿẓam barakatan min yadī, al-Muḥarrar*, II, 681, no. 1304].
A *ruqya* used by the Prophet during the illness of Thābit b. Shammās was coupled with a special treatment which consisted of blowing water [*nafatha ʿalayhi bi-māʾin*], using dust from Buṭḥān and pouring water on the patient [Ibn Daybaʿ, *Taysīru l-wuṣūl*, III, 179, no. 8].

See further on *ruqā*: Aḥmad b. Ḥanbal, *al-Musnad*, Beirut 1398/ 1978 [repr.] III, 334 [*ruqyatu l-ʿaqrab*].

Ibn Ḥajar al-ʿAsqalānī, *Taghlīq al-taʿlīq ʿalā ṣaḥīḥi l-bukhārī*, ed. Saʿīd ʿAbd al-Raḥmān Mūsā al-Qazaqī, Beirut 1405/1985, V, 46–50.

Noteworthy is the invocation enjoined by Abū l-Dardāʾ to a man who came to him complaining of inability to pass water; the Prophet had advised to use it in cases of illness: *rabbunā llāhu lladhī fī l-samāʾi taqaddasa smuka, amruka fī l-samāʾi wa-l-arḍi kamā raḥmatuka fī l-samāʾi, fa-jʿal raḥmataka fī l-arḍi wa-ghfir lanā ḥūbanā wa-khaṭāyānā, anta rabbu l-ṭayyibīna inzil raḥmatan min raḥmatika wa-shifāʾan min shifāʾika ʿalā hādhā l-wajʿi fa-yabraʾu* [Ibn Daybaʿ, *Taysīru l-wuṣūl*, III, 179, no. 11].

A tradition gives information about a change in the employment of healing incantations by the Prophet: when the two last *sūras* were revealed to him, he stopped using his former healing formulae and confined himself to healing by the recitation of these two *sūras* [Ibn Daybaʿ, *Taysīru l-wuṣūl*, III, 179, no. 9].

ad note 52: See Ibn Kathīr, *Tuḥfatu l-ṭālib bi-maʿrifati aḥādīthi mukhtaṣari bni ḥājib*, ed. ʿAbd al-Ghaniyy b. Ḥumayd b. Maḥmūd al-Kubaysī, Makka l-mukarrama 1406, p. 236, no. 123 [and see the references of the editor].

Contradictory traditions are recorded in: Ibn Ḥajar al-ʿAsqalānī, *al-Maṭālibu l-ʿāliya bi-zawāʾidi l-masānīdi l-thamāniya*, ed. Ḥabību l-Raḥmān al-Aʿẓamī, Beirut n. d., I, 39–41, nos. 127–137; also e. g. Ibn Abī Ḥātim, *ʿIlal al-ḥadīth*, Cairo 1343, I, nos. 63, 64, 175, 191.

ad note 53: Aḥmad b. ʿAbdallah al-Samdī l-Nazwī, *al-Muṣannaf*, ed. Abd al-Munʿim ʿĀmir and Jādallah Aḥmad, ʿUmān 1980, IV, 132: *fa-qāla ʿalayhi l-salam: a-laysa aṭharu ṭaʿāmikum mā massathu l-nāru.*

and see this tradition: Ibn Ḥajar al-ʿAsqalānī, *al-Maṭālibu l-ʿāliya*, I, 40, no. 135.

al-Daʿīs, *al-Maqṣad al-ʿaliyy fī zawāʾid abī yaʿlā l-mauṣiliyy*, p. 234, no. 153.

ad note 56: See e. g. al-Daʿīs, al-Maqṣad al-ʿaliyy fī zawāʾid abī yaʿlā l-mauṣiliyy, pp. 229–236, nos. 146–156.

Muḥammad b. Aḥmad al-Qaṭṭān, *al-Juzʾu l-awwal mina l-fawāʾid*, MS. Ẓāhiriyya 18 [*majmūʿa*], fol. 24 a, inf.–24 b.

ad note 58: See Ibn Kathīr, *Tuḥfatu l-ṭālib*, p. 237, no. 124: *qāla bnu ʿabbāsin: lā natawaḍḍaʾu mimmā massat al-nāru, innamā l-nāru barakatun, mā tuḥillu min shayʾin wa-lā tuḥarrimuhu* [and see the references of the editor].

Ibn Ḥazm states plainly that the traditions concerning the prohibition of food "touched by fire" [*al-wuḍū' mimmā massat al-nār*] were abrogated [Ibn Ḥazm, *al-Muḥallā*, I, 343, no. 164].

ad note 59: As to the controversial question of *wuḍū'* after touching the genitalia, see Ibn Kathīr, *Tuḥfat al-ṭālib*, pp. 217–218, nos. 107–108; al-Bayhaqī, *Ma'rifat al-sunan*, I, 327–363 [and see the references of the editor; according to the traditions stating that *wuḍū'* in the case of touching the genitalia is not mandatory the Prophet is said to have stated: *ibid.* p. 356, ... *innamā huwa minka,* and *ibid.* p. 358: *lā ba'sa bihi, innama huwa ka-ba'ḍi jasadihi*]; Ibn Ḥajar al-'Asqalānī, *al-Maṭālib al-'āliya*, I, 41–43, nos. 139–146 [the traditions stating that the *wuḍū'* is not obligatory are formulated like the traditions quoted above: ... Ḥudhayfa: *mā ubālī masistu iyyāhu au anfī au udhunī* (no. 145), the Prophet: ... *mā ubālī iyyāhu masistu au anfī* (no. 146)]; Aḥmad b. al-Ḥusayn al-Bayhaqī, *Bayān khaṭa'i man akhṭa'a 'alā l-shāfi'ī*, ed. al-Sharīf Nāyif al-Da'īs, Beirut 1402/ 1983, pp. 312–315 [and see the numerous references and comments of the editor]; Ibn 'Adiyy, *al-Kāmil*, VI, 2159, 2160, 2161; al-Fasawī, *al-Ma'rifa wa-l-ta'rīkh*, ed. Akram Ḍiyā' al-'Umarī, Beirut 1401/1981, II, 658 [see e. g. the saying ... *mā huwa illā biḍ'atun minka*]; Ibn Abī Shayba, *al-Muṣannaf*, I, 163; al-Khaṭīb al-Baghdādī, *Ta'rīkh*, Cairo 1349/1931, IX, 332, sup.; Idem, *Talkhīṣu l-mutashābih fī l-rasm*, ed. Sukayna al-Shihābī, Damascus 1958, II, 859, no. 1414 [*idhā massa aḥadukum dhakarahu fa-l-yatawaḍḍa'*- and see the references of the editor].
Ibn Dayba', *Taysīru l-wuṣūl*, III, 102–103; al-Shaybānī, *Kitābu l-ḥujja 'alā ahli l-madīnati*, I, 59–64 [and comp. *ibid.* p. 68, ll. 4–3 from bottom].

ad note 64: al-Ṭabarānī, *al-Mu'jam al-kabīr*, II, 210–212, nos. 1859–1868.
al-Da'īs, *al-Maqṣad al-'aliyy fī zawa'id abī ya'lā l-mauṣiliyy*, p. 227, no. 77.
al-Muttaqī l-Hindī, *Kanz al-'ummāl*, VIII, 127, no. 900.
Ibn Ḥazm, *al-Muḥallā*, II, 242, no. 164.

ad note 68: al-Nasā'ī, *Sunan*, n. d. , V, 222.
al-'Aynī, *'Umdat al-qārī*, IX, 263 sup.

ad note 98: See the verses of Ḥumayd al-Amajī in Samhūdī's *Wafā'u l-wafā*, ed. Muḥyī l-Dīn 'Abd al-Ḥamīd, p. 1131.

ad note 100: Ibn Abī l-Dunyā, *al-Ishrāf fī manāzili l-ashrāf*, MS. Chester Beatty 4427, fol. 43 a [a woman accompanied by her six sons, who shielded her from other people performing the circumambulation] and fol. 44 a penult.-b [a Bedouin carried his wife on his neck during his *ṭawāf*; verses spoken by him and his conversation with 'Umar].

ad note 102: al-Sinjārī, *Manā'iḥu l-karam bi-akhbāri makka wa-l-ḥaram*, MS. Leiden Or. 7018, fols. 92 b., inf.-93 a: Khalid b. 'Abdallah al-Qasrī established guards at the building of the Ka'ba in order to prevent women from mixing with men during the circumambulation.

ad note 103: al-Sinjārī, *Manā'iḥu l-karam*, MS. fols. 89 b.-90 a; and see other traditions attributing these arrangements to al-Ḥajjāj.

ad note 104: al-Sinjārī, *Manā'iḥu l-karam*, MS. fol. 122 a [quoted from al-Fākihī].

ad note 121: Ibn Ḥajar, *al-Iṣāba*, I, 307 inf.-308 sup.
al-'Aynī, *'Umdat al-qārī*, IX, 263-264.
al-Ḥakim al-Naysābūrī, *al-Mustadrak*, al-Riyāḍ, n. d. [reprint], I, 460.

ad note 124: al-Dhahabī, *Mīzān al-i'tidāl*, III, 7 inf.-8 sup., no. 5359.
Ibn al-Athīr, *Jami' al-uṣūl min aḥādīthi l-rasūl*, XII, 185-186, nos. 9100 -9106.

XIV

The interpretation of dreams

An unknown manuscript of Ibn Qutayba's "ʿIbārat al-Ruʾyā"

In memory of
Gustave von Grunebaum

A manuscript of Ibn Qutayba's compilation on dreams[1] hitherto considered lost has recently turned up in the Library of the Hebrew University.[2]

The manuscript contains 67 folios of text (15 lines to each page), carefully written in small, vowelled, clear script; three additional folios contain a list of contents written by a later scribe, a remark of a reader and a *waqf* note. The colophon records the date of copying and the place: Damascus, 20 Dhū l-qaʿda 845 H.[3]

The title of the book as given on the title page and in the colophon is "*ʿIbārat al-ruʾyā*". But the title recorded on fol. 1b and at the end of the book is "*Taʿbīr al-ruʾyā*". The book seems to have been known by both titles. Ibn al-Nadīm mentions the compilation as "*Kitāb taʿbīr al-ruʾyā*",[4] Ibn Khayr records it as "*Kitāb ʿibārat al-ruʾyā*".[5]

[1] See G. Lecomte, *Ibn Qutayba* (Damas, 1965), p. 157; T. Fahd, *La Divination Arabe* (Leiden, 1966), pp. 316–328, 350, no. 97. Lengthy passages from Ibn Qutayba's work are quoted in Ps. Ibn Sīrīn's *Muntakhab al-kalām fī tafsīr al-aḥlām*, Cairo 1382/1963.

[2] Collection Yahuda, Ms. Ar. 196. I should like to express my gratitude to Dr. M. Nadav and Mr. E. Wust who kindly let me read the manuscript and provided me with the needed photographs. An edition of the text is now in course of preparation. I should also like to thank the following libraries and their librarians: the British Museum, Cambridge University Library, the Chester Beatty Collection, the Bodleian Library, London University Library, the Sulaymaniyya and Ankara University.

[3] Fol. 67a: *...ammā baʿdu qad waqaʿa l-farāghu min kitābati hādhihi l-nuskhati l-sharīfati l-mausūmati bi-kitābi ʿibārati l-ruʾyā ʿalā yadi l-ʿabdi l-ḍaʿīfi l-naḥīfi l-rāji ilā raḥmati llāhi l-bārī yaḥyā bni muḥammadin il-bukhārī fī ʿishrīna min dhi l-qaʿdati sanata khamsin wa-arbaʿīna wa-thamānī miʾatin bi-dimashqa l-maḥrūsati ṣānahā llāhu taʿālā ʿan il-āfāt wa-l-nakabāt. al-lāhumma ghfir li-kātibihi wa-li-man naẓara fīhi āmīn, yā rabba l-ʿālamīn.*

[4] *Al-Fihrist* (Cairo, 1348), p. 439 ult.

[5] *Fahrasa*, ed. F. Codera, J. Ribera Tarrago (Saragossa, 1893; reprint Baghdād 1963), p. 266. Al-Zurqānī refers evidently to our manuscript quoting from Ibn Qutayba's *Kitāb uṣūli l-ibāra* (al-Zurqānī, *Sharḥ ʿalā l-mawāhib al-ladunniyya*, Cairo, 1328, VII, 173). The compilation of al-Kirmānī is quoted by al-Qāḍī ʿIyāḍ, *Tartīb al-madārik*, ed. Aḥmad Bakīr

The chain of the transmitters of the book is given as follows: Abū l-Ḥasan ʿAbd al-Bāqī b. Fāris b. Aḥmad al-Muqri', known as Ibn Abī l-Fatḥ al-Miṣrī;[6] Abū Ḥafṣ ʿUmar b. Muḥammad b. ʿArāk;[7] Abū Bakr Aḥmad b. Marwān al-Mālikī.[8] The Ms begins: *qara'tu ʿalā l-shaykhi l-ṣāliḥi abī l-ḥasani ʿabdi l-bā qī...* The name of the scholar who read the Ms aloud to Abū l-Ḥasan is not mentioned throughout the book. The remark on the margin of the colophon: *qābalnāhā ʿalā nuskhati l-aṣli bi-qadri l-imkāni* may support the assumption that the scribe copied it from the copy of the student who read it to Abū l-Ḥasan. It may be worthwhile to remark that Aḥmad b. Marwān al-Mālikī, the first person in the chain of the transmitters of our manuscript, is also recorded by Ibn Khayr as the transmitter of his manuscript.[9]

Our manuscript is thus the earliest extant Muslim compilation on dreams. Ibn Qutayba stresses that he derived his material from the "science of al-Kirmāni[10] and others" and undertakes to explain the principles of oneiromancy overlooked by the former scholars.[11] This passage indicates that Ibn Qutayba's compilation forms in fact a continuation of an earlier Muslim tradition of oneiromancy, which may be traced to the first half of the second century. The continuity of transmission of the lore of oneiromancy in later centuries is represented by the personality of Abū Muḥammad ʿAbd al-Raḥmān b. Muḥammad b. ʿAttāb[12] who transmitted to Ibn Khayr the compilations of al-Kirmānī and Ibn Qutayba, the commentary on the book of al-Kirmānī compiled by Abū ʿAbdallah Muḥammad b. Yaḥya b. al-Ḥadhdhā',[13]

Maḥmūd (Beirut–Tripoli 1387/1967), IV, 734, as *Kitāb al-ʿibāra* (mentioning the commentary on it "*al-Bushrā fī ʿibārat al-ru'yā*" by Muḥammad b. Yaḥyā al-Ḥadhdhā'; this commentary is mentioned in an abbreviated manner as "al-Bushrā" *ib.*, IV, 429); it is also recorded as *Kitāb al-ʿibāra* by Ibn Khayr, *op. cit.*, p. 266 (he records however the commentary of al-Ḥadhdhā' under the title "*Kitāb al-bushrā fī ta'wīl al-ru'yā*", *ib.*, p. 267).

6 See on him al-Jazarī, *Ghāyat al-nihāya fī ṭabaqāt al-qurrā'*, ed. G. Bergsträsser (Cairo, 1932), I, 357, no. 1529; he was a student of ʿUmar b. ʿArāk; d. ca. 450 H.

7 See on him al-Jazarī, *op. cit.* I, 597, no. 2431 (d. 388 H).

8 See on him Ibn Ḥajar, *Lisān al-mīzān*, I, 309, no. 931. He was the most prolific transmitter of the lore of Ibn Qutayba (*wa-kāna min arwā l-nāsi ʿan ibni qutayba*). D. 333 H; but see al-Qāḍī ʿIyāḍ, *op. cit.*, I, 27, l. 19.

9 *Fahrasa*, p. 267, l. 1.

10 In text: Ibrāhīm b. ʿAbd al-Malik, which seems to be an error; read: b. ʿAbdallah; see on him Fahd, *op. cit.*, pp. 316, 345 no. 67.

11 *ʿIbāra*, fol. 17a: *...qāla abū muḥammadin: wa-sa-ukhbiruka ʿan ta'wīli l-aḥādīthi mā najʿaluhu laka mithālan, thumma naṣīru ilā ikhbārika ʿan al-uṣūli nakhtasiru* (text *yahtaḍiru*) *li-dhālika min ʿilmi ibrāhīma bni ʿabdi llāhi* (text: *ʿabdi l-maliki*) *l-kirmānī wa-ghayrihi wa-mufaḍḍalin* (perhaps: *mufaṣṣalin*) *min al-akhbāri muḥtawin ʿalā jumalin jāmiʿatin kāfiyatin li-man aḥsana tadbīrahā wa-uʿīna bi-l-tafsīri ʿalayhā wa-ubayyinu min ʿilali tilka l-uṣūli mā aghfalahu l-mutaqaddimūna fa-lam yadhkurūhu in shā'a* [*llāhu*] *wa-lā quwwata illā bi-llāhi.*

12 See on him al-Dhahabī, *Tadhkirat al-ḥuffāẓ*, Hyderabad 1377/1958, IV, 1271 (d. 520 H).

13 See on him al-Qāḍī ʿIyāḍ, *op. cit.*, IV, 429, 733–734 (d. 416 H).

the book of Abū Dharr al-Harawī[14] and the book of Nu'aym b. Ḥammād.[15]

The compilation of Ibn Qutayba is divided into two parts: an extensive introduction (fols. 1b–25a) followed by a compendium of oneiromancy containing forty six chapters (fols. 25a–67b). Lists of chapter headings are given in the Appendix.

Our manuscript is, however, not complete. It is, therefore, fortunate that another Ms of this work, Ms. Ankara, Is. Saib Sincer I, 4501 (fols. 180a–217b) could be consulted. This Ms contains only the first part of our manuscript, i.e. the introduction; the last folios of this Ms are missing. This missing part of the Ms corresponds to fols. 23a, l. 10 – 25a, l. 11 of our manuscript. A former owner of Ms. Ankara rightly noted on the margin of fol. 217b: "*nuqṣānuhu waraqun au waraqayn* (!) *bi-shahādati wuquʿi hādhā l-bābi fī ākhiri l-fihrisi l-thāniyati l-wāqiʿati fī raqmi* 179." On fol. 180a there is in fact a list of twenty three (actually twenty four) chapters into which the introduction is divided; every chapter in this Ms is indeed preceded by a headline which conforms to this list. The missing chapter is No. 24: *bāb adab al-ta'wīl*; only the beginning of this chapter is found on fol. 217b; it can however be supplemented from our manuscript.

The missing passage in our manuscript, fol. 1b, l. 12, should be supplied from Ms. Ankara fols. 180b, l. 8 – 182a ult.; the missing passage on fol. 3a, l. 10 has to be supplied from Ms. Ankara fols. 184a, l. 7 – 185b ult. On fol. 5a, l. 8 of our manuscript the short chapter "*bāb al-ta'wīl bi-l-maʿnā*" from Ms. Ankara fols. 188b–189a ought to be added. On fol. 17a, l. 4 seven chapters from Ms. Ankara (fols. 203a–212b) have to be supplemented.

The missing material on fol. 1b of Ms. Jerusalem, which can be supplemented from Ms. Ankara, is of some importance. Counting the wonders and signs of God's creation, Ibn Qutayba stresses the Oneness of God and the grace granted to man by the fact that he has been enabled to smell, see, hear and taste in dream as well as to laugh and to cry, to cross countries while his own body is reclining, his senses inactive and his legs motionless.

These wonders associated with dream which were granted to man by God caused some unbelieving people in ancient times (*taḥayyara qaumun min mutaqaddimī l-mulḥidīn*) to be in a state of perplexion. They drew the conclusion that everything in the world has to be considered as the effect of phantasy and imagination. The sleeping person is indeed certain that the appearances of his dream are realities exactly as he who is awake considers the objects which he perceives to be realities. Ibn Qutayba quotes arguments already adduced in ancient times against this opinion.

Ibn Qutayba stresses that the majority of people in the period of the Jāhi-

14 See on him al-Qāḍi 'Iyāḍ, *op. cit,*. IV, 696–698 (d. 435 H).

15 Ibn Khayr, *op. cit.*, pp. 266–267.

liyya and Islam believed in dreams with the exception of a group of atheistic materialists (*qaumun min al-zanādiqa yaqūlūna bi-l-dahri*) and a group of physicians in ancient times. Another group of physicians who were upholders of religion (*al-dayyānūna min al-aṭibbā'*) partly accepted and partly refuted the veracity of dreams. The reality of dreams was based on the story of Joseph recounted to the People of the Book as well as on the stories recorded by transmitters (of stories) and prophets. The denial of the truth of dreams was based on the assumption that content and form of dreams are conditioned by the difference in the temperaments of men and the preoccupation of their mind.[16] Ibn Qutayba admits the existence of such dreams, argues however that they belong to the category of "confused dreams (*aḍghāth*). True dreams are brought by angels; they are copied from the Tablet in Heaven and contain good tidings or warnings against performing bad deeds. The truth of these dreams can only be denied by a stubborn man or an apostate.

The passage missing in our manuscript, fol. 3a, and which has to be inserted from Ms. Ankara fols. 184a–185b deals with the denotations of the words "*nafs*" and "*rūḥ*".

The additional chapters in Ms. Ankara, fols. 203a–212b, contain anecdotes about dreams of the Prophet, his Companions and pious men.

Initially, the field of dream interpretation had to obtain recognition as legitimately Islamic and to get the approval of the orthodox circles by reference to the permission or injunction of the Prophet. The Prophet is indeed said to have commented on Sūra x 64 ("Those who believe and are godfearing for them is good tidings in the present life and in the world to come") and stated that "good tidings in the present life" refer to good dreams which they have in their sleep.[17]

The importance of dreams was emphasized by the utterance attributed to the Prophet in which he established the relation between prophecy and dream: "Prophecy has passed", said the Prophet, "and there remain only bearers of good tidings, good dreams which a man sees or which are shown to him in sleep."[18]

[16] See N. Bland, "On the Muhammedan Science of Tabīr, or Interpretation of Dreams" *JRAS*, 1856, p. 128; Ps. Ibn Sīrīn, *Muntakhab al-kalām fī tafsīr al-aḥlām* (Cairo, 1382/1963), p. 7.

[17] *'Ibāra*, fol. 2, ll. 1–2; al-Ṭabarī, *Tafsīr*, ed. Maḥmūd Muḥammad Shākir (Cairo, 1960), XV, 124–139, nos. 17717–17756; al-Qurṭubī, *Tafsīr* ([reprint] Cairo, 1387/1967), VIII, 358; al-Suyūṭī, *al-Durr al-manthūr* (Cairo, 1314), III, 311–313; al-Ḥākim al-Naysābūrī, *al-Mustadrak* (Hyderabad, 1342), IV, 391; al-Khargūshī, *al-Bishāra wa-l-nidhāra fī ta'bīr al-ru'yā wa-l-murāqaba*, Ms. Br. Mus., Or. 6262, fol. 2b.

[18] *'Ibāra*, fol. 1b, penult. (reported on the authority of Umm Kurz al-Ka'biyya; see on her Ibn Ḥajar, *al-Iṣāba* (Cairo, 1325/1907), VIII, 272, no. 1459); al-Ḥākim, *op. cit.*, IV, 391;

The interpretation of dreams

An early[19] and widely current tradition gives an evaluation of a good dream by stating, on the authority of the Prophet, that it is one out of forty six parts of prophecy.[20]

True, sound and good dreams were of course those of the Prophet. The Prophet saw in his dream that he rode a camel with a ram behind him and that the edge of his sword was broken. The Prophet predicted that he would kill a leader of the (troops of the) enemy (= the ram – K) and that a man from his family will be killed (= the broken edge of his sword – K). In fact the leader of the enemy Ṭalḥa b. abī Ṭalḥa and the uncle of the Prophet, Ḥamza, were both killed (in the battle of Uḥud).[21]

The Prophet dreamt that two bracelets were put on his arms; he threw

al-Suyūṭī, *al-Durr*, III, 312; al-Rāghib al-Iṣfahānī, *Muḥādarāt al-udabā'* (Beirut, 1961) I, 149; al-Tibrīzī, *Mishkāt al-maṣābīḥ* (Karachi, 1350), p. 394; al-Zurqānī, *op. cit.*, VII, 163; al-Majlisī, *Biḥār al-anwār* (Tehrān, 1390), LXI, 177, 192; al-Khargūshī, *op. cit.*, fol. 2a; G. E. von Grunebaum, "The Cultural Function of the Dream as Illustrated by Classical Islam", in: G. E. von Grunebaum and Roger Caillois, *The Dream and Human Societies* (Berkeley and Los Angeles, 1966), p. 7, note 2.

19 Recorded in Ma'mar b. Rāshid's *Jāmi'*, Feyzullah 541, fol. 152a penult.–152b.

20 *'Ibāra*, fol. 2a; Muḥammad Fu'ād 'Abd al-Bāqī, *al-Lu'lu' wa-l-marjān fīmā ttafaqa 'alayhi l-shaykhān* (Cairo, 1368/1949), III, 102–103, nos. 1457–1460; al-Haythamī, *Majma' al-zawā'id* (Beirut, 1967), VII, 172; al-Ḥākim, *op. cit.*, IV, 390; al-Rāghib al-Iṣfahānī, *op. cit.*, I, 149; al-Tibrīzī, *op. cit.*, pp. 394, 396; al-Suyūṭī, *al-Durr*, III, 312–313; al-Majlisī, *op. cit.*, LXI, 175, 178, 191; al-Jarrāḥī, *Kashf al-khafā'* (Beirut, 1351), I, 436, no. 1407; al-'Azīzī, *al-Sirāj al-munīr* (Cairo, 1377/1957), II, 322; al-Ḥanafī, *al-Mu'taṣar min al-mukhtaṣar* (Hyderabad, 1362), II, 231; and see other versions: Abū Nu'aym, *Ḥilyat al-auliyā'* (Cairo, 1351/1932), VIII, 196 (a ninetieth part); al-Majlisī, *op. cit.*, LXI, 167, 177 (a seventieth part); Ma'mar b. Rāshid, *op. cit.*, fol. 152b (a seventieth part); al-Ṭabarānī, *al-Mu'jam al-ṣaghīr*, ed. 'Abd al-Raḥmān Muḥammad 'Uthmān (al-Madīna, 1388/1968), II, 56 (a seventieth part); al-Suyūṭī, *al-Durr*, III, 312–313 (a seventieth part); al-Ḥanafī, *op. cit.*, II, 231 (a seventieth or fiftieth part); al-Ṭabarī, *op. cit.*, XV, 132, no. 17730 (a part of forty four parts, or a sixtieth part); *ib.*, p. 131, no. 17729 (a part of forty nine parts); al-Zurqānī, *op. cit.*, VII, 162–165 (a part of forty four, forty five, twenty four, twenty five, fifty, seventy, seventy six parts of prophecy); and see al-Haythamī, *op. cit.*, VII, 173–174 (a fortieth, a fiftieth, a sixtieth part of prophecy); al-Qasṭallānī, *Irshād al-sārī* (Cairo, 1323), X, 123–127 (a part of forty six, forty four, forty, fifty, seventy, seventy six, twenty six parts of prophecy); cf. A. Kristianpoler, *Monumenta Talmudica* II, I: "Traum und Traumdeutung" (Wien-Berlin, 1923), p. 25, no. 69 (*ḥalom eḥad mi-shishīm li-nbu'a*); and see *ibid.*, no. 70, and see *ibid.*, p. XI); A. Löwinger, *Der Traum in der jüdischen Literatur* (Leipzig, 1908), p. 4.

21 *'Ibāra*, fol. 52b, inf.; al-Wāqidī, *al-Maghāzī*, ed. M. Jones (London, 1966), I, 209, 225–226, 307; al-Suyūṭī, *al-Khaṣā'iṣ al-kubrā*, ed. Muḥammad Khalīl Harās (Cairo, 1386/1967), I, 529; al-Haythamī, *op. cit.*, VII, 180; al-Zurqānī, *op. cit.*, VII, 174, 184–185; Ps. Ibn Sīrīn, *Muntakhab al-kalām fī tafsīr al-aḥlām* (Cairo, 1382/1963), p. 186 inf.; al-Majlisī *op. cit.*, LXI, 179; Fahd, *op. cit.*, p. 282; al-Khargūshī, *op. cit.*, fol. 142a.

them away and they fell down. He expounded this dream by the appearance of the two false prophets Musaylima and al-ʿAnsī.[22]

The Prophet saw in a dream reddish-white and black sheep (*ghanam*) coming to him. He interpreted the reddish-white ones as referring to non-Arabs, the black ones as referring to the Arabs and predicted that non-Arabs will embrace Islam and join the Arabs.[23]

The fate of Islam was revealed to the Prophet in another dream: he saw himself seated in the house of ʿUqba b. Rāfiʿ where dates of Ibn Ṭāb[24] were served. He interpreted it by using verbal associations, predicting that Islam will gain excellence in this and in the next world (*ʿrāfiʿ – rifʿa*) and that the faith of Islam has already become pure (*ṭāb – ṭāba*).[25]

A tradition attributed to the Prophet divided dreams into good and evil; good dreams come from God, evil ones from Satan. "If you see a displeasing appearance in your dream, seek refuge from Satan in God and spit three times at your left side, then it will not harm you", said the Prophet. A special prayer was devised: "I seek refuge in the God of Mūsā, ʿĪsā and Ibrāhīm from the evil of the dream, lest it harm me in my faith or in (my dealings in) this world or in my sustenance. Strong is the man protected by God, glory and power are His. There is no God but Him."[26]

22 *ʿIbāra*, fol. 46b, sup.; Ibn al-Athīr, *al-Nihāya*, ed. Maḥmūd Muḥammad al-Ṭanāḥī (Cairo, 1385/1965), V, 90; al-Haythamī, *op. cit.*, VII, 181; Ibn Kathīr, *Shamāʾil al-rasūl* ed. Muṣṭafā ʿAbd al-Wāḥid (Cairo, 1386/1967), p. 387; Ibn al-Jauzī, *al-Wafā bi-aḥwāli, l-muṣṭafā*, ed. Muṣṭafā ʿAbd al-Wāḥid (Cairo, 1386/1966), II, 633; Ibn al-Athīr, *Jāmiʿ al-uṣūl*, ed. Muḥammad Ḥāmid al-Fiqī (Cairo, 1374/1955), XII, 376, no. 4980; al-Qasṭallānī, *op. cit.*, X, 154–156; Hammām b. Munabbih, *al-Ṣaḥīfa al-ṣaḥīḥa*, ed. Muḥammad Ḥamīdullah (Hyderabad, 1375/1956), p. 119, no. 134.

23 *ʿIbāra*, fol. 53a; al-Ḥākim, *op. cit.*, IV, 395; al-Suyūṭī, *Taʾrīkh al-khulafāʾ*, ed. Muḥammad Muḥyi l-Dīn ʿAbd al-Ḥamīd (Cairo, 1371/1952), p. 105; al-Haythamī, *op. cit.*, VII, 183; Ibn al-Jauzī, *op. cit.*, II, 631; al-Majlisī, *op. cit.*, LXI, 231; I. Goldziher, *Muslim Studies*, transl. C. R. Barber and S. M. Stern (London, 1967), I, 112; Aḥmad b. Ḥajar al-Haytamī, *al-Ṣawāʿiq al-muḥriqa fī l-raddi ʿalā ahli l-bidaʿi wa-l-zandaqa*, ed. ʿAbd al-Wahhāb ʿAbd al-Laṭīf (Cairo, 1375), p. 33; al-Khargūshī, *op. cit.*, fol. 170a.

24 See about this kind of dates al-Thaʿālibī, *Thimār al-qulūb*, ed. Muḥammad Abū l-Faḍl Ibrāhīm (Cairo, 1384/1965), p. 266, no. 387; al-Bakrī, *Muʿjam mā staʿjam*, ed. Muṣṭafā al-Saqā (Cairo, 1364/1945), I, 37, note 2.

25 *ʿIbāra*, fol. 4b, sup.; al-Tibrīzī, *op. cit.*, p. 395; Ibn Ḥajar, *al-Iṣāba*, IV, 250; al-Zurqānī, *op. cit.*, VII, 186; Ibn al-Jauzī, *op. cit.*, II, 631; Ps. Ibn Sīrīn, *op. cit.*, p. 9.

26 *ʿIbāra*, fol. 24b; cf. Maʿmar b. Rāshid, *op. cit.*, fol. 152a–b; al-Haythamī, *op. cit.*, VII, 174–175, 181; al-Ḥākim, *op. cit.*, IV, 392; al-Khaṭīb al-Baghdādī, *Taʾrīkh Baghdād* (Cairo, 1349/1931), XII, 484; al-Suyūṭī, *al-Durr*, III, 313; al-Tibrīzī, *op. cit.*, p. 394; al-Zurqānī, *op. cit.*, VII, 168–169; al-Shiblī, *Ākām al-marjān*, ed. ʿAbdallah Muḥammad al-Ṣadīq (Cairo, 1376), pp. 182–184; al-Majlisī, *op. cit.*, LXI, 174, 188, 193; Ibn al-Sunnī, *ʿAmal al-yaum wa-l-layla* (Hyderabad, 1358), pp. 207–208; Ps. Ibn Sīrīn, *op. cit.*, p. 15; Muḥammad Fuʾād ʿAbd al-Bāqī, *op. cit.*, III, 102, no. 1456; N. Bland, "On the Muhammedan Science of Tabīr,

The interpretation of dreams

A dream in which the Prophet appears is considered sound and good. The Prophet is said to have stated: "He who sees me in a dream sees me in reality, because Satan does not take up my appearance".[27] Seeing the Prophet in dream is like seeing him in reality.

or Interpretation of Dreams" *JRAS*, 1856, p. 130; cf. Kristianpoler, *op. cit.*, p. 17, nos. 42–43 (and see p. IX); Löwinger, *op. cit.*, pp. 32–33.

[27] *'Ibāra*, fol. 2a; Ibn Abī l-Dunyā, *Kit. al-manām*, Ms. al-Jazzār (*majmū'a*), Acre, p. 321; al-Rāghib al-Iṣfahānī, *op. cit.*, I, 149; Aḥmad b. Ḥanbal, *Musnad*, ed. Aḥmad Muḥammad Shākir (Cairo, 1370/1950), V, 138, no. 3410 and p. 304, no. 3798; al-Haythamī, *op. cit.*, VII, 173, 181–183; al-Sharīf al-Murtaḍa, *Amālī*, ed. Muḥammad Abū l-Faḍl Ibrāhīm (Cairo, 1373/1954), II, 394; al-Ḥākim, *op. cit.*, IV, 393; al-Suyūṭī, *al-Khaṣā'iṣ*, III, 339; Abū Nu'aym, *op. cit.*, VII, 246; al-Shiblī, *op. cit.*, pp. 184–186 ("*fī bayāni anna l-shayṭāna lā yatamaththalu bi-l-nabiyyi -ṣ-*"); cf. Ma'mar b. Rāshid, *op. cit.*, fol. 153a (*man ra'ānī fī l-manāmi fa-huwa l-ḥaqqu*); al-Tibrīzī, *op. cit.*, p. 394 (*...fa-qad ra'ā l-ḥaqqa*); al-Qasṭallānī, *op. cit.*, X, 133–135, 139 (and see *ibid.*, the version: *man ra'ānī fī l-manāmi fa-sa-yarānī fī l-yaqẓa*); Ibn 'Asākir: *Tahdhīb ta'rīkh*, ed. Aḥmad 'Ubayd (Damascus, 1349), VI, 380 ult. (*man ra'ānī fī l-manāmi fa-innahu lā yadkhulu l-nāra*); al-Khargūshī, *op. cit.*, fol. 16b. Some scholars included in this category of sound and true dreams the appearance in dreams of prophets, angels, the sun, the lighting stars and clouds containing rain. (See al-Majlisī, *op. cit.*, LXI, 238, quoted from al-Baghawī's *Sharḥ al-sunna*). A remarkable *ḥadīth* transmitted by al-Ṭabarānī reports that the Prophet stated that Abū Bakr would interpret (scil. truly – K) the dreams and that his true dreams would form his lot of prophecy. (Aḥmad b. Ḥajar al-Haytamī, *al-Ṣawā'iq al-muḥriqa*, ed. 'Abd al-Wahhāb 'Abd al-Laṭīf (Cairo, 1375), p. 67 with a comment of the author on this tradition: *inna abā bakrin yu'awwilu l-ru'yā wa-inna ru'yāhu l-ṣāliḥata ḥaẓẓuhu min al-nubuwwati*).

Shī'ī sources record the tradition about the appearance of the Prophet in a dream with some significant additions. Satan will not appear in the form of the Prophet or of one of the trustees (*auṣiyā'*, i.e. the Shī'ī *imāms*), nor in the form of anyone of the Shī'a. (See this tradition: al-Majlisī, *op. cit.*, LXI, 176; and see the discussion of this tradition *ibid.*, pp. 211, 216, 234–236).

Shī'ī tradition reports that 'Alī saw the Prophet every night in a dream. The Prophet revealed to him that five of his Companions (among them Abū Bakr and 'Umar) plotted against him and decided to deprive him of the Caliphate, thus violating the injunction of the Prophet. The Prophet informed 'Alī in a dream about the pains suffered by Abū Bakr and 'Umar on their death-beds in connection with their mischievous deed. (See Sulaym b. Qays, *Kitāb al-saqīfa*, al-Najaf, n.d., pp. 96, 181; quoted by al-Majlisī, *op. cit.*, LXI, 240–241).

A sunnī tradition reported that Anas b. Mālik used to see the Prophet almost every night in his dream (Al-Haythamī, *op. cit.*, VII, 182).

There are interesting stories about dreams in which the Prophet expresses his opinion concerning religious leaders and scholars, commending, permitting or rejecting their teachings. Yazīd b. Ḥakīm saw the Prophet in a dream. He asked him about Sufyān al-Thaurī and the Prophet gave a favourable opinion about him. (Ibn Kathīr, *Tafsīr*, Beirut 1385/1966, IV, 259).

Zayd b. Dāwūd saw in a dream the Prophet granting Mālik b. Anas musk and asking him to divide it among the people. Zayd interpreted musk as representing knowledge (Ibn Abī l-Dunyā, *al-Manām*, p. 348; al-Qāḍī 'Iyād, *op. cit.*, I, 375). Abū 'Abdallah saw in a

The seriousness of dreams and their interpretation was stressed, as usual, by a *ḥadīth*. "He who lies about his dream will be ordered (at the Day of Judgement – K) to join two barley corns and will be put on burning coal."[28]

Ibn Qutayba defines the dream as a "kind of revelation and a sort of prophecy" (*li-annahu jinsun min al-waḥyi wa-ḍarbun min al-nubuwwati*).[29] The art of oneiromancy, argues Ibn Qutayba, is shrouded in mystery, very complicated and intricate; it is distinguished and sublime. Consequently, the requirements imposed on an interpreter of dreams are manifold as regards qualifications, knowledge and character. While the way to every other science is straight, its principles not being diverse and its standards (*maqāyīs*) not liable to change, the principles of oneiromancy are changeable according to the position of the person who dreams, his belief, profession, ambitions and the time and period of dreaming. Sometimes a dream is a coined proverb, which has to be interpreted according to the meaning of its words, sometimes it

dream a person coming out of a *maqṣūra* in the mosque of Ṭarsūs, quoting the utterance of the Prophet: "Imitate those who will come after me, Aḥmad b. Ḥanbal" (Abū Nuʿaym, *op. cit.*, IX, 185; and see *ib.*, p. 187: a man saw al-Khiḍr in a dream; he stated that Aḥmad b. Ḥanbal was a truthful person [*ṣiddīq*]; and see other dreams about Aḥmad b. Ḥanbal, *ib.*, pp. 187–193).

Ibrāhīm b. Mūsā al-Farrā' saw the Prophet in a dream and asked him about the *ḥadīths* reported by al-Qāsim b. ʿAbd al-Raḥmān on the authority of Abū Umāma; the Prophet disapproved of them (Ibn Ḥajar, *Tahdhīb*, VIII, 324, no. 581).

The Prophet recommended Muḥammad b. Muslim to record the knowledge of Yaḥyā b. Yaḥyā al-Ḥanzalī (Al-Qāḍī ʿIyāḍ, *op. cit.*, I, 408).

The Prophet ordered in a dream Salama b. Shabīb at the age of fifty to refrain from transmission of *ḥadīth*; afterwards the Prophet ordered him to transmit traditions (Ibn ʿAsākir, *Tahdhīb ta'rīkh*, ed. Aḥmad ʿUbayd, Damascus 1349, VI, 229).

A dream served as means for establishing the Prophet's approval of a Shīʿī poet. Saʿd al-Asadī saw the Prophet in a dream. The Prophet asked him to recite a poem of al-Kumayt (Qaṣida 2 of the *Hāshimiyyāt*, ed. J. Horowitz, Leiden, 1904, p. 27). After the Prophet had heard the *qaṣīda* he ordered Saʿd to inform al-Kumayt that as a reward for this poem God forgave him his sins (Al-Mauṣilī, *Ghāyat al-wasā'il*, Ms. Cambridge Qq 33 (10), fols. 181b inf. — 182a).

The authority of al-Thaʿlabī, the author of *Qiṣaṣ al-anbiyā'*, was established by God. Abū l-Qāsim al-Qushayrī, the author of the well-known "*Risāla*", saw God in a dream. While God was talking with al-Qushayrī He remarked: "The righteous man has come"; it was al-Thaʿlabī (Al-Ṣafadī, *al-Wāfī bi-l-wafayāt*, VII, 308, Beirut 1389/1969, ed. Iḥsān ʿAbbās).

[28] *ʿIbāra*, fol. 24b; Aḥmad b. Ḥanbal, *op. cit.*, V, 130, no. 3383; al-Ḥākim, *op. cit.*, IV, 392; al-Haythamī, *op. cit.*, VII, 174; al-Majlisī, *op. cit.*, LXI, 183; Ibn al-Athīr, *Jāmiʿ al-uṣūl*, XII, 332–333, nos. 9348–9350; al-ʿAzīzī, *op. cit.*, III, 386; Bland, *op. cit.*, p. 131. (And see another version of this tradition *ʿIbāra*, fol. 24b); Anonymous, *al-Dhakhīra wa-kashfu l-tauqīʿ li-ahli l-baṣīra*, Ms. Br. Mus., Or. 3922, fol. 29b; al-Khargūshī, *op. cit.*, fol. 8a.

[29] *ʿIbāra*, fol. 2a, l. 4.

has to be interpreted antithetically. Sometimes the content of the dream refers to another person (like the dreamer's brother, or his superior or peer).[30] Sometimes the dreams are confused (*aḍghāth*).

Due to the intricate character of dreams the requirements from the interpreter are wider than in the field of any other science. "For every scholar of some branch of the sciences", says Ibn Qutayba, "the tool of his science can be sufficient for practising it; but the oneirocritic has to be a scholar of Qur'ān and *ḥadīth* in order to interpret dreams according to their ideas, to be acquainted with Arab proverbs and rare verses of poetry, to have a knowledge of Arabic etymology and of current colloquial speech. Besides, he has to be an "*adīb*", gentle, sagacious, endowed with a capacity to judge the countenance of the people, their character-features, their rank and state, to have a knowledge of analogy and an acquaintance with the principles of oneiromancy".[31] Only with God's guidance and help will he be pious and pure of sins and get his lot of the heritage of the prophets, says Ibn Qutayba.[32]

Ibn Qutayba's intent in his introduction is to set out the ways of oneiromancy and to supply examples of dreams dealt with according to different methods: etymological, antithetical, symbolical and the ones based on Qur'ān, *ḥadīth*, current verses or proverbs.[33] The many dreams recorded by Ibn Qutayba contain forebodings, stories about reward in Paradise and punishment in Hell, judgements about character and behaviour of people; they reveal some hidden facts, edify and admonish and touch upon a wide range of subjects like religious tenets, political conditions, cultural life and moral ideas.

The attitude of the orthodox circles towards the heterodox factions in Islam is reflected in the dream of Yazīd b. Hārūn.[34] He saw a man who uttered *fatwās* in the mosque of Mecca. He inquired about the man and was told that he was the prophet Joseph. Yazīd asked him about drinking *nabīdh*.[35] Joseph stated that it was not forbidden, but disliked. Yazīd asked about the *khawārij* and Joseph answered: "They are Jews." Joseph gave the same

30 *'Ibāra*, fols. 16b inf. – 17a sup.: Abū Jahl was seen in a dream embracing Islam; this referred to his son 'Ikrima. (See Ma'mar b. Rāshid, *op. cit.*, fol. 153a inf.; Muṣ'ab b. 'Abdallah al-Zubayrī, *Nasab Quraysh*, ed. E. Lévi-Provençal (Cairo, 1953), p. 311; Ibn Ḥajar, *al-Iṣāba*, IV, 258, no. 5632). The Prophet saw in a dream Asīd b. Abī l-'Iṣ entering Paradise; this referred to his son 'Attāb b. Asīd (*al-'Ibāra, ibid.*; cf. Ibn Ḥajar, *al-Iṣāba*, IV, 211, no. 5383); cf. Ps. Ibn Sīrīn, *op. cit.*, p. 7, ll. 3–4.

31 *'Ibāra*, fol. 2a inf. – 2b sup.; cf. Ps. Ibn Sīrīn, *op. cit.*, p. 7; Bland, *op. cit.*, p. 132.

32 *'Ibāra*, fol. 2b.

33 *'Ibāra*, fol. 4a; Ps. Ibn Sīrīn, *op. cit.*, p. 9.

34 See on him Ibn Ḥajar, *Tahdhīb*, XI, 366, no. 711.

35 About drinking *nabīdh* see e.g.: al-Ṭaḥāwī, *Sharḥ mushkil al-āthār*, ed. Muḥammad Zuhrī al-Najjār (Cairo, 1388/1968), IV, 215–229; Muḥammad Fu'ād 'Abd al-Bāqī, *op. cit.*, III, 17–18, nos. 1304–1306.

answer when asked about the *rāfiḍa*: "They are Jews." Yazīd could not remember what Joseph said about the *Murjiʿa*. "What about a man praying, fasting, carrying out his duties, not trespassing in these things whatsoever?" asked Yazīd. "That is my message and that of my fathers," said Joseph.[36]

The *khawārij* are, as is usual,[37] depicted as dogs in another story. The sister of the Khārijī leader Abū Bilāl Mirdās b. Udayya saw her brother in dream in the form of a dog, weeping. He told her that he had been turned after his death into one of the dogs of Hell.[38]

The activity of the *khawārij* is mirrored in another dream, interpreted by Ibn Sīrīn. A woman told him that her patroness saw in her dream that two snakes came out from two holes in her house. Two men approached the snakes and milked them from their heads. Ibn Sīrīn remarked that a snake cannot give milk;[39] the men milked poison. They were leaders of the *khawārij* who were visiting the woman. They claim that their tenets are the *sunna* and *fiṭra*; but in fact their tenets are poison. The woman (who recounted the dream – K) confirmed that her lady had been a righteous woman until the two leaders of the *khawārij* came to her and changed her mind.[40]

The murder of Ḥusayn was also predicted in a dream. Ibn ʿAbbās saw in his dream the Prophet with dishevelled hair, dust coloured, holding in his hand a bottle filled with blood. When asked about it the Prophet said: "It is the blood of al-Ḥusayn; I am collecting it through the night." Later the date of the dream was checked; that night al-Ḥusayn was in fact killed.[41]

[36] *ʿIbāra*, fol. 13a.

[37] See the tradition *al-khawārij kilāb al-nār*: Maʿmar b. Rāshid, *op. cit.*, fol. 4a; al-Muttaqī l-Hindī, *Kanz al-ʿummāl* (Hyderabad, 1383/1963), XI, 182, no. 886; al-Thaʿālibī, *Thimār al-qulūb*, p. 394, no. 622.

[38] *ʿIbāra*, fol. 14b; al-Jāḥiẓ, *al-Ḥayawān*, ed. ʿAbd al-Salām Hārūn (Cairo, 1384/1965), I, 271.

[39] Milk denotes in Muslim oneiromancy true belief, the *fiṭra*; see *ʿIbāra*, fol. 36b, ult.: *wa-man raʾā annahu shariba labanan fa-hiya l-fiṭratu*; al-Haythamī, *op. cit.*, VII, 183.

[40] *ʿIbāra*, fol. 17b; al-Jāḥiẓ, *al-Ḥayawān*, IV, 269; Ps. Ibn Sīrīn, *op. cit.*, p. 208; cf. Abū Nuʿaym, *op. cit.*, II, 277.

[41] *ʿIbāra*, fol. 20b; Ibn Abī l-Dunyā, *al-Manām*, p. 320; al-Ḥākim, *op. cit.*, IV, 398; al-Ghazzālī, *Iḥyāʾ ʿulūm al-dīn* (Cairo, 1352/1933), IV, 431; cf. Haythamī, *op. cit.*, IX, 193 ult. – 194 sup.; Ibn Kathīr, *Shamāʾil al-rasūl*, ed. Muṣṭafā ʿAbd al-Wāḥid (Cairo, 1386/1967), p. 447; al-Majlisī, *op. cit.*, XLIV, 239; Ps. Ibn Sīrīn, *op. cit.*, p. 282; Fahd, *op. cit.*, p. 296; Muḥammad b. Aḥmad al-Tamīmī, *al-Miḥan*, Ms. Cambridge Qq. 235 (8), fol. 48a; al-Suyūṭī, *al-Khaṣāʾiṣ al-kubrā*, II, 452; al-Dhahabī, *Taʾrīkh al-Islām* (Cairo, 1367), II, 349; al-Yāfiʿī, *Mirʾāt al-jinān* (Hyderabad, 1339), I, 134; al-ʿIṣāmī, *Simṭ al-nujūm al-ʿawālī* (Cairo, 1380), III, 78; al-Ṭabarsī, *Iʿlām al-warā* (Tehran, 1338), p. 217; al-Ganjī, *Kifāyat al-ṭālib fī manāqib ʿAlī b. abī Ṭālib*, ed. Muḥammad Hādī l-Amīnī (al-Najaf, 1390/1970), p. 428.

The interpretation of dreams

The attitude of the orthodox circles towards compilations of *nasab* is reflected in the story of the dream of al-Kalbī. He saw himself on the Day of Judgement. He was brought into the presence of God, Who rebuked him for "compiling genealogies which he did not know" and ordered to lead him to Hell. On his way al-Kalbī met the Prophet and asked him to intercede for him with God, mentioning the merit of having compiled a commentary on the Qur'ān. The Prophet ordered ʿAlī, who was in his company, to interrogate al-Kalbī. Al-Kalbī having answered the questions well, ʿAlī reported the fact to the Prophet, who interceded for him and he was let free. He sat down with the Prophet and asked him when the Umayyad rule was going to end. The fall of the Umayyad dynasty happened in fact at the date fixed by the Prophet in his answer to al-Kalbī.[42] The opposition of orthodox circles to dubious genealogies, the esteem for commentaries of the Qur'ān, the desire to know the dates of the rise and fall of dynasties and the belief in the intercession of the Prophet are reflected in this story.

The negative attitude towards the Umayyads is mirrored in a passage dealing with the meanings of "soul" and "spirit". The spirits of the wicked people gather in Barhūt.[43] On the cornice of a large house in ʿUmān there used to shelter an owl. Some night another owl came and stood at its side. The ʿUmāni owl asked it who it was and it said: "I am the spirit of al-Walīd b. ʿAbd l-Malik and I am on my way to Barhūt."[44] When the date was checked it tallied with the date of the death of al-Walīd. Ibn Qutayba states that the story resembles *jāhilī*-beliefs about the *hāma* as reflected in the verse of Abū Duwād al-Iyādī:

sulliṭa l-mautu wa-l-manūnu ʿalayhim
wa-lahum fī ṣadā l-maqābiri hāmu
Death and fate were imposed upon them
and they have in the birds of graves their (embodied) spirits.

and stresses that the Prophet abolished this belief.[45]

42 *ʿIbāra*, fols. 10b–11a.

43 See Yāqūt, *Muʿjam al-buldān* (Beirut, 1374/1955), I, 405; and see al-Majlisī, *op. cit.*, LX, 206, 239.

44 *ʿIbāra*, fols. 3b–4a; al-Samarqandī, *Qurrat al-ʿuyūn* (Cairo, 1354/1935), p. 93 (on margin of *Mukhtaṣar Tadhkirat al-Qurṭubī*; but here the owl is the spirit of ʿAbd al-Malik). Another anti-Umayyad interpretation of a dream is reported on the authority of Ibn al-Musayyab. A girl saw in her dream that Moses appeared in Syria. He held in his hand a stick and walked on the surface of the water. Ibn al-Musayyab stated that if this dream be true — ʿAbd al-Malik died this night. He explained how he arrived at this conclusion: God sent Moses in order to shatter the tyrants. He did not find a tyrant (to whom this dream might refer – K) except ʿAbd al-Malik (Al-Khargūshī, *op. cit.*, fol. 15a).

45 The *ḥadīth*: *lā ʿadwā wa-lā hāma wa-lā ṣafara* is analysed by Abū ʿUbayd in his *Gharīb al-ḥadīth*, I, 27 (the verse of Abū Duwād is recorded there); cf. Ibn Athīr, *al-Nihāya*, V, 283.

The story of the dream of Ghālib al-Qaṭṭan[46] reflects the struggle of the orthodoxy against innovators. He saw in his dream Mālik b. Dīnār wearing clothes like those which he used to wear in mosque. Mālik advised him to refrain from the company of rich worldly people and unlawful innovators.[47]

Qur'ān versus poetry is symbolized in the dream of Aʿshā Hamdān,[48] which he told to al-Shaʿbī. He saw in his dream that he exchanged wheat for barley. Al-Shaʿbī interpreted it that he exchanged Qur'ān for poetry. Ibn Qutayba remarks: "The meaning of wheat and barley was here interpreted by Qur'ān and poetry. Would a man of the *ahl al-ra'y*[49] dream this dream it would be interpreted as exchange of *ḥadīth* for *ra'y*."[50]

The role of Abū Ḥanīfa in Islam is attested in the following dream: Abū Ḥanīfa saw in a dream that he was digging the bones of the Prophet; (he collected them and pressed them to his breast). Ibn Sīrīn was told this dream and said: "This is a man who will revive the *sunna* of the Prophet.[51]

The dream served sometimes as confirmation of the truth and reliability of a *ḥadīth*. ʿUbaydullah b. ʿAdī b. al-Khiyār[52] considered a lie the *ḥadīth*: "The molar-tooth of the unbeliever in Hell is like the mountain of Uḥud",[53] which was reported by Abū Hurayra. ʿUbaydullah dreamt that he had an ulcer on his finger; he scratched it and it grew and became like the mountain of Uḥud. He went to Abū Hurayra and asked him to beg for him God's pardon, which Abū Hurayra did.[54]

Ibn Qutayba relates his own dream about a *ḥadīth*. He saw in a dream Abū Dharr who transmitted to him the following utterance of the Prophet: "God said: 'He who approaches Me by the measure of a span I shall approach him by the measure of an arm; he who approaches Me by the measure of an arm I shall approach him by the measure of two arms; he who comes forth to Me walking I shall hurry to him'." When Ibn Qutayba woke up he asked about

[46] See on him al-Dhahabī, *Mīzān al-iʿtidāl*, ed. ʿAlī Muḥammad al-Bijāwī (Cairo, 1382/1963), III, 330, no. 6642; Ibn Ḥajar, *Tahdhīb*, VIII, 242, no. 444.

[47] *ʿIbāra*, fol. 15a; Abū Nuʿaym, *op. cit.*, II, 380 sup.

[48] See on him al-Āmidī, *al-Mu'talif wa-l-mukhtalif*, ed. F. Krenkow (Cairo, 1354), p. 14, no. 15; Ibn Ḥabīb, *Asmā' al-mughtālīn* (*Nawādir al-makhṭuṭāt*, ed. ʿAbd al-Salām Hārūn (Cairo, 1374/1955), VII, 265–266).

[49] See Aṣḥāb al-ra'y, EI², 692 (J. Schacht).

[50] *ʿIbāra*, fol. 9b.

[51] *ʿIbāra*, fol. 34b; al-Ibshīhī, *al-Mustaṭraf* (Cairo, 1308), II, 80. (See the striking remark of Ibn Sīrīn: *mā yanbaghī li-aḥadin min ahli hādhā l-zamāni an yarā hādhihi l-ru'yā*).

[52] See on him Ibn Ḥajar, *Tahdhīb*, VIII, 36, no. 67.

[53] See al-ʿAzīzī, *op. cit.*, II, 410; al-Suyūṭī, *al-Khaṣā'iṣ*, III, 9; al-Jarrāḥī, *op. cit.*, II, 34, no. 1637.

[54] *ʿIbāra*, fol. 11a.

the *ḥadīth* and was told that Abū Dharr and Abū Hurayra transmitted this *ḥadīth*.[55]

Sometimes a peculiar word, or a curious one, is revealed and elucidated in a dream. ʿAbdallah b. ʿĀʾidh al-Thumālī[56] promised Ghuḍayf b. al-Ḥārith[57] on his death-bed to tell him what befell him after death. ʿAbdallah appeared to him in a dream and said: "We barely escaped (scil., pain – K); we met the Lord, Who forgave the sins and did not punish for the bad deeds except the *aḥrāḍ*" (whom He did punish – K); Ghuḍayf asked who were the *aḥrāḍ*. ʿAbdallah explained the word as denoting people who are pointed at with the fingers secretly. Ibn Qutayba discusses several words of this root (*ḥ r ḍ*) and accepts ʿAbdallah's definition of this word.[58]

There is a dream which shows how faithful a believer Abū Bakr was. The Prophet, says the story, fraternized between Salmān and Abū Bakr. One night Salmān had a dream after which he turned away from Abū Bakr. When asked by Abū Bakr about his behaviour Salmān told him that he had seen him (i.e. Abū Bakr) in a dream, his hands fastened to his neck. Abū Bakr explained the dream as denoting that he had his hands fettered so as to prevent him from doing evil deeds until the Day of Judgement. The truth of this interpretation was subsequently established by the Prophet.[59]

A similar tendency can be discerned in the following story: Rabīʿa b. Umayya recounted a dream of his to Abū Bakr: "I was in a fertile land, then I moved into a land struck by barrenness. Your hands (i.e. Abū Bakr's) were fastened to your neck and you were at the side of Sarīr b. Abī l-Ḥashr."

55 *ʿIbāra*, fol. 12a; al-Mundhirī, *al-Targhīb wa-l-tarhīb*, ed. Muḥammad Muḥyī l-Dīn ʿAbd al-Ḥamīd (Cairo, 1381/1962), V, 289, no. 4532 (and see *ibid.*, no. 4531); al-Sharīf al-Raḍiyy, *al-Majāzāt al-nabawiyya*, ed. Maḥmūd Muṣṭafā (Cairo, 1356/1937), p. 272, no. 287 (with an interpretation of the *ḥadīth*); Abū Nuʿaym, *op. cit.*, IV, 101; Maʿmar b. Rāshid, *op. cit.*, fol. 170a. The reliability of the ḥadīth: *inna aḥadakum yujmaʿu khalquhu...*, transmitted by Ibn Masʿūd, was established by the Prophet in a dream. Muḥammad b. Yazīd al-Asfāṭī (see on him Ibn Ḥajar, *Tahdhīb*, IX, 525, no. 861) saw the Prophet in a dream and asked him about this *ḥadīth*, reported by al-Aʿmash on the authority on Ibn Masʿūd. The Prophet stated that he himself reported this utterance to Ibn Masʿūd and repeated this statement three times. "May God forgive al-Aʿmash, as he transmitted it, and may God forgive those who transmitted it before him and those who will transmit it after him", said the Prophet. (Ibn Rajab, *Jāmiʿ l-ʿulūm wa-l-ḥikam*, ed. Muḥammad al-Aḥmadī Abū l-Nūr, Cairo, 1970, I, 103; on al-Aʿmash [Sulaymān b. Mihrān] see al-Dhahabī, *Tadhkirat al-ḥuffāẓ*, I, 154, no. 149; Ibn Ḥibbān, *Kitāb al-thiqāt*, ed. ʿAbd al-Khāliq al-Afghānī (Hyderabad, 1388/1968), p. 90).

56 See on him Ibn Saʿd. *Ṭabaqāt* (Beirut, 1377/1958), VII, 415.

57 See on him Ibn Ḥajar, *al-Iṣāba*, V, 189, no. 6906; Ibn Saʿd, *op. cit.*, VII, 443.

58 *ʿIbāra*, fol. 16a; Ibn Saʿd, *op. cit.*, VII, 415; Ibn Abī l-Dunyā, *al-Manām*, pp. 297, 327; see al-Zamakhsharī, *al-Fāʾiq*, ed. ʿAlī Muḥammad al-Bijāwī and Muḥammad Abū l-Faḍl Ibrāhīm (Cairo, 1971), I, 276; LʿA, s.v. *ḥ r ḍ*.

59 *ʿIbāra*, fol. 9a.

Abū Bakr interpreted the dream as follows: "Your dream is true. You will abandon belief for unbelief; my affairs were destined for me righteously (i.e., my hands will not reach out for anything wrong – K) and I shall remain in a state of joy (*sarīr* → *surūr*) until the Day of Resurrection (*ḥashr*)." It is told that Rabīʿa indeed embraced Christianity and left for Byzantium.[60]

Many stories of dreams predict the rule of the first Caliphs, the rise of the Umayyad-dynasty and the *fitan*, reflecting often the conflicting religio-political views of the various factions of Muslim society.[61]

60 *ʿIbāra*, fol. 19a; Ibn Ḥajar, *al-Iṣāba*, II, 224, no. 2746.

61 The succession of the two caliphs after the Prophet was predicted according to his dream in which he saw himself drawing a bucket from a well. He was followed in this action by Abū Bakr, who drew however no more than two buckets with little force. Then he was followed by ʿUmar. The bucket grew in his hands very large and he drew it with the greatest energy. See this story, Maʿmar b. Rāshid, *op. cit.*, fol. 18a; Abū ʿUbayd, *Gharīb al-ḥadīth*, I, 87; Ibn Abī Ḥātim, *Kit. al-ʿilal*, Ms. Chester Beatty 3516, fol. 286b; al-Bayhaqī, *Maʿrifat al-sunan wa-l-āthār*, ed. Aḥmad Ṣaqr, Cairo 1389/1969, I, 119; Ibn Ḥajar al-Haytamī, *op. cit.*, p. 22; al-Zurqānī, *op. cit.*, VII, 187–188; al-Zamakhsharī, *al-Fāʾiq*, III, 61; Abū Bakr Ibn al-ʿArabī, *al-ʿAwāṣim min al-qawāṣim*, ed. Muḥibb al-Dīn al-Khaṭīb (Judda, 1387), p. 188; al-Suyūṭī, *al-Khaṣāʾiṣ al-kubrā*, II, 417–418; Muḥammad Fuʾād ʿAbd al-Bāqī, *op. cit.*, III, 165–166, nos. 1548–1549; al-Qastallāni, *op. cit.*, X, 147–149; Ps. Ibn Sīrīn, *op. cit.*, p. 292; al-Muttaqī al-Hindī, *op. cit.*, XII, 176–177, nos. 930–933 (the *ḥadīth* no. 932 and Suyūṭī, *Khaṣāʾiṣ*, II, 418 combines the tradition of succession with the tradition about the *ʿAjam* embracing Islam, mentioned above p. 72, note 23), 183–184, nos. 972–973; Fahd, *op. cit.*, p. 277. The succession of the three first Caliphs was foreseen in a dream of the Prophet. He saw in a dream Abū Bakr attached (*nīṭa bihi*) to him; ʿUmar was attached to Abū Bakr. and ʿUthmān to ʿUmar (al-Ḥākim, *op. cit.*, III, 71, 102; al-Suyūṭī, *al-Khaṣāʾiṣ al-kubrā*, II 417).

Abū Bakr saw himself in a dream clad in a yemenī garment and treading on human excrements; he had two moles on his chest. The Prophet interpreted it by saying that for two years he would rule as Caliph. (al-Muttaqī al-Hindī, *op. cit.*, XII, 162–163, no. 827. Ibn Saʿd' *op. cit.*, III, 176–177; Ibn Ḥajar al-Haytamī, *op. cit.*, p. 24).

ʿAuf b. Mālik saw in a dream a man in a crowd taller than the rest of the people. He was told that the man was ʿUmar. ʿUmar, he was told, surpasses them because he is not wary of being blamed while acting for God's sake, he will be an appointed Caliph by the predecessor and will die as martyr. ʿAuf told Abū Bakr the dream, who summoned ʿUmar and ordered ʿAuf to relate him the dream. When he said "he will be an appointed Caliph" (by the predecessor), ʿUmar silenced him and pulled him away roughly. When he became Caliph, he met ʿAuf, admitted that one part of the dream has been fulfilled, expressed his wish to act fearlessly for God's sake, but wondered how he could gain the death of a martyr if he remains in the Arab peninsula (Ibn Saʿd, *op. cit.*, III, 331; al-Muḥibb al-Ṭabarī, *al-Riyāḍ al-naḍira*, Cairo 1372/1953, I, 212).

Abū Mūsā al-Ashʿarī saw himself in a dream facing many highways, which, however, dwindled away. He went on the one which had been left and reached a mountain on which he saw the Prophet; on his side stood Abū Bakr. The Prophet pointed at ʿUmar ordering him to draw near. Abū Mūsā understood that the dream foreboded the death of ʿUmar (Ibn Saʿd, *op. cit.*, III, 332).

ʿUthmān saw the Prophet in a dream when he was besieged in his court. ʿUthmān was fasting and the Prophet told him that he would break the fast in his company in the morning. In the morning, while still fasting, ʿUthmān was indeed killed, (al-Ḥākim, *op. cit.*, III, 94, 103; al-Suyūṭī, *al-Khaṣāʾiṣ al-kubrā*, II, 443–444; Muḥammad b. Yaḥyā b. Abī Bakr, *al-Tamhīd wa-l-bayān*, ed. Maḥmūd Yūsuf Zāyid, Beirut, 1964, p. 175; al-Muḥibb al-Ṭabarī, *al-Riyāḍ*, II, 161, 167–168; and see another version *ibid.*, 167: ʿUthmān, when besieged, saw in a dream the Prophet who asked him: "Have they besieged you, have they caused you intense thirst?" "Yes", said ʿUthmān. The Prophet gave him a bucket with cold water and ʿUthmān drank until he quenched his thirst. Then the Prophet said: "If you want I shall help you against them [i.e. against the besiegers] or if else you will break the fast with us." ʿUthmān preferred to break the fast in the company of the Prophet [i.e. in Paradise] and was killed next day).

The Prophet interpreted the fire seen by Zurāra b. ʿAmr al-Nakhaʿī as indicating the *fitna* which will flame up after the Prophet's death. (See *ʿIbāra*, fol. 47b ult. — 48a; Ibn Ḥajar, *al-Iṣāba*, III, 8; Ibn ʿAbd al-Barr, *al-Istīʿāb*, ed. ʿAlī Muḥammad al-Bijāwī, Cairo, n.d., II, 517, no. 811; al-Zamakhsharī, *op. cit.*, II, 182–183; al-Zurqānī, *op. cit.*, VII, 193–194; Fahd, *op. cit.*, p. 286; and see *ʿIbāra*, fol. 51a, inf.).

The neutrality of Saʿd b. Abī Waqqāṣ was approved of in a dream. Ḥusayn b. Khārija al-Ashjaʿī became perplexed when the *fitna* broke out (i.e. after the murder of ʿUthmān). He asked God to grant him a sign how to act righteously. He saw in a dream this world and the next world and was guided by angels to a place where Ibrāhīm and the Prophet stayed. He heard the Prophet asking Ibrāhīm to beg God to pardon the sins of his people. Ibrāhīm said: "You know what your people invented (*aḥdathū*; for the meaning of *aḥdatha* see Goldziher, *op. cit.*, II, 27–31) after your death; they spilled their blood and killed their *imām*; why did they not act like my friend Saʿd?" Ḥusayn b. Khārija went to Saʿd and related him his dream. Saʿd was pleased that Ibrāhīm had named him his friend. When asked which of the two factions he joined, Saʿd stated that he kept away from both parties. He advised Ḥusayn to buy a flock and stay far away until the *fitna* came to an end (al-Dhahabī, *Siyar aʿlām al-nubalāʾ*, ed. Ṣalāḥ al-Dīn al-Munajjid, I, 81, al-Ḥakim, *al-Mustadrak*, III, 501).

The heated discussion about the position of ʿAlī is reflected in a story about a *muḥaddith* who appeared in a dream to his friend and told him about the privileged status of Muḥammad b. ʿUbayd in Paradise, because he preferred ʿUthmān to ʿAlī (al-Khaṭīb al-Baghdādī, *op. cit.*, II, 367). Muḥammad b. ʿUbayd, when alive, used to warn his audience not to listen to the Kufians who scoff at the people (*ibid.*, the Kufians were known as the partisans of ʿAlī).

The negative attitude towards the Umayyad rulers was reflected in a story according to which the Prophet saw the Umayyads in a dream jumping like apes on his minbar (al-Suyūṭī, *al-Khaṣāʾiṣ al-kubrā*, II, 427–428; al-Majlisī, *op. cit.*, LXI, 156).

The attitude of the orthodoxy towards the conflict between ʿAlī and Muʿāwiya (comp.: *idhā dhukira aṣḥābī fa-amsikū*, al-Suyūṭī, *Taʾrīkh al-khulafāʾ*, p. 176; Aḥmad b. Ḥajar al-Haytamī, *op. cit.*, p. 214) is mirrored in the story of the dream of ʿUmar b. ʿAbd al-ʿAzīz. He saw in a dream the Prophet in the company of Abū Bakr and ʿUmar. ʿAlī and Muʿāwiya were brought in and entered a house the door of which was closed behind them. After a time ʿAlī went out and stated that a verdict was given in his favour; then Muʿāwiya went out and said that God forgave him his sins (Ibn Abī l-Dunyā, *al-Manām*, p. 319).

The personality of ʿUmar b. ʿAbd al-ʿAzīz and his orthodox rule are emphasized in a story in which he tells of a dream which he dreamt. He saw the Prophet in the company of Abū Bakr and ʿUmar, and the Prophet ordered him to follow the path of Abū Bakr and ʿUmar when he will be entrusted with government (Ibn Saʿd, *op. cit.*, III, 291; al-Suyūṭī, *Taʾrīkh al-khulafāʾ*, p. 230).

A cloud flowing with butter and honey, which a man saw in a dream, was interpreted by Abū Bakr as Islam (the cloud) and Qur'ān (butter and honey).[62]

The esteem for scholars occupied with the study of the Qur'ān is reflected in the story of a dream in which al-Kisā'ī appeared and stated that God had forgiven his sins because he was dedicated to the study of the Qur'ān.[63]

The preceding tradition belongs in fact to a particular kind of stories about the rewards in Paradise granted to the pious and godfearing for their good deeds. A fine specimen of a collection of this genre of stories is the *Kitāb al-manām* of Ibn Abī l-Dunyā,[64] a contemporary of Ibn Qutayba.[65] Similar in content are some chapters on this subject in Ibn Abī Ḥātim's *Taqdimat al-ma'rifa li-kitābi l-jarḥ wa-l-ta'dīl.*[66] Our *'Ibāra* contains many stories of this kind. In some cases the tendency is to stress the specific virtues by which the pious gained Paradise, to guide the living and to admonish.

Mālik b. Dīnār saw al-Ḥasan al-Baṣrī in a dream and asked him about his experiences in the other world. Al-Ḥasan told him that he was guided by God's grace to the abode of the righteous in reward for his sorrow and weeping in this world. He accordingly said: "The longer the man's saddness in this world the longer is his joy in the life to come."[67] Ibn Qutayba remarks that this utterance is expressed in a manner which resembles al-Ḥasan's own style.[68]

Mālik b. Dīnār also saw Muslim b. Yasār[69] in a dream. Muslim told him that he had been subjected after his death to dreadful experiences, but that later God had forgiven him his sins and accepted his good deeds. Mālik sobbed and fainted. After a few days he died.[70]

62 *'Ibāra*, fol. 36a; see the different versions of this story: Ma'mar b. Rāshid, *op. cit.*, fols. 152b–153a; Muḥammad Fu'ād 'Abd al-Bāqī, *op. cit.*, III, 42–43, no. 1462; Aḥmad b. Ḥanbal, *op. cit.*, III, 357, no. 2113; Ps. Ibn Sīrīn, *op. cit.*, p. 130; al-Ḥanafī, *op. cit.*, II, 265; al-Qasṭallānī, *op. cit.*, X, 160–161; al-Muḥibb al-Ṭabarī, *al-Riyāḍ*, I, 107; Abū Bakr Ibn al-'Arabī, *op. cit.*, p. 189; cf. al-Khargūshī, *op. cit.*, fol. 120b.

63 *'Ibāra*, fol. 15a; al-Khaṭīb al-Baghdādī, *op. cit.*, XI, 410, 414.

64 Ms. al-Jazzār, Acre, *majmū'a.*

65 D. 280 H. F. Meier's statement "Die Welt der Urbilder bei 'Alī Hamadani", (*Eranos Jahrbuch*, 1950), p. 125, that the earliest collection of such stories is in the *Risāla* of al-Qushayrī must thus be altered.

66 Ibn Abī Ḥātim, *Taqdimat al-ma'rifa* (Hyderabad, 1371/1952), pp. 119–122, 311–312.

67 *'Ibāra, op. cit.*, fol. 12b; Ibn Abī l-Dunyā, *al-Manām*, p. 301; comp. a similar dream of Ibn Sīrīn in al-Dhahabī's *Ta'rīkh al-Islām* (Cairo, 1367), IV, 198.

68 *Ibid., ...aṭwalu l-nāsi ḥuznan aṭwaluhum faraḥan fī l-ākhirati*; *qāla abū muḥammadin*: *wa-hādhā kamā tarā ashbahu bi-jayyidi kalāmi l-ḥasani.*

69 See on him Ibn Sa'd, *op. cit.*, VII, 186.

70 *'Ibāra*, fol. 13a, ult. — 13b sup.; Ibn Abī l-Dunyā, *al-Manām*, p. 299, ll. 5–12; Abū Nu'aym, *op. cit.*, II, 294 inf.

Mālik b. Dīnar appeared after his death in a dream to Suhayl Akhū Ḥazm[71] and informed him that he had come to the presence of God with many sins, but that God had forgiven him because of his confidence in God (*ḥusnu l-ẓanni bi-llāhi*).[72]

Sufyān al-Thaurī appeared in a dream to Abū Khālid al-Aḥmar and informed him that he had found rest from the troubles of this world and came at the Mercy of God. According to another story Sufyān said that God had forgiven him his sins because of his *ṭalab al-ḥadīth*.[73]

Ṣāliḥ al-Barrād saw in a dream Zurāra b. Aufā.[74] Zurara told him that the best things by which to reach Paradise are trust in God and hope of little duration.[75]

Another class of dreams contain predictions about the death of pious men and how they will enter Paradise. A pious woman in Mecca dreamt about maid-servants, dressed in yellow clothes and holding sweet basil in their hands, encircling the Kaʿba. She was shocked by what she saw and said to herself: "Such a thing around the Kaʿba?" She was told in her dream that ʿAbd al-ʿAzīz b. Abī Rawwād[76] was getting married. That night, when she woke up, she was informed that he had died the same night.[77]

A woman saw in her dream a beautiful garden in which there was placed a golden throne. On this throne sat a man surrounded by servants with cups in their hands. She was told that the man was Marwān al-Muḥallimī. When

71 See on him Ibn Ḥajar, *Tahdhīb*, IV, 261, no. 449.

72 *ʿIbāra*, fol. 13b; Ibn Abī l-Dunyā, *Majmūʿat rasāʾil* (Cairo, 1354/1935), p. 41, no. 7 (*Kitāb ḥusni l-ẓanni bi-llāhi*).

73 *ʿIbāra*, fol. 14a; Ibn Abī Ḥātim, *op. cit.*, p. 121; comp. Ibn Abī l-Dunyā, *al-Manām*, p. 351: A man saw Yazīd b. Hārūn after his death in a dream and asked him whether God forgave him his sins because he studied Qurʾān. "No", said Yazīd, "because (my study of) *ḥadīth*". And see al-Fasawī, *Kit. al-maʿrifa wa-l-taʾrīkh*, Esad Ef. 2391, fol. 190b inf.: ʿAmr b. Murra hesitated whether to choose *ḥadīth* or Qurʾān. He saw in a dream a man granting gifts to the readers of Qurʾān, not to the transmitters of *ḥadīth* and he decided to prefer Qurʾān. See about *ṭalab al-ḥadīth*: Goldziher, *Muslim Studies*, II, 164 seq.; ʿAbdallah b. al-Mubārak told his friend in a dream that God forgave him his sins because of *ṭalab al-ḥadīth* (*Majmūʿat rasāʾil fī ʿulūm al-ḥadīth*, ed. Ṣubḥī al-Badrī al-Samarrāʾī, al-Madīna al-Munawwara 1389/1969, p. 47).

74 See on him Wakiʿ, *Akhbār al-quḍāt*, ed. ʿAbd al-ʿAzīz Muṣṭafā al-Marāghī (Cairo, 1366/1947), I, 292–297; Ibn Saʿd, *op. cit.*, VII, 150.

75 *ʿIbāra*, fol. 13a; Ibn Abī l-Dunyā, *al-Manām*, p. 298, cf. al-Thaʿlabī, *Kitāb qatlā l-Qurʾān*, Ms. Leiden, Or. 9981 (*majmūʿa*), fol. 9a–b.

76 See on him al-Shaʿrānī, *al-Ṭabaqāt al-kubrā* (Cairo, [n.d.]), p. 52; Abū Nuʿaym, *op. cit.*, VIII, 191.

77 *ʿIbāra*, fol. 11b; al-Yāfiʿī, *Mirʾāt al-jinān* (Hyderabad, 1338), I, 339 ult.–240 sup.; Ps. Ibn Sīrīn, *op. cit.*, p. 76.

she woke up in the morning, she was informed that the funeral of Marwān al-Muḥallimī passed by her door at that time.[78]

Ḥafṣa bint Rāshid was moved by the death of her neighbour Marwān al-Muḥallimī. She then saw him in a dream and asked him what God's decision about him was. He told her that he had been introduced into Paradise, that he had then joined the "People of the Right" (*aṣḥāb al-yamīn*) and been finally raised to "those near the Presence" (*al-muqarrabīn*). When asked whom he had met in Paradise, he answered that he had seen there al-Ḥasan (al-Baṣrī), Maymūn b. Siyāh,[79] and Muḥammad b. Sīrīn.[80]

The stories adduced above may give an idea about the dreams recorded by Ibn Qutayba concerning the pious in Paradise.

Yet another group of dreams contain injunctions, warnings and forebodings. Ismāʿīl al-Ḥaḍramī became blind. In a dream he was taught a supplication and, having recited it, he regained his eyesight.[81]

Wahb b. Munabbih fell into destitution. One night he dreamt that a man brought him a thing resembling an almond or a pistachio nut. Having opened it, he found a piece of silk on which there was an inscription saying that it was not fitting for a man who knows the justice of God, or his affair by God's mercy, to consider the sustenance given by God as too slow. Later God gave him indeed plentiful sustenance.[82]

A pious man from Hamdān saw in a dream a piece of paper on which an injunction was written ordering him to practise submission and fear of God in order to reach the rank of the righteous.[83]

A secretary of al-Ḥasan b. Sahl[84] resigned from his post and became a pious man. In his dream he saw a man who told him that his Lord called

78 *ʿIbāra*, fol. 10a–b; Ibn Abī l-Dunyā, *al-Manām*, p. 300, ll. 10–16; Ps. Ibn Sīrīn, *op. cit.*, p. 70; al-Khargūshī, *op. cit.*, fol. 62b.

79 See on him Abū Nuʿaym, *op. cit.*, III, 106; Ibn Saʿd, *op. cit.*, VII, 152.

80 *ʿIbāra*, fol. 10a; Ibn Abī l-Dunyā, *al-Manām*, p. 300, ll. 7–10; Ps. Ibn Sīrīn, *op. cit.*, pp. 69–70; al-Khargūshī, *op. cit.*, fol. 62b.

81 *ʿIbāra*, fol. 11a. Cf. Ibn Ḥanbal, *Kit. al-ʿilal*, ed. T. Kacyigit and I. Cerrahoglu (Ankara, 1963), I, 68, no. 401: Simāk became blind. He saw in his dream Abraham who stroked his eyes, ordered him to enter the Euphrates and to open his eyes in the river. He did it and regained his sight.

82 *ʿIbāra*, fol. 13a; al-Tanūkhī, *al-Faraj baʿda l-shidda* (Cairo, 1357/1938), I, 168; comp. Ibn Nāsir al-Dīn al-Dimashqī, *Jāmiʿ al-āthār fī maulidi l-mukhtār*, Ms. Cambridge Or. 913, fol. 75a sup. (It was the Prophet who saw the inscription in his dream; the story is transmitted on the authority of Wahb. b. Munabbih).

83 *ʿIbāra*, fol. 12b.

84 See on him al-Jahshiyārī, *al-Wuzarāʾ wa-l-kuttāb*, ed. al-Saqā, al-Abyārī, Shalabī (Cairo, 1357/1938), pp. 230–231.

him. He understood the hint, made the necessary preparations and set out for a pilgrimage to Mecca. He died in fact on his journey.[85]

ʿUmar saw in a dream a cock which pecked him once or twice. He interpreted it that an alien (a Persian) would kill him.[86]

ʿĀ'isha bint Ṭalḥa (and another man) saw Ṭalḥa in a dream. He complained of dampness discomforting him in his grave and asked to be removed into another place. When his grave was opened, the people found it exactly as described by Ṭalḥa. His body was found unchanged except for some of the hair in his beard.[87]

A woman saw her deceased daughter in a dream. The daughter ordered her mother to divide walnuts amongst the poor. Ibn Sīrīn interpreted the dream as follows: the woman should take out her hidden treasure and divide it among the poor. The woman admitted that she had buried this treasure at the time of a plague.[88]

A woman told Ibn Sīrīn that she dreamt the moon was entering into the Pleiades; a herald from behind her ordered her to go to Ibn Sīrīn and to tell him the story. Ibn Sīrīn's interpretation was that he would die within seven days; he died in fact on the seventh day.[89]

A man saw in a dream a bird coming down from heaven, alighting on a shrub of jasmin and picking it, then flying back towards heaven. Ibn Sīrīn explained it as referring to the death of scholars. In fact a number of scholars died in that year, among them al-Ḥasan and Ibn Sīrīn.[90]

Laylā bint Aufā al-Ḥarashiyya, the wife of Furāt al-Bakkā'ī, had a daughter who saw in her dream that she would break three banners. Her mother asked Ibn Sīrīn about it, and he interpreted the dream by saying that three of her husbands would be killed. In fact Yazīd b. al-Muhallab, ʿAmr b. Yazīd al-Taymī, and al-ʿAbbās b. ʿAbdallah b. al-Ḥārith b. Naufal b. al-Ḥārith b. ʿAbd

85 *ʿIbāra*, fol. 14a.

86 *ʿIbāra*, fol. 19a; Ibn Saʿd, *op. cit.*, III, 335–336; al-Ḥākim, *op. cit.*, III, 90; Ibn al-Jauzī, *Ta'rīkh ʿUmar*, ed. Ḥasan al-Hādī Ḥusayn (Cairo, [n.d.]), p. 166; al-Muḥibb al-Ṭabarī, *op. cit.* (Cairo, 1372/1953), II, 99; Ps. Ibn Sīrīn, *op. cit.*, p. 201; al-Majlisī, *op. cit.*, LXI, 231; Fahd, *op. cit.*, 291; Ibn Saʿd, *op. cit.*, III, 355; Muḥammad b. Aḥmad al-Tamīmī, *op. cit.*, fols. 5b, 8a, 10b, 12b.

87 *ʿIbāra*, fol. 11b; ʿAbd al-Razzāq, *al-Muṣannaf*, Ms. Murad Molla 604, fol. 60b; Ibn Abī l-Dunyā, *al-Manām*, p. 332; Ibn ʿAbd al-Barr, *op. cit.*, II, 768–769; al-Muḥibb al-Tabarī, *op. cit.*, II, 348 (quoted on the authority of Ibn Qutayba); Fahd, *op. cit.*, p. 290; Cf. Ibn Abī Shayba, *al-Muṣannaf*, ed. ʿAbd al-Khāliq al-Afghānī (Hyderabad, 1388/1968), III, 389.

88 *ʿIbāra*, fol. 18b; Ps. Ibn Sīrīn, *op. cit.*, p. 274.

89 *ʿIbāra*, fol. 18b; al-Ṣafadī, *al-Wāfī bi-l-wafayāt*, ed. Sven Dedering (Damascus, 1953), III, 146, no. 1095; al-Dhahabī, *Ta'rīkh al-islām*, IV, 196; Abū Nuʿaym, *op. cit.*, II, 277; al-Ibshīhī, *op. cit.*, II, 79; Ps. Ibn Sīrīn, *op. cit.*, p. 221; Cf. Ibn Ḥanbal, *ʿIlal*, I, 6, no. 17: Saʿīd b. Jubayr was told in his dream that al-Ḥajjāj would kill him.

90 *ʿIbāra*, fol. 20b; Ibn Kathīr, *al-Bidāya wa-l-nihāya* (Beirut–Riyāḍ, 1966), IX, 275.

al-Muṭṭalib were killed. Al-Ḥasan b. ʿUthmān b. ʿAbd al-Raḥmān b. ʿAuf succeeded to divorce her when he heard about the story of her dream and saved his life.[91]

ʿĀ'isha saw in a dream three moons falling in her bossom. Her father, Abū Bakr, interpreted it by saying that three men, the best people in the world, would be buried in her home.[92]

Of special interest are sections of the manuscript reporting about dreams in which verses unknown to the dreamer were recited. These verses, underlining the true Arabic-Islamic character of these sections, serve in some cases as predictions, in others for recording some *gharīb* versions, or for purposes of admonition.

It may be of some interest to gain more insight[93] into the dreams of Ibn Qutayba himself, he being a man of outstanding knowledge in Arabic literature, language and religious lore. Ibn Qutayba reports[94] that he saw in his youth a dream in which there were many books containing many *gharīb* expressions. He remembered some of them, but later forgot them except the expression *wa-balaghat ilayhi ṣallatu l-hawā'i*. At that time he did not know the meaning of *ṣalla*; afterwards he learnt that it meant dryness.[95]

Ibn Qutayba describes another dream which he dreamt as "a marvel" (*uʿjūba*). A man asked him one day about the word *junahiyy*, which he did not know. In a dream a person explained to him the word as a synonym of *khayzurān* (bamboo). After a while Ibn Qutayba heard a man reciting:

fī kaffihi junahiyyun rīḥuhu ʿabiqun
min kaffi arwaʿa fī ʿirnīnihi shamamu
idhā ra'athu qurayshun qāla qā'iluhā
ilā makārimi hādhā yantahī l-karamu[96]

Ibn Qutayba knew before that this verse in the version: *fī kaffihi khayzurānun*; when he heard it in the new version he understood that the explanation in the dream was right.[97]

[91] *ʿIbāra*, fol. 21a; see Ibn Ḥabīb, *al-Muḥabbar*, ed. Ilse Lichtenstaedter (Hyderabad, 1361/1942), p. 443; Ps. Ibn Sīrīn, *op. cit.*, p. 152; cf. al-Khargūshī, *op. cit.*, fol. 142b, penult.

[92] *ʿIbāra*, fol. 29a; al-Rāghib al-Iṣfahānī, *op. cit.*, I, 150; al-Suyūṭī, *Ta'rīkh al-khulafā'*, p. 105; al-Haythamī, *op. cit.*, VII, 185; Ps. Ibn Sīrīn, *op. cit.*, p. 220; al-Ibshībī, *op. cit.*, II, 79; al-Muttaqī l-Hindī, *op. cit.*, XII, 176, no. 927; *Al-Manāsik*, ed. Ḥamad al-Jāsir (al-Riyāḍ, 1389/1969), p. 374.

[93] See Ibn Qutayba's dream in connection with a *ḥadīth*, above, note 55.

[94] *ʿIbāra*, fol. 16b. [95] See L'A, s.v. *ṣ l l*.

[96] *ʿIbāra*, fol. 16b; cf. Muṣʿab b. ʿAbdallah al-Zubayrī, *op. cit.*, p. 164; *Rijāl al-Kashshī*, ed. Aḥmad al-Ḥusaynī (Karbalā', [n.d.]), p. 119; Ṣadr al-Dīn ʿAlī Khān al-Shīrāzī al-Madanī, *al-Darajāt al-rafīʿa* (al-Najaf, 1382/1962), p. 549.

[97] See L'A, s.v. *j n h*.

The interpretation of dreams

A man from Ghassān dreamt that he saw on the wall of Damascus a person who recited verses predicting the death of ʿAmr b. Saʿīd who "considered the fortress as a place of rescue from death, sought refuge in the fortress, but the fate of death visited him in the fortress." The Ghassānī recounted the dream to ʿAbd al-Malik who asked him to keep the dream in secret. After some time the dream was fulfilled: ʿAbd al-Malik killed ʿAmr b. Saʿīd (al-Ashdaq) in the fortress of Damascus.[98]

At the time of ʿUthmān a man saw in a dream a person reciting verses predicting the death of ʿUthmān. A short time afterwards ʿUthmān was killed.[99]

A man saw in a dream ʿAlī b. Hishām. He played a lute and sang:

By my life, if Khurāsān causes me to forfeit my head
so I was indeed far from the gates of Khurāsān.

After some time al-Ma'mūn sent al-ʿUjayf and ordered to kill ʿAlī b. Hishām.[100]

Ascetic poetry is represented in verses recited by girls in Paradise (*ḥūrīs*) whom a man saw in his dream:

God of men, the Lord of Muḥammad, created us
for people standing on their feet sleepless (praying – K)
Whispering to their God, the Lord of all Being
the worries of this people, circulate during the night, while (other) men sleep.[101]

Of the same character are the verses recited in a dream to Rābiʿa al-ʿAdawiyya, when she was ill:

Your prayer, when people sleep, is light

98 *ʿIbāra*, fol. 15b; Ibn Abī l-Dunyā, *Manām*, p. 347; Ibn Kathīr, *al-Bidāya*, VIII, 311 (all the sources recording the verses:

alā yā la-qaumī li-l-safāhati wa-l-wahni
wa-li-l-ʿājizi l-mauhūni wa-l-ra'yi dhī l-afni.
wa-li-bni saʿīdin baynamā huwa qā'imun
ʿalā qadamayhi kharra li-l-wajhi wa-l-baṭni.
ra'ā l-ḥiṣna manjātan fa-ltajā
ilayhi fa-zārathu l-maniyyatu fī l-ḥiṣni.)

and see the story of his killing al-Ṭabarī, *Ta'rīkh* (Cairo, 1358/1939), IV, 598–600. See *ibid.*, p. 598: ʿAmr b. Saʿīd saw in a dream ʿUthmān on the night before he was murdered; ʿUthmān dressed him in his gown.

99 *ʿIbāra*, fol. 15b; Ibn Abī l-Dunyā, *al-Manām*, p. 347:

la-ʿamru abīka fa-lā taʿjalan
laqad dhahaba l-khayru illā qalīlā
wa-qad safiha l-nāsu fī dīnihim
wa-khallā bnu ʿaffāna sharran ṭawīlā.

100 *ʿIbāra*, fol. 20b; see the story of his execution al-Ṭabarī, *Ta'rīkh*, VII, 192–193.

101 *ʿIbāra*, fol. 15b, inf. – 16a sup.

your sleep is diverse, opposed to prayer.
Your life is a plunder and a respite
it goes on and passes away steadily and ceases.[102]

Different in content is a story about a couple who promised each other to refrain from marriage in case one of them should die. The husband was the first to die. The widow kept her promise, but was persuaded by some women to remarry. On the night of her second marriage she saw in a dream her first husband who said: "How quickly did you forget the obligation, o Rabāb!" He recited the following verses:

I greeted the dwellers of this house, all of them
except Rabāb, for I am not greeting her.
She became married, while my abode
became a grave, indeed graves hide people who dwell in them.[103]

Besides the prognostic interpretations of dreams, a great number of interpretations are concerned with unknown facts of the past or the present, mainly details of private life, which would never have come to the person's knowledge without the help of the oneirocritic.

A man dreamt that he drank from a bottle with two heads, one sweet and one salty. Ibn Sīrīn said in his interpretation that he sought the favours of his wife's sister and bade him desist. The man admitted that the interpretation was a true one.[104]

A man saw in a dream that he drank from a bottle with a narrow neck. Ibn Sīrīn interpreted it by saying that the man was enticing a girl.[105]

A man dreamt a dream that he owned an ostrich that was grinding. Ibn Sīrīn said that it denoted that the man bought a slave-girl and hid her amongst the tribe of Banū Ḥanifa.[106]

A man dreamt a dream that his hand was cut off. Ibn Sīrīn interpreted it that he was a carpenter and changed his occupation.[107]

A man dreamt a dream that a pebble fell into his ear and he shook it off. Ibn Sīrīn interpreted it by saying that the man was associated to people of unorthodox innovations and heard vicious words, which his ear shook off.[108]

102 *ʿIbāra*, fol. 16a; al-Sarrāj, *Maṣāriʿ al-ʿushshāq*, Cairo, 1325/1907, pp. 146–147.

103 *ʿIbāra*, fol. 15a–b; Ibn Abī l-Dunyā, *al-Manām*, p. 344; Ibn Qayyim al-Jauziyya, *Akhbār al-nisāʾ*, ed. Nizār Riḍā, Beirut 1964, pp. 127–128.

104 *ʿIbāra*, fol. 17a; Abū Nuʿaym, *op. cit.*, II, 276–277; al-Khargūshī, *op. cit.*, fol. 125b.

105 *ʿIbāra*, fol. 17b.

106 *ʿIbāra*, fol. 17b; and see the version of al-Jāḥiẓ, *al-Ḥayawān*, IV, 368–369 (Parts of the Banū Ḥanīfa were peasants [they supplied Mecca with their agricultural products]. See EI², s.v. Ḥanīfa b. Ludjaym. And see Aḥmad b. Ḥanbal, *op. cit.*, XIII, 92, no. 7355; Ibn ʿAsākir, *op. cit.*, VI, 170).

107 *ʿIbāra*, fol. 18b; Ps. Ibn Sīrīn, *op. cit.*, p. 115; al-Khargūshī, *op. cit.*, fol. 106b.

108 *ʿIbāra*, fol. 20a.

A man saw in a dream Qatāda swallowing small pearls and spitting them out larger than those which he swallowed. Qatāda, according to Ibn Sīrīn's interpretation, transmitted more *ḥadīth* than he heard.[109]

A similar symbolism underlies Abū Bakr's interpretation of a dream, in which a man saw a big bull who came out from a small hole and could not enter it when he tried to return. Abū Bakr interpreted it as a grievous expression which cannot be taken back.[110]

A man heard in a dream a child shouting in his house. Ibn Sīrīn ordered him to stop playing on the guitar; it was in fact a singer.[111]

Drinking from a vessel symbolizes, as we have seen above,[112] sexual intercourse. The same interpretation is applied by Ibn Sīrīn in the following dream: a man saw in a dream a woman from his family lifting to her mouth a vessel of milk, but, outspeeded by a pressure to urinate, she had to put down the vessel at every attempt to drink. The woman, according to Ibn Sīrīn, was a righteous woman who longed for a man. Ibn Sīrīn advised to find for her a husband.[113]

A similar subject is dealt with in another story: Khālid b. Yazīd (or Yazīd) dreamt that he put three times a knife on the neck of a *ṭīṭawā*-bird trying unsuccessfully to slaughter it;[114] he managed to slaughter it only on the fourth time. An interpreter of dreams was summoned and explained that it refers to a virgin girl whom the dreamer failed to deflower three times, but succeeded on the fourth time. The interpreter added that the girl broke wind during the intercourse, which he deduced from the name of the bird "*ṭīṭawā*". Khālid admitted the facts.[115]

Sagacity was shown by Ibn Sīrīn in the interpretation of the following dream: A man saw in a dream that Yazīd b. al-Muhallab put up an arch between his house and that of the dreamer. Ibn Sīrīn asked the man: "Did your mother cohabit with Ibn al-Muhallab?" The man asked his mother and she admitted that she had been a slave-girl of Ibn al-Muhallab (scil. his concubine – K), later marrying the dreamer's father.[116]

109 *'Ibāra*, fol. 20b. Cf. al-Ṣafadī, *al-Wāfī bi-l-wafayāt*, ed. S. Dedering (Damascus, 1953), p. 146.

110 *'Ibāra*, fol. 20a; Ps. Ibn Sīrīn, *op. cit.*, p. 183; al-Khargūshī, *op. cit.*, fol. 168a.

111 *'Ibāra*, fol. 20b; Abū Nu'aym, *op. cit.*, II, 277; Ps. Ibn Sīrīn, *op. cit.*, p. 75.

112 See above notes 104, 105.

113 *'Ibāra*, fol. 21a; Ps. Ibn Sīrīn, *op. cit.*, p. 105.

114 See slaughter as symbol of sexual intercourse in the story recorded by al-Ibshīhī, *op. cit.*, II, 79 (a man saw in a dream a woman, who was his neighbour, slaughtered...); and see *'Ibāra*, fol. 54a, l. 10: *wa-man dhabaḥa ẓabyan iftaḍḍa jāriyatan...*; and see *ibid*, fol. 57b, l. 9: *...wa-man dhabaḥa dajājatan iftaḍḍa jāriyatan 'adhrā'a.*

115 *'Ibāra*, fol. 21b; Ps. Ibn Sīrīn, *op. cit.*, p. 12; al-Damīrī, *op. cit.*, II, 102; Abdel Daim, *op. cit.*, p. 85.

116 *'Ibāra*, fol. 21a; Ps. Ibn Sīrīn, *op. cit.*, p. 253.

A significant dream of Abū ʿAmr al-Nakhaʿī reflects the feeling of the victory of the Arabs over the Persians in the early period of Islam and their sense of self-identification with the past. Abū ʿAmr saw al-Nuʿmān b. al-Mundhir, the king of al-Ḥīra, in a dream, wearing two earrings and bracelets. When he informed the Prophet about his dream, the Prophet said: "This indicates that the kingdom of the Arabs returned to its splendour and beauty."[117]

The "Arab-character" of an object helps Saʿīd b. al-Musayyab to give an interpretation of a dream. A man saw in a dream on the battlements of the mosque a beautiful white pigeon, which was snatched away by a falcon. Ibn al-Musayyab interpreted it by saying that al-Ḥajjāj married the daughter of ʿAbdallah b. Jaʿfar. His explanation as to how he reached his conclusion is as follows: the pigeon denotes a woman, the whiteness denotes her pure pedigree; the falcon is an Arab bird, not an alien one (*laysa min ṭayri l-aʿājim*); among the Arabs he did not find anyone more closely resembling a falcon than al-Ḥajjāj.[118]

The Islamic character of Ibn Qutayba's compilation is underlined by the frequent quotations from Qur'ān and *ḥadīth*, which serve as the basis for the interpretations.

Abundance of mushrooms denote sustenance and wealth without fatigue, according to the utterance of the Prophet that mushrooms stem from *Manna*.[119]

The mouse denotes a profligate woman, because the Prophet called the mouse "*al-fuwaysiqa*" (the small profligate).[120]

According to this utterance, Ibn Sīrīn interpreted a dream in which a man saw himself having sexual intercourse with a mouse which gave birth to a date. Ibn Sīrīn asked the man whether he had at home a profligate wife. "Yes", the man answered. Further he asked: "Is she pregnant?" "Yes", the man answered. Ibn Sīrīn predicted that she would give birth to a righteous boy. He based his prognostic on the utterance of the Prophet about the mouse and his favourable saying about dates.[121]

117 *ʿIbāra*, fol. 45b; Ibn Ḥajar, *al-Iṣāba*, III, 8, no. 2789; al-Zurqānī, *op. cit.*, VII, 194; Fahd, *op. cit.*, p. 286, note 1.

118 *ʿIbāra*, fol. 57a; al-Rāghib al-Iṣfahānī, *op. cit.*, I, 150; al-Damīrī, *op. cit.*, II, 181; Ps. Ibn Sīrīn, *op. cit.*, p. 196; Fahd, *op. cit.*, p. 311, no. 6.

119 *ʿIbāra*, fol. 39b; al-Damīrī, *op. cit.*, II, 345–346; Ibn Qayyim al-Jauziyya, *Zād al-maʿād* (Beirut, [n.d.]), III, 181, 183; al-Ḥanafī, *op. cit.*, II, 366; Ibn al-Athīr, *al-Nihāya*, IV, 199; al-ʿAzīzī, *op. cit.*, III, 109; Ibn al-Athīr, *Jāmiʿ al-uṣūl*, VIII, 327, nos. 5636–5637.

120 *ʿIbāra*, fol. 5b ult.; al-Damīrī, *op. cit.*, II, 201 inf.; Ps. Ibn Sīrīn, *op. cit.*, p. 209; Ibn al-Athīr, *Jāmiʿ al-uṣūl*, XII, 367, no. 9449; about black and white mice denoting days and nights see *ʿIbāra*, fol. 8a; al-Damīrī, *op. cit.*, II, 202; Ps. Ibn Sīrīn, p. 209.

121 *ʿIbāra*, fol. 19a; Ps. Ibn Sīrīn, *op. cit.*, p. 209; cf. Ibn Kathīr, *al-Bidāya*, IX, 275.

The raven symbolizes, according to a *ḥadīth*, a profligate man.[122]

Bottles denote women, according to the utterance of the Prophet to Anjasha.[123]

A long right hand in a dream is to be interpreted as a generous helping person, as the Prophet said, addressing his wives: "The first of you who will join me (i.e. to die after me – K) will be the one with the longest hand." The first who died after the Prophet was Zaynab bint Jaḥsh.[124]

A rib seen in a dream denotes a woman according to the recommendation of the Prophet to treat woman gently because woman was created from a crooked rib and cannot be set aright.[125]

The liver denotes a treasure according to the saying of the Prophet about the troops of Mecca: *hādhihi makkatu qad ramatkum bi-aflādhi akbādihā.*[126]

Watering a garden and seeds denotes sexual intercourse, according to the prohibition of the Prophet to water the seeds of another man (referring to sexual intercourse with pregnant women).[127]

Many interpretations of dreams are based on verses of the Qur'ān, on expressions of the Qur'ān or meanings attached to them. Eggs denote women according to Sūra xxxvii 49, in which the women in Paradise are compared to hidden eggs.[128]

Timber denotes hipocrisy according to Sūra lxiii 4: "... but when they speak thou listenest to their speech, and it is as if they were propped up timbers."[129]

Stones in a dream symbolize hardness according to Sūra ii 74.[130]

Water denotes sometimes trial and allurement (*fitna*) according to Sūra lxxii 16.[131]

A king entering a locality not suiting his rank and honour (because of its smallness) denotes that the locality will be afflicted by humiliation or calamity,

122 *ʿIbāra*, fols. 5b, 24a; al-Damīrī, *op. cit.*, II, 180; al-Majlisī, LXI, 173.

123 *ʿIbāra*, fol. 6a; Ibn Ḥajar, *al-ʿIṣāba*, I, 68, no. 259; al-Bukhārī, *al-Adab al-mufrad*, ed. Muḥibb al-Dīn al-Khaṭīb (Cairo, 1379), p. 305, no. 883; Ibn ʿAbd al-Barr, *op. cit.*, I, 140; al-Jurjānī, *al-Muntakhab min kināyāt al-udabā'*, ed. Muḥammad Badr al-Dīn al-Naʿsānī (Cairo, 1326/1908), p. 7; al-Thaʿālibī, *al-Kināyāt*, ed. al-Naʿsānī (Cairo, 1326/1908), p. 4.

124 *ʿIbāra*, fol. 7a; Ibn ʿAbd al-Barr, *op. cit.*, IV, 1850, no. 3355; Ibn Saʿd, *op. cit.*, VIII, 108; al-Haythamī, *op. cit.*, IX, 248; al-Ḥanafī, *op. cit.*, II, 250; Ibn Kathīr, *Shamā'il*, p. 389; Ibn al-Athīr, *Jāmiʿ al-uṣūl*, XII, 66, no. 8850; al-Suyūṭī, *al-Khaṣā'iṣ al-kubrā*, II, 462.

125 *ʿIbāra*, fols. 6a, 31a inf.; al-Sulamī, *Ādāb al-ṣuḥba*, Jerusalem 1954, p. 82, note 245; al-Majlisī, *op. cit.*, LXI, 173.

126 *ʿIbāra*, fol. 31a; al-Sharīf al-Raḍiyy, *op. cit.*, p. 22, no. 1 (and see *ib.*, p. 226, no. 231)

127 *ʿIbāra*, fol. 37b.

128 *ʿIbāra*, fol. 5a.

129 *ʿIbāra*, fol. 5a; and see al-Qurṭubī, *Tafsīr*, XVIII, 125; al-Sharīf al-Raḍiyy, *op. cit.*, p. 293, no. 320.

130 *ʿIbāra*, fol. 5a. 131 *ʿIbāra*, fol. 5a.

according to Sūra xxvii 34: "Kings when they enter a city disorder it and make the mighty ones of its inhabitants abased."[132]

Dress denotes women according to Sūra ii 187: "Permitted to you upon the night of the fast is to go to your wives; they are a vestment to you and you are a vestment for them."[133]

A wood-carrier denotes a slanderer, according to Sūra cxi 5: "... and his wife, the carrier of the firewood" (i.e. the slanderous woman – K).[134]

The rope denotes a pact according to Sūra iii 103, 113: "And hold you fast to God's bond together..."; "Abasement shall be pitched on them wherever they are come upon except they be in a bond of God and a bond of the people."[135]

Scattered pearls denote servants according to Sūra lii 24: "... and there go round them youths, their own, as if they were hidden pearls."[136]

Fresh dates (*ruṭab*) denote good and pleasant sustenance, according to Sūra xix 24: "Shake also to thee the palm-trunk, and there shall come tumbling upon thee dates fresh and ripe."[137]

Drunkenness in a dream, without drinking intoxicants, denotes fear, according to Sūra xxii 2: "... and thou shalt see mankind drunk, yet they are not drunk, but God's chastisement is terrible."[138]

Washing with cold water symbolizes repentance, recovering from disease, being freed from prison, paying a debt, or being freed from fear, according to Sūra xxxviii 42: "This is a laving-place, cool and a drink."[139]

Rain in a restricted place (a house or locality) denotes pains and calamities, according to Sūra xi 82: "... and rained on it stones and baked clay."[140]

The tongue symbolizes a (convincing) argument or fame, according to Sūra xxvi 84: "... and appoint me a tongue of truthfulness among the others."[141]

Praying with the back to the Kaʿba symbolizes renouncing Islam, according to Sūra iii 187: "... but they rejected it behind their backs."[142] Praying above the Kaʿba also denotes renouncing Islam, according to Sūra ii, 144, 150: "From whatsoever place thou issuest, turn thy face towards the Holy Mosque..."; the man praying above the Kaʿba has no *qibla*.[143]

Eating fruits in Paradise (or getting women there) predicts welfare in this world and improvement of belief, knowledge and piety, according to Sūra xv 46: "Enter you there in peace and security."[144]

132 *ʿIbāra*, fol. 5b. 133 *ʿIbāra*, fol. 5b.
134 *ʿIbāra*, fol. 6b. 135 *ʿIbāra*, fol. 5b.
136 *ʿIbāra*, fol. 45b. 137 *ʿIbāra*, fol. 40b.
138 *ʿIbāra*, fol. 38a. 139 *ʿIbāra*, fol. 36b.
140 *ʿIbāra*, fol. 36a. 141 *ʿIbāra*, fol. 30a.
142 *ʿIbāra*, fol. 27a.
143 *ʿIbāra*, fol. 27a; Ps. Ibn Sīrīn, *op. cit.*, p. 56, ll. 14–16.
144 *ʿIbāra*, fol. 26a.

Manacles (*aghlāl*) constitute a bad omen, according to Sūra v 67: "... their hands are fettered and they are accursed for saying so..." and Sūra xxxvi 8: "Surely We have put on their necks fetters."[145] Another interpretation stresses the difference between manacles and shackles (*qayd*): manacles denote unbelief, but shackles denote firm belief.[146]

ʿUmar withdrew the nomination of his governor to Syria when the latter told him his dream. He saw the sun and the moon fighting each other; some of the stars aided the sun, some of them the moon. "With which of them were you?" asked ʿUmar. "With the moon", answered the man. ʿUmar withdrew his appointment, basing his decision on Sūra xvii 12: "... then We have blotted out the sign of the night."[147]

Two different interpretations of an identical dream, both based on the Qur'ān, were issued by Ibn Sīrīn. Two different persons dreamt that they were calling to prayer as *mu'adhdhins*. Ibn Sīrīn predicted to the first one that he would perform the *ḥajj*; to the other he foretold that his hand would be cut off (as punishment for theft). When asked about this opposite interpretation of the same dream, he said: "In the first person I noticed marks of good countenance and based my interpretation on Sūra xxii 27: "And proclaim unto mankind the pilgrimage." I was not pleased with the countenance of the other man and I interpreted according to Sūra xii 70: "... then a herald proclaimed: Ho, cameleers, you are robbers."[148]

A considerable number of verses enhance, the Arabic character of the compilation. It is indeed not surprising to find so many verses in a book by Ibn Qutayba, given his profound knowledge of Arabic poetry.

In a lengthy passage, in which he discusses the meanings of spirit (*rūḥ*) and soul (*nafs*) and the differences between them, Ibn Qutayba quotes a verse of Dhū l-Rumma, who said at the point of his death:

145 *ʿIbāra*, fol. 8b (but if a pious man sees manacles in a dream it is a good omen).

146 *ʿIbāra*, fol. 47a, inf. – 47b sup.; see Maʿmar b. Rāshid, *op. cit.*, fol. 152a inf.; al-Tibrīzī, *op. cit.*, p. 394; al-Suyūṭī, *al-Durr*, III, 312. Of interest is the interpretation of the following dream: A man saw in a dream that his son tied him with a black rope and then started to slaughter him. Ibn Sīrīn interpreted the dream by saying that the son is pious in his attitude towards his father and that he would pay a debt owed by his father (*ʿIbāra*, fol. 31b inf.; and see a more detailed report of this story Ibn Abī l-Dunyā, *al-Ishrāf fī manāzil al-ashrāf*, Ms. Chester Beatty 4427, fol. 32a).

147 *ʿIbāra*, fol. 17a; Ibn Ḥajar, *al-Iṣāba*, I, 285, no. 1353; Ibn ʿAbd al-Barr, *op. cit.*, I, 279, no. 378; al-Ibshīhī, *op. cit.*, II, 79; Ibn Abī l-Dunyā, *al-Ishrāf*, fol. 49a; Ps. Ibn Sīrīn, *op. cit.*, p. 291; al-Muttaqī l-Hindī, *op. cit.*, XI, 340, no. 1341; Muḥammad b. Aḥmad al-Tamīmī, *op. cit.*, fol. 35a.

148 *ʿIbāra*, fol. 9a; Bland, *op. cit.*, p. 133; Muḥammad b. Aḥmad al-Tamīmī, *op. cit.*, fol. 22a; al-Khargūshī, *op. cit.*, fol. 36a.

O, He Who takes my spirit from my soul at the point of death
and He Who forgives the sins, remove me from fire (of Hell).[149]

and an anonymous verse:

I remain the whole day maddened by love, and there meet
at night in dream my spirit and her spirit.[150]

The interpretation of the quince (*safarjal*) and the iris (*sūsan*) are derived from the components of these words (*sū-san* = *su' sana*; *safarjal* = *safar-jal*) and illustrated by the following anonymous verses:

She sent him as gift a quince and he drew a bad omen
and remained the whole day contemplating.
He was afraid of departure, as the first of it is journey (*safar*);
right he was in that he drew a bad omen.

and about the iris:

You gave me an iris and you did not
do well in (choosing your) gifts.
The first of it is evil and its end,
is evil of a (barren) year.[151]

A surveyer (of land) is interpreted as a traveller; this is expounded by two anonymous verses:

May God render the people of Barmak ugly, for I
became associate in their journeys because of them.
If Dhū l-Qarnayn did survey the Earth
then I am indeed a keeper of the dust.[152]

Two verses of Khidāsh b. Zuhayr are quoted attesting that the word *dajjāla* denotes a caravan; an anonymous verse conveys that the word denotes camels smeared with tar.[153]

The verb *ramā*, to throw arrows, denoting also calumniation, slander (for

149 *ʿIbāra*, fol. 3b, l. 1; *Dīwān*, ed. C. H. H. Macartney (Cambridge, 1919), p. 667 (no. 47); L'A, s.v. *z ḥ ḥ*; the variants pertinent to the discussed problem may be mentioned:

ʿ*Ibāra*: *yā qābiḍa l-rūḥi min nafsī idhā ḥtuḍirat*
wa-ghāfira l-dhanbi zaḥziḥnī min al-nāri.

Dīwān: *yā mukhrija l-rūḥi min jismī idhā ḥtaḍarat*
wa-fārija l-karbi...

L'A: *yā qābiḍa l-rūḥi ʿan jismin ʿaṣā zamanan*
wa-ghāfira l-dhanbi...

150 *ʿIbāra*, fol. 3b, l. 10. See this verse in the *Dīwān* of Jamīl Buthayna, ed. Bashīr Yamūt (Beirut, 1352/1934), p. 18.

151 *ʿIbāra*, fol. 5a; Ps. Ibn Sīrīn, *op. cit.*, p. 311, 9; Bland, *op. cit.*, p. 135; al-Khargūshī, *op. cit.*, fol. 217b.

152 *ʿIbāra*, fol. 6b; Ibn al-Faqīh, *al-Buldān*, ed. de Goeje (Leiden, 1885), p. 52 ("*muwakkalun bi-l-ʿiyāri*", not "*bi-l-ghubāri*").

153 *ʿIbāra*, fols. 6b–7a.

its interpretation of dreams in the latter connotation) is attested by Sūra xxiv 4, 6, and two verses of Labīd.[154]

The symbol of a falcon (*ṣaqr*) as a courageous man is attested by a verse of Abū Ṭālib:

The courageous men (falcons) came one after the other, as if
everyone of them clad in over-long mail (were a warrior) walking heavily.[155]

Honour is symbolized in dreams by the sky. This is attested by a verse of al-Nābigha al-Jaʿdī, recited during his meeting with the Prophet:

Our glory and our greatness reached the sky
and we hope to gain an elevated place above that.[156]

The sun symbolizes in dreams the power of the king. A verse of al-Nābigha al-Dhubyānī is quoted:

So you are the sun and the kings are the stars
when it appears, no star from among the stars appears.[157]

Stars denote the noblemen from among the people. An anonymous verse testifies it:

Whomever you will meet from amongst them you will say: "I met their chief"
they are like the stars by which the travellers travel.[158]

A rib symbolizes, as already mentioned, a woman. A verse of an anonymous poet attests it:

She is a hooked rib, you will not set her aright
lo, setting aright the ribs means breaking them.[159]

Lice in dreams symbolize the welfare of the family. A verse about it is quoted:

Up to the time when your clans grew full of lice (i.e. grew large – K)
and you saw that your sons grew up...[160]

154 *ʿIbāra*, fol. 7a; see the verses *Dīwān*, ed. Iḥsān ʿAbbās (al-Kuwayt, 1962), pp. 194–195 (nos. 72, 74); and see these verses analysed by Ibn Qutayba in his *Kit. al-maʿānī l-kabīr* (Hyderabad, 1368/1949), pp. 818, 1046–1047.

155 *ʿIbāra*, fol. 7b, l. 8; Ibn Hishām, *al-Sīra al-nabawiyya*, ed. al-Saqā, al-Abyārī, Shalabī (Cairo, 1355/1936), II, 18, l. 8 (*ʿIbāra*: *tatābaʿa fīhā*; *Sīra*: *aʿāna ʿalayhā*); cf. Muṣʿab b. ʿAbdallah al-Zubayrī, *op. cit.*, p. 431.

156 *ʿIbāra*, fol. 26a; Maria Nallino, *Le Poesie di an-Nabiġa al-Ǧaʿdī* (Roma, 1953), pp. 60 (v. 66, and see the references of the editor), 70 (v. 22); Muḥammad b. Aḥmad b. Ṭabāṭabā al-ʿAlawī, *ʿIyār al-shiʿr*, ed. Ṭāhā al-Ḥājirī and Muḥammad Zaghlūl Salām (Cairo, 1956), p. 45.

157 *ʿIbāra*, fol. 28b, l. 10; al-ʿAskarī, *Dīwān al-maʿānī* (Cairo, 1352), I, 16; *Dīwān al-Nābigha*, p. 17, l. 4.

158 *ʿIbāra*, fol. 28b, l. 13; al-ʿAskarī, *op. cit.*, I, 23 ult., 41; al-Jurjānī, *op. cit.*, p. 99 ult.

159 *ʿIbāra*, fol. 31a ult., al-Muʿāfā b. Zakariyyā, *al-Jalīs al-ṣāliḥ al-kāfī*, Ms. Topkapi Saray. Ahmet III, no. 2321, fol. 103a; Ibn Abī l-Ḥadīd, *Sharḥ nahj al-balāgha*, ed. Muḥammad Abū l-Faḍl Ibrāhīm (Cairo, 1964), XVIII, 199.

160 *ʿIbāra*, fol. 32a (in text: *qabilat*; correct reading: *qamilat*); LʿA, s.v. *q m l*.

A hand-mill in a dream symbolizes war. An anonymous verse and a verse of Zuhayr b. abī Sulmā[161] are quoted.[162]

A cloth-tent in a dream symbolizes royal power. This is based on the verse of al-Aʿshā (about the killing of al-Nuʿmān b. al-Mundhir):

He introduced al-Nuʿmān into a house the roof of which
were the chests of the elephants after (he dwelt in) the cloth tent.[163]

and on an anonymous verse:

O Ḥakam b. al-Mundhir b. Jārūd
the cloth-tent of glory is pitched upon you.[164]

There is an oneirocritical utterance which says: "He whose affairs have been accomplished in a dream and who, in a dream, has got hold of this world, has to expect decline and change of state, because everything accomplished is about to decay. This is supported by the following verse:

If a thing is accomplished, its decrease is near
expect decline if people say: "it is accomplished".[165]

A tent denotes sometimes a woman. The explanation for this interpretation is based on an expression in Arabic: "he pitched a tent upon his wife." The origin of this expression, records Ibn Qutayba, is a custom according to which people used to pitch a tent upon the man who married and slept with his wife; consequently a man sleeping with his wife on the night of his marriage was called "the pitcher of the tent". This is illustrated by a verse of ʿAmr b. Maʿdīkarib:

Have'nt you remained sleepless watching this yemeni lightening
it looks as if it were a candle of a pitcher of a tent.[166]

Wearing silk brocade not in the usual way forebodes that the dreamer will be whipped or afflicted by small-pox. Two verses of a man afflicted by small-pox expound this meaning:

Hasn't she got the tidings that I clothed myself after her (i.e. after my departure from her)
with a white stripped cloth, the dyer of which is not foolish.
I was bare of it before I wore it
and my wearing it was for me bitter and hard.[167]

161 *Dīwān*, ed. ʿUmar al-Suwaydī (Leiden, 1306/1889), p. 85.

162 *ʿIbāra*, fol. 37b.

163 *ʿIbāra*, fol. 40b, l. 6; *Dīwān*, ed. R. Geyer (London, 1928), p. 251 (no. 169).

164 *ʿIbāra*, fol. 40b, l. 8.

165 *ʿIbāra*, fol. 62a inf. — 62b sup.; Ibn Abī l-Dunyā, *Kit. dhamm l-dunyā*, Ms. Ẓāhiriyya, Damascus, fol. 22a, no. 187 (The edition of the manuscript is being prepared by Mrs. E. Almagor); Al-Rāghib al-Iṣfahānī, *Muḥāḍarāt al-udabā'*, IV, 388.

166 *ʿIbāra*, fol. 40b ult.; LʿA, s.v. *b n y* (the second hemistich); al-Jurjānī, *op. cit.*, p. 16.

167 *ʿIbāra*, fol. 41b, penult.; the first verse is recorded in the *Dīwān* of Dhū l-Rumma, p. 670, l. 4 (quoted from *Aghānī*, XVI, 122); Ibn Qutayba, *al-Maʿānī l-kabīr*, I, 486 (only

The interpretation of dreams

According to the *ḥadīth*: "the man fearing God is bridled", it seems to be a good omen to see oneself bridled in a dream. A verse is quoted in connection with this interpretation:

Free from vices is only he who controlled his mouth with a bridle.[168]

The milk of hare denotes paucity, subsequently it symbolizes paucity of means of sustenance. This is attested by an anonymous verse:

Your evil is present and your welfare is (small like)
the milk of a hare after her first parturition.[169]

Girding a sword in a dream denotes being appointed as governor; what happens in a dream to the sword or to the sword-belt (*ḥamā'il*) will happen to the man in his post as governor. The sword-belt takes the position of a cloak; the Arabs called it therefore "the cloak". A verse attesting this is quoted:

And in many a calamity brought about by a culprit
you turned your cloak into a muffler.

Ibn Qutayba adds: you turned your sword in it into a muffler, i.e. you beat with it (i.e. with your sword) their heads.[170]

The mare symbolizes a noble woman. This is illustrated by a verse of the wife of Rauḥ b. Zinbaʿ, in which she scoffs at her husband:

Am I not merely an Arab filly
born from (noble) horses, mounted by a mule.[171]

A horse with a blazon on his forehead, or white in the lower parts of his legs (*muḥajjal*) denotes in a dream a noble man; a verse of al-Nābigha al-Jaʿdī attests it:

Greet you both Laylā and say to her: "be calm"
as she set out for fame and an eminent deed.[172]

These verses current in the circles of philologists and lexicographers, some of them recorded by the *udabā'* and transmitters of *akhbār*, became thus a means of interpreting dreams.

the first verse; anonymous); for the expression *amarru wa-aʿlaqu* see al-Aʿshā, *Dīwān*, p. 148, l. 1 (XXXIII, 31).

168 *ʿIbāra*, fol. 62b, penult.; see Abū Nuwās, *Dīwān*, ed. Maḥmūd Kāmil (Cairo, 1933), p. 287, l. 2; Ibn Qutayba, *ʿUyūn al-akhbār*, Cairo 1924, II, 177.

169 *ʿIbāra*, fol. 38a, ult.; Ibn Qutayba, *al-Maʿānī l-kabīr*, I, 210 (with a commentary on the verse); L'A, s.v. *kh r s*; al-Jāḥiẓ, *Rasā'il*, ed. ʿAbd al-Salām Hārūn (Cairo, 1385/1965), II, 358 (attributed to ʿAmr b. Qamī'a); al-Jurjānī, *op. cit.*, p. 129.

170 *ʿIbāra*, fol. 44b, l. 5; Ibn Qutayba, *al-Maʿānī l-kabīr*, I, 480 (with a commentary); L'A, s.v. *r d y*; cf. al-Aʿshā, *Dīwān*, p. 39 (V, 47); al-Khansā', *Dīwān* (Beirut, 1888), p. 31.

171 *ʿIbāra*, fol. 50a, l. 3 from bottom; al-Jāḥiẓ, *Rasā'il* (*Kitāb al-bighāl*), II, 358; Aḥmad b. Abī Ṭāhir, *Balāghāt al-nisā'*, al-Najaf 1361, p. 97, l. 1; al-Bakrī, *Simṭ al-la'ālī*, ed. ʿAbd al-ʿAzīz al-Maymanī (Cairo, 1354/1936), p. 179 (see the references of the editor *ibid.*).

172 *ʿIbāra*, fol. 50a; M. Nallino, *op. cit.*, p. 94; Aḥmad b. Abī Ṭāhir, *op. cit.*, p. 185.

The examples of verses of poetry, *ḥadīths*, Qur'ān-verses and pious stories adduced above, may convey some idea about the richness of the material provided by Ibn Qutayba in this compilation.

Many of the stories are recorded with *isnāds* in which the names of the scholars from whom Ibn Qutayba directly transmitted, are mentioned: Isḥāq b. Rāhawayh,[173] Aḥmad b. Khalīl,[174] Abū Ḥātim,[175] who transmitted a great number of stories from al-Aṣmaʿī,[176] al-Ḥusayn b. al-Ḥasan al-Marwazī,[177] Abū l-Khaṭṭāb[178] and others.

Ibn Qutayba's[179] detailed and elaborate compilation gives information about the different methods of interpretation: the symbolical, the reciprocal and antithetical, the etymological, the interpretation by addition and subtraction and the interpretation based on Qur'ān and *ḥadīth.*[180] The classiffication of dreams according to *jins, ṣinf, ṭabʿ* is recorded as well.[181] Instruction and advice are given to the oneirocritics about their duties, methods and practices.[182]

Ibn Qutayba's compilation is, in fact, the continuation of an earlier tradition of oneiromancy already approved of by orthodox circles and drawing on a rich treasury of historical anectodes, *adab* stories, *zuhd* traditions, poetry, *ḥadīth* and Qur'ān. The numerous stories about dreams in Ibn Isḥāq's *Sīra*, the chapter about interpretation of dreams in Maʿmar b. Rāshid's *Jāmiʿ*, the *ḥadīths* about dreams in Aḥmad b. Ḥanbal's *Musnad*, the compilation of Ibn Abī l-Dunyā about the dreams of the righteous and pious, *Kitāb al-manām*, (with a special chapter about verses recited in dreams) bear evidence to the wide currency of this material among the orthodox and pious.

It is obvious that there existed another kind of oneiromancy based on non-Islamic and non-Arabic sources. This is indicated by a remark of al-Shāfiʿī (d. 204): "I left in al-ʿIrāq a thing which was invented by the *zanādiqa*; they call it "*taʿbīr*" and they occupy themselves with it, being distracted by it from the study of Qur'ān."[183] One may suppose that al-Shāfiʿī referred to some

173 Lecomte, *op. cit.*, pp. 52–53, no. 3.

174 Lecomte, *op. cit.*, p. 57, no. 9; Ibn Abī Ḥātim, *al-Jarḥ wa-l-taʿdīl* (Hyderabad, 1271/1952), I$_{\text{I}}$, 50, no. 49.

175 Lecomte, *op. cit.*, p. 50, no. 1; al-Marzubānī, *Nūr al-qabas*, ed. R. Sellheim (Beirut, 1964), I, 225–228.

176 See e.g. *ʿIbāra*, fols. 3b, 4b, 9b, 17b, 20a, 21b, 14b, 38a, 27a, 40a, 23a, 54b, 55a.

177 Lecomte, *op. cit.*, p. 64, no. 21; Ibn Abī Ḥātim, *al-Jarḥ*, I$_{\text{II}}$, 49, no. 219.

178 Lecomte, *op. cit.*, p. 56, no. 8; Ibn Abī Ḥātim, *al-Jarḥ*, I$_{\text{II}}$, 549, no. 2479.

179 See Fahd, *op. cit.*, p. 317.

180 *ʿIbāra*, fols. 4a–8b; see Fahd, *op. cit.*, pp. 317–328; Joseph de Somogyi, "The Interpretation of Dreams in ad-Damīrī's Ḥayāt al-Ḥayawān", *JRAS*, 1940, 1–20.

181 *ʿIbāra*, fol. 23b; see Bland, *op. cit.*, p. 136.

182 See e.g. *ʿIbāra*, fol. 23a.

183 Abū Nuʿaym, *op. cit.*, IX, 146.

compilations or traditions of Greek oneiromancy. In fact the translation of Artemidoros' *The Interpretation of Dreams* was done by Ḥunayn b. Isḥāq (d. 260).[184] Ibn Qutayba's compilation seems to have been intended as a response to the unorthodox trend of oneiromancy. It was addressed to the orthodox scholar of *ḥadīth*, to the *kātib*, to the *adīb*, to the pious believer. It differs from the work of Artemidoros in that it has at its core the notion that the interpretation of dreams should be subjected to the Arabo-Islamic tradition. The duty of the oneirocritic is to explain the symbols according to these principles, to admonish and to guide. Nowhere in the compilation of Ibn Qutayba is Artemidoros mentioned, although Ibn Qutayba who died in 270, ten years after the death of Ḥunayn, might have seen Ḥunayn's translation, or at least have been acquainted with its contents; no hint is given in the compilation of the opinions of philosophers. Some of the quotations from Artemidoros recorded by Abdel Daim (compared with the text of Ps. Ibn Sīrīn)[185] can in fact be found in the compilation of Ibn Qutayba. But these interpretations of dreams might have been already current in ʿIrāq in the first centuries of Islam and might have lost their foreign character; they were probably absorbed at a very early period into the lore of Muslim oneiromancy.

In fact Muslim oneiromancy seems to have absorbed some elements of the oneiromancy of the Ancient Near East. A vestige of this kind seems to be the story of the dream of ʿAbd al-Malik.[186] The interpretation of this dream tallies with one used for an identical case in an Assyrian tablet.[187] The idea of classifying dreams by the time of night or day[188] is echoed in Muslim oneiromancy.[189]

Traces of Jewish lore are conspicous. The idea of interpretation based on the Qur'ān, followed by Ibn Qutayba, is reminiscent of Talmudic interpretation which is based on the Torah.

184 Edited by Toufic Fahd (Damascus, 1964).

185 *L'Oniromancie Arabe d'apres Ibn Sīrīn*, pp. 151–165.

186 ʿAbd al-Malik saw himself in a dream urinating four times in the *miḥrāb*. Ibn al-Musayyab interpreted it, saying that four of his sons will rule as Caliphs. The dream was in fact fulfilled, and four of his sons were Caliphs (al-Quḍāʿī, *Taʾrīkh*, Ms. Bodleiana, Pococke 270, fol. 70a; al-Rāghib al-Iṣfahānī, *op. cit.*, I, 151; Ibn Raʾs Ghanama, *Manāqil al-durar*, Ms. Chester Beatty 4254, fol. 88a; al-Qalqashandī, *Maʾāthir al-ināfa*, ed. ʿAbd al-Sattār Farrāj (al-Kuwayt, 1964), I, 128; Ibn Saʿd, *op. cit.*, V, 123; al-Ibshīhī, *op. cit.*, II, 80; Fahd, *op. cit.*, p. 310, note 2).

187 See A. L. Oppenheim, "The Interpretation of Dreams in the Ancient Near East", *Transactions of the American Philosophical Society*, vol. 46, part 3, p. 265.

188 See Oppenheim, *op. cit.*, pp. 240 inf. – 241.

189 *ʿIbāra*, fol. 8b: *...wa-aṣdaqu auqāti l-ruʾyā bi-l-layli l-asḥāru wa-bi-l-nahāri l-qāʾilatu...* This is recorded as an utterance of the Prophet by al-Ḥākim (*al-Mustadrak* IV, 392: *aṣdaqu l-ruʾyā bi-l-asḥāri*) and al-Zurqānī (*Sharḥ al-mawāhib* VII, 166 l. 1); see Oppenheim, *op. cit.*, p. 241 (quoting Bland, *op. cit.*, p. 129).

Furthermore, some passages from the Talmūd are almost verbally quoted in the Muslim compilations. A man came to Ibn Sīrīn, according to a story and told him the dream of one of his acquaintances: the man had dreamt that he split the heads of eggs, left the yolk and took the outer parts of the eggs. Ibn Sīrīn refused to interpret the dream and insisted that the dreamer come to him personally. The man admitted that it was he who had had the dream. Ibn Sīrīn stated that the dream indicated that he was a grave-digger, plundering the graves, ransacking the shrouds of the dead and leaving their bodies. The man admitted and promised to refrain from doing it again.[190] This very dream, with an identical interpretation, is recorded in the story of Rabbī Yishmaʿel talking with the heretic.[191] The passage in Berakhot contains also the story of another dream: the man saw himself pouring oil into an olive tree. Rabbī Yishmaʿel stated that the man had had sexual intercourse with his mother. The same story is recorded in the Muslim sources with an identical interpretation attributed to Ibn Sīrīn.[192]

The principle, related in the Talmūd,[193] whereby the dream is fulfilled according to its interpretation is recorded as an utterance of the Prophet.[194] This principle is illustrated in the Talmūd by a story of a woman, who saw twice in her dream that a beam broke down from her roof. She came twice to Rabbī Elʿazar and he interpreted it saying that she would give birth to a male child; so it happened in fact in both cases. Then she dreamt again that the beam of her roof broke down; she came to Rabbī Elʿazar but did not meet him. His students interpreted the dream by saying that her husband would die. When Rabbī Elʿazar heard about it, he accused his students of having caused the death of the man by their interpretation, because dreams are fulfilled according to their interpretation.[195] Closely reminiscent is the story recorded in Muslim sources about a woman who came to the Prophet and told him that she saw in a dream a beam of the roof of her house breaking down; he interpreted it by saying that her husband would return; so it happened. After some time she saw in her sleep the same dream; she came

190 *ʿIbāra*, fols. 22b, 23b, ll. 5–8; al-Ibshīhī, *op. cit.*, II, 79.

191 Bab. Berakhot, 56b.

192 Ps. Ibn Sīrīn, *op. cit.*, p. 305; al-Ibshīhī, *op. cit.*, II, 79; al-Majlisī, *op. cit.*, LXI, 206.

193 Berakhot, 55b; see Löwinger, *op. cit.*, p. 25, note 9; Kristianpoler, *op. cit.*, p. XII, and p. 37, no. 107, note 1.

194 Maʿmar b. Rāshid, *op. cit.*, fol. 152b sup.; al-Ḥākim, *op. cit.*, IV, 391; al-Majlisī, *op. cit.*, LXI, 173, 175 (*al-ruʾyā ʿalā mā tuʿabbaru*).

195 Kristianpoler, *op. cit.*, pp. 51–52, nos. 164–165; Löwinger, *op. cit.*, pp. 25 inf. – 26 sup.

196 According to another version she told her dream to ʿĀʾisha. See al-Zurqānī, *op. cit*. VII, 171.

to the Prophet but did not meet him, and related the story of her dream to Abū Bakr.[196] He interpreted it by saying that her husband would die.[197]

The stories, recorded in Jewish sources, about the pious in Paradise[198] and about gaining knowledge of religious precepts and guidance in dreams,[199] are closely reminiscent of similar passages in Muslim oneiromancy.

The continuity of the Hebrew oneiromancy[200] can be gauged from the story of a man who found a book on oneiromancy written in Hebrew in the ruins of a house in al-Baṣra.[201]

The various elements of oneiromancy were successfully absorbed and combined in the Muslim literature on dreams. Enriched by genuine Arabic and Islamic material, thoughtfully developed by Muslim scholars, it reflects the various ideas and trends in Muslim society and became a popular topic of Arabic literature.

Ibn Qutayba's compilation is the earliest extant composition in the field of Muslim oneiromancy, a fine and rich specimen of this genre of literature.

197 *'Ibāra*, fol. 9a inf. – 9b sup. (Ibn Qutayba attempts to justify the two different interpretations by the fact that either the countenance of the woman changed or the times of the two dreams were different); the version recorded by al-Zurqānī (see above note 196) ends with the Prophet's admonition to 'Ā'isha to give good interpretations to the dreams of the Muslims, because dreams are fulfilled according to their interpretations. This reminds closely the account of the story in Jewish sources. And see al-Zamakhsharī, *op. cit.*, I, 243–244; al-Majlisī, *op. cit.*, LXI, 164–165 (quoted from *al-Kāfī*. The woman came twice to the Prophet; in both cases he interpreted the dream by saying that her husband would return safely. At the third time she met an unlucky man [*A'sar*] who predicted that her husband would die. Al-Majlisī eagerly gives the Sunnī version identifying the "unlucky man" as Abū Bakr).

198 Kristianpoler, *op. cit.*, p. 31, no. 93 and p. 32, no. 96.

199 Cf. Kristianpoler, *op. cit.*, pp. 29–30, nos. 88–91.

200 About the dependence of the Talmudic material on Greek sources see S. Liebermann, *Greek and Hellenism in Jewish Palestine* (Jerusalem, 1962), pp. 202 seq. [Hebrew].

201 Ps. Ibn Sīrīn, *op. cit.*, p. 274.

APPENDIX

A. List of chapters of the Jerusalem Ms.:

39.	*al-fīlu wa-l-jāmūsu wa-l-khinzīru*	fol. 54b
40.	*al-ḥasharātu*	fol. 55a
41.	*al-sibāʿu*	fol. 55a
42.	*fī taʾwīli l-ṭayri*	fol. 56b
43.	*banātu l-māʾi min al-samaki wa-ghayrihi*	fol. 58b
44.	*al-ʿaqāribu wa-l-ḥayyātu wa-l-hawāmmu*	fol. 59a
45.	*taʾwīlu l-ṣunnāʿi*	fol. 59b
46.	*taʾwīlu l-nawādiri*	fol. 62a

B. List of chapters of the Ankara Ms.:

1. *Dhikru l-nafsi wa-l-rūḥ*
2. *Al-taʾwīl bi-l-asmāʾ*
3. *Al-taʾwīl bi-l-maʿnā*
4. *Al-taʾwīl bi-l-Qurʾān*
5. *Al-taʾwīl bi-l-aḥādīth*
6. *Al-taʾwīl bi-l-mathal al-sāʾir*
7. *Al-taʾwīl bi-l-ḍidd wa-l-maqlūb*
8. *Taʿbīru l-ruʾyā bi-l-ziyāda wa-l-nuqṣān*
9. *Taʿbīru l-ruʾyā bi-l-auqāt*
10. *Taʿbīru l-ruʾyā bi-khtilāfi l-hayʾāt*
11. *ʿAjāʾib al-ruʾyā*
12. *Wa-min ʿajībi l-ruʾyā*
13. *Intihāʾu l-ruʾyā*
14. *Wa-min nawādirihi mā rawā Jābiru bnu Ḍamra*
15. *Wa-min nawādirihi mā rawā Marwānu bnu Muʿāwiyata*
16. *Wa-nawādir aṣḥābihi ʿalayhi l-salām*
17. *Nādira fī l-ruʾyā*
18. *Wa-min nawādir al-ruʾyā*
19. *Wa-min nawādirihi ʿalā ghayri aṣlin*
20. *Wa-min nawādirihi wa-ʿajāʾibihi*
21. *Wa-min nawādirihi fī l-ruʾyā*
22. *Amthilat al-ruʾyā*
23. *Wa-min ʿajāʾibi bni Sīrīn*
24. *Adab al-taʾwīl*

INDEX

al-Anṣār, Anṣārī: III 52; V 322; VIII 86, 87, 95, 96; IX 39, 40n, 49; XIII 11
ʿArafa, ʿArafāt: I 36n, 44; XIII 7, 29–33, 35
Arwā bint Umayya b. ʿAbdshams: VII 259n
al-ʿĀṣ b. Wāʾil: II 53; VII 248
Asad (Banū): I 44; II 39, 40; III 54; VII 256n
Asad b. ʿAbd al-ʿUzzā (Banū): II 53
al-Aṣbagh b. ʿAmr b. Thaʿlaba b. al-Ḥārith b. Ḥiṣn b. Ḍamḍam:V 325, 326
al-Aʿshā (Maymūn): II 52; XIV 96
Ashʿar (Banū), al-Ashʿariyyūn: I 34, 43; IX 40n
al-Ashʿath b. Qays: III 66
Ashjaʿ (Banū): II 40
ashrāf: VII 263
al-Ashtar: VII 271
Asīd b. Abī l-ʿĪṣ: XIV 75n
Aslam (Banū): III 52n; VII 256
Asmāʾ bint Salāma b. Mukharriba b. Jandal: V 326–330
al-Aṣbagh b. ʿAmr b. Thaʿlaba b. al-Ḥārith b. Ḥiṣn b. Ḍamḍam b. ʿAdiyy b. Janāb al-Kalbī: V 326
al-Aswad al-ʿAnsī: IX 36; XIV 72
al-Aswad b. Yaʿfur: I 41
ʿAṭāʾ b. Abī Rabāḥ: XIII 25–27
ʿAttāb b. Asīd: XIV 75n
ʿAwf b. Luʾayy: II 42
ʿAwf b. Kināna b. ʿAwf b. ʿUdhra...b. Kalb: II 48
ʿAwf b. Mālik: XIV 80n
Aws (Banū): VIII 62, 88, 90, 95
ʿAyyāsh b. Abī Rabīʿa b. al-Mughīra: V 326, 327, 330; VII 252
Ayyūb: XI 21
ʿAzāzīl: XII 6n
Azd (Banū): III 52, 55
Badr (Banū): II 38
Badr (Battle of): II 50n; V 328; VII 247, 248, 252n, 253n, 258, 259n; VIII 83
Baghīḍ (Banū): II 44
Bajīla: III 57
Bājir, see idols
Bakr (Banū): II 46, 50
Bakr b. Wāʾil (Banū): I 37, 45; II 46; III 52n
Banū Isrāʾīl: XIII 10
Baqīʿ: VIII 93
Baqīʿ al-Gharqad: XI 34
Baradān: V 322, 323
Barhūt: XIV 77
Barmakids: XI 32; XIV 94
Barra bint Murr b. Udd:III 59
al-Bāsa, see *ḥaram*
basl: II 42, 45
basmala: IX 51
Baṣra: V 325; XI 31; XIII 4n, 31; XIV 101
Basūs (war of): II 48
al-Bāssa (sanctuary): II 44
bidʿa: VII 270, 271; XI 30, 33, 34n; XIII 32
Bilāl: III 53
Biʾr ʿAbd al-Muṭṭalib: VIII 90
Biʾr Maʿūna: VII 255–257, 264, 267
Biʾr Muṭṭalib: VIII 90n
Bishr b. Saʿīd: XIII 11
the Black Stone: II 53, 55
Burayda al-Aslamī: XII 12
Buss (sanctuary): II 43–45, 50–52
Byzantium, Byzantine: II 37, 44, 45, 50; VI 164n; IX 33, 34; XII 3; XIV 80
the Camel (Battle of): IX 39
Christianity, Christian: I 48; II 45; V 330; VII 243; VIII 75, 76n, 88; XI 30, 36; XIII 6, 35, 36; XIV 80
Constantinopole: III 57
Ḍabba (Banū): V 324, 325
Damascus: VIII 74n; XIV 87
dār al-islām: VIII 67
dār al-nadwa: II 53
Dārim (Banū): V 327, 329
Daws (Banū): I 38, 40
Dāwūd: IX 44; XI 21
Dāwūd b. Hubāla: II 45
Day of Judgement: III 53; VII 267; XIV 74, 77, 79
Day of Resurrection: IX 39, 40; XI 21, 22; XII 3, 4, 21; XIV 80
al-Dayyān (Banū):I 43
deities, see idols
the Devil: X 63, 64n, 66; XII 6–8; XIII 3n; XIV 72, 73n
Dhakwān (Banū): II 39n; VII 256n
Dhakwān (Abū ʿAmr): III 65
Dhū Aṣbaḥ (Banū): VIII 78

Dhū l-Kaffayn, see idols
Dhū l-Lība, see idols
Dhū i-Qarnayn: XIV 94
Dhū l-Ra'sayn, see Khushayn b. La'y al-Fazārī al-Samkhī
Dhū l-Rumma: XIV 93
Dhū l-Ruqayba (mountain): II 41
Dhubyān (Banū): II 40
Ḍirār b. 'Amr al-Ḍabbi: V 323-325
Ḍirār b. al-Khaṭṭāb: VIII 86
the Ditch (Battle of): II 40; VII 253, 258, 260, 264; VIII 81, 89
dīwān: III 50
the Dome of the Rock, see Mosques
du'ā': VII 268, 269n; XIII 31
Ḍubā'a bint 'Āmir: I 41
the Elephant: II 51
the End of the Days: XIII 35
Euphrates: XIII 33; XIV 84n
faḍā'il: XI 22, 33
Fadak: I 33n; V 321-323, 325, 326, 328-330
fa'l: XII 11-13n
al-Fāri'a bint Hammām b. 'Urwa b. Mas'ūd: III 64
Fāṭima: VIII 80; XIII 15
fatwa: XIV 75
Fazāra: II 34-36, 38-42, 45, 49, 50
fiqh: VIII 74, 75, 92; IX 36
fitna, fitan: XIV 80, 81n, 91
al-Fiṭr (Yawm): VII 269
fiṭra: X 63, 68, 70; XIV 76
al-Furāfiṣa b. al-Aḥwaṣ b. 'Amr b. Tha'laba b. al-Ḥārith b. Ḥiṣn b. Ḍamḍam: V 326, 328
Fusṭāṭ: XIII 31
Gabriel, see Jibrīl
the Gazelle of the Ka'ba: V 329n
genealogy (see also *nasab*): II 52; III passim; IV 590; VIII 79; XIV 77
Ghassān: I 37; II 47; XIV 87
Ghaṭafān (Banū): I 44; II 35, 39, 40, 42-45; III 52; VII 256n
al-Ghayyān (Banū): XII 18
al-Ghawiyy (Banū): XII 18
Ghifār (Banū): III 52n; VII 256
God of the Ka'ba (Mecca), see Allāh
supreme God of Mecca: I 34, 47, 48
Ghuzayya (Banū): IV 590
Ḥabīb b. Maslama: VII 271; XIII 14
Haddāj b. Mālik: II 45
Haddāj b. Mālik b. Taymallāh b. Tha'laba b. 'Uqāba: II 45
Ḥaḍramawt (Banū): I 38
Ḥafṣa bint 'Umar b. al-Khaṭṭāb: III 67n, 68n
Hajar: I 45
Ḥājib b. Zurāra: VII 246
ḥajj, see pilgrimage
al-Ḥajjāj b. Yūsuf: II 54; III 60, 64; XIII 34n; XIV 90
ḥakam: VIII 90
al-Ḥakam b. al-'Āṣ: XII 16Ḥakam b. Marwān b. Zinbā' al-'Absī: II 39, 40
Ḥakam b. al-Mundhir b. Jārūd: XIV 96
Ḥakīm b. Ḥizām: IX 45
the Hall (Day of): IX 39
hāma: XIV 77
Ḥamal: II 39n
Hamdān: xiv 84
Hammām b. Murra: II 48
Ḥamza: XIV 71
Ḥanīfa (Banū): XIV 88
Ḥanẓala b. Nahd: II 47
al-ḥaram, House, Sanctuary: III 60
--of Abraha: II 44
--al-Bāsa: II 44
--of Buss: II 43, 44, 45
--of Mecca: I 42, 47, 48; II 33, 34, 44, 45, 54, 55, 57; III 60; VII 260; XI 33, 35, 36; XIII 12, 24, 26, 28
--of Qawdam: II 44
Ḥarb b. Umayya: II 38, 53
ḥarīm: II 34, 35
al-Ḥārith b. 'Abdallah b. 'Ayyāsh: V 327
al-Ḥārith b. 'Abd al-Raḥmān b. Abī Dhubāb: XIII 27
al-Ḥārith b. Fihr: III 55
al-Ḥārith b. Hishām b. al-Mughīra al-Makhzūmī: V 326, 328, 329; VII 253, 254
al-Ḥārith b. Ḥiṣn b. Ḍamḍam al-Kalbī (al-Ḥarshā): II 48; V 321-326, 330
al-Ḥārith b. Lu'ayy: III 56
al-Ḥārith b. Māriya: II 47